First Language Acquisition

Linguistics: The Essential Readings

This series consists of comprehensive collections of classic and contemporary reprinted articles in a wide range of fields within linguistics. The primary works presented in each book are complemented by outstanding editorial material by key figures in the field. Each volume stands as an excellent resource on its own, as well as an ideal companion to an introductory text.

First Language Acquisition

The Essential Readings

Edited by
Barbara C. Lust
and
Claire Foley

Blackwell
Publishing

350 Main Street, Malden, MA 02148-5020, USA
108 Cowley Road, Oxford OX4 1JF, UK
550 Swanston Street, Carlton, Victoria 3053, Australia

First published 2004 by Blackwell Publishing Ltd

Library of Congress Cataloging-in-Publication Data

First language acquisition : the essential readings / edited by Barbara
C. Lust and Claire Foley.
p. cm. — (Linguistics ; 4)
Includes bibliographical references and index.
ISBN 0-631-23254-0 (hard. : alk. paper) — ISBN 0-631-23255-9 (pbk. : alk. paper)
1. Language acquisition. I. Lust, Barbara, 1941– II. Foley, Claire. III. Series:
Linguistics (Malden, Mass.) ; 4.

P118 .F548 2004
401′.92—dc21   2003013381

A catalogue record for this title is available from the British Library.

Set in $10\frac{1}{2}/12\frac{1}{2}$ pt Ehrhardt
by Graphicraft Limited, Hong Kong
Printed and bound in the United Kingdom
by TJ International, Padstow, Cornwall

For further information on
Blackwell Publishing, visit our website:
http://www.blackwellpublishing.com

Contents

Acknowledgments

The editors and publisher gratefully acknowledge the permission granted to reproduce the copyright material in this book:

1 Noam Chomsky, pp. 1–14 from *Knowledge of Language: Its Nature, Origin, and Use.* New York: Praeger, 1986.
2 Noam Chomsky, A review of B. F. Skinner's *Verbal Behavior* from *Language* 35:1 (1959), pp. 26–58.
3 Jean Piaget and Bärbel Inhelder, pp. 51–7 and 84–91, from "The Semiotic or Symbolic Function," chapter 3 in *The Psychology of the Child*, trans. Helen Weaver. New York: Basic Books, 1969. English language version © 1969 by Basic Books, Inc. Reprinted by permission of Basic Books, a member of Perseus Books, L. L. C. Originally published in French as *La Psychologie de l'enfant* by Presses Universitaires de France, Paris, 1966.
4 Massimo Piattelli-Palmarini (ed.), pp. 23–52, 57–61, 64–5, 81, 138, 164–73, from *Language and Learning: The Debate between Jean Piaget and Noam Chomsky.* Cambridge, Mass.: Harvard University Press, 1980.
5 Hermine Sinclair, pp. 97, 98–9, 103–5, from "Comparative Linguistics and Language Acquisition" in Ramón Arzápalo and Yolanda Lastra (eds.), *Vitalidad e influencia de las lenguas indigenas en Latinoamerica*. México, D. F.: Instituto de Investigaciones Antropológicas, 1995.
6 Eric H. Lenneberg, pp. 125–31 from *Biological Foundations of Language*. New York: John Wiley, 1967.
7 Norman Geschwind, "Language and the Brain" from *Scientific American* 226:4 (1972), pp. 76–83. Reprinted with permission. © 1972 by Scientific American, Inc. All rights reserved.
8 Michael S. Gazzaniga, pp. 25–8 from *The Bisected Brain*. New York: Appleton-Century-Crofts, 1970.
9 Susan Curtiss, Victoria Fromkin, Stephen Krashen, David Rigler, and Marilyn Rigler, "The Linguistic Development of Genie" from *Language* 50:3 (September 1974), pp. 528–54.

10   Roger Brown and Camille Hanlon, pp. 11–21 and 37–53 from "Derivational Complexity and Order of Acquisition in Child Speech," chapter 1 in John R. Hayes (ed.), *Cognition and the Development of Language*. New York: John Wiley, 1970. © 1970 by John Wiley & Sons, Inc. Used by permission of John Wiley & Sons, Inc.

11   Charles A. Ferguson, "Talking to Children: A Search for Universals," pp. 203–24 from Joseph H. Greenberg (ed.), *Universals of Human Language, Volume 1: Method and Theory* (associate editors, Charles A. Ferguson and Edith A. Moravcsik). Stanford, Calif.: Stanford University Press, 1978. © 1978 by the Board of Trustees of the Leland Stanford Junior University. Reprinted with the permission of Stanford University Press, www.sup.org.

12   James L. Gould and Peter Marler, "Learning by Instinct" from *Scientific American* 255:1 (1987), pp. 74–85. © 1987 by Scientific American, Inc. All rights reserved. Reprinted with permission.

13   Barbara Landau and Lila R. Gleitman, pp. 1–5, 54–64, and 121–6 from *Language and Experience: Evidence from the Blind Child*. Cambridge, Mass.: Harvard University Press, 1985. © 1985 by the President and Fellows of Harvard College. Reprinted by permission of the publisher.

14   Steven Pinker, pp. 39–47 from *Language Learnability and Language Development*. Cambridge, Mass.: Harvard University Press, 1984. © 1984 by the President and Fellows of Harvard College. Reprinted by permission of the publisher.

15   Steven Pinker, pp. 360–4 from *Learnability and Cognition: The Acquisition of Argument Structure*. Cambridge, Mass.: MIT Press, 1989. © 1989 by the MIT Press.

16   Hermine Sinclair-deZwart, p. 25 from "Language Acquisition and Cognitive Development" in Timothy E. Moore (ed.), *Cognitive Development and the Acquisition of Language*. New York: Academic Press, 1973. © 1973 by Academic Press.

17   Dan Isaac Slobin, pp. 175–6, 179–83, 191–4, and 208 from "Cognitive Prerequisites for the Development of Grammar" in Charles A. Ferguson and Dan Isaac Slobin (eds.), *Studies of Child Language Development*. New York: Holt, Rinehart, and Winston, 1973.

18   Jean Berko Gleason, "The Child's Learning of English Morphology" from *Word* 14 (Aug.–Dec. 1958), pp. 150–77. Reprinted by courtesy of Jean Berko Gleason.

19   Roger Brown, pp. 270–5 from *A First Language: The Early Stages*. Cambridge, Mass.: Harvard University Press, 1973. © 1973 by the President and Fellows of Harvard College. Reprinted by permission of the publisher.

20   Peter D. Eimas, Einar R. Siqueland, Peter Jusczyk, and James Vigorito, "Speech Perception in Infants" from *Science* 171 (January 1971), pp. 303–6. © 1971 by the American Association for the Advancement of Science. Reprinted with permission.

21   Roman Jakobson, pp. 294–304 from "The Sound Laws of Child Language and their Place in General Phonology" in Linda R. Waugh and Monique Monville-Burston (eds.), *On Language: Roman Jakobson*. Cambridge, Mass.: Harvard University Press, 1990. This translation by R. B. Sangster and L. R. Waugh was originally published in Roman Jakobson, *Studies on Child Language and Aphasia*. The Hague: Mouton, 1971. © by the Roman Jakobson Trust.

22   N. V. Smith, pp. 47–60 and 65 from "Universal Tendencies in the Child's Acquisition of Phonology" in Neil O'Connor (ed.), *Language, Cognitive Deficits, and*

Retardation. London: Butterworth, 1975. Reproduced with permission of the author.

23 David Stampe, "The Acquisition of Phonemic Representation," pp. 443–54 in *Proceedings of the 5th Regular Meeting of the Chicago Linguistic Society*. Chicago: Chicago Linguistic Society, 1969.

24 Karl Lashley, selections from "The Problem of Serial Order in Behavior," pp. 112–36 in L. A. Jeffress (ed.), *Cerebral Mechanisms in Behavior*. New York: John Wiley, 1951.

25 Roger Brown, "The Study of Adam, Eve, and Sarah," pp. 51–9 in *A First Language: The Early Stages*. Cambridge, Mass.: Harvard University Press, 1973. © 1973 by the President and Fellows of Harvard College. Reprinted by permission of the publisher.

26 Edward S. Klima and Ursula Bellugi-Klima, "Syntactic Regularities in the Speech of Children," pp. 183–208 in J. Lyons and R. J. Wales (eds.), *Psycholinguistic Papers*. Edinburgh: Edinburgh University Press, 1966. Reproduced by permission of Ursula Bellugi-Klima.

27 Lois Bloom, "The Reduction Transformation and Constraints on Sentence Length," chapter 6, pp. 135–69 in *Language Development: Form and Function in Emerging Grammar*. Cambridge, Mass.: MIT Press, 1970. © 1970 by the MIT Press.

28 Eve V. Clark, pp. 390–418 from "The Young Word Maker: A Case Study of Innovation in the Child's Lexicon," in Eric Wanner and Lila R. Gleitman (eds.), *Language Acquisition: The State of the Art*. New York: Cambridge University Press, 1982. © 1982 by Cambridge University Press. Reprinted with the permission of Cambridge University Press.

29 Eve V. Clark, "Strategies for Communicating" in *Child Development* 49 (1978), pp. 953–9. Reprinted with permission of the Society for Research in Child Development.

Every effort has been made to trace copyright holders and to obtain their permission for the use of copyright material. The publisher apologizes for any errors or omissions in the above list and would be grateful if notified of any corrections that should be incorporated in future reprints or editions of this book.

Introduction

1 Overview

In this volume, we aim to collect in one place a set of groundbreaking works which provide the foundation for the field of first language acquisition. These foundational works either explicitly or implicitly underlie current research, and their value has endured through extensive and rapid developments in the field over the last decades. Each has helped to define our current field of inquiry. They are important not only for a historical perspective, but for a true understanding of the issues and concepts which are at the center of the field today.

Our criteria for selection of papers for this volume include the following. (i) Each of the papers was in some sense "pathbreaking," that is, it led to a reconsideration or reorientation of theory, or to a new way of viewing empirical data. Each led to new leading questions and/or to a reorientation in the field, a new way of looking at the field. (ii) Each has been frequently cited by subsequent work. (iii) Each has stood the test of time: the enduring value of these works is now attested. To ensure that each article in the volume met this criterion, we selected only works whose original publication date was in the late 1980s or earlier. Some of the papers date back as many as 50 years, but maintain their significance today. (iv) A fourth criterion relates to the target audience for the volume, which includes both established scholars and beginning students: All other things being equal, we have selected articles rich in original data and/or observations – a characteristic that allows even beginning scholars to immerse themselves in the core material that feeds hypotheses and theories.

"Foundational" does not refer to a particular theoretical or empirical approach. Many of the papers here may be rejected in whole or in part by current researchers. But they led to questions and/or methods which guide research in the field today. They either clarify fundamental theoretical tensions in the field or provide basic discoveries which underlie current investigations. We have aimed to include works whose significance transcends any one particular perspective on linguistic theory. Thus, we hope to have provided foundational readings that would be useful for scholars approaching language acquisition from a variety of frameworks in linguistics and psycholinguistics.

2   A Linguistic Approach

While language acquisition, like many cognitive puzzles, can be studied from the perspective of such diverse fields as anthropology, philosophy, or behavioral or cognitive psychology, we have intentionally selected papers which are illuminated by linguistic science, i.e., which make crucial use of the insights and findings of linguistics.[1] In turn, the articles in this volume have important implications for the broader field of linguistics, both directly through their discoveries and insights, and indirectly through work that they have led to or inspired.

While current work in the field of language acquisition has recently seen intense development in studies related to specific linguistic theories, e.g., a generative theory and a theory of Universal Grammar, the more general field of linguistic science has allowed researchers over the course of decades to refine their definition of what is being acquired. From the enormous range of scholarship that has explored the essential characteristics of human language, we extract four common or recurring features.

First, the child must acquire a formal system in which discrete elements can be combined in an infinite variety of ways. From the early part of the twentieth century, linguists have attempted to describe and formalize language as a "system of voluntarily produced symbols" (Sapir 1921, 8). The discrete elements exist at several levels (for example, levels corresponding to sounds, words, and syntax), and the links between these levels must be represented abstractly. Cross-linguistic research has illuminated the range of possible ways these units may be combined. For example, agglutinative languages combine morphemes into complex words that correspond to entire sentences in non-agglutinative languages. Since any child can acquire any language, linguistic science has helped researchers delimit the task every child undertakes.

Second, the discrete combinatorial systems of language must be mapped onto meaning. Bloomfield accordingly defined grammar as the "meaningful arrangement of forms in a language" (1933, 163), pointing the way to the general notion of grammar as the function linking form and meaning. Many of the articles in this volume have advanced our knowledge of how the child begins to assemble the abstract, formal, symbolic systems that linguistics identifies as essential to language, and to map these systems onto meaning.

Third, the development of linguistics as a science in this century led to the insight that the formal mapping from symbolic systems to meaning must be subject to some deeper organization. Saussure (1959) acknowledged the symbolic, combinatorial nature of language, but also argued that an "associative and co-ordinating faculty" (13) must organize the system: "Language is a system of signs that express ideas" (16), and "beyond the functioning of the various organs there exists a more general faculty which governs signs and which would be the linguistic faculty proper" (11). Linguistics in the earlier part of the century thus laid the groundwork for the study of language as a cognitive system, and for those who study the development of language as the development of a system of representation in the child's mind. This framework is articulated in current theories, such as the theory of Universal Grammar as a model of the Initial State (Chomsky 1986).

Finally, linguistics has constantly investigated the importance of a wider linguistic community that provides language-specific input to a child. Early in this century, the view of language as the "totality of utterances that can be made in a speech community"

(Bloomfield 1926, 26) set the stage for attention to the linguistic environment in language acquisition research. Since then, the nature of the interaction with input has been and remains an area of intense debate.[2]

In a general sense, all research in language acquisition invokes these four features of human language as identified by linguistic science. For this volume, however, we have selected research whose emphasis is linguistic.[3] The articles included in this anthology thus fall into one or more of the following categories:

1   They include discoveries (and/or underlie later discoveries) about how the child acquires the abstract systems that combine discrete, symbolic elements in a language. Moreover, they are formally precise about the nature of these systems in the developing language.
2   They include discoveries about how the child maps such systems to meaning.
3   They investigate the nature of the representation of these abstract systems, and their mapping to meaning, in the child's mind.
4   They investigate the role of the linguistic input and how it interacts with the biological foundations of grammar during language acquisition.

By virtue of this linguistic emphasis, the articles in this volume have advanced our knowledge about the nature of language itself.

3   The General Structure of the Volume

In general, this volume is organized in terms of a core course in language acquisition, one which provides the student or reader with a sense of the theoretical foundations of the field (Part I), its fundamental issues, including issues related to fundamental mechanisms of language acquisition (Part II) and a basic introduction to acquisition in each of the core components of language knowledge (i.e., morphology, phonology, syntax, semantics and pragmatics) (Part III).[4] The classics collected here are selected and organized to provide an enabling framework for the study of each of these basic areas of language acquisition.

4   The Significance of the Chapters

4.1   Part I

Chomsky's theory, as exemplified in his 1986 paper, has laid the foundations for an explicit rationalist approach to the explanation of first language acquisition. In his 1959 review of Skinner's *Verbal Behavior* (1957), Chomsky argues against empiricism as an alternative paradigm. The debate with empiricist paradigms persists actively today: see, for example, Elman et al. (1996), Pinker (1994), and Braine (1994).

Piaget's theory and the work on language acquisition conducted in that paradigm by Hermine Sinclair also attacked the empiricist perspective for the acquisition of complex cognitive knowledge in the child (e.g., chapter 2, Piaget and Inhelder 1969). However, in the Chomsky–Piaget dialogues (reflected in the Piattelli Palmarini selection), a new issue of debate arises. While Chomsky pursues the precise and formal definition of the Initial State of first language acquisition, including components of modularity and innateness, Piaget and his collaborators insist on pursuing an explanation for "development" over time. In doing so they question the nature and extent of modularity and innateness. These issues of how to resolve study of the Initial State with the explanation of development over time remain central in the field today (e.g., papers collected in Ritchie and Bhatia 1999). Indeed, this difference in emphasis divides many of the researchers now working on language acquisition. Hermine Sinclair articulates both the enduring tensions and the areas of agreement: she specifies linguistic findings that must be taken into account by all psychologists studying language, but also points out the need for psycholinguistics to aim for even clearer experimental demonstration of children's basic grammatical competence and the development of grammar.

4.2   Part II

Controversies regarding the relative roles of biological and environmental determinants of language acquisition persist today. Study of the biological underpinnings of language knowledge has exploded over the last decade with the advance of new neuroscientific brain imaging methodologies. (Recent examples include Posner and Raichle 1994/1997 and Brown and Hagoort 1999.) This field of study was set by the seminal work by Lenneberg (1967), long before the availability of these new methods. In *Biological Foundations of Language*, Lenneberg catalogues four hallmarks of maturationally guided development, and considers the development of language in light of these four characteristics. The selection included here chiefly discusses the first hallmark: developmental changes appear in regular sequences that tend to correlate with age and with milestones of development in other areas. Lenneberg's famous chart showing language and motor milestones illustrates his argument that language fits this first hallmark of maturationally guided behavior.

Gazzaniga's research (1970), based on earlier work by Sperry (1968), confirmed through modern experimental means perhaps the most basic biological foundation, i.e., the left hemisphere dominance for language. This finding remains the focus of studies in young children today, bearing critically on debates regarding the nature and degree of early brain plasticity (e.g., Neville 1995, Dehaene et al. 2002). Geschwind's paper summarizes foundational discoveries regarding areas of the left hemisphere which are correlated with specific aspects of language knowledge. It introduces the concept of "dissociation" in language knowledge and brain organization through its revelation of various aphasia types. The body of research it reviews and the classic "Wernicke-Geschwind" model of brain organization it hypothesizes have focused scientific inquiry ever since. While this model of brain organization is being questioned now (e.g., Posner and Raichle, 1994/1997), its basic discoveries and the issues it raised provide the foundation for current work, which is now aided by powerful brain imaging methods (e.g., Brown and Hagoort 1999).

Curtiss, Fromkin, Krashen, Rigler, and Rigler (1974) review the classic study of the case of "Genie," reflecting an exceptionally careful, sensitive analysis of one child's language and cognitive knowledge and development in the face of horrific deprivation and possible biological deficits. The dissociations revealed between cognitive maturation and various aspects of specific linguistic knowledge in Genie have provided invaluable scientific insights to the field, and a paradigm for studying exceptional cases to probe modularity in language acquisition. (Yamada 1990, and Smith and Tsimpli 1995 are examples of more recent studies.) At the same time, they accentuate the difficulties in separating nature and nurture in the organism.[5]

Study of the role of "input" experienced by the child remains central in the field today. (For example, see Saffran et al. 1996, and "statistical learning" paradigms based on it, and Kuhl et al. 1997. See Valian 1999 for a comprehensive review.) The critical issue of the nonexistence of "negative evidence" in language acquisition is raised and examined empirically in the classic paper by Brown and Hanlon (1970). Subsequent study evaluated the role of "positive evidence," targeting special properties of mother or caretaker speech, i.e., the "Baby Talk Register." Ferguson (1978) attempts to define precisely the properties of this special register and thus lays essential foundations for its study ever since (e.g., Pye 1986).

Gould and Marler's (1987) paper generalizes across other forms of learning in other species, and provides a model in which nature and nurture are not opposed, but wherein nature (i.e., biological programming specialized to each species for each aspect of learning) is responsible for both the possibility of and efficiency in learning. The discoveries in Gould and Marler's paper moved the field beyond the simpler Skinnerian view of learning in which no internal structure was assumed within the organism. They provide an alternative theoretical paradigm which can be extended to the study of language acquisition as well as other forms of learning. (See Gallistel 1990 for similar advances in the study of learning.)

The next set of papers in part II proposes and exemplifies various approaches to understanding the mechanisms of language acquisition and development more precisely: they consider how the child may be using the environmental input in conjunction with biological programming. "Semantic bootstrapping" is developed in the two papers by Pinker (1984 and 1989). "Syntactic bootstrapping" is first motivated in Landau and Gleitman's (1985) study of a young blind child who, marvelously, acquires the verbs "look" and "see" with ease. These two approaches, which are not necessarily mutually exclusive, emphasize early developmental mechanisms in either the semantic or the syntactic dimensions of developing language knowledge. More generally, these two approaches underlie more recent attempts to specify developmental mechanisms in which one form of linguistic knowledge builds upon another: examples include "prosodic bootstrapping," which may be reformulated as "phonological bootstrapping." (See Morgan and Demuth 1996, Gerken 1996, and Jusczyk and Kemler-Nelson 1996).

Hermine Sinclair, in her (1973) paper, raises the challenge of studying a relation between linguistic structures and Piaget's proposed abstract universal cognitive structures, and confronts the inherent difficulty in this task. In contrast, Slobin (1973) proposes a "Language Making Capacity" consisting of a set of inductive principles and/or procedures to guide the child working directly on input in the form of concrete language data. Scholars continue today to debate the degree to which such an LMC (or related system of inductive principles) could function independently of a Language Faculty consisting of specifically linguistic deductive principles.

4.3   Part III

In the area of *acquisition of morphology*, Berko Gleason's (1958) paper provides a linguistic analysis of aspects of the acquisition problem and a new method for working with children to establish their language knowledge. The "Wug test," which demonstrated children's ability to form plurals of previously unknown (nonsense) words, yielded stunning results which to this day influence the field. For example, they remain central to current debates regarding whether the child's knowledge and behavior discovered in this paper require postulating linguistic "rules" or can be accounted for by mechanical connections or associations (e.g., Rummelhart and McClelland 1987, Pinker 1999, Marcus et al. 1992, Clahsen 1999).

Roger Brown's (1973) book laid the foundation for the empirical study of language acquisition based on systematic analyses of children's language, including their natural speech. On the basis of these analyses, he and his students began to characterize regular properties of the "structure" of the child's language systems, including morphological structure, linking these properties to what was called the "telegraphic speech" phenomenon in children's early language. The databank Brown and his students began to develop (focusing on three children Adam, Eve, and Sarah) is still studied today (e.g., through CHILDES, Child Language Data Exchange System, MacWhinney and Snow 1990). The morphological phenomena observed in these data remain central to current debates about the nature of early grammatical knowledge.

In the area of *acquisition of phonology*, Eimas, Siqueland, Jusczyk, and Vigorito (1971) not only exemplify a scientific method of testing very young infants with regard to language sensitivities, but also provide a groundbreaking result, confirming that the infant's speech perception, like the adult's, is characterized by "categorical perception." Decades of research since have built on this foundation (e.g., Jusczyk 1997).

Jakobson's (1949) paper establishes theoretical foundations for the study of the acquisition of phonology. It provides a first comprehensive attempt to link formal linguistic theory to empirical study of language acquisition, i.e., to predictions and observations, including analyses of errors children make in their speech production and a theory of developmental order of acquisition. While many of Jakobson's specific predictions regarding language acquisition have now been overturned or questioned, they provided lasting scientific foundations for this field. Many of the linguistic concepts Jakobson proposed are debated (e.g., the phoneme, or the distinctive feature), yet they remain relevant to current empirical investigations and theoretical developments.

While Jakobson invoked a component of "maturation" to explain development of phonology, Smith (1975) recast the explanatory puzzle in terms of the child's mapping to the adult model. Smith (1973), on which Smith (1975) is based, remains the most comprehensive, theoretically based investigation of a child's acquisition of phonology which has yet been produced. The systematic, longitudinal analyses of the child's productions presented there not only yielded a wealth of data, but targeted issues which are central in the field today, such as the relation between a child's perception and production, and between a child's motor control and linguistic knowledge. Smith describes and elaborates fundamental discoveries in acquisition of phonology, seeking to define linguistically based "universal constraints" on children's acquisition of phonology. His discoveries continue to be recast in current theoretical terms (e.g., Spencer 1986).

Similarly, Stampe (1969), in a seemingly brief extension of linguistic analyses to the acquisition of phonology, laid out an explanatory theoretical framework which could account for much data from children's early speech production, and which is in some sense the foundation for much current work on language acquisition in the framework of "optimality theory" (e.g., Tesar and Smolensky 2002).

In the area of *acquisition of syntax*, Lashley's (1948/1951) paper led behavioral psychologists for the first time to confront the "problem of serial order," including order involved in language, e.g., word order in sentences, which varies across languages. Such serial order was not accountable through simple associations or paired transitions between units, the prevailing mechanisms of psychology at the time, and Lashley struggled with how to account for such order, suggesting that an overarching "schema" must be at work. This paper, to some degree provoking the field of "cognitive science," began to address these issues of serial order, which Chomsky would soon articulate in terms of syntax in linguistic knowledge. Inhelder and Piaget (1964), too, would argue for the need to postulate the reality of cognitive structure in order to account for seriation and would relate this to the child.

The application of grammatical analyses to young children's early sentences soon proliferated, led by the analyses of Roger Brown. His 1973 book attempts to define and capture "stages" in the child's acquisition of grammar. The early descriptive measure of "mean length of utterance," MLU, introduced there, remains productive in the field today, although its optimal definition and its relation to a child's grammatical knowledge are frequently debated.

Klima and Bellugi (1966/1971) continue the grammatical analyses of data from the same three children studied in Brown (1970), but extend them to precise syntactic operations: negation and question formation, which they characterize in terms of formal rules. Not only did this paper introduce a new level of precision and depth in syntactic analysis of children's natural speech, but its discoveries remain central to debates in current research today regarding the nature of early syntactic knowledge. In particular, Klima and Bellugi's observations of "stages" in children's production of negative and interrogative utterances in English have influenced subsequent research on these constructions in acquisition.

Finally, Bloom's (1970) paper moved the field to a new level of insight and analysis in both an empirical and a theoretical sense. Empirically, Bloom extended the scope and precision of the transcription and analysis of children's natural speech data with a view to probing syntax. Theoretically, Bloom's results in this paper forced her to recognize the necessity for a level of representation which captured syntactic and semantic components that went beyond the surface string uttered by the child. Her concept of "rich interpretation" and the syntactic analyses leading to a "reduction operation" were the start of much current work in syntax acquisition today, including new experimental work, which demonstrates that children's grammatical knowledge cannot be reduced to its surface manifestation in speech production (e.g., Gerken et al. 1990). Bloom's rich, precisely transcribed data continue to provide the basis for research in various theoretical paradigms (e.g., Hyams' 1986 studies of a "pro drop" parameter).

In the area of semantics, Eve Clark's (1982) paper both reports stunning results regarding the child's creative construction of words, i.e., the creative integration of meaning and form, and combines this extensive empirical work (including cross-linguistic comparisons) with significant linguistic analyses of the semantic conceptualization they involved. Clark's

(1978) paper represents an early approach to study of the child's developing pragmatic knowledge, an area which is just now coming more and more into the forefront of studies of language acquisition. For example, current studies of syntactic knowledge have begun to investigate interactions between the child's syntactic knowledge and developing pragmatic knowledge, although to date, linguistically informed studies of the child's pragmatic knowledge in first language acquisition remain relatively underdeveloped.

5   Towards the Future

The field of first language acquisition has developed rapidly during and beyond the time period represented by these works. A particularly important area of advancement has been in comparative cross-linguistic work on first language acquisition. This advancement may go hand in hand with advances in linguistic theory.

Until recently, scholarship in first language acquisition has most commonly been centered in individual languages.[6] What has emerged only relatively recently, over the past few decades, are comparative cross-linguistic approaches. Clark's (1982) paper in this volume provides an early example. These studies are important for several reasons. First, they allow researchers to dissociate language-specific and universal developmental patterns. For example, studying English alone might lead to the conclusion that passive sentences develop later than active sentences in general, but evidence from Sesotho (Demuth 1990) shows that this pattern is not universal. Such results lead researchers to seek deeper (rather than construction-specific) explanations for developmental trends – thus shedding light on the true nature of the human capacity for language. Second, comparative cross-linguistic study allows researchers to test a far wider range of hypotheses than could be tested by studying languages in isolation. For example, they permit controlled experiments selecting languages that differ in a significant way, allowing research to precisely test the reality of proposed linguistic features in language acquisition. Recent examples of comparative cross-linguistic research include Kuhl et al. (1997: comparative research in the area of phonology) and Boysson-Bardies and Vihman (1991). See Jakubowicz (1996) for discussion of cross-linguistic approaches to study of language acquisition.[7]

Comparative cross-linguistic research in first language acquisition has developed so far that several compilations of cross-linguistic studies now exist. Slobin (1985a, 1985b, 1992, 1997a, 1997b) has edited a five-volume compilation of cross-linguistic studies. Lust, Suñer, and Whitman (1994) and Lust, Hermon, and Kornfilt (1994) provide cross-linguistic research results in a generative linguistic framework.

We believe that scholars who seek to understand and investigate recent and current developments in the field will find that their work is enabled and enhanced by a familiarity with the works we have included here.

6   Acknowledgments

We thank our colleagues and students at Cornell University and Morehead State University for intellectual and practical support in gathering materials for this volume.

For extensive and valuable discussion of the selection criteria and the linguistic foundations of the volume, we thank James W. Gair. We are particularly indebted to the staff of Cornell University Albert R. Mann Library (especially Kornelia Vassileva Tancheva) for crucial assistance in locating and preparing many of the original sources for this volume. For many helpful comments and discussion, we thank Katherine Demuth, Suzanne Flynn, and four anonymous reviewers. We thank Shawn Lovelace for her administrative aid, and we are grateful to Annie Adams and Sarah Morrison for their support from the beginning of the project. Finally, for their expert guidance and constant encouragement, we thank Tami Kaplan and Sarah Coleman.

Notes

1   We assume that such core linguistic insights and findings are also foundational to these other fields of study.
2   Earlier roots of the debate are found in Harris (1955), on which Saffran et al. (1996) is based. Today, research bearing on this debate ranges from reports of created Nicaraguan Sign Language (Kegl et al. 1999) to a wide variety of attempts to define an "evaluation metric" or "triggers" for parameter setting in a generative framework (e.g., Fodor 1998, Lightfoot 1991, Frank and Kapur 1996).
3   These studies differ from research on language acquisition that ultimately aims to shed light, for example, on human social systems or on behavioral psychology. The differences exist despite the mutual dependence between linguistics and these other fields, and despite the need for these fields to inform each other's approaches.
4   *The Growth of Language* (Lust, forthcoming) represents a course in language acquisition organized around this structure.
5   The appendices in this article provide a particularly good example of the rich original data offered by many of the selections in this volume.
6   This scholarship has frequently focused on English, although it is not limited to English, as the range of work in this volume demonstrates.
7   The growing emphasis on comparative cross-linguistic work is evident in other areas of psycholinguistics as well, including second language acquisition (e.g., Flynn 1987) and language processing (e.g., Mazuka 1998).

References

Bloomfield, L. 1926. A set of postulates for the science of language. *Language* 2, 153–64. Reprinted in M. Joos (ed.), *Readings in Linguistics* (4th edn., 1966). Washington, DC: American Council of Learned Societies, pp. 26–31.

Bloomfield, L. 1993. *Language*. New York: Henry Holt.

Boysson-Bardies, B. de, and Vihman, M. M. 1991. Adaptation to language: evidence from babbling and first words in four languages. *Language* 67, 297–319.

Braine, Martin. 1994. Is nativism sufficient? *Journal of Child Language* 21:1, 9–31.

Brown, Colin M. and Hagoort, P. (eds.) 1999. *The Neurocognition of Language*. Oxford: Oxford University Press.

Chomsky, N. 1986. *Knowledge of Language*. New York: Praeger.

Clahsen, H. 1999. Lexical entries and rules of language: a multidisciplinary study of German inflection. *Behavioral and Brain Sciences* 22: 6, 991–1046.

Dehaene-Lambertz, C., Dehaene, S., and Hertz-Pannier, L. 2002. Functional neuroimaging of speech perception in infants. *Science* 298, 2013–15.

Demuth, K. 1990. Subject, topic and the Sesotho passive. *Journal of Child Language* 17, 67–84.

Elman, J., Bates, E., Johnson, M., Karmiloff-Smith, A., Parisi, D., and Plunkett, K. 1996. *Rethinking Innateness*. Cambridge, Mass.: Bradford Books/MIT Press.

Flynn, S. 1987. *A Parameter-Setting Model of L2 Acquisition: Experimental Studies in Anaphora*. Dordrecht: Reidel.

Fodor, J. D. 1998. Unambiguous triggers. *Linguistic Inquiry* 29, 1–36.

Frank, R., and Kapur, S. 1996. On the use of triggers in parameter setting. *Linguistic Inquiry* 27, 623–60.

Gallistel, C. R. 1990. *The Organization of Learning*. Cambridge, Mass.: Bradford Books/MIT Press.

Gerken, L. 1996. Phonological and distributional information in syntax acquisition. In J. Morgan and K. Demuth (eds.), *Signal to Syntax*. Hillsdale, NJ: Lawrence Erlbaum Associates, pp. 411–26.

Gerken, L. A., Landau, B., and Remez, R. E. 1990. Function morphemes in young children's speech perception and production. *Developmental Psychology* 27, 204–16.

Harris, Z. 1955. From phoneme to morpheme. *Language* 31, 190–222.

Hyams, N. 1986. *Language Acquisition and the Theory of Parameters*. Dordrecht: Reidel.

Inhelder, B., and Piaget, J. 1964. *The Early Growth of Logic in the Child*, trans. E. A. Lunzer and D. Papert. London: Routledge and Kegan Paul.

Jakubowicz, C. 1996. Crosslinguistic investigation. In D. McDaniel, C. McKee, and H. S. Cairns (eds.), *Methods for Assessing Children's Syntax*. Cambridge, Mass.: MIT Press. pp. 257–86.

Jusczyk, P. 1997. *The Discovery of Spoken Language*. Cambridge, Mass.: Bradford Books/MIT Press.

Jusczyk, P. and Kemler-Nelson, D. 1996. Syntactic units, prosody and psychological reality during infancy. In J. L. Morgan and K. Demuth (eds.), *Signal to Syntax*. Hillsdale, NJ: Lawrence Erlbaum Associates.

Kegl, J., Senghas, A., and Coppola, M. 1999. Creation through contact: sign language emergence and sign language change in Nicaragua. In M. DeGraff (ed.), *Language Creation and Language Change*. Cambridge, Mass.: MIT Press.

Kuhl, P., Andruski, J., Chistovich, I., Chistovich, L., Ryskina, V., Stolyarova, E., Sundberg, V., and Lacerda, F. 1997. Cross-language analysis of phonetic units in language addressed to infants. *Science* 277, 684–6.

Landau, B., and Gleitman, L. R. 1985. *Language and Experience: Evidence from the Blind Child*. Cambridge, Mass.: Harvard University Press.

Lightfoot, D. 1991. *How to Set Parameters: Arguments from Language Change*. Cambridge, Mass.: MIT Press/Bradford Books.

Lust, B. (forthcoming) *The Growth of Language*. Cambridge University Press.

Lust, B., Hermon, G., and Kornfilt, J. (eds.) 1994. *Syntactic Theory and First Language Acquisition: Cross-Linguistic Perspectives*. Volume 2. *Binding, Dependencies and Learnability*. Hillsdale, NJ: Lawrence Erlbaum Associates.

Lust, B., Suñer, M., and Whitman, J. (eds.) 1994. *Syntactic Theory and First Language Acquisition: Cross-Linguistic Perspectives*. Volume 1. *Heads, Projections, and Learnability*. Hillsdale, NJ: Lawrence Erlbaum Associates.

MacWhinney, B., and Snow, C. 1990. The child language data exchange system: an update. *Journal of Child Language* 17, 457–72.

Marcus, G., Pinker, S., Ullman, M., Hollander, M., Rosen, T. J., and Xu, F. 1992. *Over-regularization in Language Acquisition*. Monographs of the Society of Research in Child Development. Serial number 228. 57: 4.

Mazuka, R. 1998. *The Development of Language Processing Strategies: A Cross-Linguistic Study Between Japanese and English*. Hillsdale, NJ: Lawrence Erlbaum Associates.

Morgan, J., and Demuth, K. (eds.) 1996. *Signal to Syntax. Bootstrapping from Speech to Grammar in Early Acquisition*. Hillsdale, NJ: Lawrence Erlbaum Associates.

Neville, H. J. 1995. Developmental specificity in neurocognitive development in humans. In M. S. Gazzaniga (ed.), *The Cognitive Neurosciences*. Cambridge, Mass.: MIT Press, pp. 219–31.

Pinker, S. 1994. *The Language Instinct*. New York: William Morrow.

Pinker, S. 1999. *How the Mind Works*. New York: W. W. Norton.

Posner, M., and Raichle, M. 1994/1997. *Images of Mind*. New York: Scientific American Library.

Pye, C. 1986. Quiche Mayan speech to children. *Journal of Child Language* 13, 85–100.

Reuland, E., and Abraham, W. (eds.) 1993. *Knowledge and Language*. Volume 1: *From Orwell's Problem to Plato's Problem*. Dordrecht: Kluwer.

Ritchie, W., and Bhatia, T. (eds.) (1999) *Handbook of Child Language Acquisition*. New York: Academic Press.

Rummelhart, D., and McClelland, J. 1987. Learning the past tenses of English verbs: Implicit rules or parallel distributed processing. In B. MacWhinney (ed.), *Mechanisms of Language Acquisition*. Hillsdale, NJ: Lawrence Erlbaum Associates, pp. 195–248.

Saffran, J., Aslin, R., and Newport, E. 1996. Statistical learning by 8-month-old infants. *Science* 274, 1926–8.

Sapir, E. 1921/1949. *Language: An Introduction to the Study of Speech*. New York: Harcourt Brace Jovanovich.

Saussure, F. de 1959. *Course in General Linguistics*. New York: Philosophical Library.

Slobin, D. (ed.) 1985a. *The Crosslinguistic Study of Language Acquisition*. Volume 1. Hillsdale, NJ: Lawrence Erlbaum Associates.

Slobin, D. (ed.) 1985b. *The Crosslinguistic Study of Language Acquisition*. Volume 2. *Theoretical Issues*. Hillsdale, NJ: Lawrence Erlbaum Associates.

Slobin, D. (ed.) 1992. *The Crosslinguistic Study of Language Acquisition*. Volume 3. Hillsdale, NJ: Lawrence Erlbaum Associates.

Slobin, D. (ed.) 1997a. *The Crosslinguistic Study of Language Acquisition*. Volume 4. Hillsdale, NJ: Lawrence Erlbaum Associates.

Slobin, D. (ed.) 1997b. *The Crosslinguistic study of Language Acquisition*. Volume 5. *Expanding the Contexts*. Hillsdale, NJ: Lawrence Erlbaum Associates.

Smith, N. V. 1973. *The Acquisition of Phonology. A Case Study*. Cambridge: Cambridge University Press.

Smith, N., and Tsimpli, I.-M. 1995. *The Mind of a Savant*. Oxford: Blackwell.

Spencer, A. 1986. Towards a theory of phonological development. *Lingua* 68, 3–38.

Sperry, R. W. 1968. Mental unity following surgical disconnection of the cerebral hemispheres. *The Harvey Lecture Series 62*. New York: Academic Press, pp. 292–323.

Tesar, B., and Smolensky, P. 2000. *Learnability in Optimality Theory*. Cambridge, Mass.: MIT Press.

Valian, V. 1999. Input and language acquisition. In W. Ritchie and T. Bhatia (eds.), *Handbook of Child Language Acquisition*. New York: Academic Press, pp. 497–530.

Yamada, J. E. 1990. *Laura: A Case for the Modularity of Language*. Cambridge, Mass.: MIT Press/Bradford Books.

Part I

Theory of Language Acquisition

1

Knowledge of Language as a Focus of Inquiry

Noam Chomsky

The study of language has a long and rich history, extending over thousands of years. This study has frequently been understood as an inquiry into the nature of mind and thought on the assumption that "languages are the best mirror of the human mind" (Leibniz). A common conception was that "with respect to its *substance* grammar is one and the same in all languages, though it does vary *accidentally*" (Roger Bacon). The invariant "substance" was often taken to be the mind and its acts; particular languages use various mechanisms – some rooted in human reason, others arbitrary and adventitious – for the expression of thought, which is a constant across languages. One leading eighteenth-century rational grammarian defined "general grammar" as a deductive science concerned with "the immutable and general principles of spoken or written language" and their consequences; it is "prior to all languages," because its principles "are the same as those that direct human reason in its intellectual operations" (Beauzée). Thus, "the science of language does not differ at all from the science of thought." "Particular grammar" is not a true "science" in the sense of this rationalist tradition because it is not based solely on universal necessary laws; it is an "art" or technique that shows how given languages realize the general principles of human reason. As John Stuart Mill later expressed the same leading idea, "The principles and rules of grammar are the means by which the forms of language are made to correspond with the universal forms of thought. . . . The structure of every sentence is a lesson in logic." Others, particularly during the Romantic period, argued that the nature and content of thought are determined in part by the devices made available for its expression in particular languages. These devices may include contributions of individual genius that affect the "character" of a language, enriching its means of expression and the thoughts expressed without affecting its "form," its sound system and rules of word and sentence formation (Humboldt).

With regard to the acquisition of knowledge, it was widely held that the mind is not "so much to be filled therewith from without, like a vessel, as to be kindled and awaked" (Ralph Cudworth); "The growth of knowledge . . . [rather resembles] . . . the growth of

From *Knowledge of Language: Its Nature, Origin, and Use*. New York: Praeger, 1986, pp. 1–14.

Fruit; however external causes may in some degree cooperate, it is the internal vigour, and virtue of the tree, that must ripen the juices to their just maturity" (James Harris).[1] Applied to language, this essentially Platonistic conception would suggest that knowledge of a particular language grows and matures along a course that is in part intrinsically determined, with modifications reflecting observed usage, rather in the manner of the visual system or other bodily "organs" that develop along a course determined by genetic instructions under the triggering and shaping effects of environmental factors.

With the exception of the relativism of the Romantics, such ideas were generally regarded with much disapproval in the mainstream of linguistic research by the late nineteenth century and on through the 1950s. In part, this attitude developed under the impact of a rather narrowly construed empiricism and later behaviorist and operationalist doctrine. In part, it resulted from the quite real and impressive successes of historical and descriptive studies conducted within a narrower compass, specifically, the discovery of "sound laws" that provided much understanding of the history of languages and their relationships. In part, it was a natural consequence of the investigation of a much richer variety of languages than were known to earlier scholars, languages that appeared to violate many of the allegedly *a priori* conceptions of the earlier rationalist tradition.[2] After a century of general neglect or obloquy, ideas resembling those of the earlier tradition re-emerged (initially, with virtually no awareness of historical antecedents) in the mid-1950s, with the development of what came to be called "generative grammar" – again, reviving a long-lapsed and largely forgotten tradition.[3]

The generative grammar of a particular language (where "generative" means nothing more than "explicit") is a theory that is concerned with the form and meaning of expressions of this language. One can imagine many different kinds of approach to such questions, many points of view that might be adopted in dealing with them. Generative grammar limits itself to certain elements of this larger picture. Its standpoint is that of individual psychology. It is concerned with those aspects of form and meaning that are determined by the "language faculty," which is understood to be a particular component of the human mind. The nature of this faculty is the subject matter of a general theory of linguistic structure that aims to discover the framework of principles and elements common to attainable human languages; this theory is now often called "universal grammar" (UG), adapting a traditional term to a new context of inquiry. UG may be regarded as a characterization of the genetically determined language faculty. One may think of this faculty as a "language acquisition device," an innate component of the human mind that yields a particular language through interaction with presented experience, a device that converts experience into a system of knowledge attained: knowledge of one or another language.

The study of generative grammar represented a significant shift of focus in the approach to problems of language. Put in the simplest terms, to be elaborated below, the shift of focus was from behavior or the products of behavior to states of the mind/brain that enter into behavior. If one chooses to focus attention on this latter topic, the central concern becomes knowledge of language: its nature, origins, and use.

The three basic questions that arise, then, are these:

(i)	What constitutes knowledge of language?	(1)
(ii)	How is knowledge of language acquired?	
(iii)	How is knowledge of language put to use?	

The answer to the first question is given by a particular generative grammar, a theory concerned with the state of the mind/brain of the person who knows a particular language. The answer to the second is given by a specification of UG along with an account of the ways in which its principles interact with experience to yield a particular language; UG is a theory of the "initial state" of the language faculty, prior to any linguistic experience. The answer to the third question would be a theory of how the knowledge of language attained enters into the expression of thought and the understanding of presented specimens of language, and derivatively, into communication and other special uses of language.

So far, this is nothing more than the outline of a research program that takes up classical questions that had been put aside for many years. As just described, it should not be particularly controversial, since it merely expresses an interest in certain problems and offers a preliminary analysis of how they might be confronted, although as is often the case, the initial formulation of a problem may prove to be far-reaching in its implications, and ultimately controversial as it is developed.

Some elements of this picture may appear to be more controversial than they really are. Consider, for example, the idea that there is a language faculty a component of the mind/brain that yields knowledge of language given presented experience. It is not at issue that humans attain knowledge of English, Japanese, and so forth, while rocks, birds, or apes do not under the same (or indeed any) conditions. There is, then, some property of the mind/brain that differentiates humans from rocks, birds, or apes. Is this a distinct "language faculty" with specific structure and properties, or, as some believe, is it the case that humans acquire language merely by applying generalized learning mechanisms of some sort, perhaps with greater efficiency or scope than other organisms? These are not topics for speculation or *a priori* reasoning but for empirical inquiry, and it is clear enough how to proceed: namely, by facing the questions of (1). We try to determine what is the system of knowledge that has been attained and what properties must be attributed to the initial state of the mind/brain to account for its attainment. Insofar as these properties are language-specific, either individually or in the way they are organized and composed, there is a distinct language faculty.

Generative grammar is sometimes referred to as a theory, advocated by this or that person. In fact, it is not a theory any more than chemistry is a theory. Generative grammar is a topic, which one may or may not choose to study. Of course, one can adopt a point of view from which chemistry disappears as a discipline (perhaps it is all done by angels with mirrors). In this sense, a decision to study chemistry does stake out a position on matters of fact. Similarly, one may argue that the topic of generative grammar does not exist, although it is hard to see how to make this position minimally plausible. Within the study of generative grammar there have been many changes and differences of opinion, often reversion to ideas that had been abandoned and were later reconstructed in a different light. Evidently, this is a healthy phenomenon indicating that the discipline is alive, although it is sometimes, oddly, regarded as a serious deficiency, a sign that something is wrong with the basic approach. I will review some of these changes as we proceed.

In the mid-1950s, certain proposals were advanced as to the form that answers to the questions of (1) might take, and a research program was inaugurated to investigate the adequacy of these proposals and to sharpen and apply them. This program was one of the strands that led to the development of the cognitive sciences in the contemporary sense, sharing with other approaches the belief that certain aspects of the mind/brain can be usefully construed on the model of computational systems of rules that form and modify representations, and that are put to use in interpretation and action. From its origins (or with a longer perspective, one might say "its reincarnation") about 30 years ago, the study of generative grammar was undertaken with an eye to gaining some insight into the nature and origins of systems of knowledge, belief, and understanding more broadly, in the hope that these general questions could be illuminated by a detailed invest-igation of the special case of human language.

This research program has since been running its course, along a number of differ-ent paths. I will be concerned here with only one of these, with the problems it faced and the steps that were taken in an effort to deal with them. During the past 5–6 years, these efforts have converged in a somewhat unexpected way, yielding a rather different conception of the nature of language and its mental representation, one that offers interesting answers to a range of empirical questions and opens a variety of new ones to inquiry while suggesting a rethinking of the character of others. This is what accounts for an unmistakable sense of energy and anticipation – and also uncertainty – which is reminiscent of the period when the study of generative grammar in the modern sense was initiated about 30 years ago. Some of the work now being done is quite different in character from what had previously been possible as well as considerably broader in empirical scope, and it may be that results of a rather new kind are within reach, or at least within sight. I would like to try to explain why this may be so, beginning with some remarks about goals, achievements, and failures of the past years.

To avoid misunderstanding, I am not speaking here about all of the study of language but rather of generative grammar, and even here I will not attempt anything like a real history of the course of research but rather will give a somewhat idealized picture that is in part clearer in retrospect than it was at the time. Furthermore, what I am describ-ing has represented a minority position throughout, and probably still does, although in my view it is the correct one. A number of different current approaches share prop-erties of the sort discussed here and may be intertranslatable to a considerable extent. I will not consider this important topic here and will also make no effort to survey the range of ideas, often conflicting, that fall within the particular tendency that I will discuss – what is now sometimes called "government-binding (GB) theory."

I want to consider, then, two major conceptual shifts, one that inaugurated the contemporary study of generative grammar, and a second, more theory-internal, that is now in process and that offers some new perspectives on traditional problems.[4]

Traditional and structuralist grammar did not deal with the questions of (1), the former because of its implicit reliance on the unanalyzed intelligence of the reader, the latter because of its narrowness of scope. The concerns of traditional and generative grammar are, in a certain sense, complementary: a good traditional or pedagogical gram-mar provides a full list of exceptions (irregular verbs, etc.), paradigms and examples of regular constructions, and observations at various levels of detail and generality about the form and meaning of expressions. But it does not examine the question of how the reader of the grammar uses such information to attain the knowledge that is used to form and interpret new expressions, or the question of the nature and elements of this knowledge: essentially the questions of (1), above. Without too much exaggeration, one could describe such a grammar as a structured and organized version of the data presented to a child learning a language, with some general commentary and often insightful observations. Generative grammar, in contrast, is concerned primarily with the intelligence of the reader, the principles and procedures brought to bear to attain full knowledge of a language. Structuralist theories, both in the European and American traditions, did concern themselves with analytic procedures for deriving aspects of grammar from data, as in the procedural theories of Nikolay Trubetzkoy, Zellig Harris, Bernard Bloch, and others, but primarily in the areas of phonology and morphology. The procedures suggested were seriously inadequate and in any event could not possibly be understood (and were not intended) to provide an answer to question (1ii), even in the narrower domains where most work was concentrated. Nor was there an effort to determine what was involved in offering a comprehensive account of the knowledge of the speaker/hearer.

As soon as these questions were squarely faced, a wide range of new phenomena were discovered, including quite simple ones that had passed unnoticed, and severe problems arose that had previously been ignored or seriously misunderstood. A standard belief 30 years ago was that language acquisition is a case of "overlearning." Language was regarded as a habit system, one that was assumed to be much overdetermined by available evidence. Production and interpretation of new forms was taken to be a straightforward matter of analogy, posing no problems of principle.[5] Attention to the questions of (1) quickly reveals that exactly the opposite is the case: language poses in a sharp and clear form what has sometimes been called "Plato's problem," the problem of "poverty of stimulus," of accounting for the richness, complexity, and specificity of shared knowledge, given the limitations of the data available. This difference of perception concerning where the problem lies – overlearning or poverty of evidence – reflects very clearly the effect of the shift of focus that inaugurated the study of generative grammar.

A great many examples have been given over the years to illustrate what clearly is the fundamental problem: the problem of poverty of evidence. A familiar example is the structure-dependence of rules, the fact that without instruction or direct evidence, children unerringly use computationally complex structure-dependent rules rather than computationally simple rules that involve only the predicate "leftmost" in a linear sequence of words.[6] To take some other examples, to which we will return, consider sentences (2)–(7):

I wonder who [the men expected to see them]	(2)
[the men expected to see them]	(3)
John ate an apple	(4)
John ate	(5)
John is too stubborn to talk to Bill	(6)
John is too stubborn to talk to	(7)

Both (2) and (3) include the clause bounded by brackets, but only in (2) may the pronoun *them* be referentially dependent on the antecedent *the men*; in (3) the pronoun is understood as referring in some manner indicated in the situational or discourse context, but not to the men. Numerous facts of this sort, falling under what is now generally called "binding theory," are known without relevant experience to differentiate the cases. Such facts pose a serious problem that was not recognized in earlier work: How does every child know, unerringly, to interpret the clause differently in the two cases? And why does no pedagogic grammar have to draw the learner's attention to such facts (which were, in fact, noticed only quite recently, in the course of the study of explicit rule systems in generative grammar)?

Turning to examples (4)–(7), sentence (5) means that John ate something or other, a fact that one might explain on the basis of a simple inductive procedure: *ate* takes an object, as in (4), and if the object is missing, it is understood as arbitrary. Applying the same inductive procedure to (6) and (7), it should be that (7) means that John is so stubborn that he (John) will not talk to some arbitrary person, on the analogy of (6). But the meaning is, in fact, quite different: namely, that John is so stubborn that some arbitrary person won't talk to him (John). Again, this is known without training or relevant evidence.[7]

The situation is, in fact, more complex. Although plausible, the inductive procedure suggested for the relatively straightforward examples (4)–(5) does not seem correct. As noted by Howard Lasnik, the word *eat* has a somewhat different meaning in its intransitive usage, something like *dine*. One can say "John ate his shoe," but "John ate" cannot be understood to include this case. The observation is general for such cases. The intransitive forms differ from normal intransitives in other respects; for example, we can form "the dancing bear" (corresponding to "the bear that dances"), but not "the eating man" (corresponding to "the man who eats").[8] Such facts pose further problems of poverty of stimulus.

Children do not make errors about the interpretation of such sentences as (6)–(7) past a certain stage of development, and if they did, the errors would largely be uncorrectable. It is doubtful that even the most compendious traditional or teaching grammar notes such simple facts as those illustrated in (2)–(7), and such observations lie far beyond the domain of structural grammars. A wide variety of examples of this sort immediately come to attention when one faces the questions formulated in (1).

Knowledge of language is often characterized as a practical ability to speak and under-stand, so that questions (1i) and (1iii) are closely related, perhaps identified. Ordinary usage makes a much sharper distinction between the two questions, and is right to do so. Two people may share exactly the same knowledge of language but differ markedly in their ability to put this knowledge to use. Ability to use language may improve or decline without any change in knowledge. This ability may also be impaired, selectively or in general, with no loss of knowledge, a fact that would become clear if injury leading to impairment recedes and lost ability is recovered. Many such considerations support the commonsense assumption that knowledge cannot be properly described as a practical ability. Furthermore, even if this view could somehow be maintained, it would leave open all of the serious questions. Thus, what is the nature of the "practical ability" man-ifested in our interpretation of the sentences (2)–(7), how is it properly described, and how is it acquired?

Often it is not immediately obvious what our knowledge of language entails in par-ticular cases, a fact illustrated even with short and simple sentences such as (8)–(10):

his wife loves her husband   (8)
John is too clever to expect us to catch Bill   (9)
John is too clever to expect us to catch   (10)

In the case of (8), it takes some thought to determine whether *his* can be referentially dependent on *her husband* if *her* is dependent on *his wife* – that is, if the reference of either *he* or *she* is not somehow contextually indicated.[9] Examples (9) and (10) are, in fact, analogous to (6) and (7), respectively, but again, it takes some thought to discover that (10) means that John is so clever that an arbitrary person cannot expect us to catch him (John), although it is clear at once that it does not mean that John is so clever that he (John) cannot catch some arbitrary person, on the analogy of (9) (and (4), (5)). Our abilities seem limited somehow in such cases (and there are far more complex ones), but it would make little sense to speak of our knowledge of language as "limited" in any comparable way.

Suppose we insist on speaking of knowledge of language as a practical ability to speak and understand. Then normal usage must be revised in numerous cases such as those just discussed. Suppose that Jones takes a public speaking course and improves his ability to speak and understand without any change in his knowledge of English, as we would describe the situation in normal usage. We must now revise this commonsense usage and say, rather, that Jones has improved his ability$_1$ to use his ability$_2$ to speak and understand; similar translations are required in the other cases. But the two occurrences of "ability" in this description are hardly more than homonyms. Ability$_1$ is ability in the normal sense of the word: it can improve or decline, can be inadequate to determine consequences of knowledge, and so on. Ability$_2$, however, remains stable while our ability to use it changes, and we have this kind of "ability" even when we are unable to detect what it entails in concrete cases. In short, the neologism "ability$_2$" is invested with all the properties of knowledge. Note that there are cases when we do speak of abilities that we cannot put to use: for example, the case of swimmers who cannot swim because their hands are tied, although they retain the ability to swim. The cases in question are not of this sort, however.

The purpose of the attempt to reduce knowledge to ability is, presumably, to avoid problematic features that seem to inhere in the concept of knowledge, to show that these can be explained in dispositional or other terms more closely related to actual behavior (whether this is possible even in the case of ability$_1$, the normal sense, is another question). But nothing of the sort is achieved by this departure from ordinary usage; the problems remain, exactly as before, now embedded in terminological confusion. The task of determining the nature of our knowledge (= ability$_2$), and accounting for its origins and use, remains exactly as challenging as before, despite the terminological innovations.

Other examples similar to (8)–(10) raise further questions. Consider the following sentences:

John is too stubborn to expect anyone to talk to Bill (11)

John is too stubborn to visit anyone who talked to Bill (12)

Suppose we delete *Bill* from (11) and (12), yielding (13) and (14), respectively:

John is too stubborn to expect anyone to talk to (13)

John is too stubborn to visit anyone who talked to (14)

Sentence (13) is structurally analogous to (10), and is understood in the same manner: it means that John is so stubborn that an arbitrary person would not expect anyone to talk to him (John). "By analogy," then, we would expect sentence (14) to mean that John is so stubborn that an arbitrary person would not visit anyone who talked to him (John). But it does not have that meaning; in fact, it is gibberish. Here we have a double failure of analogy. Sentence (14) is not understood "on the analogy" of (4), (5), (6), (9), and (12) (hence meaning that John is so stubborn that he (John) would not visit anyone who talked to some arbitrary person), nor is it understood "on the analogy" of (7), (10), and (13); rather, it has no interpretation at all. And while the status of (11), (12), and (14) is immediately obvious, it takes some thought or preparation to see that (13) has the interpretation it does have, and thus to determine the consequences of our knowledge in this case.

Again, these are facts that we know, however difficult it may be to determine that our system of knowledge has these consequences. We know these facts without instruction or even direct evidence, surely without correction of error by the speech community. It would be absurd to try to teach such facts as these to people learning English as a second language, just as no one taught them to us or even presented us with evidence that could yield this knowledge by any generally reliable procedure. This is knowledge without grounds, without good reasons or support by reliable procedures in any general or otherwise useful sense of these notions. Were we to insist that knowledge is a kind of ability, we would have to claim that we lack the ability to understand "John is too stubborn to talk to" as meaning "John is too stubborn to talk to someone or other" (on the analogy of "John ate an apple" – "John ate"), and that we lack the ability to understand (14) on the analogy of "John ate an apple" – "John ate" (so that it means that John is too stubborn to visit anyone who talked to someone or other) or on the analogy of "John is too stubborn to talk to," with the "inversion strategy" that we somehow use in this case (so that (14) means that John is too stubborn for someone or other to visit anyone who talked to him, John). But these would be odd claims, to say the least. These are not failures of ability. It is not that we are too weak, or lack some special skill that could be acquired. We are perfectly capable of associating the sentence (14), for example, with either of the two meanings that would be provided "by analogy" (or others), but we know that these are not the associations that our knowledge of the language provides; ability is one thing, knowledge something quite different. The system of knowledge that has somehow developed in our minds has certain consequences, not others; it relates sound and meaning and assigns structural properties to physical events in certain ways, not others.

It seems that there is little hope in accounting for our knowledge in terms of such ideas as analogy, induction, association, reliable procedures, good reasons, and justification in any generally useful sense, or in terms of "generalized learning mechanisms" (if such exist). And it seems that we should follow normal usage in distinguishing clearly between knowledge and ability to use that knowledge. We should, so it appears, think of knowledge of language as a certain state of the mind/brain, a relatively stable element in transitory mental states once it is attained; furthermore, as a state of some distinguishable faculty of the mind – the language faculty – with its specific properties, structure, and organization, one "module" of the mind.[10]

Notes

1   On these and many other discussions, primarily in the seventeenth–nineteenth centuries, see Chomsky (1966). For discussion of some misinterpretation of this work, see Bracken (1984).

2   The alleged *a priorism* of work in this tradition has often been exaggerated. See Chomsky (1966) and more recent work for discussion of this point.

3   The tradition, in this case, is a different one, represented in its most advanced form in the early work of the Indian grammarians 2,500 years ago. See Kiparsky (1982). A modern counterpart is Bloomfield (1939), which was radically different in character from the work of the period and inconsistent with his own theories of language, and remained virtually without influence or even awareness despite Bloomfield's great prestige.

4   See Newmeyer (1980) for one view of the history of this period prior to the second major conceptual shift; and for some more personal comments, the introduction to Chomsky (1975a), a somewhat abbreviated version of a 1956 revision of a 1955 manuscript, both unpublished. See Lightfoot (1982) and Hornstein and Lightfoot (1981) for discussion of the general backgrounds for much current work, and Radford (1981) for an introduction to the work that led to the second conceptual shift. See Chomsky (1981) for a more technical presentation of some of the ideas that entered into this conceptual shift and van Riemsdijk and Williams (1985) for an introductory study of this current work.

5   Although basically adopting this point of view, W. V. Quine, however, argued that there is a very severe, in fact, insuperable problem of underdetermination affecting all aspects of language and grammar, and much of psychology more generally (Quine, 1960, 1972). I do not think that he succeeded in showing that some novel form of indeterminacy affects the study of language beyond the normal underdetermination of theory by evidence; his own formulations of the thesis furthermore involve internal inconsistency (see Chomsky, 1975b, 1980). There seems no reason on these grounds, then, to distinguish linguistics or psychology in principle from the natural sciences in accordance with what Hockney (1975) calls Quine's "bifurcation thesis." A similar conclusion is reached by Putnam (1981) in his abandonment of metaphysical realism on Quinean grounds. His step also abandons the bifurcation thesis, although in the opposite direction.

6   See Chomsky (1975a). See Crain and Nakayama (1984) for empirical study of this question with 3–5-year-old children.

7   The reaction to such phenomena, also unnoticed until recently, again illustrates the difference of outlook of structuralist-descriptive and generative grammar. For some practitioners of the former, the statement of the facts, which is straightforward enough once they are observed, is the answer – nothing else is necessary; for the latter, the statement of the facts poses the problem to be solved. Cf. Ney (1983), particularly, his puzzlement about the "peculiar view of grammar [that] unnecessarily complicates the whole matter" by seeking an explanation for the facts. Note that there is no question of right or wrong here, but rather of topic of inquiry.

8   In early work, such facts were used to motivate an analysis of intransitives such as *eat* as derived from corresponding transitives by a system of ordered rules that excluded the unwanted cases; see Chomsky (1962).

9   On structures of this type, and problems of binding theory, more generally, see Higginbotham (1983), among much other work.

10 See Fodor (1983). But it is too narrow to regard the "language module" as an input system in Fodor's sense, if only because it is used in speaking and thought. We might consider supplementing this picture by adding an "output system," but plainly this must be linked to

the input system; we do not expect a person to speak only English and understand only Japanese. That is, the input and output systems must each access a fixed system of knowledge. The latter, however, is a central system which has essential problems of modularity, a fact that brings the entire picture into question. Furthermore, even regarded as an input system, the language module does not appear to have the property of rapidity of access that Fodor discusses, as indicated by (8)–(14). Note also that even if Fodor is right in believing that there is a sharp distinction between modules in his sense and "the rest," which is holistic in several respects, it does not follow that the residue is unstructured. In fact, this seems highly unlikely, if only because of the "epistemic boundedness" that he notes. Many other questions arise concerning Fodor's very intriguing discussion of these issues, which I will not pursue here.

References

Bloomfield, L. 1939. Meromini Morphophonemics. *Travaux du cercle linguistique de Prague*.

Bracken, H. 1984. *Mind and Language*. Dordrecht: Foris.

Chomsky, N. 1962. A transformational approach to syntax. In A. A. Hill (ed.), *Proceedings of the Third Texas Conference on Problems of Linguistic Analysis in English (1958)*. Austin: University of Texas Press.

Chomsky, N. 1966. *Cartesian Linguistics*. New York: Harper and Row.

Chomsky, N. 1975a. *Logical Structure of Linguistic Theory*. New York: Plenum. [Drawn from an unpublished 1955–6 manuscript.]

Chomsky, N. 1975b. *Reflections on Language*. New York: Pantheon.

Chomsky, N. 1980. *Rules and Representations*. New York: Columbia University Press.

Chomsky, N. 1981. *Lectures on Government and Binding*. Dordrecht: Foris.

Crain, S., and Nakayama, M. 1984. Structure dependence in grammar formation. Unpublished manuscript, University of Connecticut.

Fodor, J. 1983. *The Modularity of Mind*. Cambridge, Mass.: MIT Press.

Higginbotham, J. 1983. Logical form, binding, and nominals. *Linguistic Inquiry* 14:3, 395–420.

Hockney, D. 1975. The bifurcation of scientific theories and indeterminacy of translation. *Philosophy of Science* 42:4, 411–27.

Hornstein, D., and Lightfoot, D. (eds.) 1981. *Explanation in Linguistics*. London: Longman.

Kiparsky, P. 1982. *Some Theoretical Problems in Panini's Grammar*. Poona: Bhandarkar Oriental Research Institute.

Lightfoot, D. 1982. *The Language Lottery*. Cambridge, Mass.: MIT Press.

Newmeyer, F. J. 1980. *Linguistic Theory in America*. New York: Academic Press.

Ney, J. 1983. Review of Chomsky (1982). *Language Sciences* 5:2, 219–32.

Putnam, H. 1981. *Reason, Truth and History*. Cambridge: Cambridge University Press.

Quine, W. V. 1960. *Word and Order*. Cambridge, Mass.: MIT Press.

Quine, W. V. 1972. Methodological reflections on current linguistic theory. In D. Davidson and G. Harman (eds.), *Semantics of Natural Language*. New York: Humanities Press, pp. 442–54.

Radford, A. 1981. *Transformational Syntax*. Cambridge: Cambridge University Press.

Riemsdijk, H. van, and Williams, E. 1985. *Introduction to the Theory of Grammar*. Cambridge, Mass.: MIT Press.

2

A Review of B. F. Skinner's
Verbal Behavior

Noam Chomsky

1. A great many linguists and philosophers concerned with language have expressed the hope that their studies might ultimately be embedded in a framework provided by behaviorist psychology, and that refractory areas of investigation, particularly those in which meaning is involved, will in this way be opened up to fruitful exploration. Since this volume is the first large-scale attempt to incorporate the major aspects of linguistic behavior within a behaviorist framework, it merits and will undoubtedly receive careful attention. Skinner is noted for his contributions to the study of animal behavior. The book under review is the product of study of linguistic behavior extending over more than twenty years. Earlier versions of it have been fairly widely circulated, and there are quite a few references in the psychological literature to its major ideas.

The problem to which this book is addressed is that of giving a "functional analysis" of verbal behavior. By functional analysis, Skinner means identification of the variables that control this behavior and specification of how they interact to determine a particular verbal response. Furthermore, the controlling variables are to be described completely in terms of such notions as stimulus, reinforcement, deprivation, which have been given a reasonably clear meaning in animal experimentation. In other words, the goal of the book is to provide a way to predict and control verbal behavior by observing and manipulating the physical environment of the speaker.

Skinner feels that recent advances in the laboratory study of animal behavior permit us to approach this problem with a certain optimism, since "the basic processes and relations which give verbal behavior its special characteristics are now fairly well understood . . . the results [of this experimental work) have been surprisingly free of species restrictions. Recent work has shown that the methods can be extended to human behavior without serious modification" (3).[1]

It is important to see clearly just what it is in Skinner's program and claims that makes them appear so bold and remarkable. It is not primarily the fact that he has set functional analysis as his problem, or that he limits himself to study of "observables", i.e.

A review of B. F. Skinner's *Verbal Behavior* (New York: Appleton-Century-Crofts, 1957) from *Language* 35:1 (1959), pp. 26–58.

input–output relations. What is so surprising is the particular limitations he has imposed on the way in which the observables of behavior are to be studied, and, above all, the particularly simple nature of the "function" which, he claims, describes the causation of behavior. One would naturally expect that prediction of the behavior of a complex organism (or machine) would require, in addition to information about external stimulation, knowledge of the internal structure of the organism, the ways in which it processes input information and organizes its own behavior. These characteristics of the organism are in general a complicated product of inborn structure, the genetically determined course of maturation, and past experience. Insofar as independent neurophysiological evidence is not available, it is obvious that inferences concerning the structure of the organism are based on observation of behavior and outside events. Nevertheless, one's estimate of the relative importance of external factors and internal structure in the determination of behavior will have an important effect on the direction of research on linguistic (or any other) behavior, and on the kinds of analogies from animal behavior studies that will be considered relevant or suggestive.

Putting it differently, anyone who sets himself the problem of analyzing the causation of behavior will (in the absence of independent neurophysiological evidence) concern himself with the only data available, namely the record of inputs to the organism and the organism's present response, and will try to describe the function specifying the response in terms of the history of inputs. This is nothing more than the definition of his problem. There are no possible grounds for argument here, if one accepts the problem as legitimate, though Skinner has often advanced and defended this definition of a problem as if it were a thesis which other investigators reject. The differences that arise between those who affirm and those who deny the importance of the specific "contribution of the organism" to learning and performance concern the particular character and complexity of this function, and the kinds of observations and research necessary for arriving at a precise specification of it. If the contribution of the organism is complex, the only hope of predicting behavior even in a gross way will be through a very indirect program of research that begins by studying the detailed character of the behavior itself and the particular capacities of the organism involved.

Skinner's thesis is that external factors consisting of present stimulation and the history of reinforcement (in particular the frequency, arrangement, and withholding of reinforcing stimuli) are of overwhelming importance, and that the general principles revealed in laboratory studies of these phenomena provide the basis for understanding the complexities of verbal behavior. He confidently and repeatedly voices his claim to have demonstrated that the contribution of the speaker is quite trivial and elementary, and that precise prediction of verbal behavior involves only specification of the few external factors that he has isolated experimentally with lower organisms.

Careful study of this book (and of the research on which it draws) reveals, however, that these astonishing claims are far from justified. It indicates, furthermore, that the insights that have been achieved in the laboratories of the reinforcement theorist, though quite genuine, can be applied to complex human behavior only in the most gross and superficial way, and that speculative attempts to discuss linguistic behavior in these terms alone omit from consideration factors of fundamental importance that are, no doubt, amenable to scientific study, although their specific character cannot at present be precisely formulated. Since Skinner's work is the most extensive attempt to accommodate human behavior involving higher mental faculties within a strict behaviorist schema of the type that has attracted many linguists and philosophers, as well as psychologists, a detailed documentation is of independent interest. The magnitude of the failure of this attempt to account for verbal behavior serves as a kind of measure of the importance of the factors omitted from consideration, and an indication of how little is really known about this remarkably complex phenomenon.

The force of Skinner's argument lies in the enormous wealth and range of examples for which he proposes a functional analysis. The only way to evaluate the success of his program and the correctness of his basic assumptions about verbal behavior is to review these examples in detail and to determine the precise character of the concepts in terms of which the functional analysis is presented. §2 of this review describes the experimental context with respect to which these concepts are originally defined. §§3–4 deal with the basic concepts "stimulus", "response", and "reinforcement", §§6–10 with the new descriptive machinery developed specifically for the description of verbal behavior. In §5 we consider the status of the fundamental claim, drawn from the laboratory, which serves as the basis for the analogic guesses about human behavior that have been proposed by many psychologists. The final section (§11) will consider some ways in which further linguistic work may play a part in clarifying some of these problems.

2. Although this book makes no direct reference to experimental work, it can be understood only in terms of the general framework that Skinner has developed for the description of behavior. Skinner divides the responses of the animal into two main categories. *Respondents* are purely reflex responses elicited by particular stimuli. *Operants* are emitted responses, for which no obvious stimulus can be discovered. Skinner has been concerned primarily with operant behavior. The experimental arrangement that he introduced consists basically of a box with a bar attached to one wall in such a way that when the bar is pressed, a food pellet is dropped into a tray (and the bar press is recorded). A rat placed in the box will soon press the bar, releasing a pellet into the tray. This state of affairs, resulting from the bar press, increases the *strength* of the bar-pressing operant. The food pellet is called a *reinforcer*; the event, a reinforcing event. The strength of an operant is defined by Skinner in terms of the rate of response during extinction (i.e. after the last reinforcement and before return to the preconditioning rate).

Suppose that release of the pellet is conditional on the flashing of a light. Then the rat will come to press the bar only when the light flashes. This is called *stimulus discrimination*. The response is called a *discriminated operant* and the light is called the *occasion* for its emission; this is to be distinguished from elicitation of a response by a stimulus in the case of the respondent.[2] Suppose that the apparatus is so arranged that bar-pressing of only a certain character (e.g. duration) will release the pellet. The rat will then come to press the bar in the required way. This process is called *response differentiation*. By successive slight changes in the conditions under which the response will be reinforced it is possible to shape the response of a rat or a pigeon in very surprising ways in a very short time, so that rather complex behavior can be produced by a process of successive approximation.

A stimulus can become reinforcing by repeated association with an already reinforcing stimulus. Such a stimulus is called a *secondary reinforcer*. Like many contemporary behaviorists, Skinner considers money, approval, and the like to be secondary reinforcers which have become reinforcing because of their aasociation with food, etc.[3] Secondary reinforcers can be *generalized* by associating them with a variety of different primary reinforcers.

Another variable that can affect the rate of the bar-pressing operant is drive, which Skinner defines operationally in terms of hours of deprivation. His major scientific book, *Behavior of organisms*, is a study of the effects of food-deprivation and conditioning on the strength of the bar-pressing response of healthy mature rats. Probably Skinner's most original contribution to animal behavior studies has been his investigation of the effects of intermittent reinforcement, arranged in various different ways, presented in *Behavior of organisms* and extended (with pecking of pigeons as the operant under investigation) in the recent *Schedules of reinforcement* by Ferster and Skinner (1957). It is apparently these studies that Skinner has in mind when he refers to the recent advances in the study of animal behavior.[4]

The notions "stimulus", "response", "reinforcement" are relatively well defined with respect to the bar-pressing experiments and others similarly restricted. Before we can extend them to real-life behavior, however, certain difficulties must be faced. We must decide, first of all, whether any physical event to which the organism is capable of reacting is to be called a stimulus on a given occasion, or only one to which the organism in fact reacts; and correspondingly, we must decide whether any part of behavior is to be called a response, or only one connected with stimuli in lawful ways. Questions of this sort pose something of a dilemma for the experimental psychologist. If he accepts the broad definitions, characterizing any physical event impinging on the organism as a stimulus and any part of the organism's behavior as a response, he must conclude that behavior has not been demonstrated to be lawful. In the present state of our knowledge, we must attribute an overwhelming influence on actual behavior to ill-defined factors of attention, set, volition, and caprice. If we accept the narrower definitions, then behavior is lawful by definition (if it consists of responses); but this fact is of limited significance, since most of what the animal does will simply not be considered behavior. Hence the psychologist either must admit that behavior is not lawful (or that he cannot at present show that it is – not at all a damaging admission for a developing science), or must restrict his attention to those highly limited areas in which it is lawful (e.g. with adequate controls, bar-pressing in rats; lawfulness of the observed behavior provides, for Skinner, an implicit definition of a good experiment).

Skinner does not consistently adopt either course. He utilizes the experimental results as evidence for the scientific character of his system of behavior, and analogic guesses (formulated in terms of a metaphoric extension of the technical vocabulary of the laboratory) as evidence for its scope. This creates the illusion of a rigorous scientific theory with a very broad scope, although in fact the terms used in the description of real-life and of laboratory behavior may be mere homonyms, with at most a vague similarity of meaning. To substantiate this evaluation, a critical account of his book must show that with a literal reading (where the terms of the descriptive system have something like the technical meanings given in Skinner's definitions) the book covers almost no aspect of linguistic behavior, and that with a metaphoric reading, it is no more scientific than the traditional approaches to this subject matter, and rarely as clear and careful.[5]

3. Consider first Skinner's use of the notions "stimulus" and "response". In *Behavior of organisms* (9) he commits himself to the narrow definitions for these terms. A part of

the environment and a part of behavior are called stimulus (eliciting, discriminated, or reinforcing) and response, respectively, only if they are lawfully related; that is, if the "dynamic laws" relating them show smooth and reproducible curves. Evidently stimuli and responses, so defined, have not been shown to figure very widely in ordinary human behavior.[6] We can, in the face of presently available evidence, continue to maintain the lawfulness of the relation between stimulus and response only by depriving them of their objective character. A typical example of "stimulus control" for Skinner would be the response to a piece of music with the utterance *Mozart* or to a painting with the response *Dutch*. These responses are asserted to be "under the control of extremely subtle properties" of the physical object or event (108). Suppose instead of saying *Dutch* we had said *Clashes with the wallpaper, I thought you liked abstract work, Never saw it before, Tilted, Hanging too low, Beautiful, Hideous, Remember our camping trip last summer?*, or whatever else might come into our minds when looking at a picture (in Skinnerian translation, whatever other responses exist in sufficient strength). Skinner could only say that each of these responses is under the control of some other stimulus property of the physical object. If we look at a red chair and say *red*, the response is under the control of the stimulus "redness"; if we say *chair*, it is under the control of the collection of properties (for Skinner, the object) "chairness" (110), and similarly for any other response. This device is as simple as it is empty. Since properties are free for the asking (we have as many of them as we have nonsynonymous descriptive expressions in our language, whatever this means exactly), we can account for a wide class of responses in terms of Skinnerian functional analysis by identifying the "controlling stimuli". But the word "stimulus" has lost all objectivity in this usage. Stimuli are no longer part of the outside physical world; they are driven back into the organism. We identify the stimulus when we hear the response. It is clear from such examples, which abound, that the talk of "stimulus control" simply disguises a complete retreat to mentalistic psychology. We cannot predict verbal behavior in terms of the stimuli in the speaker's environment, since we do not know what the current stimuli are until he responds. Furthermore, since we cannot control the property of a physical object to which an individual will respond, except in highly artificial cases, Skinner's claim that his system, as opposed to the traditional one, permits the practical control of verbal behavior[7] is quite false.

Other examples of "stimulus control" merely add to the general mystification. Thus a proper noun is held to be a response "under the control of a specific person or thing" (as controlling stimulus, 113). I have often used the words *Eisenhower* and *Moscow*, which I presume are proper nouns if anything is, but have never been "stimulated" by the corresponding objects. How can this fact be made compatible with this definition? Suppose that I use the name of a friend who is not present. Is this an instance of a proper noun under the control of the friend as stimulus? Elsewhere it is asserted that a stimulus controls a response in the sense that presence of the stimulus increases the probability of the response. But it is obviously untrue that the probability that a speaker will produce a full name is increased when its bearer faces the speaker. Furthermore, how can one's own name be a proper noun in this sense? A multitude of similar questions arise immediately. It appears that the word "control" here is merely a misleading paraphrase for the traditional "denote" or "refer". The assertion (115) that so far as the speaker is concerned, the relation of reference is "simply the probability that the speaker will emit a response of a given form in the presence of a stimulus having specified properties" is surely incorrect if we take the words "presence", "stimulus", and "probability" in their literal sense. That they are not intended to be taken literally is indicated by many examples, as when a response is said to be "controlled" by a situation or state of affairs as "stimulus". Thus, the expression *a needle in a haystack* "may be controlled as a unit by a particular type of situation" (116); the words in a single part of speech, e.g. all adjectives, are under the control of a single set of subtle properties of stimuli (121); "the sentence *The boy runs a store* is under the control of an extremely complex stimulus situation" (335); "*He is not at all well* may function as a standard response under the control of a state of affairs which might also control *He is ailing*" (325); when an envoy observes events in a foreign country and reports upon his return, his report is under "remote stimulus control" (416); the statement *This is war* may be a response to a "confusing international situation" (441); the suffix *-ed* is controlled by that "subtle property of stimuli which we speak of as action-in-the-past" (121) just as the *-s* in *The boy runs* is under the control of such specific features of the situation as its "currency" (332). No characterization of the notion "stimulus control" that is remotely related to the bar-pressing experiment (or that preserves the faintest objectivity) can be made to cover a set of examples like these, in which, for example, the "controlling stimulus" need not even impinge on the responding organism.

Consider now Skinner's use of the notion "response". The problem of identifying units in verbal behavior has of course been a primary concern of linguists, and it seems very likely that experimental psychologists should be able to provide much-needed assistance in clearing up the many remaining difficulties in systematic identification. Skinner recognizes (20) the fundamental character of the problem of identification of a unit of verbal behavior, but is satisfied with an answer so vague and subjective that it does not really contribute to its solution. The unit of verbal behavior – the verbal operant – is defined as a class of responses of identifiable form functionally related to one or more controlling variables. No method is suggested for determining in a particular instance what are the controlling variables, how many such units have occurred, or where their boundaries are in the total response. Nor is any attempt made to specify how much or what kind of similarity in form or "control" is required for two physical events to be considered instances of the same operant. In short, no answers are suggested for the most elementary questions that must be asked of anyone proposing a method for description of behavior. Skinner is content with what he calls an "extrapolation" of the concept of operant developed in the laboratory to the verbal field. In the typical Skinnerian experiment, the problem of identifying the unit of behavior is not too crucial. It is defined, by fiat, as a recorded peck or bar-press, and systematic variations in the rate of this operant and its resistance to extinction are studied as a function of deprivation and scheduling of reinforcement (pellets). The operant is thus defined with respect to a particular experimental procedure. This is perfectly reasonable, and has led to many interesting results. It is, however, completely meaningless to speak of extrapolating this concept of operant to ordinary verbal behavior. Such "extrapolation" leaves us with no way of justifying one or another decision about the units in the "verbal repertoire".

Skinner specifies "response strength" as the basic datum, the basic dependent variable in his functional analysis. In the bar-pressing experiment, response strength is defined in terms of rate of emission during extinction. Skinner has argued[8] that this is "the only datum that varies significantly and in the expected direction under conditions which are relevant to the 'learning process'." In the book under review, response strength is defined as "probability of emission" (22). This definition provides a comforting impression of objectivity, which, however, is quickly dispelled when we look into the matter more closely. The term "probability" has some rather obscure meaning for Skinner in this book.[9] We are told, on the one hand, that "our evidence for the contribution of each variable [to response strength] is based on observation of frequencies alone" (28). At the same time, it appears that frequency is a very misleading measure of strength, since, for example, the frequency of a response may be "primarily attributable to the frequency of occurrence of controlling variables" (27). It is not clear how the frequency of a response can be attributable to anything BUT the frequency of occurrence of its controlling variables if we accept Skinner's view that the behavior occurring in a given situation is "fully determined" by the relevant controlling variables (175, 228). Furthermore, although the evidence for the contribution of each variable to response strength is based on observation of frequencies alone, it turns out, that we base the notion of strength upon several kinds of "evidence" (22), in particular (22–8): emission of the response (particularly in unusual circumstances), energy level (stress), pitch level, speed and delay of emission, size of letters etc. in writing, immediate repetition, and – a final factor, relevant but misleading – over-all frequency.

Of course, Skinner recognizes that these measures do not co-vary, because (among other reasons) pitch, stress, quantity, and reduplication may have internal linguistic functions.[10] However, he does not hold these conflicts to be very important, since the proposed factors indicative of strength are "fully understood by everyone" in the culture (27). For example, "if we are shown a prized work of art and exclaim *Beautiful!*, the speed and energy of the response will not be lost on the owner." It does not appear totally obvious that in this case the way to impress the owner is to shriek *Beautiful* in a loud, high-pitched voice, repeatedly, and with no delay (high response strength). It may be equally effective to look at the picture silently (long delay), and then to murmur *Beautiful* in a soft, low-pitched voice (by definition, very low response strength).

It is not unfair, I believe, to conclude from Skinner's discussion of response strength, the "basic datum" in functional analysis, that his "extrapolation" of the notion of probability can best be interpreted as, in effect, nothing more than a decision to use the word "probability", with its favorable connotations of objectivity, as a cover term to paraphrase such low-status words as "interest", "intention", "belief", and the like. This interpretation is fully justified by the way in which Skinner uses the terms "probability" and "strength". To cite just one example, Skinner defines the process of confirming an assertion in science as one of "generating additional variables to increase its probability" (425), and more generally, its strength (425–9). If we take this suggestion quite literally, the degree of confirmation of a scientific assertion can be measured as a simple function of the loudness, pitch, and frequency with which it is proclaimed, and a general procedure for increasing its degree of confirmation would be, for instance, to train machine guns on large crowds of people who have been instructed to shout it. A better indication of what Skinner probably has in mind here is given by his description of how the theory of evolution, as an example, is confirmed. This "single set of verbal responses . . . is made more plausible – is strengthened – by several types of construction based upon verbal responses in geology, paleontology, genetics, and so on" (427). We are no doubt to interpret the terms "strength" and "probability" in this context as paraphrases of more familiar locutions such as "justified belief" or "warranted assertability", or something of the sort. Similar latitude of interpretation is presumably expected when we read that "frequency of effective action accounts in turn for what we may call the listener's 'belief'" (88) or that "our belief in what someone tells us is similarly a function of, or identical with, our tendency to act upon the verbal stimuli which he provides" (160).[11]

I think it is evident, then, that Skinner's use of the terms "stimulus", "control", "response", and "strength" justify the general conclusion stated in the last paragraph of §2 above. The way in which these terms are brought to bear on the actual data indicates that we must interpret them as mere paraphrases for the popular vocabulary commonly used to describe behavior, and as having no particular connection with the homonymous expressions used in the description of laboratory experiments. Naturally, this terminological revision adds no objectivity to the familiar "mentalistic" mode of description.

4. The other fundamental notion borrowed from the description of bar-pressing experiments is "reinforcement". It raises problems which are similar, and even more serious. In *Behavior of organisms*, "the operation of reinforcement is defined as the presentation of a certain kind of stimulus in a temporal relation with either a stimulus or response. A reinforcing stimulus is defined as such by its power to produce the resulting change [in strength]. There is no circularity about this: some stimuli are found to produce the change, others not, and they are classified as reinforcing and non-reinforcing accordingly" (62). This is a perfectly appropriate definition[12] for the study of schedules of reinforcement. It is perfectly useless, however, in the discussion of real-life behavior, unless we can somehow characterize the stimuli which are reinforcing (and the situations and conditions under which they are reinforcing). Consider first of all the status of the basic principle that Skinner calls the "law of conditioning" (law of effect). It reads: "if the occurrence of an operant is followed by presence of a reinforcing stimulus, the strength is increased" (*Behavior of organisms* 21). As "reinforcement" was defined, this law becomes a tautology.[13] For Skinner, learning is just change in response strength.[14] Although the statement that presence of reinforcement is a sufficient condition for learning and maintenance of behavior is vacuous, the claim that it is a necessary condition may have some content, depending on how the class of reinforcers (and appropriate situations) is characterized. Skinner does make it very clear that in his view reinforcement is a necessary condition for language learning and for the continued availability of linguistic responses in the adult.[15] However, the looseness of the term "reinforcement" as Skinner uses it in the book under review makes it entirely pointless to inquire into the truth or falsity of this claim. Examining the instances of what Skinner calls "reinforcement", we find that not even the requirement that a reinforcer be an identifiable stimulus is taken seriously. In fact, the term is used in such a way that the assertion that reinforcement is necessary for learning and continued availability of behavior is likewise empty.

To show this, we consider some examples of "reinforcement". First of all, we find a heavy appeal to automatic self-reinforcement. Thus, "a man talks to himself . . . because of the reinforcement he receives" (163); "the child is reinforced automatically when he duplicates the sounds of airplanes, streetcars . . ." (164); "the young child alone in the nursery may automatically reinforce his own exploratory verbal behavior when he produces sounds which he has heard in the speech of others" (58); "the speaker who is also an accomplished listener 'knows when he has correctly echoed a response' and is reinforced thereby" (68); thinking is "behaving which automatically affects the behaver and is reinforcing because it does so" (438; cutting one's finger should thus be reinforcing, and an example of thinking); "the verbal fantasy, whether overt or covert, is automatically reinforcing to the speaker as listener. Just as the musician plays or composes what he is reinforced by hearing, or as the artist paints what reinforces him visually, so the speaker engaged in verbal fantasy says what he is reinforced by hearing or writes what he is reinforced by reading" (439); similarly, care in problem solving, and rationalization, are automatically self-reinforcing (442–3). We can also reinforce someone by emitting verbal behavior as such (since this rules out a class of aversive stimulations, 167), by not emitting verbal behavior (keeping silent and paying attention, 199), or by acting appropriately on some future occasion (152: "the strength of [the speaker's] behavior is determined mainly by the behavior which the listener will exhibit with respect to a given state of affairs"; this Skinner considers the general case of "communication" or "letting the listener know"). In most such cases, of course, the speaker is not present at the time when the reinforcement takes place, as when "the artist . . . is reinforced by the effects his works have upon . . . others" (224), or when the writer is reinforced by the fact that his "verbal behavior may reach over centuries or to thousands of listeners or readers at the same time. The writer may not be reinforced often or immediately, but his net reinforcement may be great" (206; this accounts for the great "strength" of his behavior). An individual may also find it reinforcing to injure someone by criticism or by bringing bad news, or to publish an experimental result which upsets the theory of a rival (154), to describe circumstances which would be reinforcing if they were to occur (165), to avoid repetition (222), to "hear" his own name though in fact it was not mentioned or to hear nonexistent words in his child's babbling (259), to clarify or otherwise intensify the effect of a stimulus which serves an important discriminative function (416), etc.

From this sample, it can be seen that the notion of reinforcement has totally lost whatever objective meaning it may ever have had. Running through these examples, we see that a person can be reinforced though he emits no response at all, and that the reinforcing "stimulus" need not impinge on the "reinforced person" or need not even exist (it is sufficient that it be imagined or hoped for). When we read that a person plays what music he likes (165), says what he likes (165), thinks what he likes (438–9), reads what books he likes (163), etc., BECAUSE he finds it reinforcing to do so, or that we write books or inform others of facts BECAUSE we are reinforced by what we hope will be the ultimate behavior of reader or listener, we can only conclude that the term "reinforcement" has a purely ritual function. The phrase "X is reinforced by Y (stimulus, state of affairs, event, etc.)" is being used as a cover term for "X wants Y", "X likes Y", "X wishes that Y were the case", etc. Invoking the term "reinforcement" has no explanatory force, and any idea that this paraphrase introduces any new clarity or objectivity into the description of wishing, liking, etc., is a serious delusion. The only effect is to obscure the important differences among the notions being paraphrased. Once we recognize the latitude with which the term "reinforcement" is being used, many rather startling comments lose their initial effect – for instance, that the behavior of the creative artist is "controlled entirely by the contingencies of reinforcement" (150). What has been hoped for from the psychologist is some indication how the casual and informal description of everyday behavior in the popular vocabulary can be explained or clarified in terms of the notions developed in careful experiment and observation, or perhaps replaced in terms of a better scheme. A mere terminological revision, in which a term borrowed from the laboratory is used with the full vagueness of the ordinary vocabulary, is of no conceivable interest.

It seems that Skinner's claim that all verbal behavior is acquired and maintained in "strength" through reinforcement is quite empty, because his notion of reinforcement has no clear content, functioning only as a cover term for any factor, detectable or not, related to acquisition or maintenance of verbal behavior.[16] Skinner's use of the term "conditioning" suffers from a similar difficulty. Pavlovian and operant conditioning are processes about which psychologists have developed real understanding. Instruction of human beings is not. The claim that instruction and imparting of information are simply matters of conditioning (357–60) is pointless. The claim is true, if we extend the term "conditioning" to cover these processes, but we know no more about them after having revised this term in such a way as to deprive it of its relatively clear and object-ive character. It is, as far as we know, quite false, if we use "conditioning" in its literal sense. Similarly, when we say that "it is the function of predication to facilitate the trans-fer of response from one term to another or from one object to another" (361), we have said nothing of any significance. In what sense is this true of the predication *Whales are mammals*? Or, to take Skinner's example, what point is there in saying that the effect of *The telephone is out of order* on the listener is to bring behavior formerly controlled by the stimulus *out of order* under control of the stimulus *telephone* (or the telephone itself) by a process of simple conditioning (362)? What laws of conditioning hold in this case? Furthermore, what behavior is "controlled" by the stimulus *out of order*, in the abstract? Depending on the object of which this is predicated, the present state of motivation of the listener, etc., the behavior may vary from rage to pleasure, from fixing the object to throwing it out, from simply not using it to trying to use it in the normal way (e.g. to see if it is really out of order), and so on. To speak of "conditioning" or "bringing previously available behavior under control of a new stimulus" in such a case is just a kind of play-acting at science. Cf. also note 43.

5. The claim that careful arrangement of contingencies of reinforcement by the verbal community is a necessary condition for language learning has appeared, in one form or another, in many places.[17] Since it is based not on actual observation, but on analogies to laboratory study of lower organisms, it is important to determine the status of the underlying assertion within experimental psychology proper. The most common char-acterization of reinforcement (one which Skinner explicitly rejects, incidentally) is in terms of drive reduction. This characterization can be given substance by defining drives in some way independently of what in fact is learned. If a drive is postulated on the basis of the fact that learning takes place, the claim that reinforcement is necessary for learning will again become as empty as it is in the Skinnerian framework. There is an extensive literature on the question of whether there can be learning without drive-reduction (latent learning). The "classical" experiment of Blodgett indicated that rats who had explored a maze without reward showed a marked drop in number of errors (as compared to a control group which had not explored the maze) upon introduction of a food reward, indicating that the rat had learned the structure of the maze without reduction of the hunger drive. Drive-reduction theorists countered with an exploratory drive which was reduced during the prereward learning, and claimed that a slight decrement in errors could be noted before food reward. A wide variety of experiments, with somewhat

conflicting results, have been carried out with a similar design.[18] Few investigators still doubt the existence of the phenomenon. Hilgard, in his general review of learning theory,[19] concludes that "there is no longer any doubt but that, under appropriate circumstances, latent learning is demonstrable."

More recent work has shown that novelty and variety of stimulus are sufficient to arouse curiosity in the rat and to motivate it to explore (visually), and in fact, to learn (since on a presentation of two stimuli, one novel, one repeated, the rat will attend to the novel one);[20] that rats will learn to choose the arm of a single-choice maze that leads to a complex maze, running through this being their only "reward";[21] that monkeys can learn object discriminations and maintain their performance at a high level of efficiency with visual exploration (looking out of a window for 30 seconds) as the only reward;[22] and, perhaps most strikingly of all, that monkeys and apes will solve rather complex manipulation problems that are simply placed in their cages, and will solve discrimination problems with only exploration and manipulation as incentives.[23] In these cases, solving the problem is apparently its own "reward". Results of this kind can be handled by reinforcement theorists only if they are willing to set up curiosity, exploration, and manipulation drives, or to speculate somehow about acquired drives[24] for which there is no evidence outside of the fact that learning takes place in these cases.

There is a variety of other kinds of evidence that has been offered to challenge the view that drive-reduction is necessary for learning. Results on sensory-sensory conditioning have been interpreted as demonstrating learning without drive-reduction.[25] Olds has reported reinforcement by direct stimulation of the brain, from which he concludes that reward need not satisfy a physiological need or withdraw a drive stimulus.[26] The phenomenon of imprinting, long observed by zoologists, is of particular interest in this connection. Some of the most complex patterns of behavior of birds, in particular, are directed towards objects and animals of the type to which they have been exposed at certain critical early periods of life.[27] Imprinting is the most striking evidence for the innate disposition of the animal to learn in a certain direction, and to react appropriately to patterns and objects of certain restricted types, often only long after the original learning has taken place. It is, consequently, unrewarded learning, though the resulting patterns of behavior may be refined through reinforcement. Acquisition of the typical songs of song birds is, in some cases, a type of imprinting. Thorpe reports studies that show "that some characteristics of the normal song have been learnt in the earliest youth, before the bird itself is able to produce any kind of full song".[28] The phenomenon of imprinting has recently been investigated under laboratory conditions and controls with positive results.[29]

Phenomena of this general type are certainly familiar from everyday experience. We recognize people and places to which we have given no particular attention. We can look up something in a book and learn it perfectly well with no other motive than to confute reinforcement theory, or out of boredom, or idle curiosity. Everyone engaged in research must have had the experience of working with feverish and prolonged intensity to write a paper which no one else will read or to solve a problem which no one else thinks important and which will bring no conceivable reward – which may only confirm a general opinion that the researcher is wasting his time on irrelevancies. The fact that rats and monkeys do likewise is interesting, and important to show in careful experiment. In fact, studies of behavior of the type mentioned above have an independent and positive significance that far outweighs their incidental importance in bringing into question the claim that learning is impossible without drive-reduction. It is not at all unlikely that insights arising from animal behavior studies with this broadened scope may have the kind of relevance to such complex activities as verbal behavior that reinforcement theory has, so far, failed to exhibit. In any event, in the light of presently available evidence, it is difficult to see how anyone can be willing to claim that reinforcement is necessary for learning, if reinforcement is taken seriously as something identifiable independently of the resulting change in behavior.

Similarly, it seems quite beyond question that children acquire a good deal of their verbal and nonverbal behavior by casual observation and imitation of adults and other children.[30] It is simply not true that children can learn language only through "meticulous care" on the part of adults who shape their verbal repertoire through careful differential reinforcement, though it may be that such care is often the custom in academic families. It is a common observation that a young child of immigrant parents may learn a second language in the streets, from other children, with amazing rapidity, and that his speech may be completely fluent and correct to the last allophone, while the subtleties that become second nature to the child may elude his parents despite high motivation and continued practice. A child may pick up a large part of his vocabulary and "feel" for sentence structure from television, from reading, from listening to adults, etc. Even a very young child who has not yet acquired a minimal repertoire from which to form new utterances may imitate a word quite well on an early try, with no attempt on the part of his parents to teach it to him. It is also perfectly obvious that, at a later stage, a child will be able to construct and understand utterances which are quite new, and are, at the same time, acceptable sentences in his language. Every time an adult reads a newspaper, he undoubtedly comes upon countless new sentences which are not at all similar, in a simple, physical sense, to any that he has heard before, and which he will recognize as sentences and understand; he will also be able to detect slight distortions or misprints. Talk of "stimulus generalization" in such a case simply perpetuates the mystery under a new title. These abilities indicate that there must be fundamental processes at work quite independently of "feedback" from the environment. I have been able to find no support whatsoever for the doctrine of Skinner and others that slow and careful shaping of verbal behavior through differential reinforcement is an absolute necessity. If reinforcement theory really requires the assumption that there be such meticulous care, it seems best to regard this simply as a *reductio ad absurdum* argument against this approach. It is also not easy to find any basis (or, for that matter, to attach very much content) to the claim that reinforcing contingencies set up by the verbal community are the single factor responsible for maintaining the strength of verbal behavior. The sources of the "strength" of this behavior are almost a total mystery at present. Reinforcement undoubtedly plays a significant role, but so do a variety of motivational factors about which nothing serious is known in the case of human beings.

As far as acquisition of language is concerned, it seems clear that reinforcement, casual observation, and natural inquisitiveness (coupled with a strong tendency to imitate) are important factors, as is the remarkable capacity of the child to generalize, hypothesize, and "process information" in a variety of very special and apparently highly complex ways which we cannot yet describe or begin to understand, and which may be largely innate, or may develop through some sort of learning or through maturation of the nervous system. The manner in which such factors operate and interact in language acquisition is completely unknown. It is clear that what is necessary in such a case is research, not dogmatic and perfectly arbitrary claims, based on analogies to that small part of the experimental literature in which one happens to be interested.

The pointlessness of these claims becomes clear when we consider the well-known difficulties in determining to what extent inborn structure, maturation, and learning are responsible for the particular form of a skilled or complex performance.[31] To take just one example,[32] the gaping response of a nestling thrush is at first released by jarring of the nest, and, at a later stage, by a moving object of specific size, shape, and position relative to the nestling. At this later stage the response is directed towards the part of the stimulus object corresponding to the parent's head, and characterized by a complex configuration of stimuli that can be precisely described. Knowing just this, it would be possible to construct a speculative, learning-theoretic account of how this sequence of behavior patterns might have developed through a process of differential reinforcement, and it would no doubt be possible to train rats to do something similar. However, there appears to be good evidence that these responses to fairly complex "sign stimuli" are genetically determined and mature without learning. Clearly, the possibility cannot be discounted. Consider now the comparable case of a child imitating new words. At an early stage we may find rather gross correspondences. At a later stage, we find that repetition is of course far from exact (i.e. it is not mimicry, a fact which itself is interesting), but that it reproduces the highly complex configuration of sound features that constitute the phonological structure of the language in question. Again, we can propose a speculative account of how this result might have been obtained through elaborate arrangement of reinforcing contingencies. Here too, however, it is possible that ability to select out of the complex auditory input those features that are phonologically relevant may develop largely independently of reinforcement, through genetically determined maturation. To the extent that this is true, an account of the development and causation of behavior that fails to consider the structure of the organism will provide no understanding of the real processes involved.

It is often argued that experience, rather than innate capacity to handle information in certain specific ways, must be the factor of overwhelming dominance in determining the specific character of language acquisition, since a child speaks the language of the group in which he lives. But this is a superficial argument. As long as we are speculating, we may consider the possibility that the brain has evolved to the point where, given an input of observed Chinese sentences, it produces (by an "induction" of apparently fantastic complexity and suddenness) the "rules" of Chinese grammar, and given an input of observed English sentences, it produces (by, perhaps, exactly the same process of induction) the rules of English grammar; or that given an observed application of a term to certain instances it automatically predicts the extension to a class of complexly related instances. If clearly recognized as such, this speculation is neither unreasonable nor fantastic; nor, for that matter, is it beyond the bounds of possible study. There is of course no known neural structure capable of performing this task in the specific ways that observation of the resulting behavior might lead us to postulate; but for that matter, the structures capable of accounting for even the simplest kinds of learning have similarly defied detection.[33]

Summarizing this brief discussion, it seems that there is neither empirical evidence nor any known argument to support any SPECIFIC claim about the relative importance of "feedback" from the environment and the "independent contribution of the organism" in the process of language acquisition.

6. We now turn to the system that Skinner develops specifically for the description of verbal behavior. Since this system is based on the notions "stimulus", "response", and "reinforcement", we can conclude from the preceding sections that it will be vague and arbitrary. For reasons noted in §1, however, I think it is important to see in detail how far from the mark any analysis phrased solely in these terms must be and how completely this system fails to account for the facts of verbal behavior.

Consider first the term "verbal behavior" itself. This is defined as "behavior reinforced through the mediation of other persons" (2). The definition is clearly much too broad. It would include as "verbal behavior", for example, a rat pressing the bar in a Skinner-box, a child brushing his teeth, a boxer retreating before an opponent, and a mechanic repairing an automobile. Exactly how much of ordinary linguistic behavior is "verbal" in this sense, however, is something of a question: perhaps, as I have pointed out above, a fairly small fraction of it, if any substantive meaning is assigned to the term "reinforced". This definition is subsequently refined by the additional provision that the mediating response of the reinforcing person (the "listener") must itself "have been conditioned *precisely in order to reinforce* the behavior of the speaker" (225, italics his). This still covers the examples given above, if we can assume that the "reinforcing" behavior of the psychologist, the parent, the opposing boxer, and the paying customer are the result of appropriate training, which is perhaps not unreasonable. A significant part of the fragment of linguistic behavior covered by the earlier definition will no doubt be excluded by the refinement, however. Suppose, for example, that while crossing the street I hear someone shout *Watch out for the car* and jump out of the way. It can hardly be proposed that my jumping (the mediating, reinforcing response in Skinner's usage) was conditioned (that is, I was trained to jump) precisely in order to reinforce the behavior of the speaker. Similarly for a wide class of cases. Skinner's assertion that with this refined definition "we narrow our subject to what is traditionally recognized as the verbal field" (225) appears to be grossly in error.

7. Verbal operants are classified by Skinner in terms of their "functional" relation to discriminated stimulus, reinforcement, and other verbal responses. A *mand* is defined as "a verbal operant in which the response is reinforced by a characteristic consequence and is therefore under the functional control of relevant conditions of deprivation or aversive stimulation" (35). This is meant to include questions, commands, etc. Each of the terms in this definition raises a host of problems. A mand such as *Pass the salt* is a class of responses. We cannot tell by observing the form of a response whether it belongs to this class (Skinner is very clear about this), but only by identifying the controlling variables. This is generally impossible. Deprivation is defined in the bar-pressing experiment in terms of length of time that the animal has not been fed or permitted to drink. In the present context, however, it is quite a mysterious notion. No attempt is made here to describe a method for determining "relevant conditions of deprivation" independently of the "controlled" response. It is of no help at all to be told (32) that it can be characterized in terms of the operations of the experimenter. If we define deprivation in terms of elapsed time, then at any moment a person is in countless states of deprivation.[34]

It appears that we must decide that the relevant condition of deprivation was (say) salt-deprivation, on the basis of the fact that the speaker asked for salt (the reinforcing community which "sets up" the mand is in a similar predicament). In this case, the assertion that a mand is under the control of relevant deprivation is empty, and we are (contrary to Skinner's intention) identifying the response as a mand completely in terms of form. The word "relevant" in the definition above conceals some rather serious complications.

In the case of the mand *Pass the salt*, the word "deprivation" is not out of place, though it appears to be of little use for functional analysis. Suppose however that the speaker says *Give me the book*, *Take me for a ride*, or *Let me fix it*. What kinds of deprivation can be associated with these mands? How do we determine or measure the relevant deprivation? I think we must conclude in this case, as before, either that the notion "deprivation" is relevant at most to a minute fragment of verbal behavior, or else that the statement "X is under Y-deprivation" is just an odd paraphrase for "X wants Y", bearing a misleading and unjustifiable connotation of objectivity.

The notion "aversive control" is just as confused. This is intended to cover threats, beating, and the like (33). The manner in which aversive stimulation functions is simply described. If a speaker has had a history of appropriate reinforcement (e.g. if a certain response was followed by "cessation of the threat of such injury – of events which have previously been followed by such injury and which are therefore conditioned aversive stimuli") then he will tend to give the proper response when the threat which had previously been followed by the injury is presented. It would appear to follow from this description that a speaker will not respond properly to the mand *Your money or your life* (38) unless he has a past history of being killed. But even if the difficulties in describing the mechanism of aversive control are somehow removed by a more careful analysis, it will be of little use for identifying operants for reasons similar to those mentioned in the case of deprivation.

It seems, then, that in Skinner's terms there is in most cases no way to decide whether a given response is an instance of a particular mand. Hence it is meaningless, within the terms of his system, to speak of the *characteristic* consequences of a mand, as in the definition above. Furthermore, even if we extend the system so that mands can somehow be identified, we will have to face the obvious fact that most of us are not fortunate enough to have our requests, commands, advice, and so on characteristically reinforced (they may nevertheless exist in considerable "strength"). These responses could therefore not be considered mands by Skinner. In fact, Skinner sets up a category of "magical mands" (48–9) to cover the case of "mands which cannot be accounted for by showing that they have ever had the effect specified or any similar effect upon similar occasions" (the word "ever" in this statement should be replaced by "characteristically"). In these pseudo mands, "the speaker simply describes the reinforcement appropriate to a given state of deprivation or aversive stimulation". In other words, given the meaning that we have been led to assign to "reinforcement" and "deprivation", the speaker asks for what he wants. The remark that "a speaker appears to create new mands on the analogy of old ones" is also not very helpful.

Skinner's claim that his new descriptive system is superior to the traditional one "because its terms can be defined with respect to experimental operations" (45) is, we see once again, an illusion. The statement "X wants Y" is not clarified by pointing out a relation between rate of bar-pressing and hours of food-deprivation; replacing "X wants Y" by

"X is deprived of Y" adds no new objectivity to the description of behavior. His further claim for the superiority of the new analysis of mands is that it provides an objective basis for the traditional classification into requests, commands, etc. (38–41). The traditional classification is in terms of the intention of the speaker. But intention, Skinner holds, can be reduced to contingencies of reinforcement, and, correspondingly, we can explain the traditional classification in terms of the reinforcing behavior of the listener. Thus a question is a mand which "specifies verbal action, and the behavior of the listener permits us to classify it as a request, a command, or a prayer" (39). It is a request if "the listener is independently motivated to reinforce the speaker"; a command if "the listener's behavior is . . . reinforced by reducing a threat"; a prayer if the mand "promotes reinforcement by generating an emotional disposition". The mand is advice if the listener is positively reinforced by the consequences of mediating the reinforcement of the speaker; it is a warning if "by carrying out the behavior specified by the speaker the listener escapes from aversive stimulation"; and so on. All this is obviously wrong if Skinner is using the words "request", "command", etc., in anything like the sense of the corresponding English words. The word "question" does not cover commands. *Please pass the salt* is a request (but not a question), whether or not the listener happens to be motivated to fulfill it; not everyone to whom a request is addressed is favorably disposed. A response does not cease to be a command if it is not followed; nor does a question become a command if the speaker answers it because of an implied or imagined threat. Not all advice is good advice, and a response does not cease to be advice if it is not followed. Similarly, a warning may be misguided; heeding it may cause aversive stimulation, and ignoring it might be positively reinforcing. In short, the entire classification is beside the point. A moment's thought is sufficient to demonstrate the impossibility of distinguishing between requests, commands, advice, etc., on the basis of the behavior or disposition of the particular listener. Nor can we do this on the basis of the typical behavior of all listeners. Some advice is never taken, is always bad, etc., and similarly with other kinds of mands. Skinner's evident satisfaction with this analysis of the traditional classification is extremely puzzling.

8. Mands are operants with no specified relation to a prior stimulus. A *tact*, on the other hand, is defined as "a verbal operant in which a response of given form is evoked (or at least strengthened) by a particular object or event or property of an object or event" (81). The examples quoted in the discussion of stimulus control (§3) are all tacts. The obscurity of the notion "stimulus control" makes the concept of the tact rather mystical. Since, however, the tact is "the most important of verbal operants", it is important to investigate the development of this concept in more detail.

We first ask why the verbal community "sets up" tacts in the child – that is, how the parent is reinforced by setting up the tact. The basic explanation for this behavior of the parent (85–6) is the reinforcement he obtains by the fact that his contact with the environment is extended; to use Skinner's example, the child may later be able to call him to the telephone. (It is difficult to see, then, how first children acquire tacts, since the parent does not have the appropriate history of reinforcement.) Reasoning in the same way, we may conclude that the parent induces the child to walk so that he can make some money delivering newspapers. Similarly, the parent sets up an "echoic repertoire" (e.g. a phonemic system) in the child because this makes it easier to teach him new vocabulary, and extending the child's vocabulary is ultimately useful to the parent. "In all these cases we explain the behavior of the reinforcing listener by pointing to an improvement in the possibility of controlling the speaker whom he reinforces" (56). Perhaps this provides the explanation for the behavior of the parent in inducing the child to walk: the parent is reinforced by the improvement in his control of the child when the child's mobility increases. Underlying these modes of explanation is a curious view that it is somehow more scientific to attribute to a parent a desire to control the child or enhance his own possibilities for action than a desire to see the child develop and extend his capacities. Needless to say, no evidence is offered to support this contention.

Consider now the problem of explaining the response of the listener to a tact. Suppose, for example, that B hears A say *fox* and reacts appropriately, looks around, runs away, aims his rifle, etc. How can we explain B's behavior? Skinner rightly rejects analyses of this offered by Watson and Bertrand Russell. His own equally inadequate analysis proceeds as follows (87–8). We assume (1) "that in the history of [B] the stimulus *fox* has been an occasion upon which looking around has been followed by seeing a fox" and (2) "that the listener has some current 'interest in seeing foxes' – that behavior which depends upon a seen fox for its execution is strong, and that the stimulus supplied by a fox is therefore reinforcing". B carries out the appropriate behavior, then, because "the heard stimulus *fox* is the occasion upon which turning and looking about is frequently followed by the reinforcement of seeing a fox"; i.e. his behavior is a discriminated operant. This explanation is unconvincing. B may never have seen a fox and may have no current interest in seeing one, and yet may react appropriately to the stimulus *fox*.[35] Since exactly the same behavior may take place when neither of the assumptions is fulfilled, some other mechanism must be operative here.

Skinner remarks several times that his analysis of the tact in terms of stimulus control is an improvement over the traditional formulations in terms of reference and meaning. This is simply not true. His analysis is fundamentally the same as the traditional one, though much less carefully phrased. In particular, it differs only by indiscriminate paraphrase of such notions as denotation (reference) and connotation (meaning), which have been kept clearly apart in traditional formulations, in terms of the vague concept "stimulus control". In one traditional formulation a descriptive term is said to denote a set of entities and to connote or designate a certain property or condition that an entity must possess or fulfil if the term is to apply to it.[36] Thus the term *vertebrate* refers to (denotes, is true of) vertebrates and connotes the property "having a spine" or something of the sort. This connoted defining property is called the meaning of the term. Two terms may have the same reference but different meanings. Thus it is apparently true that the creatures with hearts are all and only the vertebrates. If so, then the term *creature with a heart* refers to vertebrates and designates the property "having a heart". This is presumably a different property (a different general condition) from having a spine; hence the terms *vertebrate* and *creature with a heart* are said to have different meanings. This analysis is not incorrect (for at least one sense of meaning), but its many limitations have frequently been pointed out.[37] The major problem is that there is no good way to decide whether two descriptive terms designate the same property.[38] As we have just seen, it is not sufficient that they refer to the same objects. *Vertebrate* and *creature with a spine* would be said to designate the same property (distinct from that designated by *creature with a heart*). If we ask why this is so, the only answer appears to be that the terms are synonymous. The notion "property" thus seems somehow language-bound, and appeal to "defining properties" sheds little light on questions of meaning and synonymy.

Skinner accepts the traditional account *in toto*, as can be seen from his definition of a tact as a response under control of a property (stimulus) of some physical object or event. We have found that the notion "control" has no real substance, and is perhaps best understood as a paraphrase of "denote" or "connote" or, ambiguously, both. The only consequence of adopting the new term "stimulus control" is that the important differences between reference and meaning are obscured. It provides no new objectivity. The stimulus controlling the response is determined by the response itself; there is no independent and objective method of identification (see §3 above). Consequently, when Skinner defines "synonymy" as the case in which "the same stimulus leads to quite different responses" (118), we can have no objection. The responses *chair* and *red* made alternatively to the same object are not synonymous, because the stimuli are called different. The responses *vertebrate* and *creature with a spine* would be considered synonymous because they are controlled by the same property of the object under investigation; in more traditional and no less scientific terms, they evoke the same concept. Similarly, when metaphorical extension is explained as due to "the control exercised by properties of the stimulus which, though present at reinforcement, do not enter into the contingency respected by the verbal community" (92; traditionally, accidental properties), no objection can be raised which has not already been levelled against the traditional account. Just as we could "explain" the response *Mozart* to a piece of music in terms of subtle properties of the controlling stimuli, we can, with equal facility, explain the appearance of the response *sun* when no sun is present, as in *Juliet is [like] the sun.* "We do so by noting that Juliet and the sun have common properties, at least in their effect on the speaker" (93). Since any two objects have indefinitely many properties in common, we can be certain that we will never be at a loss to explain a response of the form *A is like B,* for arbitrary A and B. It is clear, however, that Skinner's recurrent claim that his formulation is simpler and more scientific than the traditional account has no basis in fact.

Tacts under the control of private stimuli (Bloomfield's "displaced speech") form a large and important class (130–46), including not only such responses as *familiar* and *beautiful*, but also verbal responses referring to past, potential, or future events or behavior. For example, the response *There was an elephant at the zoo* "must be understood as a response to current stimuli, including events within the speaker himself" (143).[39] If we now ask ourselves what proportion of the tacts in actual life are responses to (descriptions of) actual current outside stimulation, we can see just how large a role must be attributed to private stimuli. A minute amount of verbal behavior, outside the nursery, consists of such remarks as *This is red* and *There is a man.* The fact that "functional analysis" must make such a heavy appeal to obscure internal stimuli is again a measure of its actual advance over traditional formulations.

9. Responses under the control of prior verbal stimuli are considered under a different heading from the tact. An *echoic operant* is a response which "generates a sound pattern similar to that of the stimulus" (55). It covers only cases of immediate imitation.[40] No attempt is made to define the sense in which a child's echoic response is "similar" to the stimulus spoken in the father's bass voice; it seems, though there are no clear statements about this, that Skinner would not accept the account of the phonologist in this

respect, but nothing else is offered. The development of an echoic repertoire is attributed completely to differential reinforcement. Since the speaker will do no more, according to Skinner, than what is demanded of him by the verbal community, the degree of accuracy insisted on by this community will determine the elements of the repertoire, whatever these may be (not necessarily phonemes). "In a verbal community which does not insist on a precise correspondence, an echoic repertoire may remain slack and will be less successfully applied to novel patterns". There is no discussion of such familiar phenomena as the accuracy with which a child will pick up a second language or a local dialect in the course of playing with other children, which seem sharply in conflict with these assertions. No anthropological evidence is cited to support the claim that an effective phonemic system does not develop (this is the substance of the quoted remark) in communities that do not insist on precise correspondence.

A verbal response to a written stimulus (reading) is called "textual behavior".

Other verbal responses to verbal stimuli are called "intraverbal operants". Paradigm instances are the response *four* to the stimulus *two plus two* or the response *Paris* to the stimulus *capital of France*. Simple conditioning may be sufficient to account for the response *four* to *two plus two*,[41] but the notion of intraverbal response loses all meaning when we find it extended to cover most of the facts of history and many of the facts of science (72, 129); all word association and "flight of ideas" (73–6); all translations and paraphrase (77); reports of things seen, heard, or remembered (315); and, in general, large segments of scientific, mathematical, and literary discourse. Obviously the kind of explanation that might be proposed for a student's ability to respond with *Paris* to *capital of France*, after suitable practice, can hardly be seriously offered to account for his ability to make a judicious guess in answering the questions (to him new) *What is the seat of the French government?*, . . . *the source of the literary dialect?*, . . . *the chief target of the German blitzkrieg?*, etc., or his ability to prove a new theorem, translate a new passage, or paraphrase a remark for the first time or in a new way.

The process of "getting someone to see a point", to see something your way, or to understand a complex state of affairs (e.g. a difficult political situation or a mathematical proof) is, for Skinner, simply a matter of increasing the strength of the listener's already available behavior.[42] Since "the process is often exemplified by relatively intellectual scientific or philosophical discourse", Skinner considers it "all the more surprising that it may be reduced to echoic, textual, or intraverbal supplementation" (269). Again, it is only the vagueness and latitude with which the notions "strength" and "intraverbal response" are used that save this from absurdity. If we use these terms in their literal sense, it is clear that understanding a statement cannot be equated to shouting it frequently in a high-pitched voice (high response strength), and a clever and convincing argument cannot be accounted for on the basis of a history of pairings of verbal responses.[43]

10. A final class of operants, called *autoclitics*, includes those that are involved in assertion, negation, quantification, qualification of responses, construction of sentences, and the "highly complex manipulations of verbal thinking". All these acts are to be explained "in terms of behavior which is evoked by or acts upon other behavior of the speaker" (313). Autoclitics are, then, responses to already given responses, or rather, as we find in reading through this section, they are responses to covert or incipient or potential verbal behavior. Among the autoclitics are listed such expressions as *I recall*,

I imagine, for example, assume, let X equal . . . , the terms of negation, the *is* of predication and assertion, *all, some, if, then,* and, in general, all morphemes other than nouns, verbs, and adjectives, as well as grammatical processes of ordering and arrangement. Hardly a remark in this section can be accepted without serious qualification. To take just one example, consider Skinner's account of the autoclitic *all* in *All swans are white* (329). Obviously we cannot assume that this is a tact to all swans as stimulus. It is suggested, therefore, that we take *all* to be an autoclitic modifying the whole sentence *Swans are white. All* can then be taken as equivalent to *always,* or *always it is possible to say.* Notice, however, that the modified sentence *Swans are white* is just as general as *All swans are white.* Furthermore, the proposed translation of *all* is incorrect if taken literally. It is just as possible to say *Swans are green* as to say *Swans are white.* It is not always possible to say either (e.g. while you are saying something else or sleeping). Probably what Skinner means is that the sentence can be paraphrased "*X is white* is true, for each swan X". But this paraphrase cannot be given within his system, which has no place for *true.*

Skinner's account of grammar and syntax as autoclitic processes (Chapter 13) differs from a familiar traditional account mainly in the use of the pseudoscientific terms "control" or "evoke" in place of the traditional "refer". Thus in *The boy runs,* the final *s* of *runs* is a tact under control of such "subtle properties of a situation" as "the nature of running as an *activity* rather than an object or property of an object".[44] (Presumably, then, in *The attempt fails, The difficulty remains, His anxiety increases,* etc., we must also say that the *s* indicates that the object described as the attempt is carrying out the activity of failing, etc.) In *the boy's gun,* however, the *s* denotes possession (as, presumably, in *the boy's arrival,* . . . *story,* . . . *age,* etc.) and is under the control of this "relational aspect of the situation" (336). The "relational autoclitic of order" (whatever it may mean to call the order of a set of responses a response to them) in *The boy runs the store* is under the control of an "extremely complex stimulus situation", namely, that the boy is running the store (335). *And* in *the hat and the shoe* is under the control of the property "pair". *Through* in *the dog went through the hedge* is under the control of the "relation between the going dog and the hedge" (342). In general, nouns are evoked by objects, verbs by actions, and so on.

Skinner considers a sentence to be a set of key responses (nouns, verbs, adjectives) on a skeletal frame (346). If we are concerned with the fact that Sam rented a leaky boat, the raw responses to the situation are *rent, boat, leak,* and *Sam.* Autoclitics (including order) which qualify these responses, express relations between them, and the like, are then added by a process called "composition" and the result is a grammatical sentence, one of many alternatives among which selection is rather arbitrary. The idea that sentences consist of lexical items placed in a grammatical frame is of course a traditional one, within both philosophy and linguistics. Skinner adds to it only the very implausible speculation that in the internal process of composition, the nouns, verbs, and adjectives are chosen first and then are arranged, qualified, etc., by autoclitic responses to these internal activities.[45]

This view of sentence structure, whether phrased in terms of autoclitics, syncategorematic expressions, or grammatical and lexical morphemes, is inadequate. *Sheep provide wool* has no (physical) frame at all, but no other arrangement of these words is an English sentence. The sequences *furiously sleep ideas green colorless* and *friendly young dogs seem harmless* have the same frames, but only one is a sentence of English (similarly, only one of the sequences formed by reading these from back to front). *Struggling artists can be a nuisance* has the same frame as *marking papers can be a nuisance*, but is quite different in sentence structure, as can be seen by replacing *can be* by *is* or *are* in both cases. There are many other similar and equally simple examples. It is evident that more is involved in sentence structure than insertion of lexical items in grammatical frames; no approach to language that fails to take these deeper processes into account can possibly achieve much success in accounting for actual linguistic behavior.

11. The preceding discussion covers all the major notions that Skinner introduces in his descriptive system. My purpose in discussing the concepts one by one was to show that in each case, if we take his terms in their literal meaning, the description covers almost no aspect of verbal behavior, and if we take them metaphorically, the description offers no improvement over various traditional formulations. The terms borrowed from experimental psychology simply lose their objective meaning with this extension, and take over the full vagueness of ordinary language. Since Skinner limits himself to such a small set of terms for paraphrase, many important distinctions are obscured. I think that this analysis supports the view expressed in §1 above, that elimination of the independent contribution of the speaker and learner (a result which Skinner considers of great importance, cf. 311–2) can be achieved only at the cost of eliminating all significance from the descriptive system, which then operates at a level so gross and crude that no answers are suggested to the most elementary questions.[46] The questions to which Skinner has addressed his speculations are hopelessly premature. It is futile to inquire into the causation of verbal behavior until much more is known about the specific character of this behavior; and there is little point in speculating about the process of acquisition without much better understanding of what is acquired.

Anyone who seriously approaches the study of linguistic behavior, whether linguist, psychologist, or philosopher, must quickly become aware of the enormous difficulty of stating a problem which will define the area of his investigations, and which will not be either completely trivial or hopelessly beyond the range of present-day understanding and technique. In selecting functional analysis as his problem, Skinner has set himself a task of the latter type. In an extremely interesting and insightful paper,[47] K. S. Lashley has implicitly delimited a class of problems which can be approached in a fruitful way by the linguist and psychologist, and which are clearly preliminary to those with which Skinner is concerned. Lashley recognizes, as anyone must who seriously considers the data, that the composition and production of an utterance is not simply a matter of stringing together a sequence of responses under the control of outside stimulation and intraverbal association, and that the syntactic organization of an utterance is not something directly represented in any simple way in the physical structure of the utterance itself. A variety of observations lead him to conclude that syntactic structure is "a generalized pattern imposed on the specific acts as they occur", and that "a consideration of the structure of the sentence and other motor sequences will show . . . that there are, behind the overtly expressed sequences, a multiplicity of integrative processes which can only be inferred from the final results of their activity". He also comments on the great difficulty of determining the "selective mechanisms" used in the actual construction of a particular utterance.

Although present-day linguistics cannot provide a precise account of these integrative processes, imposed patterns, and selective mechanisms, it can at least set itself the problem of characterizing these completely. It is reasonable to regard the grammar of a language L ideally as a mechanism that provides an enumeration of the sentences of L in something like the way in which a deductive theory gives an enumeration of a set of theorems. ("Grammar", in this sense of the word, includes phonology.) Furthermore, the theory of language can be regarded as a study of the formal properties of such grammars, and, with a precise enough formulation, this general theory can provide a uniform method for determining, from the process of generation of a given sentence, a structural description which can give a good deal of insight into how this sentence is used and understood. In short, it should be possible to derive from a properly formulated grammar a statement of the integrative processes and generalized patterns imposed on the specific acts that constitute an utterance. The rules of a grammar of the appropriate form can be subdivided into the two types, optional and obligatory; only the latter must be applied in generating an utterance. The optional rules of the grammar can be viewed, then, as the selective mechanisms involved in the production of a particular utterance. The problem of specifying these integrative processes and selective mechanisms is non-trivial and not beyond the range of possible investigation. The results of such a study might, as Lashley suggests, be of independent interest for psychology and neurology (and conversely). Although such a study, even if successful, would by no means answer the major problems involved in the investigation of meaning and the causation of behavior, it surely will not be unrelated to these. It is at least possible, furthermore, that such notions as "semantic generalization", to which such heavy appeal is made in all approaches to language in use, conceal complexities and specific structure of inference not far different from those that can be studied and exhibited in the case of syntax, and that consequently the general character of the results of syntactic investigations may be a corrective to oversimplified approaches to the theory of meaning.

The behavior of the speaker, listener, and learner of language constitutes, of course, the actual data for any study of language. The construction of a grammar which enumerates sentences in such a way that a meaningful structural description can be determined for each sentence does not in itself provide an account of this actual behavior. It merely characterizes abstractly the ability of one who has mastered the language to distinguish sentences from nonsentences, to understand new sentences (in part), to note certain ambiguities, etc. These are very remarkable abilities. We constantly read and hear new sequences of words, recognize them as sentences, and understand them. It is easy to show that the new events that we accept and understand as sentences are not related to those with which we are familiar by any simple notion of formal (or semantic or statistical) similarity or identity of grammatical frame. Talk of generalization in this case is entirely pointless and empty. It appears that we recognize a new item as a sentence not because it matches some familiar item in any simple way, but because it is generated by the grammar that each individual has somehow and in some form internalized. And we understand a new sentence, in part, because we are somehow capable of determining the process by which this sentence is derived in this grammar.

Suppose that we manage to construct grammars having the properties outlined above. We can then attempt to describe and study the achievement of the speaker, listener, and learner. The speaker and the listener, we must assume, have already acquired the capacities characterized abstractly by the grammar. The speaker's task is to select a particular compatible set of optional rules. If we know, from grammatical study, what choices are available to him and what conditions of compatibility the choices must meet, we can proceed meaningfully to investigate the factors that lead him to make one or another choice. The listener (or reader) must determine, from an exhibited utterance, what optional rules were chosen in the construction of the utterance. It must be admitted that the ability of a human being to do this far surpasses our present understanding. The child who learns a language has in some sense constructed the grammar for himself on the basis of his observation of sentences and nonsentences (i.e. corrections by the verbal community). Study of the actual observed ability of a speaker to distinguish sentences from nonsentences, detect ambiguities, etc., apparently forces us to the conclusion that this grammar is of an extremely complex and abstract character, and that the young child has succeeded in carrying out what from the formal point of view, at least, seems to be a remarkable type of theory construction. Furthermore, this task is accomplished in an astonishingly short time, to a large extent independently of intelligence, and in a comparable way by all children. Any theory of learning must cope with these facts.

It is not easy to accept the view that a child is capable of constructing an extremely complex mechanism for generating a set of sentences, some of which he has heard, or that an adult can instantaneously determine whether (and if so, how) a particular item is generated by this mechanism, which has many of the properties of an abstract deductive theory. Yet this appears to be a fair description of the performance of the speaker, listener, and learner. If this is correct, we can predict that a direct attempt to account for the actual behavior of speaker, listener, and learner, not based on a prior understanding of the structure of grammars, will achieve very limited success. The grammar must be regarded as a component in the behavior of the speaker and listener which can only be inferred, as Lashley has put it, from the resulting physical acts. The fact that all normal children acquire essentially comparable grammars of great complexity with remarkable rapidity suggests that human beings are somehow specially designed to do this, with data-handling or "hypothesis-formulating" ability of unknown character and complexity.[48] The study of linguistic structure may ultimately lead to some significant insights into this matter. At the moment the question cannot be seriously posed, but in principle it may be possible to study the problem of determining what the built-in structure of an information-processing (hypothesis-forming) system must be to enable it to arrive at the grammar of a language from the available data in the available time. At any rate, just as the attempt to eliminate the contribution of the speaker leads to a "mentalistic" descriptive system that succeeds only in blurring important traditional distinctions, a refusal to study the contribution of the child to language learning permits only a superficial account of language acquisition, with a vast and unanalyzed contribution attributed to a step called "generalization" which in fact includes just about everything of interest in this process. If the study of language is limited in these ways, it seems inevitable that major aspects of verbal behavior will remain a mystery.

Notes

1   Skinner's confidence in recent achievements in the study of animal behavior and their applicability to complex human behavior does not appear to be widely shared. In many recent publications of confirmed behaviorists there is a prevailing note of skepticism with

regard to the scope of these achievements. For representative comments, see the contributions to *Modern learning theory* (by Estes et al.; New York, 1954); Bugelski, *Psychology of learning* (New York, 1956); Koch, in *Nebraska symposium on motivation* 58 (Lincoln, 1956); Verplanck, Learned and innate behavior, *Psych. rev.* 52.139 (1955). Perhaps the strongest view is that of Harlow, who has asserted (Mice, monkeys, men, and motives, *Psych. rev.* 60.23–32 [1953]) that "a strong case can be made for the proposition that the importance of the psychological problems studied during the last 15 years has decreased as a negatively accelerated function approaching an asymptote of complete indifference." Tinbergen, a leading representative of a different approach to animal behavior studies (comparative ethology), concludes a discussion of "functional analysis" with the comment that "we may now draw the conclusion that the causation of behavior is immensely more complex than was assumed in the generalizations of the past. A number of internal and external factors act upon complex central nervous structures. Second, it will be obvious that the facts at our disposal are very fragmentary indeed" – *The study of instinct* 74 (Oxford, 1951).

2   In *Behavior of organisms* (New York, 1938), Skinner remarks that "although a conditioned operant is the result of the correlation of the response with a particular reinforcement, a relation between it and a discriminative stimulus acting prior to the response is the almost universal rule" (178–9). Even emitted behavior is held to be produced by some sort of "originating force" (51) which, in the case of operant behavior is not under experimental control. The distinction between eliciting stimuli, discriminated stimuli, and "originating forces" has never been adequately clarified, and becomes even more confusing when private internal events are considered to be discriminated stimuli (see below).

3   In a famous experiment, chimpanzees were taught to perform complex tasks to receive tokens which had become secondary reinforcers because of association with food. The idea that money, approval, prestige, etc. actually acquire their motivating effects on human behavior according to this paradigm is unproved, and not particularly plausible. Many psychologists within the behaviorist movement are quite skeptical about this (cf. n. 23). As in the case of most aspects of human behavior, the evidence about secondary reinforcement is so fragmentary, conflicting, and complex that almost any view can find some support.

4   Skinner's remark quoted above about the generality of his basic results must be understood in the light of the experimental limitations he has imposed. If it were true in any deep sense that the basic processes in language are well understood and free of species restrictions, it would be extremely odd that language is limited to man. With the exception of a few scattered observations (cf. his article, A case history in scientific method, *The American psychologist* 11.221–33 [1956]), Skinner is apparently basing this claim on the fact that qualitatively similar results are obtained with bar-pressing of rats and pecking of pigeons under special conditions of deprivation and various schedules of reinforcement. One immediately questions how much can be based on these facts, which are in part at least an artifact traceable to experimental design and the definition of "stimulus" and "response" in terms of "smooth dynamic curves" (see below). The dangers inherent in any attempt to "extrapolate" to complex behavior from the study of such simple responses as bar-pressing should be obvious, and have often been commented on (cf. e.g. Harlow, op.cit.). The generality of even the simplest results is open to serious question. Cf. in this connection Bitterman, Wodinsky, and Candland, Some comparative psychology, *Am. jour. of psych.* 71.94–110 (1958), where it is shown that there are important qualitative differences in solution of comparable elementary problems by rats and fish.

5   An analogous argument, in connection with a different aspect of Skinner's thinking, is given by Scriven in *A study of radical behaviorism* – *Univ. of Minn. studies in philosophy of science.* Vol. 1. Cf. Verplanck's contribution to *Modern learning theory* (283–8) for more general discussion of the difficulties in formulating an adequate definition of "stimulus" and "response".

He concludes, quite correctly, that in Skinner's sense of the word, stimuli are not object-ively identifiable independently of the resulting behavior, nor are they manipulable. Verplanck presents a clear discussion of many other aspects of Skinner's system, comment-ing on the untestability of many of the so-called "laws of behavior" and the limited scope of many of the others, and the arbitrary and obscure character of Skinner's notion of "lawful relation"; and, at the same time, noting the importance of the experimental data that Skinner has accumulated.

6   In *Behavior of organisms*, Skinner apparently was willing to accept this consequence. He insists (41–2) that the terms of casual description in the popular vocabulary are not validly descrip-tive until the defining properties of stimulus and response are specified, the correlation is demonstrated experimentally, and the dynamic changes in it are shown to be lawful. Thus, in describing a child as hiding from a dog, "it will not be enough to dignify the popular vocabulary by appealing to essential properties of 'dogness' or 'hidingness' and to suppose them intuitively known." But this is exactly what Skinner does in the book under review, as we will see directly.

7   253 f. and elsewhere, repeatedly. As an example of how well we can control behavior using the notions developed in this book, Skinner shows here how he would go about evoking the response *pencil*. The most effective way, he suggests, is to say to the subject "Please say *pencil*" (our chances would, presumably, be even further improved by use of "aversive stimulation", e.g. holding a gun to his head). We can also "make sure that no pencil or writing instrument is available, then hand our subject a pad of paper appropriate to pencil sketching, and offer him a handsome reward for a recognizable picture of a cat." It would also be useful to have voices saying *pencil* or *pen and . . .* in the background; signs reading *pencil* or *pen and . . .* ; or to place a "large and unusual pencil in an unusual place clearly in sight". "Under such circumstances, it is highly probable that our subject will say *pencil*." "The available techniques are all illustrated in this sample." These contributions of behavior theory to the practical control of human behavior are amply illustrated elsewhere in the book, as when Skinner shows (113–14) how we can evoke the response *red* (the device suggested is to hold a red object before the subject and say "Tell me what color this is").

In fairness, it must be mentioned that there are certain nontrivial applications of "operant conditioning" to the control of human behavior. A wide variety of experiments have shown that the number of plural nouns (for example) produced by a subject will increase if the experimenter says "right" or "good" when one is produced (similarly, positive attitudes on a certain issue, stories with particular content, etc.; cf. Krasner, Studies of the condi-tioning of verbal behavior, *Psych. bull.*, Vol. 55 [1958], for a survey of several dozen experi-ments of this kind, mostly with positive results). It is of some interest that the subject is usually unaware of the process. Just what insight this gives into normal verbal behavior is not obvious. Nevertheless, it is an example of positive and not totally expected results using the Skinnerian paradigm.

8   Are theories of learning necessary?, *Psych. rev.* 57.193–216 (1950).

9   And elsewhere. In his paper Are theories of learning necessary?, Skinner considers the prob-lem how to extend his analysis of behavior to experimental situations in which it is impos-sible to observe frequencies, rate of response being the only valid datum. His answer is that "the notion of probability is usually extrapolated to cases in which a frequency analysis cannot be carried out. In the field of behavior we arrange a situation in which frequencies are available as data, but we use the notion of probability in analyzing or formulating instances of even types of behavior which are not susceptible to this analysis" (199). There are, of course, conceptions of probability not based directly on frequency, but I do not see how any of these apply to the cases that Skinner has in mind. I see no way of interpreting the quoted

passage other than as signifying an intention to use the word "probability" in describing behavior quite independently of whether the notion of probability is at all relevant.

10   Fortunately, "In English this presents no great difficulty" since, for example, "relative pitch levels . . . are not . . . important" (25). No reference is made to the numerous studies of the function of relative pitch levels and other intonational features in English.

11   The vagueness of the word "tendency", as opposed to "frequency", saves the latter quotation from the obvious incorrectness of the former. Nevertheless, a good deal of stretching is necessary. If "tendency" has anything like its ordinary meaning, the remark is clearly false. One may believe strongly the assertion that Jupiter has four moons, that many of Sophocles' plays have been irretrievably lost, that the earth will burn to a crisp in ten million years, etc., without experiencing the slightest tendency to act upon these verbal stimuli. We may, of course, turn Skinner's assertion into a very unilluminating truth by defining "tendency to act" to include tendencies to answer questions in certain ways, under motivation to say what one believes is true.

12   One should add, however, that it is in general not the stimulus as such that is reinforcing, but the stimulus in a particular situational context. Depending on experimental arrangement, a particular physical event or object may be reinforcing, punishing, or unnoticed. Because Skinner limits himself to a particular, very simple experimental arrangement, it is not necessary for him to add this qualification, which would not be at all easy to formulate precisely. But it is of course necessary if he expects to extend his descriptive system to behavior in general.

13   This has been frequently noted.

14   See, for example, Are theories of learning necessary? 199. Elsewhere, he suggests that the term "learning" be restricted to complex situations, but these are not characterized.

15   "A child acquires verbal behavior when relatively unpatterned vocalizations, selectively reinforced, gradually assume forms which produce appropriate consequences in a given verbal community" (31). "Differential reinforcement shapes up all verbal forms, and when a prior stimulus enters into the contingency, reinforcement is responsible for its resulting control . . . The availability of behavior, its probability or strength, depends on whether reinforcements *continue* in effect and according to what schedules" (203–4). Elsewhere, frequently.

16   Talk of schedules of reinforcement here is entirely pointless. How are we to decide, for example, according to what schedules covert reinforcement is "arranged", as in thinking or verbal fantasy, or what the scheduling is of such factors as silence, speech, and appropriate future reactions to communicated information?

17   See, for example, Miller and Dollard, *Social learning and imitation* 82–3 (New York, 1941), for a discussion of the "meticulous training" that they seem to consider necessary for a child to learn the meanings of words and syntactic patterns. The same notion is implicit in Mowrer's speculative account of how language might be acquired, in *Learning theory and personality dynamics*, Chapter 23 (New York, 1950). Actually, the view appears to be quite general.

18   For a general review and analysis of this literature, see Thistlethwaite, A critical review of latent learning and related experiments, *Psych. bull.* 48.97–129 (1951). MacCorquodale and Meehl, in their contribution to *Modern learning theory*, carry out a serious and considered attempt to handle the latent learning material from the standpoint of drive-reduction theory, with (as they point out) not entirely satisfactory results. Thorpe reviews the literature from the standpoint of the ethologist, adding also material on homing and topographical orientation (*Learning and instinct in animals* [Cambridge, 1956]).

19   *Theories of learning* 214 (1956).

20   Berlyne, Novelty and curiosity as determinants of exploratory behavior, *Brit. jour. of psych.* 41.68–80 (1950); id., Perceptual curiosity in the rat, *Jour. of comp. physiol. psych.* 48.238–46

(1955); Thompson and Solomon, Spontaneous pattern discrimination in the rat, ibid. 47.104–7 (1954).

21 Montgomery, The role of the exploratory drive in learning, ibid. 60–3. Many other papers in the same journal are designed to show that exploratory behavior is a relatively independent primary "drive" aroused by novel external stimulation.

22 Butler, Discrimination learning by Rhesus monkeys to visual-exploration motivation, ibid. 46.95–8 (1953). Later experiments showed that this "drive" is highly persistent, as opposed to derived drives which rapidly extinguish.

23 Harlow, Harlow, and Meyer, Learning motivated by a manipulation drive, *Jour. exp. psych.* 40.228–34 (1950), and later investigations initiated by Harlow. Harlow has been particularly insistent on maintaining the inadequacy of physiologically based drives and homeostatic need states for explaining the persistence of motivation and rapidity of learning in primates. He points out, in many papers, that curiosity, play, exploration, and manipulation are, for primates, often more potent drives than hunger and the like, and that they show none of the characteristics of acquired drives. Hebb also presents behavioral and supporting neurological evidence in support of the view that in higher animals there is a positive attraction in work, risk, puzzle, intellectual activity, mild fear and frustration, etc. (Drives and the CNS, *Psych. rev.* 62.243–54 [1955]). He concludes that "we need not work out tortuous and improbable ways to explain why men work for money, why children learn without pain, why people dislike doing nothing."

In a brief note (Early recognition of the manipulative drive in monkeys, *British journal of animal behaviour* 3.71–2 [1955]), W. Dennis calls attention to the fact that early investigators (Romanes, 1882; Thorndike, 1901), whose "perception was relatively unaffected by learning theory, did note the intrinsically motivated behavior of monkeys", although, he asserts, no similar observations on monkeys have been made until Harlow's experiments. He quotes Romanes (*Animal intelligence* [1882]) as saying that "much the most striking feature in the psychology of this animal, and the one which is least like anything met with in other animals, was the tireless spirit of investigation." Analogous developments, in which genuine discoveries have blinded systematic investigators to the important insights of earlier work, are easily found within recent structural linguistics as well.

24 Thus J. S. Brown, in commenting on a paper of Harlow's in *Current theory and research in motivation* (Lincoln, 1953), argues that "in probably every instance [of the experiments cited by Harlow] an ingenious drive-reduction theorist could find some fragment of fear, insecurity, frustration, or whatever, that he could insist was reduced and hence was reinforcing" (53). The same sort of thing could be said for the ingenious phlogiston or ether theorist.

25 Cf. Birch and Bitterman, Reinforcement and learning: The process of sensory integration, *Psych. rev.* 56.292–308 (1949).

26 See, for example, his paper A physiological study of reward in McClelland (ed.), *Studies in motivation* 134–43 (New York, 1955).

27 See Thorpe, op.cit., particularly 115–8 and 337–76, for an excellent discussion of this phenomenon, which has been brought to prominence particularly by the work of K. Lorenz (cf. Der Kumpan in der Umwelt des Vogels, parts of which are reprinted in English translation in Schiller (ed.), *Instinctive behavior* 83–128 (New York, 1957).

28 Op.cit. 372.

29 See e.g. Jaynes, Imprinting: Interaction of learned and innate behavior, *Jour. of comp. physiol. psych.* 49.201–6 (1956), where the conclusion is reached that "the experiments prove that without any observable reward young birds of this species follow a moving stimulus object and very rapidly come to prefer that object to others."

30 Of course it is perfectly possible to incorporate this fact within the Skinnerian framework. If, for example, a child watches an adult using a comb and then, with no instructions, tries

to comb his own hair, we can explain this act by saying that he performs it because be finds it reinforcing to do so, or because of the reinforcement provided by behaving like a person who is "reinforcing" (cf. 164). Similarly, an automatic explanation is available for any other behavior. It seems strange at first that Skinner pays so little attention to the literature on latent learning and related topics, considering the tremendous reliance that he places on the notion of reinforcement; I have seen no reference to it in his writings. Similarly, Keller and Schoenfeld, in what appears to be the only text written under predominantly Skinnerian influence, *Principles of psychology* (New York, 1950), dismiss the latent-learning literature in one sentence as "beside the point", serving only "to obscure, rather than clarify, a fundamental principle" (the law of effect, 41). However, this neglect is perfectly appropriate in Skinner's case. To the drive-reductionist, or anyone else for whom the notion "reinforcement" has some substantive meaning, these experiments and observations are important (and often embarrassing). But in the Skinnerian sense of the word, neither these results nor any conceivable others can cast any doubt on the claim that reinforcement is essential for the acquisition and maintenance of behavior. Behavior certainly has some concomitant circumstances, and whatever they are, we can call them "reinforcement".

31   Tinbergen (op.cit., Chapter VI) reviews some aspects of this problem, discussing the primary role of maturation in the development of many complex motor patterns (e.g. flying, swimming) in lower organisms, and the effect of an "innate disposition to learn" in certain specific ways and at certain specific times. Cf. also Schiller, *Instinctive behavior* 265–88, for a discussion of the role of maturing motor patterns in apparently insightful behavior in the chimpanzee.

Lenneberg (*Language, evolution, and purposive behavior*, unpublished) presents a very interesting discussion of the part that biological structure may play in the acquisition of language, and the dangers in neglecting this possibility.

32   From among many cited by Tinbergen, op.cit. (this on page 88).

33   Cf. Lashley, In search of the engram, *Symposium of the Society for Experimental Biology* 4.454–82 (1950). Sperry, On the neural basis of the conditioned response, *British journal of animal behaviour* 3.41–4 (1955), argues that to account for the experimental results of Lashley and others, and for other facts that he cites, it is necessary to assume that high-level cerebral activity of the type of insight, expectancy, etc. is involved even in simple conditioning. He states that "we still lack today a satisfactory picture of the underlying neural mechanism" of the conditioned response.

34   Furthermore, the motivation of the speaker does not, except in the simplest cases, correspond in intensity to the duration of deprivation. An obvious counter-example is what Hebb has called the "salted-nut phenomenon" (*Organization of behavior* 199 [New York, 1949]). The difficulty is of course even more serious when we consider "deprivations" not related to physiological drives.

35   Just as he may have the appropriate reaction, both emotional and behavioral, to such utterances as *The volcano is erupting* or *There's a homicidal maniac in the next room* without any previous pairing of the verbal and the physical stimulus, Skinner's discussion of Pavlovian conditioning in language (154) is similarly unconvincing.

36   Mill, *A system of logic* (1843). Carnap gives a recent reformulation in Meaning and synonymy in natural languages, *Phil. studies* 6.33–47 (1955), defining the meaning (intension) of a predicate "Q" for a speaker X as "the general condition which an object y must fulfill in order for X to be willing to ascribe the predicate 'Q' to y". The connotation of an expression is often said to constitute its "cognitive meaning" as opposed to its "emotive meaning", which is, essentially, the emotional reaction to the expression.

Whether or not this is the best way to approach meaning, it is clear that denotation, cognitive meaning, and emotive meaning are quite different things. The differences are often obscured in empirical studies of meaning, with much consequent confusion. Thus Osgood has set himself the task of accounting for the fact that a stimulus comes to be a sign for another stimulus (*a buzzer becomes a sign for food, a word for a thing, etc.*). This is clearly (for linguistic signs) a problem of denotation. The method that he actually develops for quantifying and measuring meaning (cf. Osgood, Suci, Tannenbaum, *The measurement of meaning* [Urbana, 1957]) applies, however, only to emotive meaning. Suppose, for example, that A hates both Hitler and science intensely, and considers both highly potent and "active", while B, agreeing with A about Hitler, likes science very much, although he considers it rather ineffective and not too important. Then A may assign to "Hitler" and "science" the same position on the semantic differential, while B will assign "Hitler" the same position as A did, but "science" a totally different position. Yet A does not think that "Hitler" and "science" are synonymous or that they have the same reference, and A and B may agree precisely on the cognitive meaning of "science". Clearly it is the attitude toward the things (the emotive meaning of the words) that is being measured here. There is a gradual shift in Osgood's account from denotation to cognitive meaning to emotive meaning. The confusion is caused, no doubt, by the fact that the term "meaning" is used in all three senses (and others). [See Carroll's review of the book by Osgood, Suci, and Tannenbaum in this number of LANGUAGE.]

37 Most clearly by Quine. See *From a logical point of view* (Cambridge, 1953), especially Chapters 2, 3, and 7.

38 A method for characterizing synonymy in terms of reference is suggested by Goodman, On likeness of meaning, *Analysis* 10.1–7 (1949). Difficulties are discussed by Goodman, On some differences about meaning, ibid. 13.90–6 (1953). Carnap (op.cit.) presents a very similar idea (§6), but somewhat misleadingly phrased, since he does not bring out the fact that only extensional (referential) notions are being used.

39 In general, the examples discussed here are badly handled, and the success of the proposed analyses is overstated. In each case, it is easy to see that the proposed analysis, which usually has an air of objectivity, is not equivalent to the analyzed expression. To take just one example, the response *I am looking for my glasses* is certainly not equivalent to the proposed paraphrases: "When I have behaved in this way in the past, I have found my glasses and have then stopped *behaving in this way*", or "*Circumstances have arisen* in which I am inclined to emit any behavior which in the past has led to the discovery of my glasses; such behavior includes the behavior of looking in which I am now engaged." One may look for one's glasses for the first time; or one may emit the same behavior in looking for one's glasses as in looking for one's watch, in which case *I am looking for my glasses* and *I am looking for my watch* are equivalent, under the Skinnerian paraphrase. The difficult questions of purposiveness cannot be handled in this superficial manner.

40 Skinner takes great pains, however, to deny the existence in human beings (or parrots) of any innate faculty or tendency to imitate. His only argument is that no one would suggest an innate tendency to read, yet reading and echoic behavior have similar "dynamic properties". This similarity, however, simply indicates the grossness of his descriptive categories.

  In the case of parrots, Skinner claims that they have no instinctive capacity to imitate, but only to be reinforced by successful imitation (59). Given Skinner's use of the word "reinforcement", it is difficult to perceive any distinction here, since exactly the same thing could be said of any other instinctive behavior. For example, where another scientist would say that a certain bird instinctively builds a nest in a certain way, we could say in Skinner's terminology (equivalently) that the bird is instinctively reinforced by building the nest in this way. One is therefore inclined to dismiss this claim as another ritual introduction of the word "reinforce". Though there may, under some suitable clarification, be some truth in it, it is difficult to see how many of the cases reported by competent observers can be handled if "reinforcement" is given some substantive meaning. Cf. Thorpe, op.cit. 353 f.; Lorenz, *King Solomon's ring* 85–8 (New York, 1952); even Mowrer, who tries to show how imitation might develop through secondary reinforcement, cites a case, op.cit. 694, which he apparently believes, but where this could hardly be true. In young children, it seems most implausible to explain imitation in terms of secondary reinforcement.

41 Though even this possibility is limited. If we were to take these paradigm instances seriously, it should follow that a child who knows how to count from one to 100 could learn an arbitrary 10×10 matrix with these numbers as entries as readily as the multiplication table.

42 Similarly, "the universality of a literary work refers to the number of potential readers inclined to say the same thing" (275; i.e. the most "universal" work is a dictionary of clichés and greetings); a speaker is "stimulating" if he says what we are about to say ourselves (272); etc.

43 Similarly, consider Skinner's contention (362–5) that communication of knowledge or facts is just the process of making a new response available to the speaker. Here the analogy to animal experiments is particularly weak. When we train a rat to carry out some peculiar act, it makes sense to consider this a matter of adding a response to his repertoire. In the case of human communication, however, it is very difficult to attach any meaning to this terminology. If A imparts to B the information (new to B) that the railroads face collapse, in what sense can the response *The railroads face collapse* be said to be now, but not previously, available to B? Surely B could have said it before (not knowing whether it was true), and known that it was a sentence (as opposed to *Collapse face railroads the*). Nor is there any reason to assume that the response has increased in strength, whatever this means exactly (e.g. B may have no interest in the fact, or he may want it suppressed). It is not clear how we can characterize this notion of "making a response available" without reducing Skinner's account of "imparting knowledge" to a triviality.

44 332. On the next page, however, the *s* in the same example indicates that "the objest described as *the boy* possesses the property of running." The difficulty of even maintaining consistency with a conceptual scheme like this is easy to appreciate.

45 One might just as well argue that exactly the opposite is true. The study of hesitation pauses has shown that these tend to occur before the large categories – noun, verb, adjective; this finding is usually described by the statement that the pauses occur where there is maximum uncertainty or information. Insofar as hesitation indicates on-going composition (if it does at all), it would appear that the "key responses" are chosen only after the "grammatical frame". Cf. C. E. Osgood, unpublished paper; Goldman-Eisler, Speech analysis and mental processes, *Language and speech* 1.67 (1958).

46 E.g. what are in fact the actual units of verbal behavior? Under what conditions will a physical event capture the attention (be a stimulus) or be a reinforcer? How do we decide what stimuli are in "control" in a specific case? When are stimuli "similar"? And so on. (It is not interesting to be told e.g. that we say *Stop* to an automobile or billiard ball because they are sufficiently similar to reinforcing people [46].)

The use of unanalyzed notions like "similar" and "generalization" is particularly disturbing, since it indicates an apparent lack of interest in every significant aspect of the learning or the use of language in new situations. No one has ever doubted that in some sense, language is learned by generalization, or that novel utterances and situations are is some way similar to familiar ones. The only matter of serious interest is the specific "similarity". Skinner has, apparently, no interest in this. Keller and Schoenfeld (op.cit.) proceed to incorporate these notions (which they identify) into their Skinnerian "modern objective psychology" by defining two stimuli to be similar when "we make the same sort of response to them" (124; but when are responses of the "same sort"?). They do not seem to notice that this definition converts their "principle of generalization" (116), under any reasonable interpretation of this, into a tautology. It is obvious that such a definition will not be of much help in the study of language learning or construction of new responses in appropriate situations.

47   The problem of serial order in behavior, in Jeffress (ed.), *Hixon symposium on cerebral mechanisms in behovior* (New York, 1951).

48   There is nothing essentially mysterious about this. Complex innate behavior patterns and innate "tendencies to learn in specific ways" have been carefully studied in lower organisms. Many psychologists have been inclined to believe that such biological structure will not have an important effect on acquisition of complex behavior in higher organisms, but I have not been able to find any serious justification for this attitude. Some recent studies have stressed the necessity for carefully analyzing the strategies available to the organism, regarded as a complex "information-processing system" (cf. Bruner, Goodnow, and Austin, *A study of thinking* [New York, 1956]; Newell, Shaw, and Simon, Elements of a theory of human problem solving, *Psych. rev.* 65.151–66 [1958]), if anything significant is to be said about the character of human learning. These may be largely innate, or developed by early learning processes about which very little is yet known. (But see Harlow, The formation of learning sets, *Psych. rev.* 56.51–65 (1949), and many later papers, where striking shifts in the character of learning are shown as a result of early training; also Hebb, *Organization of behavior* 109 ff.) They are undoubtedly quite complex. Cf. Lenneberg op.cit., and Lees, review of Chomsky's *Syntactic structures in Lg.* 33.406 f. (1957), for discussion of the topics mentioned in this section.

3

The Semiotic or Symbolic Function

Jean Piaget and Bärbel Inhelder

At the end of the sensori-motor period, at about one and a half to two years, there appears a function that is fundamental to the development of later behavior patterns. It consists in the ability to represent something (a signified something: object, event, conceptual scheme, etc.) by means of a "signifier" which is differentiated and which serves only a representative purpose: language, mental image, symbolic gesture, and so on. Following H. Head and the specialists in aphasia, we generally refer to this function that gives rise to representation as "symbolic." However, since linguists distinguish between "symbols" and "signs," we would do better to adopt their term "semiotic function" to designate those activities having to do with the differentiated signifiers as a whole.

I The Semiotic Function and Imitation

The sensori-motor mechanisms are prerepresentational, and behavior based on the evocation of an absent object is not observed until during the second year. When the scheme of the permanent object is in process of being formed, from about nine to twelve months, there is certainly a search for an object that has disappeared; but since it has just been perceived, the search is part of an action already under way, and a series of clues remains to aid the child to find the object again.

Although representation does not yet exist, the baby forms and uses significations, since every sensori-motor assimilation (including perceptual assimilations) already implies the attribution of a signification, of a meaning. Significations and consequently also a duality between "signified" (the schemes themselves with their content; that is, the action) and "signifiers" are already present. However, these "signifiers" remain perceptual and are not yet differentiated from the "signified." This makes it impossible to talk about

From "The Semiotic or Symbolic Function," chapter 3 of *The Psychology of the Child*, translated by Helen Weaver. New York: Basic Books, 1969, pp. 51–7 and 84–91. English language version © 1969 by Basic Books Inc. Reprinted by permission of Basic Books, a member of Perseus Books, L.L.C. Originally published in French as *La Psychologie de l'enfant*. Paris: Presses Universitaires de France, 1966.

semiotic function at this level. An undifferentiated signifier is, in fact, as yet neither a "symbol" nor a "sign" (in the sense of verbal signs). It is by definition an "indicator" (including the "signals" occurring in conditioning, like the sound of the bell that announces food). An indicator is actually undifferentiated from its signified in that it constitutes an aspect of it (whiteness for milk), a part (the visible section for a semi-hidden object), a temporal antecedent (the door that opens for the arrival of Mama), a causal result (a stain), etc.

1   The appearance of the semiotic function

In the course of the second year (and continuing from Stage 6 of infancy), however, certain behavior patterns appear which imply the representative evocation of an object or event not present and which consequently presuppose the formation or use of differentiated signifiers, since they must be able to refer to elements not perceptible at the time as well as to those which are present. One can distinguish at least five of these behavior patterns whose appearance is almost simultaneous and which we shall list in order of increasing complexity:

1. First there is *deferred imitation*, that is, imitation which starts after the disappearance of the model. In a behavior pattern of sensori-motor imitation the child begins by imitating in the presence of the model (for example, a movement of the hand), after which he may continue in the absence of the model, though this does not imply any representation in thought. But in the case of a little girl of sixteen months who sees a playmate become angry, scream, and stamp her foot (new sights for her) and who, an hour or two after the playmate's departure, imitates the scene, laughing, the deferred imitation constitutes the beginning of representation, and the imitative gesture the beginning of a differentiated signifier.

2. Then there is *symbolic play* or the game of pretending, which is unknown at the sensori-motor level. The same little girl invented her first symbolic game by pretending to sleep – sitting down and smiling broadly, but closing her eyes, her head to one side, her thumb in her mouth, and holding a corner of the tablecloth, pretending that it was the corner of her pillow, according to the ritual she observes when she goes to sleep. Shortly afterward she put her stuffed bear to sleep and slid a shell along a box while saying "meow" (she had just seen a cat on a wall). In all these cases the representation is clear-cut and the deferred signifier is an imitative gesture, though accompanied by objects which are becoming symbolic.

3. The *drawing* or graphic image is at first an intermediate stage between play and mental image. It rarely appears before two or two and a half.

4. Then, sooner or later, comes the *mental image*, no trace of which is observed on the sensori-motor level (otherwise discovery of the permanent object would be greatly facilitated). It appears as an internalized imitation.

5. Finally, nascent language permits *verbal evocation* of events that are not occurring at the time. When the little girl says "meow" after the cat has disappeared, verbal representation is added to imitation. When, some time afterward, she says "Anpa bye-bye" (Grandpa went away), pointing to the sloping path he took when he left, the representation is supported either by the differentiated signifier, consisting of the signs of the nascent language, or by both language and mental image.

2   The role of imitation

Given these first manifestations of the semiotic function, the problem is to understand the mechanism of its formation. This is greatly simplified by the fact that the first four of these five forms of behavior are based on imitation. Moreover, language itself, which, contrary to the preceding behavior patterns, is not invented by the child, is necessarily acquired in a context of imitation. (If it were learned solely by means of a series of conditionings, as is often maintained, it would appear as early as the second month.) Imitation constitutes both the sensori-motor prefiguration of representation and the transitional phase between the sensori-motor level and the level of behavior that may properly be called representative.

Imitation is first of all a prefiguration of representation. That is to say, it constitutes during the sensori-motor period a kind of representation in physical acts but not yet in thought.[1]

At the end of the sensori-motor period the child has acquired sufficient virtuosity in the mastery of the imitation thus generalized for deferred imitation to become possible. In fact, representation in action is then liberated from the sensori-motor requirements of direct perceptual copy and reaches an intermediary level where the action, detached from its context, becomes a differentiated signifier and consequently already constitutes in part a representation in thought. With symbolic play and drawing, this transition from representation in action to representation in thought is reinforced. The "pretending to sleep" of the example cited above is still only an action detached from its context, but it is also a symbol capable of generalization. With the mental image, which follows, imitation is no longer merely deferred but internalized, and the representation that it makes possible, thus dissociated from any external action in favor of the internal sketches or outlines of actions which will henceforth support it, is now ready to become thought. The acquisition of language, rendered accessible in these contexts of imitation, finally overlays the whole process, providing a contact with other people which is far more effective than imitation alone, and thus permitting the nascent representation to increase its powers with the aid of communication.

3   Symbols and signs

Broadly speaking, the semiotic function gives rise to two kinds of instruments: *symbols*, which are "motivated" – that is, although they are differentiated signifiers, they do present some resemblance to the things signified; and *signs*, which are arbitrary or conventional. Symbols, being motivated, may be created by the individual by himself. The first symbols of the child's play are good examples of these individual creations, which obviously do not exclude later collective symbolisms. Deferred imitation, symbolic play, and the graphic or mental image thus depend directly on imitation, not as transmissions of ready-made external models (for there is an imitation of oneself as well as of others, as is shown by the example of the game of simulating sleep), but rather as transitions from prerepresentation in action to internal representation, or thought. Signs, on the other hand, being conventional, are necessarily collective. The child receives them, therefore, through the medium of imitation, but this time as an acquisition of external models. However, he immediately fashions them to suit himself and uses them, as we shall see later.

VI   Language

In the normal child, language appears at about the same time as the other forms of semi-otic thought. In the deaf-mute, on the other hand, articulate language does not appear until well after deferred imitation, symbolic play, and the mental image. This seems to indicate that language is derived genetically, since its social or educational transmission presupposes the preliminary development of these individual forms of *semiosis*. How-ever, this development, as is proved by the case of deaf-mutes, can occur independent of language.[2] Furthermore, deaf-mutes, in their collective life, manage to elaborate a gestural language which is of keen interest. It is both social and based on imitative signifiers that occur in an individual form in deferred imitation, in symbolic play, and the image, which is relatively close to symbolic play. Because of its adaptive properties rather than its playful purpose, this gestural language, if it were universal, would constitute an independent and original form of semiotic function. In normal individuals it is rendered unnecessary by the transmission of the collective system of verbal signs associated with articulate language.

1   Evolution

Articulate language makes its appearance, after a phase of spontaneous vocalization (com-mon to children of all cultures between six and ten or eleven months) and a phase of differentiation of phonemes by imitation (from eleven or twelve months), at the end of the sensori-motor period, with what have been called "one-word sentences" (C. Stern). These single words may express in turn desires, emotions, or observations (the verbal scheme becoming an instrument of assimilation and generalization based on the sensori-motor schemes).

From the end of the second year, two-word sentences appear, then short complete sentences without conjugation or declension, and next a gradual acquisition of gram-matical structures. The syntax of children from two to four has been observed in some extremely interesting studies by R. Brown, J. Berko, and others at Harvard and S. Ervin and W. Miller at Berkeley.[3] These studies, which were inspired by Noam Chomsky's hypothesis of the structure of grammatical rules, have shown that the acquisition of syntactical rules cannot be reduced to passive imitation. It involves not only an import-ant element of generalizing assimilation, which was more or less known, but also cer-tain original constructions. R. Brown isolated models of these. Moreover, he has shown that reductions of adult sentences to original infantile models obey certain functional requirements, such as the conservation of a *minimum* of necessary information and the tendency to add to this *minimum*.

2   Language and thought

In addition to this problem of the relationship of infantile language to linguistic theory, and to information theory, the great genetic problem raised by the development of infantile language concerns its relationship to thought, and in particular to the logical operations. Language may increase the powers of thought in range and rapidity, but it is controversial whether logico-mathematical structures are themselves essentially linguistic or non-linguistic in nature.

As to the increasing range and rapidity of thought, thanks to language we observe in fact three differences between verbal and sensori-motor behavior. (1) Whereas sensori-motor patterns are obliged to follow events without being able to exceed the speed of the action, verbal patterns, by means of narration and evocation, can represent a long chain of actions very rapidly. (2) Sensori-motor adaptations are limited to immediate space and time, whereas language enables thought to range over vast stretches of time and space, liberating it from the immediate. (3) The third difference is a consequence of the other two. Whereas the sensori-motor intelligence proceeds by means of successive acts, step by step, thought, particularly through language, can represent simultaneously all the elements of an organized structure.

These advantages of representative thought over the sensori-motor scheme are in reality due to the semiotic function as a whole. The semiotic function detaches thought from action and is the source of representation. Language plays a particularly important role in this formative process. Unlike images and other semiotic instruments, which are created by the individual as the need arises, language has already been elaborated socially and contains a notation for an entire system of cognitive instruments (relationships, classifications, etc.) for use in the service of thought. The individual learns this system and then proceeds to enrich it.

3   Language and logic

Must we then conclude, as has been suggested, that since language possesses its own logic, this logic of language constitutes not only an essential or even a unique factor in the learning of logic (inasmuch as the child is subject to the restrictions of the linguistic group and of society in general), but is in fact the source of all logic for the whole of humanity? These views derive from the pedagogical commonsense characteristic of the sociological school of Durkheim and also the logical positivism still adhered to in many scientific circles. According to logical positivism, in fact, the logic of the logicians is itself nothing but generalized syntax and semantics (Carnap, Tarski, etc.).

We have available two sources of important information on this subject: (1) The comparison of normal children with deaf-mutes, who have not had the benefit of articulate language but are in possession of complete sensori-motor schemes, and with blind persons, whose situation is the opposite. (2) The systematic comparison of linguistic progress in the normal child with the development of intellectual operations.

The logic of deaf-mutes has been studied by M. Vincent[4] and P. Oléron,[5] in Paris, who have applied the operatory tests of the Genevan school, and by F. Affolter in Geneva.

The results indicate a systematic delay in the emergence of logic in the deaf-mute. One cannot speak of deficiency as such, however, since the same stages of development are encountered, although with a delay of one to two years. Seriation and spatial operations are normal (perhaps a slight delay in the case of the former). The classifications have their customary structures and are only slightly less mobile in response to suggested changes of criteria than in hearing children. The learning of arithmetic is relatively easy. Problems of conservation (an index of reversibility) are solved with a delay of only one or two years compared with normal children. The exception is the conservation of liquids, which gives rise to special technical difficulties in the presentation of the assignment, since the subjects must be made to understand that the questions have to do with the contents of the containers and not with the containers themselves.

These results are even more significant when compared with the results obtained in studies of blind children. In studies made by Y. Hatwell, the same tests reveal a delay of up to four years or more compared with normal children, even in elementary questions dealing with relationships of order (succession, position "between," etc.). And yet in the blind children verbal seriations are normal (*A* is smaller than *B*, *B* smaller than *C*, therefore . . .). But the sensory disturbance peculiar to those born blind has from the outset hampered the development of the sensori-motor schemes and slowed down general coordination. Verbal coordinations are not sufficient to compensate for this delay, and action learning is still necessary before these children develop the capacity for operations on a level with that of the normal child or the deaf-mute.

4   Language and operations

The comparison of progress in language with progress in the intellectual operations requires both linguistic and psychological competence. Our collaborator, H. Sinclair, who fulfills both conditions, undertook a group of studies of which we offer one or two samples.

Two groups of children were chosen. The first was clearly preoperatory; that is, these children did not possess the least notion of conservation. The children in the second group accepted one of these notions and justified it by arguments of reversibility and compensation. Both groups were shown several pairs of objects (a large object and a small one; a group of four or five marbles and a group of two; an object that is both shorter and wider than another, etc.) and were asked to describe the pairs when one element of the pair is offered to one person and the other to a second person. This description is thus not related to a problem of conservation. The language of the two groups differs systematically. The first group uses "scalars" almost exclusively (in the linguistic sense): "this man has a big one, that man a small one; this one has a lot, that one little." The second group uses "vectors": "this man has a bigger one than the other man"; "he has more," etc. Whereas the first group describes only one dimension at a time, the second group says: "This pencil is longer and thinner," etc. In short, there is a surprising degree of correlation between the language employed and the mode of reasoning. Similarly, a second study shows a close connection between the stages of development of seriation and the structure of the terms used.

How should this relationship be interpreted? A child at the preoperatory level understands the expressions of the higher level when they are integrated into orders or assignments ("Give that man a longer pencil," etc.), but he does not use them spontaneously. If you train him to use these expressions, he learns them but with difficulty, and the training seldom influences his notions of conservation (it does in approximately one case in ten). Seriation, on the other hand, is somewhat improved by verbal training, because then the linguistic process also relates to the act of comparison and therefore to the concept itself.

These data, combined with those described on pages 60–1, indicate that language does not constitute the source of logic but is, on the contrary, structured by it. The roots of logic are to be sought in the general coordination of actions (including verbal behavior), beginning with the sensori-motor level, whose schemes are of fundamental importance. This schematism continues thereafter to develop and to structure thought, even verbal thought, in terms of the progress of actions, until the formation of the logico-mathematical operations. This is the culmination of the logic implied in the coordinations of actions, when these actions are ready to be internalized and organized into unified structures. We shall now attempt to explain this.

5   Conclusion

In spite of the astonishing diversity of its manifestations, the semiotic function presents a remarkable unity. Whether it is a question of deferred imitation, symbolic play, drawing, mental images and image-memories or language, this function allows the representative evocation of objects and events not perceived at that particular moment. The semiotic function makes thought possible by providing it with an unlimited field of application, in contrast to the restricted boundaries of sensori-motor action and perception. Reciprocally, it evolves under the guidance of thought, or representative intelligence. Neither imitation nor play nor drawing nor image nor language nor even memory (to which we might have attributed a capacity for spontaneous reproduction comparable to that of perception) can develop or be organized without the constant help of the structuration characteristic of intelligence. Let us now examine the evolution of intelligence, starting with the stage of representation which is the product of this semiotic function.

Notes

1   Imitation makes its appearance (with Stages 2 and 3 of infancy) through a kind of contagion or echopraxis. When someone performs in front of the child a gesture the child has just made, the child will repeat the gesture. A little later, the child will imitate any gesture made by an adult, provided that at some time or other this gesture has been performed by the child himself. There is thus at first an assimilation of what the child sees to his own schemes, and a triggering of these schemes. Then a little later the subject attempts to reproduce these models for the sake of the reproduction itself and no longer by automatic assimilation. This marks the appearance of the "prerepresentative" function fulfilled by imitation. Then the child advances rather quickly to the point where he copies gestures that are new to him, but only if they can be performed by visible parts of his own body. An important new phase begins with the imitation of facial movements (opening and closing the mouth or eyes, etc.). The difficulty is then that the child's own face is known to him only by touch and the face of the other

person by sight, except for a few rare tactile explorations of the other person's face. Such explorations are very interesting to note at this level, when the child is forming correspondences between the visual and tactilo-kinesthetic sensations in order to extend imitation to the non-visible parts of his body. Until these correspondences are elaborated, imitation of facial movements remains impossible or is accidental. For example, yawning, so contagious later, is not imitated until about the age of one, if it is silent. Once the correspondences have been established by means of a series of indications (auditory, etc.), imitation is generalized and plays an important role in the child's knowledge of his own body in analogy with the bodies of others. It is no exaggeration, therefore, to regard imitation as a kind of representation in action. Baldwin goes one step further, seeing it as an essential instrument in the complementary formation of the other and the self.

2   One finds in the chimpanzee a beginning of symbolic function which enables him, for example, to save tokens with which to obtain fruits from an automatic dispenser (experiment by J. B. Wolfe) and even to offer them as gifts to less fortunate companions (H. W. Nissen and M. P. Crawford).

3   U. Bellugi and R. Brown, eds., *The Acquisition of Language*, Monographs of the Society for Research in Child Development, No. 92 (1964).

4   M. Vincent and M. Borelli, "La Naissance des opérations logiques chez des sourd-muets," *Enfance* (1951), pp. 222–38, and *Enfance* (1956), pp. 1–20.

5   P. Oléron, "L'Acquisition des conservations et le langage," *Enfance* (1961), pp. 201–19.

4

Language and Learning: The Debate between Jean Piaget and Noam Chomsky

The Psychogenesis of Knowledge and Its Epistemological Significance

Jean Piaget

Fifty years of experience have taught us that knowledge does not result from a mere recording of observations without a structuring activity on the part of the subject. Nor do any a priori or innate cognitive structures exist in man; the functioning of intelligence alone is hereditary and creates structures only through an organization of successive actions performed on objects. Consequently, an epistemology conforming to the data of psychogenesis could be neither empiricist nor preformationist, but could consist only of a constructivism, with a continual elaboration of new operations and structures. The central problem, then, is to understand how such operations come about, and why, even though they result from nonpredetermined constructions, they eventually become logically necessary.

Empiricism

The critique of empiricism is not tantamount to negating the role of experimentation, but the "empirical" study of the genesis of knowledge shows from the onset the insufficiency of an "empiricist" interpretation of experience. In fact, no knowledge is based on perceptions alone, for these are always directed and accompanied by schemes of action. Knowledge, therefore, proceeds from action, and all action that is repeated or generalized through application to new objects engenders by this very fact a "scheme," that is, a kind of practical concept. The fundamental relationship that constitutes all knowledge

From *Language and Learning: The Debate between Jean Piaget and Noam Chomsky*, edited by Massimo Piattelli-Palmarini, pp. 23–52, 57–61, 64–5, 81, 138, 164–73. Cambridge, Mass.: Harvard University Press, 1980.

is not, therefore, a mere "association" between objects, for this notion neglects the active role of the subject, but rather the "assimilation" of objects to the schemes of that subject. This process, moreover, prolongs the various forms of biological "assimilations," of which cognitive association is a particular case as a functional process of integration. Conversely, when objects are assimilated to schemes of action, there is a necessary "adaptation" to the particularities of these objects (compare the phenotypic "adaptations" in biology), and this adaptation results from external data, hence from experience. It is thus this exogenous mechanism that converges with what is valid in the empiricist thesis, but (and this reservation is essential) adaptation does not exist in a "pure" or isolated state, since it is always the adaptation of an assimilatory scheme; therefore this assimilation remains the driving force of cognitive action.

These mechanisms, which are visible from birth, are completely general and are found in the various levels of scientific thought. The role of assimilation is recognized in the fact that an "observable" or a "fact" is always interpreted from the moment of its observation, for this observation always and from the beginning requires the utilization of logico-mathematical frameworks such as the setting up of a relationship or a correspondence, proximities or separations, positive or negative quantifications leading to the concept of measure − in short, a whole conceptualization on the part of the subject that excludes the existence of pure "facts" as completely external to the activities of this subject, all the more as the subject must make the phenomena vary in order to assimilate them.

As for the learning processes invoked by the behaviorist empiricists on behalf of their theses, Inhelder, Sinclair, and Bovet have shown that these processes do not explain cognitive development but are subject to its laws, for a stimulus acts as such only at a certain level of "competence" (another biological notion akin to assimilation). Briefly, the action of a stimulus presupposes the presence of a scheme, which is the true source of the response (which reverses the SR schema or makes it symmetrical [$S \rightleftarrows R$]). Besides, Pribram has demonstrated a selection of inputs existing even at the neurological level.

Preformation

Is it necessary, then, to turn in the direction of the preformation of knowledge? I will return later to the problem of innateness and will limit myself for the moment to the discussion of the hypothesis of determination. If one considers the facts of psychogenesis, one notes first the existence of stages that seem to bear witness to a continual construction. In the first place, in the sensorimotor period preceding language one sees the establishment of a logic of actions (relations of order, interlocking of schemes, intersections, establishment of relationships, and so on), rich in discoveries and even in inventions (recognition of permanent objects, organization of space, of causality). From the ages of 2 to 7, there is a conceptualization of actions, and therefore representations, with discovery of functions between covariations of phenomena, identities, and so forth, but without yet any concept of reversible operations or of conservation. These last two concepts are formed at the level of concrete operations (ages 7 to 10), with the advent of logically structured "groupings," but they are still bound to the manipulation of objects. Finally, around the age of 11 to 12, a hypothetico–deductive propositional logic is formed, with a combinatorial lattice, "sums of parts," algebraic four-groups, and so on.

However, these beautiful successive and sequential constructions (where each one is necessary to the following one) could be interpreted as the progressive actualization (related to factors such as neurological maturity) of a set of preformations, similar to the way in which genetic programming regulates organic "epigenesis" even though the latter continues to interact with the environment and its objects. The problem is therefore to choose between two hypotheses: authentic constructions with stepwise disclosures to new possibilities or successive actualization of a set of possibilities *existing from the beginning*. First, let us note that the problem is similar in the history of science: are the clearly distinct periods in the history of mathematics the result of the successive creations of mathematicians, or are they only the achievement through progressive thematizations of the set of all possibilities corresponding to a universe of Platonic ideas? Now, the set of all possibilities is an antinomic notion like the set of all sets, because the set is itself only a possibility. In addition, today's research shows that, beyond the transfinite number "kappa zero" (which is the limit of predicativity), some openings into new possibilities are still taking place, but are in fact unpredictable since they cannot be founded on a combinatorial lattice. Thus, either mathematics is a part of nature, and then it stems from human constructions, creative of new concepts; or mathematics originates in a Platonic and suprasensible universe, and in this case, one would have to show through what psychological means we acquire knowledge of it, something about which there has never been any indication.

This brings us back to the child, since within the space of a few years he spontaneously reconstructs operations and basic structures of a logico-mathematical nature, without which he would understand nothing of what he will be taught in school. Thus, after a lengthy preoperative period during which he still lacks these cognitive instruments, he reinvents for himself, around his seventh year, the concepts of reversibility, transitivity, recursion, reciprocity of relations, class inclusion, conservation of numerical sets, measurements, organization of spatial references (coordinates), morphisms, some connectives, and so on – in other words, all the foundations of logic and mathematics. If mathematics were preformed, this would mean that a baby at birth would already possess virtually everything that Galois, Cantor, Hilbert, Bourbaki, or MacLane have since been able to realize. And since the child is himself a consequence, one would have to go back as far as protozoa and viruses to locate the seat of "the set of all possibilities."

In a word, the theories of preformation of knowledge appear, for me, as devoid of concrete truth as empiricist interpretations, for the origin of logico-mathematical structures in their infinity cannot be localized either in objects or in the subject. Therefore, only constructivism is acceptable, but its weighty task is to explain both the mechanisms of the formation of new concepts and the characteristics these concepts acquire in the process of becoming logically necessary.

Reflective abstraction

If logico-mathematical structures are not preformed, one must, in contrast, go far back to discover their roots, that is, the elementary functioning permitting their elaboration; and as early as the sensorimotor stages, that is to say, much before language, one finds such points of departure (though without any absolute beginning, since one must then go back as far as the organism itself; see the section on the biological roots of knowledge). What are the mechanisms, then, that provide the constructions from one stage to the other? The first such mechanism I will call "reflective abstraction."

It is, in fact, possible to distinguish three different kinds of abstraction. (1) Let us call "empirical abstraction" the kind that bears on physical objects external to the subject. (2) Logico-mathematical abstraction, in contrast, will be called "reflective"* because it proceeds from the subject's actions and operations. This is even true in a double sense; thus we have two interdependent but distinct processes: that of a projection onto a higher plane of what is taken from the lower level, hence a "reflecting," and that of a "reflection" as a reorganization on the new plane – this reorganization first utilizing, only instrumentally, the operations taken from the preceding level but aiming eventually (even if this remains partially unconscious) at coordinating them into a new totality. (3) We will speak finally of "reflected abstraction" or "reflected thought" as the thematization of that which remained operational or instrumental in (2); phase (3) thus constitutes the natural outcome of (2) but presupposes in addition a set of explicit comparisons at a level above the "reflections" at work in the instrumental utilizations and the constructions in process of (2). It is essential, therefore, to distinguish the phases of reflective abstractions, which occur in any construction at the time of the solution of new problems, from reflected abstraction, which adds a system of explicit correspondences among the operations thus thematized.

Reflective and reflected abstractions, then, are sources of structural novelties for the following reasons: In the first place, the "reflecting" on a higher plane of an element taken from a lower level (for example, the interiorization of an action into a conceptualized representation) constitutes an establishment of correspondences, which is itself already a new concept, and this then opens the way to other possible correspondences, which represents a new "opening." The element transferred onto the new level is then constituted from those that were already there or those that are going to be added, which is now the work of the "reflection" and no longer of the "reflecting" (although initially elicited by the latter). New combinations thus result which can lead to the construction of new operations operating "on" the preceding ones, which is the usual course of mathematical progress (an example in the child: a set of additions creating multiplication).[1] As a rule, all reflecting on a new plane leads to and necessitates a *reorganization*, and it is this reconstruction, productive of new concepts, that we call "reflection"; yet well before its general thematization, reflection comes into action through a set of still instrumental assimilations and coordinations without any conceptual awareness of structures as such (this is to be found all through the history of mathematics). Finally reflected abstraction or retrospective thematization become possible, and although they are found only on preconstructed elements, they naturally constitute a new construction in that their transversal correspondences render simultaneous that which was until now elaborated by successive longitudinal linkings (compare, in scientific thought, the thematization of "structures" by Bourbaki).

---

* Translator's note: Piaget distinguishes two types of abstractions: *abstraction réfléchissante* and *abstraction réfléchie*. We have translated these two terms as "reflective" and "reflected" abstraction, respectively. Reflective abstraction is the result of "reflectings" (*réfléchissements*) and reflected abstraction is the result of "reflections" (*réflexions*).

Constructive generalization

Abstraction and generalization are obviously interdependent, each founded on the other. It results from this that only inductive generalization, proceeding from "some" to "all" by simple extension, will correspond to empirical abstraction, whereas constructive and "completive" generalizations in particular will correspond to reflective and reflected abstractions.

The first problem to be solved, then, is that of the construction of successive steps that have been established in the preceding paragraphs. Now, each one of them results from a new assimilation or operation aimed at correcting an insufficiency in the previous level and actualizing a possibility that is opened by the new assimilation. A good example is the passage of action to representation due to the formation of the semiotic function. Sensorimotor assimilation consists only of assimilating objects to schemes of action, whereas representative assimilation assimilates objects to each other, hence the construction of conceptual schemes. Now, this new form of assimilation already was virtual in sensorimotor form since it bore on multiple but successive objects; it was then sufficient to complete these successive assimilations by a simultaneous act of setting into transversal correspondence before passing to the next level. But such an action implies the evocation of objects not presently perceived, and this evocation requires the formation of a specific instrument, which is the semiotic function (deferred imitations, symbolic play, mental image which is an interiorized imitation, sign language, and so on, in addition to vocal and learned language). Now, sensorimotor signifiers already exist in the form of cues or signals, but they constitute only one aspect or a part of the signified objects; on the contrary, the semiotic function commences when signifiers are differentiated from what is thereby signified and when signifiers can correspond to a multiplicity of things signified. It is clear, then, that between the conceptual assimilation of objects between themselves and semiotization, there is a mutual dependence and that both proceed from a completive generalization of sensorimotor assimilation. This generalization embeds a reflective abstraction bearing on elements directly borrowed from sensorimotor assimilation.

Likewise, it would be easy to show that the new concepts inherent in the levels of initially concrete, then hypothetico-deductive operations proceed from completive generalizations as well. It is thus that concrete operations owe their new abilities to the acquisition of reversibility, which has already been prepared by preoperative reversibility; but the reversibility, in addition, requires a systematic adjustment of affirmations and negations, that is to say, an autoregulation which, by the way, is always working within the constructive generalizations (I will return to the subject of autoregulation in the section on necessity and equilibration). As for the hypothetico-deductive operations, these are made possible by the transition from the structures of "groupings" devoid of a combinatorial lattice (the elements of which are disjoint), to the structures of the "set of components" embedding a combinatorial lattice and full generalization of partitions.[2]

These last advances are due to a particularly important form of constructive generalizations, which consist of raising an operation to its own square or a higher power: thus, combinations are classifications of classifications, permutations are seriations of seriations, the sets of components are partitions of partitions, and so on.

Finally, let us call attention to a simpler but equally important form which consists of generalizations by synthesis of analogous structures, such as the coordination of two systems of references, internal and external to a spatial or cinematic process (the 11- to 12-year-old level).

The biological roots of knowledge

What we have seen so far speaks in favor of a systematic constructivism. It is nonetheless true that its sources are to be sought at the level of the organism, since a succession of constructions could not admit of an absolute beginning. But before offering a solution, we should first ask ourselves what a preformationist solution would mean biologically; in other words, what *a priorism* would look like after having been rephrased in terms of innateness.

A famous author has demonstrated this quite clearly: it is Konrad Lorenz, who considers himself a Kantian who maintains a belief in a hereditary origin of the great structures of reason as a precondition to any acquisition drawn from experience. But as a biologist, Lorenz is well aware that, except for "general" heredity common to all living beings or major groups, specific heredity varies from one species to another: that of man, for instance, remains special to our own particular species. As a consequence, Lorenz, while believing as a precondition that our major categories of thought are basically inborn, cannot, for that very reason, assert their generality: hence his very enlightening formula according to which the *a prioris* of reason consist simply of "innate working hypotheses." In other words, Lorenz, while retaining the point of departure of the *a priori* (which precedes the constructions of the subject), sets aside necessity which is more important, whereas we are doing exactly the opposite, that is, insisting on necessity (see the next section), but placing it at the end of constructions, without any prerequisite hereditary programming.

Lorenz's position is therefore revealing: if reason is innate, either it is general and one must have it go back as far as the protozoa, or it is specific (species-specific or genus-specific, for instance) and one must explain (even if it is deprived of its essential character of necessity) through which mutations and under the influence of which natural selections it developed. Now, as research stands at present, current explanations would be reduced for this particular problem to a pure and simple verbalism; in fact, they would consist of making reason the product of a random mutation, hence of mere chance.

But what innatists surprisingly seem to forget is that there exists a mechanism which is as general as heredity and which even, in a sense, controls it: this mechanism is autoregulation, which plays a role at every level, as early as the genome, and a more and more important role as one gets closer to higher levels and to behavior. Autoregulation, whose roots are obviously organic, is thus common to biological and mental processes, and its actions have, in addition, the great advantage of being directly controllable. It is therefore in this direction, and not in mere heredity, that one has to seek the biological explanation of cognitive constructions, notwithstanding the fact that by the interplay of regulations of regulations, autoregulation is eminently constructivist (and dialectic) by its very nature.[3]

It is understandable, therefore, that while fully sympathizing with the transformational aspects of Chomsky's doctrine, I cannot accept the hypothesis of his "innate fixed nucleus." There are two reasons for this. The first one is that this mutation particular to the human species would be biologically inexplicable; it is already very difficult to see why the randomness of mutations renders a human being able to "learn" an articulate language, and if in addition one had to attribute to it the innateness of a rational linguistic structure, then this structure would itself be subject to a random origin and would make of reason a collection of mere "working hypotheses," in the sense of Lorenz. My second reason is that the "innate fixed nucleus" would retain all its properties of a "fixed nucleus" if it were not innate but constituted the "necessary" result of the constructions of sensorimotor intelligence, which is prior to language and results from those joint organic and behavioral autoregulations that determine this epigenesis. It is indeed this explanation of a non-innate fixed nucleus, produced by sensorimotor intelligence, that has been finally admitted by authors such as Brown, Lenneberg, and McNeill. This is enough to indicate that the hypothesis of innateness is not mandatory in order to secure the coherence of Chomsky's beautiful system.

Necessity and equilibration

We still have to look for the reason why the constructions required by the formation of reason become progressively necessary when each one begins by various trials that are partly episodic and that contain, until rather late, an important component of irrational thought (non-conservations, errors of reversibility, insufficient control over negations, and so on). The hypothesis naturally will be that this increasing necessity arises from autoregulation and has a counterpart with the increasing, parallel equilibration of cognitive structures. Necessity then proceeds from their "interlocking."

Three forms of equilibration can be distinguished in this respect. The most simple, and therefore the most precocious, is that of assimilation and accommodation. Already at the sensorimotor level, it is obvious that in order to apply a scheme of actions to new objects, this scheme must be differentiated according to the properties of these objects; therefore one obtains an equilibrium aimed at both preserving the scheme and taking into account the properties of the object. If however, these properties turn out to be unexpected and interesting, the formation of a subscheme or even of a new scheme has to prove feasible. Such new schemes will then necessitate an equilibration of their own. But these functional mechanisms are found at all levels. Even in science, the assimilation between linear and angular speeds involves two joint operations: common space-time relationships are assimilated while one accommodates for these nonetheless distinct solutions; similarly, the incorporation of open systems to general thermodynamic systems requires differentiating accommodation as well as assimilations.

A second form of equilibrium imposes itself between the subsystems, whether it is a question of subschemes in a scheme of action, subclasses in a general class, or subsystems of the totality of operations that a subject has at his disposal, as for example, the equilibration between spatial numbers and measurement during calculations in which both can intervene. Now, since subsystems normally evolve at different speeds, there can be conflicts between them. Their equilibration presupposes in this case a distinction between their common parts and their different properties, and consequently a compensatory adjustment between partial affirmations and negations as well as between direct or inverted operations, or even the utilization of reciprocities. One can see, then, how equilibration leads to logical necessity: the progressive coherence, sought and finally attained by the subject, first comes from a mere causal regulation of actions of which the results are revealed, after the fact, to be compatible or contradictory; this progressive coherence then achieves a comprehension of linkings or implications that have become deductible and thereby necessary.

The third form of equilibration relies upon the previous one but distinguishes itself by the construction of a new global system: it is the form of equilibration required by the very process of differentiation of new systems, which requires then a compensatory step of integration into a new totality. Apparently, there is here a simple balance of opposing forces, the differentiation threatening the unity of the whole and the integration jeopardizing the necessary distinctions. In fact, the originality of the cognitive equilibrium (and, by the way, further down in the hierarchy, also of organic systems) is to ensure, against expectations, the enrichment of the whole as a function of the importance of these differentiations and to ensure their multiplication (and not only their consistency) as a function of intrinsic (or having become such) variations of the totality of its own characteristics. Here again one clearly sees the relationship between equilibration and progressive logical necessity, that is, the necessity of the *terminus ad quem* resulting from the final integration or "interlocking" of the systems.

In summary, cognitive equilibration is consequently "accretive" (*majorante*); that is to say, the disequilibria do not lead back to the previous form of equilibrium, but to a better form, characterized by the increase of mutual dependencies or necessary implications.

As for experimental knowledge, its equilibration admits, in addition to the previous laws, of a progressive transfer (*passage*) from the exogenous to the endogenous, in the sense that perturbations (falsifications of expectations) are first nullified or neutralized, then progressively integrated (with displacement of equilibrium), and finally incorporated into the system as deducible intrinsic variations reconstructing the exogenous by way of the endogenous. The biological equivalent of this process (compare "from noise to order" in von Foerster)[4] is to be sought in the "phenocopy," as I have endeavored to interpret and to generalize this notion in a recent paper.[5]

Psychogenesis and history of science

As Holton said, one can recognize certain convergences between psychogenesis and the historical development of cognitive structures; this is what I will attempt to define in an upcoming work with the physicist Rolando Garcia.

In some cases, before seventeenth-century science, one can even observe a stage-by-stage parallelism. For instance, in regard to the relationship between force and movement, one can distinguish four periods: (1) the Aristotelian theory of the two motors with, as a consequence, the model of *antiperistasis*; (2) an overall explanation in which force, movement, and impetus remain undifferentiated; (3) the theory of impetus (or *élan*), conceived by Buridan as a necessary intermediary between force and movement; and (4) a final and pre-Newtonian period in which impetus tends to conflate with acceleration. Now, one notes a succession of four very similar stages in the child. The first one is that one in which the two motors remain rather systematic as residues of animism, but with a large number of spontaneous examples of *antiperistasis* (and this often occurs in very unexpected situations, and not only for the movement of projectiles). During a second stage, an overall notion comparable to "action" intervenes and can be symbolized by mve, in which m represents the weight, v the speed, and e the distance covered. During a third period (ages 7 to 10), the "impetus" in the sense of Buridan's middle term spontaneously appears, but with, in addition, the power of "passing through" motionless intermediaries by passing through their "interior" when a movement is transmitted through their mediation. Finally, in a fourth phase (around the age of 11 to 12), the first inklings of the notion of acceleration appear.

For larger periods of history, obviously one does not find any stage-by-stage parallelism, but one can search for common mechanisms. For instance, the history of Western geometry bears witness to a process of structuration whose steps are those of a centration on an emphasis by Euclid on simply intrafigural relationships, then a construction of interfigural relationships with Cartesian coordinate systems, and then finally a progressive algebrization by Klein. Now one finds, on a small scale, a similar process in children, who naturally begin with the "intrafigural," but who discover around their seventh year that in order to determinate a point on a plane, one measurement is not sufficient, but two are necessary, and they must be orthogonally arranged. After this "interfigural" stage (which is necessary also for the construction of horizontal lines) follows that which we can call the "transfigural" stage, in which the properties to be discovered cannot be read on a single diagram, but necessitate a deduction or a calculation (for example, mechanical curves, relative motions, and so on).

Now, these analogies with the history of science assuredly speak in favor of my constructivism. *Antiperistasis* was not transmitted hereditarily from Aristotle to the little Genevans, but Aristotle began by being a child; for childhood precedes adulthood in all men, including cavemen. As for what the scientist keeps from his younger years, it is not a collection of innate ideas, since there are tentative procedures in both cases, but a constructive ability; and one of us went so far as to say that a physicist of genius is a man who has retained the creativity inherent to childhood instead of losing it in school.

On Cognitive Structures and Their Development: A Reply to Piaget

Noam Chomsky

In his interesting remarks on the psychogenesis of knowledge and its epistemological significance, Jean Piaget formulates three general points of view as to how knowledge is acquired: empiricism, "preformation" ("innatism"), and his own "constructivism." He correctly characterizes my views as, in his terms, a variety of "innatism." Specifically, investigation of human language has led me to believe that a genetically determined language faculty, one component of the human mind, specifies a certain class of "humanly accessible grammars." The child acquires one of the grammars (actually, a system of such grammars, but I will abstract to the simplest, ideal case) on the basis of the limited evidence available to him. Within a given speech-community, children with varying experience acquire comparable grammars, vastly underdetermined by the available evidence. We may think of a grammar, represented somehow in the mind, as a system that specifies the phonetic, syntactic, and semantic properties of an infinite class of potential sentences. The child knows the language so determined by the grammar he has acquired. This grammar is a representation of his "intrinsic competence." In acquiring language, the child also develops "performance systems" for putting this knowledge to use (for example, production and perception strategies). So little is known about the general properties of performance systems that one can only speculate as to the basis for their development. My guess would be that, as in the case of grammars, a fixed, genetically determined system of some sort narrowly constrains the forms that they can assume. I would also speculate that other cognitive structures developed by humans might profitably be analyzed along similar lines.

Against this conception Piaget offers two basic arguments: (1) the mutations, specific to humans, that might have given rise to the postulated innate structures are "biologically inexplicable"; (2) what can be explained on the assumption of fixed innate structures can be explained as well as "the 'necessary' result of constructions of sensorimotor intelligence."

Neither argument seems to me compelling. As for the first, I agree only in part. The evolutionary development is, no doubt, "biologically unexplained." However, I know of no reason to believe the stronger contention that it is "biologically inexplicable." Exactly the same can be said with regard to the physical organs of the body. Their evolutionary development is "biologically unexplained," in exactly the same sense. We can, *post hoc*, offer an account as to how this development might have taken place, but we cannot provide a theory to select the actual line of development, rejecting others that appear to be no less consistent with the principles that have been advanced concerning the evolution of organisms. Although it is quite true that we have no idea how or why random mutations have endowed humans with the specific capacity to learn a human language, it is also true that we have no better idea how or why random mutations have led to the development of the particular structures of the mammalian eye or the cerebral cortex. We do not therefore conclude that the basic nature of these structures in the mature individual is determined through interaction with the environment (though such interaction is no doubt required to set genetically determined processes into motion and of course influences the character of the mature organs). Little is known concerning evolutionary development, but from ignorance, it is impossible to draw any conclusions. In particular, it is rash to conclude either (A) that known physical laws do not suffice in principle to account for the development of particular structures, or (B) that physical laws, known or unknown, do not suffice in principle. Either (A) or (B) would seem to be entailed by the contention that evolutionary development is literally "inexplicable" on biological grounds. But there seems to be no present justification for taking (B) seriously, and (A), though conceivably true, is mere speculation. In any event, the crucial point in the present connection is that cognitive structures and physical organs seem to be comparable, as far as the possibility of "biological explanation" is concerned.

The second argument seems to me a more important one. However, I see no basis for Piaget's conclusion. There are, to my knowledge, no substantive proposals involving "constructions of sensorimotor intelligence" that offer any hope of accounting for the phenomena of language that demand explanation. Nor is there any initial plausibility to the suggestion, as far as I can see. I might add that although some have argued that the assumption of a genetically determined language faculty is "begging the question," this contention is certainly unwarranted. The assumption is no more "question-begging" in the case of mental structures than is the analogous assumption in the case of growth of physical organs. Substantive proposals regarding the character of this language faculty are refutable if false, confirmable if true. Particular hypotheses have repeatedly been challenged and modified in the light of later research, and I have no doubt that this will continue to be the case.

It is a curiosity of our intellectual history that cognitive structures developed by the mind are generally regarded and studied very differently from physical structures developed by the body. There is no reason why a neutral scientist, unencumbered by traditional doctrine, should adopt this view. Rather, he would, or should, approach cognitive structures such as human language more or less as he would investigate an organ such as the eye or heart, seeking to determine: (1) its character in a particular individual; (2) its general properties, invariant across the species apart from gross defect; (3) its place in a system of such structures; (4) the course of its development in the individual; (5) the genetically determined basis for this development; (6) the factors that gave rise to this mental organ in the course of evolution. The expectation that constructions of sensorimotor intelligence determine the character of a mental organ such as language seems to me hardly more plausible than a proposal that the fundamental properties of the eye or the visual cortex or the heart develop on this basis. Furthermore, when we turn to specific properties of this mental organ, we find little justification for any such belief, so far as I can see.

I will not attempt a detailed argument here, but will merely sketch the kind of reasoning that leads me to the conclusions just expressed.

Suppose that we set ourselves the task of studying the cognitive growth of a person in a natural environment. We may begin by attempting to delimit certain cognitive domains, each governed by an integrated system of principles of some sort. It is, surely, a legitimate move to take language to be one such domain, though its exact boundaries and relations to other domains remain to be determined. In just the same way, we might proceed to study the nature and development of some organ of the body. Under this quite legitimate assumption, we observe that a person proceeds from a genetically determined initial state S_0 through a sequence of states S_1, S_2, . . . , finally reaching a "steady state" S_s which then seems to change only marginally (say, by the addition of new vocabulary). The steady state is attained at a relatively fixed age, apparently by puberty or somewhat earlier. Investigating this steady state, we can construct a hypothesis as to the grammar internally represented. We could try to do the same at intermediate stages, thus gaining further insight into the growth of language.

In principle, it is possible to obtain as complete a record as we like of the experience available to the person who has achieved this steady state. We make no such attempt in practice, of course, but we can nevertheless focus on particular aspects of this experience relevant to specific hypotheses as to the nature of S_s and S_0. Assuming a sufficient record E of relevant experience, we can then proceed to construct a second-order hypothesis as to the character of S_0. This hypothesis must meet certain empirical conditions: It cannot be so specific as to rule out attested steady states, across languages; it must suffice to account for the transition from S_0 to S_s, given E, for any (normal) person. We may think of this hypothesis as a hypothesis with regard to a function mapping E into S_s. For any choice of E sufficient to give rise to knowledge of some human language L, this function must assign an appropriate S_s in which the grammar of L is represented. We might refer to this function as "the learning theory for humans in the domain language" – call it LT(H,L). Abstracting away from individual differences, we may take

S_0 – which specifies LT(H,L) – to be a genetically determined species character. Refinements are possible, as we consider stages of development more carefully.

More generally, for any species O and cognitive domain D that have been tentatively identified and delimited, we may, correspondingly, investigate LT(O,D), the "learning theory" for the organism O in the domain D, a property of the genetically determined initial state. Suppose, for example, that we are investigating the ability of humans to recognize and identify human faces. Assuming "face-recognition" to constitute a legitimate cognitive domain F, we may try to specify LT(H,F), the genetically determined principles that give rise to a steady state (apparently some time after language is neurally fixed, and perhaps represented in homologous regions of the right hemisphere, as some recent work suggests). Similarly, other cognitive domains can be studied in humans and other organisms. We would hardly expect to find interesting properties common to LT(O,D) for arbitrary O,D; that is, we would hardly expect to discover that there exists something that might be called "general learning theory." As far as I know, the prospects for such a theory are no brighter than for a "growth theory," intermediate in level between cellular biology and the study of particular organs, and concerned with the principles that govern the growth of arbitrary organs for arbitrary organisms.

Again, we may refine the investigation, considering intermediate states as well.

Returning to the case of language, to discover the properties of S_0 we will naturally focus attention on properties of later states (in particular, S_s) that are not determined by E, that is, elements of language that are known but for which there appears to be no relevant evidence. Consider a few examples.

The structure-dependent property of linguistic rules

Consider the process of formation of simple yes-or-no questions in English. We have such declarative-question pairs as (1):

(1)   The man is here – Is the man here?
      The man will leave. – Will the man leave?

Consider the following two hypotheses put forth to account for this infinite class of pairs:

H_1:   process the declarative from beginning to end (left to right), word by word, until reaching the first occurrence of the words *is*, *will*, etc.; transpose this occurrence to the beginning (left), forming the associated interrogative.

H_2:   same as H_1, but select the first occurrence of *is*, *will*, etc., following the first noun phrase of the declarative.

Let us refer to H_1 as a "structure-independent rule" and H_2 as a "structure-dependent rule." Thus, H_1 requires analysis of the declarative into just a sequence of words, whereas H_2 requires an analysis into successive words and also abstract phrases such as "noun phrase." The phrases are "abstract" in that their boundaries and labeling are not in general physically marked in any way; rather, they are mental constructions.

A scientist observing English speakers, given such data as (1), would naturally select hypothesis H_1 over the far more complex hypothesis H_2, which postulates abstract mental processing of a nontrivial sort beyond H_1. Similarly, given such data as (1) it is reasonable to assume that an "unstructured" child would assume that H_1 is valid. In fact, as we know, it is not, and H_2 is (more nearly) correct. Thus consider the data of (2):

(2)   The man who is here is tall. – Is the man who is here tall?
      The man who is tall will leave. – Will the man who is tall leave?

These data are predicted by H_2 and refute H_1, which would predict rather the interrogatives (3):

(3)   Is the man who here is tall?
      Is the man who tall will leave?

Now the question that arises is this: how does a child know that H_2 is correct (nearly), while H_1 is false? It is surely not the case that he first hits on H_1 (as a neutral scientist would) and then is forced to reject it on the basis of data such as (2). No child is taught the relevant facts. Children make many errors in language learning, but none such as (3), prior to appropriate training or evidence. A person might go through much or all of his life without ever having been exposed to relevant evidence, but he will nevertheless unerringly employ H_2, never H_1, on the first relevant occasion (assuming that he can handle the structures at all). We cannot, it seems, explain the preference for H_2 on grounds of communicative efficiency or the like. Nor do there appear to be relevant analogies of other than the most superficial and uninformative sort in other cognitive domains. If humans were differently designed, they would acquire a grammar that incorporates H_1, and would be none the worse for that. In fact, it would be difficult to know, by mere passive observation of a person's total linguistic performance, whether he was using H_1, or H_2.

Such observations suggest that it is a property of S_0 – that is, of LT(H,L) – that rules (or rules of some specific category, identifiable on quite general grounds by some genetically determined mechanism) are structure-dependent. The child need not consider H_1; it is ruled out by properties of his initial mental state, S_0. Although this example is very simple, almost trivial, it illustrates the general problem that arises when we attend to the specific properties of attained cognitive states.

The specified subject condition

Let us consider a slightly more complex example. The sentences (4) and (5) are near synonyms:

(4)   Each of the men likes the others.
(5)   The men like each other.

More generally, the pairs *each of the men . . . the others* and *the men . . . each other* are interchangeable without change of meaning (to a good approximation). In some contexts, however, this is not true at all. Consider, for example, the sentences of (6):

(6) (a) Each of the men expects [John to like the others].
     (b) Each of the men was surprised at [John's hatred of the others].
     (c) Each of the men liked [John's stories about the others].

Replacing *each of the men . . . the others* by *the men . . . each other* in (6), we derive, respectively, the sentences of (7) (with the automatic change of verbal inflection, which we may ignore):

(7) (a) The men expect [John to like each other].
     (b) The men were surprised at [John's hatred of each other].
     (c) The men liked [John's stories about each other].

But the examples of (7) are not near synonyms of the corresponding examples of (6). In fact, they are not well-formed English sentences at all, though if forced to assign an interpretation, we might do so – presumably, the interpretations of the corresponding examples of (6). The grounds for this judgment cannot be "semantic incoherence" or the like; look again at sentences (6a–c), which are perfectly coherent but do not, for some reason, express the meaning of (7a–c). How does the speaker of English know this to be true? Why does his grammar, in state S_s, determine these facts?

The answer, I believe, lies in a general principle of language structure that I will call the "specified subject condition" (SSC). This condition concerns rules that relate X and Y in a structure such as (8), where the bracketed embedded structure is a sentence or a noun phrase:

(8) $\ldots X \ldots [\ldots Y \ldots] \ldots$

SSC asserts roughly that no rule can apply to X and Y if the embedded phrase contains a subject distinct from Y.

Consider now sentence (7a). The brackets enclose an embedded sentence; hence (7a) is of the form (8). Take the reciprocal phrase *each other* to be Y and its proposed antecedent, *the men*, to be X. But the embedded sentence contains a subject *John* distinct from *each other*, so that the relation between X and Y is blocked by SSC. The same is true of other cases of so-called "bound anaphora." Note that the sentence (9) is quite all right, because the reciprocal phrase *each other* is itself the subject:

(9) The candidates expect [each other to win].

What of (7b)? Exactly the same condition will block (7b) if we take *John* to be the "subject" of the noun *hatred* (as it would be in a corresponding sentence *John hates . . .*) in the noun phrase contained within brackets. Similarly, (7c) is accounted for if we take *John* to be the "subject" of *stories* in the bracketed noun phrase. Observe that sentence (10) is well formed, because the embedded noun phrase contains no subject at all, and thus no subject distinct from *each other* (Y of (8)):

(10) The men heard [stories about each other].

Notice that the notion "subject" involved in SSC is rather abstract, a generalization of the corresponding notion of traditional grammar. There are good reasons, quite independent of these considerations, for generalizing the traditional notion in this way.

SSC applies not only to bound anaphora, but also to rules of quite different sorts. Consider, for example, the *wh*-questions of (11):

(11)   (a)   Who did the men hear [stories about]?
       (b)   Who did the men hear [John's stories about]?

(11a) is a grammatical sentence of English, but (11b) is not, because the rule of interrogative-formation is blocked by SSC ((11b) might also be blocked in a style that imposes more stringent conditions on stranding of prepositions).

This explanation is controversial, and I am now avoiding many further questions and a few problems. But I believe that it is essentially correct.

We may now ask exactly the same questions raised with respect to the structure-dependent property of rules. How does the language learner know that SSC applies to the bound anaphor *each other* but not to *the others* in (6)? Again, it cannot be imagined that the language learner is taught these facts or the relevant principles. No one ever makes mistakes to be corrected. As in the case of the structure-dependent principle, passive observation of a person's total performance might not enable us to determine whether the principles are in fact being observed (just as experience would not suffice, normally, to provide this information to the language learner), though "experiment" will quickly reveal that this is so. The only rational conclusion is that the SSC and the relevant abstract notion of "subject" and "bound anaphor" are properties of S_0, that is, part of LT(H,L).

It remains to determine the difference between the bound anaphor *each other* and the free anaphor *the others*, the difference that is revealed in a comparison of (6) and (7). This is straightforward. Notice that the antecedent of *each other* is strictly determined by a property of the grammar of sentences, whereas the antecedent of *the others* may, in general, be determined outside of the sentence in which it appears, by some feature of situational context or background knowledge. Thus the sentence (12) is quite possible, but (13) is not:

(12)   The others left.
(13)   Each other left.

The sentence (12) may appear in a discourse, if the participants know somehow what set is being referred to; for example, in the discourse (14):

(14)   Some of the men stayed. The others left.

In contrast, there is no discourse in which (13) may appear. Correspondingly, in sentences such as (4) and (6), the phrase *the others* might be unrelated to the phrase *each of the men*. Consider the discourse (15):

(15)   Each of the women likes some of the books. Each of the men likes the others.

We may understand *the others* to refer to the other books. There is no such possibility if (4) is replaced by (5) in (15). Thus it was not quite correct to say, as I did before, that (4) and (5) are near synonyms. They do not have the same range of meaning, as these examples demonstrate.

These are among the basic properties that distinguish free from bound anaphora. A person must have knowledge of this distinction to know the range of application of SSC. Again, it seems that such knowledge must be a property of S_0, though as in the case of many other genetically determined properties (for example, the onset of puberty, the termination of growth) the appearance of this mental characteristic may be delayed many years after birth, and may be conditional on the triggering effect of relevant experience (again, as in the case of other innate processes and structures).

"Mentally present" subjects

Let us consider next the following slightly more complex examples. Consider the sentences (16) and (17):

(16)   John seems to each of the men [to like the others].
(17)   John seems to the men [to like each other].

Sentence (16) is well formed, but (17) is not. What is the explanation for this fact?

Again, the answer is provided by SSC. The bracketed expressions in (16) and (17) do not have the full form of sentences, since they lack a subject. But they are understood as sentences with subjects, or, to use the traditional term, they each have an "understood subject," namely, *John*. The understood subject *John* of the embedded sentence fragment of (17) suffices to block the rule of reciprocal interpretation, by SSC, just as the subject *John* of the embedded sentence blocked the same rule in (7a). The only difference between (7a) and (17) is that the subject is physically present in the former case, but only "mentally present" in the second. As the example shows, mentally present subjects behave just like physically present ones with respect to SSC.

As in the earlier cases discussed, it is unimaginable that every speaker of English who can distinguish between (16) and (17) has been taught that mentally present subjects suffice to put the principle SSC into operation, or has been exposed to relevant experience. Once again, we could not know, from passive observation, that a person is aware of the relevant principle (unconsciously, to be sure). Furthermore, if English did not abide by this particular principle, it would be no "worse" a language; rather, in this pseudo-English, (17) would mean (16). Every speaker who has reached his steady state does know the principle that mentally present subjects suffice to put SSC into operation. We apparently must assume, again, that the principle is a property of S_0, coming into operation at some point in mental development.

On the notion "specified subject"

In the preceding examples, SSC served to block the application of rules to an embedded sentence or noun phrase with a subject distinct from the phrase (Y of (8)) to which the rule applied within this embedded structure. Other examples show that the "speci-fied subject" must also be distinct from X of (8). Consider, for example, the following sentences:

(18) (a)   John seems to the men [to like each other]. [same as (17)]
      (b)   The men seem to John [to like each other].
      (c)   John ordered the men [to kill each other].
      (d)   John promised the men [to kill each other].

Sentences (18b) and (18c) are well formed, and have about the same meaning as the cor-responding sentences with *each of the men . . . the others* in place of *the men . . . each other*. But (18a) and (18d) are not well formed. The explanation is transparent. In (18b) and (18c) the understood, mentally present subject of the embedded sentence fragments is identical to the antecedent *the men*, and therefore SSC does not apply, as it does in (18a) and (18d), where the mentally present subject is distinct from the antecedent. We see, then, that a "specified subject" in the embedded phrase of the sentences in (18) is one that is distinct from X of (8). Just what "distinct" means here must be made more precise; I omit this refinement here.

Again there is no *a priori* reason why any of this should be so, nor is it imaginable that the principle has been learned or derived from some sensorimotor construction or the like.

In all of these cases we are, it seems, dealing with knowledge that derives "from the original hand of nature," in Hume's phrase – that is, "innate knowledge." In order to avoid a pointless terminological dispute, I will avoid the term, simply noting that an inquiry into language leads us to attribute to the invariant state S_0 certain properties such as structure-dependence of rules, SSC, the notions of "bound anaphor" and "abstract sub-ject," the condition that mentally present subjects behave like physically present ones with respect to SSC, the conditions on the specified subject, and so forth. More gen-erally, we have tacitly presupposed throughout this discussion a certain framework of rules and principles, all of which must be attributed to S_0 as part of the schematism that determines the form of the resulting knowledge of language. Specific details result, of course, from experience.

As humans functioning in a social environment, we are naturally concerned with differences among individuals and cultures, and tend to ignore or be unaware of uni-formities. The latter are regarded as "natural" or "necessary" or are just taken for granted, just as we take for granted "obvious" properties of the natural environment. But a sci-entist who is trying to understand the nature and origin of human cognitive capacities must, in contrast, be concerned with just those invariant properties that he may safely and properly ignore in his interaction with other people. His task is to determine LT(H,D), for each D; in particular, to determine LT(H,L), the "learning theory" for humans in the domain of language, a property of the initial state S_0. I have suggested some of the characteristics that it seems appropriate to attribute to S_0. These characteristics are rather abstract; they are what I have called elsewhere "formal universals," conditions on the form and function of the system of rules and principles that constitutes our theory of the structure of some cognitive domain. In comparison, there is, to my knowledge, much less to say about "substantive universals," fixed elements that enter into particu-lar grammars.

These examples have been drawn from the domain of syntax and semantic interpretation of syntactic structures. One may find similar examples in phonology and phonetics, or in semantics proper. For example, consider the intricate properties of rule ordering and application in phonology that have been investigated in recent years. As in the cases just discussed, it seems that these are unlearned, hence properties of S_0. Or consider some of the usages that are permissible in cases of "systematic ambiguity" as compared with "accidental" or "syntactically determined" ambiguity. Compare examples (19) and (20):

(19) (a) John wrote a book.
     (b) This book weighs five pounds.
(20) (a) Flying planes are a nuisance (are dangerous).
     (b) Flying planes is a nuisance (is dangerous).

In (19a), the word *book* has an abstract reference. In saying sentence (19a), we may have no concrete object in mind (in fact, John may have just written the book in his head, committing nothing to paper). If there are two copies of the book before us, I can point to either one and say, "John wrote this book," but I cannot conclude that John wrote two books. In (19b), in contrast, the reference of *book* is concrete, or at least it would normally be. Thus there is a certain ambiguity in the usage of *book*; it can be used with either abstract or concrete reference. Though in the current state of descriptive semantics, caution is necessary, it still seems a fair guess that this ambiguity is quite systematic, not an idiosyncratic property of the word *book*, as it is an idiosyncratic property of the word *trunk* that it may refer to an oversize suitcase or an appendage of an elephant.

In the sentences of (20), the phrase *flying planes* is used in two ways, to refer to certain objects that fly in (a) and to the act of piloting in (b). But this ambiguity is syntactically determined, not a general property of phrases with these semantic functions.

The two sentences of (19) can be "combined" in a relative clause construction on *book*, despite its ambiguity, as in (21):

(21) (a) John wrote a book that weighs five pounds.
     (b) The book that John wrote weighs five pounds.
     (c) This book, which John wrote, weighs five pounds.

In (a), for example, the reference of *book* is abstract in the main clause and concrete in the embedded relative clause, but the sentence is well formed. In contrast, there can be no such relative clause construction as (22), based on (20):

(22) (a) Flying planes, which is a nuisance, are dangerous.
     (b) Flying planes, which is dangerous, are a nuisance.

The property of systematic ambiguity just noted, while rather curious, seems quite general. Consider the following sentences (23):

(23) (a) John's intelligence, which is his most remarkable quality, exceeds his foresight.

(b)   The temperature, which was 70 degrees this morning, will rise rapidly.

(c)   The price of bread, which was fixed at $1.00 a loaf by the monopoly, will rise rapidly.

In (23a), *intelligence* refers to a quality in the embedded clause and to a degree of intelligence in the main clause. Examples (23b) and (23c) illustrate a different sort of systematic ambiguity. Terms such as *temperature* or *price of bread* designate functions, which may rise or fall, and so on. But terms designating functions can be used ambiguously to designate their values as well. Thus in (23b) and (23c) the terms in question designate a function in the main clause and its value at a certain point of time in the relative clause, but the process of relativization nevertheless is not blocked.

Presumably, what I have called "systematic ambiguity" is determined within the lexical component of the grammar, by general and perhaps universal principles. Syntactically determined ambiguity (or idiosyncratic lexical ambiguity, as in the case of *trunk*) is not established by general lexical principles. Thus in the case of *book, intelligence, temperature*, or *the price of bread*, there is a single formal element with a fixed (range of) meaning, so that relativization is permitted. But in the case of *flying planes* or *trunk* we really have two formal elements with the same phonetic form; thus relativization is impermissible.

It seems reasonable to surmise that general principles of semantic representation, elements of the initial state S_0, are involved in these judgments. As is generally the case in dealing with examples drawn from the domain of meaning and reference, these cases are less striking than the syntactic or phonological cases, perhaps because the domain of semantics is simply less rich in deeper principles or perhaps because these principles, whatever they may be, have so far eluded us. If there are semantic principles of the depth and generality of those that are now partially understood in the domains of syntax, phonology, and semantic interpretation of syntactic structures, then these principles too will be natural candidates for the learning theories for humans in particular cognitive domains, hence properties of the general initial cognitive state.

The pattern of inference in the preceding examples is, I believe, entirely legitimate, though of course nondemonstrative. In each case, we begin by determining certain properties of the attained linguistic competence, the attained steady state S_s. We ask how these properties develop on the basis of an interplay of experience and genetic endowment. The properties were sought and selected in such a way as to minimize the likely role of experience, and thus to reflect genetic endowment as closely as a property of an attained steady state can do so. Thus, in the cases in question, it seems most unlikely that relevant experience is directly available, in all (or perhaps any) instances in which the steady state is attained by a language learner. It might, of course, be argued that relevant evidence is *indirectly* available, in the sense that experience has led to the development of certain generalized capacities of which the linguistic property in question is a special case; I presume that something of the sort is proposed in the "constructivist" theory. But no specific proposals exist, to my knowledge, concerning such "generalized capacities," and it does not seem very likely, to me at least, that the linguistic properties in question reflect constructions of sensorimotor intelligence or the like.

In the examples just reviewed, I have not hesitated to propose a general principle of linguistic structure on the basis of observation of a single language. The inference is legitimate, on the assumption that humans are not specifically adapted to learn one rather than another human language, say English rather than Japanese. Assuming that the genetically determined language faculty is a common human possession, we may conclude that a principle of language is universal if we are led to postulate it as a "precondition" for the acquisition of a single language. Thus, SSC may be proposed as a universal principle on the grounds that investigation of English, along the lines just reviewed, leads us to postulate this principle as an element of the initial state S_0, a precondition for language learning, a property of the general language faculty, one faculty of the mind.

To test such a conclusion, we will naturally want to investigate other languages in comparable detail. We may find that our inference is refuted by such investigation. Consider, for example, the following argument, patterned on those presented above. We may have sentences such as (24) and (25), but not (26):

(24) (a) John, who likes math, goes to MIT.
      (b) People who like math are likely to get jobs.
      (c) John, who goes to MIT, likes math.
      (d) People who go to MIT are likely to get jobs.
(25) People who like math who go to MIT are likely to get jobs.
(26) John, who likes math, who goes to MIT, is likely to get a job.

In short, restrictive relative clauses can "stack" (as in (25)), whereas nonrestrictive relative clauses cannot (compare (26)). We may, as before, inquire into the origin of this principle. A reasonable proposal is that it is a general principle of language, determined by the language faculty. Thus, as before, it is difficult to believe that relevant information is invariably presented to individuals capable of making these distinctions in English. But in this case, the conclusion is too strong, it appears. It seems that in Japanese and Korean, for example, nonrestrictive relative clauses *can* stack, giving an analogue to (26) (furthermore, the two types of relatives do not seem to be distinguished in these languages). Therefore, we must search for some modified form of the original proposal to explain the property of English just noted, perhaps in terms of some other feature of the languages in question that determines whether relatives may or may not stack.

Our earlier inferences, being nondemonstrative, are subject to the same kind of check. The structure that we attribute to the genetically determined language faculty must meet two empirical conditions: it must be sufficiently rich and specific to account for the attainment of linguistic competence in particular languages, but it must not be so rich and specific that it excludes attested cases. The theory of "universal grammar" must fall between these empirical bounds.

When a particular proposal concerning universal grammar is advanced, we must subject it to empirical confirmation in this dual manner. In principle, straightforward tests are possible; namely, we might raise a person in a controlled environment in which information concerning the proposal in question is lacking and then determine whether behavior conforms to the proposal or not. Of course, such experiments are excluded. Part of the intellectual fascination of the study of language is that it is necessary to devise complex arguments to overcome the fact that direct experimentation is rarely possible. This unavoidable contingency in no way threatens the empirical status of the questions raised, though it does affect the credibility and force of particular theories.

Perhaps a comment might be in order on the matter of empirical confirmation of grammars. In the preceding discussion, I have based my argument on data from English; for example, the fact that the well-formed interrogatives are those of (2) and not (3), the fact that (7a) is not a paraphrase of (6a) (and, in fact, is not well formed), and so on. These factual observations are not the result of careful experimentation, though there would be no problem of principle in devising experiments to provide such observations over quite an interesting range. Of course, any proposed experiment would have to meet certain conditions of adequacy. Suppose that someone devised an experimental procedure, offering an operational criterion of "well-formedness," that assigned this property to the forms of (3) rather than (2). We would know that he had simply devised a bad experiment; his "operational criterion" was not a criterion for well-formedness, whatever else it might have been. It is very easy to design bad experiments, which provide meaningless results; to design experiments that provide useful data is much more difficult.

A related problem is that experimental data necessarily relate to behavior (performance) and thus bear only indirectly on the nature of the linguistic competence – the knowledge of language – that is only one factor in performance. The problem, of course, is not unique to the study of language. In physics, and indeed throughout the natural sciences, the problem always exists of determining how given experimental evidence bears on theories that involve crucial idealizations. From these inescapable contingencies of rational inquiry one cannot, of course, conclude that experimental data – in this case, studies of performance – are irrelevant to the postulated theories, nor has this absurd proposal ever been advanced, to my knowledge. Rather, we always face the problem of determining the import of observations on theoretical constructions, whether these observations derive from experiment or simply introspection.

Ultimately, we hope to construct a comprehensive integrated theory of performance that will spell out in precise detail the interaction of various systems, with knowledge of language (linguistic competence, grammar) among them. Observations of performance bear directly on this comprehensive system, hence indirectly on its postulated components. At the moment, we have only the glimmerings of such a comprehensive integrated theory, and therefore must always view observations of performance with care, naturally. Again, I note that this is true whether these observations derive from introspection, psycholinguistic experiment, neurophysiology, or whatever. All such observations are in principle of great importance and interest. Their bearing on theories of cognitive structure and function is rarely crystal clear and is often quite obscure.

These general observations, which should be fairly obvious, have often been made in the past. Still, there persists much misunderstanding about what has been proposed. As a case in point, consider the paper "Logic and the Theory of Mind" by Carol Fleisher Feldman and Stephen Toulmin, which appeared in the *Proceedings of the Nebraska Symposium on Motivation* (1974–75). Feldman and Toulmin assert that I have dealt with the "evidential problem in a dismissive manner," taking the "extreme position" that the "language behavior of laboratory subjects . . . can neither verify nor falsify the 'psychological reality' of structures in Chomskian grammar," thus regarding "observable data about behavior" as "unsuitable evidence" in contrast to " 'intuitions' of a native speaker" which are the "only appropriate substitute." This step, they conclude, "revolutionize[s] the ground rules of scientific inquiry."[2] But in fact this point of view is one that I have always explicitly rejected, for just the reasons outlined here.

It is quite true that no observations, whether of introspection or experiment, can conclusively verify or falsify the hypotheses of linguistic theory. It is also true that experimental results must meet certain conditions of intuitive adequacy to determine their import; consider, again, a hypothetical experiment that would class (3) rather than (2) as well formed. Furthermore, as I have repeatedly stressed, all observations must be judged with care for their relevance concerning theoretical hypotheses, for the reasons just outlined. Far from "revolutioniz[ing] the grounds of scientific inquiry," these comments simply indicate that inquiry into language is quite comparable to all nontrivial research in the natural sciences, in that it is always necessary to evaluate the import of experimental data on theoretical constructions, and in particular, to determine how such data bear on hypotheses that in nontrivial cases involve various idealizations and abstractions. But that experiment and observation of behavior can provide "suitable evidence" is a truism that I (and others) have never questioned and have repeatedly stressed.

I have touched on only a few examples. In each case, when we investigate the particular properties of human cognition, we find principles that are highly specific and narrowly articulated, structures of a marvelous intricacy and delicacy. As in the case of physical organs, there seems to be no possibility of accounting for the character and origin of basic mental structures in terms of organism-environment interaction. Mental and physical organs alike are determined, it seems, by species-specific, genetically determined properties, though in both cases interaction with the environment is required to trigger growth and will influence and shape the structures that develop. Our ignorance – temporary, let us hope – of the physical basis for mental structures compels us to keep to abstract characterization, in this case, but there is no reason to suppose that the physical structures involved are fundamentally different in character and development from other physical organs that are better understood, though a long tradition has tacitly assumed otherwise.

What of other cognitive abilities and achievements – say, the growth of our system of "common-sense" beliefs about physical space and the objects in it, about human action and the structure of personality, the nature and function of artifacts, and the like? Or what of the principles, now unknown, that underlie what Peirce called "abduction," that is, the principles by which humans construct scientific theories to explain phenomena that intrigue them? I see no reason to doubt that here too there are highly specific innate capacities that determine the growth of cognitive structures, some of which remain unconscious and beyond the bounds of introspection, while others, probably quite different in kind, are explicitly articulated and put to test. Our ignorance of these matters is profound, but it may be that the results of investigation of such relatively well defined cognitive domains as human language will suggest a useful model for further inquiry.

About the Fixed Nucleus and its Innateness:
Introductory Remarks

Jean Piaget

I should like to begin by expressing to Noam Chomsky the admiration that I have for his works and listing the essential points on which I think I am in agreement with him.

These points are so essential and so fundamental that the question of the heredity or innateness of language appears very minor to me. First of all, I agree with him on what I see as Chomsky's main contribution to psychology, which is that language is the product of intelligence or reason and not the product of learning in the behaviorist sense of the term. I also agree with him on the fact that this rational origin of language presupposes the existence of a fixed nucleus necessary to the elaboration of all languages, and presupposing, for example, the subject-to-predicate relation or the ability to construct relations. Finally, I naturally agree with him regarding the partial constructivism of his works, that is, the transformational grammars. I think, therefore, that we agree on the basic points, and I do not see any major conflict between Chomsky's linguistics and my own psychology. I can go so far as to say that on the issue relating to the relationships between language and thought, I consider myself to be in symmetry with Chomsky.

Why, then, is there a disagreement on the question of the innateness of the fixed nucleus? First, I would like to say that I believe I understand why Chomsky proposed this hypothesis: simply because it is a very common opinion to presuppose that a behavior is more stable if it is firmly rooted, that is, if it is hereditary and not simply a product of autoregulation. In other words, Chomsky's fixed nucleus would appear more stable, more important, and thus of higher value, if it were hereditarily fixed. If that opinion were true, I myself would adhere to the innateness of rational and linguistic structures. However, we know today that the problem of the innateness of behavior is a much more complex problem than that of any morphological character of the organism, and that it is very difficult to agree on innateness when one is dealing with the development of behaviors. It was a long time ago in psychology that McGraw wrote in *Carmichael's Manual*[6] that the alternative between maturation and experience was a false alternative that complicated discussions instead of enlightening them. In ethology as well, we have become very careful today for the same reasons; in this domain, we no longer speak of instinct in the same sense as that of Konrad Lorenz, because we have not found any stable limits between what is innate and what is acquired. Wickler, one of Lorenz's successors from Seewiesen, recently wrote an article[7] in which one passage really struck me: he said that the development of specific behaviors (for the term *instinct* is now replaced by the term *species-specific behavior*) is not only a product of selection, but in many cases, a product of phenocopy, a problem with which I will deal later on.

In regard to the innate fixed nucleus of language, I have been impressed with the recent works of Roger Brown,[8] Lenneberg,[9] and McNeill,[10] who became converted to explaining it by sensorimotor intelligence; McNeill in particular had been initially a very strong defender of innateness, and subsequently changed his opinion. Furthermore, I should like to recall the very profound remark made by James M. Baldwin[11] (obviously not a very recent remark), who said that the child is older than all the adults and that he is anterior to prehistoric man himself, which is perfectly obvious. Consequently, what is general in the child is not necessarily inherited from the adult. For instance, while studying in Geneva notions of physics held by young children, I discovered numerous examples of explanations of movement by Aristotle's *antiperistasis*, a hypothesis according to which the air that flows back behind a body whose own motion creates that airflow, pushes the body forward; this *antiperistasis* is a common notion in a 7- to 9-year-old child. I have also discovered in detail the notion of *impetus* as conceived by Buridan, hence of "impulse" as a necessary intermediary between force and movement. Now, it is perfectly clear that there is no hereditary link between Aristotle and Buridan, or between the little Genevans on whom I conducted my research in Geneva and the little Poles studied by Szeminska[12] in Poland.

In the case of Chomsky's innate fixed nucleus, it seems to me that a major objection is added to the difficulty: this innateness is not needed to ensure the formation and the stability of this nucleus; sensorimotor intelligence is sufficient for that. Sensorimotor intelligence, which can be studied between birth and the age of $1\frac{1}{2}$ to 2 years (that is, the beginnings of language), is distributed according to six successive stages which are characterized by schemes of action interrelated by virtue of a process of extremely regular autoregulation, with corrections, reinforcements, and so on. It is only at the sixth of these stages – that is, when the assimilation of objects to the schemes of action is able to be completed by an assimilation of objects themselves, in other words, by means of representation – that language begins; and at this sixth stage, these beginnings of language profit from a whole construction achieved previously and to which I shall refer later.

But what especially bothers me about the innateness hypothesis is that the current explanations of the neo-Darwinians concerning the formation of any new character trait in the organism are based solely on notions of mutation and selection. Now, a mutation necessarily occurs at random; therefore, if there were innateness, reason and language would be the result of selected accidents, but selected subsequently, after the fact, whereas the formation itself would be the result of mutations and would therefore occur at random. I claim that in that case, it would be tantamount to shaking the solidity of the fixed nucleus, and generally speaking the solidity of knowledge, instead of consolidating it, as one might wish to do by invoking the innateness hypothesis. Konrad Lorenz, who was both a Kantian and a biologist, understood this very well when he said that Kant's a priori notions are the equivalent of what is innate from the biological point of view, adding nevertheless: this is true, but heredity is specific, therefore it can vary from one species to another and thus has nothing necessary. He eventually translated Kant's a priori categories into simple "innate working hypotheses." I absolutely refuse, for my part, to think that logico-mathematical structures would owe their origin to chance; there is nothing fortuitous about them. These structures could not be formed by survival selection but by an exact and detailed adaptation to reality.

But let us suppose now that this innateness is demonstrated. The following could happen: genes or loci could be discovered that would allow the reality of such innateness to be demonstrated. In that case, I would answer that this is not a random mutation, but that the only possible explanation would have to be sought in the direction of phenocopies, that is, in the phenomenon that I have endeavored to explain as follows: The notion of phenocopy is a biological process in which certain behaviors – for it is mostly valid in the area of behaviors – or else a certain form or a morphological structure is first acquired by the phenotype, but without being genetically determined. The phenotype, by contrast, modifies the internal environment and the upper levels of the epigenetic environment, and in this way, the variations or the mutations which can occur in the genome will be selected, not by the external environment, but by that internal or epigenetic environment which will then channel it in the same direction as the trend already acquired by the phenotype; in other words, there would be a genetic or gene-linked reconstruction of an acquisition made by the phenotype. Therefore, demonstrating innateness would still not be proof of a random mutation. You will answer me, of course,

that I have no competence in biology; I am only a novice in that field, a novice, however, who has recently received two or three encouragements: the main one is to be found
in the book written by the late Waddington, which was, regrettably, his last one, *The
Evolution of an Evolutionist*.[13] He devotes the entire ninth chapter to the example of my
Limnea living in ponds or in the large lakes of Sweden or Switzerland;[14] he sees there
the best example of what he calls "genetic assimilation," which is an equivalent of
phenocopy. Waddington calls the Limnea the best case of genetic assimilation because
it was observed in nature and not produced in a laboratory, as for example in the case of
drosophila. Likewise, in a recent ethology symposium in Parma,[15] the Italian geneticist,
Francesco Scudo, referred to these same studies on Limnea and to other similar works
in order to explain their possible meaning in the case of the formation of an innate
behavior. In other words – and I am approaching my conclusion – there are two things
to consider: (1) there is no clear and total opposition, with well-defined boundaries, between
what is innate and what is acquired: all cognitive behavior includes a portion of innateness, in its functioning at least, whereas the structure appears to me to be constructed
bit by bit by autoregulation; (2) the real problem is not to decide whether such a fixed
nucleus or other cognitive structures are innate or not; the real question is: what has
been their formation process? And, in the case of innateness, what is the biological mode
of formation of that innateness? Are we dealing with random mutations, or with more
complex processes like that of phenocopy to which I just alluded?

If it were a question of phenocopy, it goes without saying that the initial construction
would be the result of behaviors, and, consequently, innateness becomes useless again
because, among the kinds of acquisition of behavior assured by the phenotype of any
species, some give rise later on to a phenocopy, but a very large number of others do not
give rise to any such gene-linked reconstructions – the phenotypic action and behavior
are simply formed anew at each generation without necessitating a hereditary fixation.

I will conclude my discussion by saying that innateness appears useless to me as far
as our present goal is concerned, which is to emphasize the stability and the importance
of cognitive structures and, in particular, of the fixed nucleus in the field of linguistics.
I believe that the processes of autoregulation are as stable and as capable of providing
the same importance in any formation as heredity itself. The following remark must be
made, however, as a final note: as a rule, autoregulation in the organism limits itself to
preserving a certain state of equilibrium and, in the case of deviation or of a new formation, to bringing it back to its initial state; whereas, on the contrary, autoregulation in
the realm of behaviors constantly pushes the organism – or the subject, if a cognitive
behavior is involved – toward new extensions. The physiological organism has no reason
at all to change; and as Monod very aptly wrote, there is no "necessity" in evolutionary
changes. Conservation is the supreme rule for physiological equilibrium. Whereas, on
the contrary, as soon as we approach the field of behavior, we find that two goals are
being pursued: the first one is the extension of the environment, that is, the surpassing
of that environment which now encompasses the organism, through explorations and
research in new environments; the second goal is the reinforcement of the organism's
power over that environment. An autoregulation that is capable of preserving the past
as well as constantly surpassing itself through the double end of extending the environment
and reinforcing the organism's power, appears to me, when we are dealing with behaviors and cognitive processes, a much more fundamental mechanism than heredity itself.

Chomsky Let me just say what I see as the question. First, is there a fixed cognitive structure, a fixed nucleus (*noyau fixe*)? The answer is yes – we all seem to agree on that. Second, on the question we are discussing, does this fixed nucleus – which I guess is what I have been calling universal grammar in this specific case – does it arise as a result of structural properties of the organism that are genetically determined, or does it arise in each particular case through self-regulating mechanisms? We ought to know how to pursue the answer to that question, not by philosophical discussion, but by looking at specific properties of the fixed nucleus and asking how they might arise from self-regulating mechanisms, from sensorimotor constructions, and so forth. Now, just to state my own view, it seems to me inconceivable that there is any significant relationship between these specific structures and any structures of sensorimotor intelligence or general properties of self-regulatory mechanisms. However, I am entirely open-minded on this issue: if somebody could show that some of the elementary properties of language that I discussed in my paper do result from self-regulatory mechanisms I would be delighted, but I don't anticipate it.

Another point that I think ought to be stated a little more sharply is this: the issue is not to account for the stability of the fixed nucleus; rather it is to account for its specific character. Piaget is quite right to say that there are many possible explanations for stability, but that is not even in question; the question is how do we account for the specific structures that we are led to attribute to the mature organism (and indirectly to the neonate) through the study of what it does, the way it acts, and so on. I think we ought to be able to try to find the answer to that problem by looking at the specific cases and looking at all the possible explanations, exactly as we would deal with the quite comparable question of the structure of the liver or the heart or the complex mechanisms of the visual cortex. We wouldn't have philosophical debates about them; we would simply ask whether the specific structures which we are led to believe exist and function in such and such a way with particular properties in organisms are genetically determined or result from the activity of individual self-regulatory mechanisms.

Piaget I will attempt to respond to Chomsky later by trying to show how sensorimotor intelligence prepares the semiotic function in general.

Piaget I would like to make a brief remark concerning what has just been said: "general" and "innate" should not be confused; the whole weakness of the works of Jung lies in the fact that he believed that because a myth is general it corresponds to an innate archetype. Now, first of all, generality alone is no proof of innateness; and second, the question is to know whether generality is common to all levels of development or whether it becomes so. In many cases structures become general, but they do not appear as general before the proper level comes under consideration, before we hit upon a level that can be studied very easily through experimentation.

Chomsky I agree with both of these points: the fact that a thing is general is only evidence that it is innate, but it doesn't demonstrate that it is innate. If something is not general then it is certainly not innate. But what we are interested in discovering here is properties that are biologically necessary, and generality is a necessary but not a sufficient property. Again, we run into the difficulty that we can't do experimental control; to distinguish between something that is just general and something that is biologically necessary, the obvious experiment is to construct a perfectly controlled environment; since that is ruled out we have to find out indirect ways of overcoming this nondemonstrative inference. The second point that I think is valid is a point I would like to emphasize, namely, that there are certain properties that are general and, I assume, biologically determined, but only at specific levels of development. For example, at a particular advanced level of development of some organ, some complicated thing will happen necessarily at that level, and correspondingly I would assume that specific properties of language structure, for instance, simply won't come into operation at all unless a certain level of complexity has been reached.

Chomsky   There are two proposals that have been made from the Geneva group presentations: one is Inhelder's statement that *some*, but not all, of the properties of language use and structure derive from sensorimotor construction; I don't dispute this statement in any way. The other proposal is that of Piaget, in which *all* of the properties of language use and structure derive from sensorimotor construction, or to put it in Piaget's logically equivalent terms, "This innateness is not needed to ensure the formation and the stability of [the fixed] nucleus; sensorimotor intelligence is sufficient for that." This second assertion seems false to me: I know of no reason to believe that the principles of sensorimotor construction or any other general developmental methods will suffice to account for all properties of the fixed nucleus. But one cannot deny that there are some properties of what people do in regard to language that relate to other aspects of their cognitive development. That is specifically why I have been interested in trying to find the properties of language structures and their use in the area of semantics (where there are a number) and in the area of syntax and phonology; precisely, I want to find those properties that cannot be plausibly related to other aspects of cognitive development, and I want to do this because I am interested in human nature.

Schemes of Action and Language Learning

Jean Piaget

I would like to explain in a few words why I believe language to be all of a piece with acquisitions made at the level of sensorimotor intelligence. In fact, sensorimotor intelligence already possesses a logic, but a logic in action, since there is not yet either thought, representation, or language. But these actions are coordinated according to a logic that already contains multiple structures, which will develop later in a spectacular manner. First there is, of course, a generalization of actions. For example, take a child in front of a hanging object: he tries to grasp it and fails, but this makes the object swing; then he becomes very interested, he continues to hit it to make it swing, and after that, every time he sees a hanging object he pushes it and makes it swing. Here is an act of generalization that obviously shows a beginning of logical generalization or intelligence. The fundamental phenomenon at the level of this logic of actions is the phenomenon of assimilation, and I will define assimilation as *the integration of new objects or new situations and events into previous schemes*; I define "scheme" as the result of those generalizations of which I just gave an example when talking about the hanging object. These schemes of assimilation are somewhat like concepts, but of a practical kind. They are concepts in the sense that they imply comprehension (comprehension as opposed to extension, to use the French vocabulary of logic);* they are concepts of comprehension, that is, they bear on qualities and predicates, but there is no extension yet. In other words, the child recognizes a hanging object, this is comprehension, but he does not have the means of representing to himself the totality of hanging objects. And if there is no extension, it is for lack of evocation, for in order to be able to represent to oneself the totality of objects with the same quality, one must naturally have a capacity of evocation, in other words, representation. This will be the role of the symbolic or semiotic function, which will come into existence much later on, but which is not present at the beginning, hence the limitations of these practical concepts which I call schemes of assimilation.

In contrast, if there is not yet any extension, there are coordinations of schemes, and it is these coordinations that are going to constitute all of sensorimotor logic. Here is an example of coordination: let us imagine an object placed on another one; the relation "placed on" can be coordinated with the action of "pull," and the child will pull toward himself an object placed on the blanket in order to be able to reach it. As for the way to verify if there is indeed coordination, one needs only to place the object a bit farther than its base; if the child continues to pull, this means he did not understand at all and there is no coordination, whereas if he waits for the object to be on top and then pulls, there is indeed coordination. In addition, one finds in this sensorimotor logic all sorts of correspondences or practical morphisms, morphisms in the mathematical sense; one finds relationships of order, of course: the means precede the arrival at the goal, and they have to be ordered in a certain sequence; one finds interdependencies, which means that a scheme can be interlocked with another as a particular scheme or a subscheme. In short, one finds a structure that announces the structure of logic.

Let us return to my first problem: how will the subject pass from this logic of action to a conceptual logic? Conceptual logic is, for me, the logic that comprises representation and thought, thus concepts defined in extension and not only in comprehension. This passage to conceptual logic is essentially a transformation of assimilation. Up to now, assimilation was the integration of an object to a scheme of action; for example, this object can be grasped, that other object can be grasped, and so on – all the objects to be grasped are assimilated, incorporated into a scheme of action which is the action of grasping. Whereas the new form of assimilation that is going to develop and allow conceptual logic is an assimilation between objects, and no longer only between objects and a scheme of action; in other words, the objects will be directly assimilated to each other, which will permit extension. But this presupposes evocation, of course; for this, there must be a necessity to evoke, that is, to think of something that is not actually and perceptibly present. Now, where does this evocation come from? It is here that we see the formation of the symbolic or semiotic function I just mentioned.

---

* Translator's note: In French logico-mathematical terminology, the word "comprehension" is frequently used to convey the notion of "intension" as opposed to extension.

The symbolic or semiotic function is formed during the second year and appears to me to be of great importance for our problem. Naturally, language is a particular case of this function, but it is *only* a particular case – particularly important, I do not deny – but a limited case within the totality of manifestations of the symbolic function.[16]

Chomsky perhaps will object that this is semantics, and that semantics is less interesting than syntax as far as our problem is concerned, but I claim that there is a syntax here, a logical syntax of course, since we are dealing with coordinations of schemes, coordinations playing a basic role in the logic to come. Imitation appears to me to play a very large role in the formation of the semiotic function. I mean by imitation not the imitation of a person – the child may not imitate someone's gesture – but the imitation of an object, that is, the copying by gestures of the characteristics of that object (for example, the object has a hole that must be enlarged, and this enlargement is imitated by the motion of opening and closing the mouth). This imitation plays a very large role because it can be motive at the outset, as in the case I have just mentioned, but it continues later on as an interiorized imitation. I claim that the mental image is nothing more, at the beginning, than an interiorized imitation that creates the ensuing representations.

Another form of symbolic function is symbolic play. There is, of course, some playing before the age we are concerned with; a baby plays very early, but his initial games are games involving the repetition of an action that is serious elsewhere. The child can exercise his ability, for example, by swinging a hanging object; then he simply plays with it for the pleasure of exercising his ability. This kind of play is a game of simple exercise or repetition in which there is as yet no symbolism, whereas at the level we are now examining, symbolic play begins, that is to say, play that evokes by means of gestures a situation that is not current, not perceptible.[17]

A third example that I would like to cite is deferred imitation; we call in psychology deferred imitation that which begins in the absence of the model.

Here is the context in which language begins. You can see my hypothesis: that the conditions of language are part of a vaster context, a context prepared by the various stages of sensorimotor intelligence. Six of these stages can be distinguished, which are notably different in terms of their successive acquisitions, but I found it sufficient to characterize sensorimotor logic in a rough way and then the appearance of this symbolic function. It is at this moment that language appears, and it can profit from all that was acquired by sensorimotor logic and by the symbolic function in the broad sense that I give to this term, of which language is only a particular case. I think, therefore, that there is a reason for this synchrony, and that there is a link between sensorimotor intelligence and language formation. I further believe that the formation of the symbolic function, which is a necessary derivative of sensorimotor intelligence, allows the acquisition of language, and this is the reason why, for my part, I do not see the necessity of attributing innateness to those structures (subject, predicate, relationships, and so on) which Chomsky calls the "fixed nucleus." I agree with Chomsky as to its necessity, but I do not believe in innateness given the fact that there is everything that is needed, it seems to me, in what I just said to explain its formation. In other words, and here I totally agree with Chomsky, language is a product of intelligence rather than intelligence being a product of language. These are the few facts I wanted to present to you for the discussion on the relationships between language and intelligence or thought.

One more point: this synchrony is meaningful as a synchronization because in the hypothesis of innateness, one does not see why language would not appear six months earlier or a year earlier or later. Why this synchronization? It does not appear to me to be the result of chance. Furthermore, if one wants to introduce innateness into language, why not introduce it into the symbolic function in its totality, and finally into anything that is general?

Discussion

Chomsky There is no question at all that the child is doing many things before he learns language. The question that has to be raised is what is the relationship between the things the child is doing prior to the development of language and the particular aspects of the structure of the system that develops. Now, Piaget's position is radically different from Inhelder's position, and I think that is an important point to keep in mind because a lot hinges on it. Inhelder's position is that certain aspects of the nature of language relate to constructions of sensori-motor intelligence or other elements of intellectual development. I have no argu-ment with that position. But Piaget's position is much stronger: he feels that it is unnecessary to postulate an innate structure to account for the particular aspects of the semantic structure of language or, he would doubtless say, of its syntactic or its phonological structure (I'm just projecting from what he said).

Piaget I have already said that all behaviors contain something innate and something acquired, but that we do not know where the separation should be placed. I have never denied that there was something innate as far as functioning (but not structure) is concerned; no one has ever been able to make an intelligent man out of an idiot.

Chomsky I agree, but that is inconsistent with your other point of view, because if there are elements of innateness involved in the structure of language, then it is false that it is unnecessary to postulate innate structures. We can't have it both ways – it is one or the other. At any rate, let's put aside the issue of logic and turn to the concrete question at hand.

We agreed that a certain number of things happen prior to the development of language; we want to know what is the relationship, if any, between these things that happen prior to the development of language and the system that emerges. And just to correct something that I think has been a persistent misunderstanding throughout much of this discussion, it is not true that I (or linguists in general) have special reasons for wanting to exclude semantics or pragmatics or whatever from the discussion. In fact, the examples in my paper all have to do with semantics in some manner. So I wouldn't agree with Piaget's remark or other remarks made earlier that to me syntax is intrinsically more interesting than semantics. Nevertheless, there is one respect in which this is true, and it is an important point that has a bearing on this discussion: Why is syntax, or the areas of interaction between syntax and semantics, more inter-esting? The reason is that in these areas there are results, there are principles that have been proposed, and naturally the field becomes intellectually more interesting to the extent that one obtains results. There are other areas of seman-tics in which we would like to have results – we would like to have principles about the nature of the concepts of language – but unfortunately such results are lacking beyond the most superficial level. *It is for this reason, and this reason alone, that many areas of semantics are not of much interest to me in relation to this discussion.* Now, we might ask why we don't have results in these other areas. It is possible that there are no results to be had, that is, it may be that semantics, over much of its range, is just an uninteresting subject, that there is nothing deep to discover in it. Or it is possible that there is something deep to discover in it and we haven't yet found it. But whatever the answer might be, I think that for the purpose of this discussion we should be concerned with those aspects of language for which we possess significant results, that is, some nontrivial general principles of considerable empirical import and explanatory power that are not superficially obvious (I have mentioned a few principles that I think are of this sort and that involve syntax and semantics).

If we focus on the areas in which there are a certain number of results (and as I suggested earlier, what we have is a picture of an integrated system with some moderately complex principles that lead to rather surprising phenomena and offer an explanation of an interesting range of facts), the question we have to ask is as follows: how is the specific structure of this particular mental organ related to the things that the child is doing before the system emerges? There are a number of possible answers to this question: one answer might be that there is no relation; the fact that there is a temporal succession, a regular progression, is not very impressive. Sexual maturation follows the acquisition of language, but we would not conclude from that that the acquisition of language determines the form of sexual maturation, for instance. There are a number of reasons why things happen in a regular order, which may have to do with the development of dendrites, for example. Lots of strange things are happening in the brain between the ages of 2 and 4; there is a very rich growth of dendritic structures, and this may have something to do with the fact that language is developing. Lots of other things are happening about which very little is known, but certainly it would not be at all surprising if the regular progression that we observe relates to biological phenomena having to do with this extraordinarily complex physical organ about which remarkably little is known, perhaps because of its complexity. So the order of progression seems to me to show very little.

Let's return to our question: what is the relationship between these early achievements of the child and the specific structure of the system that emerges? One could, perhaps, eventually adopt, at least sometimes, Piaget's stronger position, namely, that all aspects of this mental organ are determined by the constructions of sensorimotor intelligence (this is what I take to be the meaning of the statement that it is unnecessary to postulate any specific forms of innateness). From my point of view, the arguments against that position are, for the moment, overwhelming; it seems to me that in all the cases in which there is a principle that seems plausible with regard to the nature of this system, that principle has no demonstrable (or even suggestive) relationship to the constructions of sensorimotor intelligence. Therefore, the strong form of the thesis seems to me unacceptable. I have no objection if someone proposes it as a hypothesis with regard to something that may be discovered in the future, but I see no force whatsoever to that hypothesis today. What about a weaker concept? Could it be, for example, that the constructions of sensorimotor intelligence are a necessary condition for the emergence of language? There are different ways for investigating that, for example the way Jacques Monod suggested earlier. If in fact the constructions of sensorimotor intelligence are a necessary condition for the development of language, then it should turn out that insofar as those sensorimotor constructions are impeded, the intelligence that leads to the acquisition of language should also be impeded; and if they are drastically reduced, language ought to be virtually eliminated. So if one adopts this weaker position (one that may be true, but I have no doctrine on the matter), which claims that the constructions of sensorimotor intelligence are a necessary condition for the acquisition of language, then one must make a certain number of conjectures and go on to investigate them, for example the case of paraplegics. I don't know if anyone has investigated this, but my own prediction is that it would turn out that there is no relation whatsoever, or at best the most marginal relation, between even extreme defects that would make it virtually impossible for a child to develop and do all the various things that Piaget was discussing, and his acquisition of language. Again, I don't know if this has been studied systematically, but there are at least some suggestive results. For example, there have been numerous studies on the rate of acquisition of language in blind children, who have, if not one hundred percent reduction, at least a significant reduction in their capacity to develop constructions of sensorimotor intelligence, especially those constructions that involve the visual world. Yet in this case it appears that blind children acquire language more rapidly than sighted children, which isn't so surprising in certain respects because they are more dependent on it. In any event, there is no linguistic impairment in such cases, and if a child were paralyzed, for example, my prediction would be that it would have no noticeable effect on his language development. If this is true, it is hard to see in what sense one might maintain the weaker thesis, namely, that the constructions of sensorimotor intelligence are a necessary condition for the acquisition of language. However, this thesis might be true in a still weaker sense, as Fodor suggested earlier: it could turn out that the development of schemes of action has a *triggering function*. This is something that is understood in biology – for example, let's take something that is analogous in some way to the problem of acquisition of language: the Hubel-Wiesel structures, the structures that underlie visual space. Since the studies begun ten or fifteen years ago on determining the reactions of single cells with microelectrodes, a vast amount of information has been accumulated about the highly specific structure of the most superficial processing in the visual cortex. One of the by-products of this work has been the theory that these structures degenerate; they simply don't function unless there is a certain triggering experience. In other words, unless the kitten has patterned stimulation presented to it at the appropriate age, these systems will simply degenerate – a neuronal degeneration takes place. Diffuse light will not suffice to keep the systems functioning, and naturally blindness will destroy them very significantly. Of course, the pattern of stimulation does not determine what the system does, the latter is just going to do essentially what it is designed to do. Experience won't turn a kitten into an octopus. But the pattern of stimulation will determine the activation of the system. It's a little bit like turning on the ignition in an automobile: it's necessary that you turn the key for the car to run, but the structure of the internal combustion engine is not determined by this act. This structure will do what it has to do when you start it with the key. It is perfectly possible and conceivable that certain kinds of interaction with the external world serve a triggering function for the acquisition of language; this is a still weaker theory, in terms of what one might propose, and I have no idea whether it is true or false. There is no reason to believe it at the moment, to my knowledge. The only reason that has been proposed, as far as I can see, is the matter of orderly progression, which as I have said is not very important evidence in my view, and also the fact that there are some not very general similarities between some of the things that happen in language and some of the things that happen elsewhere: representation, schemata, embedding, temporal order, and so on. However, as soon as we look at any of the particular aspects of language, whether semantic or syntactic, about which there are any nontrivial results (again, by that I mean principles of some generality that have an explanatory power), it appears that there is no resemblance, no similarity, no relationship between these principles and any known constructions of sensorimotor intelligence. That is not to say that somebody may not discover such relationships someday; I just don't *see* any relationship, and to my knowledge, no one has offered a plausible case that there is such a relationship. I would say, then, that a rational approach would be to assume that in the domain where we have some nontrivial results concerning the structure of language, the principles of organization that determine the specific structures of language are simply part of the initial state of the organism. As far as we know these principles don't generalize, that is, there are no known analogues in other domains of intelligence (it is possible that such analogues are partially there, but this remains to be seen). I think that it is rational to draw this conclusion on the basis of what little we know. And furthermore, to pick up a remark of Fodor's, this is in a way the null hypothesis. Even if there were no evidence at all, I would say that it is a reasonable conjecture because it is very hard to imagine anything else. For example, if there are constructions of sensorimotor intelligence or particular concepts that develop in particular ways, then I would think, as Fodor argued, that *in those cases too we will just have to assume that the concepts themselves are essentially innately determined, since we know of no other way of accounting for their acquisition.* Thus the discovery (if it is a discovery; to me it seems to be) of what I regard as strong evidence that particular aspects of language are innately determined simply seems to me to be a confirmation of the null hypothesis, interesting but not surprising.

Notes

1   Considering the number of these additions and not only their result.
2   Let us recall that completive generalization is a constructive process essential in mathematics: for example, the transition from passages of groupoids to semigroups, then from there to monoids, then to groups, to rings, and to bodies.

3   It is true that autoregulation is in part innate, but more in terms of functioning than in terms of structures.

4   H. von Foerster, "On Self-organizing Systems and their Environments," in *Self-organizing Systems*, ed. M. Yovitz and S. E. Cameron (Elmsford, NY: Pergamon Press, 1960).

5   J. Piaget, *Adaptation vitale et psychologie de l'intelligence: Sélection organique et phénocopie* (Paris: Hermann, 1974).

6   P. H. Mussen, ed., *Carmichael's Manual of Child Psychology* (New York: Wiley, 1970).

7   W. Wickler, "Vergleigende Verhaltensforschung und Phylogenetik," in G. Heberer, *Die Evolution der Organismen*, vol. 1 (Stuttgart: Fisher, 1967).

8   R. W. Brown, *Psycholinguistics: Selected Papers by Roger Brown* (New York: Free Press, 1970).

9   E. E. Lenneberg, *Biological Foundations of Language* (New York: Wiley, 1967); see also "On Explaining Language," *Science* 164: 635–43, 1969.

10 D. McNeill, in *Sentences as Biological Systems*, ed. P. Weiss (1971), pp. 59–68.

11 J. M. Baldwin, *Dictionary of Philosophy and Psychology* (Gloucester, Mass.: Smith, 1960).

12 A. Szeminska, in J. Piaget et al., *Etudes d'épistémologie génétique*, vol. 27, *La Transmission des mouvements* (Paris: Presses Universitaires de France, 1972).

13 C. Waddington, *The Evolution of an Evolutionist* (Ithaca, NY: Cornell University Press, 1975).

14 In Lake Geneva, at a depth of 900 feet, lives a small Limnea that appears to be completely different from any littoral species. As recently as a few years ago, when we were able to obtain live specimens and raise them in an aquarium, there was an immediate return to the initial type. In that particular case, we were dealing only with a phenotypic variation that recurred in each generation, with no necessity for genotypic reconstruction.

15 A. Belestrieri, D. De Martis, and O. Siciliani, eds., *Etologia e Psichiatria* (Rome: Laterza, 1974).

16 I was able to observe a beginning of this symbolic function in two of my children. First, in one of my daughters: I showed her a half-opened box of matches, and while she watched I put an object in it (a thimble; I must specify that it was not something to eat, and we shall see why). The child tried to open the box to reach the object that was inside. She pulled on all sides, but nothing happened; finally she stopped, looked at the box, and opened and closed her mouth. This was the symbolization of what she had to do (since there was nothing good to eat inside). A new fact confirmed this interpretation: I repeated the experiment four years later with my son, at the same age, and he, instead of opening and closing his mouth when he did not succeed in opening the box, looked at the slit and at his hand, and then opened and closed his hand. It was, therefore, the same symbolization. This time, the hand was used instead of the mouth, but one immediately sees that it is again the representation of the goal to be reached (besides, once this evocation was over, he stuck his finger in the slit and started to pull). The two children, four years apart, resolved the problem only after this symbolic evocation.

17 The first symbolic play I observed was in one of my daughters. This child, in order to fall asleep, needed to grab the corner of a cloth, and then take her thumb and suck on it. One morning, when she was wide awake in her crib, her mother took her in her bed. The girl did not want to go back to sleep and remained sitting in bed, but she noticed a corner of the sheet, took it in her hand, put her thumb in her mouth, and then bent her head and closed her eyes. She made believe she was asleep while smiling and without lying down. This time, she imitated herself; she imitated the whole ritual that she used every night to fall asleep. This is an example of symbolic play; several days later, there was a huge proliferation, and the symbolic play became much more complex.

5

Comparative Linguistics and Language Acquisition

Hermine Sinclair[-deZwart]

Let me start by limiting the scope of my paper: it will only be concerned with grammar, i.e. morphology and syntax. I believe that what is specific to language as a system of representation and communication in comparison with other ways of representation and communication is its grammatical structure. I also believe that the acquisition of grammar cannot be studied fruitfully without taking into account cognitive development in general.

For grammar, I will refer to the theory elaborated by Chomsky and his colleagues, since it is explicitly proposed as a theory of acquisition as well as a linguistic theory. For cognitive development in general, I will refer to what I consider to be the most coherent theory of the acquisition of knowledge, i.e. Piaget's psychogenetic and epistemological theory.

Briefly, Chomsky and his followers are constructing a theory of language knowledge that aims to be universal and at the same time to be a model of acquisition of language by the child. It is not a theory of how speakers use language in various situations of communication.

Though universal grammar and core-grammar are proposed as a model for acquisition, this theory remains strictly linguistic in the sense that the linguists work backwards from their own expert knowledge of one or a few languages, deriving increasingly general rules and principles that capture the regularities of what appear to be very disparate phenomena. Strictly speaking, only data from other languages can invalidate the hypothesized structures. Data from child-language, pathology or non-expert adult judgments of well-formedness can at best provide supporting evidence only. Some Chomskyan linguists, however, think that such evidence could be important. The theory remains structuralist and lacks a functional component. Nonetheless, the work done in the last 10 years or so in the framework of this theory has yielded many insights which, in my opinion,

From "Comparative Linguistics and Language Acquisition" in *Vitalidad e influencia de las lenguas indígenas en Latinoamérica*, edited by Ramón Arzápalo and Yolanda Lastra, pp. 97, 98–9, 103–5. México, D.F.: Instituto de Investigaciones Antropológicas, 1995.

cannot be ignored by psycholinguists: its search for universal principles that have reper-
cussions and implications throughout the total system of a language, and its endeavour
to give abstract structural representations of different layers of a linguistic system are
in certain ways compatible with Piaget's epistemological and psychological theory, which
can also be thought of as universalist and structuralist.

Piaget's theory is universalist, because all human beings are supposed to make sense
of the physical and social environment they live in by universal processes of reasoning
resulting in universal structures of thought; though speed and outcome of the process
may vary considerably according to socio-cultural factors, processes and structures are
fundamentally the same. This universality underlying socio-cultural variety has been
confirmed by many intercultural studies in child development.

It is structuralist, because Piaget and his collaborators captured the ways humans make
sense of the world of objects and people, i.e. their reasoning patterns in systems of a
logic of actions and thinking, systems that can be described as abstract structures.

There are, however, important differences between Piaget's epistemological and
psychological theory of knowledge and that of Chomskyan grammar. Piaget's theory is
focused on the problem of progress and development of knowledge. It uses three sources
of data:

1]   the study of the development of basic concepts in the child,
2]   the history of science,
3]   formal models of the state of scientific knowledge at a particular time.

Thus it not only aims at providing abstract representations of successive structures
that capture privileged stages in knowledge, but it also proposes universal functional
processes of development and progress.

I certainly do not think that it is as yet possible to give a clear summary of the constructivist view of language acquisition. First, we all agree that the analysis of spontaneous production of utterances may not give a correct picture of knowledge of language,
even if this is restricted to grammar. The child also understands utterances, and understanding exceeds production, as has been demonstrated by Sachs and Truswell (1978);
understanding is also based on knowledge. Moreover, in both the production and the
comprehension of utterances, knowledge of language is interacting with many other
kinds of knowledge, as well as with beliefs and emotions – this is true for the child in
interaction with an adult or with another child as it is for the adult in everyday conversation or when preparing a paper. Experimentation always introduces some artificiality,
but experiments certainly seem necessary if we want to investigate the acquisition of
grammar. Very few psycholinguistic experiments have as yet been carried out that
captured basic grammatical competence in the way Piaget's well-known experiments captured the underlying patterns of reasoning and their development in situations bearing
on fundamental concepts. Nonetheless, the guiding principle of progressive changes in
the relation between the knowing subject and the object of his knowledge, through the
construction of, first, structural fragments, then differentiations and integrations into
increasingly varied and more powerful systems by means of abstraction would seem to
be equally fruitful for developmental psycholinguistics.

References

Chomsky, N. 1980. *Rules and Representations*. New York: Columbia University Press.

Chomsky, N. 1985. *Knowledge of Language*. New York: Praeger.

Dore, J. 1985. "Holophrases revisited" in M. D. Barret, ed., *Children's Single Word Speech*. New York, Wiley, pp. 23–55.

Hyams, N. 1986. *Language Acquisition and the Theory of Parameters*. Dordrecht: Reidel.

Lust, B. 1983. "On the notion 'principal branching direction', a parameter of universal grammar" in Y. Otsu, H. van Riemsdijk, K. Inoue, A. Kamio and N. Kawasaki, eds., *Studies in Generative Grammar and Language Acquisition*. Tokyo: International Christian University, pp. 137–151.

Piaget, J. 1936. *La Naissance de l'intelligence chez l'enfant*. Neuchâtel: Delachaux et Niestlé.

Piaget, J. 1937. *La Construction du réel chez l'enfant*. Neuchâtel: Delachaux et Niestlé.

Piaget, J. 1945. *La Formation du symbole chez l'enfant*. Neuchâtel: Delachaux et Niestlé.

Piaget, J. A. and R. García. 1983. *Psychogenèse et histoire des sciences*. Paris: Flammarion.

Piaget, J. A. and R. García. 1987. *Vers une logique des significations*. Geneva: Murionde.

Sachs, J. and L. Truswell. 1978. "Comprehension of two-word instructions by children in the one-word stage." *Journal of Child Language*, 5: 17–24.

Sinclair, H., I. Berthoud-Papandropoulou, J. P. Bronckart, H. Chipman, E. Ferreiro and E. Rappe du Cher. 1976. "Recherche en psycho-linguistique génétique." *Archives de Psychologie*, 44: 157–75.

Sinclair, H., M. Stambak, I. Lézine, S. Rayna and M. Verba. 1982. *Les Bébés et les choses*. Paris: Presses Universitaires de France.

Veneziano, E., H. Sinclair and I. Berthoud. 1990. "From one word to two words." *Journal of Child Language*, 17: 633–50.

Part II

The Nature–Nurture Controversies

6

Language in the Context of Growth and Maturation

Eric H. Lenneberg

I Characteristics of Maturation of Behavior

Why do children normally begin to speak between their 18th and 28th month? Surely it is not because all mothers on earth initiate language training at that time. There is, in fact, no evidence whatever that any conscious and systematic teaching of language takes place, just as there is no special training for stance or gait. Superficially, it is tempting to assume that a child begins to speak as soon as he has a need for it. However, there is no way of testing this assumption because of the subjectivity of the notion of need. We have here the same logical difficulties as in testing the universality of the pleasure principle as the prime motivation.

To escape the inevitable circularity of the argument we might ask: Do the child's needs change at 18 months because his environment regularly changes at that time, or because he himself undergoes important and relevant changes? Society and parents do behave somewhat differently to an older child, and thus there are some environmental innovations introduced around the time of the onset of speech; yet the changes of the social environment are to a great extent in response to changes in the child's abilities and behavior. Quite clearly the most important differences between the prelanguage and postlanguage phases of development originate in the growing individual and not in the external world or in changes in the availability of stimuli. Therefore, any hypothesis that pivots on an assumption of need may be restated: the needs that arise by eighteen months and cause language to develop are primarily due to maturational processes within the individual. Since needs *per se* can be defined only in a subjective and logically circular manner, it is futile to begin an inquiry into the relevant factors of speech development by the adoption of a need-hypothesis. Instead, we must try to understand the nature of the maturational processes. The central and most interesting problem is whether the emergence of language is due to very general capabilities that mature to a critical minimum at about eighteen months to make language, and many other skills, possible, or whether there might be some factors specific to speech and language that

From *Biological Foundations of Language*. New York: John Wiley, 1967, pp. 125–31.

come to maturation and that are somewhat independent from other, more general processes.

Unfortunately, the importance and role of maturation in the development of language readiness cannot be explored systematically by direct experiment, and we are reduced to making inferences from a variety of observations and by extrapolation. The difficulty is that we cannot be certain what kind of experiments or observations to extrapolate from. Behavior is far from the monolithic, clear-cut, self-evident phenomenon postulated by psychologists a generation ago. Different aspects of behavior make their emergence at different periods in the life cycle of an individual and for a variety of causes. Furthermore, the spectrum of causes changes with species.

The hallmarks for maturationally controlled emergence of behavior are the following (1) regularity in the sequence of appearance of given milestones, all correlated with age and other concomitant development facts; (2) evidence that the opportunity for environmental stimulation remains relatively constant throughout development, but that the infant makes different use of such opportunities as he grows up; (3) emergence of the behavior either in part or entirely, before it is of any immediate use to the individual; (4) evidence that the clumsy beginnings of the behavior are not signs of goal-directed practice.

Points (1) and (2) are obvious and need no elaboration. Point (3) is commonplace in the embryology of behavior. A vast array of motor patterns may be observed to occur spontaneously or upon stimulation in embryos long before the animal is ready to make use of such behavior. The so-called *Leerlaufreaktion* or vacuum activity observed by ethologists is another example of emergence of behavior at given developmental stages and in the absence of any use or externally induced need-fulfillment (for details see Hess, 1962; Lorenz, 1958).

Point (4), the relatively unimportant role of practice for the emergence of certain types of behavior with maturation, has been amply demonstrated in animals by Carmichael (1926, 1927), Grohmann (1938), and by Thomas and Schaller (1954). Similarly, children whose legs had been immobilized by casts (for correcting congenital hip deformations) at the time that gait normally develops can keep perfect equilibrium and essentially appear "to know" how to walk when released from the mechanical handicap even though their muscles may be too weak during the first weeks to sustain weight over many steps.

Generally, there is evidence that species-specific motor coordination patterns (*Erbkoordination*) emerge according to a maturational schedule in every individual raised in an adequate environment. The emergence of such patterns is independent of training procedures and extrinsic response shaping. Once the animal has matured to the point at which these patterns are present, the actual occurrence of a specific pattern movement may depend upon external or internal stimuli (for instance, certain hormone levels in the blood) or a combination of the two (Lehrman, 1958a and 1958b).

The aim of these comments is to direct attention to *potentialities* of behavior – the underlying matrix for behaving – instead of to a specific *act*. If we find that emergence of a certain behavior may be partially or wholly attributed to changes within the organism rather than causative changes in the environment, we must at once endeavor to discover what organic changes there are. Unless we can demonstrate a somatic basis, all our speculations are useless.

The four characteristics of maturationally controlled emergence of behavior will now be employed as touchstones, so to speak, in discussing whether the onset of language may reasonably be attributed to a maturational process.

II Emergence of Speech and Language

(1) The regularity of onset

The onset of speech consists of a gradual unfolding of capacities; it is a series of generally well-circumscribed events which take place between the second and third year of life. Certain important speech milestones are reached in a fixed sequence and at a relatively constant chronological age. Just as impressive as the age constancy is the remarkable synchronization of speech milestones with motor-developmental milestones, summarized in Table 4.1.

The temporal interlocking of speech milestones and motor milestones is not a logical necessity. There are reasons to believe that the onset of language is not simply the consequence of motor control. The development of language is quite independent of articulatory skills (Lenneberg, 1962); and the perfection of articulation cannot be predicted simply on the basis of general motor development. There are certain indications for the existence of a peculiar, language-specific maturational schedule. Many children have learned a word or two before they start to toddle, and thus must be assumed to possess a sufficient degree of motor skill to articulate, however primitive; yet the expansion of their vocabulary is still an extremely slow process. Why could they not rapidly increase their lexicon with "sloppy" sound-symbols much the way a child with a cleft palate does at age three? Similarly, parents' inability to train their children at this stage to join the words *daddy* and *by-by* into a single utterance cannot be explained on the grounds of motor incompetence, because at the same age children babble for periods as long as the duration of a sentence. In fact, the babbled "sentence" may be produced complete with intonation patterns. The retarding factor for language acquisition here must be a psychological one, or perhaps better, a cognitive one and not mechanical skill. About age three manual skills show improved coordination over earlier periods, but dexterity is still very immature on an absolute scale. Speech, which requires infinitely precise and swift movements of tongue and lips, all well-coordinated with laryngeal and respiratory motor systems, is all but fully developed when most other mechanical skills are far below their levels of future accomplishment. The evolvement of various motor skills and motor coordinations also has specific maturational histories; but the specific history for speech control stands apart dramatically from histories of finger and hand control.

The independence of language development from motor coordination is also underscored by the priority of language comprehension over language production. Ordinarily the former precedes the latter by a matter of a few months (especially between the ages of 18 to 36 months). In certain cases this gap may be magnified by many years (Lenneberg, 1964). Careful and detailed investigations of the development of understanding by itself have been undertaken only in more recent years (Brown and Bellugi, 1964;

Table 6.1 Developmental milestones in motor and language development

At the completion of:	Motor development	Vocalization and language
12 weeks	Supports head when in prone position; weight is on elbows; hands mostly open; no grasp reflex	Markedly less crying than at 8 weeks; when talked to and nodded at, smiles, followed by squealing-gurgling sounds usually called *cooing*, which is vowel-like in character and pitch-modulated; sustains cooing for 15–20 seconds
16 weeks	Plays with a rattle placed in his hands (by shaking it and staring at it), head self-supported; tonic neck reflex subsiding.	Responds to human sounds more definitely; turns head; eyes seem to search for speaker; occasionally some chuckling sounds
20 weeks	Sits with props	The vowel-like cooing sounds begin to be interspersed with more consonantal-sounds; labial fricatives, spirants and nasals are common; acoustically, all vocalizations are very different from the sounds of the mature language of the environment
6 months	Sitting: bends forward and uses hands for support; can bear weight when put into standing position, but cannot yet stand with holding on; reaching: unilateral; grasp: no thumb apposition yet; releases cube when given another	Cooing changing into babbling resembling one-syllable utterances; neither vowels nor consonants have very fixed recurrences; most common utterances sound somewhat like ma, mu, da, or di
8 months	Stands holding on; grasps with thumb apposition; picks up pellet with thumb and finger tips	Reduplication (or more continuous repetitions) becomes frequent; intonation patterns become distinct; utterances can signal emphasis and emotions
10 months	Creeps efficiently; takes side-steps, holding on; pulls to standing position	Vocalizations are mixed with sound-play such as gurgling or bubble-blowing; appears to wish to imitate sounds, but the imitations are never quite successful; beginning to differentiate between words heard by making differential adjustment
12 months	Walks when held by one hand; walks on feet and hands – knees in air; mouthing of objects almost stopped; seats self on floor	Identical sound sequences are replicated with higher relative frequency of occurrence and words (mamma or dadda) are emerging; definite signs of understanding some words and simple commands (show me your eyes)
18 months	Grasp, prehension and release fully developed; gait stiff, propulsive and precipitated; sits on child's chair with only fair aim; creeps downstairs backward; has difficulty building tower of 3 cubes	Has a definite repertoire of words – more than three, but less than fifty; still much babbling but now of several syllables with intricate intonation pattern; no attempt at communicating information and no frustration for not being understood; words may include items such as thank you or come here, but there is little ability to join any of the lexical items into spontaneous two-item phrases; understanding is progressing rapidly

Table 6.1   (cont'd)

At the completion of:	Motor development	Vocalization and language
24 months	Runs, but falls in sudden turns; can quickly alternate between sitting and stance; walks stairs up or down, one foot forward only	Vocabulary of more than 50 items (some children seem to be able to name everything in environment); begins spontaneously to join vocabulary items into two-word phrases; all phrases appear to be own creations; definite increase in communicative behavior and interest in language
30 months	Jumps up into air with both feet; stands on one foot for about two seconds; takes few steps on tip-toe; jumps from chair; good hand and finger coordination; can move digits independently; manipulation of objects much improved; builds tower of six cubes	Fastest increase in vocabulary with many new additions every day; no babbling at all; utterances have communicative intent; frustrated if not understood by adults; utterances consist of at least two words, many have three or even five words; sentences and phrases have characteristic child grammar, that is, they are rarely verbatim repetitions of an adult utterance; intelligibility is not very good yet, though there is great variation among children; seems to understand everything that is said to him
3 years	Tiptoes three yards; runs smoothly with acceleration and deceleration; negotiates sharp and fast curves without difficulty; walks stairs by alternating feet; jumps 12 inches; can operate tricycle	Vocabulary of some 1000 words; about 80% of utterances are intelligible even to strangers; grammatical complexity of utterances is roughly that of colloquial adult language, although mistakes still occur
4 years	Jumps over rope; hops on right foot; catches ball in arms; walks line	Language is well-established; deviations from the adult norm tend to be more in style than in grammar

Ervin, 1964; Ervin and Miller, 1963). The evidence collected so far leaves little doubt that there is also an orderly and constant progression in this aspect of language development.

References

Brown, R. W. and Bellugi, U. 1964. Three processes in the child's acquisition of syntax. In E. H. Lenneberg (ed.), *New Directions in the Study of Language*. Cambridge, Mass.: MIT Press, pp. 131–61.

Carmichael, L. 1926. The development of behavior in vertebrates experimentally removed from the influence of external stimulation. *Psychol. Rev.*, 33, 51–8.

Carmichael, L. 1927. A further development of the development of behavior in vertebrates experimentally removed from the influence of external stimulation, *Psychol. Rev.*, 34, 34–47.

Ervin, S. M. 1964. Imitation and structural change in children's language. In E. H. Lenneberg (ed.), *New Directions in the Study of Language*. Cambridge, Mass.: MIT Press, pp. 163–89.

Ervin, S. M. and Miller, W. R. 1963. Language development. *Child Psychology* (62nd Yearbook, National Society for the Study of Education). Chicago: University of Chicago Press, pp. 108–43.

Grohmann, J. 1938. Modifikation oder Funktionsregung? Ein Beitrag zur Klärung der wechsel-eitigen Beziehungen zwischen Instinkthandlung und Erfahrung, *Z. Tierpsychol.*, 2, 132–44.

Hess, E. H. 1962. Ethology: an approach toward the complete analysis of behavior. In R. W. Brown, E. Galanter, E. H. Hess, and G. Mandler (eds), *New Directions in Psychology*. New York: Holt, Rinehart, and Winston.

Lehrman, D. S. 1958a. Induction of broodiness by participation in courtship and nest-building in the Ring Dove (*Streptopelia risoria*). *J. Comp. Physiol. Psychol.*, 51, 32–6.

Lehrman, D. S. 1958b. Effect of female sex hormones on incubation behavior in the Ring Dove (*Streptopelia risoria*). *J. Comp. Physiol. Psychol.*, 51, 142–5.

Lenneberg, E. H. 1962. Understanding language without ability to speak: a case report. *J. Abnorm. Soc. Psychol.*, 65, 419–25.

Lenneberg, E. H. 1964. Speech as a motor skill with special reference to non-aphasic disorders. In U. Bellugi and R. Brown (eds), *The Acquisition of Language* (Monograph of the Society for Research in Child Development, no. 92; vol. 29, no. 1), pp. 115–27.

Lorenz, K. H. 1958. The evolution of behavior. *Scientific American*, 119 no. 6 (December), 67–78.

Thomas, E. and Schaller, F. 1954. Das Spiel der optisch isolierten, jungen Kasper-Hauser-Katze. *Naturwiss.*, 41, 557–8.

7

Language and the Brain

Norman Geschwind

Virtually everything we know of how the functions of language are organized in the human brain has been learned from abnormal conditions or under abnormal circumstances: brain damage, brain surgery, electrical stimulation of brains exposed during surgery and the effects of drugs on the brain. Of these the most fruitful has been the study of language disorders, followed by postmortem analysis of the brain, in patients who have suffered brain damage. From these studies has emerged a model of how the language areas of the brain are interconnected and what each area does.

A disturbance of language resulting from damage to the brain is called aphasia. Such disorders are not rare. Aphasia is a common aftereffect of the obstruction or rupture of blood vessels in the brain, which is the third leading cause of death in the US. Although loss of speech from damage to the brain had been described occasionally before the 19th century, the medical study of such cases was begun by a remarkable Frenchman, Paul Broca, who in 1861 published the first of a series of papers on language and the brain. Broca was the first to point out that damage to a specific portion of the brain results in disturbance of language output. The portion he identified, lying in the third frontal gyrus of the cerebral cortex, is now called Broca's area [see illustration on page 00].

Broca's area lies immediately in front of the portion of the motor cortex that controls the muscles of the face, the jaw, the tongue, the palate and the larynx, in other words, the muscles involved in speech production. The region is often called the "motor face area." It might therefore seem that loss of speech from damage to Broca's area is the result of paralysis of these muscles. This explanation, however, is not the correct one. Direct damage to the area that controls these muscles often produces only mild weakness of the lower facial muscles on the side opposite the damage and no permanent weakness of the jaw, the tongue, the palate or the vocal cords. The reason is that most of these muscles can be controlled by either side of the brain. Damage to the facial motor face area on one side of the brain can be compensated by the control center on the opposite

From *Scientific American* 226: 4 (1972), pp. 76–83. Reprinted with permission. © 1972 by Scientific American, Inc. All rights reserved.

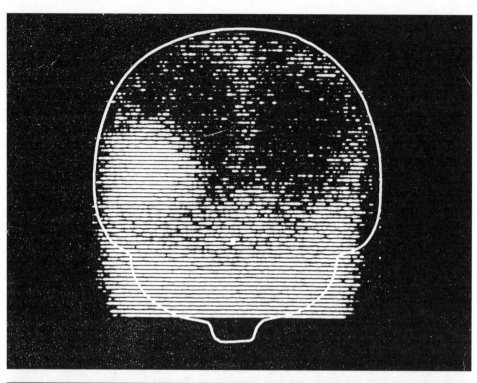
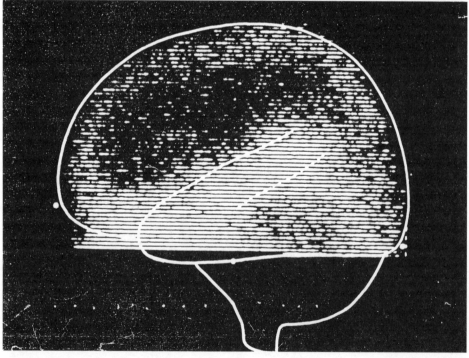

side. Broca named the lesion-produced language disorder "aphemia," but this term was soon replaced by "aphasia," which was suggested by Armand Trousseau.

In 1865 Broca made a second major contribution to the study of language and the brain. He reported that damage to specific areas of the left half of the brain led to disorder of spoken language but that destruction of corresponding areas in the right side of the brain left language abilities intact. Broca based his conclusion on eight consecutive cases of aphasia, and in the century since his report his observation has been amply confirmed. Only rarely does damage to the right hemisphere of the brain lead to language disorder; out of 100 people with permanent language disorder caused by brain lesions approximately 97 will have damage on the left side. This unilateral control of certain functions is called cerebral dominance. As far as we know man is the only mammal in which learned behavior is controlled by one half of the brain. Fernando Nottebohm of Rockefeller University has found unilateral neural control of birdsong. It is an interesting fact that a person with aphasia of the Broca type who can utter at most only one or two slurred words may be able to sing a melody rapidly, correctly and even with elegance. This is another proof that aphasia is not the result of muscle paralysis.

In the decade following Broca's first report on brain lesions and language there was a profusion of papers on aphasias of the Broca type. In fact, there was a tendency to believe all aphasias were the result of damage to Broca's area. At this point another great pioneer of the brain appeared on the scene. Unlike Broca, who already had a reputation at the time of his first paper on aphasia, Carl Wernicke was an unknown with no previous publications; he was only 26 years old and a junior assistant in the neurological service in Breslau. In spite of his youth and obscurity his paper on aphasia, published in 1874, gained immediate attention. Wernicke described damage at a site in the left hemisphere outside Broca's area that results in a language disorder differing from Broca's aphasia.

In Broca's aphasia speech is slow and labored. Articulation is crude. Characteristically, small grammatical words and the endings of nouns and verbs are omitted, so that the speech has a telegraphic style. Asked to describe a trip he has taken, the patient may say "New York." When urged to produce a sentence, he may do no better than "Go . . . New York." This difficulty is not simply a desire to economize effort, as some have suggested. Even when the patient does his best to cooperate in repeating words, he has difficulty with certain grammatical words and phrases. "If he were here, I would go" is more difficult than "The general commands the army." The hardest phrase for such patients to repeat is "No ifs, ands or buts."

The aphasia described by Wernicke is quite different. The patient may speak very rapidly, preserving rhythm, grammar and articulation. The speech, if not listened to closely,

Figure 7.1   (opposite) Location of some lesions in the brain can be determined by injecting into the bloodstream a radioactive isotope of mercury, which is taken up by damaged brain tissue. The damaged region is identified by scanning the head for areas of high radioactivity. The top scan was made from the back of the head; the white area on the left shows that the damage is in the left hemisphere. The bottom scan is of the left side of the head and shows that the uptake of mercury was predominantly in the first temporal gyrus, indicating damage to Wernicke's speech area by occlusion of blood vessels. David Patten and Martin Albert of the Boston Veterans Administration Hospital supplied the scan.

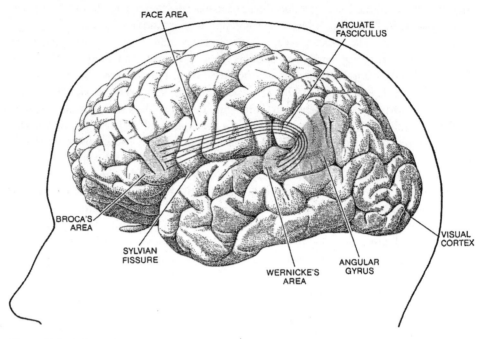

Figure 7.2 Primary language areas of the human brain are thought to be located in the left hemisphere, because only rarely does damage to the right hemisphere cause language disorders. Broca's area, which is adjacent to the region of the motor cortex that controls the movement of the muscles of the lips, the jaw, the tongue, the soft palate, and the vocal cords, apparently incorporates programs for the coordination of these muscles in speech. Damage to Broca's area results in slow and labored speech, but comprehension of language remains intact. Wernicke's area lies between Heschl's gyrus, which is the primary receiver of auditory stimuli, and the angular gyrus, which acts as a way station between the auditory and the visual regions. When Wernicke's area is damaged, speech is fluent but has little content and comprehension is usually lost. Wernicke and Broca areas are joined by a nerve bundle called the arcuate fasciculus. When it is damaged, speech is fluent but abnormal, and patient can comprehend words but cannot repeat them.

may almost sound normal. For example, the patient may say: "Before I was in the one here, I was over in the other one. My sister had the department in the other one." It is abnormal in that it is remarkably devoid of content. The patient fails to use the correct word and substitutes for it by circumlocutory phrases ("what you use to cut with" for "knife") and empty words ("thing"). He also suffers from paraphasia, which is of two kinds. Verbal paraphasia is the substitution of one word or phrase for another, sometimes related in meaning ("knife" for "fork") and sometimes unrelated ("hammer" for "paper"). Literal or phonemic paraphasia is the substitution of incorrect sounds in otherwise correct words ("kench" for "wrench"). If there are several incorrect sounds in a word, it becomes a neologism, for example "pluver" or "flieber."

Wernicke also noted another difference between these aphasic patients and those with Broca's aphasia. A person with Broca's aphasia may have an essentially normal comprehension of language. Indeed, Broca had argued that no single lesion in the brain could cause a loss of comprehension. He was wrong. A lesion in Wernicke's area can produce a severe loss of understanding, even though hearing of nonverbal sounds and music may be fully normal.

Perhaps the most important contribution made by Wernicke was his model of how the language areas in the brain are connected. Wernicke modestly stated that his ideas were based on the teachings of Theodor Meynert, a Viennese neuroanatomist who had attempted to correlate the nervous system's structure with its function. Since Broca's area was adjacent to the cortical region of the brain that controlled the muscles of speech, it was reasonable to assume, Wernicke argued, that Broca's area incorporated the programs for complex coordination of these muscles. In addition Wernicke's area lay adjacent to the cortical region that received auditory stimuli [see illustration above]. Wernicke made the natural assumption that Broca's area and Wernicke's area must be connected. We now know that the two areas are indeed connected, by a bundle of nerve fibers known as the arcuate fasciculus. One can hypothesize that in the repetition of a heard word the auditory patterns are relayed from Wernicke's area to Broca's area.

Comprehension of written language would require connections from the visual regions to the speech regions. This function is served by the angular gyrus, a cortical region just behind Wernicke's area. It acts in some way to convert a visual stimulus into the appropriate auditory form.

We can now deduce from the model what happens in the brain during the production of language. When a word is heard, the output from the primary auditory area of the cortex is received by Wernicke's area. If the word is to be spoken, the pattern is transmitted from Wernicke's area to Broca's area, where the articulatory form is aroused and passed on to the motor area that controls the movement of the muscles of speech. If the spoken word is to be spelled, the auditory pattern is passed to the angular gyrus, where it elicits the visual pattern. When a word is read, the output from the primary visual areas passes to the angular gyrus, which in turn arouses the corresponding auditory form of the word in Wernicke's area. It should be noted that in most people comprehension of a written word involves arousal of the auditory form in Wernicke's area. Wernicke argued that this was the result of the way most people learn written language. He thought, however, that in people who were born deaf, but had learned to read, Wernicke's area would not be in the circuit.

According to this model, if Wernicke's area is damaged, the person would have difficulty comprehending both spoken and written language. He should be unable to speak, repeat and write correctly. The fact that in such cases speech is fluent and well articulated suggests that Broca's area is intact but receiving inadequate information. If the damage were in Broca's area, the effect of the lesion would be to disrupt articulation. Speech would be slow and labored but comprehension should remain intact.

This model may appear to be rather simple, but it has shown itself to be remarkably fruitful. It is possible to use it to predict the sites of brain lesions on the basis of the type of language disorder. Moreover, it gave rise to some definite predictions that lesions in certain sites should produce types of aphasia not previously described. For example, if a lesion disconnected Wernicke's area from Broca's area while leaving the two areas intact, a special type of aphasia should be the result. Since Broca's area is preserved, speech should be fluent but abnormal. On the other hand, comprehension should be intact because Wernicke's area is still functioning. Repetition of spoken language, however,

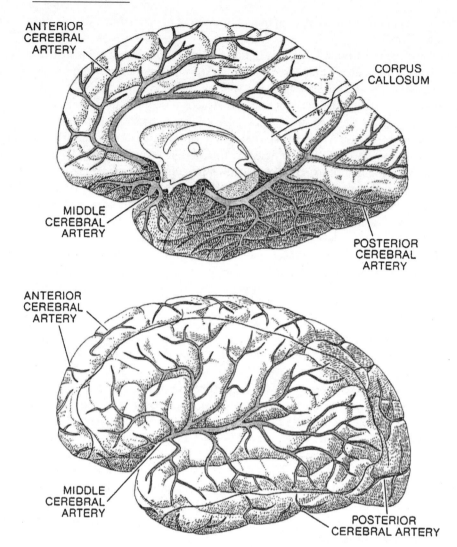

Figure 7.3 Cerebral areas are nourished by several arteries, each supplying blood to a specific region. The speech and auditory region is nourished by the middle cerebral artery. The visual areas at the rear are supplied by the posterior cerebral artery. In patients who suffer from inadequate oxygen supply to the brain the damage is often not within the area of a single blood vessel but rather in the "border zones." These are the regions between the areas served by the major arteries where the blood supply is marginal.

should be grossly impaired. This syndrome has in fact been found. It is termed conduction aphasia.

The basic pattern of speech localization in the brain has been supported by the work of many investigators. A. R. Luria of the USSR studied a large number of patients who suffered brain wounds during World War II [see "The Functional Organization of the Brain," by A. R. Luria; *Scientific American*, March, 1970]. When the wound site lay over Wernicke's or Broca's area, Luria found that the result was almost always severe and

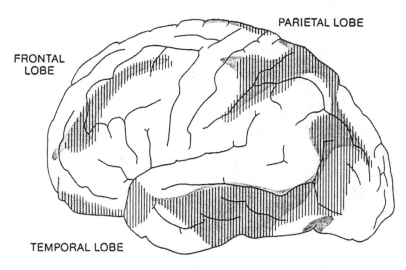

Figure 7.4   Isolation of speech area by a large C-shaped lesion produced a remarkable syndrome in a woman who suffered from severe carbon monoxide poisoning. She could repeat words and learn new songs but could not comprehend the meaning of words. Postmortem examination of her brain revealed that in the regions surrounding the speech areas of the left hemisphere, either the cortex or the underlying white matter (*hatched areas*) was destroyed but that the cortical structures related to the production of language (Broca's area and Wernicke's area) and the connections between them were left intact.

permanent aphasia. When the wounds were in other areas, aphasia was less frequent and less severe.

A remarkable case of aphasia has provided striking confirmation of Wernicke's model. The case, described by Fred Quadfasel, Jose Segarra, and myself, involved a woman who had suffered from accidental carbon monoxide poisoning. During the nine years we studied her she was totally helpless and required complete nursing care. She never uttered speech spontaneously and showed no evidence of comprehending words. She could, however, repeat perfectly sentences that had just been said to her. In addition she would complete certain phrases. For example, if she heard "Roses are red," she would say "Roses are red, violets are blue, sugar is sweet and so are you." Even more surprising was her ability to learn songs. A song that had been written after her illness would be played to her and after a few repetitions she would begin to sing along with it. Eventually she would begin to sing as soon as the song started. If the song was stopped after a few bars, she would continue singing the song through to the end, making no errors in either words or melody.

On the basis of Wernicke's model we predicted that the lesions caused by the carbon monoxide poisoning lay outside the speech and auditory regions, and that both Broca's area and Wernicke's area were intact. Postmortem examination revealed a remarkable lesion that isolated the speech area from the rest of the cortex. The lesion fitted the prediction. Broca's area, Wernicke's area, and the connection between them were intact. Also intact were the auditory pathways and the motor pathways to the speech organs. Around the speech area, however, either the cortex or the underlying white matter was

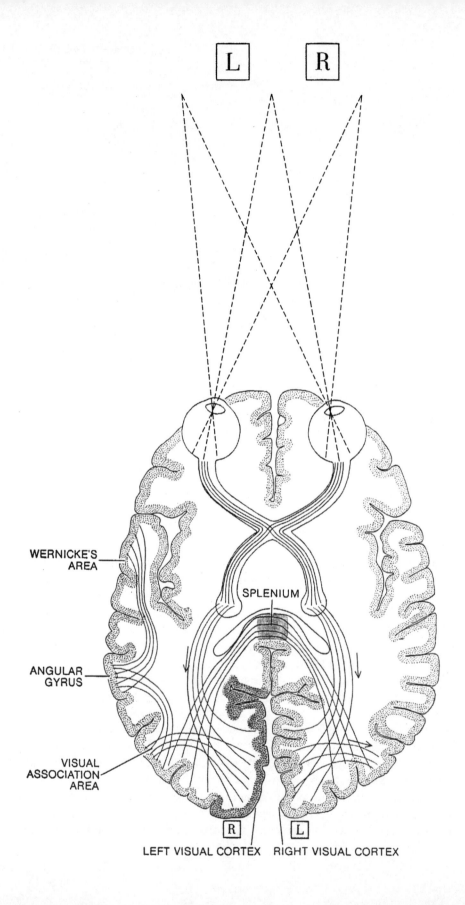

L R

WERNICKE'S
AREA

SPLENIUM

ANGULAR
GYRUS

VISUAL
ASSOCIATION
AREA

R L

LEFT VISUAL CORTEX   RIGHT VISUAL CORTEX

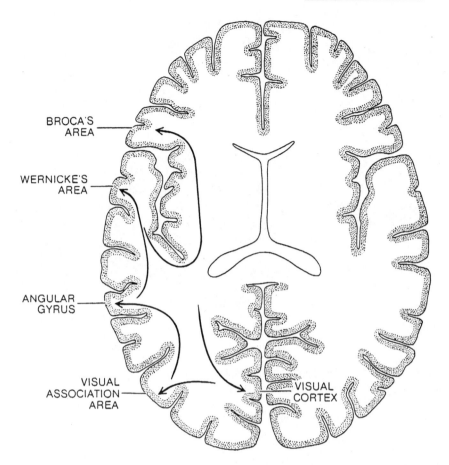

Figure 7.6 Saying the name of a seen object, according to Wernicke's model, involves the transfer of the visual pattern to the angular gyrus, which contains the "rules" for arousing the auditory form of the pattern in Wernicke's area. From here the auditory form is transmitted by way of the arcuate fasciculus to Broca's area. There the articulatory form is aroused, is passed to the face area of the motor cortex, and the word is spoken.

destroyed [see figure 7.4]. The woman could not comprehend speech because the words did not arouse associations in other portions of the cortex. She could repeat speech correctly because the internal connections of the speech region were intact. Presumably well-learned word sequences stored in Broca's area could be triggered by the beginning phrases. This syndrome is called isolation of the speech area.

Figure 7.5 (*opposite*) Classic case of a man who lost the ability to read even though he had normal visual acuity and could copy written words was described in 1922 by Joseph Jules Dejerine. Postmortem analysis of the man's brain showed that the left visual cortex and the splenium (*dark colored areas*) were destroyed as a result of an occlusion of the left posterior cerebral artery. The splenium is the section of the corpus callosum that transfers visual information between the two hemispheres. The man's left visual cortex was inoperative, making him blind in his right visual field. Words in his left visual field were properly received by the right visual cortex, but could not cross over to the language areas in the left hemisphere because of the damaged splenium. Thus words seen by the man remained as meaningless patterns.

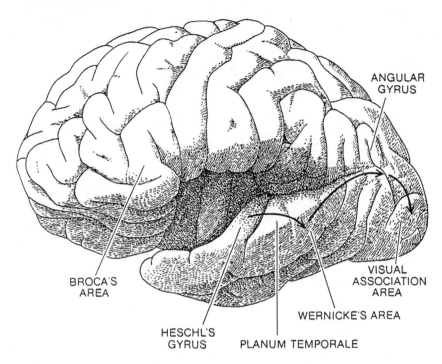

Figure 7.7   Understanding the spoken name of an object involves the transfer of the suditory stimuli from Heschl's gyrus (the primary auditory cortex) to Wernicke's area and then to the angular gyrus, which arouses the comparable visual pattern in the visual association cortex. Here the Sylvian fissure has been spread apart to show the pathway more clearly.

Two important extensions of the Wernicke model were advanced by a French neurologist, Joseph Jules Dejerine. In 1891 he described a disorder called alexia with agraphia: the loss of the ability to read and write. The patient could, however, speak and understand spoken language. Postmortem examination showed that there was a lesion in the angular gyrus of the left hemisphere, the area of the brain that acts as a way station between the visual and the auditory region. A lesion here would separate the visual and auditory language areas. Although words and letters would be seen correctly, they would be meaningless visual patterns, since the visual pattern must first be converted to the auditory form before the word can be comprehended. Conversely, the auditory pattern for a word must be transformed into the visual pattern before the word can be spelled. Patients suffering from alexia with agraphia cannot recognize words spelled aloud to them nor can they themselves spell aloud a spoken word.

Dejerine's second contribution was showing the importance of information transfer between the hemispheres. His patient was an intelligent businessman who had awakened one morning to discover that he could no longer read. It was found that the man was blind in the right half of the visual field. Since the right half of the field is projected to the left cerebral hemisphere, it was obvious that the man suffered damage to the visual pathways on the left side of the brain [see figure 7.5]. He could speak and comprehend spoken language and could write, but he could not read even though he had normal visual acuity. In fact, although he could not comprehend written words, he could copy them correctly. Postmortem examination of the man's brain by Dejerine revealed two lesions that were the result of the occlusion of the left posterior cerebral artery. The visual cortex of the left hemisphere was totally destroyed. Also destroyed was a portion of the corpus callosum: the mass of nerve fibers that interconnect the two cerebral hemispheres. That portion was the splenium, which carries the visual information between the hemispheres. The destruction of the splenium prevented stimuli from the visual cortex of the right hemisphere from reaching the angular gyrus of the left hemisphere. According to Wernicke's model, it is the left angular gyrus that converts the visual pattern of a word into the auditory pattern; without such conversion a seen word cannot be comprehended. Other workers have since shown that when a person is blind in the right half of the visual field but is still capable of reading, the portion of the corpus callosum that transfers visual information between the hemispheres is not damaged.

In 1937 the first case in which surgical section of the corpus callosum stopped the transfer of information between the hemispheres was reported by John Trescher and Frank Ford. The patient had the rear portion of his corpus callosum severed during an operation to remove a brain tumor. According to Wernicke's model, this should have resulted in the loss of reading ability in the left half of the visual field. Trescher and Ford found that the patient could read normally when words appeared in his right visual field but could not read at all in his left visual field.

Hugo Liepmann, who was one of Wernicke's assistants in Breslau, made an extensive study of syndromes of the corpus callosum, and descriptions of these disorders were a standard part of German neurology before World War I. Much of this work was neglected, and only recently has its full importance been appreciated. Liepmann's analysis of corpus callosum syndromes was based on Wernicke's model. In cases such as those described by Liepmann the front four-fifths of the corpus callosum is destroyed by occlusion of the cerebral artery that nourishes it. Since the splenium is preserved the patient can read in either visual field. Such a lesion, however, gives rise to three characteristic disorders. The patient writes correctly with his right hand but incorrectly with the left. He carries out commands with his right arm but not with the left; although the left hemisphere can understand the command, it cannot transmit the message to the right hemisphere. Finally, the patient cannot name objects held in his left hand because the somesthetic sensations cannot reach the verbal centers in the left hemisphere.

The problem of cerebral dominance in humans has intrigued investigators since Broca first discovered it. Many early neurologists claimed that there were anatomical differences between the hemispheres, but in the past few decades there has been a tendency to assume that the left and right hemispheres are symmetrical. It has been thought that cerebral dominance is based on undetected subtle physiological differences not reflected in gross structure. Walter Levitsky and I decided to look again into the possibility that the human brain is anatomically asymmetrical. We studied 100 normal human brains, and we were surprised to find that striking asymmetries were readily visible. The area we studied was the upper surface of the temporal lobe, which is not seen in the intact brain because it lies within the depths of the Sylvian fissure. The asymmetrical area we found and measured was the planum temporale, an extension of Wernicke's area. This region was larger on the left side of the brain in 65 percent of the cases, equal in 24 percent and larger

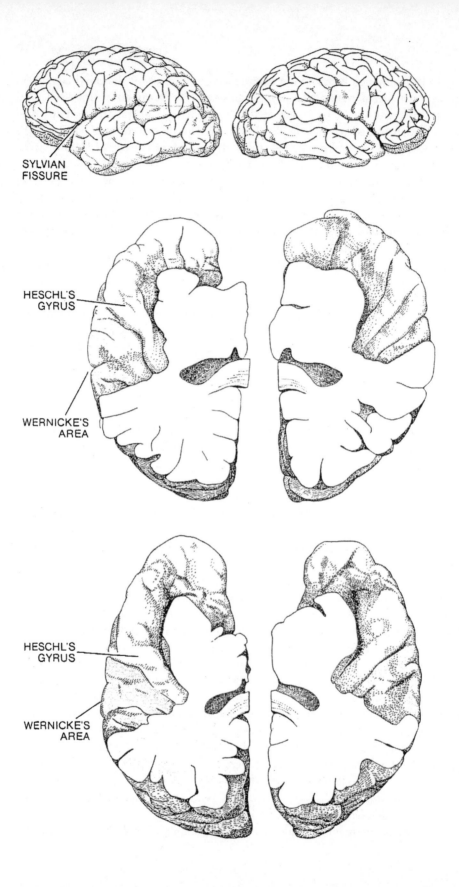

MEANING	BROCA'S APHASIA				WERNICKE'S APHASIA
	KANA		KANJI		
	PATIENT'S	CORRECT	PATIENT'S	CORRECT	
INK	インヌ (KINSU)	インキ (INKI)	墨 (SUMI)	墨	参 答 微 圦 久 (LONG TIME) 矢 (SOLDIER) 美
UNIVERSITY	ガイ (TAI)	ダイガク (DAIGAKU)	大学	大学 (GREAT LEARNING)	
TOKYO	トウ (TOU)	トウキヨウ (TOKYO)	東京	東京 (EAST CAPITAL)	

Figure 7.9   Japanese aphasics display some characteristics rarely found in Western patients because of the unique writing system used in Japan. There are two separate forms of such writing. One is Kana, which is syllabic. The other is Kanji, which is ideographic. Kana words are articulated syllable by syllable and are not easily identified at a glance, whereas each Kanji character simultaneously represents both a sound and a meaning. A patient with Broca's aphasia, studied by Tsuneo Imura and his colleagues at the Nihon University College of Medicine, was able to write a dictated word correctly in Kanji but not in Kana (*top left*). When the patient was asked to write the word "ink," even though there is no Kanji character for the word, his first effort was the Kanji character "sumi," which means India ink. When required to write in Kana, the symbols he produced were correct but the word was wrong. Another patient who had Wernicke's aphasia wrote Kanji quickly and without hesitation. He was completely unaware that he was producing meaningless ideograms, as are patients who exhibit paraphasia in speech. Only two of the characters had meaning (*top right*).

on the right side in 11 percent. In absolute terms the left planum was nine millimeters longer on the average than the right planum. In relative terms the left planum was one-third longer than the right. Statistically all the differences were highly significant. Juhn A. Wada of the University of British Columbia subsequently reported a study that confirmed our results. In addition Wada studied a series of brains from infants who had died soon after birth and found that the planum asymmetry was present. It seems likely that the asymmetries of the brain are genetically determined.

It is sometimes asserted that the anatomical approach neglects the plasticity of the nervous system and makes the likelihood of therapy for language disorders rather hopeless. This is not the case. Even the earliest investigators of aphasia were aware that

Figure 7.8   (*opposite*) Anatomical differences between the two hemispheres of the human brain are found on the upper surface of the temporal lobe, which cannot be seen in an intact brain because it lies within the Sylvian fissure. Typically the Sylvian fissure in the left hemisphere appears to be pushed down compared with the Sylvian fissure on the right side (*top illustration*). In order to expose the surface of the temporal lobe a knife is moved along the fissure (*broken line*) and then through the brain, cutting away the top portion (*solid line*). The region studied was the planum temporale, an extension of Wernicke's area. The middle illustration shows a brain with a larger left planum; the bottom illustration shows left and right planums of about the same size. In a study of about 100 normal human brains planum temporale was larger on the left side in 65 percent of the cases, equal on both sides in 24 percent of the cases, and larger on the right side in 11 percent.

some patients developed symptoms that were much milder than expected. Other patients recovered completely from a lesion that normally would have produced permanent aphasia. There is recovery or partial recovery of language functions in some cases, as Luria's large-scale study of the war wounded has shown. Of all the patients with wounds in the primary speech area of the left hemisphere, 97.2 percent were aphasic when Luria first examined them. A follow-up examination found that 93.3 percent were still aphasic, although in most cases they were aphasic to a lesser degree.

How does one account for the apparent recovery of language function in some cases? Some partial answers are available. Children have been known to make a much better recovery than adults with the same type of lesion. This suggests that at least in childhood the right hemisphere has some capacity to take over speech functions. Some cases of adult recovery are patients who had suffered brain damage in childhood. A number of patients who have undergone surgical removal of portions of the speech area for the control of epileptic seizures often show milder language disorders than had been expected. This probably is owing to the fact that the patients had suffered from left temporal epilepsy involving the left side of the brain from childhood and had been using the right hemisphere for language functions to a considerable degree.

Left-handed people also show on the average milder disorders than expected when the speech regions are damaged, even though for most left-handers the left hemisphere is dominant for speech just as it is for right-handers. It is an interesting fact that right-handers with a strong family history of left-handedness show better speech recovery than people without left-handed inheritance.

Effective and safe methods for studying cerebral dominance and localization of language function in the intact, normal human brain have begun to appear. Doreen Kimura of the University of Western Ontario has adapted the technique of dichotic listening to investigate the auditory asymmetries of the brain. More recently several investigators have found increased electrical activity over the speech areas of the left hemisphere during the production or perception of speech. Refinement of these techniques could lead to a better understanding of how the normal human brain is organized for language. A deeper understanding of the neural mechanisms of speech should lead in turn to more precise methods of dealing with disorders of man's most characteristic attribute, language.

8

The Bisected Brain

Michael S. Gazzaniga

It is of special interest to study intermodal mechanisms in split-brain man, especially in the language-weak, disconnected right hemisphere. Results of these tests allow two main points. First, the nondominant, speechless, but semiverbal, right hemisphere is clearly capable of making high-order intersensory associations. Whether these match in extent and kind all those operations clearly present in the left, dominant hemisphere, has not been determined. In brief, the tests go something like this. Visual stimuli are quickly flashed into one or the other visual half-fields. If pictures are flashed into the left field, only the right hemisphere views the stimulus. Because these patients have had their cerebral commissures sectioned, the left hemisphere remains completely uninformed about the nature of the stimulus. Similarly, when stimuli are flashed in the right visual field, only the left hemisphere is privy to the information.

The objects to be matched through touch are placed out of view, underneath the table, as shown in Figure 8.1. When the left hand is used, only the right hemisphere has access to the incoming stereognostic information. When the right hand palpates objects, only the left hemisphere is privy to the stereognostic information. (There are exceptions to these latter two statements, and they will be discussed below.)

Using this general testing procedure, stimuli were flashed to the right and to the left hemisphere, and tactual matches were subsequently requested with the appropriate hand. In all of the following tests, the left hemisphere proved capable of carrying out all operations requested. For example, when a picture of an orange was flashed to the left hemisphere, the subject would correctly retrieve with the right hand an orange from a series of objects presented out of view. The subject would then say in a normal fashion that the stimulus had been an orange. If the subject had used the left hand, with its major sensory projection going to the right hemisphere, and the visual stimuli were exclusively projected to the left hemisphere, intermodal associations would have failed. In order for an association of this kind to succeed in brain-bisected man, incoming visual and tactual information must be projected to the same hemisphere.

From *The Bisected Brain*. New York: Appleton-Century-Crofts, 1970, pp. 25–8.

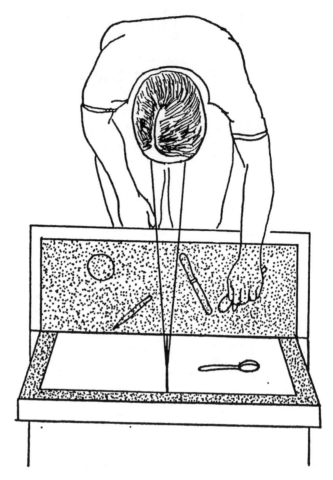

Figure 8.1   Visual-tactile association is performed by a split-brain patient. A picture of a spoon is flashed to the right hemisphere; with the left hand he retrieves a spoon from behind the screen The touch information from the left hand projects mainly to the right hemisphere, but a weak "ipsilateral" component goes to the left hemisphere. This is usually not enough to enable him to say (using the left hemisphere) what he has picked up.

What is of more interest is that the speechless, nondominant, right hemisphere was also capable of making high–order intermodal matches. When visual stimuli such as triangles, ovals, squares, or pictures of objects such as pencils, spoons, apples, oranges, and so forth, were presented exclusively to the right hemisphere, the subjects would claim they saw nothing (i.e., the left hemisphere was talking), as it were – but then, with the left hand, they would retrieve the match from a series of objects. After each correct response, the subject was asked what had been retrieved. All replied they didn't know. Here again, it was the left hemisphere "talking," and it did not "know." It neither "saw" the visual stimulus nor had direct access to the tactual information. But because the right hemisphere performs consistently and well on such tests over a long period of time, it is assumed that it "knows" and is "aware" of the test stimulus: it isn't able to "talk" about it.

Again, because the visual information was exclusively flashed to the right hemisphere, the right hand (with its major sensory projections going to the left hemisphere) worked at only chance level.

Tactual-visual associations were also performed by each hemisphere. The subjects were first given something to palpate with either the left or the right hand, and were subsequently asked to point to a matching stimulus from a series placed in full view. All proved capable of doing this.

The conclusion from this sort of study is that as long as sensory and sensory-motor processes are featured in the same hemisphere, intermodal responses are possible not only in the dominant, language-strong, left hemisphere, but also in the disconnected, language-weak, right hemisphere. When the visual information is presented to one hemisphere and the tactual information to the other, no intermodal associations could be demonstrated. Further, in two patients who showed no linguistic competence whatsoever, intermodal matches were consistently performed at above chance level.

9

The Linguistic Development of Genie

Susan Curtiss, Victoria Fromkin, Stephen Krashen David Rigler, and Marilyn Rigler

Interest in cases of children reared in environments of extreme social isolation can be traced back at least to the 18th century. At that time the interest was stimulated by the debates concerning the theory of innate ideas and the struggle between the "geneticists" and the "environmentalists". In 1758, Carl Linnaeus first included *Homo ferus* as a subdivision of *Homo sapiens*. One of the defining characteristics of *Homo ferus*, according to Linnaeus, was his lack of speech or overt language. All the cases in the literature attest to the correctness of this observation.

The most dramatic cases of children reared under severe conditions of social isolation and stimulus deprivation are those described as "wild" or "feral" children, children who have reportedly been reared with wild animals or have lived alone in the wilderness. Two such children, Amala and Kamala, found in 1920, were supposedly reared by wolves. Information on the prior history of these children is lacking (Singh & Zingg 1966). A more celebrated case is that of Victor, the "wild boy" of Aveyron, discovered in 1798 (Itard 1962). The study of Victor was limited by methods available at the end of the 18th century, as well as by a limited understanding of the nature of language. But Itard's anecdotal account of Victor's training and development has provided useful insights into language acquisition, as well as other areas of perceptual and cognitive development.

There are also reported cases of children whose isolation has been associated with congenital or acquired sensory loss (e.g. Howe & Hall 1903, Dahl 1965, Fraiberg & Freedman 1964). In addition, there are cases of children whose isolation resulted from deliberate efforts to keep them from normal social intercourse (Von Feuerbach 1833, Mason 1942, Davis 1940, 1947, Freedman & Brown 1968, Koluchova 1972). The present paper deals with a child in this category.

Nowhere in modern scientific literature is there a systematic study of the effects of very long-term isolation in childhood. The only cases comparable to the one reported here are those of Victor (Itard) and Caspar Hauser (e.g. von Feuerbach), which date back about a century and a half. All the other children reported had been isolated for much shorter periods and emerged from their isolation at a much younger age. Even in

From *Language* 50: 3 (September 1974), pp. 528–54.

these cases, the opportunity for careful observation was lacking; and in the earlier cases, the reports omit information on just those questions of interest to linguists.

The case of Genie assumes even more importance, then, because of its unique character, and because, from the time she emerged from isolation, a team of psychologists, psychiatrists, neurologists, and linguists have been working with this amazing child. In this paper we shall discuss only questions of linguistic concern, with emphasis on Genie's acquisition of phonology and syntax.

1. Case history. Genie was born in April 1957. When we first encountered her, she was 13 years and 7 months old – a painfully thin child who appeared six or seven years old. When hospitalized for malnutrition, Genie could not stand erect or chew food; she was not toilet trained; and she did not speak, cry, or produce any vocal sounds. The reconstruction of her previous life presents a bizarre and inhuman story. From the age of 20 months, Genie had been confined to a small room under conditions of apparently increasing physical restraint. In this room she received minimal care from a mother who was herself rapidly losing her sight. She was physically punished by her father if she made any sounds. Most of the time she was kept harnessed into an infant's potty chair; otherwise she was confined in a homemade sleeping bag in an infant's crib covered with wire mesh. She was fed only infant food.

The details of her discovery are not pertinent to this discussion, nor is speculation concerning the psychotic reasons behind the parents' actions. We have little information on the nature and extent of Genie's linguistic input during her isolation. The father's intolerance of noise is known, and there was no television or radio in the home. The periods of any human contact during the day were extremely limited. We know that her father and older brother did not speak to her, but at times barked at her like dogs. For the most part, hour after hour, day after day, year after year she was alone and constrained in her prison.

When Genie was discovered, she was taken into protective custody by the police and admitted into the Children's Hospital of Los Angeles. During her stay in the hospital she showed remarkable development. Physically she improved dramatically. She rapidly gained weight and height, and breast development signaled oncoming sexual maturation. Her cognitive growth was quite rapid. In a seven-month period, her Vineland score (a non-verbal cognitive development test) increased from 15 to 42 months; six months after admission, on the Leiter scale (another such test) she passed all the items at the four-year level, two at the five-year level, and two out of four at the seven-year level. Genie's emotional growth was reflected not only in her changing relationships with things and people, but also in her increasing capacity for emotional expression.

In July 1971, Genie left the hospital to live with a foster family, of which she now functions as a member. In all aspects of her life – psychological, physical, mental, and linguistic – Genie continues to develop.

2. Had Genie acquired any language? When Genie was first admitted to the hospital, there was little evidence that she had acquired any language; she did not speak. Furthermore, she seemed to have little control over the organs of speech. Even for non-speech functions, she showed great deficits in muscular control when chewing, swallowing etc. In the earliest period it was almost impossible to determine the extent of her

comprehension of spoken language. In the absence of detailed information on her earlier linguistic input, either before or during her period of isolation, no meaningful predictions could be made concerning her linguistic development.

One of the first questions which required an answer was whether Genie's inability to speak represented merely a "performance" deficit. It was thought that, if she was able to comprehend spoken language, this would reflect some linguistic knowledge of language, even though physiological and psychological factors were preventing her from using this knowledge to produce speech. If this were the case, whatever linguistic development occurred would be less a process of acquiring the basic linguistic system than of learning to utilize her knowledge. But if Genie did not comprehend spoken language, she was faced with the task of first-language acquisition, a task normally completed before age five.

The attempt to determine the extent of her linguistic competence (specifically, comprehension) was full of difficulties. Her lack of responses did not necessarily mean that she failed to understand what was said to her. On the other hand, when she did respond, it was not always easy to determine whether or not her understanding depended primarily on extra-linguistic cues. There were some clues, however, all pointing toward lack of comprehension of language beyond the domain of a few single words; e.g., she often responded to words clearly out of the context of their environment – and, at the other extreme, failed to respond to simple commands. It appeared, therefore, that Genie was a child who did not have linguistic competence; i.e., who had not yet acquired language. Any controlled comprehension tests, however, had to wait until Genie was willing and able to participate and respond.

On 3 March 1971, Genie was visited by Ursula Bellugi-Klima and Edward Klima. Their report of this visit states: "(Genie) seems to understand a good deal more than she says of language, but it is not always clear what cues she is using to respond to sentences." They recommended "the use of tests and games [to establish] how much and what aspects of spoken language she understands and responds to [which would be] a far better index of her knowledge of language than the handful of words she uses spontaneously." Furthermore, to distinguish between her understanding which depended on "tone of voice, gestures, hints, guidance, facial and bodily expressions" and her understanding based on linguistic knowledge, they suggested that, "In the situations reserved for testing and evaluating her understanding of spoken language alone, all these [extra-linguistic cues] must be eliminated."

A number of comprehension tests and games were developed and administered to Genie each week. It was clear from the outset that Genie's comprehension of language was only slightly in advance of her speech production. Systematic testing of her comprehension did not begin until October 1971, however, and Genie had already begun to acquire language by then.

3. Comprehension development. The tests which were constructed to evaluate Genie's progress in learning to use grammatical information in the comprehension of language, and their results, are presented in Appendix 1, below. The results of these tests show that Genie is acquiring language. She has learned (though not by imitation or by prescribed "rules") to process or understand constructions involving negation, coördinating conjunctions, many prepositional relations, pluralization of nouns, modification, possessives, the comparative and superlative, and several relational adjectives.

Several of these tests have revealed continual comprehension of the particular aspect of syntax being tested. Such tests include a negative/affirmative sentence test (with or without relativization, and with or without contraction of the negative element), a conjunction test with *and*, tests on the comprehension of *next to* and *beside*, a test of the comprehension of the possessive in both its syntactic forms, and tests concerning modification (as well as the comprehension of the comparative and superlative, which, however, were not tested before January 1972).

Other tests show inconsistent or incorrect responses, indicating Genie's lack of comprehension of the syntactic feature or rule being tested. Her performance on the active/passive test and on the "WH-question" test has been totally inconsistent. Both are tests of word order to some extent. This is peculiar and confusing, since Genie has used consistent and correct word order (in terms of the adult model) to indicate SVO relations, as well as modification and possessive relations, in her own productive speech.

Some of the tests reveal acquisition of syntactic features or rules which were totally lacking at the onset of testing. The "conjunction test" reveals this. All along, Genie's test performance has indicated knowledge of the conjunction *and*. But for the first year, 1972, she responded to *or* and *and* as if they were identical. She showed neither hesitation nor confusion when presented with a sentence in which two nouns were conjoined by *or*, responding to such a sentence in the same manner as if *and* were used. In August 1972, Genie began to respond differently to the test items with *or*. Now, after a long delay, she responds by doing a number of different things (e.g. piling up all the test items, or manipulating the objects mentioned in the sentence in a strange way); her gestures and facial expressions reveal confusion, uncertainty, and, at times, great frustration. It seems clear that Genie is now aware that *or* does not mean *and*, but she does not yet know its meaning. The acquisition of the concept of disjunction may in any case be more reflective of logical development than of language acquisition per se (see Furth 1966).

Genie acquired the ability to distinguish between singular and plural count nouns during the period of testing. Until July 1972, she made no consistent responses to indicate comprehension of this distinction; her test performance was never better than chance. In July, one of us (Susan Curtiss) embarked on a program to teach her this distinction.

Because Genie had so many physical and psychological problems associated with speaking, we decided early in our work to try the visual/written mode as linguistic input, in addition to the speech mode. We introduced printed words on 3×5 index cards used with a pocket-board. We aimed at teaching her to recognize printed words and to use them to form syntactic constructions. In teaching Genie the plural, test pictures were used along with printed words designating the pictured nouns; in addition, a large red S and the numbers *1*, *2*, and *3* were used. A game was played in which Genie learned to match the test pictures with a string of the following sort: $1 + N, 2 + N + S, 3 + N + S$, where N was the printed word signifying one of the objects in the pictures. From there, Genie learned to construct such a string as a match to the spoken phrase only: Curtiss would say *Three dishes*, and Genie would construct the string *3 dish S*. In both tasks, the following pluralization rule was taught: "If there is more than one, you need an *S*." Articulation of the regular plural morpheme (in its three phonetic variants) was also practiced. A final step was to introduce nouns other than those on which Genie was drilled, as the oral stimuli to which she would respond with written strings. In three weeks (5 lessons), Genie had mastered the plural concept, and since that time her performance on this test has been perfect.

The motivation for designing such teaching methods, to help Genie learn language, is to aid her in her social relations with the world in which she lives. Children learn such structures at an early age. At sixteen, Genie has constructed some rules on her own; but where this process can be aided, we believe it is our responsibility to do so.

4. Phonological development. Genie's phonetic and phonological output has been complicated by both psychological and physiological factors. As stated above, it appears that she was punished for making sounds, and thus learned early in life to repress any sound production. After her emergence, Genie had to learn to acquire control over her vocal organs as part of her learning to articulate the different sounds which represent the phonological elements of spoken language. Many of her early utterances (both imitative and spontaneous) were produced as "silent" or whispered articulations; and her strange voice quality was noted by all the consultants who visited her. She still has enormous difficulty in controlling air volume, air flow, glottal structures, and glottal vibrations.

In normal quiet breathing, only the inspiratory muscles are utilized; but in speaking, both inspiration and expiration involve muscular controls. Since speech is an "overlaid function" (in Sapir's terms), we learn very early in life to use the respiratory mechanism simultaneously for speaking as well as breathing. Maintaining the proper air pressure across the glottis, to permit vocal-cord vibration, requires that we learn to control air flow and air volume. But Genie's lack of speech during the many years of her isolation prevented her from learning these necessary controls. In fact, it would appear that what she learned was to prevent sound production rather than to produce sounds. This conditioning prevented any sound whatever from being made even in her tantrums, during uncontrolled thrashing and scratching. Her lack of pitch control, and the body tension which is observed when she attempts to control the expiration of air during speech, are therefore not surprising.

There has been some improvement in Genie's ability to produce speech, although her speech production is still far from normal. The intensity of the acoustic signal is very low; there is little variation of pitch (fundamental frequency); her general pitch level is very high.

Many researchers have concluded that children learn the intonation contours of the language prior to the non-prosodic segmental speech sounds (Weir 1962, Miller & Erwin 1964). Bever, Fodor & Weksel (1965: 479) claim: "It is widely accepted in the literature that the child effectively masters the intonation pattern of his language BEFORE HE HAS LEARNED ANY WORDS AT ALL" (their emphasis). While Braine 1970 suggests that evidence is lacking for the claim that intonation (as a linguistic feature) is controlled before speech, it is certainly the case that even during the babbling stage a wide variation in pitch contours is noted. This has not been the case for Genie, for the reasons given above. Auditory tests and impressionistic observations show that the problem is not her inability to perceive different pitch changes or pitch contours. Rather, it is her inability to control pitch variations in her own speech production. Further tests are being conducted to determine her ability to respond to grammatically determined differences in intonation contours.

Genie's supra-glottal articulatory abilities show more normal development. Here too, however, there are ups and downs in her ability to produce intelligible utterances. For her segmental inventory, see Appendix 2, below.

Genie's first basic "words" were monosyllabic consonant–vowel sequences; the consonant was a non-aspirated labial or dental stop, and the vowel a monophthong. Her first disyllabic words differed from what some researchers have considered to be the second stage of phonological development. E.g., Moskowitz 1971 suggests that the first disyllabic utterances are "reduplications" of the whole CV syllable. But Genie's first disyllabic words did not follow this pattern; instead they closely paralleled the adult forms in the consonants and vowels appearing in both syllable positions.

For a number of months, her basic syllable structure was of the form (C)(L)V(C). The vowel could be either short or long. The initial consonant (when there was no following liquid) was any of the possible initial consonants found in Standard American English, except the affricates. As of June 1972, however, the voiced and voiceless interdental fricatives, [θ] and [ð], were used only in imitations, and the affricates [č] and [ǰ] varied with the corresponding stops. In this period, more often than not she deleted final consonants; but since this was not consistent, the internal representation of the words and syllables must have included these consonants, and her grammar must have included an optional rule deleting final consonants. One could say that at this stage she had not yet learned to "suppress" the natural syllable structure (Stampe 1972). When a final nasal was "unpronounced", its presence was often shown in the nasalization of the preceding vowel. Since the nasal was sometimes present, rule 1 includes nasal as well as oral consonants:

(1)   (optional) C → Ø / ____$ (where $ = syllable boundary)

Since a word like *can* was pronounced either as [kæn] or [kæ̃], one might conclude that Genie's grammar included a constraint such that, in lexical representations, all vowels preceding nasal consonants were redundantly nasal. But this does not seem to be the case, since Genie would sometimes substitute a non-nasal consonant for the nasal, and in such cases the vowel was not nasalized. E.g., at times *funny* was pronounced [fʌ̃nːɪ] and at other times as [fʌtɪ]. If the vowel were basically nasal, one would expect *[fʌ̃tɪ]. It appears, then, that vowel nasalization occurred as a rule (or process, cf. Stampe), that all vowels were phonologically oral, and that the replacement of nasals by oral consonants blocked the vowel-nasalization rule.

Initial voiceless stops were produced with or without aspiration, more often unaspirated. But when the initial consonant corresponded to an *s*-stop cluster, the stop was always unaspirated. This would make it appear that aspiration was not "applied by rule", but stored as a feature of the segments; otherwise one might expect the voiceless stop corresponding to /sp sk st/ to be randomly aspirated or unaspirated. Although the initial consonant could be any of those listed, the medial and final consonants in words produced by Genie have been more restricted: [t] has substituted for medial [n], and for medial and final [k] and [s]. Only recently have final [k] and [s] emerged with consistency.

In the last few months, Genie has begun to produce words with initial *s* followed by stop, inserting an epenthetic shwa-like vowel to break up the cluster. Since English reduced vowels are for the most part "shwa-like", her use of [ə] as the epenthetic vowel may show her increasing knowledge of English phonology: she could just as well insert an [a] or [ɪ] or a copy of the first vowel. One might also suggest, however, that the [ə] is the universally unmarked neutral vowel.

Genie can pronounce many sound sequences in imitation which she does not use in spontaneous speech. It is clear that her output is more constrained by her own phonological "realization" rules than by her inability to articulate the sounds and sound sequences of English. This shows that, even in an abnormal case of language acquisition, one must differentiate between a child's phonological system and phonetic ability.

A child's phonological development does not proceed totally separate from syntactic development. This is particularly clear in the area of morphophonemic alternations; e.g., plurality is expressed both syntactically and morphologically. On 20 October 1971, Genie was tested for the first time on her comprehension of simple singular vs. plural nouns. Two pictures were presented to her, one with a single object and the other with several similar objects. The items were balloons, turtles, and pails, all objects which she knew, could recognize and point to, and even name. The investigator said each time: "Point to the ____", with the blank filled by either the singular or the plural form. Of twelve responses, seven were incorrect, showing a random response.

This singular–plural test was administered regularly in the months which followed. Three additional objects were added – noses, dishes, and horses – but the same random responses resulted. Although Genie could appropriately use and understand utterances including numbers and *many* or *lots of*, she could not distinguish plurality by linguistic means, either by the addition of the plural morpheme ($/z/$: [z] [s] [ɨz]) or by the plural form of the copula (*are* vs. *is*).

In July 1972, however, she began to show that she had acquired the linguistic plural. In eight tests her responses were 100% correct. This "learning" resulted from specific "teaching" techniques as explained above.

5. Spontaneous "sentence" production. About five months after Genie's admission to the hospital, she began to use single words spontaneously. Her early vocabulary included mainly color words, numbers from 1 to 5, the noun *mama*, and the verb forms *stop it* and *spit*. Already at this stage one can note a difference between this inventory of words and the first words of a normal child, which are typically nouns, plus particles like *up* and *down* (Velten 1943). In none of the descriptions of the early child's vocabulary does one find items as cognitively sophisticated as color words or numbers.

Genie's vocabulary grew rapidly and steadily; by the time she began combining two words, she had learned and was producing close to two hundred words. Again one may note the size of Genie's vocabulary, before two-word sentences appeared, as compared with that of normal children's vocabulary (about 50 words) at this same stage. Genie's vocabulary approached the dimensions found in aphasic children before they begin to construct two-word sentences (see Eisenson and Ingram 1972).

Genie's two-word "grammar" emerged around June 1971. There was never a point at which these utterances could be described adequately by a Pivot–Open system (Braine 1963, Miller & Ervin). Braine observed, in the children he studied, that "a few individual words are singled out and used in a particular utterance position in combination with a variety of words . . . The words singled out have been called PIVOT WORDS . . . the words that are combined with the pivots also occur as single-word utterances, whereas the pivot words themselves may not occur alone." No stage in Genie's development parallels this; but perhaps Braine's generalization fails to apply to many normal children as well (see Bowerman 1973: 68–70). In Genie's grammar (at that stage) one would be hard pressed to decide what was "pivot" and what was "open". Furthermore, a Pivot–Open grammar would fail to capture the semantic and syntactic relations clearly involved in her two-word utterances. When the two-word "sentences" are analysed as to their specific semantic and syntactic structures, Genie's knowledge of different semantic and syntactic relations is revealed. In addition, even words that seem to be good candidates for "pivots" occur alone, and have more than one possible position in Genie's utterances – e.g. *Hurt cat* and *Cat hurt*, or *No more father* and *Father no more*. This differs from the utterances noted by Miller & Ervin which ended with either *on* or *off*, and those which began with *this*, *that*, *more*, *a*, *the*, or *other*, with these "pivot" words used in a fixed position.

Bloom 1970 discusses the various relations which may be expressed by a two-word sentence. In Genie's case, a verb + noun construction may express a verb–object or subject–verb relation, as in *Want milk* (verb + object) vs. *Hurt hospital* (verb + subject). But from June 1971 to September 1971, Genie's two-word utterances were primarily *modifier + noun* or possessive constructions of *noun + noun*. The modifier, in the modifier + noun constructions, could be either a number, or an adjective of size, quantity, or emotional quality. The last type was combined only with animate nouns. Sample utterances are:

(2)   a.   yellow balloon, wet blouse, big feet, bad boy(s).
      b.   Butler shampoo, Dave back, Curtiss chin, Marilyn bike.

The possessive constructions manifested, in every instance, fixed word order: N_1 was the possessor, and N_2 the possessed item, as shown in 2b.

In September 1971, Genie began to produce two-word utterances with verbs: subject + verb, verb + object. First-person subjects never appeared in surface sentences. Examples are:

(3)   SV
      a.   Dave hurt   10/11/71
      b.   Mark paint   10/27/71
      c.   Curtiss come   11/24/71
(4)   VO
      a.   love Marilyn   10/8/71
      b.   like powder   10/14/71
      c.   shake hand   11/24/71

Sentences of the form noun + predicate adjective followed shortly:

(5)   a.   stocking white   11/4/71
      b.   Curtiss sick   12/15/71

In November 1971, Genie was observed on rare occasions to produce sentences of three or four words. These sentences were of various types: subject + verb + object; subject + object, with a complex NP as either subject or object; three- or four-word noun phrases; and predicatives of the form NP + NP. The first-person subject, always omitted in two-word utterances, now appeared in some of these longer strings:

(6)   Genie love Curtiss [cf. earlier *Love Curtiss.*]

Also, two-word strings which had earlier been complete sentences now served as NP's in longer sentences:

(7)   a.   Want more soup [earlier *More soup.*]
      b.   Mark mouth hurt [earlier *Mark mouth.*]

An interesting aspect of this stage of development is that Genie's three- and four-word NP's seem to display a cognitive complexity normally not found in early child speech. The following examples illustrate this:

(8)   a.   Valerie mother coat
      b.   Valerie mother purse
      c.   Little white clear box.

Another important characteristic of these utterances is that a number of the complex NP's display obvious non-imitative order, i.e. order not heard in the adult model. Two examples of these are:

(9)   a.   small two cup
      b.   little bad boy.

Such utterances provide clear evidence that Genie, like normal children, is not learning language by imitation alone. They also reveal that the length of Genie's utterances does not directly reflect her syntactic capabilities. That is, given the fact that she does on occasion produce utterances of more than three or four morphemes, the infrequency of such utterances may be explained by her difficulties – both physiological and emotional – in producing speech, rather than by limitations of her linguistic competence. Thus, when Genie fails to communicate her message with one- or two-word utterances, she can expand the sentences, revealing a more extensive syntactic system than usually appears on the surface.

   In February 1972, negative sentences emerged (it should be noted that Genie was able to comprehend negative sentences much earlier). Such sentences consisted of the negative element *no more* affixed to either a noun or a noun + verb. In July, negative sentences with *no more* attached only to a verb appeared:

(10)   a.   No more father.
       b.   No more take wax.
       c.   No more have.

Locative sentences emerged at the same time, consisting of either noun + noun or verb + noun. Only nouns denoting locations were used:

(11)   a.   Cereal [in] kitchen.
       b.   Play [in] gym.

In July 1972, the first examples of an expanded verb phrase were observed, initially of the form verb + VP:

(12) a. Want go shopping.
      b. Like chew meat.

Later, around October 1972, these strings were expanded to include complex NP's and more complex VP's:

(13) a. Want buy toy refrigerator.
      b. Want go walk [to] Ralph[s].

In all the above constructions, Genie used only one mechanism for expressing grammatical relations – that of word order. In November 1972, her first grammatical markers emerged, when she began to use the preposition *on*:

(14) Question: Where is your toy radio?
      Genie: On chair.

It is possible that, in this period, *on* was used (or understood) to mean either "on" or "in"; it is not clear that Genie was aware of the distinction. Except for *no more*, this use of the preposition is the first example of what may be called grammatical morphemes.
      Genie has now also begun to use the progressive aspect marker *-ing* with verbs:

(15) a. Genie laughing.
      b. Curtiss coughing.
      c. Tori eating bone.

In every case she has appropriately used the progressive marker to denote ongoing action. It is interesting to note that Brown, Cazden & Bellugi 1969 have found *on* and *-ing* to be among the earliest grammatical markers in normal language acquisition.
      Genie has produced a few sporadic plurals (e.g. *bears, noses, swings*); but the fact that she still simplifies final clusters may account for the general lack of overt plurals in [s] and [z]. She also now imitates the past-tense forms of strong verbs such as *gave* and *fell*, and on a few occasions has incorporated them into her spontaneous utterances:

(16) a. Grandma gave me cereal.
      b. Took off.

It is not clear, of course, whether these forms represent the past tense.
      Genie has also begun to use the prepositions *in, at, behind, front*, and *after*:

(17) a. Like horse behind fence.
      b. Like good Harry at hospital.
      c. I like wheelchair in hospital.
      d. Marilyn front.

She also produces possessives which are phonologically marked:

(18)   a.   Joel's room.
     b.   Mark's room.
     c.   I like Dave's car.

All these markers are used appropriately, being affixed only to the "correct" word category, and are used in an appropriate semantic context.

Besides the emergence of individual prepositions, Genie now uses prepositions in adverbial phrases:

(19)   a.   In hospital, shot hurt arm.
     b.   After dinner have cookie.

She still speaks in shorter strings than she is capable of constructing, and thus often deletes these items; but the syntactic markers are appearing more frequently in her spontaneous speech.

In addition, Genie has begun to use the vocative, and to produce imperative sentences. The vocative (or "nominative of address") is present very early in normal child language, and it is of interest that it remained absent from Genie's speech for so long. Its appearance is probably more the result of emotional development than of syntactic acquisition. Perhaps the syntactic structures emerge only when the necessary psychological factors are present: in order to request or demand something from specific individuals, the speaker must have enough of a self-concept to feel she has the power and right to so address people and to make direct demands. We now find sentences like those below as part of Genie's everyday speech:

(20)   a.   Go way, Joel, finish story!
     b.   Get out baby buggy!

Verb particles are now used, as shown by regularly occurring utterances like *Get out*, *Take off*, *Put down*, and *Put back*. Indirect objects also appear in recent sentences:

(21)   a.   Curtiss give me valentine.
     b.   Give valentine Mr. James.
     c.   Grandma gave me cereal.
     d.   Grandpa give me cookie chew.

Another addition to Genie's grammar is a determiner category. She often imitates the definite article, e.g. *In the hospital, In the backyard*; and she frequently uses the determiner *another*:

(22)   a.   Another house have dog.
     b.   Another house blue car.

No definite–indefinite distinction has appeared.

As stated above, in the discussion of the two-word sentence stage, Genie produced "genitive" constructions at an early period. These show her continuing syntactic development. As mentioned, she now uses the possessive marker, and has also begun to use the possessive pronoun *my*:

(23)   a.   Willie slap my face.
       b.   My house.
       c.   My pennies.

Such utterances exemplify her advancement from using word order alone to express syntactic relations to the use of explicit and appropriate grammatical formatives. More recently, possession is expressed by the verb *have*:

(24)   a.   Bears have sharp claw.
       b.   Bus have big mirror.
       c.   Bathroom have big mirror.
       d.   Curtain have flower.
       e.   Father have flower curtain.

She has also added *no* and *not* as negation elements to her earlier *no more*. The three now seem to be used appropriately:

(25)   a.   No more have.
       b.   No more ear hurt.
       c.   No like hospital.
       d.   No stay hospital.
       e.   Not have orange record.
       f.   Not good fish tank.

There is still no movement of the NEG into the sentence; in fact no movement transformations of any kind are revealed in her speech to date.

Further syntactic complexities are revealed by Genie's use of compound NP's. In talking about cats and dogs, she said *Cat hurt*, then *Dog hurt*, and then *Cat dog hurt*; when asked what was in a snapshot, she replied *Curtiss, Genie, swimming pool*, naming the three important features of the picture. Prior to December 1971, she would name only one thing at a time, and would have to be asked *What else?* before providing an additional word.

Genie has begun to give consistently appropriate answers to *when*-questions:

(26)   a.   Q: When do you see Mama?
             Genie: Friday.
       b.   Q: When does Curtiss come?
             Genie: Monday.

In addition, Genie seems now to comprehend *why*-questions; e.g., when Curtiss was ill and unable to see her at the regular time, Genie said: *Disappointed.* Her foster mother asked *Why?* and Genie replied: *Curtiss sick.*

Genie comprehends questions with *who*, *what*, *where*, *whose*, and *how*, although there are no WH-words in her own utterances. It would seem that she has the ability to "decode" the syntactic structures of WH-questions (but note the test in Appendix 1).

A recent development (December 1972) is her comprehension of personal pronouns and her own use of *I*. This pronoun seems to be limited to co-occurrences with the verbs *want* and *like*, but it is definitely present in strings with these verbs, and even receives stress (reflected by greater intensity and duration).

At the beginning of December, Genie produced a sentence with greater syntactic complexity than those exemplified above. Curtiss and Genie were accidentally locked out of Genie's foster home, and had to wait until someone arrived with a key. When her foster family arrived, Curtiss said to Genie: *Tell them what happened*. Genie said: *Tell door lock*, as she nodded knowingly and pointed to the door. It seemed quite clear that the sentence meant "Tell them that the door was locked, huh." If this is indeed how the sentence is to be interpreted, it would seem that Genie now has a recursive property in her grammar, as shown by this sentence and by the combining of the two sentences *Cat hurt* and *Dog hurt* to produce *Cat dog hurt*. If this is so, she has acquired the two essential aspects of syntax that permit the generation of an infinite set of sentences: the ability to combine a finite set of linguistic elements in new combinations, and the ability to generate sentences consisting of more than one base sentence.

6. Comparison of Genie's syntactic development with that of normal children. The language development to date is encouraging, but it is important to note some of the differences which exist between Genie's development and that of normal children. The size and nature of her vocabulary is different. For one thing, her vocabulary is much larger than that of children at the same stage of syntactic development. She learns new words rapidly, and seems to be able to add constantly to the store of words in long-term memory. This illustrates the distinction between storage of lists of elements and rules of grammar.

The rate of Genie's syntactic acquisition, however, is much slower than normal. The two-word stage, which normally lasts from two to six weeks (see Eisenson & Ingram), lasted for more than five months in Genie's case. In addition, negative sentences (which, along with affirmative active-declarative sentences, constitute the only types occurring), remain in the earliest stage of development, i.e. NEG + S (see Brown, Cazden & Bellugi 1969, Klima & Bellugi-Klima 1966). This is despite the fact that negative sentences have occurred in Genie's speech for more than a year and a half. In fact, as noted above, there are as yet no movement transformations of any kind in Genie's grammar; nor are there any question words, demonstratives, catenatives, rejoinders (*yes*, *no*, *please* etc.), or pronouns of any kind other than first-person pronouns.

Yet there are areas where Genie's language appears to be more sophisticated, cognitively, than is found in normal language acquisition. The inclusion of color words and numbers in her early vocabulary was noted above (see Castner 1940, Denckla 1972). Normally, children's vocabularies are expanded a great deal before colors or numbers are learned. Moreover, Genie's use of vocabulary items has never involved the kind of semantic over-generalizations found in the speech of very young children (Clark 1973). But phonological extension is present; e.g., she often uses gestures to accompany her verbalization of certain words, stooping to a sitting position when she says *sit* and also when she says *sick*. She does not abstract specific semantic features; i.e., the name for some round object like *moon* is not used for other round objects, as described by Clark. But she is able to extend generic features correctly; thus, when she learned the word *dog*, she used it appropriately for all dogs, and never for a cat or a horse. But except in such generic terms there is no semantic extension.

Genie's comprehension of all the WH-questions is also of interest. Normal children ordinarily learn *how*, *why*, and *when* questions much later than *who*, *what*, and *where* questions, despite the fact that syntactically they present identical problems (Brown 1968, Ervin-Tripp 1970). One may hypothesize that this disparity can be attributed to non-linguistic cognitive asymmetries rather than linguistic rules: the former group appears to require more sophisticated inferences about the way objects and events are to he understood or integrated. The fact that Genie is able to understand all these questions shows a more developed cognitive ability than is found in children whose grammars are more highly developed, but whose cognitive age is below hers. This is also revealed by Genie's ability to comprehend the comparative, the superlative, and the differences between *more* and *less* (see Appendix 1) – all this, of course, without any WH-words or comparative or superlative markers in her own speech. These indications of cognitive sophistication, in the absence of linguistic (especially syntactic) development, suggest a possible independence of cognition and linguistic development, and perhaps also the independence of semantics and syntax.

The difference between Genie's linguistic competence (her grammar) and her performance is sharply apparent in the differences between her comprehension and production. But this is not too different from what is found in normal language acquisition. Even at the earliest stage, between 18 and 24 months, children appear to comprehend structures greater in complexity than those which they produce. In a number of experiments concerned with comprehension, C. Smith 1970 has shown that children aged approximately 18 months to 2 years "apparently handle only the high-stress content words that they utter themselves". She suggests that "perhaps their listening is mainly an attempt to 'find' words they know", and that "The linguistic competence of these children does not differ markedly from their performance" (118). But older children (aged $2\frac{1}{2}$) already display a competence which differs greatly from their speech behavior: these children attend to "function words", even though they do not use them in spontaneous speech. Children from 3 to 4 years show an even greater difference between the spontaneous utterances they produce and the structures which they are able to decode.

Right from the start, Genie appeared to understand words which she did not produce herself. This, of course, does not refer specifically to a difference between competence and performance, since "comprehension" is also performance. But what is most evident in Genie's language is that she does indeed have greater abilities than she frequently displays, as shown by her sentence expansions when she had to go beyond two-word utterances in order to be understood.

It has been suggested that a speaker's linguistic competence includes the knowledge of what strings are well-formed, i.e., what are "grammatical" sentences in the language. It is clear that one cannot ask Genie to separate grammatical from non-grammatical sentences; one can't do this with normal children, either, or in many cases with mature speakers, although Fischer 1971 has noted that children of 7 years may respond to ungrammatical strings by giggling. One incident, however, seems to show that Genie, despite her slow development and overly-simple grammar, does know the meaning of grammaticality.

This was revealed in a session where printed words were being used. In February 1973, we decided to work with the written mode to help Genie learn to ask and understand WH-questions. Prior to this time, when she attempted to construct sentences with the "word cards", she frequently produced blatantly ungrammatical strings and seemed entirely satisfied with her efforts, expecting to be praised in all cases. During the session under discussion, the first WH-question that Genie constructed was *What is under?* She sat back, read it to herself, then said *Silly!*, and added the NP object *the green box*, thereby changing her ill-formed string to a grammatical question. In constructing the answer to that question, she first replaced the question mark with a period, and then removed the WH-word, leaving, *is under the green box*. Again she read it to herself, again said *Silly*, and added *the orange box*, to form the grammatical string *The orange box is under the green box*. It is true that, semantically, the uncorrected sentences have no content, and Genie's corrections may merely reflect this cognitive awareness; but the order of all the words was in keeping with her knowledge of "well-formedness". The fact that she can form questions in printed words, but not in speech, may, then, not only show a competence/performance distinction, but may also show that she is learning what constitutes a well-formed string.

7. Critical-age hypothesis and language lateralization. Genie began to learn language when she was close to fourteen years of age. As stated above, she was already pubescent. Thus she has been learning her "first language" at an age beyond the "critical age for first-language acquisition" proposed by Lenneberg 1967. The critical period concept does not pertain solely to language acquisition. The concept itself derives from experimental embryology, but has been generalized by ethologists to apply to the development of certain animal behaviors. The term refers to innately determined behavior, the appearance of which is dependent upon environmental facilitation during some developmentally critical period. Whether critical periods exist for human beings is a matter of controversy. There is, of course, no question but that certain environmental conditions are necessary for the acquisition of certain knowledge and behavior. But crucial evidence is not available, since no one today would attempt to replicate the apocryphal experiments conducted by Psammetichus or King John to determine the language used by children when all linguistic input is cut off. One reason for the controversy about critical periods in man is the difficulty of adequate definition of the innate behavior to be elicited, and the time and nature of the required environmental facilitation.

One of the clearest statements about critical periods in man concerns the emergence of language. Lenneberg suggests that language is an innately determined behavior dependent upon certain neurological events, but obviously also dependent upon some unspecified minimal exposure to language at a certain stage in the child's development. According to him, language acquisition is precluded when lateralization of cerebral function is complete, which he believes occurs about the time of puberty. Hence the critical period for language acquisition is presumed to be during some period prior to onset of puberty; subsequent to this time, primary language by "mere exposure" is hypothesized to be impossible. On the other hand, Krashen & Harshman 1972 argue that the development of lateralization of language is complete well before puberty, and suggest that lateralization and language acquisition may go hand in hand. If this is so, we would expect a greater left-hemisphere lateralization in Genie as she progresses with language.

In an effort to establish whether or not lateralization was complete, specially devised dichotic listening tests (Kimura 1967) were administered to Genie. In such tests the subject hears simultaneous differing stimuli, one to each ear. In right-handed normal subjects, the right ear excels for verbal stimuli (nonsense syllables, words etc.), the left ear excels for certain non-verbal stimuli (musical chords, environmental sounds etc.) Genie is right-handed; hence, if lateralization for language had already occurred, it was anticipated that verbal stimuli presented to her right ear would be "preferred" to those received by the left ear.

Two sets of stimuli were used.[1] The "verbal" type consisted of 15 pairs of "point to" words; i.e., each pair of words was preceded by the binaural instructions *Point to the____*. Genie pointed to toys or pictures representing the words, which were familiar to her: *baby*, *boy*, *car*, *mirror*, *table*, and pig. The non-verbal tape consisted of pairs of environmental sound stimuli recorded from Genie's actual environment (piano chords, car horn, water running, telephone ringing, squeal of toy chimp). She responded by pointing to snapshots of the sound source.

In monaural testing of all stimuli, Genie scored 100%. The results of these tests are surprising, since her verbal dichotic scores show an extreme left-ear advantage; this points to right-hemisphere dominance for language, unusual in a right-handed subject. The right ear performed at a chance level. Such extreme ear differences have been found only in split-brain and hemispherectomized subjects (Milner, Taylor & Sperry 1968, Curry 1968). The results of the dichotic tests using environmental sounds also show a left-ear advantage, but only to a degree found in normal subjects. This "normal" result shows that Genie is not simply one of those rare individuals with reversed dominance, but instead is one in whom all auditory processing currently appears to be taking place in the right hemisphere. (For more detailed description of these tests, see Krashen, Fromkin and Curtiss 1972; Krashen and Harshman 1972; and Fromkin et al. 1974.)

One tentative hypothesis to explain this performance is that inadequate language stimulation during her early life inhibited or interfered with language aspects of left-hemisphere development. One may speculate as follows: At the time of her confinement, Genie was developing into a "normal" right-handed, left-dominant speaker. The confinement and resulting lack of linguistic stimulation prevented the language areas in the left hemisphere from developing further. In learning language, Genie is utilizing a right hemisphere that is already developed and specialized for other things. (It should be noted here that Genie is very proficient in what are considered right-hemisphere functions, e.g. gestalt pattern-recognition, spatial perception etc.) What occurred may be described as a kind of functional atrophy of the usual language centers, brought about by disuse or suppression. This left-hemisphere atrophy may be "blocking" right-ear stimuli, preventing them from reaching language centers in the right hemisphere, thus accounting for the low right-ear score.

If this hypothesis is true, it would support to some extent the "critical age" position. The implication would be that Genie's capacity for language acquisition is limited and that it will cease at some point in the near future, as seems to be the case in the few adult patients who have suffered left-hemisphere damage.

A. Smith 1966, studying a left-hemispherectomized man who incurred a left lesion during adulthood, reports that the mature right hemisphere can attain some propositional language. This patient, however, remained severely aphasic eight months after surgery (see also Bogen 1969). Similarly, Hillier 1954 reported a left hemispherectomy on a 14-year-old boy and found early progress; after 19 months, however, there was a stable deficit. Adult left-hemispherectomies, however, have a head start over Genie – namely, the limited but definite linguistic competence of the right hemisphere (simple nouns, verbs, positive–negative distinction etc. in visual comprehension; see Gazzaniga 1970).

One cannot tell what is meant in these brief reports by "progress in propositional language". Genie has already gone beyond the stages reported in the literature for such cases. Her comprehension of WH-questions, relative clauses, singular–plural distinctions, negatives etc., and her production of complex NP's, sentence conjunctions etc. provide evidence that there is steady if modest progress in first-language acquisition.

Genie's continuing linguistic development may show that language acquisition, or at least language input, is a prerequisite for lateralization, and that language acquisition and lateralization do not go hand in hand; or it may show that hemispheric specialization is prerequisite to language. Should we find that the degree of lateralization changes as Genie acquires more language – i.e., if she begins to use the left hemisphere for language processing – this would be strong evidence that it is man's genetic language mechanisms which "trigger" hemispheric specialization. There is much evidence that the left hemisphere is specialized for more than language (Efron 1963, Carmon and Nachson 1971, Papçun, Krashen and Terbeek, 1971). If we find that Genie is "left lateralized" for other cognitive functions, but not for language, this may reveal the independence of the language mechanism from other cognitive functions. We are just now attempting to find ways to investigate other aspects of behavior which may be left-lateralized for Genie.

This paper is a progress report on Genie's linguistic development. Her language acquisition so far shows that, despite the tragic isolation which she suffered, despite the lack of linguistic input, despite the fact that she had no language for almost the first fourteen years of her life, Genie is equipped to learn language and she is learning it. No one can predict how far she will develop linguistically or cognitively. The progress so far, however, has been remarkable, and is a tribute to the human capacity for intellectual achievement.

Appendix 1.   Comprehension Tests

The words used in all the tests were nouns, verbs, and adjectives used in Genie's own utterances. The response required was principally "pointing" – a gesture familiar to Genie before the onset of testing. At first, each test was specifically made very short, requiring only 6 or 8 responses, so that all the stimuli could be presented, and so that the testing session could be as long or short as Genie's particular mood suggested. At a later period, revisions were made – tests were lengthened, made more complex, added, or dropped. A summary of the tests and test results follows.

(1) SINGULAR–PLURAL DISTINCTION IN NOUNS. Pairs of pictures were used – a single object on one picture, three of the same objects on the other. The test sentences differed only by absence or presence of plural markers on the nouns. Genie was asked to point to the appropriate picture.

Sample item: Point to the $\begin{cases} \text{balloon.} \\ \text{balloons.} \end{cases}$

Words used: *balloon(s)*, *pail(s)*, *turtle(s)*, *tree(s)*, *umbrella(s)*, *nose(s)*, *box(es)*, *rose(s)*, *horse(s)*, *dish(es)*, *pot(s)*, *book(s)*, *cup(s)*, *carrot(s)*, *jacket(s)*, *hat(s)*.
Results: Test administered 34 times – 10/71 to 10/73.

	Correct	Incorrect
10/71–7/72	80	74
8/72–10/73	338	0

(2) CONJUNCTION. Five familiar objects were placed in a row in front of Genie. She was asked to point to one or more of them in response to the test sentences.
Sample items: Show me the fork and pencil.
Show me the crayon or the knife.
Show me either the spoon or the crayon.
Results: Early responses to *or* conjunction treated same as *and* sentences. Later responses to *or* showed differentiation between *and* and *or* but non–comprehension of meaning of *(either)/or*.

10/71–12/73	Correct	Incorrect	Unanalysable responses
and sentences	100	3	0
or sentences	7	51	6

(3) MORPHOLOGICAL NEGATION WITH *un*. Pairs of pictures depicting objects in opposing states were presented. Genie had to point to the picture corresponding to the item specified in the test sentence. There were two forms of this test: without relativization and with relativization. Both forms were presented at each test session. In addition, the revised version also tested responses to the same pictures with *not* used instead of *un*.
Sample items: Show me the tied shoe.
Show me the untied shoe.
Show me the box that is wrapped.
Show me the box that is unwrapped.
Show me the box that is not wrapped.
Results:

		Correct	Incorrect
with *un*	11/71–9/72	30	32
	7/73–9/73	25	11
with *not*	7/73–9/73	34	2

(4) PREPOSITIONS *in*, *into*, *on*, AND *under*. A dish, a button, a pencil, and two small glasses, one turned upside-down, were laid on a flat surface Genie was instructed to manipulate the objects.
Sample items: Put the button into the glass.
Put the button on the glass.
Results: Comprehension only of *in*.

		Correct	Incorrect
11/71–3/73	*in*	37	8
	on	25	23
	under	28	21

A logistics problem (one of manipulating and moving the particular objects involved) may have affected her performance. This test, along with all other preposition tests, was replaced by Test 21.

(5) NEGATIVE VS. AFFIRMATIVE STATEMENTS. Four pairs of pictures identical except for the presence or absence of some element were presented. Genie had to point to the picture corresponding to the test sentence. There were four forms of this test: (a) without contraction or relativization, (b) with relativization only, (c) with contraction only, (d) with relativization and contraction.

Sample items: (a) Show me "The girl is wearing shoes."
   Show me "The girl is not wearing shoes."
   (b) Show me the bunny that has a carrot.
   Show me the bunny that does not have a carrot.
   (c) Show me "The girl is wearing shoes."
   Show me "The girl isn't wearing shoes."
   (d) Show me the bunny that has a carrot.
   Show me the bunny that doesn't have a carrot.

Results: Performance on this test was 100% correct at all times, regardless of the test form. A more complex negation test was then substituted for it; see Test 25.

(6) ACTIVE VS. PASSIVE.
Part (i): A set of three pictures with the same elements in different relationship to each other was presented. Genie had to point to the appropriate picture. There were two forms of this test: (a) with progressive aspect (*be* + *ing*), and (b) with simple present.
Part (ii): The revised version added another picture set and the box task from Test 15, to which Genie was allowed to point.

Sample items: (a) Point to "The boy (is) pulling the girl."
   (b) Point to "The girl is pulled by the boy."
   (c) What is $\begin{cases} \text{the blue box on?} \\ \text{on the blue box?} \end{cases}$.

Results: Totally inconsistent performance. Most of the time no better than a chance level of correct responses; at times all incorrect responses.

	Correct	Incorrect
11/71–7/72	59	52
10/72–10/73	37	38

(7) PREPOSITIONS I: *beside, in front of, behind, next to.* A set of three pictures in which the same items appeared in different arrangements was presented. Genie had to point to the appropriate picture. The test had two forms: (a) without relativization, and (b) with relativization. Form (b) was usually the one presented.

Sample items: (a)   Show me "The tree (is) behind the house."
Show me "The house (is) beside the tree."
    (b)   Show me the house that is next to the tree.
Show me the house that is in front of the tree.

Results: Inconsistent responses to *behind* and *in front of*; clear comprehension of *beside* and *next to*. The test was replaced by Test 21.

		Correct	Incorrect
11/71–3/73	*behind*	14	22
	in front	15	19
	beside	31	0
	next to	4	0

(8) MODIFICATION. In first version, red plastic circles, squares, and triangles of three different sizes each were arranged in rows in random order. In later version, yellow circles, squares, and triangles are added to the array. Genie's task was to point to the named object.

Sample items: Point to the $\begin{Bmatrix} \text{big} \\ \text{little} \end{Bmatrix} \begin{Bmatrix} \text{red} \\ \text{yellow} \end{Bmatrix} \begin{Bmatrix} \text{circle.} \\ \text{triangle.} \\ \text{square.} \end{Bmatrix}$

Results:

	Correct	Incorrect
11/71–12/71	40	25
1/72–5/72	26	10
5/72–12/73	144	0

(Genie's response to the modifier *little* was to select the medium-sized object, indicating that for her a size adjective without a superlative or comparative marker had an absolute, rather than a relative, meaning. She would point to the smallest-sized object only when the word *tiny* was substituted for *little* in the test presentation.)

(9) SUPERLATIVE I. Five white buttons (all small and similar in size) and three strips of paper all the same width, each varying approximately $\frac{1}{2}$ inch in length from the next in size, were presented. Genie's task was to point to the appropriate object.

Sample items: Point to the $\begin{Bmatrix} \text{biggest} \\ \text{smallest} \end{Bmatrix}$ button.

                Point to the $\begin{Bmatrix} \text{longest} \\ \text{shortest} \end{Bmatrix}$ paper.

Results:

	Correct	Incorrect
11/71–1/72	14	6
8/72–12/72	11	2

(10) SUPERLATIVE II. Same test procedures as in 8, usually administered directly after or in conjunction with Test 8. (Since Genie consistently selected the medium-sized shape

in response to the word *little*, her responses to the word *littlest* would clearly indicate whether or not she comprehended the superlative morpheme *-est*.)

Sample item: Point to the $\left\{\begin{array}{l}\text{biggest}\\\text{littlest}\end{array}\right\}$ red $\left\{\begin{array}{l}\text{circle.}\\\text{triangle.}\\\text{square.}\end{array}\right\}$

Results: Consistently correct responses. Clear comprehension of the relational adjectives used and the function and meaning of the superlative marker.

	Correct	Incorrect
12/72–12/73	84	0

(11) COMPARATIVE. Two white buttons, with small difference in size, and two strips of paper with slight length difference were presented. Genie had to point to the appropriate item.

Sample items: Which button is $\left\{\begin{array}{l}\text{bigger?}\\\text{smaller?}\end{array}\right\}$

Which paper is $\left\{\begin{array}{l}\text{shorter?}\\\text{longer?}\end{array}\right\}$

Results: All responses correct.

	Correct	Incorrect
1/72–3/73	20	0

(12) COMPARATIVE AND SUPERLATIVE. Seven circles of different sizes were lined up in unseriated order and pasted to a piece of colored paper. Tester pointed to a circle and told Genie: "Point to one that's bigger/littler." In the case of the superlative, Genie was told: "Point to the biggest/littlest circle." (The circles were not aligned by size).
Results 10/73–1/74:

	Correct	Incorrect
Comparative	24	0
Superlative	6	2

(13) POSSESSIVE. First two different sets of pictures were presented. Set 1 showed (a) a cat missing one foot, (b) a human foot, (c) a cat's foot. Set 2 showed (a) a wagon missing one wheel, (b) a wheel much too large for the wagon, (c) a wheel that would fit the wagon. Later three more picture sets were added. Genie had to point to the appropriate picture.

Sample items: Point to the cat's foot.
Point to the foot of the cat.

Results:

	Correct	Incorrect
1/72–2/72	4	4
3/72–9/73	41	0

(14) Pronouns. Pictures of children sitting and eating or being fed were used. Genie had to point to the appropriate picture. The test included reflexive and reciprocal pronouns as well as simple personal pronouns.

Sample items: Show me "The boy is feeding himself."
          Show me "He is feeding himself."
          Show me "He is feeding him."
          Show me "He is feeding her."

Results:

	PN's correct	Incorrect
9/72–8/73	35	54
10/73–2/74	46	27
(same sentences with nouns)		
9/72–8/73	24	6
10/73–2/74	22	11

(15) Wh-questioning of subject vs. object. Picture task: two pictures were presented – (a) a boy pulling a girl in a wagon, (b) a girl pulling a boy in a wagon. Box (object) task: four plastic boxes of different sizes were used, including two red boxes, one blue box, and one white box. The boxes were arranged so that one was either *in* or *on* another.

Sample items: Picture task: Who is the girl pulling?
                    Who is pulling the girl?
          Box task: What is on the red box?
                    What is the red box on?

Results: Performance inconsistent. Genie was usually unable to respond at all, even though she had been answering various types of wh-questions for more than a year. The responses she did give did not reveal any consistent strategy. This test was discontinued because the verbal responses caused too many problems for Genie.

(16) Prepositions II: *under, over, in, on, behind, in front of.* Buttons and plastic boxes of different colors and sizes were used. Genie's task was to manipulate the buttons and boxes in accordance with the instructions.

Sample item: Put the red box behind the blue box.
Results 10/72–8/73:

	Correct	Incorrect
on	36	9
in	37	4
over	11	2
under	17	7
in front of	20	6
in back of	7	3
next to	7	1
behind	12	5

(17) Yes AND *no*; *in, on,* AND *under*. This test was devised because Genie frequently gave no response to "yes/no" questions. At times the questions were answered by appropriate head gestures, but often simply by repetition of the last word(s) of the question.

Part (a): The words *yes* and *no* were printed on index cards and set before Genie. Genie was asked to answer questions by pointing to one of the two cards.

Results: Consistently correct responses.

Part (b): Using the same cards as in (a), Genie was asked to respond to questions with the prepositions given above.

Sample questions: Is the button on my hand?
Is the button in my hand?
Is the red box in the white box?

Results: Consistent correct responses. In the few isolated cases where she gave wrong responses, she seemed to be teasing.

	Correct	Incorrect
yes	12	4
no	8	2

(18) *Come here* vs. *Go there*.

Part (a): Two circles, both large enough for two people to stand in, were drawn on the floor. An adult stood in one circle telling Genie either *Come here* or *Go there*.

Results: In every case except one, Genie went into the empty circle.

Part (b): Two circles were drawn in a row, some distance from each other. One adult stood in each circle. Genie stood in the middle between the two circles. The adults, in turn, instructed Genie to *Go there* or *Come here*.

Results: In all cases, Genie joined the adult who had issued the instruction, treating *Go there* identically with *Come here*.

Part (c): Same circles as in (b). Genie was not in line with the circles. An adult stood in one circle; the other circle was empty. The adult in the circle told Genie to *Go there* or *Come here*.

Results: Genie joined the adult in the circle each time.

Part (d): Same circles; no one in circles; one adult stood closer to one circle than the other; Genie stood several feet away, equidistant from both circles. Adult issued same requests as above.

Results: Genie in every instance went to circle farthest from the speaker.

Results of all four test situations: no comprehension of *here-there* distinction.

(19) *More* AND *less*.

Part (a): A different number of buttons (sometimes almost equal) was placed in each of Genie's hands. Genie was asked to look at each hand and point to the one that had *more*, or *less* buttons.

Results: Correct responses with no difficulty or hesitation.

Part (b): Plastic shapes of different size and thickness were used. Different combinations of sizes and numbers of these shapes were put into each hand. Genie had to point to the one containing more or less. (Triangles were always matched, against triangles, etc.)

Sample item: Which hand has $\left\{\begin{array}{l}\text{more?}\\\text{less?}\end{array}\right\}$

Results 8/73–12/73:

	Correct	Incorrect
more	21	0
less	21	0

(20) *Some, one, all.* Five plastic circles, 5 plastic squares, 8 plastic triangles were placed on a table, which also held an empty box and a tin dish. Genie had to follow the instructions in the test sentences.

Sample items: Put $\left\{\begin{array}{l}\text{some}\\\text{one}\\\text{all}\end{array}\right\}$ of the $\left\{\begin{array}{l}\text{triangles}\\\text{circles}\\\text{squares}\end{array}\right\}$ $\left\{\begin{array}{l}\text{in the dish.}\\\text{in the box.}\\\text{on the table.}\end{array}\right\}$

Results:

some	Correct	Incorrect
10/73–11/73	5	4 interpreted as *all*
1/74	5(?); 4 of these were *one* responses.	1 *all* response
all		
10/73–1/74	15	0
one		
10/73–1/74	11	1

(21) PREPOSITIONS, Plastic boxes of different sizes and colors were used. Genie had to manipulate them according to the prepositional relation expressed in the test item (40–50 test items in all).

Sample items: Put the $\left\{\begin{array}{l}\text{yellow}\\\text{blue}\\\text{green}\\\text{white}\\\text{orange}\end{array}\right\}$ box $\left\{\begin{array}{l}\text{under}\\\text{over}\\\text{in}\\\text{on}\\\text{behind}\\\text{beside}\\\text{next to}\\\text{in front of}\\\text{in back of}\end{array}\right\}$ the ____ box.

Results 9/73–2/74:

	Correct	Incorrect
in	40	0
on	31	5
over	15	11
under	13	14
in back of	18	8
in front of	22	3
behind	11	9
beside	20	0
next to	10	0

(22) POSSESSIVE PRONOUNS. A picture of a boy and girl was used. Genie had to point to named items either on the picture or on the tester's body.

Sample items: Point to his hand.
               Point to your mouth.
               Point to my chin.

Results 10/73–12/73: Correct, 26; Incorrect, 31.

(23) *Before* AND *after*. Genie had to touch parts of her body according to instructions.

Sample items: $\begin{Bmatrix} \text{Before} \\ \text{After} \end{Bmatrix}$ you touch your ____, touch your ____.

              Touch your ____ $\begin{Bmatrix} \text{before} \\ \text{after} \end{Bmatrix}$ you touch your ____.

Results 10/73–2/74:

	Correct	Incorrect
Before you touch ____, touch ____.	3	18
After you touch ____, touch ____.	17	0
Touch ____ before you touch ____.	24	3
Touch ____ after you touch ____.	21	6

(24) TENSE AND ASPECT. Genie was shown 6 picture sets, 3 pictures in a set, depicting action sequences. She had to point to the picture (one of the three) described by the test sentence. The test sentences varied only with respect to the tense/aspect of the verb. (The sets were randomly presented, so that process of elimination did not enter as a variable.)

Sample items: Point to "The girl will open the umbrella."
               Point to "The girl opened the umbrella."
               Point to "She is pouring the juice."
               Point to "She is going to pour the juice."

Results 10/73–1/74:

	Correct	Incorrect
Future with *will*	3	15
Future with *going to*	17	1
Progressive (*-ing*)	10	8
Past	9	9

(25) COMPLEX NEGATION. Four pictures were presented: (a) a red book on a chair, (b) a red book on a table, (c) a blue book on a chair, (d) a blue book on a table. Genie had to point to the picture described by the test sentence.

Sample items: The book that is on the table is not red.
               The book that is not on the table is red.

Results 10/73–12/73: Correct, 59; Incorrect, 1.

(26) COMPLEX SENTENCE PROCESSING. Two sets of pictures were used: (a) a boy sitting on a chair looking at a girl who is also looking at him; a boy sitting on a chair, turned away from a girl also turned away from him; a girl on a chair looking at a boy facing

her; (b) a smiling boy looking at a frowning girl turned away from him; a smiling girl looking at a frowning boy facing her; a frowning girl looking at a smiling boy turned away from her; a frowning boy and a smiling girl turned away from each other. Genie had to point to the picture described by the test sentence.

   Sample items: The girl who is sitting is looking at the boy.
                 The boy who is smiling is looking at the girl.

   Results:

	Correct	Incorrect
11/7/73	18	10
11/14/73	21	7
12/5/73	11	3

Appendix 2.   Genie's Phonological and Phonetic Inventory

VOWELS

/i/   [tʰi] "teeth", [síbə] "zebra".
/ɪ/   [fɪ] "fish", [pɪ] "pig".
/e/   [kəréy] "crayon", [tey] "stay".
/ɛ/   [lɛ] "lets", [síɣərɛ] "cigarette".
/æ/   [rǽbɪ] "rabbit", [bæ] "bath".
/u/   [yu] "you", [tu / tʰu] "tooth".
/ʊ/   [bʊ] "book" (also [bʊx], imitation).
/o/   [no] "no", [to] "stove".
/ɔ/   [hɔ / hɔr] "horse", [dɔ] "dog", [mɔ / mɔr] "more".
/a/   [kʰaː / kaː] "car", [har] "hard".
/ʌ/   [bʌ] "bus", [bʌ́l] "bubble", [wər] "word".
/ə/   [pʰər] "purse".
/ay/   [ray] "right", [fáydə] "Friday", [láyə̃] "lion".
/æw/   [hǽwə] "house", [æw] "out" ([ǽwət], imitation).
/ɔy/   [bɔy] "boy".

NASALIZED VOWELS

[ĩ]   [gərĩ] "green".
[ĩ]   [jĩ] "gym".
[õ]   [kõ / kõm] "comb".
[ɛ̃]   [pʰɛ̃́sɪ] "pencil", [dɛ̃́tʰɪ] "dentist".
[æ̃]   [kʰæ̃ / kæ̃n] "can", [pæ̃] "pants".
[ʌ̃]   [gʌ̃] "gun" (also [gʌd / gʌ́nːə]), [tʰʌ̃ / tʌ̃] "tongue".
[ã]   [bənã́nã] "banana".
[ũ]   [pũ] "spoon".
[ẽ]   [gẽ] "game".

CONSONANTS

/b/   [bɪː] "big", [bʌ] "bus".
/p/   [pʰɪ / pɪ] "pig", [pũ] "spoon", [sup] "soup".
/d/   [dátə] "doctor", [dɔ] "dog".
/t/   [tʰiy] "teeth", [to / sətó] "stove", [bǽːət] "basket".

/g/   [gɪ] "give", [go] "go", [dɔ́əɣ] "dog".
/k/   [kʰar] "car", [mʌ̃́ki] "monkey", [ku] "school", [bʊx] "book".
/s/   [saʔ] "sock", [su] "soup", [suzæ̃́] "Susan", [səpú / pṹ / pṹn] "spoon".
/z/   [suzæ̃́] "Susan" (cf. [síbə] "zebra").
/š/   [šɔr] "short", [šápi] "shopping".
/θ/   [tʰʌ̃] "thumb" ([θʌ̃] imitation).
/f/   [fõ] "phone", [fɪ] "fish".
/v/   [víkʰiː] "Vicki" (or [fíkʰiː]).
/m/   [mʌ̃́ki] "monkey", [mar] "Mark", [mɔːl] "small".
/n/   [no] "no", [bʌ́ni] "bunny".
/ŋ/(?)   [díŋkĩŋ] "thinking" (imitation).
/ǰ/   [ǰɪ / ǰĩ] "gym", [dʸi] "jeans".
/č/(?)   [tʰi] "cheek", [tʸɛ] "chair".
/r/   [rǽbɪ] "rabbit", [har] "hard", [brɛ] "bread".
/l/   [láyə̃] "lion", [ɛ́lbo] "elbow", [lay] "like", [bʌ́l̩] "bubble".
/w/   [wər] "word", [wa/wã] "want".
/h/   [har] "hard", [hɔr] "horse", [hæw] "how".
/y/   [yu] "you".
CONSONANT CLUSTERS (reduced, produced, broken-up)
/st/   [to / sətó] "stove".
/sp/   [pu / səpú] "spoon".
/sk/   [ke·ʔ] "scale".
/sm/   [mɔːl / s·mɔ·] "small".
/sn/   [neyt / s·ney] "snake".
/sl/   [səló· / slo·] "slow".
/sw/   [səwɛ́t] "sweat".
/bl/   [bley] "blade".
/gl/   [gəlǽ] "glass", [sʌ̃́glæt] "sunglasses".
/br/   [brɛ] "bread".
/gr/   [grĩ] "green".
/dr/   [drĩ] "dream", [dɔrʌ̃́] "drum".
/fr/   [frɛ̃] "friend".
/kr/   [krey / kəréy] "crayon".
/tr/   Absent?
/pr/   [prayz] "surprise".
/skw/   [gwɛ / səgwéw] "square".
/str/   [tərɛ́tʸ] "stretch".
/gl/   [gəlǽ] "glass".
/kl/   [klaː] "clock", [tla] "closet".
/pl/   [ɛ́dəplǽ] "eggplant".
/kw/   [kwɛ́tʸəma·r] "question mark".

Note

1   Stimuli were prepared with the assistance of Sarah Spitz at the UCLA Phonetics Laboratory, using PDP-12 computer programs developed by Lloyd Rice.

References

Bever, T. G., J. A. Fodor; and W. Weksel. 1965. On the acquisition of syntax: a critique of contextual generalizations. *Psychological Review* 72, 467–82.

Bloom, L. 1970. Language development: form and function in emerging grammars. Cambridge, Mass.: MIT Press.

Bogen, J. 1969. The other side of the brain, II: an appositional mind. *Bull. L.A. Neurol. Soc.* 34, 135–62.

Bowerman, M. F. 1973. *Early Syntactic Development: A Cross-linguistic Study with Special Reference to Finnish*. Cambridge: Cambridge University Press.

Braine, M. D. S. 1963. The ontogeny of English phrase structure: the first phase. *Lg.* 39, 1–14.

Braine, M. D. S. 1970. The acquisition of language in infant and child. In *The Learning of Language*, ed. C. Reed. New York: Appleton, pp. 7–95.

Brown, R. 1968. The development of wh-questions in child speech. *Journal of Verbal Learning and Verbal Behavior* 7, 279–90.

Brown, R., C. Cazden, and U. Bellugi. 1969. The child's grammar from I to III. *Minnesota Symposia on Child Psychology*, ed. John P. Hill, 2, 28–73. Minneapolis: University of Minnesota Press.

Carmon, A., and I. Nachson. 1971. Effect of unilateral brain-damage on perception of temporal order. *Cortex* 7, 410–18.

Castner, B. M. 1940. Language development. In *The First Five Years of Life*, ed. A. Gesell et al. New York: Harper & Row, pp. 189–237.

Clark, E. 1973. What's in a word? On the child's acquisition of semantics in his first language. *In Cognitive Development and the Acquisition of Language*, ed. Timothy E. Moore. New York: Academic Press, pp. 65–110.

Curry, F. 1968. A comparison of the performance of a right-hemispherectomied subject and twenty-five normals on four dichotic listening tasks. *Cortex* 4, 144–53.

Dahl, H. 1965. Observations on a natural experiment: Helen Keller. *Journal of the American Psychoanalytic Association* 13, 533–50.

Davis, K. 1940. Extreme social isolation of a child. *American Journal of Sociology* 45, 554–65.

Davis, K. 1947. Final note on a case of extreme isolation. *American Journal of Sociology* 52, 431–7.

Denckla, M. B. 1972. Performance on color tasks in kindergarten children. *Cortex* 8, 177–90.

Efron, R. 1963. The effect of handedness on the perception of simultaneity and temporal order. *Brain* 86, 261–84.

Eisenson, J., and D. Ingram. 1972. Childhood aphasia: an updated concept based on recent research. *Papers and Reports on Child Language Development, Stanford University*, 4, 103–20.

Ervin-Tripp, S. 1970. Discourse agreement: how children answer questions. In *Cognition and the Development of Language*, ed. J. R. Hayes. New York: John Wiley, pp. 79–107.

Fischer, S. 1971. The acquisition of verb–particle and dative constructions. MIT dissertation.

Fraiberg, S., and D. A. Freedman. 1964. Studies in the ego development of the congenitally blind child. *Psychoanalytic Study of the Child* 19, 113–69.

Freedman, D. A., and S. L. Brown. 1968. On the role of coenesthetic stimulation in the development of psychic structure. *Psychoanalytical Quarterly* 37, 418–38.

Fromkin, V., S. Krashen, S., Curtiss, D. Rigler, and M. Rigler. 1974. The development of language in Genie: a case of language acquisition beyond the "critical period." *Brain and Language* 1, 81–107.

Furth, H. 1966. *Thinking without Language: Psychological Implications of Deafness*. New York: Free Press.

Gazzaniga, M. 1970. *The Bisected Brain*. New York: Appleton–Century–Crofts.

Hillier, W. 1954. Total left hemispherectomy for malignant glioma. *Neurology* 4, 718–21.

Howe, M., and F. H. Hall. 1903. *Laura Bridgman*. Boston: Little Brown.

Itard, J. 1962. *The Wild Boy of Aveyron*. New York: Appleton–Century–Crofts.

Kimura, D. 1967. Functional asymmetry of the brain in dichotic listening. *Cortex* 3, 163–78.

Klima, E., and U. Bellugi-Klima. 1966. Syntactic regularities in the speech of children. In *Psycholinguistics Papers*, ed. J. Lyons and R. J. Wales. Edinburgh: Edinburgh University Press, pp. 183–208.

Koluchova, J. 1972. Severe deprivation in twins. *Child Psychology and Psychiatry* 13, 107 ff.

Krashen, S., V. Fromkin, and S. Curtiss. 1972. A neurolinguistic investigation of language acquisition in the case of an isolated child. Paper presented at LSA winter meeting.

Krashen, S., and R. Harshman. 1972. Lateralization and the critical period. Paper presented at the 83rd meeting of the Acoustical Society of America.

Lenneberg, E. 1967. *Biological Foundations of Language*. New York: John Wiley.

Mason, M. K. 1942. Learning to speak after six and one-half years. *Journal of Speech Disorders* 7, 295–304.

Miller, W. and S. Ervin. 1964. The development of grammar in child language. In *The Acquisition of Language*, ed. U. Bellugi and R. Brown. Chicago: University of Chicago Press, pp. 9–34.

Milner, B., L. Taylor, and R. Sperry. 1968. Lateralized suppression of dichotically presented digits after commissural section in man. *Science* 161, 184–6.

Moskowitz, A. 1971. Acquisition of phonology. University of California, Berkeley, dissertation.

Papçun, G., S. Krashen, and D. Terbeek. 1971. Is the left hemisphere specialized for speech, language, or something else? *Working Papers in Phonetics, UCLA*, 19, 69–77.

Singh, J. A. L., and R. M. Zingg. 1966. *Wolf-children and Feral Man*. London: Archon Books.

Smith, A. 1966. Speech and other functions after left (dominant) hemispherectomy. *Journal of Neurological and Neurosurgical Psychiatry* 29, 467–71.

Smith, C. 1970. An experimental approach to children's linguistic competence. In *Cognition and the Development of Language*, ed. J. R. Hayes. New York: John Wiley, pp. 109–35.

Stampe, D. 1972. A dissertation on natural phonology. University of Chicago dissertation.

Velten, H. V. 1943. The growth of phonemic and lexical patterns in infant language. *Language* 19, 281–92.

Von Feuerbach, A. 1833. *Caspar Hauser*. London: Simpkin & Marshall.

Weir, R. 1962. *Language in the Crib*. The Hague: Mouton.

10

Derivational Complexity and Order of Acquisition in Child Speech

Roger Brown and Camille Hanlon

Editors' note: In the omitted section of this paper, Brown and Hanlon present a working set of formal rules in a generative framework to derive the sentence types they study. The missing section also includes some of the data that established the order of acquisition (for example, tables presenting the number of occurrences across time of the relevant utterance types in Adam, Eve, and Sarah).

Fodor and Garrett (1966) have made a useful retrospective analysis of the experiments done in the past five years to test the "psychological reality" of transformational grammar. It seems to them that investigators in this tradition have been testing the proposition that the complexity of derivation of a sentence, measured by the number of optional transformational rules applied, corresponds with the psychological complexity of processing the sentence. The idea that derivational complexity ought to correspond with psychological complexity derives, Fodor and Garrett suggest, from a notion that the grammar of a language might function as an actual component of the psychological programs involved in understanding sentences. The grammar could be a literal component if, at one implausible extreme, a listener assigned a structural description to a received sentence by synthesizing all possible sentences up to the point (some months later) at which he generated a match. The grammar could also be a literal component if, somewhat more plausibly, a received sentence were assigned a structure through the rewriting of less general symbols into more general ones utilizing a set of reversed phrase structure rules in reverse order.

    The early experiments on the psychological reality of transformational grammar seemed to provide impressive evidence for a rather direct relation between derivational and psychological complexity. Later on, the grammar moved from beneath these early experiments, changing the character of the derivational complexities involved and calling attention to the fact that changes of meaning were also involved. In the early experiments, complexity was often confounded with sentence length, frequency, and naturalness as well as with

From chapter 1 of *Cognition and the Development of Language*, ed. John R. Hayes. New York: John Wiley, 1970, pp. 11–21 and 37–53. ©1970 by John Wiley & Sons, Inc. Used by permission of John Wiley & Sons, Inc.

meaning; replications controlling for one or more of these variables have generally yielded results in which the importance of derivational complexity seems much reduced.

The early experiments stayed nervously close to a small family of sentences: the simple, active, affirmative, declarative (SAAD), the negative (N), the question (Q), the passive (P), and such compounds of these as passive-negative (PN), negative question (NQ) and so on. Later experiments broadened the range of sentences studied and, at the same time, complicated the idea of derivational complexity. When separable verbs in transformed position (*Put your coat on*) are compared with separable verbs in non-transformed position (*Put on your coat*), we have a difference of one optional, singulary, meaning-preserving transformation. When the negative (*I don't see it*) is compared with a corresponding SAAD (*I see it*), we have a difference in the morphemes generated by the phrase structure rules as well as a difference of obligatory transformations (T*do*) and optional transformations (T*not*). When verbal auxiliaries of varying complexity are compared (for example, *He was going* and *He would have been going*) we have, among other things, a difference in the number of times a particular obligatory transformation must be applied in a single derivation. The only cases in which an increase in derivational complexity is at all reliably associated with an increase in psychological difficulty seem to be those in which meaning is also changed.

The earliest experiments in the tradition (those George Miller did with McKean and Slobin, 1962) undertook to assess complexity by measuring the time required to transform sentences of one type into sentences of another type. Later on, other indices of psychological complexity were utilized: time to understand a sentence well enough to judge it true or false; and ability accurately to recall sentences in a free-recall situation and in a single-sentence, immediate-recall situation with buffer material added to make it possible to measure the storage space required for the sentence. For this range of tasks, it is not surprising that a difference of derivational complexity, even when it is of a single fixed type, does not show a stable relationship to psychological complexity. With respect to an SAAD and its corresponding negative (N) and passive (P), for instance, it takes more time to transform from SAAD to P than from SAAD to N, but the N takes longer to comprehend than does the P.

Fodor and Garrett draw the one general conclusion that it is now possible to draw from this literature: derivational complexity, in the sense of the number of rules applied in deriving a sentence, does not correspond in any simple way to the psychological complexity involved in understanding and retaining the sentence. Fodor and Garrett also accept the one clear implication of their conclusion: transformational grammars are not actual components of the routines by which sentences are processed; the relation between the formalization of the native speaker's presumed competence (the grammar) and his psycholinguistic performances must be less direct than had been imagined. The Fodor and Garrett conclusions are the ones the experimental literature now justifies, but these conclusions are probably not the last or the most interesting statements that will be made about these results. The complex pattern of evidence that now speaks wholly negatively may find an affirmative voice in the future.

In this chapter we propose to ask whether derivational complexity is related to the order in which constructions emerge in child speech. In view of the outcome of the experimental literature on adult processing of sentences, it is necessary to say why any relation of the kind described should be expected in child speech.

We shall, in the first place, limit ourselves to relations of derivational complexity of the type we call "cumulative". When the derivation of a sentence "Y" follows all the rules applied in the derivation of a sentence "X" plus at least one rule not applied in X, then Y has greater cumulative derivational complexity than X (X < Y). The negative passive sentence in English has greater cumulative derivational complexity than both its negative active counterpart and its affirmative passive counterpart. However, the negative passive does not have a similar status with respect to the *yes-no* question, even though more rules are applied in deriving the former than in deriving the latter. The crucial point is that the negative-passive utilizes some rules not utilized in the question, but the question also utilizes at least one rule not utilized in the negative-passive.

Some of the experimenters who have studied adult processing of sentences have explicitly limited their predictions to the cumulative case (for example, Savin and Perchonock, 1965), but others have simply calculated derivational complexity in terms of the number of rules applied, without requiring the rules to stand in a cumulative relation. The difference is, of course, that when psychological complexity is predicted to follow derivational complexity calculated simply in terms of the number of rules, an assumption is made that any one rule equals any other in adding a constant increment of psychological complexity. This assumption is rather improbable, even when the only consideration is the fact that one rule may employ just one of the elementary transformations (deletion, substitution, adjunction, and permutation), while another rule employs several. When psychological complexity is predicted from *cumulative* derivational complexity, there is no assumption that one rule equals another. The suggestion is simply that, when the derivation of one sentence involves everything that the derivation of another involves, plus something more, then the something-more sentence will be more complex psychologically.

But why should derivations, which are more like proofs in geometry than like programs for speaking or understanding, have anything to do with the order in which children begin to understand and speak sentences of various kinds? A generative grammar is intended to represent the linguistic knowledge of the native speaker even though it does not represent the *manner* in which such knowledge is brought to bear in speaking and understanding. The native speaker's feeling for the way that a sentence splits into a hierarchy of sub-wholes is represented by the phrase-structure rules, which also represent his feeling for such relations in a sentence as subject-predicate and verb-object. Transformational rules represent the native speaker's sense that large sets of sentences are related to one another in such a way that, for each member of one set, there is a specific counterpart in the other set. One sometimes has the feeling, as generative grammars undergo their own historical transformations, that the powerful systematic requirements of the whole structure are moving the formalization a long way from "untrained" intuition. Still, through 1965 at least (Chomsky, 1965; Katz and Postal, 1964; Klima, 1964), the main lines of M.I.T. intuition are similar to our own.

Since a grammar formalizes adult knowledge, it is reasonable to hypothesize that the child's knowledge of the structure of his language grows from derivationally less complex grammar to derivationally more complex grammar. The hypothesis is reasonable, but not necessarily true. To test it, we should have good experimental techniques for inquiring about the young child's knowledge of the structure of sentences. Since we do not have such techniques, we propose to infer – with much uncertainty – the points at which grammatical knowledge emerges, from the study of naturally occurring linguistic interaction between child and mother. We propose to treat the child's production of a construction, in quantity and over a good part of its proper range, together with evidence that he understands the construction when others use it, as *signs* that he has the grammatical knowledge represented formally by the derivation of the construction in the adult grammar. It seems possible to us that the order of emergence of such knowledge would reflect derivational complexity even when the *speed* and *accuracy* with which such knowledge is employed in understanding and retaining sentences does not.

Probably the derivation is no nearer to being a description of performance for the child than it is for the adult. There may be numerous kinds of strategies of speaking and understanding which, from the first, make the relation between grammar and performance an indirect one. We do not mean to suggest otherwise, but rather to suggest that when performance over a range of sentences and situations attains a near-adult level of excellence, the performance may be taken as a sign of the acquisition of knowledge. Between knowledge and the grammar there may be a fairly direct relation.

There is reason to think that for some of the sentence types on which we shall report, it is particularly reasonable to treat performance as a sign of the acquisition of structural knowledge. The total set comprises *yes-no* questions (Q), negatives (N), truncated predicates (Tr), truncated questions (Tr Q), negative questions (NQ), truncated negatives (Tr N), and truncated negative questions (TrNQ). Although there are some knotty derivational problems (discussed at a later point), the sentences in this set may be partially ordered in terms of cumulative derivational complexity. The most complex in the set are the truncated negative questions, which are such negative tags as: *The old man drives well, doesn't he?* One of the more complex types is the truncated question, which is an affirmative tag like: *The old man doesn't drive well, does he?* With respect to these tags in particular, the inference from performance to structural knowledge seems strong.

Introduction to Tag Questions

When he was four years and seven months old, the boy we call Adam produced 32 tags in a two-hour sample of conversation. Included among them were the following sentences.

Ursula's my sister, isn't she?	*He can't beat me, can he?*
I made a mistake, didn't I?	*He doesn't know what to do, does he?*
Me and Diandros are working, aren't we?	

The truncated questions at the ends of these all seem to have the same semantic; they are requests for confirmation. There is one minor variation. The negative questions appended to affirmative propositions convey a presumption that the answer will be affirmative and, in fact, the most common answers to these were *Yes* and *That's right*. The affirmative questions appended to negative propositions convey a presumption that the answer will be negative, and *No* was the most common answer.

There are simpler mechanisms than the tag question for requesting confirmation. English speakers can use *huh?* or *right?*, and the children we have studied used these forms much earlier than they used the tags. In some languages even the mature tags are, like *huh?*, forms that do not vary with the structure of the sentences to which they are appended; the Germans can always ask *nicht wahr?* and the French *n'est-ce pas?* We would suppose that forms like these could be learned as fixed routines, but mature English tags cannot be. Adam requests confirmation with *isn't she?*, *didn't I?*, *does he?*, *aren't you?* and in many other ways. This variation of form occurs with no appreciable variation of semantic, but it is not a free variation; the form of the tag is fixed by the structure of the declarative.

Suppose Adam gave us the sentence *Me and Diandros are working*, without the question, and, on a different occasion, as an independent utterance, the question *Aren't we?* and we wondered how much the child knew of the structure of these sentences. Did he know that the subject of the first was *Me and Diandros* and that this subject was plural in number? Did he know that his second sentence could be derived from a declarative counterpart (*We aren't*) by interchanging the subject and the first member of the auxiliary (plus *n't*)? Did he know, that this second sentence could be derived from an affirmative counterpart (*Are we?*) by adjunction of the negative morpheme? In the record itself there would be nothing to go on but the fact that the sentences were produced. Even if there had been time to prepare experimental tests to inquire about Adam's knowledge, it is doubtful that such tests could have been invented. Suppose that we imagine the situation changed to the actual case in which the two sentences were produced as one, as the tag question *Me and Diandros are working, aren't we?* The fact of such production now offers fairly powerful evidence of grammatical knowledge.

The negative truncated question in the tag is a complex derivative of the antecedent declarative. It may be said loosely that the question is derived by the following processes: pronominalization, negation, interrogation, and truncation. Still speaking loosely, the processes go like this. As it is the subject that must be pronominalized, the child must know that *Me and Diandros* constitutes the subject. This is the kind of knowledge one would represent in the tree structure of the sentence by showing that *Me and Diandros* constitutes an "NP" directly dominated by "S." Clearly, the subject of a sentence cannot, in the few examples from Adam – let alone in English generally – be identified with any surface feature of the sentence such as the first word in the sentence or the first noun. To select the correct pronoun *we*, it is necessary to know that the subject is plural and inclusive of the speaker. In other cases it would be necessary to know the gender of the subject. From *Me and Diandros are working*, by the process of pronominalization alone, the sentence *We are working* is obtained, and that is still a long way from the ultimate tag form.

Negation can be roughly said to adjoin *n't* to the first member of the auxiliary. To do that Adam must have had the auxiliary properly bracketed and labeled. In deriving *didn't I?* from *I made a mistake*, Adam seems to have known something like the fact that the first member of the auxiliary is the morpheme "Past," which requires *do* support in the absence of any other auxiliary. By adding negation to pronominalization, we arrive at *We aren't working*.

Interrogation interchanges the first member of the auxiliary plus *n't* with the subject, yielding *Aren't we working?* Predicate truncation deletes all of the predicate except the first member of the auxiliary plus *n't*, and so at length we obtain the truncated negative question *Aren't we?* This loose derivation is summarized as follows.

Sentence	Grammatical Change
Me and Diandros are working.	Pronominalization
We are working.	Negation
We aren't working.	Interrogation
Aren't we working?	Truncation
Aren't we?	

The structure of English sentences is so obvious to the native speaker that he can scarcely realize how difficult it would be to derive truncated questions from declaratives without knowledge of sentence structure. Consider the following numerical parallel in which the string of digits following the comma can be derived from the string before the comma by using a constant function.

321118596,6210
95617,5227
2242139128746,6224
34229997,____ ?

Is there anyone who feels able to complete the last utterance? The rules are as follows.

1   Consider the subject to be the first set of digits summing to 5 or more. To pronominalize, if the subject is exactly 5, double it. If more than 5, triple it. Place after the comma and follow it with the rest of the antecedent string.
2   The first member of the auxiliary is the first set of numbers following the subject that sums to 3 or more. To adjoin the negative, insert the number "2" after the first member of the auxiliary.
3   The interrogative is created by interchanging the subject and the first member of the auxiliary together with the negative "2." If the first member of the auxiliary sums to exactly 3, double it (for *do* support).
4   Truncate the predicate by deleting the string after the subject.

So the step-by-step derivation of the last tag goes like this.

Sentence	Grammatical Change
34229997	Pronominalization
21229997	Negation
212229997	Interrogation
222219997	Truncation
22221	

It is difficult to see how Adam could produce the variety of tags that he does if he did not have all the structural knowledge described, which is a large part of the knowledge formally represented in the derivation of tags. To be sure, one could argue that, since the form of the truncated question is fixed by the form of the declarative, Adam could have learned all his 32 sentences in the one sample as fixed routines. However, the unlikeliness of this possibility becomes increasingly evident as more and more tags are studied, practically all of which are one-time occurrences.

For both negative and affirmative tags, the fact of production is strong evidence of grammatical knowledge. For the other kinds of sentences to be considered, one cannot feel as sure that correct production and evidence of comprehension are signs that the child has all the knowledge represented by the derivations in the adult grammar. The evidence is unevenly strong across sentence types and situations. A truncated negative declarative (TrN) like I *can't* produced in response to a parental sentence like *You can lift it* strongly suggests knowledge of the negation and truncation rules as well as correct bracketing of the verbal auxiliary. With respect to *yes-no* questions (Q), one can get fairly convincing evidence of comprehension, since these sentences are produced by others and tend to elicit responses from the child. For a full discussion of all the evidence, readers should consult the full grammatical discussions prepared by the project. In this paper we propose to simply present production figures for sentence types, since that is the aspect of the evidence that is easily made public. For all the sentence types, there is evidence of comprehension which appears in advance of production.

Sentence Derivations and the Order of Complexity

We will start with an overview of the loose grammatical conception guiding the study, and then introduce formal rules as refinements of this conception.

An overview

The kinds of sentences to be considered are as follows.

1   Simple, active, affirmative, declarative (SAAD). For example, *We had a ball.*
2   Simple, active, affirmative, interrogative (Q). For example, *Did we have a ball?*
3   Simple, active, negative, declarative (N). For example, *We didn't have a ball.*
4   Simple, active, affirmative, declarative, truncated (Tr). For example, *We did.*
5   Simple, active, negative, interrogative (NQ). For example, *Didn't we have a ball?*
6   Simple, active, affirmative, interrogative, truncated (Tr Q). For example, *Did we?* (Also used as affirmative tag.)
7   Simple, active, negative, declarative, truncated (TrN). For example, *We didn't.*
8   Simple, active, negative, interrogative, truncated (TrNQ). For example, *Didn't we?* (Also used as negative tag.)

Examining the above scheme a reader may wonder why we did not rotate sentence types in all the slots, including, for instance, passives as well as actives and complex sentences as well as simple ones. In the case of passives, the answer is that well-formed passives, not truncated but complete with agents, had only just begun to appear at the point where our records presently terminate – about age five. In the case of complex sentences, which include the various kinds of embeddings and conjoinings, the problems of analysis and interpretation are so complicated as to call for an independent study.

The cumulative derivational complexity of the seven types of sentences named and exemplified above works out roughly like this.

SAAD < Q < NQ,TrQ,TrNQ	4 predictions
SAAD < N < NQ,TrN,TrNQ	4 predictions
SAAD < Tr < TrQ,TrN,TrNQ	4 predictions
SAAD < NQ < TrNQ	2 predictions
SAAD < TrQ < TrNQ	2 predictions
SAAD < TrN < TrNQ	2 predictions
SAAD < TrNQ	1 prediction

The notation "A < B" means that A is less derivationally complex than B. Sentence symbols separated by commas (for example, NQ,TrQ,TrNQ) are not ordered relative to one another in this writing. In the listing above, each independent prediction is listed only once; since we have Q < NQ in the first line, we do not repeat it in the fourth. It should be noted that the sentence types are not completely ordered in terms of derivational complexity; we do not have an order for the pairs Q and N, Q and Tr, N and Tr; Q and TrN, N and TrQ, Tr and NQ; and NQ and TrQ, NQ and TrN, TrQ and TrN. If the facts of partial ordering are kept in mind, then the following representation of the overall order is helpful.

$$Q\ NQ$$
$$SAAD\ N\ TrQ\ TrNQ$$
$$Tr\ TrN$$

Why should the complexity order be as we have represented it? SAAD sentences are not, of course, uniform in the number of rules applied in their derivations; there may be from one to four auxilaries, and the more there are, the more often the obligatory affixation transformation must be applied. Likewise, a noun phrase may have one or several determiners, and predeterminers as well; an SAAD may have none, one, or many adverbials; an SAAD may involve complex selection rules and transformations to accomplish number agreement and it may not. However, for each SAAD there is a Q counterpart which employs all the rules of the SAAD plus the rule that transposes subject and elements of the auxiliary. Similarly, for each SAAD there is a negative counterpart which applies the rules of the SAAD; the rule that accomplishes preverbal placement of the negative morpheme; and sometimes also the rule contracting the negative. Finally, for each SAAD there is a truncated counterpart which may apply all the rules of the SAAD – if it is derived from a specific full declarative – plus the rule which cuts the predicate back to the first member of the auxiliary. It can then be said that Q, N, and Tr, though not in that order, are all more complex than SAAD. Thus, the increments of derivational complexity are clearly not uniform. The added rules are all different, and negatives often involve contraction when the other types do not. In addition, there is a difference of meaning between SAAD and either N or Q but not between SAAD and Tr. The deep structures of N and Q contain morphemes missing from otherwise corresponding SAAD sentences.

This is perhaps the right point at which to call attention to an important difference between the naturalistic study of child speech and the experimental studies mentioned at the start of this paper. In an experimental study of derivational complexity, sentences that are exact counterparts of one another can be compared; for example, *The boy hit the ball; Did the boy hit the ball?; The boy didn't hit the ball;* etc. To simplify our above description of the sentence types that concern us, we carried a single example *We had a ball* across all types. In fact, however, only one of these sentences actually came within the empirical compass of the study; the little girl we call Sarah did produce the tag *We had a ball, didn't we?* It is not possible to study exact counterpart sentences in a naturalistic study in the way that one can in an experiment. We shall be comparing frequencies of sentences of any one type (for example, negatives) with frequencies of entirely different specific sentences of other types. We must, therefore, make the large assumption that the population of sentences of one type (such as negatives), with respect to all grammatical features except those defining the type, is of the same average complexity as the population of sentences of each other type.

The sentence types N, Q, and Tr are more complex than SAAD sentences because each of the first three types adds at least one new rule, not only to particular sentences, but also to the grammar as a whole. The rules are Tnot, Tq, and Ttr. According to our rough general conception, the remaining differences of complexity arise from the application of additional rules in particular derivations but not from the addition of new rules to the grammar. We think of NQ, TrQ, and TrN as combinations of two rules employed one at a time in N, Q, and Tr. We think of TrNQ as a triadic combination from the same set. There is then a qualitative difference between the predictions of the first level (comparing Q, N, and Tr with SAAD) and those of the later levels, and it will be interesting to see if this qualitative line can be seen in the data. In addition, some of the comparisons of the later levels, like some of those on the first level, involve semantic changes (for example, Q and NQ), whereas others do not (Q and TrQ). . . .

Sentence Length, Frequency, and Semantic

What factors other than derivational complexity could account for the order of emergence of SAAD, Q, N, Tr, TrN, TrQ, and TrNQ? Length and frequency are not cognitive variables, but we cannot be sure that they will, on that account, fail to influence results obtained by cognitive psychologists. In experimental studies of sentence comprehension and recall, sentence length has often been confounded with complexity, the two increasing together. For example, Savin and Perchonock (1965), in their study of immediate recall, made 17 predictions on the basis of cumulative derivational complexity; 13 of these 17 would also be made if one simply used sentence length as an index of complexity. For the *wh* question in their experiment, Savin and Perchonock decide that there are no predictions from cumulative complexity, but they fail to note that sentence length makes 10 predictions in this case, of which 9 are confirmed.

Sutherland (1966) and others have suggested that complexity is also likely to be confounded with frequency in such favorite sets of sentences as SAAD, Q, N, P (passives), NQ, NP, and NPQ. Since no one seems to have cited any actual counts of sentence types, we may as well do so. We have made many such counts in our study for the speech parents use to children. In a sample of 700 sentences, the number of SAAD sentences will run between one and two hundred; Q and N will both be something like one half to one quarter as frequent as SAAD; of passives, negative questions, negative passives, and the like there will typically be between none and half a dozen. Of course we do not know how representative such counts are of adult speech generally, but in parent-to-child speech, at any rate, complexity is confounded with frequency in the kinds of sentences that have been most often used in experiments.

Are length and frequency confounded with complexity in the sentences we have studied? Consider length in the following sample set.

SAAD.	*We had a ball.*	(4 words)
Q.	*Did we have a ball?*	(5 words)
N.	*We didn't have a ball.*	(6 words)
Tr.	*We did.*	(2 words)
TrN.	*We didn't.*	(3 words)
TrQ.	*Did we?*	(2 words)
TgQ.	*We didn't have a ball, did we?*	(8 words)
NQ.	*Didn't we have a ball?*	(6 words)
TrNQ.	*Didn't we?*	(3 words)
TgNQ.	*We had a ball, didn't we?*	(7 words)

Of the 19 predictions from derivational complexity that apply when we have TrQ and TrNQ, rather than complete tags, 7 would go the same way if sentence length were used as an index of complexity, but 12 would go differently. Of the 16 predictions from derivational complexity that apply when we have the tags TgQ and TgNQ, sentence length predicts the same way in 11 cases and differently in 5. So, in our sentences, length and derivational complexity are partially but not completely confounded. Examining the outcomes of the 12 predictions for which length and complexity predict differently (when we have Tr and TrQ) across the 3 children, we find that complexity is correct in 31 instances. The outcome is unsettled in 4 instances and length is correct just once. The results are about the same with tags included. So it does look as if sentence length will not explain the order of emergence, even though sentence length is a variable that increases with age. One of the reasons this family of constructions caught our eye in the first place was that we were surprised to find such short utterances as tags and truncations developing quite late in the child's speech.

Frequency turns out to be a more serious variable than length. In order to see whether differential construction frequencies in parental speech could affect order of emergence in child speech, we wanted a count of parental frequencies that antedated emergence and was relatively free of influence from the children. So we used two samples of 700 utterances each taken immediately prior to II and III. At III the children were not regularly producing any of the constructions except the SAAD sentences. We counted the 8 major constructions in the two samples for each of the three mothers and used just those sentences of the mother that were neither imitations nor expansions of sentences produced by the children.

As in all counts we have made for parental speech, the frequency profiles of the three mothers were highly correlated. Of the results we will report the average value per 700 utterances, across mothers and samples, for each main sentence type. They are:

	Q (53)	TrQ (2)	
SAAD(139)	N(56)	TrN(2)	TrNQ (4)
	Tr(13)	NQ (4)	

Clearly, frequency and derivational complexity are closely related.

The apparently quite general correlation between grammatical complexity and frequency has a certain independent interest. It is not, to begin with, simply an artifact of a system of sentence classification. Potentially there are as many different sentences of one type as of any other type. Any SAAD is susceptible of, for instance, negation, truncation, interrogation, and tagging. Apparently, however, there are many more occasions calling for declaration than for interrogation, for affirmation than for negation, and relatively few occasions calling for truncation and requests for confirmation. One is reminded of Zipf's (1949) empirical law relating word length inversely to word frequency, and also of his general idea that the relation exists because of a Principle of Least Effort that causes our frequently used tools to be kept simple and close to hand. The derivationally simple sentence types seem to be those we most often need, and the derivationally complex types those we need less often. If psychological complexity is related to derivational complexity, then it may not be inappropriate to invoke a Principle of Least Effort.

Of the 19 main predictions made by derivational complexity, 17 are also made by frequency, and the two predictions on which complexity and frequency do not agree are based on very small frequency differences in our counts. It is possible, then, that the order in which the child's knowledge of the sentences develops is determined by the frequency with which parents model the sentences.

We have often found before that parental frequencies predict the order in which constructions will "emerge," in terms of some frequency criterion, in successive samples of child speech. In the early months of our study we had to consider seriously a really radical alternative to the notion that frequent modelling of a sentence type facilitates learning its structure. Suppose the children had known everything from the beginning but emitted constructions according to a frequency profile like that of the parents. The chance that any particular construction would attain an arbitrary frequency criterion in an early sample would be greater for frequent constructions than for infrequent constructions. So what looked like a pattern of successive "emergences" might simply be a kind of sampling phenomenon. Up to a point that is true. But when you have more than two years of zero frequency for something like the negative and affirmative tags, you can be confident, when they eventually appear, that something new has been learned. You can be particularly confident when you see the sudden overproduction we have seen in Adam's sample #50. So we think that at least we no longer need seriously to consider the possibility that the children were learning nothing new, but we must still consider the possibility that modelling frequency affects the order of learning.

In addition to the differences of length and frequency among sentence types, there are semantic differences. Interrogatives, negatives, and tags all differ from SAAD sentences in the meanings they communicate. Is it perhaps the meanings that account for the order of emergence? As it happens, the children have primitive ways of asking questions, negating, and requesting confirmation, and the primitive forms are present even in I and II. The primitive negative is created by preposing a negative word, *no* or *not*, to a sentence: *No want, Not Sarah's*, and the like. Primitive *yes-no* questions are created by using a rising interrogative intonation for any sentence or sentence fragment. Primitive requests for confirmation are chiefly *huh*? and *right*? Of course, the mature grammatical forms provide for semantic refinements that the primitive forms miss; the difference, for instance, between *Do you see him?* and *Will you see him?* Still, it cannot be the basic semantics of interrogation, negation, and confirmation that defer the acquisition of the mature grammatical structures. The basic meanings have been expressed from the beginning of our records. What has happened developmentally is that immature means of expression have been displaced by mature means.

We must now distinguish between two sorts of order of emergence in child speech. The first sort is an order among constructions that are all mature adult forms. This is the sort of order with which the present paper has been concerned. We have asked whether the order of emergence of some eight types of well-formed adult sentences reflects the derivational complexity of the types in terms of the adult grammar, and found that it does. The second sort of order concerns constructions which are equivalent semantically but which exist in one or more immature or childish forms as well as, eventually, the adult form. This kind of sequence exists for questions, negatives, and tags and for many other constructions. The children we have studied asked *wh* questions with preposed question word, but without interposing subject and auxiliary, long before they made *wh* questions in which they did both. They said *Why you went* and *What he's doing* before they said *Why did you go?* and *What is he doing?* The children combined negation and indeterminates to form sentences like *I didn't see something* and *It don't have some tapioca in it* before they learned to make indeterminates into indefinites in negative sentences and so to say *I didn't see anything* and *It don't have any tapioca in it.*

With respect to the sort of sequence that moves from immature to mature constructions, it is possible to ask again about the role of derivational complexity. However, the immature forms are not generated by adult grammar; they are ungrammatical from the adult point of view. Consequently, the notion of cumulative derivational complexity with which we have thus far operated has no application to the second sort of sequence. The relevant standard of complexity is not the adult grammar but the child's own grammar. What kinds of changes must be made in his system if it is to generate mature negatives, tags, *wh* questions, indefinites, and the like? Additional rules may be required; old rules may lose some of their generality; and rules of an entirely new type may be introduced. This is going to be a long and complicated story and we are not ready in this paper to try to tell it.

There is another interesting question about the progression from immature to mature forms. What causes it to occur at all? Why should the child relinquish old ways? Is it because they are ineffective? Does the necessity of communicating exercise a selection pressure in favor of adult forms? Or are the old ways given up simply because parents express disapproval of them and approval of more mature forms? Is there a pressure toward maturity exerted by contingent approval? Our records offer some information on these questions and we turn to that now.

Communication Pressure and Contingent Approval

The data to be reported in this section flatly contradict what most parents say about their own child-training practices. That may mean that parents do not act as they think they act. It may also mean that the parent–child interaction in our records is simply not representative; it is probably not representative of parents generally, and perhaps not even representative of the parents of Adam, Eve, and Sarah. May not the presence of a psychologist and a tape recorder have altered usual practices? It certainly may have. However, one should not assume that it must have. A single investigator stayed with each child over the course of the study, in one case for three years. The investigator became a family friend and interaction with him and in his presence seems completely without self-consciousness after the first couple of weeks.

Communication pressure

Do ill-formed constructions in child speech give way to well-formed constructions because there is a selection pressure in communication which favors the latter? Child utterances often seem to function as instrumental acts designed to accomplish effects in other persons. Surely the well-formed utterance, since it would be correctly interpreted, is a superior tool to the ill-formed utterance, which must often be misunderstood or simply not comprehended. The protocols we have permit a rough test of this proposition with respect to some of the constructions that interest us.

Yes-no questions, *wh* questions, negatives, and tags all occur in child speech in primitive or ill-formed versions before they occur as well-formed constructions. The ill-formed constructions start well in advance of the well-formed versions. Some of the primitive forms are eventually entirely displaced by mature forms (negatives and *wh* questions). Some primitive forms, the *yes-no* question that does not interpose subject and auxiliary and the *huh?* tag, are acceptable alternatives in adult speech, and these are not displaced entirely but rather simply make room for mature forms. In all cases it is possible to find samples in which primitive and mature forms are both present in quantity. What we want to know is whether there is a difference in the quality of response from adult interlocutors to the two kinds of form.

To test the proposition we used (except in the case of tags) two of the samples, corresponding to grammars, for each construction. For *yes-no* questions, we used samples III and V; for *wh* questions, and also for negatives, samples III and IV. The samples were selected so as to maximize the numbers of both primitive and well-formed constructions of the type in question for all three children. They represent times when the construction was undergoing change and the child was vacillating between primitive and well-formed versions, times when communication pressure should have operated if it ever does. Tags had to be treated somewhat differently from the other constructions. There were, in Eve's records, no well-formed tags at all; in Sarah's they start at V; and in Adam's they do not start until after V. Consequently, the study of responses to tags, primitive and well-formed, is limited to Sarah and Adam and is based on just those 2-hour samples from each child which contained the largest numbers of tags: Adam's sample 50, and Sarah's samples 100–103.

Interlocutor responses to child utterances were classified in the following terms. *Yes-no* questions, *wh* questions, and tags all request answers and such answers are one sort of comprehending response. Sometimes a response does not directly answer a question, but nevertheless clearly shows comprehension and represents a reasonable sort of continuation; for instance, in response to *Where Christmas cookies?* we have *We ate them all.* These two kinds of response to questions are grouped together in Table 10.1 as "Sequiturs" or clearly relevant and comprehending reactions. "Non Sequiturs" in

Table 10.1 represent the conjunction of several different sorts of reactions. Sometimes the interlocutor queries all or some part of the child's question; for instance, in response to *Where my spoon?* we have *Your spoon?* Sometimes the interlocutor responds with a new topic or seeming irrelevancy; for instance, in response to *Where ice cream?* we find *And the potatoes.* Sometimes a response reveals an actual misunderstanding of the child's question; *What time it is?* elicited *Uh, huh, it tells what time it is.* Sometimes there was simply no response at all to a question. Sometimes there was a response of doubtful classification. Non Sequiturs, then, are made up of "queries" plus "irrelevancies" plus "misunderstandings" plus "no responses" plus "doubtfuls." The sequiturs and non sequiturs of Table 10.1 do not always sum to 100% because there was a residual category which seemed not to belong with either of the others, a category of "repeats." Repeats of ill-formed utterances usually contained corrections and so could be instructive; repeats of well-formed utterances would not be corrections. Interlocutor responses to negatives were categorized in the same way as responses to questions, with a single exception. Negatives do not request answers in the way that questions do. Sequiturs are all simply continuations strongly suggesting comprehension of the child's utterance.

Table 10.1 presents the percentages of sequiturs and non sequiturs in response to primitive and well-formed constructions of each type for each child. The mean percentages of sequitur responses to primitive and well-formed constructions are exactly the same (45%). The mean percentage of non sequitur responses is slightly, but not significantly, higher to primitive constructions than to well-formed constructions; 47% in the former case and 42% in the latter. The obtained difference on Non Sequiturs should be interpreted in the light of the fact that a great many of the non sequiturs were "no responses," and it is not clear that these should all be considered unsatisfactory responses. In some cases the child was talking fast and scarcely seemed to expect or leave time for an answer. When non sequiturs were counted more narrowly – as instances of genuine misunderstanding – we found precisely one instance (the example given earlier) for all children and all constructions. In general, the results provide no support for the notion that there is a communication pressure favoring mature constructions.

When coding the transcriptions for communication pressure, one forms the impression that the primitive forms were understood perfectly well by adult interlocutors, who, indeed, did not notice anything primitive or ill-formed about the constructions. Rising intonation is a fairly good sign of a *yes-no* question, as is the preposed *wh* word of a *wh* question, and *no* or *not* for the negative, and *huh?* for the tag. The operations the child fails to perform on these utterances are in fact redundant as far as the meaning of the construction is concerned.

It is possible, of course, that communication pressure plays an important role in speech progression at other seasons of development and with other constructions. It may, for instance, be the force that causes the child to relinquish holophrases in favor of sentences. Unfortunately, there is a kind of paradoxical difficulty in the way of demonstrating such an effect with nonexperimental data. In order to prove that a child learns new means of expression because he has messages to communicate that cannot be handled with the means at his command, the investigator must be able to detect such uncommunicated messages. The investigator is not, however, the only person trying to "read" the child and probably not the most expert person; the child's parents or siblings are likely to be the experts. Therefore, it is usually the case that any message the investigator can make

Table 10.1 Sequiturs and non sequiturs following primitive and well-formed constructions

	Yes-No (III and V)		Wh (III and IV)		Tags (Adam 50; Sarah 100–103)		Negatives (III and IV)		Means	
	Primitive	Well-formed	Primitive	Well-formed	Primitive	Well-formed	Primitive	Well-formed	Primitive	Well-formed
Sequiturs	.70	.83	.44	.45			.70	.31	.61	.53 Eve
Non Sequiturs	.18	.13	.37	.18			.20	.49	.25	.27
Sequiturs	.48	.46	.45	.37	.54	.56	.00	.24	.31	.36 Adam
Non Sequiturs	.50	.43	.50	.52	.42	.44	.86	.52	.62	.49
Sequiturs	.47	.52	.38	.52	.52	.36	.33	.41	.42	.45 Sarah
Non Sequiturs	.53	.47	.62	.43	.48	.57	.56	.51	.55	.50
									.45	.45 Means
									.47	.42

out, the family can also make out, and so the child will in fact already be communicating any idea that we can be sure he has. In naturalistic studies we usually have to admit that we did not know a child possessed a given refinement of meaning until he started to produce the construction expressing that refinement.

Contingent approval

It might be supposed that syntactically correct utterances come to prevail over those that are incorrect, through the operation of positive reinforcement and punishment on the part of adults. A positive reinforcer is generally defined as any event which, being made contingent upon the emission of an antecedent response, increases the frequency of that response. In this sense, reinforcers can never be specified before one has observed their effect. Whether or not an event is a reinforcer waits upon information as to whether or not it has, in fact, reinforced.

The definition of *punishment*, in Skinner's sense, begins with the notion of a "negative reinforcer." An event subsequent to a response is a negative reinforcer of that response when the *withdrawal* of the event, being made contingent on the emission of the response, causes the response to increase in frequency. Shock is often a negative reinforcer. Punishment, finally, involves the *presentation* of a negative reinforcer, and while punishment does not seem to extinguish a response, it does depress the frequency of its performance.

Strictly speaking, there is no way to disconfirm the following proposition: "Syntactically correct utterances become more frequent because of reinforcement and less frequent because of punishment." To disconfirm it, one would have to show that there is no event (or better, no way of conceiving events) which increases the frequency of syntactically correct utterances when its presentation is made contingent on such utterances, and also no event which increases frequency when its withdrawal is made so contingent. Because events subsequent to child speech are indefinitely various (or better, susceptible of being conceived in indefinitely various ways) one can never be sure that there is no event which functions as a reinforcer or punishment.

In practice, of course, we know that certain events are likely to be reinforcers or punishments for a given response because we have seen that they have this effect on many other responses. Money is supposed to be such a conditioned "generalized reinforcer" and social approval is supposed to be another. In *Science and Human Behavior* (1953, p. 78), Skinner wrote: "Another person is likely to reinforce only that part of one's behavior of which he approves, and any sign of his *approval*, therefore, becomes reinforcing in its own right. Behavior which evokes a smile or the verbal response 'That's right' or 'Good' or any other commendation is strengthened. We use this generalized reinforcer to establish and shape the behavior of others, particularly in education. For example, we teach both children and adults to speak correctly by saying 'That's right' when appropriate behavior is emitted." By extension, it seems reasonable to think that signs of disapproval would be generalized punishments. The proposition "Syntactically correct utterances come to prevail over syntactically incorrect utterances through the selective administration of signs of approval and disapproval" is a testable one.

The proposition cannot possibly be true for the natural case of parents and children at home unless parental approval and disapproval are in fact appropriately contingent on syntactical correctness. If the reactions *are* appropriately contingent, then they may or may not have the effects proposed. In our materials parental reactions do not even meet the minimal circumstance of appropriate contingency and so the proposition may be discarded without testing its further implications.

The demonstration goes like this. In order to investigate contingencies at different levels of child proficiency, we worked with samples II and V. We first listed all of those exchanges in which a parent responded with such signs of approval as *That's right, Correct, Very good*, and *Yes*, and such signs of disapproval as *That's wrong* or *That's not right* or *No*. We could not, in this analysis, limit ourselves to approval and disapproval following the constructions on which we have focused in this paper (questions, negatives, tags, etc.) because such exchanges were too infrequent.

The general plan, of course, was to contrast the syntactic correctness of the population of utterances followed by a sign of approval with the population followed by a sign of disapproval. There are some problems about scoring the syntactical correctness of a child's utterance. When an utterance consists of only one word it has no syntax and so cannot be either correct or incorrect. All such were disregarded. Child utterances, like adult utterances, can be well-formed even though they are not complete subject-predicate sentences, so we do not want to measure them against some notion of the grammatically complete sentence. The indices we used are not responsive to all aspects of syntax but they are responsive to those that can be confidently scored for spontaneous speech. An error was scored whenever some grammatical marker that was obligatory in terms of the surrounding context of the utterance was missing. For instance, *He not walking* contains an error because *is* is missing. An error was also scored whenever the form of a morpheme required by the context was erroneous; for instance, *Her curl my hair* or *I throwed it*, or *I don't want something*. Finally an error was scored whenever morphemes were not in the correct order: *What he's doing*.

The results are summarized in Table 10.2 as a set of frequency tables for which an utterance was simply counted correct or incorrect – whatever the degree of incorrectness. Another analysis scores degrees of correctness and uses mean scores. In neither case is there even a shred of evidence that approval and disapproval are contingent on syntactic correctness.

What circumstances do govern statements of approval and disapproval from parents? Surely they are not emitted without reference to the child's speech. Table 10.3 provides a few examples which suggest the answer. Approval and disapproval are not primarily linked with the grammatical form of the utterance. They are rather linked to the truth value of the proposition, which the adult fits to the child's generally incomplete and often deformed sentence. And so, though Eve makes a grammatical error when she expresses the proposition that her mother is a girl with the utterance *He a girl*, the proposition itself is true and since it is the proposition rather than the grammar that governs response, the response is approving. By contrast, when Sarah points and says *There's the animal farmhouse*, her syntax is impeccable but the proposition is false, and so the reaction is disapproving.

The truth value of a presumed proposition is the most important determinant of approval and disapproval, but it is not the only determinant. When Eve says something that may be approximated as *What the guy idea*, she says something that can be neither true nor false; it is a kind of exclamation. The exclamation is identifiable as a poor performance of a familiar routine, and mother elects to disapprove phonological aspects

Table 10.2   Relations between syntactic correctness of antecedent child's utterance and approving or disapproving parental response[a]

	Sarah			Adam			Eve	
	Correct	Incorrect		Correct	Incorrect		Correct	Incorrect
App.	4	9	App.	4	3	App.	6	19
Dis.	4	6	Dis.	2	0	Dis.	3	5
				(a) At II				

	Sarah			Adam			Eve	
	Correct	Incorrect		Correct	Incorrect		Correct	Incorrect
App.	23	4	App.	13	6	App.	33	29
Dis.	12	2	Dis.	7	1	Dis.	12	15
				(b) At V				

[a] Only 1 of 6 in right direction. Remaining 1 is not significant.

Table 10.3   Examples of utterances approved and disapproved

Approval

Adam. *Draw a boot paper.*   **Adam's Mother.** *That's right. Draw a boot on paper.*

Eve.   *Mama isn't boy, he a girl.*   **Eve's Mother.**   *That's right.*
Sarah. *Her curl my hair.*   **Sarah's Mother.** *Um hmm.*

Disapproval

Adam. *And Walt Disney comes on Tuesday.*   **Adam's Mother.** *No, he does not.*
Eve.   *What the guy idea.*   **Eve's Mother.**   *No, that's not right. Wise idea.*

Sarah. *There's the animal farmhouse.*   **Sarah's Mother.** *No, that's a lighthouse.*

of the performance and to model an improved version. While there are several bases for approval and disapproval, they are almost always semantic or phonological. Explicit approval or disapproval of either syntax or morphology is extremely rare in our records and so seems not to be the force propelling the child from immature to mature forms.

Conclusions

What is the significance for child speech of the two sorts of sequence and what is the significance of the negative findings with respect to communication pressure and contingent approval? The fact that some constructions appear in one or more "ungrammatical" forms before they appear in adult form shows that children are learning rules and not simply utterances. A sentence like *I don't see something* has the same force on the syntactic level as *I goed* on the morphological. Both suggest the generalization of rules to cases that ought to be exceptions.

I see smoke.	*It is snowing.*
I don't see smoke.	*It snowed.*
I see something.	*I am going.*
I don't see something.	*I goed.*

The fact that some ungrammatical or immature forms have been used by all the children that have been studied shows that children are alike in the innate knowledge, language-processing routines, preferences and assumptions they bring to the problem of language acquisition. One such preference seems to be for a small number of rules of maximal generality (McNeill 1970). The combination of negatives and indeterminate pronouns (for example, *I don't hear someone*) treats these pronouns as other pronouns and, indeed, noun phrases generally, are so treated. The failure to make the affirmative-negative switch on tags, resulting in such sentences as *We can play, can we?* treats the tag question as if it were an echo question given in response to another speaker's production of the first proposition. It is even conceivable that children say *What he wants?* and *Why you went?* because they are trying to use a single rule for *wh* questions and embedded *wh* clauses as in: *We know what he wants* and *We know why you went*.

The immature rules for interrogation and negation may arise as McNeill (1970) has suggested because they are much closer to the base structure than are the transformed adult forms. The transformations are certainly language-specific and so must be learned. The base structure has a better chance of being universal and innate.

If the negative results for communication pressure and contingent approval are representative of parental practice, then these cannot be the forces causing the child to relinquish immature forms and adopt adult forms. In our data the two principles of response (or rule) selection fail to meet the first requirement one can set; they are not contingent in the way that they are required to be. We suspect that the only force toward grammaticality operating on the child is the occasional mismatch between his theory of the structure of the language and the data he receives. Piaget's terms, "assimilation" (the present theory), "accommodation" (the impact of the data), and "disequilibrium" (the mismatch), were created to deal with a similar lack of extrinsic motivation in the child for progressing toward operativity. Of course this formulation leaves most questions unanswered. For instance, why do data have an impact at some times and at other times no effect at all?

The fact that there is a sequence, among well-formed constructions, from those that are derivationally simple, in terms of the adult grammar, toward those that are derivationally complex, suggests that the adult grammar does, at least roughly, represent what it is that the child is learning. Of course we do not yet know how general the sequence is. It seems to be the case (when a lot of underbrush is hacked away) that control of the base structure precedes control of transformational knowledge and that simple sentences precede conjoinings and embeddings (as these were understood in the linguistics of 1965). On the other hand, in many points of detail, we do not find a progression from derivational simplicity to complexity. For instance, noun phrases with separable verbs occur in transformed position well before they occur in untransformed position.

Finally, there is the relation between parental frequency and order of emergence among well-formed constructions. Our guess is that this is an incidental consequence of the relation between frequency and complexity and that frequency, above some minimum level, does not determine the order in which structural knowledge emerges. What would happen if the parents of a child produced tags at a much higher rate than is normal? We have some basis for a guess.

The parents of Adam, Eve, and Sarah did produce certain *wh* questions at a very high rate in a period when the children did not understand the structure of *wh* questions. What happened then? The children learned to produce the two most frequently repeated *wh* questions, *What's that?* and *What doing?*, on roughly appropriate occasions. Their performance had the kind of rigidity that we have learned to recognize as a sign of incomprehension of structure; they did not produce, as their parents of course did, such structurally close variants as *What are those?* and *Who's that?* and *What is he doing?* When, much later, the children began to produce all manner of *wh* questions in the preposed form (such as *What he wants*), it was interesting to note that *What's that?* and *What are you doing?* were not at first reconstrued in terms of the new analysis. If the children had generated the sentences in terms of their new rules, they ought to have said *What that is?* and *What you are doing?* but instead they, at first, persisted with the old forms. One of us (Brown) found himself doing a comparable thing when he studied Japanese at Berlitz. Early in his lessons he learned, and made heavy use of, the form *korewa* meaning "this-one-here." Quite a bit later he learned about the particle *wa* (roughly nominative, but see McNeill, 1970, for complications) which was added to nouns and pronouns. He did not, however, reanalyze *korewa* into *kore* and *wa*, but continued to think of it as a single word, until one day he heard *kore-no* (genitive) and then *kore-o* (accusative) and thought "Why it's *kore-wa*!"

We suggest that any form that is produced with very high frequency by parents will be somehow represented in the child's performance even if its structure is far beyond him. He will find a way to render a version of it and will also form a notion of the circumstances in which it is used. The construction will become lodged in his speech as an unassimilated fragment. Extensive use of such an unanalyzed or mistakenly analyzed fragment probably protects it, for a time, from reanalysis when the structure relevant to it is finally learned. Such, we suspect, are the effects of frequency.

In closing, we would like to express the distaste experimentalists must feel for the assumptions, compromises, and qualifications involved in the use of naturalistic data. We find that naturalistic studies build an appetite for experiment – for controls, complete data, large samples, and statistical analysis. But we also find the reverse. The two kinds of research are complementary activities and complementary forms of evidence. In experimental work one uses the ingenuity he has on advance planning for data collection, whereas in naturalistic work little ingenuity goes into the data collection and all that is available goes into data analysis. The history of psychology generally and of psycholinguistics in particular shows that careful experimental work provides no sure path to the truth. Neither does naturalism. There are rich opportunities for error in either method. But on the whole, the opportunities arise at different points, and when the methods are used in combination, the truth has a chance to appear.

References

Chomsky, N. 1965. *Aspects of the Theory of Syntax*. Cambridge, Mass.: MIT Press.

Chomsky, N. 1957. *Syntactic Structures*. The Hague: Mouton.

Fodor, J. and Garrett, M. 1966. "Some reflections on competence and performance." In J. Lyons and R. J. Wales (eds.), *Psycholinguistics Papers*. Edinburgh: Edinburgh University Press, pp. 135–54.

Katz, J. J. and Postal, P. M. 1964. *An Integrated Theory of Linguistic Descriptions*. Cambridge, Mass.: MIT Press.

Klima, E. S. 1964. "Negation in English." In J. A. Fodor and J. J. Katz (eds.), *The Structure of Language*. Englewood Cliffs, NJ: Prentice-Hall, 1964.

McNeill, D. 1970. "The development of language." In P. A. Mussen (ed.), *Carmichael's Manual of Child Psychology*, 3rd edn. New York: Wiley.

Savin, H. B. and Perchonock, Ellen. 1965. "Grammatical structure and the immediate recall of English sentences." *Journal of Verbal Learning and Verbal Behavior* 4, 348–53.

Skinner, B. F. 1953. *Science and Human Behavior*. New York: Macmillan.

Sutherland, N. S. 1966. Discussion of Fodor, J. and Garrett, M. "Some reflections on competence and performance." In J. Lyons and R. J. Wales (eds.), *Psycholinguistics Papers*. Edinburgh: Edinburgh University Press.

Zipf, G. K. 1949. *Human Behavior and the Principle of Least Effort*. Cambridge, Mass.: Addison-Wesley.

11

Talking to Children:
A Search for Universals

Charles A. Ferguson

1 Baby Talk Registers

1.1 "Baby talk," the special way we sometimes talk to infants, seems an unlikely phenomenon to investigate if we want to find universals of human language, i.e. things that hold for language in general as opposed to characteristics of particular languages at particular times. We generally feel apologetic or embarrassed if caught engaging in unmistakable baby talk, and we certainly do not like to give it serious attention, except perhaps to warn parents against its use to children because it might deflect or retard their language development.

There are, however, many ways to search for language universals, and marginal phenomena in language may sometimes be just as revealing as the central topics of syntax and phonology. One way to search for universals, surprisingly enough, is to study one language in great depth. This was the path of the Indian grammarians and philosophers of language, who for centuries concentrated their attention on Sanskrit and discovered much about how human language works. It has also been the preferred path of transformational grammarians, who have spent more effort on English than on all the other languages of the world combined and have greatly extended our knowledge of human language. Another way is to work with a handful of languages that are strikingly different from one another or have some special position among the languages of the world. This was the route followed by Helwig in the seventeenth century when he wrote his universal grammar on the basis of the characteristics of Latin, Greek, Hebrew, and Aramaic – the principal language of Western civilization plus the three languages of the sacred scriptures (Helvicus 1619). A recent example of this approach is Vihman's search for universal principles of consonant harmony in child language acquisition, although her choice of six languages was dictated by the fact that these languages were the only ones

From *Universals of Human Language*. Volume 1. *Method and Theory*, ed. Joseph H. Greenberg, Charles A. Ferguson, and Edith A. Moravcsik. Stanford, Calif.: Stanford University Press, 1978, pp. 203–24. © 1978 by the Board of Trustees of the Leland Stanford Junior University. Reprinted with the permission of Stanford University Press, www.sup.org.

for which full data from at least two children were available (Vihman 1978). Another approach is to select a sizable sample of the world's languages, at least 25 or so, representing different language families and different parts of the world, in the hope that the sample will give a good approximation to the nature and extent of interlingual variation on the phenomenon being investigated. This is the approach familiar to us from Greenberg's well-known paper on basic word order (Greenberg 1966a) and a number of more recent studies in the same tradition, such as Steele's paper on word-order variation (Steele 1978), which utilize data from a large number of languages.[1]

1.2   The search for universals can focus just on matters of linguistic structure. What kinds of vowel systems do the world's languages have, and what principles explain their typological constraints (Crothers 1978)? What kinds of interrogative systems are there, and why (Ultan 1978)? How do pronoun systems work in general (Ingram 1978)? Or, the search for language universals can focus on uses of language. Do all languages have ways to show deference, to teach, to express affection? If so, are there universal principles about the occasions of these uses, the way they are acquired, and the way they vary in salience from one speech community to another? Or even, the search for universals can focus on the relation between structure and use. For example, are there universals about the relation between the showing of deference and the shape of pronoun systems (Brown and Gilman 1960)? Does teaching in all speech communities make use of questions of certain syntactic shapes to which the questioner already knows the answer (cf. Sinclair and Coulthard 1975)? Before deciding on any of these or other ways to search for language universals, let us better identify the phenomenon to be investigated: the way adults or older children modify their normal speech when addressing very young children.

1.3   In spite of our embarrassment with the topic of baby talk, it is a promising field of study. In the first place, baby talk is very widespread. People who ridicule its use and deny using it themselves may find that they use it in talking to a pet animal or in making fun of someone else, and even people who avoid most of the extreme lexical and phonological characteristics of baby talk still modify their speech extensively in talking to very young children. It is easy to tell which of two tape recordings was addressed to an infant and which to an adult, entirely apart from the subject matter of the conversation. Second, analysis of the way people generally talk to young children is relevant to the larger question of how children acquire their mother tongue. If the language addressed to children is markedly different from ordinary adult-to-adult conversation, it seems plausible that this difference might help or hinder the child in its language development, and our folk beliefs take a definite position on this question. Finally, the study of talk to children should bear on general questions of how language varies. If the variation is not random, but has recognizable regularities – as it clearly does or one could not recognize baby talk – it may be part of the speakers' linguistic competence that merits inclusion in our grammars and theories of language.

Psychologists, linguists, anthropologists and others have studied talk addressed to children from various perspectives and for various purposes.[2] Recent literature includes reports of psycholinguistic experiments about language acquisition, elicited accounts exploring marginal systems in language, and participant observation of child socialization in different cultures. Our purpose here is the search for language universals, using published studies from a selected sample of the world's languages, and focused on the relation between structure and use. The 27 languages included in the sample are (Syrian) Arabic, (Neo-)Aramaic, Bengali, Berber, Cocopa, Comanche, Dutch, (American) English, German, Gilyak, Greek, Hidatsa, Hungarian, Japanese, (Havyaka) Kannada, Kipsigis, Latvian, Luo, Maltese, Marathi, Pomo, (Brazilian) Portuguese, Romanian, Samoan, Serbo-Croatian, Spanish, and Tzeltal (see Appendix). The sample is high in Indo-European (ten languages) and low in African and Oceanic languages, but we are limited by the published sources. Most of the studies used as sources are devoted primarily to an invest-igation of baby talk lexicon and have only brief comments on other aspects. Studies that treat a full range of topics are available only for English and Dutch. The question of language universals in baby talk has been mentioned by a succession of authors, includ-ing Jakobson (1960), Ferguson (1964, 1977b), Kelkar (1964), Drachmann (1973), and Ervin-Tripp (1977). Of these, Ferguson (1977b) identifies about 30 "widespread char-acteristics" of baby talk structure and use. Snow (1977) identifies over 30 "dependent variables" in experimental studies of English and Dutch talk to children. About a third of these two lists overlap. Rūķe-Draviņa, in an article written after hearing the Ferguson and Snow papers, addresses the question of universals directly (Rūķe-Draviņa 1976). She expresses caution about the universality of the various characteristics that have been noticed, but submits six probable universals: high pitch (*Ammenton*), reduplication, hypocorism, names of body parts and events closely connected with the young child, onomatopoeia and pronoun shift. In the present paper, five of these, together with 17 other characteristics of talk addressed to young children, are examined across languages in the search for universals.

2   Characteristics of Talk to Children

2.1   The most notable characteristics of speech addressed to young children are pro-sodic. In accounts of baby talk in which intonation is mentioned, the authors comment on the overall higher pitch and/or exaggerated intonation contours used.[3] Also, people tend to speak more slowly, with exaggerated care in enunciation, and to have fewer dysfluencies in their sentences and longer pauses between them. There is, in short, a "tone of voice" appropriate for talking to young children that is surprisingly similar in every speech community where observations have been made. For English there are even careful measurements under controlled conditions that supply data on fundamental pitch, intonation contour, and extra vowel length (Garnica 1977a, b). I think it is reasonable to assume – until we have direct counterevidence – that this baby talk tone of voice is a universal of human language behavior. But where does it come from and what does it do? In the first place, the overall high pitch may be imitative of what the infant pro-duces. Babies' early vocalizations, and indeed children's vocalizations for a number of years, average much higher than normal adult pitch, in part because of the size and shape of their vocal tracts. Second, it corresponds to the perceptual sensitivities of the child. Infants even a few days after birth can discriminate pitch differences, and they pay more attention to high pitches than to low ones, so that the adults' use of higher pitch may serve the functions of getting the child's attention and marking particular stretches of speech by adults as being directed to the child, in distinction to all the lower-pitched adult-to-adult talk. In the third place, the baby talk tone may serve to give hints to the child about the grammatical structure of the utterances. Boundaries are more clearly marked, distracting false starts and interruptions are reduced, and intonation contours and extra vowel length highlight positions of primary stress in the adult language. For discussion, see Sachs 1977.

All these sources and functions that seem reasonable to assume for baby talk tone are also found in other modifications made in our speech to young children. The modifications tend to reflect the child's vocal behavior, they get the child's attention and cooperation in verbal interaction, they mark the adult's speech as child-directed, and they clarify the linguistic structure of the speech to help in comprehension and in the acquisition of control of the language.

Although the prosodic modifications in talking to children are important, they have not been as interesting to linguists as the grammatical modifications. Most of the psycholinguistic investigation of the nature of mothers' speech to children that was undertaken during the late sixties and early seventies focused on syntax. This was natural because linguistics during that period focused on syntax, and exciting claims were being made that language development was largely innate and took place almost independently of the language input to the child. Linguists pointed to the fragmentary, often non-grammatical nature of talk and emphasized the miraculous accomplishment of the child as somehow inducing from this mass of difficult data the correct grammar of the language. Accordingly, it was with considerable glee that psycholinguistic researchers in study after study, with mothers and non-mothers, children present and children absent, younger children and older children, male and female adults, male and female children, and other variables, demonstrated that the speech addressed to young children has shorter sentences, fewer subordinate clauses, fewer grammatical relations, and more repetitions than normal adult-to-adult speech. It also often omits inflectional endings, function words, and the verb "to be." It has, as we noted under prosody, fewer dysfluencies. As Snow said in her 1972 paper, it is almost as if the adult were constructing a set of lessons for the child that would afford maximum help in acquiring the grammar. Some researchers tried to see in these grammatical modifications some general simplifying processes at work. Presumably, the parents were unconsciously untangling the syntactic complexities of their normal speech in ways that reflected the linguists' notions of the derivational history of the sentences and were producing sentences closer to the "deep structure" that some felt the child's use of language begins with. Alas, it has turned out that baby talk simplifications are as much concerned with surface brevity and semantic cohesion as with transformational simplicity. The miracle of the acquisition of syntax remains, but one argument of the nativists has been weakened; the language input to children is modified in ways that seem tailored to the needs of the child in verbal interaction and must somehow be relevant to the process of language acquisition. For full discussion of syntactic modification and its effects, see Newport et al. 1977; Snow 1977 reviews both prosodic and syntactic characteristics.

There are also lexical modifications in talk to children. Every speech community seems to have a small lexicon of words used primarily with young children.[4] Four aspects of this special lexicon are worth noting as universals of a sort. The words fall into certain semantic areas, they include greater use of hypocoristic affixes, they are used more freely in different word class functions than the normal adult lexicon, and they tend to be phonologically simplified. Typical semantic areas in baby talk lexicon are body parts and functions, kin terms, food, animals, and infant games (e.g. peekaboo, pattycake). Although all these areas are usually represented in a baby talk lexicon, the exact items included may be very variable, especially in food terms, which may be as limited as one word for "food" in general or as elaborate as the more than a dozen names for different foods in Berber nursery language. Here we will check for the presence of a) at least one name for a body part and one kin term, and b) at least one word for a game. The use of diminutives and hypocoristic formations seems universal, although the nature and extent vary from the -ie on English nouns to the rich variety of diminutive formations in Latvian used with nouns, adjectives and verbs. The use of baby talk words in constructions of different word classes, reminiscent of the holophrastic utterances and early syntax of child language, is attested for several languages; here we will look specifically for the use of compound verbs made with general purpose auxiliaries (e.g. go bye-bye, faire dodo).

Phonological simplification includes a tendency toward simple canonical forms (e.g. CVCV) and the omission of more complex, difficult, "marked" sounds or their replacement by less marked substitutes (e.g. stops for fricatives, singletons for consonant clusters, semivowels for liquids). Also typical are consonant and vowel harmonies of the kind often found in child language, reduplication being an extreme example. Here we will check only for cluster reduction, liquid substitution, and reduplication. A characteristic will be counted as present if at least one incontrovertible example of it is attested. Since the phonological simplifications found in the special baby talk lexicon may be productive outside it, i.e. may be applied to adult words in new baby talk formations, these processes may be regarded as a set of phonological modifications characterizing baby talk material rather than merely a characteristic of the special lexicon. A full discussion of lexical and phonological modifications appears in Ferguson 1977b.

Finally, some of the modifications are not grammatical in traditional senses of the word; they may be called discourse features. Examples: the high percentage of questions, frequent use of tags (o.k.?, hm?), the here-and-now semantics and high semantic continuity between pairs of utterances, and striking shifts in pronoun use (especially in alternatives for you). Every study that mentions pronoun use notes that first and second person pronouns are often replaced by third person nouns; several also note the use of first plural for second singular. Savić 1974 is an example of detailed treatment of the kinds of questions used by adults in interaction with young children; Wills 1977 is a similarly detailed study of pronoun shift in talk to children.

The primary occasion of use of baby talk register is in addressing young children, and that occasion of use serves as the defining frame for the study of its structural characteristics. Like other registers, however, it may be extended to secondary uses, as when the register appropriate for legal documents and technical exchanges in the courtroom is used elsewhere to poke fun at lawyers or to give an authoritative flavor to the proceedings. Baby talk, or selected features of it, may be used to suggest the speech of children. Also, it may be used in talking to pets, in coaxing other people (or even objects) to behave the way the speaker wants, in calling attention to someone's childishness, and in talk between lovers. Some of these extensions are undoubtedly widespread or even universal, but there is considerable cross-cultural variation. At times, only a limited set of baby talk features appear in a context that does not seem to be an extension of the register as a whole, and exploration of this phenomenon leads to the identification of structural-functional components that are combined in various ways to constitute different registers (cf. Brown 1977, Ferguson 1977b). These extended uses and related registers are generally mentioned incidentally or not at all in descriptions of talk to children, but here we will check the sample languages on three secondary uses: suggesting or reporting child speech, talking to animals, and use in adult intimate interaction such as between lovers.

The characteristics of talk to children co-occur regularly enough and are so interrelated that they constitute a register, but there is so much variation in the degree to which they occur and the relative incidence of different characteristics, that a range of intraregister variability must also be recognized.[5] The most striking – and apparently universal – variability is in what can be called "degree of babyishness." Changes in the degree of babyishness may reflect the age of the addressee, the nature of the situation, the speaker's estimate of the linguistic abilities of the child, the strength of the affective bond between the interactants, and so on. This variability has been investigated experimentally (e.g. Newport 1976, Cross 1977) and is discussed in several register descriptions (cf. Ferguson 1977b).

2.2   The discussion so far has been synchronic, although with some allusions to the diachrony of child language development. Greenberg's state-and-process model of language (Greenberg 1966b) requires investigation of diachronic processes that lead to synchronic states, and the transmission (and change) of baby talk registers deserves comment. The only aspect of talk to children which has been considered diachronically is the lexicon, and it has been shown that core items of the baby talk lexicon tend to persist for long periods of time (e.g. 2000 years for Latin-Spanish *pappa* "food").

Lexical items are, however, subject to areal diffusion, perhaps spreading with patterns of child rearing across linguistic communities. The important points here are two: (a) the phonetic shapes and semantic areas tend to be universal, but the actual lexical items, i.e. the phonetic-semantic pairings, are specific to particular languages or speech communities; (b) some lexical items undergo sound changes with the rest of the language, whereas others remain marginal and are not so affected. Sample evidence for (a): English *(go) night-night, sleepy-bye*; French *(faire) dodo*; Latvian *aiju žūžū, čučēt*; Japanese *nenne (suru)*; Arabic *ninni*. Sample evidence for (b): Syrian Arabic *nkəy* "baby's first word" is *nčəy* in those dialect areas in which the change $k \rightarrow \check{c}$ has taken place; the word for "hurt, sore" is *wawa* in Middle Eastern languages that have *w* in their phonemic inventory, but *vava* in those that have *v* but not *w*. Other elements of baby talk have not been traced historically, but it would be interesting to know, for example, the history of such phenomena as ENGLISH baby talk constructions with *go* and French ones with *faire*; the omission of the copula in English, Romanian, and other baby talk, patterns of inflection reduction in particular languages, and the like. Discussion of baby talk diachrony appears in Bynon 1968, Crawford 1970, Ferguson 1964, and Oswalt 1976.

2.3   The accompanying table 11.1 presents the facts of presence (+) and absence (−) of the putative universals in the baby talk registers of the 27 sample languages. If the source gives no indication of presence or absence, the box is left open on the chart. The evidence is confirmatory as far as it goes, but the gaps in the data are numerous. Examining these

Table 11.1 Characteristics of baby talk registers.*

	Ar	Am	Bg	Br	Cc	Cm	Du	En	Ge	Gi	Gr	Hi	Hu	Ja	Ka	Ki	La	Lu	Ml	Mr	Pm	Pr	Ro	Sa	Se	Sp	Tz
PROSODY																											
1. High pitch	+						+	+	+			(+)					+	+	+	+	+	+				+	+
2. Exaggerated contours		+					+	+	+		+			+			+	+		+						+	+
3. Slow rate		+		+			+	+				+					(+)										
SYNTAX																											
4. Short sentences		+					+	+							+		+							+	+		
5. Parataxis							+	+																	+		
6. Telegraphic style			+				+	+						+		+				+			+				
7. Repetition							+	+								+				+						+	+
LEXICON																											
8. Kin terms and body parts	+	+		+		+	+	+	+		+		+	+	+		+	+	+	+	+	+		+	+	+	
9. Infant games	+	+		+		+	+	+	+		+		+	+			+	+	+	+	+	+			+	+	
10. Qualities	+	+				+	+	+	+		+		+	+			+	+	+	+	+	+				+	
11. Compound verbs							+	+	+					+	+				+	+	+	+	+			+	
12. Hypocorism	+	+		+	+	+	+	+	+	+	+			+	+		+	+	+	+	+	+	+		+	+	+
PHONOLOGY																											
13. Cluster reduction		+	(+)	+			+	+	+		+						+	+	+	+	+	+			+	+	
14. Liquid substitution		(+)	+		+		+	+	+		+	+		+			+	+	+	+	+	+			+	+	
15. Reduplication	+	+	+	+		+	+	+	+		+		+	+			+	+	+	+	+	+	+		+	+	
16. Special sounds	+	+		+	+	+	(+)	+	+		+		+	+			+	+	+	+	+	+			+	+	
DISCOURSE																											
17. Questions							+	+								+	+	+						+	+		+
18. Pronoun shift		+					+	+						+			+	+	+	+	+	+		+	+	+	
EXTENDED USES																											
19. Child speech															+		+										
20. Animals				–	+			+	+								+	+		+	+						
21. Adult intimacy		+		–				+	+			–					+	+	+	+	+	+					
VARIATION IN DEGREE											+			+		+	+		+	+		+					

*Languages are abbreviated and arranged in alphabetical order; see Appendix for their full names.

different descriptions of baby talk for comparable data is frustrating, much in the way language universals research is frustrating for grammatical phenomena. The authors of the various studies simply do not provide answers to the questions the researcher wants to ask. In spite of the gaps, however, the chart is informative, and the lack of minuses suggests that many of the gaps would be filled with plusses if the authors were asked specifically about them. In this way the chart as it now stands could serve as a minimum checklist of things to be looked for when a language researcher attempts to describe the baby talk register in a speech community, and indeed the preparation of such checklists is one of the useful by-products of universals research.

3   Summary and Conclusions

3.1   In every human society people modify their normal speech in talking to very young children. The modifications are prosodic (e.g. higher pitch), grammatical (e.g. shorter sentences), lexical (e.g. special baby words), phonological (e.g. reduplication), and discoursal (e.g. greater proportion of questions). Such modifications have an innate basis in pan-human child-care behaviors, but the details in every speech community are largely conventionalized (i.e. culturally shaped) and in part arise directly from interactional needs and imitation of children's behavior. The modificational features are variable in incidence, but constitute a surprisingly cohesive set of linguistic features that may be regarded as a "register" in the language user's repertoire. This "baby talk" register is an important factor in the socialization of children, apparently assisting in the acquisition of linguistic structure, the development of interactional patterns, the transmission of cultural values, and the expression of the user's affective relationship with the addressee.

3.2   The baby talk register in every speech community tends to be extended to uses other than addressing young children, such as reporting child speech, sarcastic attribution of childishness, and talk between lovers or to animals; such extensions are typically conventionalized and vary in detail from one community to another.

   Structural features of the baby talk register tend to occur in other registers that share features of function or use. Thus, baby talk features that are related to the limited language competence of the child who is addressed may occur in registers addressed to others who lack such competence (e.g. speakers of other languages, people with impaired hearing) and baby talk features that are related to the adult-child affective relationship may occur in registers addressed to people being tended (e.g. nurse to patient, counselor to client).

3.3   The baby talk register is variable along the dimension between normal speech and the most extreme deviation from normal, and this variation tends to reflect the speaker's estimate of the communicative competence of the child addressed and the strength of the affective bond between them; aspects of the register may vary in this dimension very subtly in "fine tuning" with slight changes in the child's behavior.

3.4   Children's ability to use aspects of this register in addressing younger children begins very early – at the latest in the third year – and develops along with their whole communicative competence.

3.5   The conventionalized details of the register for talking to young children are transmitted from one generation to the next much as the rest of language is, and the special lexicon may be very conservative, remaining essentially the same for long periods of time; it is possible and instructive to reconstruct earlier baby talk and to investigate the etymologies of baby-talk words.

The description of a special register used in talking to young children seems far from our original goal of finding language universals. Instead of discovering phonological or syntactic universals of human language, we seem to have ended with the discovery of a universal way of modifying language for interactional purposes, which cuts across the usual components of the linguist's grammar. In fact, however, our discovery suggests a different kind of language universals, a kind that ethnographers of communication take for granted, but are less appreciated by most linguists. From the universal statements about talk to children of each of the five preceding paragraphs, it is possible to extrapolate to register variation in general. In this spirit five universals are proposed for serious consideration as characterizing the nature of human language.

1   Every language has register variation.

A part of the language user's competence is the ability to vary the structure of the language in accordance with conditions of use, such as the addressee, the occasion, the topic, or the speaker's role.

2   Any register may be extended to secondary uses.

Any register may be extended, just as any lexical item, grammatical category, or genre of discourse may be used metaphorically or in derived senses, and such extensions may become conventionalized.

3   A given register is variable in extent of deviation from the least marked "natural" form of the language.

The structural and functional boundaries of a register are often blurred, and the degree of its implementation may vary. This variation in degree of deviation may itself be used as a marker of adjustment to the situation, and such use may be conventionalized.

4   Children acquire competence in register variation as they acquire the basic grammatical structure of their language.

Register variation is not something added on to the grammar or a way of using the grammar, acquired separately; it is an integral part of language that is acquired simultaneously. Individuals may acquire some registers late in life, but register variation as such begins as soon as the child produces recognizable language.

5   Registers are transmitted and changed as part of the total structure of a language.

Patterns of register variation continue through time and are subject to structural and functional change in much the same way phonological, syntactic and lexical structures continue and change.

Language universals of this kind characterize human language just as much as the usual structural universals do, and they raise the same kind of questions concerning how much is innate or acquired and how much is uniquely human or shared with other animals. In a recent paper I pointed out that all human societies seem to have verbal greetings, and that all primate species also exhibit greeting behaviors (Ferguson 1977a). Many of the functions (e.g. showing deference) and many of the actions (e.g. bowing) are similar, but human societies have, in addition, verbal routines of greeting that share in the syntactic and phonological structure of the language(s) of the society. We might hazard the guess, then, that some of our nonverbal greeting behavior has a significant biological substrate, i.e. is in some sense "wired" into the organism at birth, and that even some aspects of the verbal greeting behavior of human beings are innate in the sense that human beings do some of the same things with language that they and their primate cousins do with nonverbal behavior on occasions of greeting. The same judgment can be made about the register for talking to children, if we can show that other primates adjust their communicative behavior while interacting with not fully competent individuals. And indeed, just this kind of behavior is well attested for chimpanzees who have learned to use sign language. It is somehow reassuring to know that when Koko, the Stanford gorilla who has learned to sign, is communicating with Mike, the young novice signer, she makes her signs more slowly and carefully, in effect using her version of a baby talk register. In adjusting our speech for talking to children – even though we do it in a uniquely human way with our linguistic structure – we are essentially exercising deep-seated biological capabilities even more universal than we thought.

Appendix

List of sources by language

ARABIC (SYRIAN)	Ferguson 1956
ARAMAIC (NEO-)	Sabar 1974
BENGALI	Dil 1975
BERBER	Bynon 1968
COCOPA	Crawford 1970, 1974
COMANCHE	Casagrande 1948
DUTCH	Beheydt 1976; Snow et al. 1976; Vorster 1974
ENGLISH	Blount and Padgug 1977; Ferguson 1964; Garnica 1977a, b; Read 1946; Snow 1972, 1977 (review of others)
GERMAN	Zoeppritz 1976
GILYAK	Austerlitz 1956
GREEK	Drachmann 1973
HIDATSA	Voegelin and Robinett 1954
HUNGARIAN	MacWhinney 1974
JAPANESE	Chew 1969; Fischer 1970; Takahashi 1977
KANNADA (HAVYAKA)	Bhat 1967
KIPSIGIS	Harkness 1977

LATVIAN	Rūķe-Draviņa 1959, 1961, 1977
LUO	Blount 1972
MALTESE	Gassar-Pullicino 1957
MARATHI	Kelkar 1964
POMO	Oswalt 1976
PORTUGUESE (BRAZILIAN)	Stoel-Gammon 1976
ROMANIAN	Avram 1967
SAMOAN	Blount 1972
SERBO-CROATIAN	Jocić 1975
SPANISH	Blount and Padgug 1977; Ferguson 1964
TZELTAL	Stross 1972

Notes

1   Linguists have not yet resolved the question of how to select a suitable sample of languages (cf. Bell 1978). For research on phonological universals, the 200-language sample of the Stanford Phonology Archive (Vihman 1977) is now available and has been used for several studies in this book, but there is no comparable archived sample for other aspects of language.

2   For general reviews of the literature, see Farwell 1975 and Slobin 1975. Snow and Ferguson 1977 contains new studies, reviews, commentary, and Andersen's annotated bibliography.

3   In several studies of speech addressed to young children in AMERICAN-INDIAN speech communities, and authors have asserted that the use of overall high pitch is not as noticeable as in AMERICAN ENGLISH talk to young children, being limited chiefly to occasions of mimicking the child. Harkness 1975 also maintains that in a Guatemalan Indian community the most typical style of talking to children is in a rapid monotone, with willingness to repeat as often as the child asks for it. All these studies are fragmentary, however, and the question clearly needs further research.

4   Even Stross, who claims that there was little or no use of lexical or phonological features of a baby talk register in the village he studied, notes that two of the mothers "used three or four special words" (Stross 1972: 6–7 and footnote 2).

5   Variability across social classes in talking to children has been studied experimentally for English (Holzman 1974) and Dutch (Snow et al. 1976). Familial and individual variation in baby talk is considerable, presumably because of the nature of the interactions for which it is appropriate, but linguists generally pay little attention to individual linguistic profiles (but cf. Ferguson 1975 and Fillmore et al. 1979), and this variation will not be considered here for lack of data.

Bibliography

Austerlitz, Robert. 1956. Gilyak nursery words. *Word* 12, 200–79.

Avram, A. 1967. De la langue qu'on parle aux enfants roumains. In *To Honor Roman Jakobson*, vol. I. The Hague: Mouton, pp. 133–40.

Beheydt, L. 1976. Nederlandse baby talk. Paper presented at the colloquium Psycholinguistisch Onderzoek, in België, Gent 25–26 Nov. Preprint, Louvain: Department of Linguistics, Katholieke Universiteit te Leuven.

Bell, Alan. 1978. Language samples. In *Universals of Human Language*. Volume 1. *Method and Theory*, ed. J. H. Greenberg, C. A. Ferguson, and E. A. Moravcsik. Stanford, Calif.: Stanford University Press.

Bhat, D. N. S. 1967. Lexical suppletion in baby talk. *Anthropological Linguistics [AL]* 9, 33–6.

Blount, Ben G. 1972. Parental speech and language acquisition: some Luo and Samoan examples. *AL* 14, 119–30.

Blount, Ben G., and Elise J. Padgug. 1977. Prosodic, paralinguistic and features in parent-child speech: English and Spanish. *Journal of Child Language* 4, 67–86.

Brown, Roger. 1977. Introduction. In G. E. Snow and C. A. Ferguson (eds.), *Talking to Children*. Cambridge: Cambridge University Press, pp. 1–27.

Brown, Roger, and Albert Gilman. 1960. The pronouns of power and solidarity. In *Style in Language*, ed. T. A. Sebeok. Cambridge, Mass.: MIT Press, pp. 253–76.

Bynon, J. 1968. Berber nursery language. *Transactions of the Philological Society* (1968), 107–61.

Casagrande, Joseph B. 1948. Comanche baby language. *International Journal of American Linguistics [IJAL]* 14, 11–14.

Cassar-Pullicino, J. 1957. Nursery vocabulary of the Maltese Archipelago. *Orbis* 6, 192–8.

Chew, John J., Jr. 1969. The structure of Japanese baby talk. *Journal-Newsletter of the Association of Teachers of Japanese* 6: 1, 4–17.

Crawford, James M. 1970. Cocopa baby talk. *IJAL* 36, 9–13.

Crawford, James M. 1974. Baby talk in an American Indian language. Draft of paper for Conference on Language Input and Acquisition, Boston.

Cross, Toni G. 1977. Mothers' speech adjustments: the contribution of selected child listener variables. In C. E. Snow and C. A. Ferguson (eds.), *Talking to Children*. Cambridge: Cambridge University Press, pp. 151–88.

Crothers, John. 1978. Typology and universals of vowel systems. In *Universals of Human Language*. Volume 2. *Phonology*, ed. J. H. Greenberg, C. A. Ferguson, and E. A. Moravcsik. Stanford, Calif.: Stanford University Press, pp. 93–152.

Dil, Afia. 1975. Bengali baby talk. *Child Language* 1975, ed. W. von Raffler Engel (*Word* 27), 11–27.

Drachmann, Gaberell. 1973. Baby talk in Greek. *Ohio State University Working Papers in Linguistics* 15.

Ervin-Tripp, Susan. 1977. A psychologist's point of view. In G. E. Snow and C. A. Ferguson (eds.), *Talking to Children*. Cambridge: Cambridge University Press, pp. 335–9.

Farwell, Carol B. 1975. The language spoken to children. *Human Development* 18, 288–309.

Ferguson, Charles A. 1956. Arabic baby talk. In *For Roman Jakobson*, ed. M. Halle. The Hague: Mouton, pp. 121–9.

Ferguson, Charles A. 1964. Baby talk in six languages. *American Anthropologist* 66: 6, part 2, 103–14.

Ferguson, Charles A. 1975. Applications of linguistics. In *Survey of American Linguistics*, ed. R. Austerlitz. Lisse: De Ridder, pp. 63–75.

Ferguson, Charles A. 1977a. Structure and use of politeness formulas. *Language in Society* 5, 137–51.

Ferguson, Charles A. 1977b. Baby talk as a simplified register. In C. E. Snow and C. A. Ferguson (eds.), *Talking to Children*. Cambridge: Cambridge University Press, pp. 209–35.

Ferguson, Charles A., David B. Peizer, and Thelma E. Weeks. 1973. Model-and-replica phonological grammar of a child's first words. *Lingua* 31, 35–65.

Fillmore, G. J., Daniel Kempler, and W. S-Y. Wang (eds.) 1979. *Individual Differences in Language Ability and Language Behavior*. New York: Academic Press.

Fischer, John L. 1970. Linguistic socialization: Japan and the United States. In *Families in East and West*, ed. R. Hill and R. König. The Hague: Mouton, pp. 107–19.

Garnica, Olga K. 1977a. Some characteristics of speech to young children. *Ohio State University Working Papers in Linguistics* 22, 11–72.

Garnica, Olga K. 1977b. Some prosodic and paralinguistic features of speech to young children. In C. E. Snow and C. A. Ferguson (eds.), *Talking to Children*. Cambridge: Cambridge University Press, pp. 63–88.

Greenberg, Joseph H. 1966a. Some universals of grammar with particular reference to the order of meaningful elements. In *Universals of Language*, ed. J. H. Greenberg, 2nd edn. Cambridge, Mass.: MIT Press, pp. 73–113.

Greenberg, Joseph H. 1966b. Synchronic and diachronic universals in phonology. *Language* 42, 508–17.

Harkness, Sara. 1975. Cultural variation in mothers' language. *Child Language* 1975, ed. W. von Raffler Engel (*Word* 27), 495–8.

Harkness, Sara. 1977. Aspects of social environment and first language acquisition in Africa. In C. E. Snow and C. A. Ferguson (eds.), *Talking to Children*. Cambridge: Cambridge University Press, pp. 309–16.

Helvicus, Christophorus (Helwig, Christopher). 1619. Libri didactici, grammaticae universalis, Latinae, Graecae, Hebraicae, Chaldaicae.

Holzman, Mathilda. 1974. The verbal environment provided by mothers for their very young children. *Merill-Palmer Quarterly* 20, 33–42.

Ingram, David. 1978. Typology and universals of personal pronouns. In *Universals of Human Language*. Volume 3, *Word Structure*, ed. J. H. Greenberg, C. A. Ferguson, and E. A. Moravcsik. Stanford, Calif.: Stanford University Press, pp. 213–47.

Jakobson, Roman. 1960. Why "mama" and "papa?" In *Perspectives in Psychological Theory*, ed. B. Kaplan. New York: International University Press.

Jocić, M. 1975. Modifications in adults' speech in adult–child communication. Paper presented at the Third International Child Language Symposium, London.

Kelkar, Ashok R. 1964. Marathi baby talk. *Word* 20, 40–54.

MacWhinney, Brian. 1974. How Hungarian children learn to speak. Doctoral dissertation, University of California, Berkeley, pp. 446–57.

Moskowitz, Breyne Arlene. 1972. The acquisition of phonology and syntax: a preliminary study. Approaches to natural languages, ed. K. Hintikka et al. Dordrecht, Netherlands: Reidel.

Newport, Elissa. 1976. Motherese: the speech of mothers to young children. *Cognitive Theory*, ed. N. Castellan et al. Volume II. Hillsdale, NJ: Lawrence Erlbaum Associates.

Newport, Elissa, Henry Gleitman and Lila R. Gleitman. 1977. Mother, I'd rather do it myself: some effects and non-effects of maternal speech style. In C. E. Snow and C. A. Ferguson (eds.), *Talking to Children*. Cambridge: Cambridge University Press, pp. 109–49.

Oswalt, Robert L. 1976. Baby talk and the genesis of some basic Pomo words. *IJAL* 42, 1–13.

Read, Allen Walker. 1946. The social setting of hypocoristic speech (so-called baby talk). Paper presented at the annual meeting of the Modern Language Association, Washington, DC.

Rūķe-Draviņa, Velta. 1959. Ammensprache. Chapter V, §2 of Diminutive im Lettischen. *Acta Universitatis Stockholmiensis, Etudes de Philologie Slaves* 8, 25–34.

Rūķe-Draviņa, Velta. 1961. Ns. lastenhoitajain kielestä ("On so-called nursery language"). *Virittäjä* 1, 85–91.

Rūķe-Draviņa, Velta. 1976. Gibt es Universalien in der Ammensprache? Akten des 1. Salzburger Kolloquiums über Kindersprache (= *Salzburger Beiträge zu Linguistik* 2), 3–16.

Rūķe-Draviņa, Velta. 1977. Modifications of speech addressed to young children in Latvian. In C. E. Snow and C. A. Ferguson (eds.), *Talking to Children*. Cambridge: Cambridge University Press, pp. 237–53.

Sabar, Yona. 1974. Nursery rhymes and baby words in the Jewish Neo-Aramaic dialect of Zakoh (Iraq). *Journal of the American Oriental Society* 94, 329–36.

Sachs, Jacqueline. 1977. The adaptive significance of linguistic input to children. In C. E. Snow and C. A. Ferguson (eds.), *Talking to Children*. Cambridge: Cambridge University Press, pp. 51–61.

Savić, Svenka. 1974. Aspects of adult-child communication: the problem of question acquisition. Paper presented at the symposium: Structure and Function of Utterances, Cracow, Poland, October 1974.

Sinclair, J. M. and R. M. Coulthard. 1975. *Towards an Analysis of Discourse: The English used by Teachers and Pupils*. London: Oxford University Press.

Slobin, Dan I. 1975. On the nature of talk to children. In *Foundations of Language Development*, vol. I, ed. E. H. Lenneberg and E. Lenneberg. New York: Academic Press, pp. 283–97.

Snow, Catherine E. 1972. Mothers' speech to children learning language. *Child Development* 43, 549–65.

Snow, Catherine E. 1977. Mothers' speech research: from input to interaction. In C. E. Snow and C. A. Ferguson (eds.), *Talking to Children*. Cambridge: Cambridge University Press, pp. 31–49.

Snow, Catherine E., and Charles A. Ferguson (eds.). 1977. *Talking to Children*. Cambridge: Cambridge University Press.

Snow, Catherine E., A. Arlman-Rupp, Y. Hassing, J. Jobse, J. Joosten, and J. Vorster. 1976. Mothers' speech in three social classes. *Journal of Psycholinguistic Research* 5, 1–20.

Steele, Susan. 1978. Word order variation: a typological study. In *Universals of Human Language*. Volume 4. *Syntax*, ed. J. H. Greenberg, C. A. Ferguson, and E. A. Moravcsik. Stanford, Calif.: Stanford University Press, pp. 585–623.

Stoel-Gammon, Caroline. 1976. Baby talk in Brazilian Portuguese: *Papers and Reports on Child Language Development* 11, 83–8.

Stross, Brian. 1972. Verbal processes in Tzeltal speech socialization. *AL* 14, 1–13.

Takahashi, Kunitoshi. 1977. Some characteristics of baby talk in Japanese. Unpublished paper, University of Tsukuba, Ibaraki, Japan.

Ultan, Russell. 1978. Some general characteristics of interrogative systems. In *Universals of Human Language*. Volume 4. *Syntax*, ed. J. H. Greenberg, C. A. Ferguson, and E. A. Moravcsik. Stanford, Calif.: Stanford University Press, pp. 11–49.

Voegelin, C. F. and Florence M. Robinett. 1954. "Mother language" in Hidatsa. *IJAL* 20, 65–70.

Vihman, Marilyn May. 1977. A reference manual and users' guide to the Stanford Phonology Archive, part I. Department of Linguistics, Stanford University.

Vihman, Marilyn May. 1978. Consonant harmony: its scope and function in child language. In *Universals of Human Language*. Volume 2. *Phonology*, ed. J. H. Greenberg, C. A. Ferguson, and E. A. Moravcsik. Stanford, Calif.: Stanford University Press, pp. 00–00.

Vorster, Jan. 1974. Mothers' speech to children: some methodological considerations (= Publikaties van het Instituut voor Algemene Taalwetenschap 8). Universiteit van Amsterdam.

Wills, Dorothy Davis. 1977. Participant deixis in English and baby talk. In C. E. Snow and C. A. Ferguson (eds.), *Talking to Children*. Cambridge: Cambridge University Press, pp. 271–95.

Zoeppritz, Magdalena. 1976. Babysprache im Deutschen. In *A Bunch of Mayflowers (Broder Carstensen zum 50. Geburtstag am 27. Mai 1976)*, ed. D. Lehmann et al., pp. 264–72.

12

Learning by Instinct

James L. Gould and Peter Marler

Learning is often thought of as the alternative to instinct, which is the information passed genetically from one generation to the next. Most of us think the ability to learn is the hallmark of intelligence. The difference between learning and instinct is said to distinguish human beings from "lower" animals such as insects. Introspection, that deceptively convincing authority, leads one to conclude that learning, unlike instinct, usually involves conscious decisions concerning when and what to learn.

Work done in the past few decades has shown that such a sharp distinction between instinct and learning – and between the guiding forces underlying human and animal behavior – cannot be made. For example, it has been found that many insects are prodigious learners. Conversely, we now know that the process of learning in higher animals, as well as in insects, is often innately guided, that is, guided by information inherent in the genetic makeup of the animal. In other words, the process of learning itself is often controlled by instinct.

It now seems that many, if not most, animals are "preprogrammed" to learn particular things and to learn them in particular ways. In evolutionary terms innately guided learning makes sense: very often it is easy to specify in advance the general characteristics of the things an animal should be able to learn, even when the details cannot be specified. For example, bees should be inherently suited to learning the shapes of various flowers, but it would be impossible to equip each bee at birth with a field guide to all the flowers it might visit.

Innately guided learning – learning by instinct – is found at all levels of mental complexity in the animal kingdom. In this article our examples will be drawn primarily from the behavior of bees and birds, our respective fields of particular expertise, but the results can be generalized to the primates, even to man. There is strong evidence, for example, that the process of learning human speech is largely guided by innate abilities and tendencies.

From *Scientific American* 255:1 (1987), pp. 74–85. © 1987 by Scientific American, Inc. All rights reserved. Reprinted with permission.

Two Theoretical Frameworks

The distinction often made between learning and instinct is exemplified by two theoretical approaches to the study of behavior: ethology and behaviorist psychology. Ethology is usually thought of as the study of instinct. In the ethological world view most animal behavior is governed by four basic factors: sign stimuli (instinctively recognized cues), motor programs (innate responses to cues), drive (controlling motivational impulses) and imprinting (a restricted and seemingly aberrant form of learning).

Three of these factors are found in the egg-rolling response of geese, a behavior studied by Konrad Z. Lorenz and Nikolaas Tinbergen, who together with Karl von Frisch were the founders of ethology. Geese incubate their eggs in mound-shaped nests built on the ground, and it sometimes happens that the incubating goose inadvertently knocks an egg out of the nest. Such an event leads to a remarkable behavior. After settling down again on its nest, the goose eventually notices the errant egg. The animal then extends its neck to fix its eyes on the egg, rises and rolls the egg back into the nest gently with its bill. At first glance this might seem to be a thoughtful solution to a problem. As it happens, however, the behavior is highly stereotyped and innate. Any convex object, regardless of color and almost regardless of size, triggers the response; beer bottles are particularly effective.

In this example the convex features that trigger the behavior are the ethologists' sign stimuli. The egg-rolling response itself is the motor program. The entire behavior is controlled by a drive that appears about two weeks before the geese lay eggs and persists until about two weeks after the eggs hatch. Geese also exhibit imprinting: during a sensitive period soon after hatching, goslings will follow almost any receding object that emits an innately recognized "kum-kum" call and thereafter treat the object as a parent.

Classical behaviorist psychologists see the world quite differently from ethologists. Behaviorists are primarily interested in the study of learning under strictly controlled conditions and have traditionally treated instinct as irrelevant to learning. Behaviorists believe nearly all the responses of higher animals can be divided into two kinds of learning called classical conditioning and operant conditioning.

Classical conditioning was discovered in dogs by the Russian physiologist Ivan P. Pavlov. In his classic experiment he showed that if a bell is rung consistently just before food is offered to a dog, eventually the dog will learn to salivate at the sound of the bell. The important factors in classical conditioning are the unconditioned stimulus (the innately recognized cue, equivalent to the ethological sign stimulus, which in this case is food), the unconditioned response (the innately triggered behavioral act, equivalent to the ethological motor program, which in this case is salivation) and the conditioned stimulus (the stimulus the animal is conditioned to respond to, which in this case is the bell). Early behaviorists believed any stimulus an animal was physically capable of sensing could be linked, as a conditioned stimulus, to any unconditioned response.

In operant conditioning, the other major category of learning recognized by most behaviorists, animals learn a behavior pattern as the result of trial-and-error experimentation they undertake in order to obtain a reward or avoid a punishment. In the classic example a rat is trained to press a lever to obtain food. The experimenter shapes the behavior by rewarding the rat at first for even partial performance of the desired response. For example, at the outset the rat might be rewarded simply for facing the end of the cage in which the lever sits. Later the experimenter requires increasingly precise behavior, until the response is perfected. Early behaviorists thought any behavior an animal was physically capable of performing could be taught, by means of operant conditioning, as a response to any cue or situation.

Challenges to Behaviorism

By 1970 several disturbing challenges to the behavioristic world view had appeared. The idea that any perceptible cue could be taught, by classical conditioning, as a conditioned stimulus was dealt a severe blow by John Garcia, now at the University of California at Los Angeles. He showed that rats could not associate visual and auditory cues with food that made them ill, even though they could associate olfactory cues with such food. On the other hand, he found that quail could associate not auditory or olfactory cues but visual ones – colors – with dangerous foods. Later work by other investigators extended these results, showing, for example, that pigeons readily learn to associate sounds but not colors with danger and colors but not sounds with food. The obvious conclusion was that these animals are predisposed to make certain associations more easily in some situations than in others.

The same kind of pattern was discovered in experiments in operant conditioning. Rats readily learn to press a bar for food, but they cannot learn to press a bar in order to avoid an electric shock. Conversely, they can learn to jump in order to avoid a shock but not in order to obtain food. Similarly, pigeons easily learn to peck at a spot for a food reward but have great difficulty learning to hop on a treadle for food; they learn to avoid shock by hopping on a treadle but not by pecking. Once again it seems that in certain behavioral situations animals are innately prepared to learn some things more readily than others.

The associations that are most easily learned have an adaptive logic. In the natural world odor is a more reliable indicator than color for rats (which are notoriously nocturnal) trying to identify dangerous food; the color of a seed is a more useful thing for a pigeon to remember than any sounds the seed makes. Similarly, a pigeon is more likely to learn how to eat novel seeds if it experiments on food with its beak rather than with its feet. Animals that have innate biases concerning which cues they rely on and which

Figure 12.1 (opposite) Training and testing apparatus teaches bees to land on particular targets and checks their ability to remember the targets. Pairs of targets are arranged on each side of a rotatable box (top). The box is covered so that only one pair is visible at a time. Each target has a feeder at the center, which can be filled with sugar solution. To train the bee, the investigator supplies food to one target but not the other and lets the bee feed there (bottom, a). To keep the bee from simply memorizing the location of the target bearing food, the box is rotated so that the bee can also be trained on a second pair of targets that is a mirror image of the first (b). After the bee has been fed about 10 times, it is tested; the box is rotated to expose a pair of targets that both contain no food (c), and the bee is watched to see which it chooses to land on first. The apparatus can test the bee's ability to remember such characteristics as a target's color, pattern, shape, and odor.

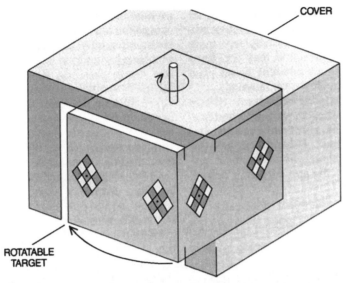

COVER

ROTATABLE TARGET

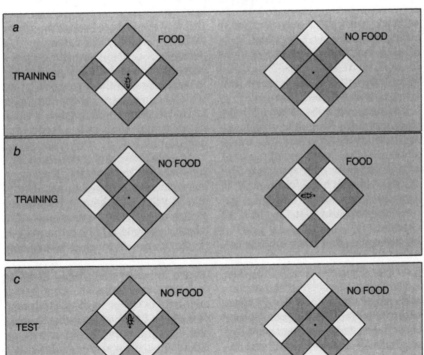

a

TRAINING

FOOD

NO FOOD

b

TRAINING

NO FOOD

FOOD

c

TEST

NO FOOD

NO FOOD

procedures they attempt are more likely to ignore spurious cues, and they will learn faster than animals without inherent biases. The idea that animals are innately programmed to attend to specific cues in specific behavioral contexts and to experiment in particular ways in other contexts suggests a mutually reinforcing relation between learning and instinct. This relation helps to explain the once anomalous phenomenon of imprinting and to reconcile the approaches of behaviorists and ethologists.

Instinctive Learning in Bees

The convergence of the two perspectives is illustrated by the ways honey bees learn about flowers. Bees inherently learn certain characteristics of a flower more easily than they learn others. Perhaps even more significant, once bees have acquired knowledge about a flower the ways in which they organize and refer to that knowledge are entirely instinctive.

Bees make their living by collecting nectar and pollen. Both of these essential foods are found in flowers, which offer them as a bribe to attract pollinating insects. Bees recognize flowerlike objects instinctively: they land spontaneously on small, brightly colored objects that have a high spatial frequency, or ratio of edges to unbroken areas (the spatial frequency of an object is high, for example, if the object has petals), and centers that (like the center of a flower) absorb ultraviolet light and so appear dark to bees.

Although bees recognize flowerlike objects innately, they have to learn which of those objects are likely to hold food. The initial flowerlike characteristics constitute an unconditioned stimulus: a set of sign stimuli. They trigger the unconditioned responses of landing and probing with the proboscis, behaviors that represent two innate motor programs. If a flowerlike object rewards a bee with food, the flower's specific characteristics may be learned – imprinted – as conditioned stimuli.

The first thing honey bees learn about a flower is its odor. Von Frisch showed early in his career that after a bee has been trained by being fed at a feeder that has a particular odor, it selects flowers of like odor from among hundreds of alternatives. Randolf Menzel of the Free University of Berlin showed that even one training visit is enough to teach the bee to choose the same odor 90 percent of the time in later visits; after only three training visits the rate of success is higher than 98 percent [see "Learning and Memory in Bees," by Randolf Menzel and Jochen Erber; *Scientific American*, July, 1978]. Bees do not learn all odors with equal ease. Nonfloral odors take longer to learn, although it is unclear whether the bias results from insensitivity to inappropriate odors or from some problem in remembering them.

The next thing honey bees learn about a flower is its color. Menzel has shown that roughly three training visits to flowers of the same color are necessary before bees select that color over an alternative color 90 percent of the time. After about 10 training trips the bees choose the correct color more than 95 percent of the time. As with odors, bees do not learn all colors equally quickly, but enough is known about the vision of bees to rule out the possibility that this bias is based on an unevenness in the bees' ability to see different colors.

Honey bees also learn the shapes and color patterns of flowers, but they need more training visits in order to reach the level of 90 percent accuracy in remembering shape;

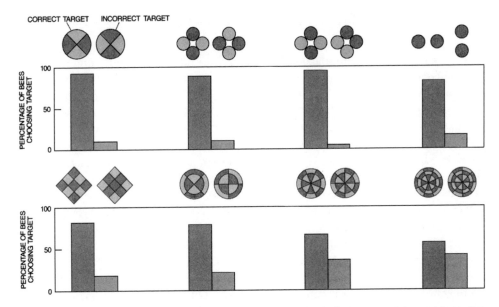

Figure 12.2 Targets provided evidence that bees remember a flower as a picture, not as a list of characteristics. The targets in each pair differ from each other only in the arrangement of their components (often one is merely a rotation of the other), and so they would be represented by identical lists of characteristics. Bees would be able to distinguish the targets in a pair only if they remember a target as a picture. Bees remembered the target they had been trained on except when it was very intricate; their memory may not have fine enough resolution to distinguish such targets. The targets shown are a few of many used in experiments.

about five or six visits suffice to enable them to distinguish a square "flower" (a plastic square containing a feeder) from a triangular one.

As with odor and color, bees inherently prefer some shapes over others. They particularly prefer busy patterns to simple ones. Until recently most investigators had thought bees do not remember a pattern as a picture (unlike human beings, and vertebrates in general) but rather as a list of defining characteristics, in much the same way as advertisements for real estate often depend not on photographs but on verbal lists: "Red Cape Cod, three bedrooms, two baths, detached garage." Such a list might enable bees to distinguish among species of flowers, and it would not require as large and complex a central nervous system as a picture memory would. Recent experiments by one of us (Gould) indicate, however, that bees do store low-resolution pictures of flowers.

Bees learn many things about flowers, but there are some cues that cannot be stored as part of flower memory even though bees can learn them in other behavioral contexts. For example, honey bees are famous for their exquisite sensitivity to polarized light (by which they navigate), but they cannot learn the polarization patterns of flowers. They are also adept at learning which way a hive faces (to the point where rotating the hive by 90 degrees leaves most foragers unable to find the entrance until other bees provide strong chemical cues), but they will not learn in what direction a free-standing flower faces.

Organization of Bee Knowledge

The cues bees do remember about flowers, such as odor, color and pattern, are not remembered with equal weight. For example, if a bee that has been trained to feed at a peppermint-scented blue triangular target is presented with a choice between an orange-scented blue triangular target and a peppermint-scented yellow circular target, it will inevitably choose the peppermint-scented target even though that target has neither the color nor the shape the bee has been trained on. It is only when two targets have the same odor that bees pay much attention to color or shape; under those conditions color takes precedence over shape. This hierarchy corresponds to the relative reliability of the cues in nature. The odor of a flower is usually constant, whereas color can fade or appear different under different lighting conditions, and shape changes with damage from wind and herbivores, and even with viewing angle.

The hierarchy is an important factor in the organization of the bees' memory, but there is an even more important organizational element: the time of day at which each flower provides nectar. Bees learn the time at which food is available from each flower more slowly than they learn odor, color or shape, but once they have learned it, that knowledge serves to organize their use of the rest of their memory.

The organizational role of time was clearly shown by Franz Josef Bogdany of the University of Würzburg. For several days he trained a set of foragers to feed at two different feeders at differing times of day. From 10:00 to 11:00 A.M., for example, he fed them at a peppermint-scented blue triangular feeder; from 11:00 A.M. until noon he fed them at an orange-scented yellow circular feeder that was placed on the site the blue feeder had occupied. One day he put both feeders out at 9:00 A.M. and noticed an interesting pattern. Trained foragers began to appear at the blue feeder at about 9:45. They foraged exclusively at that feeder for about an hour. At roughly 10:45 some foragers began to shift to the yellow feeder, and by 11:15 the blue feeder – which was still full of food – was completely abandoned.

Bees behave as though they have an appointment book by which they schedule their visits; no more than one entry can be made for any specific time. The resolution of the book is about 20 minutes; that is, bees cannot remember two separate appointments if they are less than 20 minutes apart. Bees have been able to remember as many appointments as experimenters have tried to teach them. The standing record, set by R. Koltermann of the University of Frankfurt, is nine appointments in eight hours.

Another experiment by Bogdany shows finer details in the structure of honey-bee memory. After days of being trained to the peppermint-scented blue triangular feeder, bees were presented with an orange-scented blue triangular feeder. The foragers learned the new odor in one visit, but they completely forgot the color and shape, even though these characteristics had not been changed. On the other hand, when bees were trained to an odorless blue triangle and then presented with a peppermint-scented blue triangle, they learned the new odor without forgetting the color and shape. Apparently the appointment book has an entry for each cue; the entries are structured in such a way that blanks can always be filled in but that if even one item is changed, the entire entry is erased.

Such results suggest that honey bees, guided to particular targets by instinctively recognized cues, memorize certain specific features of the targets and store that memory

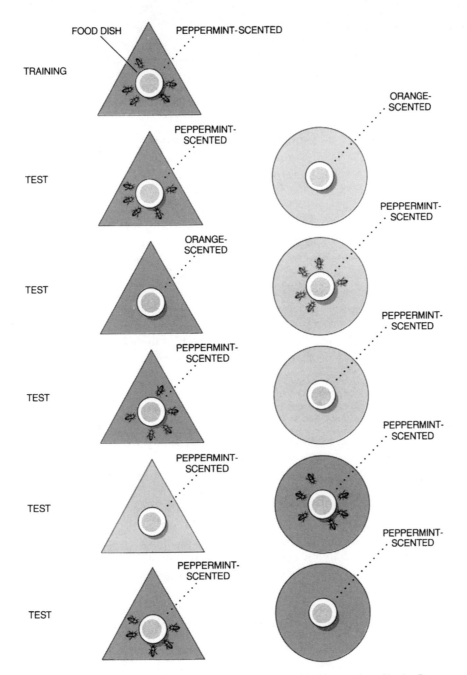

Figure 12.3 Hierarchical structure of bees' memory is revealed in a series of tests. Bees were trained to land on peppermint-scented blue triangles. Their training was confirmed by a test in which they preferred a peppermint-scented blue triangle to an orange-scented yellow circle, even when both targets bore full food dishes. Then they were offered an orange-scented blue triangle and a peppermint-scented yellow circle. They chose the latter, showing they are more likely to be guided by the memory of a scent than by the memory of a shape or color. Later tests, interspersed with controls, showed bees are more likely to rely on a remembered color than a remembered shape. The structure of bees' memory shows that instinct guides a bee's use of the knowledge it gains through learning.

in a "prewired," hierarchical memory array. The cues that are memorized, the speed with which each cue is memorized and the way the memorized data are stored are all innate characteristics of the bee.

Learning about Enemies

Animals need to learn many things other than how to find food. For example, they must learn how to recognize and respond to various kinds of predators and enemies. For some animals it is enough merely to identify a very general class of predators. Flying moths and crickets automatically begin evasive maneuvers when they hear the high-pitched sounds characteristic of hunting bats. Other animals must be able to make finer distinctions among friends and potential foes. Nesting birds are a particularly apt example. They must learn to distinguish harmless birds, such as robins, from birds such as crows and jays, which hunt for eggs and nestlings. The "fill in the blanks" strategy adopted by bees as they learn about flowers is also applicable to this kind of learning.

When nesting birds detect nest predators, they attack en masse, a phenomenon commonly known as "mobbing." How do birds know whom to mob and whom to ignore? Eberhard Curio of the University of the Ruhr has shown that the process of learning which species to mob is innately guided.

In Curio's experiments groups of birds (most often European blackbirds) were kept in separate cages. Between the cages was placed a rotatable box with four compartments. At any given time the birds in one cage could see into only one compartment of the rotatable box, while the birds in the other cage saw a different compartment [see illustration]. The birds could see into each other's cages.

Curio began by rotating the central box to present a stuffed Australian honeycreeper – a harmless species – to each cage. The live birds showed no reaction. He then put a stuffed owl in one compartment and a honeycreeper in the opposite compartment. When the box was rotated so that each model was in view of one of the two sets of birds, the birds in the cage exposed to the owl began to emit the species' innate mobbing call and tried to attack the model. The other group observed the mobbing for a moment and then, responding to this powerful set of sign stimuli, began trying to attack the stuffed honeycreeper, at the same time emitting the mobbing call. On later occasions this group of birds always tried to mob honeycreepers, a species they had never seen attack a nest. Curio found that the baseless aversion to honeycreepers was passed on from generation

Figure 12.4 (opposite) Mobbing behavior of the European blackbird demonstrates the instinctive way the species learns to recognize predators. Between the cages in which the birds sit is a rotatable, four-chambered box (1). Each bird can see only one chamber of the box, but it can also see into the other bird's cage. First each bird is shown a stuffed Australian honeycreeper, a harmless species (2); neither bird shows any interest. Then one bird is shown a stuffed owl (a predator of small birds) and the other is shown a honeycreeper. The bird shown an owl tries to chase it away and gives the characteristic "mobbing call" (3). The other bird at first watches and then (4) joins in the mobbing behavior. It has learned to mob honeycreepers. When both birds are shown honeycreepers (5), it teaches the other to mob honeycreepers as well (6).

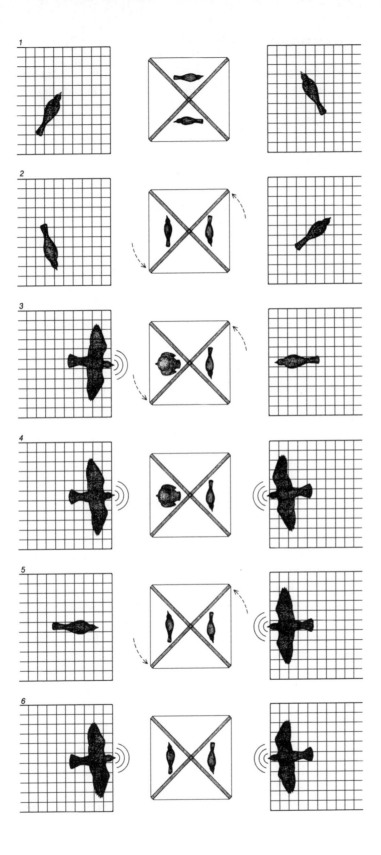

to generation. The young birds learned to mob honeycreepers by watching their parents. In later experiments Curio was able to teach his birds to mob bottles of laundry detergent.

There is good reason to think variations of this strategy of learning about enemies are at work in many mammalian species as well as in birds. Perhaps the most elaborate version is found in vervet monkeys. As was shown by Robert M. Seyfarth, Dorothy L. Cheney (both now at the University of Pennsylvania) and one of us (Marler), vervets have special alarm calls for each of four kinds of predators: aerial predators such as eagles, four-legged predators such as leopards, predatory primates such as baboons, and snakes. Each alarm call elicits a different kind of response. For example, an eagle alarm sends vervets on the ground toward cover and causes those in the exposed tops of trees to drop like stones into the protective interior, whereas a snake call is ignored by vervets in trees but induces those on the ground to rear up on their hind legs and scan the ground around them.

Young vervets instinctively emit alarm calls in response to a wide but specific range of stimuli. For example, any object within certain size limits moving in free space at a certain angular velocity causes the young monkeys to give the eagle call; the call can be elicited by a stork or even a falling leaf. With time the infants learn which species cause the adults to call. Hence vervets growing up in one region might learn to give alarm calls on seeing baboons, leopards and a certain species of eagle, whereas those in another region might react to human beings, hunting dogs and a certain species of hawk. Like the bees' system of learning about flowers, this innate system is efficient for learning essential information about predictably unpredictable situations: predictable kinds of threat posed by animals whose exact species cannot be predicted.

Song Learning in Birds

Another task an animal must perform that often requires learning is recognizing others of its own species. Perhaps the richest and best understood use of learning in species recognition is the learning of songs by birds. All birds have a repertoire of perhaps one or two dozen calls that are innately produced and recognized. These calls need not be learned and can be produced even by birds hatched and reared in isolation. Several kinds of birds also have more complex vocal patterns – songs for attracting mates and defending territory – that must to some extent be learned from adults of the same species.

The white-crowned sparrow, which has been studied extensively by one of us (Marler), is a good example. Adults of this species produce a three-part or four-part courtship song rich in melodic detail. Different individuals produce recognizably different songs, but the organization of the song is common to the species. The song produced by each male white-crown is similar to (but not identical with) the songs heard near the place it was reared. (There are actually local dialects.)

Experiments in manipulating the sensory experience of young sparrows have revealed much about the organization of the process of song learning. A bird kept in auditory isolation, for example, begins to produce and experiment with song notes by the time it is about a month old. This period of experimentation, known as subsong, waxes and wanes for roughly two months. By about the bird's 100th day it "crystallizes" its

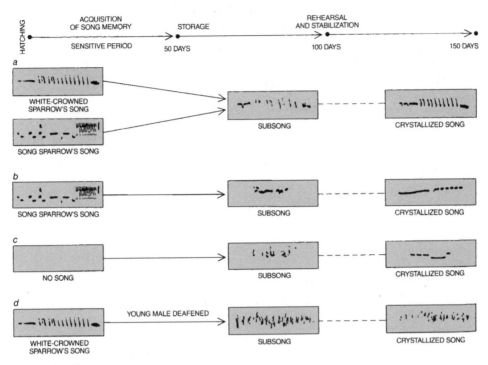

Figure 12.5 Song learning in the white-crowned sparrow exhibits great specificity: young male birds can instinctively identify and preferentially learn the song of their own species. If a young male white-crown is played tape recordings of adult white-crown song and adult song-sparrow song (a), it first begins a period of experimentation, known as subsong, and then produces a crystallized song very similar to the white-crown song it has heard. If it is played only a tape recording of song-sparrow song (b), it will not learn the song: it still goes through subsong, but its final, crystallized song does not resemble either the song-sparrow song or the white-crown song. A bird that is played no song (c) also learns nothing. If the young bird hears a white-crown song but is deafened before subsong begins (d), it is unable to learn how to produce the song it heard; it produces an amorphous song with no melodic structure.

song into a form that will not change significantly; the song is highly schematic, but it bears many of the basic features of normal adult white-crown song. Such experiments show that the chick is born with a basic innate song, which it learns to elaborate when it is raised in the wild.

In another experiment we play tape-recorded songs of other species to isolated young birds. Such songs have little effect on the final, crystallized song produced by the bird (although Luis Baptista of the California Academy of Sciences has shown that a live tutor can sometimes successfully indoctrinate young white-crowns). On the other hand, when we play a medley of tape recordings, one of which reproduces a real white-crown song, the young male somehow manages to pick out the white-crown song and learns to produce a tolerable imitation. If it is to produce a perfect imitation, the bird must hear the song before it is about seven weeks old. (The actual period varies with experimental conditions.) The "window" for learning (the time in which the drive to learn is high) is called the sensitive period.

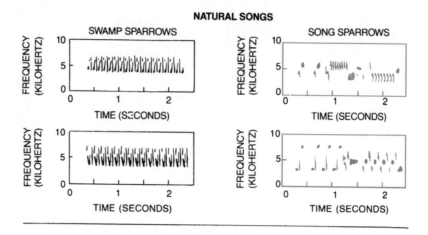

NATURAL SONGS

SWAMP SPARROWS

SONG SPARROWS

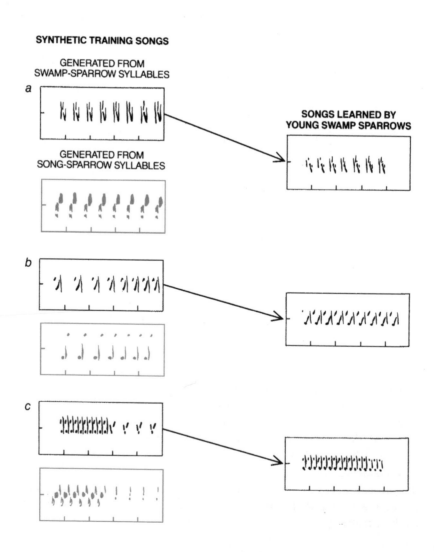

SYNTHETIC TRAINING SONGS

GENERATED FROM
SWAMP-SPARROW SYLLABLES

a

GENERATED FROM
SONG-SPARROW SYLLABLES

SONGS LEARNED BY
YOUNG SWAMP SPARROWS

b

c

Taken together, these experiments show that learning of the local song dialect in the white-crowned sparrow is innately controlled, irreversible and restricted to a sensitive period; these are exactly the characteristics of classical imprinting. Starting with some form of innate song, the young male depends on innately recognized cues to trigger the learning process and later learns to imitate the more elaborate, memorized song.

The actual process of developing the bird's own version of the local dialect seems to be done by trial-and-error learning. In the case of the white-crowned sparrow, weeks or months may pass between the end of the sensitive period (during which the bird memorizes the song) and the bird's first experiments with recognizable imitations, which come at the end of subsong. Masakazu Konishi, now at the California Institute of Technology, has demonstrated that when a young male white-crown that has been exposed to white-crown song is deafened before any crystallization, it never sings anything melodic – not even its innate song. Apparently a bird must experiment with its beak, syrinx and pulmonary muscles, listening to the sounds that result from various manipulations and trying to match them to its mental record. During the progression from subsong to crystallization the bird shapes its song to match the record stored in its brain, whether that record consists of only the rough, innate song or of a song memorized during the sensitive period. Konishi found that by the time the bird has crystallized its song the singing has become so routine that deafening has little or no effect.

The Cues within Adult Birdsong

How do the young songbirds pick out their own species' song from a world full of sounds? What specific cues do the sparrows rely on to determine which song to learn? One of us (Marler) and his colleagues have investigated this question in experiments with swamp sparrows and song sparrows, two species that nest within earshot of one another.

Of the two species, swamp sparrows have the simpler song. It consists of a single series of regularly repeated syllables; the kinds of syllables vary from theme to theme, bird to bird and region to region. The song sparrow's song is more complex: it consists of at

Figure 12.6 (opposite) Synthetic songs identified the cues young song sparrows rely on in identifying their own species' song. The natural swamp-sparrow song (top left; two songs are shown because the exact song varies from bird to bird) consists of one syllable repeated at a steady rate. The song-sparrow song (top right) contains several syllables, beginning with an accelerating trill. In one pair of synthetic songs (a) both songs had the steady rate of swamp-sparrow songs but one was constructed from swamp-sparrow syllables and the other from song-sparrow syllables. In another pair (b) each song still consisted of a single syllable, but the syllables were repeated at an accelerating rate; in one song the syllable was from swamp-sparrow song and in the other it was from song-sparrow song. Swamp sparrows learned the swamp-sparrow syllable and restructured the tempo to match the natural swamp-sparrow song. In another pair (c) each song consisted of two syllables, arranged as they would be in a song-sparrow song; again one song was made up of swamp-sparrow syllables and the other of song-sparrow syllables. Young swamp sparrows learned one of the syllables in the song generated from swamp-sparrows syllables and delivered that syllable at their characteristic rate. The experiments show young swamp sparrows rely on cues within individual syllables when determining which song to learn.

least four types of syllables, often beginning with an accelerating trill. Although the innate songs of the two species reflect some of these structural differences, the syllables from which the innate songs are constructed are much simpler.

The auditory cues that guide learning might include elements of the syllables themselves, elements of the tempo and phrase structure or elements of both. As a first stage in determining which of these elements are important, we gave hand-reared sparrows of both species a chance to learn from tapes of their own species or tapes of the other species. As we had expected, the birds learned almost exclusively from tapes of their own species. The rare cross-species imitations are important, however: they show that songs of other species can physically be sung, and that the normal tendency not to learn the song of another species comes from the birds' inattentiveness to such songs rather than from inability to produce them.

To investigate further the role of different aspects of song structure in learning preferences, we put together synthetic training songs that varied in structure and played them to young birds of both species. For example, we fabricated one song from a slow, steady repetition of song-sparrow syllables and another from a slow, steady repetition of swamp-sparrow syllables. The tempo of these songs was like that of swamp-sparrow song. Swamp sparrows readily learned the steady song with swamp-sparrow syllables but not the other song, and song sparrows learned only the song containing song-sparrow syllables. These results indicated that cues lie within syllables.

By itself that experiment did not indicate whether or not tempo and phrase structure might be important as well. To investigate this issue we synthesized a variety of other songs. The new songs were created from syllables of both species, but the syllables were organized in a variety of patterns. Some of the patterns were like those of the swamp sparrow and others were like those of the song sparrow.

One of the songs, for example, was made up of swamp-sparrow syllables but had the accelerating rate of delivery characteristic of song sparrows. Would young swamp sparrows reject the song because it had the wrong tempo? Or would they accept it because it had the correct sign stimulus for learning (the right syllables) and so sing an abnormally paced song? In fact, the young swamp sparrows did neither. They learned the syllables of the song, but in their own singing they actually changed the tempo, so that they delivered the learned syllables at the constant rate typical of their own species.

In another variation we fabricated songs even more similar in structure to song-sparrow songs. Each song had two segments; each segment consisted of a different type of syllable, and in one segment the syllables were delivered at an accelerating rate. When the songs were made up of different kinds of swamp-sparrow syllables, young swamp sparrows learned to sing a steady repetition of one of the two syllable types, regardless of the temporal pattern in which the syllables had been presented. Swamp sparrows thus seem to focus entirely on the syllabic structure when searching for cues, paying scant attention to the organization of the song as a whole.

Song sparrows are different. They are readier to accept the alien syllables of the swamp sparrow if the syllables are presented in song models that have complex phrase structures (although they reject swamp-sparrow syllables when they are delivered at a steady tempo). The two attributes – syllable type and syntactic structure – apparently have additive effects.

These experiments show that although the song sparrow and the swamp sparrow are closely related, the innate mechanisms that control learning in the two species are different. No doubt the white-crowned sparrow is different in its own way.

Speech Learning in Humans

The learning of songs in birds has a number of parallels with the learning of speech in human beings. In swamp sparrows, song learning involves the innate recognition of certain elements in the species-specific syllables. There is now abundant evidence that human infants innately recognize most or all of the more than two dozen consonant sounds characteristic of human speech, including consonants not present in the language they normally hear. The innate ability to identify sign stimuli present in consonants confers several advantages: it allows the infant to ignore a world full of irrelevant auditory stimuli in order to focus on speech sounds, it starts the child on the right track in learning to decode the many layers of meaning buried in the immensely complex and variable sounds of speech, and it provides an internal standard for the child to use in judging and shaping speech sounds.

Another aspect of human speech learning parallels the subsong phase, the period during which birds of species that learn to sing begin to experiment with sound production. The subsong phase begins right on schedule even if the bird has been deafened (although such birds learn nothing from their vocal experimentation). Human infants also have a phase of babbling, in which they develop, through trial-and-error learning, the ability to produce the set of consonants found in their own language. As with birds, babbling begins and ends on schedule even in deaf children.

Birds have an innate, templatelike structure that specifies the rules for producing syllables in song. On a vastly different scale, there is good reason to believe that the rhythms in which words and sentences are assembled in speech and the set of rules known as grammar (in particular the division of words into such categories as nouns, verbs, adjectives and adverbs) are at some deep level also innate. This idea, argued most persuasively by Noam Chomsky of the Massachusetts Institute of Technology, helps to explain why the learning of speech proceeds so easily compared with the learning of such inherently simpler tasks as addition and subtraction.

Sophisticated Learning

Although much of animal learning (and probably more of human learning than is yet suspected) is innately guided by learning programs, much human behavior clearly cannot be explained so simply. For example, imagining a solution before exploring it physically is a behavior outside the two traditional forms of learning originally studied by behaviorists. This kind of cognitive learning, called cognitive trial and error, comes much closer than programmed learning to one's intuitive sense of what intelligence is. It requires the ability to recall and combine separate bits of learned information and from such mental recombination to formulate new behavioral solutions.

The first evidence that animals have such an ability came in 1948 in a series of experiments by Edward C. Tolman of the University of California at Berkeley. In one experiment Tolman allowed rats to explore a maze that had two alternative goals, a white box and a black box, both containing food; rats learned the routes to both boxes, and chose them with equal frequency. Later Tolman took the rats to another room, where a black box and a white box were put side by side, and he gave them a shock when they entered the black box. When the rats were released in the maze the next day, they entered only the white box. Tolman concluded that they had combined information from the two entirely different experiments, generalizing about black boxes and remembering that one route led to a black box. Tolman also found that rats have an ability to form mental maps of familiar areas and from the maps to plan novel routes. Tolman's finding was subsequently confirmed and explored by David S. Olton of Johns Hopkins University.

The ability to form maps is by no means limited to rats and human beings. Emil W. Menzel of the State University of New York at Stony Brook has found the same ability in captive chimpanzees; John R. Krebs of the University of Oxford and Sara J. Shettleworth of the University of Toronto have shown that seed-caching birds can form cognitive maps registering the locations of hundreds of hidden seeds.

Mental Maps and Categories

In an effort to determine how common this sophisticated cognitive ability is, one of us (Gould) investigated whether honey bees also have mental maps. When bees travel a familiar route, they rely on prominent landmarks. The usual explanation of how bees use landmarks is that they remember the series of landmarks encountered en route to each site and can refer to the landmarks only in the same way as Hansel and Gretel would have referred to their trail of breadcrumbs. In that case bees would have no idea how one set of landmarks leading to one site is related spatially to the set that leads to any other site.

We tested whether bees do navigate this way or whether they in fact put landmarks in the context of a mental map of their home area. We trained certain bees to feed in one area and then, on subsequent days, captured them as they flew from the hive to that area and carried them (in the dark) to another location.

We thought that when the bees were released in the new area, they might adopt any of several courses of action. They could be disoriented and fly at random. Alternatively, they could fail to understand that they had been displaced; they would then fly off at the same compass bearing they would normally follow to get to the food site from the hive. If bees can navigate only by specific strings of landmarks, they might recognize the landmarks around the new location as part of a route different from the one they were on when they were captured; they would then follow that route back to the hive and from there fly to the food site. Finally, if bees do have cognitive maps, they should be able to determine where they were in relation to the food site and to select the appropriate bearing to reach the food, even though they had never flown from the hive to the food site before by such a roundabout route.

We found that bees overwhelmingly followed the last of these alternatives: when the area to which they were displaced was within their home area (the four or so square kilometers immediately surrounding the hive), they flew directly to the food site. It seems, then, that for bees cognitive map making is an innate part of route learning.

Another sophisticated ability involved in the process of learning is the formation of abstract concepts and categories. Is this ability found in animals? One suggestive hint comes from the work of Richard J. Herrnstein of Harvard University. He showed thousands of slides to laboratory-reared pigeons and rewarded them when they pecked at slides in which some specific kind of object, say a tree, was in the picture; these birds, of course, had never seen a real tree. The birds learned the task remarkably quickly, which suggests that they had a strong innate disposition to form generalized conceptual categories. When they were later tested with slides showing new species of trees, the birds reliably picked out the slides with trees, including some slides the experimenters had at first thought were treeless. The birds' occasional errors were also revealing: they sometimes identified telephone poles and television antennas as trees.

Students of human language acquisition have long known that children automatically form conceptual categories for the new words they learn. Chairs, tables and lamps are organized into a "furniture" category and the category of "chairs" is subdivided into subordinate categories such as rocking chairs and armchairs. Such categorization is essential to the rapid acquisition of words, and word storage in the brain is probably organized as a categorized filing system. The effects of small strokes, which can kill small regions of the brain, seem to reflect such a system: their victims sometimes lose an entire category of words, for instance the names of flowers.

It seems reasonable to propose that the drive to categorize is innate in at least some species. Perhaps it is the ability to make and manipulate categories that underlies the ability of animals to perform cognitive trial and error: to evaluate alternatives and formulate simple plans.

A New Synthesis

The emerging picture of learning in animals represents a fundamental shift from the early days of behaviorism, when animals were supposed to be limited to learning by classical conditioning and operant conditioning and were expected to be able to learn any association or behavior by those processes. It is now understood that much learning, even though it is based on conditioning, is specialized for the learning of tasks the animal is likely to encounter. The animal is innately equipped to recognize when it should learn, what cues it should attend to, how to store the new information and how to refer to it in the future. Even the ability to categorize and perform cognitive trial and error, a process that may be available to the higher invertebrates, may depend on innate guidance and specialization – specialization that enables the chickadee, with its tiny brain, to remember the locations of hundreds of hidden seeds, whereas human beings begin to forget after hiding about a dozen.

This perspective allows one to see that various animals are smart in the ways natural selection has favored and stupid where their life-style does not require a customized learning program. The human species is similarly smart in its own adaptive ways and almost embarrassingly stupid in others. The idea that human learning evolved from a few processes, which are well illustrated in other animals, to fit species-specific human needs helps to bring a new unity to the study of animal behavior and a new promise for understanding human origins.

13

Language and Experience

Barbara Landau and Lila R. Gleitman

If we will observe how children learn languages, we shall find that, to make them understand what the names of simple ideas or substances stand for, people ordinarily show them the thing whereof they would have them have the idea; and then repeat to them the name that stands for it, as "white", "sweet", "milk", "sugar", "cat", "dog".
(John Locke, An Essay Concerning Human Understanding, *1690, Book 3.IX.9)*

To know a language is to know the relations between sounds and their meanings. Since these relations vary over the languages of the world – in English /si/ means "gaze with the eyes" but in Spanish /si/ means "yes" – it follows that the child must acquire them by induction from specific experience. Common sense requires us to agree with Locke that the relevant inductions have to do with ascertaining how heard speech relates to objects, scenes, and events the learner is experiencing as he listens. After all, how could it be otherwise? If you saw rhinoceroses when we said "giraffes," you might learn a language, but it wouldn't be *our* language. All parties who have thought about language learning – from the early empiricists such as Locke and Berkeley to rationalists such as Leibniz, and from behaviorists such as Bloomfield (1933) and sociocommunicative theorists such as Bruner (1974–5) to learnability theorists such as Wexler and Culicover (1980) – agree thus far: Some interpretive context, paired with speech events, is required if language learning is to get off the ground floor.

   No disagreement arises, then, about the *necessity* for extralinguistic experience. But despite this agreement, the theorists just mentioned vary considerably in their conceptions of how language is attained by the young child. Their disagreements have to do with the *sufficiency* of experience for learning a language. Exactly how is the relevant external experience to be internally represented? How could anyone *use* this experience to learn a language? How could seeing a dog while hearing "dog" determine that /dɔg/ means "dog"?[1]

From *Language and Experience: Evidence from the Blind Child*. Cambridge, Mass.: Harvard University Press, 1985, pp. 1–5, 54–64, and 121–6. © 1985 by the President and Fellows of Harvard College. Reprinted by permission of the publisher.

In this book, we take up the case of language learning by blind children. This topic seems relevant to questions about the role of experience in language learning because, at least on first inspection, the blind seem to confront a world quite different from our own. To the extent that blind children's extralinguistic contexts for the words and sentences they hear differ from those of sighted children, one might expect their language learning to differ as well. And to the extent that learning really does differ, the role of experience in building a mental lexicon may be clarified. This is because the problem of language learning for any individual, however circumstanced, is a problem of learning from partial information. No one requires experience of every dog to acquire the word *dog*. It is this strikingly uniform acquisition of language, based on only partial and sometimes quite impoverished relevant experiences, that makes a mystery of language induction. We expect to gain insight into the nature of this problem by examining language learning in the blind child, who evidently must work with a different inductive base.

In our studies we focused on three questions about how experiential deprivations might affect blind children:

(1) Is their language acquisition seriously delayed or grossly distorted because of limits on available contextual support?

(2) Are their difficulties centered on linguistic items and structures that, for sighted people, describe visible things or the visual experience?

(3) Is their learning, to the extent that it is successful, a consequence of special adjustments made by their sighted caregivers?

To address the first question, we studied the standard milestones in three blind children's acquisition of a first language, comparing these with accounts in the literature for sighted children. Both for syntax and for word learning, extreme differences in what is learned early and easily by blind and sighted children might be expected, assuming that extralinguistic experience is the driving causal force in language learning. Oddly enough, our general finding is that the blind children develop much as do their sighted agemates.

To approach the second question, we investigated in detail a blind child's [Keith's] development for two apparently sight-related categories: her use and interpretation of the verbs *look* and *see* (as compared to aural and tactual verbs such as *hear* and *touch*) and her use and interpretation of the adjectives of color (*red* and *green* as opposed to other property terms such as *big* and *round*). Surely if extralinguistic experience provides the route to learning, a blind child should have maximum trouble with these terms, for they seem to refer directly to the sighted world. Nonetheless, as we will show, a congenitally blind child can acquire considerable sophistication with the sighted vocabulary.

To understand these surprising findings, we then examined the actual input circumstances of a blind learner to ascertain whether selected properties of the sentences or contexts provided by her caregivers explain the character of what she learned. The findings from this inquiry taken as a whole give little support to the view that first language attainment is explainable as a straightforward derivative of information provided in the environment of the learner. Rather, they suggest to us a learning procedure significantly modulated and constrained by the child's natural (innate) biases about the content and form of a natural language.

Before turning to our study of blind children, we want to consider the general problems learners seem to face in inducing the lexicon from observation of extralinguistic circumstances.

Three Problems for Learning from Observation

Following Locke, we have asserted that to make children understand words, people show them the thing "and then repeat to them the name that stands for it." (Of course the settings for such showing and telling usually are informal rather than overtly tutorial but this does not change the position.) Still there is a problem because of the particularities of these learning experiences as compared with the generality of what is learned. The child who has seen Fido and Rover while hearing the sound signal /dɔg/ will ultimately be able – without further language learning – to refer to Rex and Spot by producing the same sound signal. That is, the child's input consists of sound/situation pairs, but his final output is a set of form/meaning pairs, appropriate to an infinite set of novel but well-circumscribed situations. How is it that children ineluctably move from these singular experiences to general knowledge of terms, which allows their creative use? How do they project to the full set of pairings in the language – all dogs from Pekinese to Russian wolfhounds – given the small and inconclusive subset of pairings – say, Chihuahuas and poodles – provided by experience? To help understand the issues here, we now take up three problems in making good the claim that language can be learned "from" experience.

Too many encodings of experience are available

Normally circumstanced learners are exposed to objects, scenes, and events as they listen to the stream of speech. But these objects, scenes, and events are in no direct way the "meanings" that learners are seeking to pair with the language forms. They are merely what they seem to be: objects, scenes, and events. Any of them can be linguistically described in myriad ways, for language can encode a variety of descriptions of a single scene. For instance, the same creature out there is an object, a mammal, a cat, Felix. And the same event out there is the cat on the mat, the mat under the cat, and the mat and the cat on the floor. When the cat is pointed to (accompanied by the sound /kæt/), then, what is to prevent the listening-watching child from interpreting that experience (and that sound) as "object," "organism," "furriness," "white," "cute," "whiskers," "legs"?[2]

Similarly, scenes relevant to the utterance "The cat is on the mat" are just as relevant to "The mat is under the cat" or "The cat and the mat are on the floor." How is the learner to realize that the linguistic encoding (the *particular* sentence spoken) is of one of these descriptions of the scene and not the other? The real-world context available to the learner is apposite to all of them.

The problem, in short, is that there is always as much positive evidence in the external world for one of these interpretations as for the next. If no child chooses the false solutions, the question is how they all know enough to avoid them. If some of the children do choose falsely – that is, if we settle on different internal constructions of the sense of words – the problem is how we ever manage to understand each other. Thus the general acknowledgment that context is necessary should not be confused with a proof that it is sufficient for language acquisition. That is why one can't (though many do) say the child learns language from observing the world, and let it go at that.

These problems are extremely tricky. One false conjecture about the particular sentence spoken by the adult, and an escalating series of miscalculations about the language is likely to ensue. For example, suppose the child guesses the unintended mat-under-cat interpretation while she is hearing a cat-on-mat utterance. Then she might conclude (falsely, of course) that *cat* means "mat" and *on* means "under." But this simple reversal is not the only wrong direction she might take. After all, she comes equipped with no passport to tell her that the language in question is English and that therefore the subject probably comes before the verb; other languages systematically use a different ordering of thematic roles in simple sentences. Thus the learner who has made the accidentally false conjecture about the scene description (mat-under-cat) while hearing "cat on mat" may correctly conjecture that *cat* means "cat," but at the cost of the false conjecture that English is an object-first rather than a subject-first language – and, again, that *on* means "under." No wonder, in light of such problems, that the mere statement that learning relies on contextual interpretation has achieved little in the way of definite results, nor been able to explain what is learned when and under what conditions by children.[3]

False experiences

It must be true that occasionally a child is inspecting a scene while the adult is thinking and speaking of something else altogether, creating a potentially false pairing for the inductive learner. For example, a mother might say "Granny is coming for dinner" or "Time for your nap" while the child inspects a cat on the mat. What is to prevent the learner from the attempt to pair this extralinguistic experience with the sound signal /taɪmfəryərnæp/? If this problem is not qualitatively different from those mentioned just above, it certainly is an exacerbation of the real difficulties in envisaging a machinery that extracts the words and their meanings from raw confrontations with utterance/event pairs.

The problem of abstract meanings

A great many words, among them many that are easily learned by toddlers, have no direct connection with sensory-perceptual experience. Whatever the basis for learning words that refer to rabbits, waistcoats, and watchfobs, much of the lexicon traffics in concepts that overreach in abstractness what any child can be expected to induce from immediate environmental cues. Even such simple verbs as *get* or *put* require for felicitous use apprehension of a mental goal, not just an action, on the part of the speaker/listener (for discussion, see Huttenlocher, Smiley, and Charney, 1983). Even such simple nouns as *fun* and *pet*, or adjectives such as *fair* and *good*, encode descriptions not embodied in the physical substance or single material property of their extensions. In addition, some words encode highly general and often unobservable relations (*similar, brother, but*) and properties (*very, the*) or grammatical functions divorced from any experiential description (*of* or infinitival *to*). But learners evidently have little trouble in acquiring the sense of these words, which could not derive from material aspects of experience.

Plan of the Comprehension Studies

We know that sighted children explore the world predominantly by eye and that blind children explore predominantly by hand (though, to be sure, sighted children can also explore manually, and there is a panoply of ancillary haptic kinesthetic means by which blind youngsters can interact with the world outside their bodies). Therefore, at first guess, a word like *touch* or *feel* might serve for blind youngsters as *look* does for sighted children. Our aim was to discover Kelli's (and controls') glosses for the words *look* and *touch*. To do so, we tried to elicit the children's characteristic responses to requests that required observable action.

Such actions cannot, it is true, be interpreted as direct indicators of the meaning of the terms to their users. This is simply a fact about how words and sentences relate to the world. Particularly, responses to requests and commands are often affected by conversational inferences about the intent of the interlocutor that go beyond the literal meaning of words and syntactic structures (Searle, 1975; Grice, 1975). As one example, children asked to "find X" will often find it, but then give it to the interlocutor. This does not mean they don't understand *find*, but rather that they assume an intention that goes beyond what was said, i.e., that someone asked one to find something because he wanted it given to him. Far be it from us to complain of these inference-based acts – without them, communication would be even harder than it is. Nevertheless, such complications pose an interpretive difficulty for the investigator if he is trying to determine the component lexical or syntactic functioning of child subjects. But despite these difficulties in using the child's actions to reconstruct his meanings, the experiments now to be reported achieved systematic, but different, responses from Kelli and the sighted children. Moreover, the responses also differed systematically as a function of the verb (*look* or *touch*) in each command.[4]

An important detail for interpreting the results has to do with the order in which the experiments were carried out. For Kelli, the reader can easily reconstruct the order by noting her age at the time of each experiment. For the sighted children, the order of presentation of the experiments was systematically varied among the four subjects. This is crucial because they might have been learning something in one of the experiments that they used to understand how to behave in the next. As it turned out, the presentation order had no particular effect.

Experiment 1: Does *look* mean "touch" to the blind child?

Setting.   In this experiment and all that follow, Kelli and the sighted control children were tested individually in their homes or a laboratory room familiar to them during informal play periods. The experimenter gave the subject a command and waited for a response. Usually the children responded immediately; if they did not, the command was repeated. No child failed to respond after two such presentations of a command. The closest pacing of presentation of commands was one minute but often much slower, sometimes as far apart as thirty minutes. All sessions were videotaped. The analysis of the results was always based on the videotaped behaviors.

Subjects.   Kelli was 36 months old when this experiment was conducted. The four sighted blindfolded controls ranged in age from 33 to 42 months.

Stimuli and procedure.   The subjects were presented with the commands to *Look up*, *Look down*, *Look behind you*, *Look in front of you*, *Look over here by me*, and *Look over there by Mommy*. These commands were in the single order listed above to all subjects. The contexts varied: Some commands were presented when no object was in the target location (e.g., *Look up*, when no object was in the space above the subject's body), and others were presented when an object (a graduated ring tower) was in the target location (e.g., *Look behind you*, when the ring tower had been placed behind the subject's body). When there was an object in the location mentioned, sometimes the child was made aware of this and sometimes not.

Coding.   Here, as for all succeeding procedures, the videotaped behaviors, including the subject's verbal responses, were coded by the experimenter or an assistant in terms of the relevant variables (e.g., "orients head toward," "contacts with the hand"). Sample reliability checks for all coding procedures (for these and for the further procedures to be reported) were made by an independent observer and were in each case at or above .90.

Results.   The contextual circumstances (whether or not an object was at the target location or known to be there in advance) had no effect on the responses of the subjects. Blindness versus blindfoldedness, in contrast, resulted in responses so distinct as to require no tabular presentation. Kelli moved her hands in the appropriate spatial directions (that is, up, down, and so on), usually exploring to find if there was something there but *never* tilting her head to face the object, in six out of six trials. Her head remained facing forward, even when she was responding to "Look behind you." In clear contrast, each blindfolded sighted child moved her head in the appropriate spatial directions (e.g., tilting the head up to "Look up") in six out of six trials. Figures 13.1 and 13.2 show examples of these behaviors.

   This different pattern of response for blind and sighted subjects is significant ($p = .001$, Fisher exact test). A satisfactory first gloss is that *look* means "turn one's eyes toward" for a sighted child (though "turn one's nose toward" or "orient the face toward" would do as well) while *look* means "contact with the hands" to the blind child.

Experiment 2: *Look* is more like "apprehend" to the blind child

The results of Experiment 1 might simply mean that for Kelli *look* meant "touch." But this interpretation runs up against a problem. For in fact Kelli almost never used the (known) word *touch* that, in the speech of her mother, coded precisely the meaning she allegedly had in mind for her own haptic activities. So we next tried to find out whether *look* was distinct from *touch* for Kelli.

   Our first approach was to pit these two words against each other. When told "Touch X but don't look at it," Kelli would usually simply touch or stroke the object or bang it with her fist. Then told "Now you can look at it," she would manually explore it extensively, running her hands over all its surfaces (see Landau, 1982, for the full results of this procedure).

Figure 13.1 Kelli's response to "look up!" In Experiment 1, the blind child moved her hands, not her eyes and head, in the direction indicated by the command in six out of six trials.

We next asked whether certain adjectival and adverbial modifications of *look* produce still more distinctive behaviors. We reasoned that responses to, e.g., "look very hard" and "touch very hard" might be more distinguishable from one another than simply "look" and "touch." As will now be shown, the pattern of results strongly suggests a distinction between these two verbs as Kelli construed them.

Subjects.   This experiment was also performed when Kelli was 36 months, but a couple of weeks older than she was during Experiment 1. The four blindfolded sighted children ranged from 33 to 42 months.

Stimuli and procedure.   Using several toys, we asked Kelli to "look" or "touch" (1) with spatial modifiers: *up, behind you, in that* (container), *under* (some object), and *here*; (2) with intensity modifiers: *real hard, gently, real good*; and (3) with instruments of contact or perception: *with your finger, foot, nose, mouth, ear*. For each of these modifiers two commands were given, one using *look* and the other using *touch*. For example, a pair of intensity commands was "Look at (object) gently" and "Touch (object) gently." This yielded a total of twenty-six commands (thirteen pairs), presented in a randomized order over three experimental sessions.

Table 13.1   Experiment 2: *Look* is more like "apprehend" to the blind child (Kelli's behavior)

Command types	Look	Touch
Differentiated		
up	nonexploratory	exploratory
behind you	exploratory	nonexploratory
real hard	exploratory	nonexploratory
gently	exploratory	nonexploratory
with finger	exploratory	nonexploratory
with foot	exploratory	nonexploratory
with nose	exploratory	nonexploratory
with mouth	exploratory	nonexploratory
Nondifferentiated		
under	exploratory(?)[a]	exploratory(?)
in the X	exploratory	other
real good	nonexploratory	nonexploratory
with ear	exploratory(?)	exploratory(?)
here	exploratory	exploratory

a. For those marked (?) there was some doubt as to the classification. For instance, asked to look for something "under the table," she put her head down under the table and then asked for the object, "Can I have X?" But notice that these coding questions only arise among the nondifferentiated command types.

Table 13.2   Experiment 2: Summary of Kelli's behavioral types (exploratory/nonexploratory) in response to two verbs (*look/touch*)

Behavior	Look	Touch	Total
Exploratory	11	4	15
Nonexploratory	2	8	10

The sighted blindfolded children were tested for a subset of these stimuli, namely *behind you, up, with your foot, finger, mouth, nose, ear*. This yielded a total of fourteen commands (seven pairs), presented in a randomized order within a single session.

Analysis.   The behavioral descriptions were first coded for whether or not the member of a pair (*look* and *touch*) elicited different responses or the same response (*differentiated* versus *not differentiated* in Tables 13.1 and 13.3 for the blind and sighted subjects, respectively). Next all the responses for Kelli were coded as to whether they were *exploratory* or *nonexploratory*, as summarized in Table 13.2. For example, extensive manipulation of an object with examination of all its parts was called an exploratory response; banging the object with closed fist was called nonexploratory. While these two categories could be used to organize all but one of Kelli's responses without coding difficulty, the response styles of the sighted subjects were quite different and required different coding categories that we will describe later (Table 13.3).

Results and discussion

Responses of Kelli.   Inspection of Table 13.1 reveals that for eight of the thirteen command types (*up, behind you, real hard, gently, with your finger, foot, nose, mouth*), Kelli distinguished between *touch* and *look* command pairs. For the remaining five command types (*under, in the container, real good, with your ear, here*), Kelli behaved no differently for *look* versus *touch* commands, sometimes exploring and sometimes touching for each.

For the eight command types among which Kelli differentiated, the interpretive distinction is very clear. She consistently (seven out of eight trials) interpreted *touch* as "contact" (bang, scratch, tap); *look* was never interpreted this way in eight trials. In contrast, *look* was consistently interpreted as "explore" or "apprehend" (manipulate, feel all over, pretend to eat or smell): seven of eight commands to "look" elicited exploratory responses.

A few examples will make this pattern clearer. In response to "look behind you," Kelli searched around in the area behind her with her hands, but when told to "touch behind you'" she touched her back. When told to "look real hard" she rubbed the object all over, running her hand along its surfaces; when told to "touch real hard" she banged her hand against the object. Thus *touch* and *look* are distinguished by whether or not they elicit exploratory behavior. Two of Kelli's responses may hint that her interpretation of *look* is not restricted to manual exploration but may extend to any exploratory behavior. Told to "look with your mouth" she pretended to taste (held it up to her mouth), but asked to "touch with your mouth" she bent down and pressed her mouth against the object; told to "look with your nose" she sniffed at the object, but told to "touch with your nose" she bent her head down and pressed her nose against it. In general, for all differentiated responses, each response to *look* was made by moving the object to the named organ; each response to *touch* was made by moving the named organ to the object.

Thus Kelli differentiated between commands to look and commands to touch. To evaluate these results statistically, we tabulated her responses to all the stimulus commands, including the pairs where her behavior was not differentiated for *look* versus *touch*. Table 13.2 thus organizes the *exploratory/nonexploratory* responses as a function of the *look/touch* commands (omitting one uncodable response). The pattern of differentiation between *look* and *touch* commands is highly significant ($p < .025$, Fisher exact test).

Responses of the sighted children.   The results for the sighted blindfolded subjects are shown in Table 13.3. These children also usually (a mean of 9.6 of the fourteen commands) differentiated between *look* and *touch* commands. The predominant response to *touch* was simple manual contact; the predominant response to *look* was "visual," as described more fully below. The comparison of these contact responses and visual responses to the two verbs is statistically significant (Chi Square = 22.94, df = 1, $p < .01$).

In detail, the response types, where differentiated, were in some ways similar to Kelli's. The predominant interpretation of *touch* was a simple manual contact (3.5 of 4.8), while *look* was infrequently interpreted this way (0.8 of 4.8). But the responses to the *look* commands were altogether different from Kelli's. Most frequently, commands to *look* seemed to be interpreted as commands to do something visual (with the eyes), even though the eyes were covered: The children oriented their heads in the direction indicated by the command. The second most frequent response was to do something we called "analogy

Table 13.3 Experiment 2: Mean responses to *look* versus *touch* by sighted children

Behavior	Look	Touch	Total
Did differentiate	4.8	4.8	9.6
Manual			
Exploratory	0.0	0.3	0.3
Nonexploratory (contact)	0.8	3.5	4.3
Orients hands only	0.0	0.3	0.3
"Visual"			
Orients head only	2.5	0.0	2.5
Orients head plus hand movement	0.3	0.7	1.0
Makes analogy to vision	1.2	0.0	1.2
Did not differentiate	2.2	2.2	4.4
Total	7.0	7.0	14.0

to vision." Here they behaved as though the organ named could see (be used as a distance receptor), orienting that organ toward the object (e.g., bringing the foot close to but not touching the object). Finally, there was occasionally some additional activity accompanying the visual responses (orientation of eyes) whose sense we could not decipher: The child would orient the head as if to look at something but also, e.g., turn the head from side to side.

In sum, the sighted children understood *look* only when it could be interpreted as a visual experience. Since they were blindfolded in this experiment, they settled for orienting their covered eyes in the direction of the named object or (so it seemed to us), pretending that a named organ had grown an eye and orienting *this* in the direction of the named object. In contrast, they interpreted *touch* to mean "contact." Recall that Kelli also distinguished *look* from *touch* on a considerable number of commands. But her response to *look* was never a mere orientation of the named "sensor." Rather, when *look* and *touch* were differentiated, the former was most often interpreted as "explore" and the latter as "contact."

Our preliminary conclusion is that *look* is tied to the visual modality for the sighted children, while *touch* is interpreted as physical contact. For Kelli, too, *touch* implies physical contact. But from the evidence presented so far, one might suspect that for her *look* means "to perceive and apprehend, independent of modality." This interpretation would explain her responses to "look with the nose" as sniffing and "look with the mouth" as pretending to taste. It is important in this context to note that the sighted children's visual analogies were not at all like Kelli's responses to *look*. They did not seem to assume that the foot and nose could "look" in the sense that they are exploratory sensoria, albeit not really visual ones. Rather they seemed to assume that – given the bizarre situation – their feet or noses had grown an eye, which, hypothetically or metaphorically speaking, could look – visually, in the way the eye looks, by orienting the line of sight and perceiving at a distance.

But establishing the sense of these words for the blind and sighted children required further inquiry. We had to find out whether Kelli distinguished looking from other perceptions (such as listening), so as to determine whether the item *look* meant "apprehend by any modality," as just suggested, or was specific to the haptic modality. After all, only two of many commands suggested that *look* might for her have had an amodal interpretation. And we had to find out whether the sighted blindfolded children could be induced to "look" with their hands, in which case we might have to revise the conjecture that their use of the item *look* is specific to vision. . . .

What the Learner Brings to the Verb-Learning Task

Where is the learner to begin the quest for the relations between sound and meaning? We first review evidence concerning the knowledge that young learners bring into the task of learning verb meanings. (1) They seem to have at least rudimentary conceptual knowledge of the logical forms of sentences (predicate-argument structures) and are disposed to believe that nominals encode the arguments and verbs encode the predicates in such structures. (2) They can construct surface parses (phrase structural analyses) of the sentences they hear, which may serve as the representational formats on which detailed verb inductions are performed. The verb-learning scenario we shall try to defend depends on both these kinds of supposition about the child's initial state.

Initial conceptual representations

Conceptions underlying major form-class distinctions.   Many investigators (Slobin, 1981; Gentner, 1982; Braine and Hardy, 1982; Pinker, 1982, 1984; and many other sources) suggest that we must begin by granting two rather strong (and not so self-evident) conjectures to the learner. The first is that verbs encode actions and states, and the second is that nouns encode persons, places, and things. This claim is certainly not that these fourth-grade definitions of the syntactic classes describe mature language knowledge. It is rather that these are initial conjectures by means of which the child bootstraps his way toward the major lexical classes (formal distributional analysis later can add such nonactions as *seem* to the set of verbs and such nonthings as *justice* to the set of nouns; see Maratsos, 1982).[5]

A first indication of this distinction appears in the properties of the child's first rudimentary sentences (produced at about two years of age). These usually consist only of two words: a noun and a verb. As has been shown repeatedly, this noun and verb differ in their serial ordering in the young child's utterances in languages like English (Bloom, 1970; Brown, 1973; Slobin, 1973; Maratsos, 1982), or – in other languages – by the inflectional markers they select (e.g., Hebrew: see Levy, 1983b), or both (e.g., Serbo-Croatian: see Slobin, 1982).

Evidence that this noun/verb distinction comes in part from the child's preexisting biases about the nature of a language, rather than from transparent inductions over the input corpus, has been presented by Feldman, Goldin-Meadow, and Gleitman (1978; Goldin-Meadow, 1982), who studied deaf children of hearing parents who were not exposed to sign language and could not learn a spoken language owing to their deafness. As apparently often occurs with children in these circumstances, they developed manual communication systems (called "home sign" by the deaf community). Even in these informal and untutored systems, the investigators were able to show that nouns and verbs were distinguished both in their form (the kind of iconic gesture used) and in their syntactic organization (their position in gestured sentences).

We cannot say exactly how learners exposed to ordinary language data make the initial decision about which morphological items are to be the nouns (and thus encode the persons and objects) and which are to be the verbs (and thus encode the actions and states), but see Pinker, 1984, for discussion. Perhaps special properties of ostension and of the forms of maternal utterances (e.g., *That's* a man; he's *jumping*) can be shown to bear on this problem (Shipley, Kuhn, and Madden, 1983). But however it is accomplished, this partitioning of the lexical stock has already been made at the moment in development we are concerned with: when the child begins to determine the meanings of the various verbs.

The predicate-argument analysis of sentences.   Gleitman and Wanner have reviewed evidence showing that the young learner is predisposed to consider the sentence of English in terms of a predicate-argument logic in which the verb serves as the predicate itself and the various nominals surrounding it serve as its arguments. Evidence comes from an examination of young children's speech. At early stages of language learning, with only rare exceptions, each of the formatives (separate lexical items) in the child's speech encodes (a) a predicate, (b) an argument of that predicate, or (c) a logical word such as *not*. Words that serve other functions, such as auxiliary verbs, relativizers, determiners, and adjectives, are largely missing from speech during a lengthy period during development.

Most revealing, according to Gleitman and Wanner, it is occasionally true of language as used by mature individuals that some of these relational and logical items are conflated within a single formative. For instance, *not* is conflated within the subject NP for certain indefinite pronominals of standard English: We say "*No*body likes me," not "Anybody (or nobody) does *not* like me." But young children, including Kelli, resist such conflations, saying "Anybody can't see me now" or "Nobody don't like me" often despite strenuous attempts of their parents to correct them (McNeill, 1966; for further documentation, see Newport, 1982). Summarizing, the young learner seems to be predisposed to organize the sentence structure by uttering words that figure directly in the predicate-argument logic – the words that would be the heads of the semantically functioning phrases in adult well-formed sentences – omitting all else.

In addition, learners seem to know how many arguments a particular verb intent requires, without instruction (though they could not know their placement within syntactic structures, for this varies for the predicates of a single language and varies extensively across languages). One source of evidence is again the deaf isolates. Feldman et al. were able to show by a syntactic analysis of these children's gestured sentences that they conceived a single argument for a verb such as *sleep* (the experiencer of the action) and so used only a single nominal with this verb; but they conceived two arguments for *hit* (the agent and patient), providing it with two nominal phrases, and three arguments for *give* (agent, patient, recipient), providing it with three nominal phrases in their signed sentences. We shall assume that children exposed to ordinary language data have the same presuppositions: that the logic of a predicate such as *give* involves the one who gives, the one who is given, and the thing that is given, while *sleep* involves only its experiencer. It was shown that this analysis – at least for the common verbs of motion – can be constructed in terms of the positions and motions of objects relative to the learner's body (and can be mapped onto the linguistic formatives by attention to syntactic structure).

Which predicates are lexicalized?   Finally, the deaf subjects of Feldman et al. also document a point so self-evident that usually we do not notice that it *requires* documentation. Without formal linguistic exposure, children suppose that certain ideas are worth lexicalizing (e.g., "sleep," "hit", "give") while many others are not (e.g., the absurd and complex idea of "either singing or leaking out of containers", cf. Osherson, 1978). The topic of "natural" versus "absurd" lexical choices will concern us later. Here it suffices to point out that the learner must bring some such biases into the learning situation. As we have remarked before, only such presuppositions can ultimately account for why "head tilting" seems never to be considered as the construal for *look* – either for sighted children, who in principle could so encode each experience they have with this word, or for Kelli, who was deliberately tutored in this construal.

In particular, the analyses suggest some of the categories that are recruited in language learning. Kelli seems to have made use of the spatial locations and motions of objects in her environment as the experiental basis for reconstructing predicate-argument structures. If so, the tendency to observe the world according to the positions and motions of objects in space is part of the equipment the child (blind or sighted) brings into the learning situation. We pointed to experimental demonstrations of Kelli's spatial knowledge beginning earlier than any language knowledge (Landau et al., 1981, 1984) as support for the idea that even a blind child can encode her environment spatially.

Syntactic representations

We have attempted to show that the verbs cannot be individuated *solely* by inspecting the real-world situation that accompanies their use, even if it is granted that this situation is naturally conceived in ways relevant to the construction of predicate-argument logic. We proposed that acquisition of the meanings of verbs requires also that the learner make reference to a linguistic analysis of heard sentences, their parse structures. But if this is so, it must be that the child has access to this parse for the sake of learning, rather than arriving at this parse as the outcome of learning. A crucial question, then, is whether the learner has a basis for constructing the surface parse before the verbs are individuated and hence before the whole ball game is over. We presupposed this in Chapter 6, but we now present evidence that exists in its support.

Gleitman and Wanner reviewed evidence that phrase-structure analyses of heard sentences can be constructed by young learners on the basis of sentence prosody. Their initial information is derived in large from a bottom-up, perceptually automatic analysis of the speech wave in terms of the physical analysis underlying such segmental categories as *stressed syllable* and *lengthened syllable* and such suprasegmental categories as *rhythmicity* and *tone*. Syntactic as well as lexical factors influence the way these properties are manifested in the sound patterns of spoken sentences. For example, pauses and durational patterns (syllable length) in the wave form are fine-grained enough to pick out syntactic constituents and even to distinguish syntactic boundaries of varying strengths (Klatt, 1975, 1976; Liberman and Streeter, 1976; Nakatani and Dukes, 1977; Nakatani and Schaffer, 1978; Streeter, 1978; Cooper and Paccia-Cooper, 1980). These distinguishing physical properties can be expected to be even more obvious in maternal speech to young children, which is slower in overall rate and more exaggerated in prosodic contours (Fernald and Simon, 1984).

A significant body of evidence supports the idea that learners exploit these physical clues. Fernald (1982, 1984) has shown that infants prefer to listen to the exaggerated contours of Motherese (the special style characteristic of adult-to-child speech) rather than to adult-to-adult talk. Obviously this has nothing to do with the meaning of the Motherese discourse, for infants understand not a word of it. Spring and Dale (1977) have shown discrimination of linguistic stress in early infancy. Babbling in the prespeech period already shows language-specific choices among these categories (DeBoysson-Bardies, Sagart, and Durand, 1984). Early free speech (Gleitman and Wanner, 1982) and imitative speech (Blasdell and Jensen, 1970) reproduce the same salient properties of the wave form. Read and Schreiber (1982) among others have shown that older children can extract and report syntactic constituents (e.g., subject of the sentence) based on these prosodic cues. Finally, these generalizations about prosodic influences on language learning hold true across languages where the grammatical and semantic functions assigned by particular prosodic properties differ (Slobin, 1982; Pye, 1983; Mithun, forthcoming; and see Gleitman and Wanner for this analysis, based on the cross-linguistic evidence presented by the authors just cited).

Summary

Accepting the evidence just summarized, we suppose that children approach the problem of individuating the verb meanings armed with a vocabulary of simple concrete nouns, and at least rudimentary conceptual understanding of predicate-argument logic and its mapping onto the spatial properties of scenes. Learners also have biases about at least some simple predicates and substantives that are natural to lexicalize. Moreover, they can construct a surface parse of utterances heard and can place the verb within this parse on the prosodic evidence.

All this prior apparatus granted, we now return to the problem of how a child might learn which verbs encode which meanings. For after all, we have only reviewed evidence that on hearing "The ball rolls off the table" the child can parse it roughly as

$$_S(_{NP}(\text{the ball})_{VP}(_V(\text{rolls})_{PP}(\text{off}_{NP}(\text{the table}))))$$

How does she decide on the meaning of the verb?

Notes

1   The notation here adopted renders a number of distinctions we shall make throughout. An utterance of some word or sentence is rendered with double quotation marks ("dog"). Slash

marks indicate that the phonetic description of that word or sentence is intended (/dɔg/), while single quotes represent the idea, notion, or meaning of that word or sentence ("dog"). We use italics to represent mention of the word or sentence, considered as an abstract linguistic formative (*dog*). Of course no special notation is employed where a word or sentence is used as a straightforward referring expression, i.e., when the word is used to refer to some or all extensions of the term. The standard notation is used when unattested or anomalous sentences are mentioned: They are preceded by an asterisk, e.g., *House the is red*, or by a question mark if their acceptability is doubtful. Our phonetic transcriptions follow Ladefoged (1975), except that we render reduced vowels with a schwa /ə/.

2   What is worse, in the account just given we have underestimated the problem of lexical concept acquisition by restricting attention only to certain "reasonable" options for interpretation that the learner might entertain. But it seems that in principle a number of "unreasonable" options exist if the learner is unwary. Such philosophers as Quine (1960) and Goodman (1966) have pointed out the scope of problems for a truly ignorant and openminded observer trying to learn concepts and words by inspecting the information available in the ambiant environment. For example, on every occasion that an observer has positive evidence for having observed a cat (as someone points to a cat and says "cat"), he has just as good positive evidence that he has observed cat stages, or certain undetached parts of a cat or even something that is a cat until the year 2000, but will turn into a dog in the year 2001 (i.e., though observation may tell this learner that what is now visible is a cat, the observation itself says nothing about transformations this cat might undergo in future – maybe it will become a pillar of salt). There is always exactly as much positive evidence in the external world for each of these mad ideas as there is for the various nonabsurdities. But it is enough for us to consider the reasonable alternatives left open by particular experience to understand the difficulties in making good the claim (doubtless true) that learning word meanings occurs at least in part by inspecting the real world.

3   This problem is worse if the learner assumes that English, like Latin, allows free positioning of the thematic roles. Some limited freedom in this regard does exist even in English: One can say "This book collects dust" and "Dust collects on these books" or "This garden swarms with bees" and "Bees are swarming in this garden" to mean closely related things. Thus even the child learning a word-order language cannot be too secure in supposing that a stipulated phrasal position in a sentence is a good guide to its thematic role.

4   It is worth noting that the problem here posed for the investigator is just the problem we are posing for the child learners. Since they too are exposed not to sentence/meaning pairs, but only to utterance/event pairs, different for each learner and for the same learner on different exposures ("learning trials"), how do all of them use these different and indirect clues to reconstruct approximately the same word meanings? In short, how does the extralinguistic context help, since the context is not the meaning? Nonetheless, as the landmark work of Bloom (1970) showed, rich interpretation of the contexts accompanying the young child's language use does seem to provide a reliable data base for making inferences about linguistic intent. And of course, difficult as it is to state *how*, the young child's input of utterance/event pairs in practice does seem to provide a reliable data base for acquiring a grammar. Our aim is to make a contribution to the question of how this gets done in light of the logical difficulties we have reviewed.

5   Maratsos (1982) and Levy (1983a), discussing the German and Hebrew (nonnatural) gender systems, point out that very young children can extract form-class distinctions that are semantically incoherent. Nonetheless, we believe that the semantic bootstrapping hypothesis does much of the required work of getting the child into the language system.

References

Blasdell, R., and P. Jensen. 1970. Stress and word position as determinants of imitation in first language learners. *Journal of Speech and Hearing Research* 13, 193–202.

Bloom, L. 1970. *Language Development: Form and Function in Emerging Grammars*. Cambridge, Mass.: MIT Press.

Braine, M. D. S., and J. A. Hardy. 1982. On what case categories there are, why they are, and how they develop: an amalgam of *a priori* considerations, speculations, and evidence from children. In E. Wanner and L. R. Gleitman (eds.), *Language Acquisition: The State of the Art*. New York: Cambridge University Press, pp. 219–39.

Brown, R. 1973. *A First Language: The Early Stages*. Cambridge, Mass.: Harvard University Press.

Cooper, W. E., and J. Paccia-Cooper. 1980. *Syntax and Speech*. Cambridge, Mass.: Harvard University Press.

DeBoysson-Bardies, B., L. Sagart, and C. Durand. 1984. Discernible differences in the babbling of infants according to target language. *Journal of Child Language* 11, 1–15.

Feldman, H., S. Goldin-Meadow, and L. R. Gleitman. 1978. Beyond Herodotus: the creation of language by linguistically deprived deaf children. In A. Lock (ed.), *Action, Gesture, and Symbol: The Emergence of Language*. New York: Academic Press, pp. 351–414.

Fernald, A. 1982. Acoustic determinants of initial preference for "Motherese." Ph.D. dissertation, University of Oregon.

Fernald, A. 1984. The perceptual and affective salience of mothers' speech to infants. In L. Feagans, C. Garvey, and R. Golinkoff (eds.), *The Origins and Growth of Communication*. New Brunswick, NJ: Ablex, pp. 5–29.

Fernald, A., and T. Simon. 1984. Expanded intonation contours in mothers' speech to newborns. *Developmental Psychology* 20, 104–13.

Gentner, D. 1982. Why nouns are learned before verbs: linguistic relativity vs. natural partitioning. In S. Kuczaj (ed.), *Language Development: Language, Culture, and Cognition*. Hillsdale, NJ: Erlbaum, pp. 301–34.

Gleitman, L. R., and E. Wanner. 1982. Language acquisition: the state of the state of the art. In E. Wanner and L. R. Gleitman (eds.), *Language Acquisition: The State of the Art*. New York: Cambridge University Press, pp. 3–48.

Gleitman, L. R., and E. Wanner. 1984. Current issues in language learning. In M. H. Bornstein and M. E. Lamb (eds.), *Developmental Psychology: An Advanced Textbook*. Hillsdale, NJ: Erlbaum.

Goldin-Meadow, S. 1982. The resilience of recursion: a study of a communication system developed without a conventional language model. In E. Wanner and L. R. Gleitman (eds.), *Language Acquisition: The State of the Art*. New York: Cambridge University Press, pp. 51–77.

Goodman, N. 1966. *The Structure of Appearance*, 2nd edn. Indianapolis: Bobbs-Merrill.

Klatt, D. H. 1975. Vowel lengthening is syntactically determined in a connected discourse. *Journal of Phonetics* 3, 229–40.

Klatt, D. H. 1976. Linguistic uses of segmental duration in English: acoustic and perceptual evidence. *Journal of the Acoustic Society of America* 59, 1208–21.

Ladefoged, P. 1975. *A Course in Phonetics*. New York: Harcourt Brace Jovanovich.

Landau, B., H. Gleitman, and E. S. Spelke. 1981. Spatial knowledge and geometric representation in a child blind from birth. *Science* 213, 1275–8.

Landau, B., E. S. Spelke, and H. Gleitman. 1984. Spatial knowledge in a young blind child. *Cognition* 16:3, 225–60.

Lenneberg, E. H. 1967. *Biological Foundations of Language*. New York: Wiley.

Levy, Y. 1983a. It's frogs all the way down. *Cognition* 15, 75–93.

Levy, Y. 1983b. The acquisition of Hebrew plurals: the case of the missing gender category. *Journal of Child Language* 10, 107–21.

Liberman, M., and L. Streeter. 1976. List of nonsense syllable mimicry in the study of prosodic phenomena. Paper delivered at Acoustical Society of America meeting, San Diego.

McNeill, D. 1966. The creation of language by children. In J. Lyons and R. Wales (eds.), *Psycholinguistics Papers*. Edinburgh: Edinburgh University Press, pp. 99–115.

Maratsos, M. 1982. The child's construction of grammatical categories. In E. Wanner and L. R. Gleitman (eds.), *Language Acquisition: The State of the Art*. New York: Cambridge University Press, pp. 240–66.

Mithun, M. 1982. The acquisition of polysynthesis. [Manuscript cited in A. Peters, 1984.]

Nakatani, L., and K. Dukes. 1977. Locus of segmental cues for word juncture. *Journal of the Acoustic Society of America* 62:3, 714–24.

Nakatani, L., and J. Schaffer. 1978. Hearing "words" without words: prosodic cues for word perception. *Journal of the Acoustic Society of America* 63:1, 234–45.

Newport, E. L. 1982. Task specificity in language learning? Evidence from speech perception and American Sign Language. In E. Wanner and L. R. Gleitman (eds.), *Language Acquisition: The State of the Art*. New York: Cambridge University Press, pp. 450–80.

Osherson, O. 1978. Three conditions on conceptual naturalness. *Cognition* 6:4, 263–90.

Peters, A. 1984. Speech delivered at the Graduate School of Education, University of Pennsylvania.

Pinker, S. 1982. A theory of the acquisition of lexical interpretive grammars. In J. Bresnan (ed.), *The Mental Representation of Grammatical Relations*. Cambridge, Mass.: MIT Press, pp. 53–63.

Pinker, S. 1984. *Language Learnability and Language Development*. Cambridge, Mass.: Harvard University Press.

Pye, C. 1983. Mayan telegraphese. *Language* 59:3, 583–604.

Quine, W. V. 1960. *Word and Object*. Cambridge, Mass.: MIT Press.

Read, C., and P. Schreiber. 1982. Why short subjects are harder to find than long ones. In E. Wanner and L. R. Gleitman (eds.), *Language Acquisition: The State of the Art*. New York: Cambridge University Press, pp. 78–101.

Shipley, E. F., I. F. Kuhn, and E. C. Madden. 1983. Mothers' use of superordinate terms. *Journal of Child Language* 10:3, 571–88.

Slobin, D. I. 1973. Cognitive prerequisites for the development of grammar. In C. A. Ferguson and D. I. Slobin (eds.), *Studies of Child Language Development*. New York: Holt, Rinehart, and Winston, pp. 175–208.

Slobin, D. I. 1981. The origins of grammatical encoding of events. In W. Deutsch (ed.), *The Child's Construction of Language*. New York: Academic Press.

Slobin, D. I. 1982. Universal and particular in the acquisition of language. In E. Wanner and L. R. Gleitman (eds.), *Language Acquisition: The State of the Art*. New York: Cambridge University Press, pp. 128–70.

Spring, D. R., and P. S. Dale. 1977. Discrimination of linguistic stress in early infancy. *Journal of Speech and Hearing Research* 20, 224–31.

Streeter, L. A. 1978. Acoustic determinants of phrase boundary perception. *Journal of the Acoustic Society of America* 64, 1582–92.

14

The Semantic Bootstrapping Hypothesis

Steven Pinker

Grimshaw (1981), as well as Macnamara (1982), proposes a solution to the bootstrapping problem. Although grammatical entities do not have semantic definitions in adult grammars, it is possible that such entities refer to identifiable semantic classes in parent-child discourse. That is, it is plausible that, when speaking to infants, parents refer to people and physical objects using nouns, that they refer to physical actions and changes of state using verbs, that they communicate definiteness using determiners, and so on. In addition, propositions with action predicates involving the semantic relations agent-of-action and patient-of-action may be expressed using the grammatical relations SUBJ and OBJ. Presumably, such notions as physical object, physical action, agent-of-action, and so on, unlike nounhood, verbhood, and subjecthood, are available to the child perceptually and are elements of the semantic representation that I proposed as part of the input to the language acquisition mechanisms. If the child tentatively assumes these syntax-semantics correspondences to hold, and if they do hold, he or she can make the correct inferences in the example. The categorization of words can be inferred from their semantic properties, and their grammatical relations can be inferred from the semantic relations in the event witnessed. Together with the schemata in (5) this uniquely determines the correct phrase structure tree shown in Figure 14.1 and the rules and lexical entries of (7).

(7) $S \rightarrow NP_{SUBJ} \; VP$
     $NP \rightarrow det \; N$
     $VP \rightarrow V \; NP_{OBJ}$

   the: det
   boy: N
   threw: V
   rocks: N

From *Language Learnability and Language Development*. Cambridge, Mass.: Harvard University Press, 1984, pp. 39–47. ©1984 by the President and Fellows of Harvard College. Reprinted by permission of the publisher.

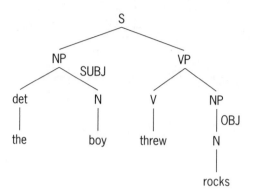

Figure 14.1

The hypothesis that the child initially uses semantic notions as evidence for the presence of grammatical entities in the input was called the "semantic bootstrapping hypothesis" in Pinker (1982), and was based on Grimshaw's (1981) proposal that syntactic entities are "canonical structural realizations" of semantic entities and Macnamara's (1982) similar proposal that object, action, and attribute are the "inductive bases" for noun, verb, and adjective. According to the version of the hypothesis I am advancing, the child assumes that the correspondences shown in Table 14.1 hold in the linguistic input.

Structure-dependent distributional learning

Of course, the child can only get so far with semantic bootstrapping, since many nouns do not refer to objects (e.g., *the flight of the bird*), many subjects do not denote agents of actions (e.g., *John sustained an injury; John received a parcel*), and so on. Grimshaw and Macnamara propose that once a basic scaffolding of semantically induced rules and lexical items is in place, the semantically neutral items and rules can be learned by observing their distribution within the known structures. For example, for the sentence *the situation justified extreme measures*, the child could inspect the grammatical rules in (7) induced from the sentence shown in Figure 14.1. Those rules state that *the* is a determiner, that determiners are only introduced by the phrase structure rule NP → det N, that sentences begin with an NP, and that therefore *situation*, the word following *the* within the NP, must be a noun. Similarly, the phrase *the situation* could be recognized as the subject of the sentence and *justified* as its verb, thanks to the rule S → NP$_{\text{SUBJ}}$ VP in the grammar, in turn leading the child to conclude that *justified* uses the function SUBJ to express one of its arguments. Affixes, once they are learned, can also be used to identify syntactic categories – for example, if the past tense marker *-ed* had been identified from semantically transparent cases similar to that shown in Figure 14.1, it too could be used to identify the verbhood of the word *justified*. This process may be called *structure-dependent distributional learning*, "structure-dependent" because it is the distribution of words within constituent or inflectional structures already acquired that triggers learning. This is in contrast to learning procedures based on the distribution of entities in particular serial positions or in particular adjacency or co-occurrence relations with other words (see Pinker, 1979, for discussion).

Table 14.1[*]

Grammatical element	Semantic inductive basis[1]
	SYNTACTIC CATEGORIES
Noun	Name of person or thing
Verb	Action or change of state
Adjective	Attribute
Preposition	Spatial relation, path, or direction
Sentence	Main proposition
	GRAMMATICAL FUNCTIONS
Subject	Agent of action; cause of causal event; subject of an attribution of location, state, or circumstance; argument with "autonomous reference"
Object and Object2	Patient or theme
Oblique	Source, goal, location, instrument
Complement	Proposition serving as an argument within another proposition
Topic	Discourse topic distinct from the arguments of the main predicate[2]
Focus	Discourse focus
	CASES[3]
Nominative or Ergative	Agent of transitive action
Accusative or Absolutive	Patient of transitive action
Nominative or Absolutive	Actor of intransitive action
Dative	Goal or beneficiary
Instrumental	Instrument
Etc.	
	GRAMMATICAL FEATURES
Tense	Relative times of event, speech act, and reference point
Aspect	Durativity
Number	Number
Human	Humanness
Animate	Animacy
Etc.	
	TREE CONFIGURATIONS
Sister of X	Argument of X
Sister of X′ (Aunt of X)	Restrictive modifier of X
Sister of X″ (Great-aunt of X)	Nonrestrictive modifier of X

The hypothesis that the child's learning strategies use a combination of semantic bootstrapping and distributional learning is subtle and controversial, and hence deserves further amplification. In particular, I will address these questions: What exactly is being claimed, anyway? Is the claim viable? What are the alternatives? What is the relevant evidence?

The Logical Status of the Semantic Bootstrapping Hypothesis

Let me begin by pointing out what the semantic bootstrapping hypothesis does not claim. It does not claim that the young child lacks formal categories, or that his or her initial categories are organized around or defined by semantic criteria. Rather, the hypothesis presupposes that the child uses formal categories at all stages, and is intended to explain how the child knows *which* formal categories to posit in response to particular input sequences. Second, it does not claim that children fail to perform distributional analyses or that they allow semantically based analyses to override distributionally based analyses. Rather, it claims that children always give priority to distributionally based analyses, and is intended to explain how the child knows *which* distributional contexts are the relevant ones to examine. In the rest of the chapter, I will spell out these points in detail.

First of all, what does it mean to say that the child has a procedure to recognize antecedently specified formal categories and relations like "nouns" and "subjects"? "Noun" is, after all, just the name for a symbol, and according to the computational theory of cognition the only significance of the name of a symbol in a cognitive account is that the process that manipulates such symbols treats all the symbols with a given name alike but differently from symbols with different names. Thus, if one replaced the symbols *noun, verb, noun phrase*, and *verb phrase* by *Ethel, Fred, Ethel phrase*, and *Fred phrase* everywhere in the adult grammar and processor, the Ethel-Fred grammar would be indistinguishable from the noun-verb grammar. Why worry, then, about how the child learns "nouns" when all he or she really needs to do is learn discriminable symbols?

The answer is that in using a single name to refer to symbols in grammars for different languages, one is committing oneself to the hypothesis that there exist symbols with universal properties across languages. On pain of circularity, this hypothesis must be translated into the hypothesis that certain phenomena tend to be correlated with one another across languages, the names themselves merely denoting the symbols that enter into the correlated set of phenomena. The correlations need not be perfect, and it is not strictly necessary for there to be some subset of phenomena that invariably accompany the symbol; a family resemblance structure will suffice to give meaning to the concept of a universal grammatical symbol.

The concept of "subject" can illustrate this point. In LFG, SUBJ is a symbol referring to (a) the agentive argument of active action predicates; (b) the noun phrase position that is usually the leftmost NP daughter of S; (c) the argument of an embedded complement that may be unexpressed and controlled by an argument of the matrix predicate; (d) the matrix argument that controls an unexpressed complement subject when there is no matrix object present; (e) the argument in active clauses receiving either nominative or ergative case marking in two-place predicates and nominative or absolutive case marking in one-place predicates; (f) the function that objects assume during passivization; (g) the function that becomes oblique during passivization; (h) the function not permitted in the phrase structure rules expanding VP, AP, and nonpredicative NP and PP; (i) the function that can be unexpressed and controlled in an adjunct (this is distinct from (c), which refers to complements as opposed to adjuncts – see Bresnan, 1982a); (j) one of the functions that may be controlled anaphorically (this is distinct from

(c) and (i), which refer to functional as opposed to anaphoric control); (k) the specific function whose binding is determined by principles of "obviation" in anaphoric control; (l) the label for one of the set of constituent positions whose grammatical features may be encoded in agreement affixes on verbs. This list could be extended by including several other phenomena such as those involving bounding nodes, reflexives and reciprocals, ellipsis, and other lexical rules. (Many of these conditions are imperfectly stated, and many are probable but not necessary in a given language. See Bresnan, 1982a, b, for further details about these conditions, and Keenan, 1976, for a similar list that is less formal but more firmly grounded in research on linguistic diversity.)

When a linguist examining a particular language uses the term SUBJ, then, to refer to an element in a rule accounting for one of the phenomena in a family resemblance structure such as (a)–(l), he or she is making the empirical prediction that the element so labeled should enter into the remaining phenomena in (a)–(l) (some necessarily, others probabilistically). The use of the term SUBJ in rules for different languages is identical to the hypothesis that (a)–(l) are universally correlated. Such a correlation is unlikely to arise again and again in historically unrelated languages unless there was some property of the minds of speakers of those languages that caused one of the correlated properties to trigger the rest. Thus, the universal correlations in (a)–(l) suggest that the symbols labeled SUBJ which one attributes to the minds of speakers of different languages are in some sense of the same psychological kind.[4] How the child identifies exemplars of that kind in the linguistic input then becomes a meaningful psychological question.

The semantic bootstrapping hypothesis, as it applies to subjects, amounts to the claim that (1) the child uses phenomenon (a) to label certain entities as SUBJs in the first rules he or she coins; (2) thereafter he or she expects the entities labeled SUBJ in those rules to enter into phenomena (b)–(l) as well; and thus (3) those entities are subject, without further learning, to any of the conditions in (b)–(l) that are universally true; and (4) the child fixes the parameters of those phenomena in (b)–(l) that admit of cross-linguistic variation by checking the input for a restricted set of properties of the SUBJ-labeled entities, and a restricted set of co-occurrence relations between the SUBJ-labeled entities and certain other entities. In other words, the child is spared from having to record all perceptible properties and correlations involving the input elements; thanks to having identified certain universal symbols, he or she can exploit formal and substantive linguistic universals to focus the learning process upon those properties and correlations that define differences among languages. Another way of putting it is that the child exploits the "rich deductive structure" (Chomsky, 1981) inherent in the family resemblance correlations defining substantive universals, and at the very start he or she uses the semantically transparent members of the family as the first "premises" of the deductions.

To extend this argument to some other grammatical symbol, it is necessary to show that (1) the symbol enters into a set of phenomena that are universally correlated, analogous to (a)–(l) above (if this is not true, then linguists' use of that same symbol in rules for different languages would be theoretically meaningless, if not downright misleading, see Steele, 1981); (2) one of those phenomena must include some notion that is perceptually available to the child in the semantic portion of his or her input (analogous to (a) above); and (3) when parents express that notion in their speech to the child, they must use the symbol in question (though this need not be true of adult-to-adult discourse). If these conditions are true, then the semantic bootstrapping hypothesis can be applied to the problem of how rules incorporating that symbol are first acquired: the child can use the phenomenon that includes the perceptually available notion as the inductive basis for the symbol in question, expecting the rest of the phenomena involving that symbol to follow (as before, subject to parametric variation).

Do the necessary correlations exist? Of course, if there are no true substantive universals – that is, no family resemblance structures involving collections of semantic and formal phenomena – then the semantic bootstrapping hypothesis cannot be true. Jane Grimshaw (personal communication) points out that there is a great deal of indirect and informal evidence for such substantive universals implicit in the practice of comparative linguists. Grimshaw points out that linguists often do not apply formal tests involving the universally valid earmarks of a category when assigning words to syntactic categories in a newly studied language. For example, even if it is true that the best diagnostic of nounhood is strictly formal, such as that complex phrases headed by nouns cannot be extracted from, comparative linguists do not generally test for extractability from various constituents before deciding whether to call the head of such a constituent a noun. Rather, they use semantic notions as their first hypothesis about the category membership of an unknown word: for example, if a word is a proper name, they call it a noun. All this is unexceptional. But what is interesting is that such a strategy rarely leads to trouble. Linguists seldom have to recategorize large sets of words after examining other phenomena in the language; for example, there do not seem to be languages in which the extraction phenomena associated with noun phrases in English pertain to action words but not names. To the extent that semantically inspired categorization of common word types (e.g., those likely to be used in parent-child discourse) does not lead to descriptive crises for the linguist, it is not unreasonable to assume that the child, too, can safely begin by categorizing words in this way.

There are also more systematic studies of substantive universals. Names for individual things and people are almost always nouns (Gleason, 1961; Greenberg, 1963; Macnamara, 1982).[5] Auxiliaries have the semantic property of designating sentence modality, tense, aspect, epistemic status, and modal concepts such as necessity, possibility, impossibility, and the like; this semantic property correlates universally with the syntactic and morphological privileges of auxiliaries, such as appearing in designated phrase structure positions, lacking productive morphology, being contractible, constituting a closed class, and signaling sentence modality by virtue of the positions they appear in (Steele, 1981). And subjects, as mentioned, have the semantic properties of designating agents of actions, causes of causal sequences, subjects of an attribution, autonomous reference, and definiteness, together with their formal properties of occurring to the left of the object, being unexpressed in complements, easily taking zero case marking, and so on (Keenan, 1976).[6]

One must place an important proviso, however, on the use of semantic information to infer the presence of syntactic symbols, especially grammatical relations. Keenan argues that the semantic properties of subjecthood hold only in what he calls "basic sentences": roughly, those that are simple, active, affirmative, declarative, pragmatically neutral, and minimally presuppositional. In nonbasic sentences, these properties may not hold. In English passives, for example, agents can be oblique objects and patients subjects, and in stylistically varied or contextually dependent sentences the agent can be found in nonsubject positions (e.g., *eats a lot of pizza, that guy*). Thus one must have the child not draw conclusions about grammatical relations from nonbasic sentences. This could be done in two ways: the parents or caretakers might filter out nonbasic sentences from their speech when they talk to infants, or the child might filter out nonbasic sentences from the input using various contextual or phonological diagnostics of nonbasicness such as special intonation, extra marking on the verb, presuppositions set up by the preceding discourse or the context, nonlinguistic signals of the interrogative or negative illocutionary force of an utterance, and so on. (Sentences perceived to be nonbasic need not be filtered out altogether, of course; the child can use them to learn aspects of grammar that are not sensitive to basicness such as the internal structure of noun phrases, while denying those inputs access to the mechanisms that learn about grammatical relations). Later in the chapter I will discuss some evidence pertaining to the speech of adults to children; I know of no research directly addressed to the question of whether children can reliably perceive the nonlinguistic correlates of basicness in Keenan's sense (though see Hoff-Ginsberg and Shatz, 1982). My guess is that both types of filtering are at work; but in any case it is important to point out that a viable version of the semantic bootstrapping hypothesis requires that the semantically driven inferences occur only on the inputs that pass through such filters, given what we know about the nature of the linguistic universals pertaining to subjects.

Notes

1   I beg the thorny question as to the proper definition of the various semantic terms I appeal to such as "agent," "physical object," and the like. All that is required for this account is that (a) there exists a definition of these notions as they enter into the perceptual and cognitive world of the child, regardless of whether such a definition is inadequate for these notions as adults understand them, and (b) the child is equipped with recognition procedures for the referents of these notions. (More specifically, the referents picked out by the child's recognition procedures should constitute a subset of those picked out by the adult definition of the relevant semantic notion. Thus the theory is compatible with Huttenlocher et al.'s findings (1983) that infants may restrict their use of subjects to themselves when they are agents of self-initiated actions, rather than to agents in general.)

2   Li and Thompson (1976) point out that in virtually every language in which the function TOPIC plays a prominent role, there exist "double subject" sentences containing distinct subject and topic constituents. Thus the child could use the presence of a topic that does not have any of the correlates of subjecthood as evidence that the target language defines a distinct topic constituent. This strategy would prevent him or her from being confused by non-topic-prominent languages, in which the discourse topic might be identifiable from context but it does not receive any special encoding within the grammar.

3   I assume that the child eventually chooses either the pair nominative/accusative or the pair ergative/absolutive, by noticing whether the case marker for the intransitive actor is identical to the marker for the transitive agent (in which case nominative/accusative will be chosen) or to the marker for the transitive patient (in which case ergative/absolutive will be chosen). An alternative would be to have only two possible cases: ergative, for subjects of transitives, and accusative, for objects of transitives; subjects of intransitives would be assigned accusative or ergative case depending on whether their markers were phonologically identical to one or another.

4   One might wonder why the existence of a correlated set of linguistic phenomena justifies posit-
ing a single symbol that enters into each phenomenon. Why not instead simply list each entity
(word or phrase) that enters into each of the phenomena, and let the pattern of correlation
itself symbolize the regularities, rather than a symbol which has no meaning other than its
behavior in the set of correlated phenomena to begin with (e.g., as in Maratsos and Chalkley,
1981)? The answer is that there is a principle of computational efficiency that Marr and Nishihara
(1978) call the Principle of Explicit Naming: when a particular data structure must be referred
to often, or by a wide range of processes, that data structure should be given an explicit label.
As it applies to grammatical symbols, this principle affords a gain in efficiency in the following way. If there were no symbol for "subject," for example, then the phenomena in (a)–(l)
would have to be listed separately for each predicate that has a subject argument. If there are
m subject phenomena and n predicates, the grammar would need mn rules. On the other hand,
if the grammar were allowed to state that the n individual predicates took SUBJ arguments,
and that the m phenomena pertained to SUBJs, it would need only $m + n$ rules. Thus we
have a reduction from multiplicative to additive complexity.

5   The following fact has been pointed out to me as a possible counterexample to these generalizations. Verbs in American Indian languages such as Navajo and Cherokee contain a great
deal of information about the objects serving as their arguments. For example, a verb might
encode whether the object is long, flat, or solid and whether it is rigid or flexible. Perhaps,
then, the child would mistakenly categorize such verbs as nouns under the semantic bootstrapping hypothesis. In fact, this is unlikely. These phenomena are not significantly different in a formal sense from English number agreement; they do not constitute cases of a verb
being a *name* for an object. The verb retains the same stem and refers to the same action regardless of the nature of its arguments; the markers for object properties take on different forms
and appear in different positions within the word depending on which semantic roles their
referents are playing with respect to the verb; and the markers are not used with particular
basic level objects but with any object in a much more inclusive class defined by the relevant
set of features. These are properties that any viable theory of name learning would have to
be sensitive to.

6   The semantic bootstrapping hypothesis is not logically tied to any single formulation of
substantive universals (for example, see Marantz, 1982, for a universal theory of grammatical
relations different from Keenan's). The hypothesis would have to be fleshed out in a different
way, but not abandoned, should it turn out that logical subjecthood, for instance, is a better
semantic inductive basis for grammatical subjecthood than is agenthood. If it should turn out
that there are no independent grammatical consequences of something being a subject at all,
then the semantic bootstrapping hypothesis would be irrelevant to the acquisition of subjects,
though it could be relevant to the identification of other universal symbols, such as those
for syntactic categories. The semantic bootstrapping hypothesis would be made totally dis-
pensable if there were *no* substantive universals, or no substantive universals with reliable
semantic inductive bases, or if all substantive universals had perceptual inductive bases other
than semantic ones (e.g., serial position, phonological properties).

References

Bresnan, J. 1982a. Control and complementation. In J. Bresnan (ed.), *The Mental Representation
of Grammatical Relations.* Cambridge, Mass.: MIT Press.

Bresnan, J. (ed.) 1982b. *The Mental Representation of Grammatical Relations.* Cambridge, Mass.:
MIT Press.

Chomsky, N. 1981. *Lectures on Government and Binding*. Dordrecht: Foris.

Gleason, H. A. 1961. *An Introduction to Descriptive Linguistics*, rev. edn. New York: Holt, Rinehart, and Winston.

Greenberg, J. H. 1963. Some universals of grammar with particular reference to the order of meaningful elements. In J. H. Greenberg (ed.), *Universals of Language*. Cambridge, Mass.: MIT Press, pp. 73–113.

Grimshaw, J. 1981. Form, function, and the language acquisition device. In C. L. Baker and J. J. McCarthy (eds.), *The Logical Problem of Language Acquisition*. Cambridge, Mass.: MIT Press, pp. 165–82.

Hoff-Ginsberg, E., and M. Shatz. 1982. Linguistic input and the child's acquisition of language. *Psychological Bulletin* 92, 3–26.

Huttenlocher, J., P. Smiley, and R. Charney. 1983. Emergence of action categories in the child: evidence from verb meanings. *Psychological Review* 90, 72–93.

Keenan, E. O. 1976. Towards a universal definition of "subject." In C. Li (ed.), *Subject and Topic*. New York: Academic Press, pp. 303–33.

Li, C., and S. A. Thompson. 1976. Subject and topic: a new typology of language. In C. Li (ed.), *Subject and Topic*. New York: Academic Press, pp. 457–89.

Macnamara, J. 1982. *Names for Things: A Study of Child Language*. Cambridge, Mass.: Bradford Books/MIT Press.

Marantz, A. 1982. On the acquisition of grammatical relations. *Linguistische Berichte: Linguistik als Kognitive Wissenschaft* 80/82, 32–69.

Maratsos, M. P., and M. Chalkley. 1981. The internal language of children's syntax: the ontogenesis and representation of syntactic categories. In K. Nelson (ed.), *Children's Language*, vol. 2. New York: Gardner Press.

Marr, D., and H. K. Nishihara. 1978. Representation and recognition of the spatial organization of three-dimensional shapes. *Proceedings of the Royal Society of London* 200, 269–94.

Pinker, S. 1979. Formal models of language learning. *Cognition* 1, 217–83.

Pinker, S. 1982. A theory of the acquisition of lexical interpretive grammars. In J. Bresnan (ed.), *The Mental Representation of Grammatical Relations*. Cambridge, Mass.: MIT Press, pp. 53–63.

Steele, S. (with A. Akmajian, R. Demers, E. Jelinek, C. Kitagawa, R. Oehrle, and T. Wasow). 1981. *An Encyclopedia of AUX: A Study of Cross-linguistic Equivalence*. Cambridge, Mass.: MIT Press.

15

Implications for the Semantic Bootstrapping Hypothesis

Steven Pinker

It is widely recognized both that syntax is correlated with semantics and that syntax is not reducible to semantics. In other work I have used this observation to try to explain a fundamental problem in language acquisition: how the child uses perceptual input (sounds and situations) to hypothesize grammatical structures (grammatical categories and relations, phrase structures, lexical entries) at the outset of the language acquisition process (Pinker, 1982, 1984, 1987). The suggestion is that children innately expect syntax and semantics to be correlated in certain ways in the speech that they attend to, can derive the semantic representation by nongrammatical means (attending to the situation, making inferences from the meanings of individually acquired words), and can thereby do a preliminary syntactic analysis of the first parental utterances they process. For example, if children know that a word refers to a thing, they can infer that it is a noun; if they know that X is a predicate and Y is its argument, they can infer that X is the head of a phrase that includes Y; if they know that a phrase is playing the role of agent, they can infer that it is the subject of the clause. With some grammatical rules under their belts, children would now be equipped to handle sentences violating these correlations as they start to be relaxed in the input speech they process (e.g., passives, where the subject is not an agent, or deverbal nouns, which do not refer to things). They can do this by classifying these nonbasic words in terms of their distribution within the grammatical structures that they are now capable of analyzing. For example, a child could now infer that Z must be a noun because it is in a noun position.

Some version of this "semantic bootstrapping hypothesis" appears to be helpful in explaining how language acquisition gets started, but it is not without problems (see Pinker, 1987, for discussion). First, like most explicit theories of language acquisition (see Pinker, 1979), it assumes that children can accurately encode from context the adult's intended meaning. Second, if the correlations between syntax and semantics are not universal, we need a special explanation for how children learn languages that violate them. Third, if the correlations are only probabilistic even in the most cooperative of languages, we

From *Learnability and Cognition: The Acquisition of Argument Structure*. Cambridge, Mass.: MIT Press, 1989, pp. 360–4. © 1989 by the MIT Press.

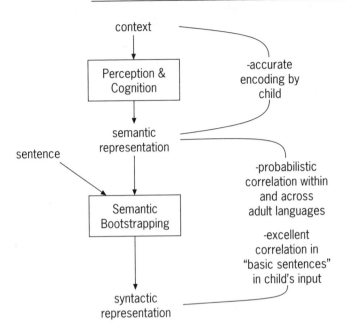

Figure 15.1

need to assume either that parents filter the noncorrelated structures (passives, deverbal nouns, etc.) out of their own speech, or that children can filter them out of parents' speech using some independent criterion such as complexity or nonstandard illocutionary force. These are strong assumptions.

In constructing the semantic bootstrapping hypothesis, I pretty much equated semantic structures with conceptual structures. This was an expedient step because I was trying to show how language acquisition got started, and so I could only allow input information that the child could possess before he or she knew a thing about the particular target language. The flow of information, and idealized assumptions about the correspondences between structures, are shown in Figure 15.1.

However, the argument I just provided for the autonomy of semantics changes the picture somewhat, making it simpler in one way and more complex in another. Since semantic representations are linguistic representations that are partially specific to a language, they cannot be inferred from context before language acquisition has started. Rather, it must be a separate conceptual structure that is created from context. The assumption that children can accurately encode the meaning of an input sentence from context would be replaced by two assumptions. First, there is the innocuous assumption that children's perceptual and cognitive mechanisms are enough like adults' (at least in situations in which they interact with their parents) that they construe the world in pretty much the same way that the adults speaking to them do. Second, there is a somewhat stronger assumption: that in parent-to-child speech, the parent uses words whose semantic representations correspond closely to the child's conceptual representation for that situation, so that event-category labeling and analogous processes for other grammatical entities will generally be accurate. Something like that assumption was behind the success of

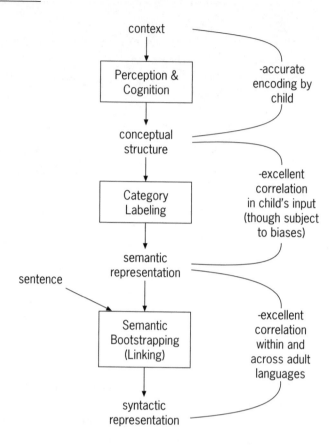

Figure 15.2

the Gropen et al. experiments in which we were able to predict (on fairly common-sense assumptions about distinctiveness) that children would set up the semantic representation for one event in terms of a state change and the semantic representation for another as a kind of motion, even though logically either encoding would have been possible for either event. Then semantic bootstrapping can take place, using syntax-semantics correspondences like the linking rules invoked throughout this book. The new picture is shown in Figure 15.2.

This new picture is more complicated in that it involves one extra link in the chain between perceptual input and grammatical output, and hence one more thing that can go wrong. However, its linguistic and psychological assumptions are simpler and more reasonable. First, the correspondences between syntax and semantics are no longer probabilistic correlations that the child exploits heuristically. Rather, they are the product of formal grammatical linking principles that may be universal and exceptionless (except for rare adjustments like those in syntactically ergative languages). This comes at the cost, of course, of making the semantic representations more abstract and language-particular and much more loosely tied to conceptual categories. Second, the assumptions about the child's effective input (or "intake," as it is sometimes called) are different: rather than parents having to use only syntactic structures that respect syntax-semantics correlations (or the child having to filter out the violations that slip through), the parents would have to use only semantic structures that correspond to the child's conceptual encoding of the situation. Though in many individual cases the assumptions would be equivalent, the revised picture is more plausible on the whole. Heuristic correlations between perceptually derivable conceptual/semantic categories and syntax are both undesirable formally and difficult to defend empirically, compared to linking regularities between syntax and an abstract semantics. (See Langacker, 1987, for an extensive attempt to link syntax to semantic categories that are highly abstract yet potentially interfaceable with nonlinguistic conceptual structure.) Furthermore, it is easier to swallow the psychological assumption that parents use words and constructions that they think their children will understand in the same way they do than that they use words and constructions that belong to a specially well-behaved subset of grammar. In fact, a main defense of the earlier version of the bootstrapping hypothesis was the hope that in many cases these two assumptions would be identical; it is clearly the former assumption that is the untendentious one.

In concrete terms, the difference would run as follows. In the simplified two-box version in Figure 15.1, the child assumed that agents of physical actions were subjects, and parents avoided sentences in which agents of physical actions weren't subjects (e.g., passives). In the more realistic three-box version in Figure 15.2, the child assumes that the first argument of an ACT semantic structure, or the first argument of a BE structure if there is no ACT structure, is a subject, and parents avoid sentences in which the child would not be likely to construe the meaning as involving an ACT or BE relation (thus they would be free to use passives in contexts in which the child was likely to realize that something was being predicated of the patient). Similarly, in the older view, the child would assume that patients of physical motion were objects, and parents would have to avoid verbs like *fill* where that is not true. In the newer view, children would assume that entities serving as the second argument of ACT and the first argument of GO were objects, and parents would have to avoid verbs whose objects were not motional patients only if the child would fail to construe that situation as involving a change of state of the motional goal. Again, note that the Gropen et al. experiments suggest that children's construals of such events can be fairly predictable by adults.

In sum, an autonomous semantics separate from conceptual structure allows the acquisition theorist to continue to exploit a correlation between syntax and the child's conception of the world, but to break up that correlation into a formal and nearly exceptionless grammatical linkage between syntax and semantics and a more probabilistic cognitive correlation between semantics in parental speech and childlike concepts. Obviously this does not eliminate the many complexities and unknown quantities in getting acquisition started on the right foot, but it involves shifting some of the burdens of explanation onto subtheories that are better able to bear them.

References

Bowerman, M. (1983). Hidden meanings: the role of covert conceptual structures in children's development of language. In D. R. Rogers and J. A. Sloboda (eds.), *The Acquisition of Symbolic Skills*. New York: Plenum, pp. 445–70.

Bowerman, M. 1990. Mapping thematic roles onto syntactic functions: are children helped by innate "linking rules"? *Linguistics* 28, 1253–89.

Langacker, R. W. 1987. Nouns and verbs. *Language* 63, 53–94.

Pinker, S. 1979. Formal models of language learning. *Cognition* 7, 217–83.

Pinker, S. 1982. A theory of the acquisition of lexical interpretive grammars. In J. Bresnan (ed.), *The Mental Representation of Grammatical Relations*. Cambridge, Mass.: MIT Press, pp. 53–63.

Pinker, S. 1984. *Language Learnability and Language Development*. Cambridge, Mass.: Harvard University Press.

Pinker, S. 1987. The bootstrapping problem in language acquisition. In B. MacWhinney (ed.), *Mechanisms of Language Acquisition*. Hillsdale, NJ: Erlbaum, pp. 399–441.

16

Language Acquisition and Cognitive Development

H. Sinclair-deZwart

It would seem that to take Piaget as a handbook for developmental psycholinguistics is not a simple task. It implies rather involved, and (to many, maybe) rather devious, reasoning. A direct transposition of his theory of cognitive development is impossible. Moreover, until recently, Piaget concentrated on logico-mathematical knowledge, and his studies of the development of physical concepts such as force, movement, etc. are as yet little known outside Geneva. These recent studies show that there are close links between knowledge in one field and that in another, but they also show that what were initially described as universal cognitive structures are more properly considered as symptoms (in the field of logical thinking) of even more general structures which also underlie concepts of causality, time, etc., where they may acquire rather different forms. Piaget (Ferreiro, 1971, Preface) himself has suggested the possible application of these ideas to language acquisition: Linguistic structures may well be yet another symptom of the very general, universal cognitive structures.

Reference

Ferreiro, E. 1971. *Les Relations temporelles dans le langage de l'enfant.* Geneva: Droz.

.

From *Cognitive Development and the Acquisition of Language*, ed. Timothy E. Moore. New York: Academic Press, 1973, p. 25. © 1973 by Academic Press.

17

Cognitive Prerequisites for the Development of Grammar

Dan I. Slobin

Editors' note: The first section omitted from this paper (see page 241) lists references to publications on the acquisition of 40 different languages. The second omitted section (see page 244) draws on Hungarian and Serbo-Croation data to argue for a developmental universal: "Post-verbal and post-nominal locative markers are acquired earlier than pre-verbal and pre-nominal locative markers." This example lays the groundwork for Slobin's Operating Principle A (page 244). Finally, in the third omitted section (page 246), Slobin presents five additional "Operating Principles."

Every normal human child constructs for himself the grammar of his native language. It is the task of developmental psycholinguistics to describe and attempt to explain the intricate phenomena which lie beneath this simple statement. These underlying phenomena are essentially cognitive. In order for the child to construct a grammar: (1) he must be able to cognize the physical and social events which are encoded in language, and (2) he must be able to process, organize, and store linguistic information. That is, the cognitive prerequisites for the development of grammar relate to both the *meanings* and the *forms* of utterances. This paper represents a preliminary attempt to explore these cognitive prerequisites in the light of cross-linguistic comparison of the ontogenesis of grammar.

The past decade in developmental psycholinguistics has brought a vast increase in our knowledge of how English-speaking children acquire their native language. The present decade promises to place those findings in broader perspective. Developmental psycholinguists are beginning to reach out to other language communities, in order to study children acquiring other native languages and in order to make contact with the findings of foreign colleagues. At the same time we are beginning to relate our work to the psychology of perceptual and cognitive development (see papers in Hayes, 1970). Developmental psycholinguistics is thus moving from particularism to universalism in two significant ways: from the particularism of English to the acquisition of language in

From *Studies of Child Language Development*, ed. Charles A. Ferguson and Dan Isaac Slobin. New York: Holt, Rinehart, and Winston, 1973, pp. 175–6, 179–83, 191–4, and 208.

general, and from the particularism of linguistic development to cognitive development in general. We are just beginning to sense the intimate relations between linguistic universals and cognitive universals, and are far from an adequate developmental theory of either.

The psychology of cognitive development promises an eventual universal theory of the growth of the mind (see, for example, papers in Mussen, 1970). The psycholinguistic aspects of this theory will require detailed information on the acquisition of a variety of native languages. The value of cross-linguistic comparison, of course, is to avoid drawing conclusions about child language development which may, in fact, be limited to the acquisition of languages like English. The hope is to find similar developmental processes in different sorts of languages.

Language-definitional Universals

In order to begin at this point, therefore, it is necessary to take as given what may be referred to as "language-definitional" universals. That is to say, children (and adults) everywhere have the same general definition of the form and function of language. Everywhere language consists of utterances performing a universal set of communicative functions (such as asserting, denying, requesting, ordering, and so forth), expressing a universal set of underlying semantic relations, and using a universal set of formal means (such as combinable units of meaning, made up of combinable units of sound, etc.). Furthermore, language – everywhere – is grammatical, in the sense that the meaning of a message is not fully determined by any combination of the meanings of its elements. In all language which I will consider – child and adult – there is a non-direct relation between the surface, acoustic form of messages and their underlying meanings. It is in no way surprising that children should define language in the same way as adults: indeed, they could not learn language if they did not share this definition. In fact, one could argue that human language could not be so defined if it were not so defined by children, because, in a profound sense, language is created anew by children in each generation. Language-definitional universals are what David McNeill calls "strong linguistic universals," and I follow his proposition that such universals reflect "a specific linguistic ability and may not be a reflection of a cognitive ability at all" (1970, p. 74). While much argument has centered on the issue as to whether language-definitional universals are innate, I will avoid this issue here, and merely point to them as basic linguistic capacities which are prerequisites to the questions which I want to consider (cf. Bever's "basic linguistic capacities" [1970]). We will meet the child at the point when he knows there are meaningful words which can be combined to produce meaningful utterances. And at this point we will pose the queston advanced above: Are there common orders of acquisition of different linguistic features across languages?

Content and Form in Child Speech

The first and most obvious point that comes to mind is that language is used to express the child's cognitions of his environment – physical and social – and so a child cannot begin to use a given linguistic form meaningfully until he is able to understand what it means. It should be possible, then, to rank linguistic forms in terms of the psychological, or cognitive complexity of the notions they express. For example, no one would expect a child to be able to form conditionals before he could make assertions, to make statements about time before making statements about place, and so on. Is it possible, then, to trace out a universal course of linguistic development on the basis of what we know about the universal course of cognitive development? (Can one take Piaget as a handbook of psycholinguistic development?)

In fact, many such expectations (including those suggested above) are supported by data. The earliest grammatical markers to appear in child speech seem to express the most basic notions available to the child mind. For example, in languages which provide a vocative inflection, this is typically one of the earliest grammatical markers to emerge in child speech (Hungarian, Serbo-Croatian [Miktès, 1967; Mikeš and Vlahović, 1966]; Polish [Shugar, 1971]). One of the earliest semantic relations to be formally marked in child speech is that of verb–object. In order languages, like English, this relation is marked early by consistent word order. In languages which provide an inflection for marking the object of action (accusative), this is typically an extremely early inflection to emerge – often the first (Finnish [Argoff, 1976], Latvian [Rūķe-Draviņa, 1959, 1963], Russian [Gvozdev, 1949; Imedadze, 1960]). In Luo the first inflections are subject and object affixes on verbs (Blount, 1969). In every language for which relevant data are available, there is an early form of negation in which a negative particle is affixed to a simple sentence. In languages as diverse as English, Arabic, Czech, Latvian, Japanese, and Samoan, early yes–no questions are formed by rising intonation.

Numerous findings such as these offer support for the notion that the first linguistic forms to appear in child speech will be those which express meanings consistent with the child's level of cognitive development. But striking surprises occur in some languages. For example, yes–no questions in adult Finnish are not formed by rising intonation, but by attachment of a question particle to the word questioned and movement of that word to the front of the sentence. And, strangely enough, Melissa Bowerman, in her recent dissertation on Finnish acquisition (1973), reports that little Finnish children simply do not ask yes–no questions – at least not in any formally marked way. And Margaret Omar, in a recent dissertation on the acquisition of Egyptian Arabic (1973), reports that the noun plural "is the most difficult and latest aspect of the language structure to be mastered; older children in this study erred in pluralizing even familiar nouns." And older children, in her study, meant children as old as 15! The reason apparently lies in the extreme complexity of plural marking in Arabic. Briefly: there is a small class of regular plurals, but most nouns fall into a large number of fairly irregular classes in regard to plural formation. There is also a special dual form; a distinction between pluralizing "counted" and "collected" nouns (for example, "trees" as a group, or "trees" as a collection of individual trees); what is more, the numerals 3–10 take the noun in the plural, while numerals above 11 take the singular.

So although one can talk about order of acquisition in terms of semantic or cognitive complexity, there is clearly a point at which formal linguistic complexity also plays a role. I think we can learn a good deal from discovering just what constitutes formal linguistic complexity for the child. If we can order linguistic devices in terms of their acquisition complexity, we can begin to understand the strategies used by the child in arriving at the grammar of his language. To put it the other way, a definition of what is simple for a child to acquire is a definition of the child's first guess as to the nature of language. The child must successively modify such first guesses until he ends up with the conception of language shared by the adults in his community.

Studies of bilingual children yield valuable suggestions as to what sorts of formal devices may be simpler to acquire than others. If a given meaning receives expression at the same time in both languages of a bilingual child, this suggests that the formal devices in the two languages are similar in complexity. For example, Imedadze (1960), studying the linguistic development of her Russian-Georgian bilingual daughter, noted the simultaneous emergence of the genitive and the instrumental in both languages. She concludes that: "The ease of acquisition and the simultaneous appearance of these forms of the genitive and instrumental cases can only be attributed to the fact that these forms express the very same semantic relationships in analogous fashion [in Russian and Georgian]."

If a given semantic domain receives expression earlier in one of the two languages, a difference in formal complexity is suggested. A useful example comes from studies by Melanie Mikeš and Plemenka Vlahović of Serbo-Croatian–Hungarian bilingual children in Northern Yugoslavia (Mikès, 1967; Mikeš and Vlahović, 1966). Well before they were two years of age, two bilingual girls were productively and appropriately using a variety of Hungarian case endings on nouns indicating such locative relations as illative, elative, sublative, and superessive – that is, in plain English, the children were using inflections to express the directional notions of "into," "out of," and "onto," and the positional notion of "on top of." At the same time they had barely begun to develop locative expressions in Serbo-Croatian, which requires a locative preposition before the noun along with some case inflection attached to the end of the noun.

Now, the fact that this cross-linguistic discrepancy occurs *within* a single child speaking both languages, rather than between two monolingual children, poses a central question in clear focus: When the child speaks Hungarian, she appropriately uses directional and positional locative inflections, and one is confident to credit her with the semantic intentions to express such notions as "into," "onto," and so forth. What are we to say of the same child, however, when she fails to grammatically signal such intentions with the corresponding prepositions when speaking Serbo-Croatian? It seems clear to me that if, for example, she puts a doll into a drawer, saying, in Serbo-Croatian, "doll drawer," we must credit her with the same semantic intention as when, describing the same situation in Hungarian, she adds an illative inflection to the word for "drawer."

The point I am trying to make, of course, does not depend on the child's bilingualism. The example merely illuminates the general proposition that a child's underlying semantic intentions can contain more information than his surface utterance. The speech of very young children is nearly always interpretable in context, and the very young child is neither able nor feels constrained to express his total intention in a single utterance. Lois Bloom (1970) has made this point abundantly clear in her recent book describing early grammatical development in three American children. For example, a child said "Mommy sock" in two different situations: when mommy was putting a sock on her, and when she picked up mommy's sock. Bloom is confident in labeling the utterance in the first situation as "subject-object," and the second as "genitive," and I think she is right. Previous descriptions of children's grammar were too bound to surface characterizations of word distribution, and failed to differentiate between the several meanings of homonymous utterances, such as "Mommy sock" (e.g., Braine, 1963b; Brown and Fraser, 1963; Miller and Ervin, 1964). More recent approaches to child language (and to linguistic theory) pay increasing attention to the semantic substratum of speech, and to the functions of utterances (e.g., Antinucci and Parisi, 0000; Bloom, 1970; Blount, 1969; Bowerman, 1970; Brown, 1973; E. Clark, 1970, 1971; H. Clark, 1970; Cromer, 1968; Ervin-Tripp, 1970a,b, 1971; Kernan, 1969; Parisi and Antinucci, 1970; Schlesinger, 1971; Slobin, 1970; Talmy, 1970).

To sum up thus far: Cognitive development and linguistic development do not run off in unison. The child must find linguistic means to express his intentions. The means can be easily accessible (as, for example, the Hungarian locative), or quite unaccessible (as, for example, the Finnish yes–no question or the Arabic noun plural). The problem is: What makes a given linguistic means of expression more or less accessible to the child?

In posing the question in these terms, I am assuming that there is a fairly autonomous development of intentions to express various semantic notions. This claim must be defended before answering the questions of relative accessibility of formal linguistic devices, for one may be tempted to pose the counterargument that grammar plays a leading role in cognitive development. . . .

Phrased roughly, one can say that the following is one of the basic "self-instructions" for language acquisition:

OPERATING PRINCIPLE A: Pay attention to the ends of words.

We have seen this operating principle reflected in data on word imitation and in the acquisition of locative expressions. It is also evident in the acquisition of other inflectional systems. For example, accusative and dative inflections are very early acquisitions in inflected languages like Russian, Polish, Serbo-Croatian, Latvian, Finnish, Hungarian, and Turkish – where they are realized as noun suffixes. But these inflections are relatively late in the acquisition of German (Stern and Stern, 1907), where they are realized as forms of pre-nominal articles. English articles are also lacking at early stages of development. It is not the semantic nature of articles which accounts for the omissions in German and English, because the Bulgarian article, which is a noun suffix, appears early in child speech (Gheorgov, 1908). Apparently Operating Principle A is at work here as well, making it relatively difficult for the child to detect German inflections. The principle also accounts for the finding (Grégoire, 1937) that the first negative element in early French speech is *pas* – the final member of the separated pair *ne* . . . *pas*.

All of these findings taken together suggest a general developmental universal, based on the supposition that Operating Principle A is one of the first operating principles employed in the ontogenesis of grammar:

Universal A1: For any given semantic notion, grammatical realizations in the form of suffixes or postpositions will be acquired earlier than realizations in the form of prefixes or prepositions.[1]

In order for this universal to be manifested, a number of language-definitional universals must be taken for granted (e.g. that there are words, that the meaningful unit is smaller than the word, that sounds can express grammatical relations as well as make reference, and so on). In addition, the emergence of inflections requires at least one other basic operating principle:

OPERATING PRINCIPLE B: The phonological forms of words can be systematically modified.

Numerous observers have reported a period of playful modification of words which precedes the emergence of inflections. Werner and Kaplan, reviewing the European diary literature, note (1963, p. 155):

> there are some indications reported in the literature which suggest that long before the child grasps the role of form-changes as grammatical devices, he grasps the fact that forms of vocables may be modified to express some qualification of, or affective reaction to an event.

They cite many examples of playful reduplication, suffixing, and so forth. In languages which provide inflectional diminutive or affectionate forms, such inflections are among the first to emerge. Shugar (1971), for example, cites early Polish diminutives for names (e.g., *tatunia* [= *tata* "father"] and *mamunia* [= *mama*]) and for other words (e.g., *śliweczka* [= *śliwka* "plum"] and *jabluszka* [= *jablko* "apple"]). Pačesová (1968, p. 216) gives remarkable examples from the early speech of a Czech boy who inserted extra syllables into adjectives in order to intensify their meanings. For example, the child had the following series for the adjective *veliký* "big": [velikej] – [velika:nskej] – [velikana:nskej] – [velikanana:nskej]; and *malý* "little" was changed to: [mali:] – [maliŋki:] – [malineŋki:] – [malilineŋki:] – [malulilineŋki:].

Children frequently experiment with the forms of words before they discover the meanings of particular formal changes. For example, Rūķe-Draviņa (1959) gives numerous examples of the early noncomprehending use of linguistic forms in Latvian:

> The inflections -*a*/-*e* (nominative) and -*u*/-*i* (accusative) are used in free variation as alternative pronunciations of nouns at age 1; 6, not being differentiated for the two case meanings until 1;8.

> The plural ending is occasionally attached to nouns referring to singular objects before the acquisition of the pluralization rule.

> Masculine and feminine adjectives are first used indiscriminately, ignoring the gender of the associated noun.

In all of these Latvian examples the form in adult speech is salient (according to Operating Principle A) and is fairly regular. A similar example is the English plural, which sometimes appears in early child speech as an alternative pronunciation of nouns.[2]

Operating Principles A and B present part of an explanation for the relative ease of acquisition of Hungarian locative inflections: the inflections are presumably perceptually salient, and the child is presumably prepared to manipulate the forms of word endings in his production. These principles both relate to ongoing speech processing – the deployment of attention in speech perception and the production of grammatical markers in speaking, although they also have implications for the kinds of linguistic rules which will be formed. Another set of determinants of ease of acquisition has to do more directly with rule organization factors – both simplicity and consistency of rules from a formal point of view, and semantic consistency. In the Hungarian system the locative marker is directly bound to the noun, while in the Serbo-Croatian system it is divided between a pre-nominal preposition and an inflection. In addition, the choice of formal markers for locative expression is semantically consistent and non-arbitrary in Hungarian, but is much less principled and orderly in Serbo-Croatian. A full answer to the question posed in our test case, therefore, will require operating principles for rule formation as well as for language processing. Principles of this sort will be advanced later in the paper, in connection with broader ranges of data. The test case has played its role in demonstrating the types of cognitive prerequisites to grammatical development which can be revealed by the method outlined above.

Broadly speaking, there are three classes of such prerequisites: (1) those related to the underlying semantics of utterances, (2) those related to the perception and production of speech under short-term constraints, and (3) those related to the organization and storage of linguistic rules.[3] The first class of prerequisites falls within the domain of the general psychology of cognitive development; the remaining prerequisites must be elaborated by developmental psycholinguistics. These are essentially *language processing variables* which can be conceptualized in terms of *operating principles* such as those proposed above. A number of such operating principles, and the predicted developmental universals which flow from them, will be proposed in the last section of this paper. Such operating principles guide the child in developing strategies for the production and interpretation of speech and for the construction of linguistic rule systems. The operating principles function within a framework of constraints on linguistic performance. These constraints must be considered before enumerating specific operating principles in more detail.

Conclusion

What has been sketched out on the preceding pages is only an outline of what some day may evolve into a model of the order of acquisition of linguistic structures. It has several major components, all of which must be elaborated. The first component, I have argued, is the development of semantic intentions, stemming from general cognitive development. The child, equipped with an inherent definition of the general structure and function of language, goes about finding means for the expression of those intentions by actively attempting to understand speech. That is to say, he must have preliminary internal structures for the assimilation of both linguistic and non-linguistic input. He scans linguistic input to discover meaning, guided by certain ideas about language, by general cognitive-perceptual strategies, and by processing limitations imposed by the constraints of operative memory. As in all of cognitive development, this acquisition process involves the assimilation of information to existing structures, and the accommodation of those structures to new input. The speech perception strategies engender the formation of rules for speech production. Inner linguistic structures change with age as computation and storage space increase, as increasing understanding of linguistic intentions leads the child into realms of new formal complexity, and as internal structures are interrelated and re-organized in accordance with general principles of cognitive organization. All of these factors are cognitive prerequisites for the development of grammar. While we can disagree about the extent to which this process of developing grammars requires a richly detailed innate language faculty, there can be no doubt that the process requires a richly structured and active child mind.

Notes

1   Greenberg (1957) presents a closely related argument in terms of the psycholinguistic bases of linguistic change. He explores Sapir's observation, corroborated by his own experience, "that prefixing is far less frequent than suffixing in the languages of the world" (p. 89). Greenberg adduces a number of possible psychological causes for a regular historical development away from prefixes to suffixes and finally to isolating linguistic systems. Greenberg examines this phenomenon as an example of the role of psychological factors in language change. The suggestions made here about attention to suffixes in child language development provide an important link to his chain of reasoning. (Of course, additional sorts of psycholinguistic factors will have to be introduced to account for development of an isolating language into either a prefixing or a suffixing one. In consonance with the present argument, however, Greenberg notes that the latter course of historical development is more frequent [p. 93].)

2   It should be noted that there are considerable individual differences between children in their propensity to play with form when not expressing meaning. For example, of the two girls studied by Roger Brown, Eve had a period of free variation of singular and plural forms, whereas Sarah did not use the plural inflection until she could use it correctly. The problem of individual differences between children in their approaches to language acquisition has not been addressed frequently in developmental psycholinguistics, but is obviously of great importance – especially in light of the typically small samples required by longitudinal research methods. Wick Miller (1964a) has made a valuable observation in this regard:

> There are individual differences in grammatical development . . . some children are more prone to invent their own grammatical patterns, patterns that have no relationship to adult patterns. The early grammatical rules for some are limited and quite regular, and for other children they are more variable and more difficult to define. Some children are quite willing to speak at almost any time, whether or not they have the appropriate grammatical structures at hand to express their thoughts, whereas others are more reserved in this regard, and will avoid talking at all, or will use a clumsy circumlocution. . . . I am inclined to think that the variations that are closely tied to formal features of language reflect innate individual differences.

3   Cf. the distinction made by Braine (1971) in his recently-proposed "discovery-procedures" model of language acquisition between (1) concept learning, (2) the scanner, and (3) the memory component. The operating principles proposed here are aimed at specifying some of the properties to which the scanner is sensitive and some of the organizational features of the memory. In addition, Braine's model posits a preferential order or hierarchy among the properties noticed by the scanner. The property hierarchy (cf. Chomsky's "simplicity metric") for a given language would result from the application of the operating principles (e.g., the suggested preference for word-final markers), as well as a possible preferential order of application of some operating principles.

Bibliography

Antinucci, F., and D. Parisi. 1970. Primi risultati di uno studio sullo sviluppo linguistico infantile. *Atti del IV Convegno della Società di Linguistica Italiana*. Rome: Bulzoni.

Argoff, H. D. 1976. The acquisition of Finnish inflectional morphology. Ph.D. dissertation, University of California, Berkeley.

Bever, T. G. 1970. The cognitive basis for linguistic structures. In J. R. Hayes (ed.), *Cognition and the Development of Language*. New York: Wiley, pp. 279–362.

Bloom, L. M. 1970. *Language Development: Form and Function in Emerging Grammars*. Cambridge, Mass.: MIT Press.

Blount, M. G. 1969. Acquisition of language by Luo children. Ph.D. dissertation, University of California, Berkeley. [Working Paper no. 19, Language Behavior Research Laboratory.]

Bowerman, M. F. 1973. *Early Syntactic Development: A Cross-linguistic Study with Special Reference to Finnish*. Now York: Cambridge University Press.

Braine, M. D. S. 1963. The ontogeny of English phrase structure: the first phase. *Language* 39, 1–13.

Braine, M. D. S. 1971. On two types of models of the internalization of grammars. In D. I. Slobin (ed.), *The Ontogenesis of Grammar: A Theoretical Symposium*. New York: Academic Press, pp. 153–86.

Brown, R. 1973. *A First Language: The Early Stages*. Cambridge, Mass.: Harvard University Press. [Chapter I: Semantic and grammatical relations. Chapter II: Grammatical morphemes and the modulation of meaning.]

Brown, R., and C. Fraser. 1963. The acquisition of syntax. In C. N. Cofer and B. S. Musgrave (eds.), *Verbal Behavior and Learning: Problems and Processes*. New York: McGraw-Hill, pp. 158–97. [Also in U. Bellagi and R. Brown (eds.), The acquisition of language. *Monogr. Soc. Res. Child Development*, 29:1 (1964), 43–79.]

Clark, E. 1970. How young children describe events in time. In G. B. Flores d'Arcais and W. J. M. Levelt (eds.), *Advances in Psycholinguistics*. Amsterdam: North Holland, pp. 275–84.

Clark, E. V. 1971. On the acquisition of the meaning of *before* and *after*. *J. Verb. Learn. Verb. Behavior* 10, 266–75.

Clark, H. H. 1970. The primitive nature of children's relational concepts. In J. R. Hayes (ed.), *Cognition and the Development of Language*. New York: Wiley, pp. 269–78.

Cromer, R. F. 1968. The development of temporal reference during the acquisition of language. Unpublished Ph.D. dissertation, Harvard University.

Ervin-Tripp, S. 1970a. Discourse agreement: How children answer questions. In J. R. Hayes (ed.), *Cognition and the Development of Language*. New York: Wiley, pp. 71–107.

Ervin-Tripp, S. 1970b. Structure and process in language acquisition. In J. E. Alatis (ed.), *Report of the Twenty-First Annual Round Table Meeting on Linguistics and Language Studies*. Washington, DC: Georgetown University Press, pp. 312–44.

Ervin-Tripp, S. 1971. An overview of theories of grammatical development. In D. I. Slobin (ed.), *The Ontogenesis of Grammar: A Theoretical Symposium*. New York: Academic Press, pp. 189–212.

Ferguson, C., and D. Slobin (eds.) 1973. *Studies of Child Language Development*. New York: Holt, Rinehart, and Winston.

Gheorgov, I. A. 1908. *Ein Beitrag zur grammatischen Entwicklung der Kindersprache*. Leipzig: Engelmann. [Also in *Arch. Ges. Psychol*. 11 (1908), 242–432.]

Grégoire, A. 1937–47. *L'apprentissage du langage*. Volume 1. *Les deux premières années*. Volume 2. *La troisième année et les années suivantes*. Paris: Droz.

Greenberg, J. H. 1957. Order of affixing: a study in general linguistics. In J. H. Greenberg, *Essays in Linguistics*. Chicago: University of Chicago Press, pp. 86–94.

Gvozdev, A. N. 1949. *Formirovaniye u rebenka grammaticheskogo stroya russkogo yazyka*. 2 parts. Moscow: Akad. Pedag. Nauk RSFSR. [Reprinted in A. N. Gvozdev, *Voprosy izucheniya detskoy rechi*. Moscow: Akad. Pedag. Nauk RSFSR, 1961, pp. 149–467.]

Hayes, J. R. (ed.) 1970. *Cognition and the Development of Language*. New York: Wiley.

Imedadze, N. V. 1960. K psikhologicheskoy prirode rannego dvuyazychiya. *Vopr. psikhol.* 6:1, 60–8.

Kernan, K. 1969. The acquisition of language by Samoan children. Ph.D. dissertation, University of California, Berkeley. [Working Paper no. 21 (1969), Language Behavior Research Laboratory.]

McNeill, D. 1970. *The Acquisition of Language: The Study of Developmental Psycholinguistics*. New York: Harper & Row. [Coincides in large part with chapter of same title in P. H. Mussen (ed.), *Carmichael's Manual of Child Psychology*, 3rd edn, volume 1. New York: Wiley, 1970, pp. 1061–1161.]

Mikeš, M. 1967. Acquisition des catégoires grammaticales dans le langage de l'enfant. *Enfance* 20, 289–98.

Mikeš, M., and P. Vlahović. 1966. Razvoj gramatickih kategorija u decjem govoru. *Prilozi proucavanju jezika, II*. Novi Sad, Yugoslavia.

Miller, W. R. 1964. The acquisition of grammatical rules by children. Paper read at a meeting of the Linguistic Society of America. [Printed in C. Ferguson and D. Slobin (eds.), *Studies of Child Language Development*. New York: Holt, Rinehart, and Winston, 1973.]

Miller, W. R., and S. M. Ervin. 1964. The development of grammar in child language. In U. Bellugi and R. Brown (eds.), The acquisition of language. *Monogr. Soc. Res. Child Development* 29:1, 9–33.

Mussen, P. H. (ed.) 1970. *Carmichael's Manual of Child Psychology*, 3rd edn. 2 vols. New York: Wiley.

Omar, M. K. 1973. *The Acquisition of Egyptian Arabic as a Native Language*. The Hague and Paris: Mouton.

Pacesova, J. 1968. *The Development of Vocabulary in the Child*. Brno: University J. E. Purkyne.

Parisi, D. 1970. *Il linguaggio come processo cognitivo*. Turin: Boringhieri.

Parisi, D., and F. Antinucci. 1970. Lexical competence. In G. B. Flores d'Arcais and W. J. M. Levelt (eds.), *Advances in Psycholinguistics*. Amsterdam: North Holland, pp. 197–210.

Rūķe-Draviņa, V. 1959. Zur Entstehung der Flexion in der Kindersprache: ein Beitrag auf der Grundlage des lettischen Sprachmaterials. *International Journal of Slavic Linguistics and Poetics* 1/2, 201–22. [Translation: On the emergence of inflection in child language: a contribution based on Latvian speech data, printed in C. Ferguson and D. Slobin (eds.), *Studies of Child Language Development*. New York: Holt, Rinehart, and Winston, 1973, pp. 00–00.]

Rūķe-Draviņa, V. 1963. *Zur Sprachentwicklung bei Kleinkindern: Beitrag auf der Grundlage lettischen Sprachmaterials. I. Syntax*. Lund: Slaviska Institutionen vid Lunds Universitet.

Schlesinger, I. M. 1971. Production of utterances and language acquisition. In D. I. Slobin (ed.), *The Ontogenesis of Grammar: A Theoretical Symposium*. New York: Academic Press, pp. 63–101.

Shugar, G. W. 1971. Personal communication re study of Polish acquisition. January 31.

Slobin, D. I. 1970. Universals of grammatical development in children. In G. B. Flores d'Arcais and W. J. M. Levelt (eds.), *Advances in Psycholinguistics*. Amsterdam: North Holland, pp. 174–86.

Stern, C., and W. Stern. 1907. *Die Kindersprache: Eine psychologische und sprachtheoretische Untersuchung*. Leipzig: Barth. [4th rev. edn., 1928.]

Talmy, T. 1970. Semantic componentry and Samoan acquisition. Working Paper no. 35, Language Behavior Research Laboratory, University of California, Berkeley.

Werner, H., and B. Kaplan. 1963. *Symbol Formation*. New York: Wiley.

Part III

Areas of Language Knowledge

18

The Child's Learning of English Morphology

Jean Berko [Gleason]

In this study we set out to discover what is learned by children exposed to English morphology. To test for knowledge of morphological rules, we use nonsense materials. We know that if the subject can supply the correct plural ending, for instance, to a noun we have made up, he has internalized a working system of the plural allomorphs in English, and is able to generalize to new cases and select the right form. If a child knows that the plural of *witch* is *witches*, he may simply have memorized the plural form. If, however, he tells us that the plural of **gutch* is **gutches*, we have evidence that he actually knows, albeit unconsciously, one of those rules which the descriptive linguist, too, would set forth in his grammar. And if children do have knowledge of morphological rules, how does this knowledge evolve? Is there a progression from simple, regular rules to the more irregular and qualified rules that are adequate fully to describe English? In very general terms, we undertake to discover the psychological status of a certain kind of linguistic description. It is evident that the acquisition of language is more than the storing up of rehearsed utterances, since we are all able to say what we have not practiced and what we have never before heard. In bringing descriptive linguistics to the study of language acquisition, we hope to gain knowledge of the systems and patterns used by the speaker.

In order to test for children's knowledge of this sort, it was necessary to begin with an examination of their actual vocabulary. Accordingly, the 1000 most frequent words in the first-grader's vocabulary were selected from Rinsland's listing (H. D. Rinsland, *A Basic Vocabulary of Elementary School Children*, New York, Macmillan, 1945). This listing contains the most common words in the elementary school child's vocabulary, as taken from actual conversations, compositions, letters, and similar documents. This list was then examined to see what features of English morphology seem to be most commonly represented in the vocabulary of the first-grade child. From this we could decide what kind of extensions we might expect the child to be able to make. All of the English inflexional morphemes were present.

The areas that seemed to be most promising from this examination were the plural and the two possessives of the noun, the third person singular of the verb, the progressive

From *Word* 14 (August–December 1958), pp. 150–77. Reprinted by courtesy of Jean Burko Gleason.

and the past tense, and the comparative and superlative of the adjective. The pronouns were avoided both because of the difficulty involved in making up a nonsense pronoun, and because the pronouns are so few in number and so irregular that we would hardly expect even adults to have any generalized rules for the handling of new pronouns. Moreover, we do not encounter new pronouns, whereas new verbs, adjectives, and nouns constantly appear in our vocabularies, so that the essential problem is not the same. The past participle of regular or weak verbs in English is identical with the past tense, and since the regular forms were our primary interest, no attempt was made to test for the past participle. A number of forms that might suggest irregular plurals and past tenses were included among the nouns and verbs.

The productive allomorphs of the plural, the possessive, and the third person singular of the verb are phonologically conditioned and identical with one another. These forms are /-s ∼ -z ∼ -əz/, with the following distribution:

/-əz/ after stems that end in /s z š ž č ǰ /, e.g. *glasses, watches*;
/-s/ after stems that end in /p t k f θ/, e.g. *hops, hits*;
/-z/ after all other stems, viz. those ending in /b d g v ð m n ŋ r l/, vowels, and semi-vowels, e.g. *bids, goes.*

The productive allomorphs of the past are /-t ∼ -d ∼ -əd/, and they are also phonologically conditioned, with the following distribution:

/-əd/ after stems that end in /t d/, e.g. *melted*;
/-t/ after stems that end in /p k č f θ š/, e.g. *stopped*;
/-d/ after stems ending in voiced sounds except /-d/, e.g. *climbed, played.*

The progressive -*ing* and the adjective -*er* and -*est* do not have variants. It might also be noted that the possessive has an additional allomorph /-ø/; this occurs after an inflexional /-s/ or /-z/, so that if the form *boy* is made plural, *boys*, the possessive of that plural form is made by adding nothing, and indicated in writing only by the addition of an apostrophe: *boys'.*

The children's vocabulary at the first-grade level also contains a number of words that are made of a free morpheme and a derivational suffix, e.g. *teacher*, or of two free morphemes, e.g. *birthday*. The difficulties encountered in this area are many. First, it might be noted that there are not many contrasts, i.e., not many cases of the same derivational suffix being added to different bases to produce forms of like function. Although *beautiful* and *thankful* both appear on the list, it does not seem that these examples are numerous enough for us to expect a young child to be able to append -*ful* to a new noun in order to produce an adjective. Word derivation and compounding are furthermore often accompanied by changes in stress and pronunciation, so that the picture is additionally complicated. There seemed to be enough examples of the stress pattern ´`, as in *bláckboàrd* as against *blàck boárd*, and of the diminutive-affectionate -*y*, the adjectival -*y*, and the agentive -*er* to warrant testing for these forms.

So far as the general picture is concerned, all speakers of the language are constrained to use the inflexional endings and apply them appropriately to new forms when they are encountered. We are not so often called upon to derive or compound new words, although by the time we are adults we can all to some extent do this. From the children's actual vocabulary we were able to make an estimate of the kind of morphological rules they might be expected to possess, and from these items a test could be constructed. It was noted, moreover, that in the child's vocabulary there are a number of compound words, like *blackboard* and *birthday*. It is entirely possible to use a compound word correctly and never notice that it is made of two separate and meaningful elements. It is also possible to use it correctly and at the same time have a completely private meaning for one or both of its constituent elements. In order to see what kind of ideas children have about the compound words in their vocabularies, it was decided to ask them directly about a selected number of these words.

Within the framework of the child's vocabulary, a test was devised to explore the child's ability to apply morphological rules to new words. He was called upon to inflect, to derive, to compound, and, lastly, to analyse compound words.

Materials and Procedure

In order to test for the child's use of morphological rules of different types and under varying phonological conditions, a number of nonsense words were made up, following the rules for possible sound combinations in English. Pictures to represent the nonsense words were then drawn on cards. There were 27 picture cards, and the pictures, which were brightly colored, depicted objects, cartoon-like animals, and men performing various actions. For reasons that will be discussed later, several actual words were also included. A text, omitting the desired form, was typed on each card. An example of the card to test for the regular plural allomorph in /-z/ can be seen in figure 18.1.

The subjects included 12 adults (seven women and five men), all of whom were college graduates. Many of these adults had also had some graduate training. All were native speakers of English.

The child subjects were obtained at the Harvard Preschool in Cambridge and the Michael Driscoll School, in Brookline, Massachusetts. At the Preschool, each child was brought to the experimenter, introduced, and told that now he was going to look at some pictures. The experimenter would point to the picture and read the text. The child would supply the missing word, and the item he employed was noted phonemically. After all of the pictures had been shown, the child was asked why he thought the things denoted by the compound words were so named. The general form of these questions was "Why do you think a blackboard is called a blackboard?" If the child responded with "Because it's a blackboard", he was asked, "But why do you think it's called that?" The children at the Preschool ranged between four and five years in age. Twelve girls and seven boys were asked all items of the completed test, and two groups, one of three boys and three girls and one of five boys and three girls, were each asked half of the inflexional items in preliminary testing.

At the Driscoll School, the experimenter was introduced to the class and it was explained that each child was going to have a turn at looking at some pictures. The procedure from this point on was the same as for the Preschool. All children in the first grade were interviewed. There were 26 boys and 35 girls in this group. Ages ranged from five and one half to seven years.

Figure 18.1   The plural allomorph in /-z/.

The following is the order in which the cards were presented. Included is a statement of what was being tested, a description of the card, and the text that was read. Pronunciation is indicated by regular English orthography; a phonemic transcription is included for first occurrences of nonsense words.

1. Plural. One bird-like animal, then two. "This is a wug /wʌg/. Now there is another one. There are two of them. There are two ____."

2. Plural. One bird, then two. "This is a gutch /gʌč/. Now there is another one. There are two of them. There are two ____."

3. Past tense. Man with a steaming pitcher on his head. "This is a man who knows how to spow /spow/. He is spowing. He did the same thing yesterday. What did he do yesterday? Yesterday he ____."

4. Plural. One animal, then two. "This is a kazh /kæž/. Now there is another one. There are two of them. There are two ____."

5. Past tense. Man swinging an object. "This is a man who knows how to rick /rik/. He is ricking. He did the same thing yesterday. What did he do yesterday? Yesterday he ____."

6. Diminutive and compounded or derived word. One animal, then a minuscule animal. "This is a wug. This is a very tiny wug. What would you call a very tiny wug? This wug lives in a house. What would you call a house that a wug lives in?"

7. Plural. One animal, then two. "This is a tor /tɔr/. Now there is another one. There are two of them. There are two ____."

8. Derived adjective. Dog covered with irregular green spots. "This is a dog with quirks /kwɔrks/ on him. He is all covered with quirks. What kind of dog is he? He is a ____ dog."

9. Plural. One flower, then two. "This is a lun /lʌn/. Now there is another one. There are two of them. There are two ____."

10. Plural. One animal, then two. "This is a niz /niz/. Now there is another one. There are two of them. There are two ____."

11. Past tense. Man doing calisthenics. "This is a man who knows how to mot /mat/. He is motting. He did the same thing yesterday. What did he do yesterday? Yesterday he ____."

12. Plural. One bird, then two. "This is a cra /kra/. Now there is another one. There are two of them. There are two ____."

13. Plural. One animal, then two. "This is a tass /tæs/. Now there is another one. There are two of them. There are two ____."

14. Past tense. Man dangling an object on a string. "This is a man who knows how to bod /bad/. He is bodding. He did the same thing yesterday. What did he do yesterday? Yesterday he ____."

15. Third person singular. Man shaking an object. "This is a man who knows how to naz /næz/. He is nazzing. He does it every day. Every day he ____."

16. Plural. One insect, then two. "This is a heaf /hiyf/. Now there is another one. There are two of them. There are two _____."

17. Plural. One glass, then two. "This is a glass. Now there is another one. There are two of them. There are two _____."

18. Past tense. Man exercising. "This is a man who knows how to gling /gliŋ/. He is glinging. He did the same thing yesterday. What did he do yesterday? Yesterday he _____."

19. Third person singular. Man holding an object. "This is a man who knows how to loodge /luwdž/. He is loodging. He does it every day. Every day he _____."

20. Past tense. Man standing on the ceiling. "This is a man who knows how to bing /biŋ/. He is binging. He did the same thing yesterday. What did he do yesterday? Yesterday he _____."

21. Singular and plural possessive. One animal wearing a hat, then two wearing hats. "This is a niz who owns a hat. Whose hat is it? It is the _____ hat. Now there are two nizzes. They both own hats. Whose hats are they? They are the _____ hats."

22. Past tense. A bell. "This is a bell that can ring. It is ringing. It did the same thing yesterday. What did it do yesterday? Yesterday it _____."

23. Singular and plural possessive. One animal wearing a hat, then two. "This is a wug who owns a hat. Whose hat is it? It is the _____ hat. Now there are two wugs. They both own hats. Whose hats are they? They are the _____ hats."

24. Comparative and superlative of the adjective. A dog with a few spots, one with several, and one with a great number. "This dog has quirks on him. This dog has more quirks on him. And this dog has even more quirks on him. This dog is quirky. This dog is _____. And this dog is the _____."

25. Progressive and derived agentive or compound. Man balancing a ball on his nose. "This is a man who knows how to zib /zib/. What is he doing? He is _____. What would you call a man whose job is to zib?"

26. Past tense. An ice cube, then a puddle of water. "This is an ice cube. Ice melts. It is melting. Now it is all gone. What happened to it? It _____."

27. Singular and plural possessive. One animal wearing a hat, then two. "This is a bik /bik/ who owns a hat. Whose hat is it? It is the _____ hat. Now there are two biks. They both own hats. Whose hats are they? They are the _____ hats."

28. Compound words. The child was asked why he thought the following were so named. (No pictures were used for these items.)

a.	afternoon	h.	handkerchief
b.	airplane	i.	holiday
c.	birthday	j.	merry-go-round
d.	breakfast	k.	newspaper
e.	blackboard	l.	sunshine
f.	fireplace	m.	Thanksgiving
g.	football	n.	Friday

It took between ten and fifteen minutes to ask a child all of these questions. Even the youngest children have had experience with picture books, if not actual training in naming things through pictures, and no child failed to understand the nature of the task before him. It was, moreover, evident that a great number of these children thought they were being taught new English words. It was not uncommon for a child to repeat the nonsense word immediately upon hearing it and before being asked any questions. Often, for example, when the experimenter said "This is a *gutch*", the child repeated, "*Gutch*". Answers were willingly, and often insistently, given. These responses will be discussed in the following section.

Results

Adult answers to the inflexional items were considered correct answers, and it was therefore possible to rate the children's answers. In general, adult opinion was unanimous – everyone said the plural of *wug* was *wugs*, the plural of *gutch* was *gutches*; where the adults differed among themselves, except in the possessives, it was along the line of a common but irregular formation, e.g. *heaf* became *heaves* in the plural for many speakers, and in these cases both responses were considered correct. If a child said that the plural of *heaf* was *heafs* or *heaves* /-vz/, he was considered correct. If he said *heaf* (no ending), or *heafès* /-fəz/, he was considered incorrect, and a record was kept of each type of response.

Sex differences

The first question to be answered was whether there is a sex difference in the ability to handle English morphology at this age level. Since it seemed entirely possible that boys entering the first grade might be on the whole somewhat older than girls entering the first grade, it was necessary to equate the two groups for age.

The children were divided into seven age groups. Since at each of these levels there were more girls than boys, a random selection of the girls was made so that they would match the boys in number. The distribution of these ages and the number in each group can be seen in Table 18.1. This distribution was utilized only in comparing the performance of the boys with that of the girls; in all other instances, the responses of the entire sample were considered.

The groups of 28 boys and 28 girls thus selected were compared with one another on all inflexional items. The chi square criterion with Yates' correction for small

Table 18.1   Distribution of children at each age level for comparison of the sexes

Age	Boys	Girls	Total
4	2	2	4
4:6	1	1	2
5	2	2	4
5:6	2	2	4
6	10	10	20
6:6	6	6	12
7	5	5	10
Total:	28	28	56

frequencies was applied to each item, and on none was there a significant difference between the boys' and girls' performance; boys did as well as girls, or somewhat better, on over half the items, so that there was no evidence of the usual superiority of girls in language matters. From this it would appear that boys and girls in this age range are equal in their ability to handle the English morphology represented by these items.

Age differences

Having ascertained that there was no difference between boys' and girls' answers, we combined the sexes and went on to compare the younger with the older children. The oldest children at the Preschool were five years old, and the youngest at the Driscoll School were five and one half years, so that the dividing line was made between the schools. Chi square corrected for small frequencies was again applied to all inflexional items. First graders did significantly better than preschoolers on slightly less than half of these. The differences can be seen in Table 18.2.

Formation of the plural

The nature of the children's answers can best be seen through a separate examination of the noun plurals, the verbs, and the possessives. The percentage of all children supplying correct plural endings can be seen in Table 18.3. The general picture indicates that children at this age have in their vocabularies words containing the three plural allomorphs /-s ~ -z ~ -əz/, and can use these words. The real form *glasses* was included here because we knew from a pretest that children at this age generally did not make correct application of /-əz/ to new forms, and we wanted to know if they used this form with a common English word. Evidently they have at least one actual English model for this contingent plural. In uncomplicated cases children at this age can also extend the use of these forms to new words requiring /-s/ or /-z/, as indicated by the high percentage of right answers for *wug* and *bik*, a form used in the pretest and answered correctly by a correspondingly high number of children. For the items *wugs* and *glasses*

Table 18.2 Age differences on inflexional items

Item	Percentage of correct pre-school answers	Percentage of correct first-grade answers	Significance level of difference
Plural			
glasses............	75	99	.01
wugs...............	76	97	.02
luns	68	92	.05
tors	73	90	–
heafs	79	80	–
cras................	58	86	.05
tasses.............	28	39	–
gutches...........	28	38	–
kazhes	25	36	–
nizzes	14	33	–
Progressive			
zibbing	72	97	.01
Past Tense			
binged	60	85	.05
glinged............	63	80	–
ricked	73	73	–
melted	72	74	–
spowed............	36	59	–
motted.............	32	33	–
bodded	14	31	.05
rang.................	0	25	.01
Third Singular			
loodges............	57	56	–
nazzes	47	49	–
Possessive			
wug's..............	68	81	–
bik's................	68	95	.02
niz's................	58	46	–
wugs'	74	97	.02
biks'................	74	99	.01
nizzes'.............	53	82	.05

there is, moreover, a significant difference between the younger and older groups. For *glasses* they progress from 75% right to 99% right in the older group, a change that is significant at the 1% level. The few wrong answers in these cases were either a complete failure to respond, or a repetition of the word in its singular form.

From this it is evident that however poorly children may do on extensions of the rule for forming the plural of *glass*, they do have this item in their vocabulary and can produce it appropriately. During the period from Preschool to the first grade, those who do not have this item acquire it. They can also extend the rule for the addition of the

Table 18.3   Percentages of children supplying correct plural forms

Item	Allomorph	Per Cent Correct
glasses	/-əz/	91
wugs	/-z/	91
luns	/-z/	86
tors	/-z/	85
heafs, -ves	/-s/ /-z/	82
cras	/-z/	79
tasses	/-əz/	36
gutches	/-əz/	36
kazhes	/-əz/	31
nizzes	/-əz/	28

/-s/ or /-z/ allomorph where the more general rules of English phonology dictate which of these forms must be used. During this period they perfect this knowledge.

The ability to add /-z/ to *wug and /-s/ to *bik does not alone prove that the child possesses the rule that tells which allomorph of the plural must be used: English phonology decrees that there cannot be a consonant cluster */-kz/ or */-gs/. The final consonant determines whether the sibilant must be voiced or unvoiced. The instances in English where there is a choice are after /l/ /n/ and /r/, and after a vowel or semivowel. Thus we have minimal pairs like: *ells* : *else*; *purrs* : *purse*; *hens* : *hence*; *pews* : *puce*. In forming the plural of *wug or *bik, the child has only to know that a dental sibilant must be added; which one it is is determined by the invariant rules of combination that govern English consonant clusters. If, however, he is faced with a new word ending in a vowel, semivowel, /-l/, /-n/, or /-r/, he himself must make the choice, because so far as English phonology is concerned he could add either a /-z/ or an /-s/ and still have a possible English word. We would expect him, therefore, to have more difficulty forming the plural of a new word ending in these sounds than in cases where phonology determines the form of the sibilant. These problems are represented by the forms *cra, *tor, and *lun. As table 3 indicates, the percentages correct on these items were respectively 79, 85, and 86. The difference between performance on *wug and *cra is significant at the 5% level.

During the period from preschool to the first grade, they improved markedly in their handling of *cra and *lun. The differences between the younger and older groups were significant at the 5% level. The case of adding /-s/ to these forms did not, however, arise. The child here, as in so many other stages of language learning, answered complexity with silence: the wrong answers were invariably the unaltered form of the singular.

The only other case to be answered correctly by the majority of the children was *heaf. Since adults responded with both *heafs and *heaves /-vz/, both of these answers were considered correct. It must be noted that although 42% of the adults gave *heaves as the plural of this item, employing what would amount to a morphophonemic change along the lines of: *knife* : *knives*; *hoof* : *hooves*, only three children out of a total of 89 answering this item said *heaves; 9, or 10% added nothing, and an additional four formed the plural with the wrong allomorph, i.e. they said /hiyfəz/, treating the /-f/ as if it belonged to the sibilant-affricate series. /f/ is, of course, phonetically very similar to

/s/, and one of the questions suggested by this problem was whether children would generalize in the direction of phonetic similarity across functional boundaries – /f/ is distinguished phonetically from /s/ only in that it is grave and /s/ is acute. It is, so to speak, no more different from /s/ than /z/ is, and it is as similar to /s/ as /ž/ is to /z/. It does not, however, so far as English phonology is concerned, function like /s š z ž č j/, none of which can be immediately followed by another sibilant within the same consonant cluster. The high percentage of correct items indicates that /f/ had already been categorized as belonging to the consonant class that can be followed by /-s/, and the phonetic similarity between /f/ and the sibilants did not lead the children to generalize the rule for the addition of the /-əz/ allomorph in that direction. Nor could any irregular formation be said to be productive for children in this case, although for adults it apparently is.

The proportion of children's right answers suddenly drops when we come to the form *tass. As table 3 shows, 91% of these children when given the form glass could produce the form glasses. When given the form *tass, a new word patterned after glass, only 36% could supply the form *tasses. The picture becomes progressively worse with the other words ending in sibilants or affricates, and by the time we reach the form *niz, only 28% answered correctly. *Niz of these four, is the only one that ends in a sound that is also the commonest plural allomorph, /-z/, and the children did the worst on this item. What is of additional interest, is that on these four items there was no significant improvement from the Preschool to the first grade. The difference between performance on *cra, the worst of the other items, and *tass, the best of these, was significant at the .1% level. Again, the wrong answers consisted in doing nothing to the word as given. It must be noted, however, that in these items, the children delivered the wrong form with a great deal of conviction: 62% of them said "one *tass, two *tass" as if there were no question that the plural of *tass should and must be *tass. From this it is evident that the morphological rules these children have for the plural are not the same as those possessed by adults: the children can add /-s/ or /-z/ to new words with a great deal of success. They do not as yet have the ability to extend the /-əz/ allomorph to new words, even though it has been demonstrated that they have words of this type in their vocabulary.

The form "kazh" /kæž/ was added here once again to see in what direction the children would generalize. /ž/, although it is in the sibilant-affricate group, is very rare as a final consonant in English: it occurs only in some speakers' pronunciation of garage, barrage, and a few other words. As table 3 indicates, the children treated this word like the others of this group. It might also be noted here that for the forms *gutch and *kazh, some few children formed the plural in /-s/, i.e., /gʌčs/ and /kæžs/. 10% did this for *gutch, and 5% for *kazh, errors that indicate that the phonological rules may not yet be perfectly learned. What is clearest from these answers dealing with the plural is that children can and do extend the /-s/ and /-z/ forms to new words, and that they cannot apply the more complicated /-əz/ allomorph of the plural to new words.

Verb inflexions

The children's performance on the verb forms can be seen in Table 18.4. It will be observed that the best performance on these items was on the progressive, where they

Table 18.4 Percentages of children supplying correct verb forms

Item	Allomorph	Percentage Correct
Progressive		
zibbing	/-iŋ/	90
Past Tense		
binged, bang	/-d ~ æ ← (i)/	78
glinged, glang	/-d ~ æ ← (i)/	77
ricked	/-t/	73
melted	/-əd/	73
spowed	/-d/	52
motted	/-əd/	33
bodded	/-əd/	31
rang	/æ ← (i)/	17
Third Singular		
loodges	/-əz/	56
nazzes	/-əz/	48

were shown a picture of a man who knew how to *zib and were required to say that he was *zibbing. The difference between *zibbing and the best of the past tense items, *binged, was significant at the 5% level. The improvement from the younger to the older group was significant at the 1% level; fully 97% of the first graders answered this question correctly. Here, there was no question of choice, there is only one allomorph of the progressive morpheme, and the child either knows this -ing form or does not. These results suggest that he does.

The results with the past tense forms indicate that these children can handle the /-t/ and /-d/ allomorphs of the past. On *binged and *glinged the percentages answering correctly were 78 and 77, and the older group did significantly better than the younger group on *binged.

Actually, the forms *gling and *bing were included to test for possible irregular formations. A check of English verbs revealed that virtually all in -ing form their past tense irregularly: sing: sang; ring: rang; cling: clung, and many others. The only -ing verbs that form a past tense in -ed are a few poetic forms like enringed, unkinged, and winged, and onomotopoeias like pinged and zinged. Adults clearly felt the pull of the irregular pattern, and 50% of them said *bang or *bung for the past tense of *bing, while 75% made *gling into *glang or *glung in the past. Only one child of the 86 interviewed on these items said *bang. One also said *glang, and two said *glanged – changing the vowel and also adding the regular /-d/ for the past.

The great majority on these forms, as well as on *ricked which requires /-t/, formed the past tense regularly. There was a certain amount of room for variation with the past tense, since there is more than one way of expressing what happened in the past. A number of children, for example said "Yesterday he was *ricking". If on these occasions the experimenter tried to force the issue by saying "He only did it once yesterday, so yesterday once he__?" The child usually responded with "once he was *ricking". Taking into account this possible variation, the percentages right on *rick, *gling and *bing represent a substantial grasp of the problem of adding a phonologically determined /-t/ or /-d/.

With *spow the child had to choose one or the other of the allomorphs, and the drop to 52% correct represents this additional complexity. Several children here retained the inflexional /-z/ and said /spowzd/, others repeated the progressive or refused to answer. No child supplied a /-t/.

On *motted, the percentage correct drops to 33, although the subjects were 73% right on the real word *melted*, which is a similar form. On *bodded they were 31% right, and on *rang* only 17% right. The older group was significantly better than the younger on *rang* and *bodded*. What this means is that the younger group could not do them at all – not one preschool child knew *rang* – and the older group could barely do them. What emerges here is that children at this age level are not able to extend the rule for forming the past tense of *melted* to new forms. They can handle the regular /-d/ and /-t/ allomorphs of the past in new instances, but not /-əd/. Nor do they have control of the irregular past form *rang*, and consequently do not form new pasts according to this pattern, although adults do. They have the /-əd/ form in actual words like *melted*, but do not generalize from it. With *ring*, they do not have the actual past *rang*, and, therefore no model for generalization. In the children's responses, the difference between *spowd, the worst of the items requiring /-t/ or /-d/, and *motted, the best requiring /-əd/ is significant at the 2% level. For *mot and *bod, the wrong answers, which were in the majority, were overwhelmingly a repetition of the present stem: "Today he *bods; yesterday he *bod." To the forms ending in /-t/ or /-d/ the children added nothing to form the past.

The third person singular forms require the same allomorphs as the noun plurals, /-s ~ -z ~ -əz/, and only two examples were included in the experiment. These were *loodge and *naz, and required the /-əz/ ending. 56% of the children supplied the correct form *loodges, and 48% supplied *nazzes. The wrong answers were again a failure to add anything to the stem, and there was no improvement whatsoever from the younger to the older group on these two items.

Formation of the possessive

The only other inflexional items statistically treated were the regular forms of the possessive. The percentages of children supplying right answers can be seen in Table 18.5. In the singular, the problem was the same as for the noun plurals, and the children's difficulty with the /-əz/ form of the allomorph is mirrored in the low percentage who were able to supply *niz's /-əz/ when told "This is a *niz who owns a hat. Whose hat is it? It is the _____?" For *bik's there was a significant improvement at the 2% level between the younger and older groups. For *niz's the younger group did no worse than the older group.

In the plural possessives the problem is somewhat different: since these words are already regularly inflected, the possessive is formed by adding a morphological zero. The children did not add an additional /-əz/ to these forms, and in the case of *nizzes', they erred on the side of removing the plural -es, e.g. for the plural possessive they said simply *niz in those cases where they gave the wrong answers.

Table 18.5 Percentages of children supplying correct possessive forms

Singular	Allomorph	Percentage Correct
wug's	/-z/	84
bik's	/-s/	87
niz's	/-əz/	49
Plural		
wugs'	/-ø/	88
biks'	/-ø/	93
nizzes'	/-ø/	76

It was the adults who had difficulty with the plural possessives: 33% of them said **wugses* /-zəz/ and **bikses* /-səz/, although none said **nizes* /-əzəz/. This is undoubtedly by analogy with proper nouns in the adults' vocabulary, i.e., no adult would say that if two dogs own hats, they are the **dogses* /-zəz/ hats. However an adult may know a family named *Lyons*, and also a family named *Lyon*. In the first instance, the family are the *Lyonses* /-zəz/ and if they own a house, it is the *Lyonses'* /-zəz/ house; in the second instance, the family are the *Lyons* and their house is the *Lyons'* /-nz/. The confusion resulting from competing forms like these is such that some speakers do not make this distinction, and simply add nothing to a proper noun ending in /-s/ or /-z/ in order to form the possessive – they say "it is Charles' /-lz/ hat". Some speakers seem also to have been taught in school that they must use this latter form. It seems likely that the children interviewed had not enough grasp of the /-əz/ form for these niceties to affect them.

Adjectival inflexion

The last of the inflexional items involved attempting to elicit comparative and super-lative endings for the adjective **quirky*. The child was shown dogs that were increasingly **quirky* and expected to say that the second was **quirkier* than the first, and that the third was the **quirkiest*. No statistical count was necessary here since of the 80 children shown this picture, only one answered with these forms. Adults were unanimous in their answers. Children either said they did not know, or they repeated the experimenter's word, and said "**quirky*, too". If the child failed to answer, the experimenter supplied the form **quirkier*, and said "This dog is *quirky*. This dog is *quirkier*. And this dog is the ——?" Under these conditions 35% of the children could supply the *-est* form.

Derivation and compounding

The children were also asked several questions that called for compounding or deriv-ing new words. They were asked what they would call a man who **zibbed* for a living, what they would call a very tiny **wug*, what they would call a house a **wug* lives in, and what kind of dog a dog covered with **quirks* is.

Adults unanimously said that a man who *zibs is a *zibber, using the common agentive pattern -er. Only 11% of the children said *zibber. 35% gave no answer. 11% said *zíbbingmàn and 5% said *zíbmàn, compounds that adults did not utilize. The rest of the children's answers were real words like clown or acrobat.

For the diminutive of *wug, 50% of the adults said *wuglet. Others offered little *wùg, *wuggie, *wugette, and *wugling. No child used a diminutive suffix. 52% of the children formed compounds like báby *wùg, teény *wùg, and little *wùg. Two children, moreover, said a little *wug is a *wig, employing sound symbolism – a narrower vowel to stand for a smaller animal. For the house a *wug lives in, 58% of the adults formed the asyntactic compound *wúghoùse. Others said *wuggery, *wúgshoùse, and *wúghùt. Again, no child used a suffix. The younger children did not understand this question, and where the older children did, they formed compounds. 18% of the first graders said *wughoùse. Others suggested birdcage and similar forms. What emerges from this picture is the fact that whereas adults may derive new words, children at this stage use almost exclusively a compounding pattern, and have the stress pattern ´` at their disposal: the adults unanimously said that a dog covered with *quirks is a *quirky dog. 64% of the children formed the compound *quírk dòg for this item, and again, no child used a derivational suffix.

Analysis of compound words

After the child had been asked all of these questions calling for the manipulation of new forms, he was asked about some of the compound words in his own vocabulary; the object of this questioning was to see if children at this age are aware of the separate morphemes in compound words. The children's explanations fall roughly into four categories. The first is identity: "a blackboard is called a blackboard because it is a blackboard." The second is a statement of the object's salient function or feature: "a blackboard is called a blackboard because you write on it." In the third type of explanation, the salient feature happens to coincide with part of the name: "a blackboard is called a blackboard because it is black"; "a merry-go-round is called a merry-go-round because it goes round and round". Finally, there is the etymological explanation given by adults – it takes into account both parts of the word, and is not necessarily connected with some salient or functional feature: "Thanksgiving is called Thanksgiving because the pilgrims gave thanks."

Of the children's answers, only 13% could be considered etymological. Most of their answers fell into the salient-feature category, while the number of identity responses dropped from the younger to the older group. Many younger children offered no answers at all; of the answers given, 23% were identity. Of the older children, only 9% gave identity answers, a difference that was significant at the 1% level.

As we might expect, the greatest number of etymological responses – 23% – was given for Thanksgiving, which is an item that children are explicitly taught. It must be noted, however, that despite this teaching, for 67% of the children answering this item, Thanksgiving is called Thanksgiving because you eat lots of turkey.

The salient feature answers at first seem to have the nature of an etymological explanation, in those instances where the feature coincides with part of the name – 72% of the answers, for instance, said that a fireplace is called a fireplace because you put fire in it. When the salient feature does not coincide with part of the name, however, the etymological aspects also drop out. For *birthday*, where to the child neither the fact that it is a day nor that it is tied to one's birth is important, the number of functional answers rises: it is called *birthday* because you get presents or eat cake. Only 2% said anything about its being a day.

The child approaches the etymological view of compound words through those words where the most important thing about the word so far as the child is concerned coincides with part of the name. The outstanding feature of a merry-go-round is that it does, indeed, go round and round, and it is the eminent appropriateness of such names that leads to the expectation of meaningfulness in other compound words.

Although the number of etymological explanations offered by the children was not great, it was clear that many children have what amounts to private meanings for many compound words. These meanings may be unrelated to the word's history, and unshared by other speakers. Examples of this can be seen in the following.

"An airplane is called an *airplane* because it is a plain thing that goes in the air."

"Breakfast is called *breakfast* because you have to eat it fast when you rush to school."

"Thanksgiving is called that because people give things to one another." (Thingsgiving?)

"Friday is a day when you have fried fish."

"A handkerchief is a thing you hold in your hand, and you go 'kerchoo'."

These examples suffice to give the general nature of the private meanings children may have about the words in their vocabulary. What is of additional interest, is that the last explanation about the handkerchief was also offered by one of the college-graduate adult subjects.

We must all learn to handle English inflexion and some of the patterns for derivation and compounding. So long as we use a compound word correctly, we can assign any meaning we like to its constituent elements.

Conclusion

In this experiment, preschool and first-grade children, ranging from four to seven years in age, were presented with a number of nonsense words and asked to supply English plurals, verb tenses, possessives, derivations and compounds of those words. Our first and most general question had been: do children possess morphological rules? A previous study of the actual vocabulary of first graders showed that they know real items representing basic English morphological processes. Asking questions about real words, however, might be tapping a process no more abstract than rote memory. We could be sure that our nonsense words were new words to the child, and that if he supplied the right morphological item he knew something more than the individual words in his vocabulary: he had rules of extension that enabled him to deal with new words. Every child interviewed understood what was being asked of him. If knowledge of English consisted of no more than the storing up of many memorized words, the child might be expected to refuse to answer our questions on the grounds that he had never before heard of a *wug, for instance, and could not possibly give us the plural form since no one had ever told him what it was. This was decidedly not the case. The children answered the questions; in some instances they pronounced the inflexional endings they had added with exaggerated care, so that it was obvious that they understood the problem and wanted no mistake made about their solution. Sometimes, they said "That's a hard one," and pondered a while before answering, or answered with one form and then corrected themselves. The answers were not always right so far as English is concerned; but they were consistent and orderly answers, and they demonstrated that there can be no doubt that children in this age range operate with clearly delimited morphological rules.

Our second finding was that boys and girls did equally well on these items. Sometimes the girls had a higher percentage of right answers on an item, and more often the boys did somewhat better, but no pattern of differences could be distinguished and the differences were never statistically significant. These findings are at variance with the results of most other language tests. Usually, girls have been shown to have a slight advantage over boys. In our experiment, girls were no more advanced than boys in their acquisition of English morphology. Since other language tests have not investigated morphology *per se*, it is easy enough to say that this is simply one area in which there are no sex differences. A reason for this lack of difference does, however, suggest itself: and that is the very basic nature of morphology. Throughout childhood, girls are perhaps from a maturational point of view slightly ahead of the boys who are their chronological age mates. But the language differences that have been observed may be culturally induced, and they may be fairly superficial. Some social factor may lead girls to be more facile with words, to use longer sentences, and to talk more. This can be misleading. A girl in an intellectual adult environment may, for instance, acquire a rather sophisticated vocabulary at an early age. This should not be taken to mean that she will learn the minor rules for the formation of the plural before she learns the major ones, or that she will necessarily be precocious in her acquisition of those rules. What is suggested here is that every child is in contact with a sufficiently varied sample of spoken English in order for him to be exposed at an early age to the basic morphological processes. These processes occur in simple sentences as well as in complex ones. Practice with a limited vocabulary may be as effective as practice with an extensive vocabulary, and the factors that influence other aspects of language development may have no effect on morphological acquisition. Since, moreover, this type of inner patterning is clearly a cognitive process, we might expect it to be related to intelligence more than to any other feature. Unfortunately, there were no IQs available for the subjects, so that a comparison could not be made, and this last must remain a speculation.

Our next observation was that there were some differences between the preschoolers and the first-graders. These were predominantly on the items that the group as a whole did best and worst on: since no child in the Preschool could supply the irregular past *rang*, and a few in the first grade could, this difference was significant. Otherwise, the improvement was in the direction of perfecting knowledge they already had – the simple plurals and possessives, and the progressive tense. The answers of the two groups were not qualitatively different: they both employed the same simplified morphological rules. Since this was true, the answers of both groups were combined for the purpose of further analysis.

Children were able to form the plurals requiring /-s/ or /-z/, and they did best on the items where general English phonology determined which of these allomorphs is required. Although they have in their vocabularies real words that form their plural in

/-əz/, in the age range that was interviewed they did not generalize to form new words in /-əz/. Their rule seems to be to add /-s/ or /-z/, unless the word ends in /s z š ž č ǰ/. To words ending in these sounds they add nothing to make the plural – and when asked to form a plural, repeat the stem as if it were already in the plural. This simplification eliminates the least common of the productive allomorphs. We may now ask about the relative status of the remaining allomorphs /-s/ and /-z/. For the items like *lun or *cra, where both of these sounds could produce a phonologically possible English word, but not a plural, no child employed the voiceless alternant /-s/. This is the second least common of the three allomorphs. The only places where this variant occurred were where the speaker of English could not say otherwise. So far as general English phonology is concerned a /-z/ cannot in the same cluster follow a /-k-/ or other voiceless sound. Once the /-k-/ has been said, even if the speaker intended to say /-z/, it would automatically devoice to /-s/. The only morphological rule the child is left with, is the addition of the /-z/ allomorph, which is the most extensive: the /-əz/ form for him is not yet productive, and the /-s/ form can be subsumed under a more general phonological rule.

What we are saying here is that the child's rule for the formation of the plural seems to be: "a final sibilant makes a word plural". The question that arises is, should we not rather say that the child's rule is: "a voiceless sibilant after a voiceless consonant and a voiced sibilant after all other sounds makes a word plural." This latter describes what the child actually does. However, our rule will cover the facts if it is coupled with a prior phonological rule about possible final sound sequences. The choice of the voiceless or voiced variant can generally be subsumed under phonological rules about final sound sequences; the exceptions are after vowels, semivowels, and /l- n- r-/. In these places where phonology leaves a choice, /-z/ is used, and so the child's conscious rule might be to add /-z/. It would be interesting to find out what the child thinks he is saying – if we could in some way ask him the general question, "how do you make the plural?"

Another point of phonology was illustrated by the children's treatment of the forms *heaf and *kazh. It was demonstrated here that the children have phonological rules, and the direction of their generalizations was dictated by English phonology, and not simple phonetic similarity. /-ž/ is a comparatively rare phoneme, and yet they apparently recognized it as belonging to the sibilant series in English, and they rarely attempted to follow it with another sibilant. The similarity between /f/ and the sibilants, did not, on the contrary cause them to treat it as a member of this class. The final thing to be noted about *heaf is that several children and many adults said the plural was *heaves. This may be by analogy with leaf: leaves. If our speculation that the /-z/ form is the real morphological plural is right, there may be cases where instead of becoming devoiced itself, it causes regressive assimilation of the final voiceless consonant.

The allomorphs of the third person singular of the verb and the possessives of the noun are the same as for the noun plural, except that the plural possessives have an additional zero allomorph. These forms were treated in the same way by the children, with one notable exception: they were more successful in adding the /-əz/ to form possessives and verbs than they were in forming noun plurals. They were asked to produce three nearly identical forms: a man who *nazzes; two *nizzes; and a *niz's hat. On the verb they were 48% right; on the possessive they were 49% right, and on the noun plural they were only 28% right. The difference between their performance on the noun plural and on the other two items was significant at the 1% level. And yet the phonological problem presented by these three forms was the same. For some reason the contingent rule for the formation of the third person singular of the verb and for the possessive is better learned or earlier learned than the same rule for the formation of noun plurals. The morphological rule implies meaning, and forms that are phonologically identical may be learned at different times if they serve different functions. These forms are not simply the same phonological rule, since their different functions change the percentage of right answers. Perhaps the child does better because he knows more verbs than nouns ending in /s z š ž č ǰ/, and it is possible that he has heard more possessives than noun plurals. It is also possible that for English the noun plural is the least important or most redundant of these inflexions. This is a somewhat surprising conclusion, since nouns must always appear in a singular or plural form and there are ways of avoiding the possessive inflexion: it is generally possible to use an *of* construction in place of a possessive – we can say *the leg of the chair* or *the chair's leg*, or *the chair leg* although in cases involving actual ownership we do not say *of*. A sentence referring to *the hat of John* sounds like an awkward translation from the French. And no child said it was *the hat of the *niz*. The children's facility with these forms seems to indicate that the possessive inflexion is by no means dying out in English.

Of the verb forms, the best performance was with the present progressive: 90% of all the children said that a man who knew how to **zib* was **zibbing*. Undoubtedly, children's speech is mostly in the present tense, and this is a very commonly-heard form. Explanations of what is happening in the present all take this form. "The man is *running*" – or *walking* or *eating* or *doing* something. The additional point is that the *-ing* forms are not only very important; this inflexion has only one allomorph. The rules for its application are completely regular, and it is the most general and regular rules that children prefer.

The children's handling of the past tense parallels their treatment of the plurals, except that they did better on the whole with the plurals. Again, they could not extend the contingent rule. Although they have forms like *melted* in their vocabulary, they were unable to extend the /-əd/ form to new verbs ending in /t d/. They treated these forms as if they were already in the past. They applied the allomorphs /-d/ and /-t/ appropriately where they were phonologically conditioned, and only /-d/ to a form like **spow*, where either was possible. This suggests that their real morphological rule for the formation of the past is to add /-d/, and under certain conditions it will automatically become /-t/. Many adult speakers feel that they are adding a /-d/ in a word like *stopped*; this may be because of the orthography, and it may be because they are adding a psychological /-d/ that devoices without their noticing it.

Whereas the children all used regular patterns in forming the past tense, we found that for adults strong pasts of the form *rang* and *clung* are productive. Since virtually all English verbs that are in the present of an *-ing* form make their pasts irregularly, this seemed a likely supposition. Adults made **gling* and **bing* into **glang* and **bang* in the past. New words of this general shape may therefore be expected to have a very good chance of being treated according to this pattern – real words like the verb *to string* for instance, have been known the vacillate between the common productive past and this strong subgroup and finally come to be treated according to the less common pattern.

The children, however, could not be expected to use this pattern since we could not demonstrate that they had the real form *rang* in their repertory. They said **ringed*. At one point, the experimenter misread the card and told the child that the bell *rang*. When the child was asked what the bell did, he said, "It **ringed*." The experimenter then corrected him and said, "You mean it *rang*." The child said that was what he had said, and when asked again what that was, he repeated, "It *ringed*," as if he had not even heard the difference between these two allomorphs. Perhaps he did not.

The adults did not form irregular pasts with any other pattern, although a form was included that could have been treated according to a less common model. This was the verb **mot*, which was of the pattern *cut* or *bet*. There are some 19 verbs in English that form their past with a zero morpheme, but this group does not seem to be productive.

The cases of **gling*, which became **glang* in the past and **mot*, which became **motted* suggest some correlates of linguistic productivity. About nineteen verbs in English form their past tense with a zero allomorph. About 14 verbs form their past like *cling*, and seven follow the pattern of *ring*. Within these last two groups there are words like *win*, which becomes *won* and *swim*, which becomes *swam*. We can also find words similar to *win* and *swim* that are quite regular in the past: *pin* and *trim*. But virtually all of the verbs that end in *–ing* form their past in *–ang* or *–ung*. There are approximately 10 of these *–ing* verbs.

The productivity of the *–ang* and *–ung* forms proves that new forms are not necessarily assimilated to the largest productive class. Where a small group of common words exist as a category by virtue of their great phonetic similarity and their morphological consistency, a new word having the same degree of phonetic similarity may be treated according to this special rule. *Ox* : *oxen* is not similarly productive, but probably would be if there were just one other form like *box* : *boxen*, and the competing *fox* : *foxes* did not exist. With **mot*, the zero allomorph is not productive because although it applies to more cases than are covered by the *–ing* verbs, it is not so good a rule in the sense that it is not so consistent. The final /-t/, which is the only common phonetic element, does not invariably lead to a zero allomorph, as witness *pit* : *pitted, pat* : *patted,* and many others.

Although the adults were uniform in their application of *–er* and *–est* to form the comparative and superlative of the adjective, children did not seem to have these patterns under control unless they were given both the adjective and the comparative form. With this information, some of them could supply the superlative.

Derivation is likewise a process little used by children at this period when the derivational endings would compete with the inflexional suffixes they are in the process of acquiring. Instead, they compound words, using the primary and tertiary accent pattern commonly found in words like *bláckboàrd*.

The last part of the experiment was designed to see if the children were aware of the separate elements in the compound words in their vocabulary. Most of these children were at the stage where they explained an object's name by stating its major function or salient feature: a blackboard is called a *blackboard* because you write on it. In the older group, a few children had noticed the separate parts of the compound words and assigned to them meanings that were not necessarily connected with the word's etymology or with the meaning the morphemes may have in later life. Not many adults feel that Friday is the day for frying things, yet a number admit to having thought so as children.

These last considerations were, however, tangential to the main problem of investig-ating the child's grasp of English morphological rules and describing the evolution of those rules. The picture that emerged was one of consistency, regularity, and simpli-city. The children did not treat new words according to idiosyncratic pattern. They did not model new words on patterns that appear infrequently. Where they provided inflexional endings, their best performance was with those forms that are the most regular and have the fewest variants. With the morphemes that have several allomorphs, they could handle forms calling for the most common of those allomorphs long before they could deal with allomorphs that appear in a limited distribution range.

19

The Order of Acquisition

Roger Brown

The order of the fourteen morphemes for Adam, Sarah, and Eve is pictured in Figure 19.1. The names of the morphemes are written from top to bottom to represent early to late. The spacing of the names relative to the stages (I to V) and to one another represents the spacing in time of the points of acquisition. The stages have, you will recall, constant central mean-length-of-utterance (MLU) values for all the children: Stage I, MLU = 1.75; Stage II, MLU = 2.25; Stage III, MLU = 2.75; Stage IV, MLU = 3.50; Stage V, MLU = 4.00. The ages of the children at each stage vary, and they appear in Figure 19.1. Through Stage V the criterion of acquisition is three successive samples in which the morpheme appears 90 percent of the time, or more, in obligatory contexts. For all children three successive samples constitute approximately six hours of transcription.

The morphemes listed below Stage V had not attained the 90 percent criterion at this point. They are ordered in terms of the percentages of the morphemes supplied in obligatory contexts in the last six hours of the records including Stage V. While this is actually an order of level of performance at V it probably corresponds quite closely with the order of ultimate acquisition. Consider, for example, the eight morphemes which in Eve, the youngest of the three children, had not attained criterion by V. The top three were all at average levels of 80 percent or more in the final six hours. These three morphemes, the uncontractible copula, the past irregular, and articles had all attained acquisition criterion before V in both Adam and Sarah. On the other hand, Eve's last three morphemes (uncontractible auxiliary, contractible copula, and contractible auxiliary), which were at levels 56 percent or below, had none of them attained criterion in Adam or Sarah by V. In further illustration, notice that the first of Adam's morphemes below V had attained criterion before V in Sarah.

While the morphemes below V are ordered with respect to one another in the particular child's performance it is not the case that a given ordinal position represents the same level of performance across children. For example, Sarah's tenth morpheme and

From *A First Language: The Early Stages*. Cambridge, Mass.: Harvard University Press, 1973, pp. 270–5. © 1973 by the President and Fellows of Harvard College. Reprinted by permission of the publisher.

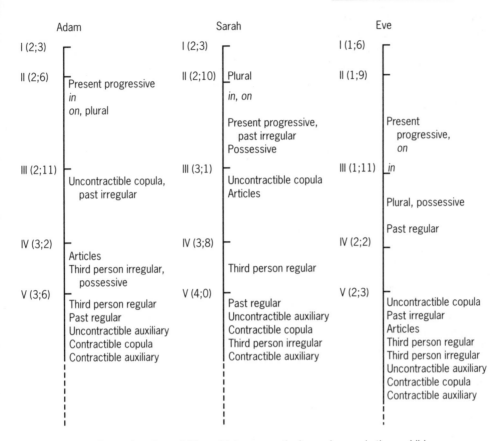

Figure 19.1   The order of acquisition of 14 grammatical morphemes in three children.

the first below V, the past regular, was present an average of 95 percent of the time in the last six hours though not yet at a consistent level across samples of 90 percent or better. Eve's tenth morpheme, on the other hand, which was the fourth below V, the third person regular, was at a 77 percent level.

There are three important conclusions to be drawn from Figure 19.1. The most important is this: the developmental order of the fourteen morphemes is quite amazingly constant across these three unacquainted American children. The constancy may be expressed in terms of Spearman rank-order correlation coefficients (rhos). The rhos, corrected for ties are as follows: Adam and Sarah, 0.88; Adam and Eve, 0.86; Sarah and Eve, 0.87. The reasons why this degree of constancy should amaze are, I am sure, quite evident. The basic data consist of uncontrolled spontaneous speech. Performance levels are not simple frequencies which might be expected to be fairly stable in conversational English for morphemes of this kind but are a genuine quality of performance or competence measure: percentages supplied in obligatory contexts. For none of the morphemes can it be said that the instances counted are entirely homogeneous. For example, there are several allomorphs of the regular plural and several kinds of grammatical agreement are involved, and so the instances entering into one sample might represent quite a different range from the instances entering into another. Nevertheless the constancy is there.

Some factor or some set of factors caused these grammatical morphemes to evolve in an approximately consistent order in these children. Of course I have known for years that this was true of grammatical devices generally because I could see it in the grammars that I wrote. But I had no idea in advance just how true it would prove to be for this set of morphemes when all were carefully scored and ordered in terms of the same criteria.

The second conclusion is that while order of development approaches invariance, rate of development varies widely. Compare Eve at age 2;3 (her Stage V) with Adam and Sarah at age 2;3 (their Stage I). Eve had attained criterion on six morphemes and was close to it on three others; all were present to some extent. Adam and Sarah had attained criterion on no morphemes at all, and most were completely absent from their speech.

The third conclusion is that MLU, or our Stages I to V, which are defined in terms of MLU, is a fairly good index of the level of development of grammatical morphemes at least through Stage V when MLU = 4.00. Adam, Eve, and Sarah at V had all attained criterion on five morphemes (present progressive, *on*, *in*, plural and possessive) and had either attained criterion or were very close to it (80 percent or better) on another four (uncontractible copula, past irregular, articles, past regular).

The third conclusion is that, while chronological age alone is a poor index of level of development, age in conjunction with MLU is a better predictor than MLU alone. Another way of putting this is that if two children at the same stage or MLU value are also at the same age they are more alike in their control of our grammatical morphemes than if they are at the same stage and the ages are quite far apart. Adam and Sarah are more like one another in terms of how much they have acquired at a given stage than either is like Eve, and Adam and Sarah are closer in age to one another than to Eve.

Acquisition Order in Other Studies of Spontaneous Speech

Until the spring of 1972 no one but Cazden and I had coded data in terms of presence in, or absence from, obligatory contexts but then Jill and Peter de Villiers (1973) did the job on a fairly large scale. They made a cross-sectional study from speech samples of 21 English-speaking children aged between 16 and 40 months. The speech samples ranged in size from 200 to 900 utterances. The de Villiers scored the 14 morphemes we have scored; they used our coding rules to identify obligatory contexts and calculated the children's individual MLU values according to our rules. Because their speech samples were much smaller than ours the problem of variability with certain morphemes was more severe and the de Villiers adopted the practice of including in the scoring of a given morpheme only transcripts which included at least five obligatory contexts for that morpheme.

Two different criteria of morpheme acquisition were used in the analyses of data. By method I, the morphemes were ranked in terms of the order of the lowest MLU sample at which each reached the 90 percent criterion; when more than one morpheme attained criterion at the same MLU the ranks were counted as tied. This is a kind of cross-sectional adaptation of our primary criterion. The second (II) way of calculating acquisition order is the same essentially as the method I used for morphemes that had not attained the 90 percent criterion by Stage V. The percentages supplied in obligatory

Table 19.1   Mean order of acquisition of 14 morphemes across three children

Morpheme	Average Rank
1. Present progressive	2.33
2–3. *in, on*	2.50
4. Plural	3.00
5. Past irregular	6.00
6. Possessive	6.33
7. Uncontractible copula	6.50
8. Articles	7.00
9. Past regular	9.00
10. Third person regular	9.66
11. Third person irregular	10.83
12. Uncontractible auxiliary	11.66
13. Contractible copula	12.66
14. Contractible auxiliary	14.00

contexts for each child were averaged across all children and the morphemes were ranked for order of acquisition. The study then yielded two morpheme acquisition rank orders: I (utilizing a 90 percent criterion); II (utilizing percentages supplied). To compare with the de Villiers' two orders it was necessary to have a single rank order for the three children: Adam, Eve, and Sarah. This I obtained by averaging the orders appearing in Figure 19.1 across the three children. This procedure yields Table 19.1 in which the average of the three ranks follows the name of each morpheme.

We have then three rank orders for the same 14 morphemes scored in the same way and using closely similar criteria of acquisition. We will call the two orders of the de Villiers', I and II, and mine, III. The degree of invariance is, even to one who expected a substantial similarity, amazing. The rank order correlations are: between I and II, .84; between II and III, .78; between I and III, .87. These relations are only very slightly below those among Adam, Eve, and Sarah themselves. Thanks to the de Villiers it has been made clear that we have a developmental phenomenon of substantial generality.

There are numerous other interesting outcomes in the de Villiers' study. The rank order correlation between age and order II is .68, while that between MLU and the same order is .92, very close to perfect. So MLU is a better predictor than age in their study as in ours of morpheme acquisition. In fact with age partialed out, using a Kendall partial correlation procedure, the original figure of .92 is only reduced to .85, suggesting that age adds little or nothing to the predictive power of MLU.

One result reverses mine: the de Villiers generally found that the contractible copula and auxiliary *be* forms attained criterion before the uncontractible forms. Neither they nor I have a really persuasive explanation of this reversal. There are many possibilities and as yet no strong evidence for any one of them.

Except for the de Villiers' study (1973), reports in the literature all concern one or another subset of the full set of 14 morphemes, and so the best we can do is check the full ordering on our explicit criterion against various partial orderings on criteria that are either not explicit or explicit but different from our own. It is, however, of some interest to know how general the order seems to be and how free it is of any single acquisition criterion.

Besides the ordering of the 14 morphemes we know that they are almost totally absent in Stage I for Adam, Eve, and Sarah. The generality of this, roughly the "telegraphic" quality of child speech, was documented for English and all languages so far studied in our Stage I, and so I shall not cite data or statements to this effect here. The inherent variability of the morphemes, being sometimes present in and sometimes absent from, obligatory contexts, during the early course of development does still need the support of other data. We proceed study by study.

Reference

De Villiers, Jill D. 1973. A cross-sectional study of the acquisition of grammatical morphemes in child speech. *Journal of Psycholinguistic Research* 2:3, 267–78.

20

Speech Perception in Infants

Peter D. Eimas, Einar R. Siqueland, Peter Jusczyk, and James Vigorito

In this study of speech perception, it was found that 1- and 4-month-old infants were able to discriminate the acoustic cue underlying the adult phonemic distinction between the voiced and voiceless stop consonants /b/ and /p/. Moreover, and more important, there was a tendency in these subjects toward categorical perception: discrimination of the same physical difference was reliably better across the adult phonemic boundary than within the adult phonemic category.

Earlier research using synthetic speech sounds with adult subjects uncovered a sufficient cue for the perceived distinction in English between the voiced and voiceless forms of the stop consonants, /b-p/, /d-t/, and /g-k/, occurring in absolute initial position.[1] The cue, which is illustrated in the spectrograms displayed in Fig. 20.1, is the onset of the first formant relative to the second and third formants. It is possible to construct a series of stimuli that vary continuously in the relative onset time of the first formant, and to investigate listeners' ability to identify and discriminate these sound patterns. An investigation of this nature[2] revealed that the perception of this cue was very nearly categorical in the sense that listeners could discriminate continuous variations in the relative onset of the first formant very little better than they could identify the sound patterns absolutely. That is, listeners could readily discriminate between the voiced and voiceless stop consonants, just as they would differentially label them, but they were virtually unable to hear intraphonemic differences, despite the fact that the acoustic variation was the same in both conditions. The most measurable indication of this categorical perception was the occurrence of a high peak of discriminability at the boundary between the voiced and voiceless stops, and a nearly chance level of discriminability among stimuli that represented acoustic variations of the same phoneme. Such categorical perception is not found with nonspeech sounds that vary continuously along physical continua such as frequency or intensity. Typically, listeners are able to discriminate many more stimuli than they are able to identify absolutely, and the discriminability functions do not normally show the same high peaks and low troughs found in the case of the voicing distinction.[3] The strong

From *Science* 171 (January 1971), pp. 303–6. ©1971 by the American Association for the Advancement of Science. Reprinted with permission.

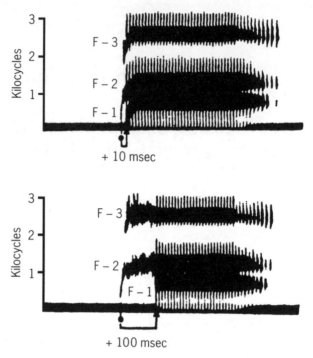

Figure 20.1   Spectrograms of synthetic speech showing two conditions of voice onset time (VOT): slight voicing lag in the upper figure and long voicing lag in the lower figure. The symbols *F-1*, *F-2*, and *F-3* represent the first three formants, that is, the relatively intense bands of energy in the spectrum. [Courtesy of L. Lisker and A. S. Abramson.]

and unusual tendency for the stop consonants to be perceived in a categorical manner has been assumed to be the result of the special processing to which sounds of speech are subjected and thus to be characteristic of perception in the speech or linguistic mode.[4]

Because the voicing dimension in the stop consonants is universal, or very nearly so, it may be thought to be reasonably close to the biological basis of speech and hence of special interest to students of language development. Though the distinctions made along the voicing dimension are not phonetically the same in all languages, it has been found in the cross-language research of Lisker and Abramson[5] that the usages are not arbitrary, but rather very much constrained. In studies of the production of the voicing distinction in 11 diverse languages, these investigators found that, with only minor exceptions, the various tokens fell at three values along a single continuum. The continuum, called voice onset time (VOT), is defined as the time between the release burst and the onset of laryngeal pulsing or voicing. Had the location of the phonetic distinctions been arbitrary, then different languages might well have divided the VOT continuum in many different ways, constrained only by the necessity to space the different modal values of VOT sufficiently far apart as to avoid confusion.

Not all languages studied make use of the three modal positions. English, for example, uses only two locations, a short lag in voicing and a relatively long lag in voicing. Prevoicing or long voicing lead, found in Thai, for example, is omitted. Of interest, however, is

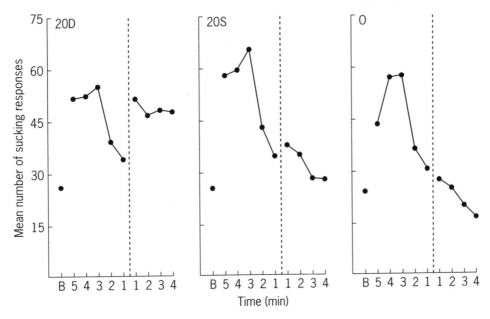

Figure 20.2   Mean number of sucking responses for the 4-month-old infants, as a function of time and experimental condition. The dashed line indicates the occurrence of the stimulus shift, or in the case of the control group the time at which the shift would have occurred. The letter *B* stands for the baseline rate. Time is measured with reference to the moment of stimulus shift and indicates the 5 minutes prior to and the 4 minutes after shift.

the fact that all languages use the middle location, short voicing lag, which, given certain other necessary articulatory events, corresponds to the English voiced stop /b/, and one or both of the remaining modal values. The acoustic consequences for two modes of production are shown in Fig. 20.2; these correspond to short and long voicing lags, /b/ and /p/, respectively.

Given the strong evidence for universal – and presumably biologically determined – modes of production for the voicing distinction, we should suppose that there might exist complementary processes of perception.[6] Hence, if we are to find evidence marking the beginnings of speech perception in a linguistic mode, it would appear reasonable to initiate our search with investigations of speech sounds differing along the voicing continuum. What was done experimentally, in essence, was to compare the discriminability of two synthetic speech sounds separated by a fixed difference in VOT under two conditions: in the first condition the two stimuli to be discriminated lay on opposite sides of the adult phonemic boundary, whereas in the second condition the two stimuli were from the same phonemic category.

The experimental methodology was a modification of the reinforcement procedure developed by Siqueland.[7] After obtaining a baseline rate of high-amplitude, nonnutritive sucking for each infant, the presentation and intensity of an auditory stimulus was made contingent upon the infant's rate of high-amplitude sucking. The nipple on which the child sucked was connected to a positive pressure transducer that provided polygraphic recordings of all responses and a digital record of criterional high-amplitude sucking responses. Criterional responses activated a power supply that increased the intensity of the auditory feedback. A sucking rate of two responses per second maintained the stimulus at maximum intensity, about 75 db (13 db over the background intensity of 62 db).

The presentation of an auditory stimulus in this manner typically results in an increase in the rate of sucking compared with the baseline rate. With continued presentation of the initial stimulus, a decrement in the response rate occurs, presumably as a consequence of the lessening of the reinforcing properties of the initial stimulus. When it was apparent that attenuation of the reinforcing properties of the initial stimulus had occurred, as indicated by a decrement in the conditioned sucking rate of at least 20 percent for two consecutive minutes compared with the immediately preceding minute, a second auditory stimulus was presented without interruption and again contingent upon sucking. The second stimulus was maintained for 4 minutes after which the experiment was terminated. Control subjects were treated in a similar manner, except that after the initial decrease in response rate, that is, after habituation, no change was made in the auditory stimulus. Either an increase in response rate associated with a change in stimulation or a decrease of smaller magnitude than that shown by the control subjects is taken as inferential evidence that the infants perceived the two stimuli as different.

The stimuli were synthetic speech sounds prepared by means of a parallel resonance synthesizer at the Haskins Laboratories by Lisker and Abramson. There were three variations of the bilabial voiced stop /b/ and three variations of its voiceless counterpart /p/. The variations between all stimuli were in VOT, which for the English stops /b/ and /p/ can be realized acoustically by varying the onset of the first formant relative to the second and third formants and by having the second and third formants excited by a noise source during the interval when the first formant is not present. Identification functions from adult listeners[8] have indicated that when the onset of the first formant leads or follows the onset of the second and third formants by less than 25 msec perception is almost invariably /b/. When voicing follows the release burst by more than 25 msec the perception is /p/. Actually the sounds are perceived as /ba/ or /pa/, since the patterns contain three steady-state formants appropriate for a vowel of the type /a/. The six stimuli had VOT values of -20, 0, $+20$, $+40$, $+60$, and $+80$ msec. The negative sign indicates that voicing occurs before the release burst. The subjects were 1- and 4-month-old infants, and within each age level half of the subjects were males and half were females.

The main experiment was begun after several preliminary studies established that both age groups were responsive to synthetic speech sounds as measured by a reliable increase in the rate of sucking with the response-contingent presentation of the first stimulus ($P < .01$). Furthermore, these studies showed that stimuli separated by differences in VOT of 100, 60, and 20 msec were discriminable when the stimuli were from different adult phonemic categories; that is, there was reliable recovery of the rate of sucking with a change in stimulation after habituation ($P < .05$). The finding that a VOT difference of 20 msec was discriminable permitted within-phonemic-category discriminations of VOT with relatively realistic variations of both phonemes.

In the main experiment, there were three variations in VOT differences at each of two age levels. In the first condition, 20D, the difference in VOT between the two stimuli to be discriminated was 20 msec and the two stimuli were from different adult phonemic categories. The two stimuli used in condition 20D had VOT values of $+20$

and +40 msec. In the second condition, 20S, the VOT difference was again 20 msec, but now the two stimuli were from the same phonemic category. In this condition the stimuli had VOT values of −20 and 0 msec or +60 and +80 msec. The third condition, 0, was a control condition in which each subject was randomly assigned one of the six stimuli and treated in the same manner as the experimental subjects, except that after habituation no change in stimulation was made. The control group served to counter any argument that the increment in response rate associated with a change in stimulation was artifactual in that the infants tended to respond in a cyclical manner. Eight infants from each age level were randomly assigned to conditions 20D and 20S, and ten infants from each age level were assigned to the control condition.

Figure 20.2 shows the minute-by-minute response rates for the 4-month-old subjects for each of the training conditions separately. The results for the younger infants show very nearly the identical overall pattern of results seen with the older infants. In all conditions at both age levels, there were reliable conditioning effects: the response rate in the third minute prior to shift was significantly greater than the baseline rate of responding ($P < .01$). As was expected from the nature of the procedure, there were also reliable habituation effects for all subjects. The mean response rate for the final 2 minutes prior to shift was significantly lower than the response rate for the third minute before shift ($P < .01$). As is apparent from inspection of Fig. 20.1, the recovery data for the 4-month-old infants were differentiated by the nature of the shift. When the mean response rate during the 2 minutes after shift was compared with the response rate for the 2 minutes prior to shift, condition 20D showed a significant increment ($P < .05$), whereas condition 20S showed a nonsignificant decrement in responding ($P > .05$). In the control condition, there was a fairly substantial decrement in responding during the first 2 minutes of what corresponded to the shift period in the experimental conditions. However, the effect failed to reach the .05 level of significance, but there was a reliable decrement when the mean response rate for the entire 4 minutes after shift was compared with the initial 2 minutes of habituation ($P < .02$). The shift data for the younger infants were quite similar. The only appreciable difference was that in condition 20S there was a nonsignificant increment in the response rate during the first 2 minutes of shift.

In Fig. 20.3 the recovery data are summarized for both age groups. The mean change in response rate (that is, the mean response rate for the initial 2 minutes of shift minus the mean response rate during the final 2 minutes before shift) is displayed as a function of experimental treatments and age. Analyses of these data revealed that the magnitude of recovery for the 20D condition was reliably greater than that for the 20S condition ($P < .01$). In addition, the 20D condition showed a greater rate of responding than did the control condition ($P < .01$), while the difference between the 20S and control conditions failed to attain the .05 level of significance.

In summary, the results strongly indicate that infants as young as 1 month of age are not only responsive to speech sounds and able to make fine discriminations but are also perceiving speech sounds along the voicing continuum in a manner approximating categorical perception, the manner in which adults perceive these same sounds. Another way of stating this effect is that infants are able to sort acoustic variations of adult phonemes into categories with relatively limited exposure to speech, as well as with virtually no experience in producing these same sounds and certainly with little, if any, differential reinforcement for this form of behavior. The implication of these findings is that the

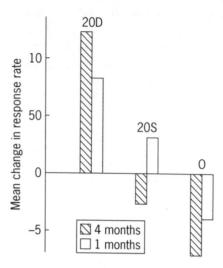

Figure 20.3   The mean change in response rate as a function of experimental treatments, shown separately for the 1- and 4-month-old infants. (See text for details.)

means by which the categorical perception of speech, that is, perception in a linguistic mode, is accomplished may well be part of the biological makeup of the organism and, moreover, that these means must be operative at an unexpectedly early age.

References and Notes

1   A. M. Liberman, P. C. Delattre, F. S. Cooper, *Language and Speech* 1, 153 (1958); A. M. Liberman, F. Ingemann, L. Lisker, P. C. Delattre, F. S. Cooper, *J. Acoust. Soc. Amer.* 31, 1490 (1959). It should be emphasized that the cues underlying the voicing distinction as discussed in the present report apply only to sound segments in absolute initial position.
2   A. M. Liberman, K. S. Harris, H. S. Hoffman, H. Lane, *J. Exp. Psychol.* 61, 370 (1961).
3   P. D. Eimas, *Language and Speech* 6, 206 (1963); G. A. Miller, *Psychol. Rev.* 63, 81 (1956); R. S. Woodworth and H. Schlosberg, *Experimental Psychology* (Holt, New York, 1954).
4   A. M. Liberman, F. S. Cooper, D. P. Shankweiler, M. Studdert-Kennedy, *Psychol. Rev.* 74, 431 (1967); M. Studdert-Kennedy, A. M. Liberman, K. S. Harris, F. S. Cooper, *ibid.* 77, 234 (1970).
5   L. Lisker and A. S. Abramson, *Word* 20, 384 (1964).
6   P. Lieberman, *Linguistic Inquiry* 1, 307 (1970).
7   E. R. Siqueland, address presented before the 29th International Congress of Psychology, London, England (August 1969); E. R. Siqueland and C. A. DeLucia, *Science* 165, 1144 (1969).
8   L. Lisker and A. S. Abramson, *Proc. Int. Congr. Phonet. Set. 6th* (1970), p. 563.
9   Supported by grants HD 03386 and HD 04146 from the National Institute of Child Health and Human Development. P.J. and J.V. were supported by the NSF Undergraduate Participation Program (GY 5872). We thank Dr. F. S. Cooper for generously making available the facilities of the Haskins Laboratories. We also thank Drs. A. M. Liberman, I. G. Mattingly, A. S. Abramson, and L. Lisker for their critical comments. Portions of this study were presented before the Eastern Psychological Association, Atlantic City (April 1970).

21

The Sound Laws of Child Language and their Place in General Phonology

Roman Jakobson

The splendid work of A. Grégoire, recently published under the title *L'Apprentissage du langage* (Liège, 1937), marks a milestone in the study of the initial stages of child language. According to this eminent Belgian linguist, the investigator ought "to have lived day by day, hour by hour, in the society of infants (p. 5), and to have been constantly on the watch for the external manifestations of their behavior," and furthermore he must be extremely precise as regards the difficult transcription of linguistic phenomena and the establishment of their conditions and their functions. The microscopic analysis of A. Grégoire combines these two qualities and permits us to evaluate and to utilize advantageously also the numerous data of earlier publications. There we find on the one hand observations by qualified linguists both precise and judicious but for the most part too concise and fragmentary, and on the other hand detailed studies of psychologists and pedologists lacking, unfortunately all too often, linguistic methodology.

The wealth of our experience makes it possible to give a structural analysis of language in its making and to look for general laws, or tendencies, if one prefers a more prudent formulation. At the beginning of this century M. Grammont stated the problem with impressive accuracy (1902, p. 262): In the child's speech, he said, there is "neither incoherence nor chance occurrences. . . . The child undoubtedly misses the mark, but he always deviates from it in the same fashion. . . . It is the consistency of the deviations which strikes us in his language and which, at the same time, allows us to understand the nature of the MODIFICATION." What, then, is the principle of this DEVIATION in the successive acquisition of phonemes?

Since the time of Buffon THE PRINCIPLE OF LEAST EFFORT has often been invoked: those sounds which are the easiest to articulate are acquired first. But there is one fact crucial to the linguistic development of the child which clearly contradicts this hypothesis. During the babbling period the child easily produces the widest variety of sounds (for example,

From Linda R. Waugh and Monique Monville-Burston (eds.), *On Language: Roman Jakobson.* Cambridge, Mass.: Harvard University Press, 1990, pp. 293–304. This translation by R. B. Sangster and L. R. Waugh was originally published in Roman Jakobson, *Studies on Child Language and Aphasia.* The Hague: Mouton, 1971. © by the Roman Jakobson Trust.

clicks, palatalized, rounded or pharyngealized consonants, affricates, sibilants, etc.) almost all of which he eliminates upon passing to the "few words" stage, to use the expression of Oscar Bloch, that is, upon assigning to his sound productions their first semantic values. It is true that some of these disappearing sounds are not maintained by the child when they do not occur in the speech of those around him, but there are other sounds which suffer the same fate despite their presence in the adult speech, and the baby re-acquires them only after much effort. Such is frequently the case with velars, sibilants, and liquids. The infant used to repeat these sounds while babbling; their motor image was thus familiar to him and the acoustic image should not have been lacking either. The son of the careful Serbian investigator M. Pavlović (1920) said *tata* for *kaka* while still distinguishing aurally between the two words *kaka* and *tata*. And P. Passy (1937) tells us of the case of a child who, while substituting the form *tosson* for both *garçon* (boy) and *cochon* (pig), became very angry when his mother, imitating him, did not differentiate these two words in her pronunciation. Occurrences of this type are well known. The loss of certain sounds has been attributed to the lack of a connection between the acoustic and the motor image, but, as some observers note, the child sometimes begins by pronouncing the [k] in the first words that he reproduces, and then all of a sudden abandons the velars, replacing them obstinately with dentals.

One can explain the selection of sounds which occurs upon passing from the babbling stage to language in the proper sense of the word only by the fact of the passage itself, that is to say, by the phonemic value that the sound acquires. The infant passes little by little from spontaneous and aimless soliloquies to a semblance of conversation. Seeking to conform to those around him, he learns to recognize the identity of the phonic phenomenon which he hears and which he emits, which he retains in his memory and which he reproduces at will. The child distinguishes this phenomenon from the other phonic phenomena he has heard, retained, and repeated, and this distinction, taking on a permanent and intersubjective value, tends toward a meaning. To the desire to communicate is now added the desire to communicate something. It is precisely these first distinctions, aiming at becoming significant, which necessitate simple, clear-cut, and stable sound oppositions, capable of being engraved in the memory and implemented at will. The PHONETIC RICHNESS of the babbling period thus gives way to a PHONOLOGICAL LIMITATION.

The close connection which exists between this selection of phonemes on the one hand and the unmotivated and clearly conventional character of the linguistic sign, on the other, is confirmed by the fact that exclamations and onomatopoetic expressions are not bound by such a limitation. These VOCAL GESTURES which, in adult speech as well, tend to form a distinct layer, seem to seek out expressly sounds not admissible elsewhere. It is precisely the expressive value of the unusual, rather than conformity to a model, which underlies the infant's use of rounded front vowels in his onomatopoetic expressions while he continues to replace them elsewhere by unrounded front vowels or by rounded back vowels. Thus an eleven-month old boy, cited in the well-known book by C. and W. Stern (1928), renders by *öö* the movement of horses and cars, the young Grégoire of nineteen months uses these same vowels to reproduce the sounding of a bell, and the little fifteen-month old daughter of Marcel Cohen (1925) imitates by similar sounds the barking of a dog. When she then changes this onomatopoeic expression into the simple designation for a dog – [oo] – she adapts the vocalism to the phonemic system at her disposal.

By eliminating these particular facts and following step by step the formation of the child's phonemic system, we discern a rigid REGULARITY in the succession of his acquisitions, which constitute for the most part a strict and invariable temporal sequence. It has been nearly a century now that this regularity has impressed observers: whether it is a question of French or English children, Scandinavian or Slavic, German or Japanese, Estonian or New Mexican Indian, every careful linguistic description provides equal confirmation of the fact that the RELATIVE CHRONOLOGY of certain innovations remains always and everywhere the same. The rate of succession is nevertheless quite variable: thus, two successive events, following each other immediately in some children, may be separated by a few years in the development of others. A kind of slowmotion film, such cases of delayed phonological development are particularly instructive.

Ordinarily the vowel system originates in a wide vowel and the consonant system simultaneously in a stop with occlusion at the front of the mouth; usually the vowel is an |a| and the consonant a labial stop. The first opposition within the consonantal system is between nasal and oral, and the second between labials and dentals (|m|-|n|, |p|-|t|).

These two oppositions constitute the MINIMAL CONSONANTAL SYSTEM of all the languages of the world; they are lacking only in those where there exist extrinsic and mechanical alterations (of the vocal apparatus). Such an instance is the lack of labials in Tlingit and similar American Indian languages (and in some female dialects of Central Africa) due to the artificial mutilation of the lips, and even in these cases the class of labials tends to be represented in the phonological system by specific substitutes.

Following the appearance of these two consonantal oppositions a narrow vowel arises in opposition to the wide vowel in the child's speech, and the ensuing stage in the development of the vowel system produces either a third degree of aperture or a split within the narrow phoneme into a front and back vowel. Each of these two processes results in a system of three vowels which is the MINIMAL VOCALIC SYSTEM of all the languages of the world. This minimal vocalic system as well as the minimal consonantal system require the presence of phonemes combining two "differential elements", in Saussurian terminology. (Thus in the "triangular" vowel system |u|-|a|-|i| the phoneme |u| is velar in contradistinction to |i| and narrow in opposition to the phoneme |a|, and in a "linear" vowel system the mid vowel is complex: wide in contradistinction to the narrow vowel and at the same time narrow in opposition to the wide vowel). If we consider the phonemes acquired in child language beyond the minimal systems discussed above, we observe that their order of acquisition corresponds exactly to the general laws of IRREVERSIBLE SOLIDARITY (IMPLICATION) which govern the synchrony of the languages of the world.

Thus, in the child's phonemic system the acquisition of velar and palatal consonants implies that of labials and dentals, and in the languages of the world the presence of palato-velars implies the simultaneous existence of labials and dentals. This solidarity is irreversible: the presence of labials and dentals does not imply the presence of palato-velars as can be shown, for example, by the total absence of the latter in Tahitian and in the Tatar language of Kasimov, and likewise the absence of velar and palatal nasals in numerous languages.

The child's acquisition of fricatives presupposes that of stops, and similarly in the phonological systems of the world's languages the existence of the former implies that of the latter. There are no languages without stops, but on the other hand one finds many languages in Oceania, Africa, and South America without a single fricative; among the languages of the Old World one can cite, for example, Karakalpak and Tamil which both lack autonomous fricative phonemes.

The acquisition by the child of affricates in distinctive opposition to the corresponding stops presupposes the acquisition of fricatives within the same series; by the same token, in the languages of the world the distinctive opposition of an affricate to a dental, labial, or palato-velar stop implies the presence of a dental, labial, or palato-velar fricative.

No horizontal (front-back) opposition in open vowels can be acquired by the child as long as he has not acquired the same opposition in close vowels. This order of succession corresponds exactly to the general synchronic law formulated by N. S. Trubetzkoy.

The acquisition of front rounded vowels, secondary vowels in the terminology of P. Rousselot (1925), presupposes the acquisition of primary vowels, i.e., back rounded and the corresponding front unrounded vowels. The secondary series implies the presence of primary vowels of the same degree of aperture in the languages of the world.

Oppositions which are relatively rare in the languages of the world are among the last acquired by the child. Thus a second liquid would be among the last acquisitions of the child's phonemic system. The sibilant liquid (ř), an extremely rare phoneme in the languages of the world, usually terminates the phonological apprenticeship of Czech children; children of the various Indian tribes which make use of glottalized consonants are late in acquiring them, and nasal vowels appear in French and Polish children's speech only after all the other vocalic phonemes have already appeared.

One could easily multiply the number of concurrences between the order of development in child language and the general laws which are brought to light by the synchronic study of the languages of the world, and one would surely find still more analogous correspondences the more one could obtain precise linguistic data about children of diverse ethnic groups. But one can nevertheless draw conclusions from the very existence of the parallelism touched upon.

Every phonological system is a STRATIFIED STRUCTURE, that is to say, is formed of superimposed layers. The hierarchy of these layers is practically universal and invariable. It occurs in the synchrony of language; consequently we have to do with a PANCHRONIC ORDERING. If there exists a relationship of irreversible solidarity between two phonological values, the secondary value can not exist without the primary and the primary cannot be eliminated without the secondary. This ordering is to be found in any EXISTING phonological system, and it governs all its mutations; the same ordering determines, as we have just observed, the acquisition of language, a system in the process of build up; and – let us now add – it reappears in language disorders, where we have to do with a system in the process of regression and disintegration.

As observations on language disorders by neurologists and psychiatrists teach us, nasal vowels tend to disappear first, as does the opposition between liquids, secondary vowels succumb before primary ones, fricatives and affricates change into stops, velar consonants are lost before consonants produced in the front part of the mouth, and labial consonants as well as the vowel |a| are the last phonemes to resist this process of disintegration, and it is these latter which are identical to the phonemes of the initial stage of child language. Higher layers are eliminated before lower ones. Aphasic impairments reproduce in reverse order the child's language acquisition. A phonological analysis of the different types of APHASIA (viz., disorders of a cerebral origin which involve no damage to the vocal apparatus itself) is what is called for to shed light upon the correspondences discussed, a study equally fruitful for the neurologist as for the linguist.

Certain points of contact between children's language on the one hand and certain so-called primitive languages on the other, had been noted a long time ago but these languages have been looked upon as survivals, reflecting, so to speak, the childhood of mankind. Appeals were made to the biogenetic law of Häckel, according to which the individual, in his own development, recapitulates phylogeny, the development of the species. The dearth of phonemes in a given language, however, is not necessarily a primordial deficiency; often, on the contrary, historical studies indicate that it is an impoverishment of recent date. What remains decisive in the correspondence between child language and the languages of the world is exclusively THE IDENTITY OF THE STRUCTURAL LAWS which underlie every modification of language, individual and social. It is, in other words, the same invariable superposition of values which is at the basis of every growth and decline in a phonological system.

It is not enough to emphasize the regularity of this superposition; it must be explained by demonstrating its necessity. The inadequacy of atomizing interpretations is obvious. The rules of child language cannot be separated from the corresponding facts in the languages of the world. Some investigators have noted, for example, that labial and dental consonants appear earlier in child language than velar ones, and the motivation for this fact has been sought in the habitual movements involved in sucking; but one could scarcely find even a fervent Freudian who would want to invoke infantile recollection to explain another manifestation of this same law, namely the loss of velars in certain Tatar or Polynesian languages. Instead of viewing the totality of the phonemic oppositions successively acquired by the child, this ordered structure has been broken up and crumbled. Thus by attributing the early appearance of labials to the protrusion of the lips or to visual imitation, it was forgotten that the primary opposition, the clearest and most stable one, between merely oral and nasal labials remains completely unexplained.

The phonological sequence of stages, however, is rigorously consistent. It follows the principle of MAXIMAL CONTRAST, and it proceeds, in the ordering of oppositions, from the SIMPLE and homogeneous to the COMPLEX and differentiated. Let us limit ourselves for the moment to citing briefly some examples.

The babbling stage begins with indeterminate sounds which observers say are neither consonants nor vowels, or else, which amounts to the same thing, are both at the same time. The babbling stage ends with a clear distinction between consonant and vowel. From the motor point of view these two categories are opposed one to the other as closure to opening. It is the low vowel |a| which affords the maximum opening, while on the other hand the stop consonants present zero opening, and among the stops it is the labials which obstruct the oral cavity completely. One might expect a priori that precisely this maximal contrast would be used at the threshold of child language to initiate the distinction between consonantal and vocalic, and experience confirms our expectation.

It is on the axis of SUCCESSION that the opposition between these two categories first arises. The labial stop forms, in combination with the vowel, the rudiment of the syllable. Opposition between phonemes on the other axis, the axis of SIMULTANEITY, in the terminology of F. de Saussure, does not yet exist. And yet it is this latter opposition which is the necessary premise for the distinctive function of phonemes. The phonemic framework of the syllable requires a phonemic content, framework and content being, as Viggo Brøndal has pointed out, two interdependent concepts.

Cavity without closure and cavity with closure – or, in other words, vowel and consonant – and then an innovation occurs: the FIRST OPPOSITION ON THE AXIS OF SIMULTANEITY, the opposition of oral and nasal stops. While the vowel remains characterized by the absence of closure, the consonant is split into two – one consonant characterized by a single cavity with closure and the other, adding to the first a subsidiary open cavity, and thus combining the specific features of an oral stop and of a vowel. This synthesis is a natural consequence of the opposition CONSONANT-VOWEL, whereas nasal vowels, which are opposed to oral vowels as a double open cavity is to a single open cavity, are a much more specialized phenomenon and a much less apparent contrast. This is why nasal vowels as well as consonants with a double closure appear only rarely in the languages of the world, and rather late in the acquisitions of infants learning to master these languages; whereas, on the other hand, the nearly universal opposition of nasal and oral consonants tends to be the first opposition with a distinctive value in child language.

In order to clarify the SECOND CONSONANTAL SPLIT, we might briefly survey the penetrating discoveries of W. Koehler (1910–15) and C. Stumpf (1926), which linguistics has yet to utilize. To these two experts in acoustics and perception of speech is due the credit for having determined and differentiated two kinds of irreducible qualities of speech sounds. Just as with colors, those sounds are, on the one hand, either ACHROMATIC or CHROMATIC to different degrees, and, on the other hand, either LIGHT (acute) or DARK (grave). The latter opposition gains in value as the chromatism decreases. Among vowels, it is the vowel |a| which is the most chromatic and the least susceptible to the opposition light–dark, while the narrow vowels are most conducive to this latter opposition and the least chromatic. The two dimensions of the vocalic triangle, whose horizontal or BASE-LINE is |u|-|i| and whose VERTICAL is |a|, correspond to the two psycho-physiological processes in the detailed analysis of Stumpf: the "U-I PROCESS" which comprises the opposition between light and dark, and the "A PROCESS" which determines the various degrees of chromatism. The first process (the wide line in the diagram) is fundamental, the second (the narrow line in the diagram) is subordinate.

Figure 21.1   Stumpf's two processes

Stumpf realized that there are no languages with a vocalic system based solely on the fundamental process. He hesitantly suggested that such a system might have existed, but in a prelinguistic era. Yet this supposition in no way solves the problem. We know that languages with linear vowel systems do in fact exist, but it is precisely the base of the triangle which is suppressed in these cases. Thus we find the vowel system reduced to the vertical dimension (1) in several West Caucasian languages analyzed by Trubetzkoy and (2) in child language (as well as in aphasia) at the stage where no distinction is made between different vowels of the same degree of aperture (for example, between |u| and |i|), in which case either they are used as contextual or stylistic variants or else only one of them is found. These facts seem to lead to an untenable paradox: one might conclude that the fundamental process is inseparably bound to the accessory yet the accessory can still occur independently!

This apparent contradiction can, however, be resolved once one considers vocalic and consonantal systems as TWO PARTS OF A WHOLE, and once one draws the necessary conclusions from Stumpf's own lucid definition (which he himself failed to do) according to which the presence of pronounced chromatism (*ausgeprägte Färbung*) is what distinguishes, in the first place, consonants from vowels. Given that chromatism is the paramount characteristic of vowel phonemes, the peak of chromatism represented by |a| thus makes this the optimal vowel, *princeps vocalium* (chief vowel) in C. Hellwag's terminology (1781). The vertical dimension *A* which differentiates the various degrees of chromatism is naturally the cardinal, sometimes even the only axis of vocalic systems. Consonants are phonemes without pronounced chromatism, and the opposition between light and dark, a contrast which increases as chromatism decreases, is consequently the cardinal axis of consonantal systems. Acoustic analysis demonstrates that labials oppose a dark timbre to the light timbre of dentals. Given that the dark timbre represents, according to Stumpf, the maximal degree of the process in question, labials thus represent the consonantal optimum.

In this way several different laws simultaneously receive an INTRINSIC explanation: to wit, the priority of labial consonants and of the vowel |a|, as well as the anteriority of the base line in oral and nasal consonants (the split into labials and dentals), the anteriority of the vertical line in the vocalic system (differentiation according to degree of aperture), and finally the order of the split within the vowels into back and front, which proceeds from narrow to wide.

In the acquisition of language the first vocalic opposition appears later than the first consonantal oppositions: hence there is a stage of development in which consonants already fulfill a distinctive function, while the lone vowel functions only as a support for the consonants and as a means of providing expressive variations. Thus we see that consonants assume phonemic value before vowels. In other words, there first appear the achromatic phonemes which divide along the horizontal axis, the axis of black and white; then arise the chromatic phonemes which divide along the vertical axis, the axis of degrees of chromatism. The ANTERIORITY OF THE FUNDAMENTAL PROCESS in relation to the accessory one is thus entirely confirmed.

Achromatic speech sounds, or more precisely sounds without pronounced chromatism, display, as Stumpf has already pointed out, diverse degrees of achromatism. Thus in the consonantal system one observes the same two dimensions as in the vocalic system, but in the opposite hierarchical order. A linear vocalic system is vertical whereas a linear consonantal system is confined to the base line. Palatovelar (= either palatal or velar) consonants present the minimum of achromatism. Being remote, just as are wide vowels, *von der Linie der blossen Helligkeiten* ("from the line of pure brightness"), to use Stumpf's expression, they show a relatively low aptitude for being split up into two distinct classes of lightness and darkness: into a class of palatals and a class of velars. Thus they form the peak of the consonantal triangle. The phonemes at the peak carry a higher degree of specific intensity than those at the base. It is noteworthy in this connection to recall that, *ceteris paribus*, low vowels are superior to high ones in their degree of perceptibility, and that palatovelar consonants are superior in their respect to the corresponding anterior consonants. As a matter of fact what is only an epiphenomenon of vocalic oppositions forms the very essence of palatovelar consonants. The acoustic filters used in Stumpf's analysis of $|k|$, $|t|$, and $|p|$ proved that when $|t|$ and $|p|$ were at the point of disappearing, the velar still subsisted as a dry knocking noise. It is a glottal stop, an indeterminate plosive phoneme, to which one finds velars reduced in languages with a leniar consonantal system, and often as well in child language (or aphasia) at a corresponding stage.

Obviously the opposition of vowels and stops, or, in other words, of opening and closure, precedes the opposition between complete and attenuated closure, i.e., between stops and fricatives. The opposition of an $|u|$ to an $|i|$ involves two parallel distinctions, which allows the combination of these two opposite properties in a rounded front palatal ($|ü|$) or an unrounded back phoneme ($|ɯ|$), is, needless to say, a secondary acquisition. The complexity of affricates is of exactly the same nature.

When continuing to compare the linguistic acquisitions of the child with the typology of the languages of the world, one comes to the conviction that also the sequential combinability of phonemes and finally the system of grammatical meanings are in turn subject to the same rule of the SUPERPOSITION OF VALUES.

The universality and the internal logic of the hierarchy observed above allow us apparently to assume the same order for the genesis of human language (glottogony). This invariability enables linguists to verify and to accept, for instance, the ingenious hypothesis recently suggested by J. van Ginneken (1907) (and previously by L. Noiré; see 1895, 1917) as to the beginnings of human language: consonantal oppositions must have preceded vocalic oppositions. It is true that this inquirer assumes a still earlier stage, one of clicks, but he himself notes that these did not function as phonemes but rather as merely vocal gestures forming, to be precise, a prelinguistic and an extratinguistic layer, to which we would only add a "postlinguistic" layer, as the study of aphasia seems to indicate. In a similar way A. Trombetti's hypothesis (1923) regarding the anteriority of stops appears to be also corroborated, whereas the priority of affricates surmised by N. Marr must be discarded.

We have tried to trace the rigorous stratification of several phonemic oppositions and to look for a tentative elucidation of this ordering. The principle is simple to the point of being trivial: it is impossible to put in place the roof without having first erected the frame, nor can one take away the frame without having first removed the roof. And it is this principle which governs both the dynamic and static aspects of language; in this way once disparate facts can now be coordinated, some supposed "unsolvable enigmas" may be eliminated, and seemingly disparate and blind laws obtain a unifying sense. The phonological development of the child as well as the aphasic regressions are in their broad outlines nothing but the corollary of this principle.

All this proves that the choice of differential elements within a language, far from being arbitrary or fortuitous, is on the contrary regulated by laws (or tendencies) of a universal and immutable nature. We have just briefly examined a few LAWS OF IMPLICATION of the type: the existence of an entity Y implies the existence of an entity X in the same phonemic system. One could just as well examine another series of laws, no less important for the typology of languages. These are LAWS OF INCOMPATIBILITY of the type: the existence of an entity Y excludes the existence of an entity X in the same phonological system.

Obsessed, despite his innovating pursuits, by that fear of goal-directed approaches which characterized the decline of the past century, F. de Saussure taught as follows (1916, p. 85): "Contrary to the false idea which we like to foist on language, the latter is not a mechanism created and aimed to express concepts." Now, however, we are in a position to reply to the devastating hypercriticism of the previous era, that it is precisely common sense, and in particular the idea that we as talking beings intuitively have about language, that is the most realistic: language is indeed a tool regulated and aimed to express concepts. It efficiently masters the sound matter and transforms these physical objects into oppositive attributes capable of bearing meaning. The rules of phonological structure sketched above are one of the proofs for this statement.

References

Bloch, Oscar. 1921. Les premiers stades du langage de l'enfant. *Journal de Psychologie* 18, 693–712.

Brøndal, Viggo. 1928. *Les Parties du discours*. Copenhagen: G. E. C. Gad.

Cohen, Marcel. 1925. Sur les langages successifs de l'enfant. In *Mélanges linguistiques offerts à M. J. Vendryès*. Paris: Champion, pp. 109–29.

Grammont, Maurice. 1902. Omomatopées et mots expressifs. In *Trentenaire de la Société pour l'Etude des Langues Romains*. Montpellier, pp. 261–322.

Grégoire, A. 1937. *L'Apprentissage du langage*. Volume 1. Paris and Liège: Droz.

Hellwag, Christopher F. 1781. *De formatione loquelae*. Tübingen.

Köhler, Wolfgang. 1910–1915. Akustische Untersuchungen. *Zeitschrift für Psychologie* 54, 241–89; 58, 59–160; 64, 92–160; 72, 1–192.

Noiré, Ludwig. 1895. *On the Origin of Language, and the Logos Theory*. Chicago: Open Court Publishing.

Passy, Paul. 1937. *Les Sons du français: leur formation – leur combinaison – leur représentation*. Paris: Didier. [First edition 1887; cf. *Lectures variées: mises en transcription phonétique*. Paris: Didier, 1897.]

Pavlovic, Milivoj. 1920. *Les Langages enfantins: acquisition du serbe et du français par un enfant serbe*. Paris: Champion.

Robins, R. H. 1968. *A Short History of Linguistics*. Bloomington: Indiana University Press.

Rousselot, Pierre Jean. 1925. *Principes de phonétique expérimentale*, 3rd edn. Paris: H. Didier. [First published in 1897.]

Saussure, Ferdinand de. 1916. *Cours de linguistique générale*, ed. C. Bally and A. Sechehaye. Paris: Payot. [2nd edn. 1922]

Stern, C., and W. Stern. 1928. *Die Kindersprache: Eine psychologische und sprachtheorische Untersuchung*. Leipzig: Barth.

Stumpf, Carl. 1907. Zur Einteilung der Wissenschaften. *Abhandlungen der Königlichen Preussischen Akademie der Wissenschaften* (Berlin), 61ff.

Trombetti, A. 1923. *Elementi di glottologia*. Bologna: N. Zanichelli.

Trubetzkoy, Nikolai S. 1929. Zur allgemeine Theorie des phonologischen Vokalsystems. *Travaux du Cercle Linguistique de Prague* 1, 39–67.

Trubetzkoy, Nikolai S. 1949. *Principes de phonologie*. Paris: Klinksieck. [Reprint 1967. Translation of *Grundzüge der Phonologie*, Prague, 1939, with appendixes added by Roman Jakobson.]

Trubetzkoy, Nikolai S. 1969. *Principles of Phonology*. Berkeley: University of California Press. [Translation of *Grundzüge der Phonologie*, Prague, 1939.]

van Ginneken, Jac. 1907. *Principes de linguistique psychologique*. Paris.

22

Universal Tendencies in the
Child's Acquisition of Phonology

N. V. Smith

1

It is a commonplace that very young children deviate from adult norms of pronunciation in their rendering of words in the vocabulary of the language they are learning. The following are typical examples of the efforts of a two-year-old learning English.[1] (The International Phonetic Alphabet is used.)

dark → g̊aːk
star → ḍaː
brush → b̥ʌt
bus → b̥ʌt
cheese → ḍiː
yellow → lɛluː

Given such performance data the immediate problem is to determine whether they also faithfully mirror the child's competence, or whether it is necessary to postulate more abstract representations for the child's lexical items which are then mapped on to the actually occurring form. To take the example of "dark"; is this word stored by the child as [g̊aːk] (i.e. his pronunciation), and produced accordingly; is it stored as [daːk] (i.e. the adult pronunciation) and subjected to specific deformations in the process of production; or is it necessary to postulate some third, more abstract or less abstract representation? For a number of reasons the second of these alternatives seems to be the correct one. I list a selection of these reasons immediately below.

(a) The child's understanding of adult speech

In addition to the obvious fact that everyone, child or adult, has a greater latent than active command of language it seems clear that children can perceive at a very early age,

From Neil O'Connor (ed.), *Language, Cognitive Deficits, and Retardation*. London: Butterworth, 1975, pp. 47–60 and 65. Reproduced with permission of the author.

contrasts they are unable to make until much later. Thus, for instance, although "brush" and "bus" were pronounced identically by A at age 2 as [bʌt] he had no difficulty at all in correctly identifying pictures of the two items when asked to "show me the____". Indeed, he was similarly able to bring me pictures of a "mouth" and a "mouse" from the adjoining room some months before the onset of speech and some years before he made the /θ–s/ contrast himself. This ability would be hard to explain if the child had only his own output as his internal representation, but is immediately accounted for if his internalization is really equivalent to the adult form.

It should also be noted that in those cases where the child's neutralization of 2 adult forms is closer to one of the model items than the other: e.g. (at age 3)

ship → sip
 sip → sip

the pronunciation of this neutralized form (in this case [sip]) either by an adult or in the form of a tape-recording of himself is first identified as that which is "correct" for the adult ("drink something") even if an alternative interpretation ("boat") can be imposed with some kind of contextualization of the sort "it goes on the water". [For further discussion cf. Morton & Smith, 1974.]

(b)   "Overlapping phonemes"

Although the relationship between the phonological segments of a child's forms and their adult models is regular[2] it is generally a many : many relation rather than a 1:1 relation; e.g.

adult /d/ → child's /d/ as in "Daddy" → [dɛdiː]
  "   /d/ →   "   /g/ " " "dark" above etc.
  "   /s/ →   "   /t/ " " "bus" above
  "   /ʃ/ →   "   /t/ " " "brush" above[3]

In a number of cases this many : many relation manifests a further complication in which one segment in a subset of the child's forms is subject to free variation while the same segment in a different subset is not subject to such free variation. For instance, at one stage adult /l/ and /r/ were neutralized as [l], e.g.

  let → lɛt
 light → lait
 write → lait
 really → liːliː etc.

Then, at a subsequent stage, when /r/ was being mastered the following distribution of data appeared:

let → lɛt
light → lait
write → rait/lait   (in free variation)
really → riːliː/liːliː   (in free variation)

Now if one postulates that the child has his own system distinct from the adult's the statement of the distribution of [l] and [r] in this system is apparently random. If, however, one assumes that the child operates the adult system with regular and definable deformations superimposed on it, then the distribution of [l/r] is perfectly natural.

(c)   The across-the-board nature of changes in the child's developing phonology

Just as hypothesizing that the child controls the adult system allows one to explain the overlapping distribution of [l/r], so also does it allow one to account for the regularity of the longitudinal changes the child makes. Thus, to take the same examples as in (b) above; if the child had internalized all the relevant forms with an [l] (as he pronounced them) then when he began to use [r] in some words one would expect that this usage would be occasionally generalized to the wrong forms – i.e. that there might be occurrences of [r] for adult /l/ – say [rait] for "light" or [riːriː] for "really". The fact that *no* such "mistakes" ever appeared and the child regularly made changes in his performance "across-the-board" to phonologically defined classes of element is a further indication that the child has mastery of the adult system, not just of his own output.

(d)   Indirect manifestations of adult contrasts superficially merged by the child

I have already stressed the regularity of the correspondence between the adult and child forms, and have also mentioned that at the age of two, phonetic voicing contrasts were non-distinctive for the child; e.g.

card ⎫
      ⎬ g̊aːt
cart ⎭

teddy ⎫
      ⎬ dɛdiː
Daddy ⎭

pea ⎫
    ⎬ b̥iː
bee ⎭

big ⎫
    ⎬ b̥ik   etc.
pig ⎭

In general plosives were voiceless lenis initially, fully voiced medially and voiceless fortis finally. However, there were environments in which it was quite obvious that the child was reproducing the adult voicing contrast, though not in this form. For instance, the child's treatment of consonant clusters consisting of a nasal followed by a plosive differed according to whether the plosive was voiced or voiceless: e.g.

tent → d̥ɛt
pink → b̥ik
lamp → wæp

i.e. before a voiceless consonant nasals are deleted. Compare

window → winuː
  finger → wiŋə
    hand → ɛn

i.e. after a nasal, voiced consonants are deleted.

    Accordingly, the child had minimal pairs where the adult distinction was one merely of voice, but his was one of nasal *v.* non-nasal consonant: e.g.

meant → mɛt
mend → mɛn

Thus, although the child's own "system" had no voicing contrast we must ascribe to him the ability to perceive and manipulate a voicing contrast if we wish to account for the regularity of the relationship between his forms and the adult forms.

(e)   Restructuring

Normally changes in the child's developing phonology took place "across-the-board"; for instance when a post-consonantal liquid was produced in say, "bread"→ [blɛd] after a long initial period in which such clusters were reduced to the initial consonantal element only, (in this case [b̥ed̥]) the comparable change was made to all and only those adult words containing such a configuration at the same time; e.g.

black → blæk (earlier [b̥æk])
blow → bluː ("   [b̥uː]) etc.
but never "bed" → *[blɛd]

    However, in a few exceptional cases it appeared that the child had "restructured" an item in terms of his own pronunciation of it, in such a way that a "primitive" form persisted after all comparable forms had changed. For instance, by a process of consonant harmony (q.v. below) words with an initial coronal consonant assimilated this segment to a following velar or labial; e.g.

dark → g̊aːk	table → b̥eːbu	
duck → g̊ʌk	stop → b̥ɔp	
neck → ŋɛk	same → weːm	
ring → g̊iŋ	take → g̊eːk	etc.

Once this process was lost by the child all the relevant items appeared in their correct form: [daːk, dʌk, nɛk, riŋ] etc. *except* for the single item "take" which remained [keik] for several months.[4] I assume that this item had been "restructured" as [keik] in its underlying (internalized) representation.

There was another small class of restructured items which provide evidence that the child's internalized representations were made in terms of elements of the adult system even though these elements were not directly controlled by the child in his performance.

As a result of the rule mentioned immediately above initial /s/ before a labial became [w]; e.g.

    same → weim
     sip → wip
    some → wʌm   etc.

whereas /s/ before another coronal was neutralized with /t/ etc; e.g.

     sat → ḍæt
    shine → ḍain   etc.

There were also two other sources for the child's [w]: first from adult /w/

    one → wʌn   etc.

and second from adult /f/ which regularly became [w] in initial position:

     fish → wit
    finger → wiŋə   etc.

(There were in fact *no* occurrences of [f] initially in the child's speech.)

Now at a stage when the consonant harmony rule was lost the /s/ before a labial was treated the same way as /s/ before a coronal consonant:

    same → ḍeim
     sip → ḍip

while sat → [ḍæt] as before.

The only exceptions to this regularization were "some" and its derivatives which remained as they were:

        some → wʌm
     somebody → wʌmbɔdiː
     something → wʌ(m) pin
     sometimes → wʌmḍaim
     somewhere → wʌmwɛ

Items like:

fish → wit
finger → wiŋgə
one → wʌn

whose initial [w] was not due to a harmonization rule also remained unchanged of course.

At this stage it looks, quite simply, as if "some" etc. have had the initial /s/ restructured as [w]. However, the next relevant change in the system was that the rule converting /f/ to [w] was lost: i.e.

fish → fit
finger → fiŋgə
foot → fut   etc.

although items with an initial /w/ in the adult form remain unchanged

one → wʌn

and items with an initial /s/ were also unaffected:

same → tʰeim
Simon → tʰaimən   etc.

But, at precisely this same stage, "some" and its derivatives also adopted an initial [f]:

some → fʌm
somebody → fʌmdɔdiː
something → fʌmpin
sometimes → fʌmtaimd
somewhere → fʌmwɛ

Thus it would appear that the restructuring of "some" etc. was not to an initial [w] – but to an initial [f] (which, of course, is phonetically far more plausible): that is to an item which did not occur as such in his own output at all – but which does occur in the adult system and which was treated exactly as one would expect such an adult segment to be treated. Unless we wish to say that the irregular behaviour of "some" etc. is random, it seems that we must accept that the child operates in terms of a system different from his output, and moreover a system which is precisely equivalent to the adult one: so much so that even his irregularities and mistakes are explicable only in the framework of this adult system.[5]

(f) Puzzles

The foregoing evidence appears to support the hypothesis that the child's internalized phonological forms are in terms of the adult system. It would also be largely consistent with the further hypothesis that the child's performance divergence from this system is attributable to his motor inability to execute certain complex movements or combinations of movements (even though the regular many : many correspondence of segments between adult and child speech might make this less attractive). This section and the next are intended to demonstrate that such an explanation is untenable.

As a result of two widespread rules the finer details of which need not concern us, we find the following kinds of example at age $2\frac{1}{2}$ or thereabouts;

bottle → bɔkəl
pedal → pɛgəl
rattle → rækəl   etc.

where /t/ and /d/ are velarized before a dark[l]; and

zoo → d̥uː
lazy → leːdiː
maze → meid   etc.

where /z/ falls together with other adult coronals as [d].

With the two rules ordered as they are here this gives rise to the following distribution of data:

puddle → pʌgəl
puzzle → pʌdəl

That is, the child is perfectly capable of producing the sequence of sounds [pʌdəl] but only as his phonological interpretation of "puzzle": whenever he attempts to produce "puddle" it comes out as [pʌgəl]. Thus although it may be the case that /z/ → [d] at least in part because the child is physically unable to pronounce [z] – this explanation will certainly NOT do for his mispronunciation of "puddle" as [pʌgəl].[6] Comparable instances of this phenomenon could be multiplied considerably.

(g) Recidivism

Further evidence of the irrelevance of the child's motor abilities to his treatment of adult words is provided by the phenomenon of recidivism, or apparent regression from a stage where a phonological contrast is mastered by the child, to a subsequent stage when this contrast is lost. For instance, by rules whose regularity I must ask you to take on trust (but for a demonstration of this regularity cf. Smith, 1973), A progressed from a stage where "lunch" and "shut" (and other comparable examples) were neutralized as [dʌt], to a stage where they were distinguished as [lʌt] and [dʌt] respectively, and then to a further stage where they fell together again as [lʌt]. That is, the child has learned to distinguish in his pronunciation two items which he then allows to fall together again, and where clearly the form of the neutralization is independent of articulatory difficulty. Again further examples could be given ad lib.

2

If it is accepted that the child's lexical representations are in terms of the adult system and not his own output,[7] but that this output is regularly related to the adult forms, then a natural way of accounting for the divergences between the two systems is by means of a set of ordered rules which take the adult surface forms as input and give the child's forms as output. The total set of these rules at any one stage then characterizes the child's speech patterns for that period, and developmental changes in his progressing phonology are accounted for by means of various changes to the set of rules. In the work mentioned I have presented a set of some 30 such realization rules for each of some 30 (arbitrarily delimited) stages in the child's developing phonology. Here I will merely give 10 of the more important rules which characterized his speech at 2 years and 2 months to give some idea of their effect, and to serve as a representative basis for the universal constraints I wish to propose for such rules in section 3. The sample rules will be followed by illustrative derivations of a couple of particular forms from A's vocabulary to show the cumulative effect of the rules. Each particular rule will be exemplified by items which for the sake of clarity presuppose the operation of the other rules listed as well as some of the rules which I have omitted here. For full details cf. Smith (1973).

(i) $[+ \text{nasal}] \rightarrow \text{ø}/\!\!-\!\!-\!\!-[- \text{voiced}]$
      e.g. tent → dɛt
            pink → b̥ik   etc.

(ii) $[+ \text{cons}] \rightarrow \text{ø}/ [+ \text{nasal}] \overline{[+ \text{voiced}]}$
      e.g. finger → wiɲə
            hand → ɛn

(iii) $\begin{bmatrix} + \text{coronal} \\ - \text{del rel} \end{bmatrix} \uparrow\!\!\rightarrow \begin{bmatrix} -\text{cor} \\ -\text{ant} \end{bmatrix} / - \begin{bmatrix} + \text{syllabic} \\ - \text{stress} \end{bmatrix} + \text{lateral]}$
      e.g. puddle → pʌgəl[8]
            bottle → bɔkəl

(iv) $\begin{bmatrix} + \text{coronal} \\ + \text{anterior} \\ + \text{continuant} \\ + \text{strident} \end{bmatrix} \rightarrow \text{ø}/ - [- \text{syllabic}]$
      (i.e. /s/ is deleted preconsonantally)
      e.g. stop → b̥ɔp
            spin → b̥in
            stay → d̥eː
            sweet → wiːt

(v) $\begin{bmatrix} + \text{coronal} \\ + \text{anterior} \\ + \text{continuant} \\ + \text{strident} \\ + \text{voiced} \end{bmatrix} \rightarrow \text{ø}/ - \#$

(i.e. /z/ is deleted finally)

e.g. cheese → ḍiː

eyes → ai

(vi)   [+ sonorant] → ø/ [+ consonantal] ——

e.g.   blow → ḅuː

bread → ḅɛḍ

new → nuː

(vii)   [+ coronal] → $\begin{bmatrix} - \text{coronal} \\ \alpha \text{ anterior} \end{bmatrix}$ /—— [+ syllabic] $\begin{bmatrix} - \text{coronal} \\ \alpha \text{ anterior} \end{bmatrix}$

e.g. dark → g̊aːk

neck → nɛk

table → ḅeːbu

sip → wip

(viii) $\begin{bmatrix} - \text{coronal} \\ + \text{anterior} \\ + \text{continuant} \\ - \text{lateral} \end{bmatrix}$ → [+ sonorant] /—— [+ syllabic]

e.g.   fish → wit

finger → wiɲə

sip → wip

room → wum

(ix)   [+ coronal] → [+ anterior]

e.g. brush → ḅʌt

white → ḍait

(x)   [+ segment] → [+ voiced]

e.g. teddy → ḍɛdiː

pig → ḅik⁹

To see how the rules work, let us assume that we have the adult form "drink". A phonemic representation of this would be: /driŋk/ which accordingly serves as input to the rules:

driŋk → drik	by rule (i)
drik → dik	by rule (vi)
dik → gik	by rule (vii)
gik → gig	by rule (x)

and then the phonetic rule mentioned in the footnote on p. 56 above would give the final phonetic form: [g̊ik].[10] No other rules can apply.

"sip" – viz.   /sip/ → "vip"   by rule (vii)[11]

"vip" → wip   by rule (viii)

wip → wib   by rule (x)

and again low-level phonetic rules will give the child's final form [wip].

3

It is of course trivially easy to write rules mapping one set of objects onto another, and such rules as the above have no value unless they are both fully motivated and rigidly constrained. I trust that section 1 of this paper constitutes sufficient motivation for the input to these rules; I have shown elsewhere (Smith, 1973) that the longitudinal development of these rules in terms of ordering and internal simplicity affords linguistic justification for their status; and in this section I wish to propose a set of putatively universal constraints on the form and function of such realization rules so as to limit their power in an interesting fashion.

Although the rules exemplified appear to perform a number of disparate functions (and it must be remembered that they represent only about one-third of the total set of rules necessary to characterize one particular stage of the child's phonology), closer examination reveals that all such rules must perform one of four functions.

These are:

(a)   to effect consonant and vowel harmony;
(b)   to bring about an "ideal" CVCV . . . canonical form;
(c)   to effect simplification in the system of phonological elements used;
(d)   to effect grammatical simplification.

Moreover these four functions are hierarchically ordered such that (a) and (b) must be maximally implemented before it is possible to implement (c) and (d).

Examples of consonant harmony are provided inter alia by rules (iii) and (vii). In the case of (vii) this is self-evident; as a result of the operation of the rule, all consonantal segments have the same point of articulation whereas previously they had differing points of articulation. In the case of (iii) the harmony is less obvious, but in fact the velarization of alveolars before a dark [l] is clearly an assimilatory process, albeit one whose nature is masked by the inadequacy of current generative formalisms. Examples of vowel harmony are provided by:

open → ubuː
broken → buguː

where all the vowels end up phonologically identical. [The length difference is positionally determined.]

It should not need stressing that consonant and vowel harmony can be implemented just as well by manner of articulation as by place of articulation, and that the "choice" of feature in terms of which the harmonization takes place and the direction (progressive or regressive) of the assimilation is an individual variable.

Examples of (b) – essentially "cluster reduction" – are provided by several of the rules listed – for instance (i) and (ii) which were discussed earlier in describing the different ways that clusters of nasal plus consonant were simplified. Again there is no particular reason why this specific solution should be selected by the child: it is predictable, however, that simplification of some kind will take place. In fact a more common solution is for all nasal clusters to be reduced the same way, e.g. by deleting either the nasal or the consonant in all cases.

By (c), systemic simplification, is meant the neutralization in the child's system, of contrasts operative in the adult system. Examples are provided by the last two rules given, the former of which, (ix), removes the contrast between alveolars and palato-alveolars, e.g.

brush/bus → bʌt
        ̥

and the latter of which, (x), eliminates the voicing contrast of the adult language.

The only example of (d) in the rules given here is afforded by (v), eliminating final /z/, where the motivation for this apparently arbitrary rule (final /s/ was retained) is the grammatical simplification given by eliminating the contrast between singular and plural, possessive and non-possessive etc. In fact final /z/ developed in five different ways depending on its morphological status and, as can be seen from the example "cheese" → [diː], gave rise to anomalous forms where the child has apparently re-analysed a singular as a plural.

When it is claimed that consonant and vowel harmony and cluster reduction must be implemented by the child before systemic (or grammatical) simplification takes place, this is to explain the superficially complex nature of the mapping between adult and child forms. For instance, at two years A's phonological system contained only 8 consonants: /b d g m n ŋ w l/ in comparison with the 24 or so consonants of the adult system: viz. /p t k b d g ʧ ʤ f θ s ʃ h v ð z ʒ r l w j m n ŋ/. Now clearly the simplest way formally to relate these systems would be merely to have a small number of neutralization rules mapping, say, all adult labials on to [b], or eliminating specific contrasts such as the voiced/voiceless distinction: a type of rule which in fact does occur – cf. (ix) and (x). It seems, however, that children are "pre-programmed" to maximize over the whole system those strategies which give rise to the least marked canonical and segmental forms – i.e. alternating sequences of consonants and vowels, where these, moreover, have articulatory features in common – before reducing the actual complexity of the system as an inventory of segments.

In addition to this functional characterization of realization rules – and perhaps it should be spelt out again that my claim is that the four tendencies[12] to consonant harmony, cluster reduction, systemic simplification and grammatical simplification are the only possible functions realization rules can have – it is also possible to state formal constraints on the rules. It will be obvious on even casual inspection that realization rules must be ordered. Thus rules (i) and (ii) above, whose formalization depends crucially on the specification of the feature [voiced], must patently precede rule (x) which neutralizes that distinction. It is also clear that rules (ix) and (x), the two rules given here which effect systemic simplification are then context-free whereas the rules which implement consonant harmony and cluster reduction are context-sensitive. This suggests at once that the formal analogue of the functional differences described above, namely the priority of (a) and (b) over (c)[13] is that all rules of type (c) will normally be context-free, whereas those of types (a) and (b) will always be context-sensitive. For those au fait with current phonological theory it might also be pointed out that rules of types (a) and (b) demonstrate precisely the properties of "conspiracies" in the sense of Kisseberth (1970).[14]

To summarize: I have attempted to show that the normal child's phonological competence is largely equivalent to the adult's, and that accordingly his deviations from the adult norm are correctly characterized by a set of rules which take the adult form as input and give the child's form as output. Further, in giving these rules a (hopefully) language-free characterization in terms both of their formal and functional properties, I suggest that they reflect in a reasonably direct way the strategies that children bring to bear in the acquisition of speech whatever the language they happen to be learning. In other words these constraints reflect universal tendencies in the acquisition of phonology.

Notes

1 Here, and throughout this paper, examples are based on observations of my son A, over a period of some two years, though conclusions reached have been corroborated by informal observations of other children learning English and other languages. For an exhaustive discussion and analysis of the issues sketched here, the reader is referred to my book (Smith, 1973).

2 The relationship is regular for about 97 per cent of the time (cf. Smith, 1973).

3 In fact at the stage under discussion [t] [ḍ] and [d] were all positional variants (allophones) of the same phoneme.

4 The transition from [g̊] to [k] in [keik] is the result of the independent appearance of a voicing contrast in the child's phonology. "taken" was also exceptional – occurring in the form [kukən].

5 It is clear that any argument based on exceptions must be backed up by massive documentation of the regular, unexceptional, cases, and that I have not presented such evidence here. However, I would point out that such documentation and further corroboration for this particular analysis of restructuring are available in the book referred to earlier (Smith, 1973).

6 I suspect that motor inabilities explain all and only those rules characterized as rules of "systemic simplification" below.

7 The third possibility mentioned on page 48, that the child's competence is equivalent neither to his output nor the adult forms is dismissed in Smith (1973).

8 For the sake of clarity I have made minor alterations in the vowels of some examples here. At the stage described "bottle" was [bɔgu] or [bɔku] rather than [bɔkəl]. Nothing depends on this.

9 The rule accounting for the allophonic variation among the stops (cf. p. 49 above) is a low-level phonetic rule which follows all the realization rules. Rule (x) here, then, merely eliminates the adult voicing contrast.

10 Note that the implication of this is that the realization rules characterize the child's "phonemic" system.

11 This is the first rule applicable. Note that the form represented as "v" is in fact an ad hoc abbreviation for a bundle of distinctive features which does not necessarily have any possible pronunciation. This is frequently the case in intermediate lines of a derivation in generative phonology.

12 For the distinction between "tendency" and "rule" cf. the discussion which follows this paper in [*Language, Cognitive Deficits, and Retardation*, ed. Neil O'Connor (1975)].

13 The position of (d) (rules of grammatical simplification) in this framework seems less clear.

14 *In nuce* rules "conspire" when they tend to produce the same output even though they have no structural properties in common (e.g. rules reducing consonant clusters either by deleting consonants or by intercalating vowels).

References

Kisseberth, C. 1970. On the functional unity of phonological rules. *Linguistic Inquiry*, 1, 291.

Morton, J. and Smith, N. 1974. Some ideas concerning the acquisition of phonology. In *Proceedings of the Centre National de Recherche Scientifique Conférence on Current Problems in Psycholinguistics*.

Smith, N. V. 1973. *The Acquisition of Phonology*. Cambridge: Cambridge University Press.

23

The Acquisition of
Phonetic Representation

David Stampe

Since 1965 I have been reporting to the Society on a theory of natural phonology, based on the assumption that the phonological system of a language is largely the residue of an innate system of phonological processes, revised in certain ways by linguistic experience. But since my previous talks have not been published, I have chosen this year to review some highlights of those talks rather than to report on more recent work.

A phonological process merges a potential phonological opposition into that member of the opposition which least tries the restrictions of the human speech capacity. Processes characteristically fall into contradictory sets, reflecting conflicting phonetic restrictions. Obstruents become voiceless irrespective of their context, because their oral constriction impedes the air-flow required by voicing, while, on the other hand, they become voiced in voiced environments by "assimilation." Where these processes overlap, for example between vowels, there is a contradiction: an obstruent cannot be both voiceless and voiced. There are three ways by which such contradictions are resolved.

The most radical resolution is by suppression of one of the contradictory processes. The mastery of voiced obstruents in all contexts entails the suppression of the devoicing process mentioned above, with a resulting opposition of voice in obstruents in all contexts except those in which the voicing process merges them.

The second resolution is by suppression of some part of a process – to limit the set of segments it applies to or the set of contexts it applies in. Implicit in each process are various subtle and strict hierarchies, ranging from the greatest generality which is phonetically motivated, to the complete suppression of the process. For example, the devoicing process may be limited to tense obstruents, but not to lax ones unless it is altogether suppressed, because tense obstruents are less favorable to voicing than lax ones. Or it may be limited to voiceless contexts, or initial and final positions, and so forth. Likewise the voicing process may be limited to contexts between vowels, between non-high vowels, or between low vowels, but it may not be limited to apply just between high vowels, for example. In this example the traditional parameter of "sonority" clearly

From *Proceedings of the 5th Regular Meeting of the Chicago Linguistic Society*. Chicago: Chicago Linguistic Society, 1979, pp. 443–54.

plays a role. Besides such phonological limitations, there are also nonphonological limitations which may be imposed, but these are not relevant to this discussion.

The third resolution is by ordered application. Many languages lack a voicing opposition in obstruents, which can be ascribed to the devoicing process, but their obstruents are voiced in certain voiced contexts by the (later) application of the voicing process. For this pair of processes, application in the opposite order would be indistinguishable from suppression of the voicing process. But many pairs of processes are manifest in either order. For example, there is an assibilation process changing *t* to *s* before *s*, and a process which I will refer to here as absorption, which changes vowel plus nasal to nasalized vowel before spirants. Both processes applied in Latin and Greek. Assibilation changed Latin *nepoːt-s* "grandson" (gen. *nepoːt-is*) to *nepoːss*, which is simplified to *nepoːs*, and Greek *oːt-s* "ear" (gen. *oːt-os*) to *oːss*, whence *oːs*. Absorption changed Latin *sanguin-s* "blood" (gen. *sanguin-is*) to *sanguis* (by subsequent denasalization) and Greek *hrin-s* "nose" (gen. *hrin-os*) to *hris*. As the Latin form *mens* from *ment-s* "mind" (gen. *ment-is*) shows, absorption could not apply after assibilation in Latin. Thus it could not apply to the *Vns* sequence which resulted from the assibilation of *Vnts*, to original *Vns*. In Greek, however, the order of these processes was not limited at all: *himant-s* "thong" (gen. *himant-os*) underwent assibilation and then absorption to yield *himas*. Since Greek does not limit the effect of either process, it can be assumed to reflect the innate relationship of these processes, whereas Latin reflects a limitation – by ordering – of the effect of the absorption process.[1]

I assume, then, that in its language-innocent state, the innate phonological system expresses the full system of restrictions of speech: a full set of phonological processes, unlimited and unordered. The most extreme processes are usually observable only in infancy: unstressed syllables are deleted, clusters and coarticulations are simplified, obstruents become lax stops, linguals become coronal, vowels merge to *a*.[2] The fullest effect of the innate system is seen in the utterances of what might be called the "post-babbling" period, which, although they are still nonsemantic, characteristically consist of well-articulated sequences of identical and stressed syllables composed of lax stop (or nasal) plus low vowel: *dadada, ŋaŋaŋa, mamama* or the like. Even this early there is some freedom, in that the stop may or may not be voiced by assimilation to the vowel, the vowel may or may not be fronted by a coronal, a coronal may or may not be palatalized, nasals may or may not be denasalized, and so forth. The first words resemble these post-babbling utterances in structure, and indeed they are often just continuations of these, with semantic import.[3]

Each new phonetic opposition the child learns to pronounce involves some revision of the innate phonological system. It appears that the mechanisms of this revision are the same as those which resolve contradictions between processes: suppression, limitation, and ordering. The child's task in acquiring adult pronunciation is to revise all aspects of the system which separate his pronunciation from the standard. If he succeeds fully, the resultant system must be equivalent to that of standard speakers.

In the view I am proposing, then, the mature system retains all those aspects of the innate system which the mastery of pronunciation has left intact. (But not *only* those, since some processes and conditions on processes are certainly learned.) The processes which survive determine what phonetic representations are pronounceable in the language. For example, there is a process devoicing word-final obstruents (presumably a limited version of the process devoicing obstruents in general) which usually manifests itself immediately upon the acquisition of word-final obstruents. English-speaking children must suppress this process if their pronunciation is to conform to the standard, but German children need not, because German permits this devoicing: *hunt/hundə* "dog/dogs". As the example shows, the devoicing process governs only the phonetic representation of German words, since the phonological representation of *hunt* is *hund*. In other languages it governs the phonological representations as well, in case there is no voicing opposition in morpheme-final obstruents. And in languages which, for example, lack morpheme-final consonants altogether, the process stays in the system but has no overt manifestation. This claim flies in the face of all phonological theories known to me, but it appears to be supported by the pronunciation, in such languages, of foreign words with final voiced obstruents, which, if they are pronounced at all, are characteristically devoiced.[4]

Students of child language have noted striking regularities in the order in which phonetic representations are mastered. My studies have convinced me that these regularities can be fully explained by independently attested properties of the innate system – its processes, their inner hierarchies, and their interrelations – and by the three mechanisms whereby the innate system is revised. In particular, it appears that there is no need to refer to "implicational laws," such as Jakobson (1940) proposed, since to the extent that these are valid they seem to result entirely from the innate system.

Consider, for example, the implicational laws that affricates imply spirants and spirants imply stops (Jakobson, 51, 55). There seem to be only two general, context-free processes affecting these obstruent articulations: obstruents become stops (which may be limited to affricates become stops) and affricates become spirants. If these processes are innate, it can readily be seen that there is no possible suppression, limitation, or ordering which could violate the implicational laws and thereby result in a different order of acquisition. In fact, even the "intermediate" levels of representation permitted by these mechanisms conform to the implicational laws. A similar account can be given for all the implicational laws of which I am aware.[5]

However, there are less general processes affricating or spirantizing palatal and even velar stops, and context-sensitive processes affricating stops before high vowels, or spirantizing them after vowels, for example. As might be expected, if these apply there may arise contradictions to the order of acquisition predicted by the implicational laws. Jakobson was able to ignore these contradictions by interpreting the implicational laws in terms of phonemic representation, which could treat palatal affricates as stops, for example, if there were no contrast. But the contradictory context-sensitive processes cannot be ignored, for they may neutralize phonemic oppositions in certain contexts. Therefore the implicational laws cannot even account for the phonemic representation but only for the phonemic inventory, which is unaffected by contextual neutralizations. This is surely a high price to pay for implicational laws, since if the processes are taken as the primitives of the theory, as I am proposing, it is possible to make predictions about representations as well as inventories, and in fact about representations at every level. And if we extended the notion implicational law to allow for the contradictory processes, then the laws would themselves be contradictory, and to resolve the contradictions we would have to appeal to suppression, limitation, and ordering. In other words, there would then be no difference between the implicational laws and the innate processes, which is just what I am arguing.

Most modern students of child phonology have assumed that the child has a phonemic system of his own, distinct from that of his standard language. So far as I am aware, no evidence whatsoever has been advanced to support this assumption. There is, on the other hand, abundant evidence that the child's representations closely conform to adult speech. Since this claim is essential to the theory I am proposing – that the child's productions result from the application of the innate phonological system to some sort of phonological representation – it is appropriate to digress briefly from strictly phonetic concerns and examine some evidence of this phonological representation. Most major works on child language agree that the child has internalized a representation of adult speech which transcends in detail his own reduced productions. The most striking evidence, I think, comes when a child masters a phonological opposition he previously had merged. From that moment he pronounces the new segment in precisely the appropriate morphemes, without rehearing them, and the old substitute does not reappear again.[6] Unless, of course, his mastery is only conditional, so that the process remains optional. But even in this case the variation between the new and old segment will take place only in morphemes which in the adult language have the former. Jakobson, discussing the emergence of *k* after the suppression of the process that makes linguals coronal, says that "when *k* finally appears, mistakes in the use of both phonemes (*k*, *t*) arise at first, especially those caused by a hypercorrect repression of the expected *t* in favor of *k*" (54). But all the cases of this which I have seen in the literature can be, in fact must be, explained as the result of some additional process whose presence was not previously apparent. In the case in question, the culprit is the infantile process which makes coronals velar if a velar occurs in the word, so that "cat" and "dog", earlier pronounced *tæt* and *dɔd*, change at the first appearance of velars to *kæk* and *gɔg*. Jakobson's example of such a hypercorrection, quoted from Nadoleczny, is clearly subject to this analysis: a child said *Duten Ta Herr Dotta*, then *Guken Gag Herr Goka*, presumably for "Guten Tag, Herr Doktor." Far from being evidence against the child's having mentally represented phonological oppositions before he can produce them, such cases actually support the claim. My son had a process deleting final stops, so that "dog" was pronounced like "doll" at first, as *da*. Immediately upon the acquisition of velars "dog" became *ga*, the coronal being assimilated to the *deleted* velar, while "doll" remained unchanged.[7]

Returning to the acquisition of phonetic representation, I will now cite some examples from children's speech illustrating the ordering, limitation, and suppression of innate processes. Examples of one child having ordered two processes which another child has not, are common, but clear examples of a child actually performing the ordering are difficult to find in the literature. However, I am aware of a few cases. For example, Hildegard Leopold at 20 months said *du(ı)ʃ* "juice", *du* "June", *do:i* "Joey", beside *dʒuıʃ* "church", *dʒudʒu* "choo-choo", by application of the processes (a) *dʒ* becomes *d*, and (b) stops become voiced before vowel (compare *du* "to, do"). But at 19 months "choo-choo" had been *dudu* (Leopold 1947: 268 and 1939: 126), by unordered application of the same processes. At 22 months Joan Velten devoiced word-final obstruents (*bat* "bad, bite") and then denasalized everything after a non-nasal consonant (*bub* "broom", *bud* "spoon"). But the only word she had previously acquired which met the conditions of both these processes, "lamb", had been pronounced *bap*, with the unordered application making *m* into *b* and then *p* (Velten 1943).[8] My son John had *kæ̃jŋ* "Channing" by

(a) flapping of *n*, flap-deletion, and desyllabification. His pronunciation of "candy" was at first *kǽĵ*, by processes (b) changing *nd* to *nn* and *nn* to *n*, applied before (a). Later "candy" became *kǽni*, by ordering (b) after (a).[9]

Examples of limitation are much easier to find. Hildegard Leopold voiced obstruents before voiced segments (*baba* "papa") and later only between voiced segments (*paba*), before she finally suppressed the process (*papa*, Leopold 1947: 31). By exactly parallel steps, at 25 months Joan Velten first distinguished between *pu:bu* "paper, people, purple" and *bu:bu* "baby", and then at 27 months between *papu* "puppy" and *pabu* "probably" (Velten 290). The denasalization process in her speech, mentioned above, was limited to nonfinal positions before being suppressed: *saˑbud* "salmon" becomes *saˑbun* and finally *saˑmun* (291). Chao's granddaughter, learning Mandarin, at first palatalized all coronals and then limited this to continuant coronals (Chao 1951: 29f).[10]

The *h*-deletion process, context-free in its most general form, was successively limited in my son's speech to syllables of decreasing stress, until he attained the standard formal pronunciation with *h* dropped only before completely stressless syllables. This is a conditional limitation even in the standard, at least in my dialect, and so it may apply to increasingly stressed syllables in increasingly relaxed speech (*his henhouse, 'is henhouse, 'is hen'ouse, 'is 'en'ouse*). The example illustrates, incidentally, the way the inner hierarchy of a process governs not only its form but its application; phonetic representations requiring a violation of the hierarchy (e.g. *'enhouse*) do not occur.

As an example of suppression, I will cite just the word "kitty" as pronounced by a two-year old boy in successive interviews. His pronunciation changed from *ki:* (*kii*) to *kii* to *kiɪ* to *kiɪ́* to *kɪti*, by successive suppression of the processes of prevocalic tensing, postsyllabic desyllabification, flap-deletion, and flapping (the boy's parents speak a New York dialect with unflapped *t*). It is extraordinary for a child to manifest all the intermediate steps between his first and last pronunciations of a form. My son's pronunciation of this word went directly from *ki:* to *kiɪ́*. This does not necessarily indicate that he suppressed all the processes at once, since suppression of the first (flap-deletion) would have resulted in the same abrupt change.

Passy believed that phonetic change arose from "imperfect imitation, by children, of the speech of adults" (1890: 225). This hypothesis explains why, except in borrowing, phonetic change does not seem to occur in adults. It also explains, as the Neogrammarian view of phonetic change as due to subconscious drifts of pronunciation does not, how change might be quite radical. And finally, to the extent that children's deformations of adult speech are regular, it explains why phonetic change is regular. If the child fails to master a certain sound, it will appear that he has changed it to the sound he regularly substituted for it.[11]

This account can readily be expressed by the theory I am proposing. A phonetic change occurs when the child fails to suppress some innate process which does not apply in the standard language. Thus if an American child fails to suppress the process devoicing word-final obstruents, for example, his speech – compared to the adult standard – will exhibit a phonetic change corresponding to the "addition" of a process to the phonology. This change has become standard in certain Appalachian dialects. The change would not affect the *phonological* representations of its originators, of course, nor would it affect those of later generations if there remained any phonological support for the original representations. In the dialects in question, "bet" and "bed", earlier *bɛt* and *bɛːd* by the

standard process making stressed vowels long or short before voiced or voiceless segments, respectively, are still distinguished by vowel length as *bɛt* and *bɛːt*.

In the above example the processes are ordered, with length adjustment before devoicing. The innate, unordered application of these can be seen in the speech of children.
For example, Joan Velten at first pronounced "back" and "bad" alike as *bat*, with length
adjustment applying after devoicing, then at 24 months distinguished these as *bat* and
baːt, respectively (Velten, 289), by ordering length adjustment before devoicing. Thus
her phonological system becomes identical, with regard to these processes, to the dialects
cited above. Three weeks later she attains the standard pronunciation by suppressing
the voicing process.

The conservative influence of the standard exerts itself by rejecting most of the innovations of children. Innovations are only gradually admitted, often just conditionally
at first. Thus it is that phonetic changes often begin as optional rather than obligatory
pronunciations. The conservatism of the standard forces the innovator to suppress a
process at least in his formal speech. Beside the dialects which have admitted obligatory
devoicing, there are many others, more conservative, which still admit it only in relaxed
speech. We must not imagine that the fact that phonetic changes are characteristically
optional before they become obligatory means that they are at first optional in child speech.
On the contrary, the child's progressions are essentially opposite to the tendencies of
change – we might say the regressions – of the standard language.

This is why the typical progression from unordered to ordered application exemplified
in the child appears in the opposite order in the corresponding phonetic change. Even
those dialects which have admitted devoicing have required that it be ordered with respect
to length adjustment. German has gone a step further in admitting unordered application, so that *bunt* has the same length whether it represents underlying *bunt* or *bund*.
The conservative ordering of assibilation after absorption, as in Latin *mens* (<*ment-s*)
was relaxed in popular Latin so that *n* was absorbed here as well.[12]

The child must limit a phonological process to the form compatible with the standard, and to the extent he fails, it will appear that he has "generalized" the process. The
generalization will therefore conform to the hierarchies implicit in the process, and it
will proceed in the opposite direction along these hierarchies from the child's limitation
of it. These hierarchies regularly assume the form of hierarchies of applicability if the
generalizations are optional ones, as in the example of *h*-deletion cited above. They are
sometimes even reflected in the isoglosses surrounding an innovating dialect. Ideally,
the innermost dialects have admitted a process in its most general form, and each
successive isogloss marks an additional limitation which has been enforced, until at the
outermost isogloss we encounter dialects which have not admitted the process in any
form. Of course, the ideal is rarely encountered. The classic example involves the isoglosses
of the "Rhenish Fan," on the boundary between High and Low German.[13]

I have dwelt on phonetic change at some length because the account of phonetic
acquisition presented here appears to explain fully all the currently known mechanisms
of regular phonetic change. The apparent addition, generalization, and unordering of
processes arise in the child's failure, respectively, to suppress, limit, or order processes
of the innate system to the extent required by the standard language.[14] In other words,
the child simply fails to master a phonetic opposition in some or all contexts. This is
really all that is involved. But we must refer to the innate system and the mechanisms

by which it is limited to understand the precise nature and the regularity of phonetic change.

The theory of the acquisition and change of phonetic representations outlined here can be extended in a natural way to account for the acquisition and change of phonological representations (Stampe 1968). And finally, it can account for the implicational regularities such as Jakobson observed in the phonological systems of the world's languages, but in much finer detail than can Jakobson's theory, which was limited just to a subset of the context-free phonological processes. The markedness theory of Chomsky and Halle (1968: chapter 9) was incidentally limited to approximately the same set of processes. As a result these theories were limited in potential just to the most underlying levels of representation, which are relatively, though not entirely, undisturbed by the remaining processes. An important difference between those theories and the theory outlined here, then, is that the latter is intended to account for all levels of phonological representation. Of course, such theories as these can succeed only insofar as they are made substantive, in the present instance by a description of the innate phonological system. It becomes increasingly obvious that this staggering task must confront any serious attempt to advance our understanding of phonology.

Notes

1 The Greek processes are unordered in that the correct forms would result if the processes applied sequentially and iteratively in random order. The notion "unordered" corresponds to the "unmarked ordering" of Kiparsky (1965) except that I extend it, as noted, to include re-application. (More on this below.) "Ordered" here corresponds to Kiparsky's "marked ordering".

2 However, most of the processes mentioned in this paragraph make limited appearances, at least, in some adult languages. For example, the palatalization of coronals observed in many children applies generally, though lightly, in Efik. It is limited to sibilants in Bengali, and to nasals in Sora.

3 "Post-babbling" utterances, as defined here, are to be distinguished from the unstructured, random vocalizations of true babbling, which, significantly, is essentially alike in deaf and hearing children. Since the structure of post-babbling utterances can be accounted for by the innate phonological system, one might further speculate that they are underlain by phonological representations, in some sense, perhaps as crude imitations of adult speech, prior to the recognition of its distinctions and semanticity.

4 This crucial issue is discussed in Stampe (1979), where it is contended that the problem of "phonological admissibility" is contained in, and therefore inseparable from, the larger problem of loan phonology.

5 Conversely, it turns out that incorrect implicational laws, like Jakobson's conjecture that spirants imply nasals (Velten 1943: 282), fail to correspond to actual processes; in this instance, there is no general process changing (non-nasal) spirants to nasals.

6 The most notable exceptions to this generalization involve words which the parents have imitated. Since we often used my son's *pibi* for "T.V." (by despirantization and labial "harmony"), this word persisted for months after he had suppressed these processes, even though he could pronounce *tivi* with ease. Later after he adopted the standard form he still occasionally used *pibi* in babytalking. The most striking cases of "frozen speech" involve elder siblings, who occasionally adopt some stage of the speech of the younger, and continue it as

a private language even after the younger sibling has attained standard pronunciation. (Jakobson 1940 cites some references.) Such exceptions support, rather than refute, the claim that the child's representations correspond to the productions of his models.

7   In "Yes, Virginia . . ." I argue that the child's phonological representations must in fact be at least as deep as a "phonemic representation" of adult speech, based on examples like *bʌdn* for adult *bʌr̃n*, each of which derive (by the application of different processes) from *bʌtn*.

8   With *b* for *w* for *l* (compare *bɪbi* for *bɪwi* for *bɪli* "Billy", reported to me by Arlene Zide). The form *bap* persisted until the 27th month, because it was adopted by the adults of the household (Velten, 282 note). Therefore the final *b* expected upon the ordering of denasalization after devoicing at 22 months did not appear on schedule in this form. (Compare note 6 above.)

9   The unordered application survives, however, in allegro speech. Further examples of optional unordering in synchronic phonology are discussed in Stampe (1979).

10 Since she ordered her palatalization process after the Mandarin allophonic process fronting vowels after palatals, pronouncing adult *ʃɛn* (<*ʃan*) and *san* as *ʃɛn* and *ʃan*, Chao is forced to conclude that her phonemic system has more vowels than the adult one. Of course, this conclusion is necessary only if one insists that the girl's phonological representations were a phonemic version of her own pronunciations.

11 This view was applied by Jakobson (1940) to the phonemic level. The more recent proposal by Halle (1962), that change reflects the addition of a process to the phonology, is not so limited, and reflects our current conviction that phonological processes are not mere descriptive devices but rather genuine components of the mental grammar. But Halle's implication that adults might spontaneously add a process is difficult to understand. Halle's general theory is based on the assumption that all phonological processes are rules which are constructed by the child to account for his linguistic experience, and that the phonological system is evaluated according to the simplicity of these rules – so that (other things being equal) the fewer rules, the better. It is not at all clear, given this view, why a process should be added in the first place.

12 On the basis of this Latin example it can be argued, contra Kiparsky (1968), that a process is not simply reordered but rather *un*ordered in this sort of change, because the absorption process had to apply twice. The first, and original, application (*sanguis* < *sanguin-s*) left no nasality behind, due to application of an unordered process denasalizing vowels. But the second application did leave nasality (*mēs* < *mens* < *ment-s*). That is, when absorption was unordered so that it could apply to the result of assibilation, the denasalization process became ordered. (The ordering is an incidental result of change, not a primary change. Similarly, an unordered process devoicing final obstruents might become ordered upon the addition of a process, deleting final vowels. Naturally, further changes might undo these conservatisms.)

  This suggests that Kiparsky's explanation of order changes as simplifications of the grammar is incorrect (compare also note 14). It is possible to avoid this result only by denying the relationship of the two absorptions, but it was to express such relationships that Kiparsky proposed the notion of change by reordering in the first place. For further examples of this sort, including "iterative" application, see Stampe (1979).

13 It should be emphasized, perhaps, that "generalization" as used in this discussion has little relation to its use in generative phonological theory, since the latter is concerned not with innate processes but rather with rules which are "internalized" by the child to represent "significant generalizations" about his language. That the child supplements the innate phonological system with rules, particularly morphological and expressive ones, is not at issue. But so little is known of such rules as yet that most recent speculations about constraints on them – such as the notational and "markedness" conventions of Chomsky and Halle (1968: chapters 8 and 9) – seem quite premature.

14 Kiparsky (1968) also proposes change by suppressing processes of the standard language, which he explains, along with generalization and reordering, as simplification of the grammar. He is thus unable to explain the addition of processes, whereas my proposal can explain addition, generalization, and ordering but not suppression. But there are less than a half dozen clear cases of change by suppression, against innumerable cases of addition.

One of the clearest cases involves the suppression of the German process devoicing word-final obstruents in certain Yiddish and northern Swiss dialects (Kiparsky 1968: 177). That the process was suppressed seems certain, but the cause appears not to have been "simplification" but rather a dilemma occasioned by the loss, in all these dialects, of most word-final schwas. This introduced thousands of voiced obstruents into word-final position and, since the last schwas lacked clear morphological support, flatly contradicted the devoicing process. Two resolutions were possible to children confronting this situation. They could apply devoicing to the newly final obstruents, and thus merge *bunt* and *bund* < *bundə* as *bunt*; or suppress it, and keep *bunt* and *bund* distinct. Some dialects took the former option and others, the ones Kiparsky cites, the latter. What this suggests is that although suppression occurs under certain circumstances, it is not a primary mechanism of change.

Of course, a process may be "suppressed" if a later process is added whose effects include its own. (This situation is exactly parallel to the unordering of a process, if there are no intervening processes – like the denasalization process in note 12 – to reveal an earlier application.) But in the theory I am proposing, the first process would not really be suppressed – since it would not interfere with the pronunciation of the language in any way – but would merely have become unobservable.

The claim that change by suppression is extraordinary is equivalent to the claim that the child does not ordinarily suppress processes which apply obligatorily in the standard language. Although this superficially appears to occur in child language, a deeper study seems invariably to reveal that such appearances are due to other factors, most typically a distinct process which, applying later, undoes the effects of the standard process.

Bibliography

Chao, Yuen-Ren. 1951. The Cantian idiolect. *University of California Publications in Semitic Philology* 2, 27–44.

Chomsky, Noam, and Morris Halle. 1968. *The Sound Pattern of English*. New York: Harper, Row.

Halle, Morris. 1962. Phonology in generative grammar. *Word* 18, 54–72.

Jakobson, Roman. 1940. *Kindersprache, Aphasie, und allgemeine Lautgesetze*. [Translated as *Child Language, Aphasia, and Phonological Universals*. The Hague: Mouton, 1968.]

Kiparsky, Paul. 1965. Phonological change. Ph. D. dissertation, M.I.T.

Kiparsky, Paul. 1968. Linguistic change and linguistic universals. In *Universals in Linguistic Theory*, ed. Emmon Bach and Robert T. Harms. New York: Holt, Rinehart, and Winston, pp. 170–202.

Leopold, Werner F. 1939–47. *Speech Development of a Bilingual Child*. 2 vols. Evanston, Ill.: Northwestern University Press.

Passy, Paul. 1890. *Étude sur les changements phonétiques*. Paris: Librairie Firmin-Didot.

Stampe, David. 1968. "Yes, Virginia . . ." Unpublished paper presented to the 4th Annual Regional Meeting of the Chicago Linguistic Society.

Stampe, David. 1979. *A Dissertation on Natural Phonology*. New York: Garland.

Velten, H. V. 1943. The growth of phonemic and lexical patterns in infant language. *Lg.* 19, 281–92.

24

The Problem of Serial Order in Behavior

K. S. Lashley

The previous speakers have approached our common problem by considering the properties of the elementary units of which we believe the cerebral structure to be built up. They have considered the kinds of neural integration or behavior which can be anticipated from those properties. The remaining members of the symposium have in their research been concerned chiefly with the analysis of complex behavior, seeking to derive general principles of neural integration from the infinitely complex products of that integration. Our common meeting ground is the faith to which we all subscribe, I believe, that the phenomena of behavior and of mind are ultimately describable in the concepts of the mathematical and physical sciences. In my discussion here, I have deliberately turned to the opposite extreme from the neuron and have chosen as a topic, one aspect of the most complex type of behavior that I know: the logical and orderly arrangement of thought and action. Our discussion so far has dealt chiefly with the conditions of input and of immediate switching in the nervous mechanism, without explicit consideration of what is already going on within the system.

My principal thesis today will be that the input is never into a quiescent or static system, but always into a system which is already actively excited and organized. In the intact organism, behavior is the result of interaction of this background of excitation with input from any designated stimulus. Only when we can state the general characteristics of this background of excitation, can we understand the effects of a given input.

The unpronounceable Cree Indian word "kekawewechetushekamikowanowow" is analyzed by Chamberlain (1911) into the verbal root, *tusheka*, "to remain," and the various particles which modify it as follows: *ke(la)wow*, the first and last syllables, indicating second person plural; *ka*, a prefix of the future tense; *we*, a sort of imperative mode expressing a wish; *weche*, indicating conjunction of subject and object; *mik*, a suffix bringing the verb into agreement with a third person subject and second person object; and *owan*, a suffix indicating that the subject is inanimate and the object animate. A literal translation: "You will I wish together remain he-you it-man you" or, freely, "may it remain with you." This difference in structure between Cree and English illustrates

From L. A. Jeffress (ed.), *Cerebral Mechanisms in Behavior*. New York: John Wiley, 1951, pp. 112–36. Also published in *The Neuropsychology of Lashley: Selected Papers*, ed. F. A. Beach, D. O. Hebb, C. T. Morgan, H. W. Nissen. New York: McGraw-Hill, 1960, pp. 506–28.

an outstanding characteristic of verbal behavior: the occurrence of predetermined, orderly sequences of action which are unique for each language. In English the adjective precedes, in French it follows the noun which it modifies. In English the movement or action of the subject is expressed as early as possible after the subject; in German the expression of action may be postponed until all qualifying thoughts have been expressed. In a sentence discussing this subject, Pick (1913) introduces fifty-five words between the subject and the principal verb. Each Chinese word, and to a lesser extent, each English word, stands as an unchanging unit. In the highly inflective languages, such as Sioux, the form of almost every word in the sentence may be altered, according to some attribute of the subject, as when two objects rather than one or several are discussed.

The study of comparative grammar is not the most direct approach to the physiology of the cerebral cortex, yet Fournié (1887) has written, "Speech is the only window through which the physiologist can view the cerebral life." Certainly language presents in a most striking form the integrative functions that are characteristic of the cerebral cortex and that reach their highest development in human thought processes. Temporal integration is not found exclusively in language; the coordination of leg movements in insects, the song of birds, the control of trotting and pacing in a gaited horse, the rat running the maze, the architect designing a house, and the carpenter sawing a board present a problem of sequences of action which cannot be explained in terms of successions of external stimuli.

Associative Chain Theories

In spite of the ubiquity of the problem, there have been almost no attempts to develop physiological theories to meet it. In fact, except among a relatively small group of students of aphasia, who have had to face questions of agrammatism, the problem has been largely ignored. It is not even mentioned in recent textbooks on neurophysiology or physiological psychology, nor is there any significant body of experimental studies bearing upon the problem. The spinal animal scarcely exhibits serial activity, so the physiologist may be excused for overlooking the phenomenon. On the other hand, psychologists have been concerned chiefly with the question of whether or not the organizing processes displayed in serial action are conscious, and very little with the organization itself. I have chosen to discuss the problem of temporal integration here, not with the expectation of offering a satisfactory physiological theory to account for it, but because it seems to me to be both the most important and also the most neglected problem of cerebral physiology. Temporally integrated actions do occur even among insects, but they do not reach any degree of complexity until the appearance of the cerebral cortex. They are especially characteristic of human behavior and contribute as much as does any single factor to the superiority of man's intelligence. A clearer formulation of the physiological problems which they raise should be of value, even though a solution of the problems is not yet in sight.

I shall consider first some of the questions raised by the structure of language, then turn to other forms of serial action for indications of the nature of the nervous mechanisms involved.

To the best of my knowledge, the only strictly physiological theory that has been explicitly formulated to account for temporal integration is that which postulates chains of reflexes, in which the performance of each element of the series provides excitation of the next. This conception underlay the "motor theories" of thinking which were advocated by several psychologists early in this century. Watson (1920) sought to identify thought with inaudible movements of the vocal organs, linked together in associative chains. The peripheral chain theory of language was developed in greatest detail by Washburn (1916). She distinguished what she called "successive movement systems" and, although she drew her examples from memorized series of nonsense syllables, her implication was that such series are typical of all language behavior. She defined a movement system as "a combination of movements so linked together that the stimulus furnished by the actual performance of certain movements is required to bring about other movements." She described speech as a succession of vocal acts in which the kinesthetic impulses from each movement serve as a unique stimulus for the next in the series (1916, pages 11 ff.). Attempts to confirm these peripheral theories by mechanical (Thorsen, 1925) or electrical (Max, 1937) recording of muscular tensions have given no valid evidence in support of them. It should be noted that, at the time when the theories were proposed, it was generally believed that conduction in the nervous system is always downstream from sense organ to muscle, and that muscular contraction must always follow promptly on stimulation. The existence of reverberatory circuits which could maintain central activity was scarcely suspected.

The introspective psychology which objected to such peripheral theories did not explicitly formulate an alternative neurological theory, but there is implicit in it a view that verbal thought is a simple chain of central processes in which each element serves to arouse the next by direct association. Titchener, for example, maintained that the meaning of a word (or of an auditory image in his system) consists of the chain of associations which it arouses; that it has no meaning until such a sequence has occurred. From this it must be inferred that he was thinking in terms of a simple associative chain, since no other relating process is suggested.

Objections to the Associative Chain Theory

A consideration of the structure of the sentence and of other motor sequences will show, I believe, that such interpretations of temporal organization are untenable and that there are, behind the overtly expressed sequences, a multiplicity of integrative processes which can only be inferred from the final results of their activity. There is an extensive controversial literature dealing with this inferred integrative activity. Pick (1913) devotes almost his entire book, *Die agrammatischen Sprachstörungen*, to reviewing discussions of the subject. Most of this literature deals with the question of whether or not the integrative processes are conscious. Much of this is irrelevant to the present topic, but the advocates of so-called imageless thought did present a great deal of material indicative of the complexity of the problem of thought structure. From this, and other evidence which I shall present, I believe that the production of speech involves the interaction of at least three, possibly four, major neurological systems which are interrelated but somewhat independently variable.

Let us start the analysis of the process with the enunciation of the word. Pronunciation of the word "right" consists first of retraction and elevation of the tongue, expiration of air and activation of the vocal cords; second, depression of the tongue and jaw; third, elevation of the tongue to touch the dental ridge, stopping of vocalization, and forceful expiration of air with depression of the tongue and jaw. These movements have no intrinsic order of association. Pronunciation of the word "tire" involves the same motor elements in reverse order. Such movements occur in all permutations. The order must therefore be imposed upon the motor elements by some organization other than direct associative connections between them. So, for the individual movements in writing or typing the word, finger strokes occur in all sorts of combinations. No single letter invariably follows *g*, and whether *gh*, *ga*, or *gu* is written depends upon a set for a larger unit of action, the word.

Words stand in relation to the sentence as letters do to the word; the words themselves have no intrinsic temporal "valence." The word "right," for example, is noun, adjective, adverb, and verb, and has four spellings and at least ten meanings. In such a sentence as "The mill-wright on my right thinks it right that some conventional rite should symbolize the right of every man to write as he pleases," word arrangement is obviously not due to any direct associations of the word "right" itself with other words, but to meanings which are determined by some broader relations.

It has been found in studies of memorization of nonsense syllables that each syllable in the series has associations, not only with adjacent words in the series, but also with more remote words. The words in the sentence have, of course, associations with more remote words as well as with adjacent ones. However, the combination of such direct associations will not account for grammatical structure. The different positions of the word "right" in the illustrative sentence are determined by the meanings which the positions in relation to other words denote, but those meanings are given by other associations than those with the words in the spoken sentence. The word can take its position only when the particular one of its ten meanings becomes dominant. This dominance is not inherent in the words themselves.

From such considerations, it is certain that any theory of grammatical form which ascribes it to direct associative linkage of the words of the sentence overlooks the essential structure of speech. The individual items of the temporal series do not in themselves have a temporal "valence" in their associative connections with other elements. The order is imposed by some other agent.

This is true not only of language, but of all skilled movements or successions of movement. In the gaits of a horse, trotting, pacing, and single footing involve essentially the same pattern of muscular contraction in the individual legs. The gait is imposed by some mechanism in addition to the direct relations of reciprocal innervation among the sensory-motor centers of the legs. The order in which the fingers of the musician fall on the keys or fingerboard is determined by the signature of the composition; this gives a *set* which is not inherent in the association of the individual movements.

The Determining Tendency

What then determines the order? The answer which seems most in accord with common sense is that the intention to act or the idea to be expressed determines the sequence. There are, however, serious difficulties for this solution. There is not much agreement among psychologists concerning the nature of the idea. The structuralist school, under the leadership of Titchener, held that the idea consists of mental images, often the auditory images of words, and the meanings are nothing but sequences of such images. Describing the role of images in his lecturing, Titchener wrote (1909), "When there is any difficulty in exposition, a point to be argued *pro* and *con* or a conclusion to be brought out from the convergence of several lines of proof, I hear my own voice speaking just ahead of me." What a solution of the lecture problem for the lazy man! He need not think but only listen to his own inner voice; to the chain of associated auditory images. A behaviorist colleague once remarked to me that he had reached a stage where he could arise before an audience, turn his mouth loose, and go to sleep. He believed in the peripheral chain theory of language. (This clearly demonstrates the superiority of behavioristic over introspective psychology. The behaviorist does not even have to listen to his own inner voice.)

Seriously, such positions offer no solution for the problem of temporal integration. Titchener finds his grammar ready made and does not even raise the question of the origin of the succession of images. The chain-reflex theory, while definite, is untenable.

The third view of the nature of the idea was developed by a group known as the "Würzburg School" (see Boring, 1929); exponents of image-less thought. It held that some organization precedes any expression that can be discovered by introspective or objective means. Thought is neither muscular contraction nor image, but can only be inferred as a "determining tendency." At most, it is discovered as a vague feeling of pregnancy, of being about to have an idea, a Bewusstseinslage. It is not identical with the words which are spoken, for quite frequently no word can be recalled which satisfactorily expresses the thought, and we search a dictionary of synonyms until a word or phrase is found which does seem appropriate.

In his discussion of the relation of thought to speech, Pick (1913) accepts this point of view, but he asserts further that the set or the idea does not have a temporal order; that all of its elements are cotemporal. Evidence in support of this conclusion comes, for example, from translation of one language into another which has a different sentence structure. I read a German sentence, pronouncing the German words with no thought of their English equivalents. I then give a free translation in English, without remembering a single word of the German text. Somewhere between the reading and free translation, the German sentence is condensed, the word order reversed, and expanded again into the different temporal order of English. According to Epstein (n.d.), the polyglot shifts readily from one language to another, expressing the same thought in either, without literal translation. The readiness with which the form of expression of an idea can be changed, the facility with which different word orders may be utilized to express the same thought, thus is further evidence that the temporal integration is not inherent in the preliminary organization of the idea.

The Schema of Order

The remaining alternative is that the mechanism which determines the serial activation of the motor units is relatively independent, both of the motor units and of the thought structure. Supporting evidence for this may be found in the mistakes of order, the slips and interferences which occur in writing and speaking. For some time I have kept records of errors in typing. A frequent error is the misplacing or the doubling of a letter. *These* is typed t-h-s-e-s, *look* as l-o-k-k, *ill* as i-i-l. Sometimes the set to repeat may be displaced by several words. The order is dissociated from the idea. Earlier, in preparing this paper, I wrote the phrase, "maintain central activities." I typed *min*, omitting the *a*, canceled this out and started again; *ama*. The impulse to insert the *a* now dominated the order. I struck out the *a* and completed the phrase, only to find that I had now also dropped the *a* from *activities*. This example suggests something of the complexity of the forces which are at play in the determination of serial order and the way in which conflicting impulses may distort the order, although the primary determining tendency, the idea, remains the same.

The polyglot, who has become proficient in a secondary language, who thinks in it and even dreams in it, may still tend to use the grammatical structure of his native tongue. If, as in French, that tongue applies gender to inanimate things, the English pronouns referring to them may take the gender of the French equivalents, though the French nouns are not thought. The German postponement of the verb or the Magyar use of the past infinitive may be incorporated in the new language. In such cases, the structuring seems to be dissociated both from the content and from the simple associative connections of the words themselves.

The case with which a new structure may be imposed on words is illustrated by the quickness with which children learn hog Latin. The form which I learned involved transposing the initial sound of each word to the end of the word and adding a long *a*. Thus – at-thay an-may oes-gay own-day e-thay eet-stray. Some children become very facile at such inversions of words, and re-structure new words without hesitation. From such considerations it seems to follow that syntax is not inherent in the words employed or in the idea to be expressed. It is a generalized pattern imposed upon the specific acts as they occur.

"Priming" of Expressive Units

There are indications that, prior to the internal or overt enunciation of the sentence, an aggregate of word units is partially activated or readied. Evidence for this comes also from "contaminations" of speech and writing. The most frequent typing errors are those of anticipation; the inclusion in the word being typed of some part of a word or word structure which should properly occur later in the sentence. It may be only a letter. Thus I wrote, *wrapid* writing, carrying the *w* from the second word to the first. Not infrequently words are introduced which should occur much later in the sentence, often five or six words in advance.

In oral speech, Spoonerisms illustrate the same kind of contamination. The Spoonerism is most frequently an inversion of subject and object: "Let us always remember that waste makes haste." But it may be only a transposition of parts of the words: "Our queer old dean" for "our dear old queen." The frequency with which such contaminations occur is increased by haste, by distraction, by emotional tension, or by uncertainty and conflict as to the best form of expression. In some types of aphasia the tendency to disordered arrangement of words is greatly increased, and, in extreme cases, the attempt to speak results in a word hash with complete loss of grammatical organization. Professor Spooner, after whom such slips are named, was probably suffering from a mild form of aphasia. In these contaminations, it is as if the aggregate of words were in a state of partial excitation, held in check by the requirements of grammatical structure, but ready to activate the final common path, if the effectiveness of this check is in any way interfered with.

In his *Psychopathology of Everyday Life*, Freud has given numerous examples of similar contaminations of action outside the sphere of language. We do not need to accept his theories of censorship and suppression to account for such slips. They are of the same order as misplacements in typing and represent contaminations of coexisting, determining tendencies to action.

Such contaminations might be ascribed to differences in the relative strength of associative bonds between the elements of the act, and thus not evidence for pre-excitation of the elements or for simultaneous pre-excitation. However, the understanding of speech involves essentially the same problems as the production of speech and definitely demands the postulation of an after–effect or after–discharge of the sensory components for a significant time following stimulation. Thus, in the spoken sentence, "Rapid righting with his uninjured hand saved from loss the contents of the capsized canoe," the associations which give meaning to righting are not activated for at least 3 to 5 seconds after hearing the word. I shall refer later to other evidence for such long after-discharge of sensory excitations. The fact of continued activation or after-discharge of receptive elements and their integration during this activation justifies the assumption of a similar process during motor organization. The processes of comprehension and production of speech have too much in common to depend on wholly different mechanisms.

Internal and Overt Speech

One other point with respect to the organization of speech: The earlier literature on aphasia emphasized the distinction of internal and overt speech. The aphemia of Broca and the pure motor aphasia of Wernicke and later writers were held to be a loss of the ability to enunciate without loss of ability to think in words and without paralysis of the organs of speech. The brain insult was assumed to affect only the transition from the thought to the enunciation of the word. We may doubt the existence of instances of such "pure" defects and question the reliability of the early clinical examinations in view of the more careful analyses that have been made since 1917, but the distinction of internal and overt speech is still valid and the transition still unexplained. Watson interpreted internal speech as inaudible movements of the vocal organs, and Jacobsen (1932) and Max (1937) have given evidence of changes in muscular tonus during verbal thinking or thought of movement. This is far from proving that the motor discharge is essential for the internal formation of words, however.

I once devised an instrument to record small movements of the tongue. Within the limits of its sensitivity, it showed that in silent thinking the tongue usually drops to the back of the mouth and shows no detectable movement. Verbal problems, such as the correct squaring of three-place numbers, could be carried out with no trace of overt movement. If, however, I urged the subject to hurry or if I slapped his face, his tongue came forward and showed movements corresponding to the syllabification of internal speech or of the computation he was performing. This I interpret as indicating that internal speech may be carried out wholly by processes within the nervous system, with some unessential discharge upon the final common path for vocal movements. Facilitation of the motor path, either by increased emotional tension or by "voluntary" reinforcement, increases its excitability until the same central circuits whose activity constitutes internal speech are able to excite the overt movements. This aspect of the language function is irrelevant to the problem of syntax or serial order, but is important as illustrating a further point in the dynamics of the cerebrum. Many activities seem to require for their performance both a specific patterning and also a general facilitation, a rise in dynamic level. There are, I think, indications that hemiplegia and motor aphasia are primarily expressions of a low level of facilitation rather than a loss of specific integrative connections which are involved in the use of language or in the patterning of our movements. A monkey, for example, after ablation of the precentral gyrus may seem unable to use the arm at all, but if emotional excitement is raised above a certain level, the arm is freely used. As soon as the excitement dies down, the arm is again hemiplegic. I have seen something of the same sort in a human hemiplegic. The problem of the availability of memories, which was raised earlier in the discussion here, may find a partial solution in such fluctuations in dynamic level. In many of the organic amnesias the pattern of integration seems to be retained but can be reactivated only by an abnormally intense sensory or central reinforcement.

Generality of the Problem of Syntax

I have devoted so much time to discussion of the problem of syntax, not only because language is one of the most important products of human cerebral action, but also because the problems raised by the organization of language seem to me to be characteristic of almost all other cerebral activity. There is a series of hierarchies of organization; the order of vocal movements in pronouncing the word, the order of words in the sentence, the order of sentences in the paragraph, the rational order of paragraphs in a discourse. Not only speech, but all skilled acts seem to involve the same problems of serial ordering, even down to the temporal coordination of muscular contractions in such a movement as reaching and grasping. Analysis of the nervous mechanisms underlying order in the more primitive acts may contribute ultimately to the solution even of the physiology of logic.

It is possible to designate, that is, to point to specific examples of, the phenomena of the syntax of movement that require explanation, although those phenomena cannot be clearly defined. A real definition would be a long step toward solution of the problem. There are at least three sets of events to be accounted for. First, the activation of the expressive elements (the individual words or adaptive acts) which do not contain the temporal relations. Second, the determining tendency, the set, or idea. This masquerades under many names in contemporary psychology, but is, in every case, an inference from the restriction of behavior within definite limits. Third, the syntax of the act, which can be described as an habitual order or mode of relating the expressive elements; a generalized pattern or schema of integration which may be imposed upon a wide range and a wide variety of specific acts. This is the essential problem of serial order; the existence of generalized schemata of action which determine the sequence of specific acts, acts which in themselves or in their associations seem to have no temporal valence.

I shall turn now to other phenomena of movement which may be more readily phrased in physiological terms and which may suggest some of the mechanisms underlying serial order.

Duration and Intensity of Nervous Discharge

A consideration of the control of extent and rate of movement supports the view that sensory factors play a minor part in regulating the intensity and duration of nervous discharge; that a series of movements is not a chain of sensory-motor reactions. The theory of control of movement which was dominant at the turn of the century assumed that, after a movement is initiated, it is continued until stopped by sensations of movement and position, which indicate that the limb has reached the desired position. This theory was opposed by a good bit of indirect evidence, such as that accuracy of movement is increased rather than diminished with speed. I had opportunity to study a patient who had a complete anesthesia for movements of the knee joint, as a result of a gunshot wound of the cord (1917). In spite of the anesthesia, he was able to control the extent and speed of movements of flexion and extension of the knee quite as accurately as can a normal person.

The performance of very quick movements also indicates their independence of current control. "Whip-snapping" movements of the hand can be regulated accurately in extent, yet the entire movement, from initiation to completion, requires less than the reaction time for tactile or kinesthetic stimulation of the arm, which is about one-eighth of a second, even when no discrimination is involved. Such facts force the conclusion that an effector mechanism can be pre-set or primed to discharge at a given intensity or for a given duration, in independence of any sensory controls.

Central Control of Motor Patterns

This independence of sensory controls is true not only of intensity and duration of contraction of a synergic muscle group but is true also of the initiation and timing of contraction of the different muscles in a complex movement. The hand may describe a circular movement involving coordinated contractions of the muscles of the shoulder, elbow, and wrist in about $\frac{1}{10}$ second, and the stopping of movement at a given position, of course, is only a small fraction of that time. The finger strokes of a musician may reach sixteen per second in passages which call for a definite and changing order of successive finger movements. The succession of movements is too quick even for visual reaction time. In rapid sight reading it is impossible to read the individual notes of an arpeggio. The notes must be seen in groups, and it is actually easier to read chords seen simultaneously and to translate them into temporal sequence than to read successive notes in the arpeggio as usually written.

Sensory control of movement seems to be ruled out in such acts. They require the postulation of some central nervous mechanism which fires with predetermined intensity and duration or activates different muscles in predetermined order. This mechanism might be represented by a chain of effector neurons, linked together by internuncials to produce successive delays in firing. In some systems the order of action may be determined by such a leader or pace-setter. Buddenbrock (1921) has shown for the stick insect, and Bethe (1931) for a number of animals from the centipede to the dog, that removal of one or more legs results in a spontaneous change in the order of stepping. Thus, for the insects, the normal order is alternate stepping of the first pair of legs with right first, left second, right third leg advancing together. With removal of the left first leg, the right first and left second alternate and the order becomes right first, left third, right third stepping together, with left second and right second advancing together, instead of alternately. These investigators were interested in spontaneity of reorganization, rather than in the mechanism of coordination, and did not propose any theory for the latter. They did show, however, that it is necessary to remove the leg completely to get the change in pattern of movement; sensory impulses from a limb stump would prevent it. Such coordination might be explained, perhaps, by a combination of loss of excitability in the centers of the absent limb, by the excitation of the remaining anterior center as a leader or pace-setter, and the spread of alternate waves of inhibition and excitation from the more anterior to the more posterior limb centers. The spontaneous change in coordination shows, however, that the coordination is not due to the action of predetermined anatomic paths but is the result of the current physiological state of the various limb centers.

Such an hypothesis implies also the assumption of a polarization of conduction along the neuraxis, with the order of excitation determined by the spatial arrangement of the centers of the legs. I see no other possibility of accounting for the facts. The examples of circular movement and of finger coordination, involving temporal integration of movements, seem to call for a similar hypothesis. They might be ascribed to an habitual linkage of the movements through a simple chain of internuncials but for two facts. First, such series are usually reversible at any point or can be started from any point. This would require the assumption of a second set of internuncials habituated to conduct in the opposite direction, and this in turn leads to the further assumption of a polarization of conduction. Second, such patterns of coordinated movement may often be transferred directly to other motor systems than the ones practiced. In such transfer, as to the left hand for writing, an analysis of the movements shows that there is not a reduplication of the muscular patterns on the two sides, but a reproduction of movements in relation to the space coordinates of the body. Try upside-down mirror writing with the left hand and with eyes closed for evidence of this. The associative linkage is not of specific movements but of directions of movement. An analysis of systems of space coordinates suggests mechanisms which may contribute to production of such series of movements in a spatial pattern.

Space Coordinate Systems

The work of Sherrington, Magnus, and others on postural tonus and reflexes has defined one level of spatial integration rather fully, yet it is doubtful if these studies have revealed the effective neural mechanism. The work has shown that the tonic discharge to every muscle in the postural system is influenced by afferent impulses from every other muscle, toward increased or decreased activity, according to its synergic or antergic action. To these influences are added vestibular and cerebellar effects. Diagrammatically these mutual influences of the muscular system may be represented by separate reflex circuits from each receptor to every muscle, as Sherrington (1906, p. 148) has done. But no neuro-anatomist would, I am sure, maintain that such separate circuits or paths exist. What the experiments on posture actually show is a correlation of sensory stimulation and of tonic changes in a network of neurons whose interconnections are still undefined. The reactions isolated experimentally have the characteristics of simple directly conducted reflexes, but their combination results in patterns of movement and posture which have definite relations to the axes of the body and to gravity.

This postural system is based on excitations from proprioceptors. The distance receptors impose an additional set of space coordinates upon the postural system, which in turn continually modifies the coordinates of the distance receptors. The dropped cat rights itself, if either the eyes or the vestibular senses are intact, but not in the absence of both. The direction of movement on the retina imposes a directional orientation on the postural system. Conversely, the gravitational system imposes an orientation on the visual field. Upright objects such as trees or the corners of a room appear upright, at no matter what angle the head is inclined. Derangement of the vestibular system can disturb the distance orientation or the orientation of the receptors, as in the apparent swaying of the vertical as a result of the after-images of motion following hours of rock-ing in a small boat.

There are other, still more generalized systems of space coordinates. We usually keep track of the compass points or of some more definite index of direction by a temporal summation of the turns made in walking, though not always with success. Finally, there is a still more plastic system in which the concepts of spatial relations can be voluntarily reversed, as when one plays blindfold chess alternately from either side of the board.

Explanation of these activities, these complex interactions, in terms of simple isolated interconnections of all of the sensory and motor elements involved seems quite improb-able on anatomic grounds and is ruled out by results of our experiments on sectioning of the spinal cord. Ingebritzen (1933) studied rats with double hemisection of the cord; one-half of the cord cut at the second, the other at the fifth cervical segment. In the best case only a small strand of the spino–cerebellar tract of one side remained intact. These rats were able to balance in walking, oriented to visual stimuli, scratched with the right or left hind foot according to the side of the face stimulated, were able to run mazes correctly, and even learned to rise on the hind feet and push down a lever with the forepaws in opening a box.

The alternative to the isolated-path theory of the space coordinates is that the vari-ous impulses which modify postural tonus are poured into a continuous network of neurons, where their summated action results in a sort of polarization of the entire sys-tem. I shall consider later the integrative properties of such a net. For the moment I wish to emphasize only the existence of these systems of space coordinates. Their influences pervade the motor system so that every gross movement of limbs or body is made with reference to the space system. The perceptions from the distance receptors, vision, hear-ing, and touch are also constantly modified and referred to the same space coordinates. The stimulus is *there*, in a definite place; it has definite relation to the position of the body, and it shifts with respect to the sense organ but not with respect to the general orientation, with changes in body posture.

Memories of objects usually give them position in the space system, and even more abstract concepts may have definite spatial reference. Thus, for many people, the cardinal numbers have definite positions on a spiral or other complicated figure. What, if anything, such space characters can contribute to temporal integration is an open question. They provide a possible basis for some serial actions through interaction of postural and timing mechanisms.

Rhythmic Action

The simplest of the timing mechanisms are those controlling rhythmic activity. T. Graham Brown (1914) first showed by his studies of deafferented preparations that the rhythmic movements of respiration and progression are independent of peripheral stimulation and are maintained by a central nervous mechanism of reciprocal innervation. He suggested that this mechanism of reciprocal innervation, rather than the simple reflex, is the unit of organization of the whole nervous system. He thus foreshadowed, in a way, the conception of reverberatory circuits which is coming to play so large a part in neurological theory today. Holst (1937) has recently shown that the rhythmic movement of the dorsal fin of fishes is a compound of two superimposed rhythms, that of its own innervation and that of the pectoral fins. These two rhythms are centrally maintained.

Musical rhythms seem to be an elaboration of the same sort of thing. The time or beat is started and maintained at some definite rate, say 160 per minute. This rate is then imposed upon various activities. The fingers of the musician fall in multiples of the basic rate. If the leader of a quartet speeds up the time or retards, all the movements of the players change in rate accordingly. Not only the time of initiation but also the rate of movement is affected. The violinist, in a passage requiring the whole bow, will draw the bow from frog to tip at a uniform rate for the required number of beats, whether the tempo is fast or slow. With practiced violinists, the rate of movement is extremely accurate and comes out on the beat at the exact tip of the bow.

Superimposed on this primary rhythm is a secondary one of emphasis, giving the character of 3/4, 4/4, 6/4, or other time. The mechanism of these rhythms can be simply conceived as the spread of excitation from some centers organized for reciprocal innervation; as a combination of the principles of Brown and of Holst. There are, however, still more complicated rhythms in all music. That of the melodic line is most uniform. In much music, the melodic progression changes in 2, 4, or some multiple of 4 measures. In improvisation, the performer keeps no count of measures, yet comes out almost invariably in a resolution to the tonic of the key after some multiple of eight measures. Here a generalized pattern is impressed on the sequence, but it is a simpler pattern than that of grammatical structure. It only requires the recurrence of a pattern at certain rhythmic intervals; a pick-up of a specific pattern after so many timed intervals.

There are, in addition, still less regular rhythms of phrasing and emphasis. Parallels to these can be found in speech. The skilled extemporaneous speaker rounds his phrases and speaks with a definite though not regular rhythm.

The rhythms tend to spread to almost every other concurrent activity. One falls into step with a band, tends to breathe, and even to speak in time with the rhythm. The all pervasiveness of the rhythmic discharge is shown by the great difficulty of learning to maintain two rhythms at once, as in three against four with the two hands. The points to be emphasized here are the widespread effects of a rhythmic discharge indicating the involvement of almost the entire effector system, the concurrent action of different rhythmic systems, and the imposition of the rate upon both the initiation and speed of movement. Consideration of rhythmic activity and of spatial orientation forces the conclusion, I believe, that there exist in the nervous organization, elaborate systems of interrelated neurons capable of imposing certain types of integration upon a large number of widely spaced effector elements; in the one case transmitting temporally spaced waves of facilitative excitation to all effector elements; in the other imparting a directional polarization to both receptor and effector elements. These systems are in constant action. They form a sort of substratum upon which other activity is built. They contribute to every perception and to every integrated movement.

Interaction of Temporal and Spatial Systems

Integration ascribed to the spatial distribution of excitations in the nervous system has been much more intensively studied than the temporal aspects of nervous activity. Theories of integration are based almost exclusively upon space properties, time entering only in theories of facilitation, inhibition, and after-discharge. In cerebral functions, however, it is difficult to distinguish between spatial and temporal functions. The eye is the only organ that gives simultaneous information concerning space in any detail. The shape of an object impressed on the skin can scarcely be detected from simultaneous pressure, but the same shape can readily be distinguished by touch when traced on the skin with a moving point or when explored by tactile scanning. The temporal sequence is readily translated into a spatial concept. Even for vision it might be questioned whether simultaneous stimulation gives rise directly to space concepts. The visual object is generally surveyed by eye movements, and its form is a reconstruction from such a series of excitations. Even with tachistoscopic exposures, the after-discharge permits a temporal survey, and, with visual fixation, shifts of attention provide an effective scanning.

Since memory traces are, we believe, in large part static and persist simultaneously, it must be assumed that they are spatially differentiated. Nevertheless, reproductive memory appears almost invariably as a temporal sequence, either as a succession of words or of acts. Even descriptions of visual imagery (the supposed simultaneous reproductive memory in sensory terms) are generally descriptions of sequences, of temporal reconstructions from very fragmentary and questionable visual elements. Spatial and temporal order thus appear to be almost completely interchangeable in cerebral action. The translation from the spatial distribution of memory traces to temporal sequence seems to be a fundamental aspect of the problem of serial order.

I spoke earlier of the probability of a partial activation or priming of aggregates of words before the sentence is actually formulated from them. There is a great deal of evidence for such preliminary facilitation of patterns of action in studies of reaction time and of word association. Reaction time, in general, is reduced by preliminary warning or by instructions which allow the subject to prepare for the specific act required. In controlled association experiments, the subject is instructed to respond to the stimulus word by a word having a certain type of relation to it, such as the opposite or a part of which the stimulus is the whole; black–white, apple–seed. The result is an attitude or set which causes that particular category to dominate the associative reaction. Whether such preliminary reinforcement is to be ascribed to accumulation of excitatory state, as defined by Sherrington (1906), or to some other physiological process, the facts of behavior assure that it is a genuine phenomenon and plays a decisive role in determining the character of the response.

Once the existence of such states of partial activation is recognized, their possible role in temporal integration must be considered. There are indications that one neural system may be held in this state of partial excitation while it is scanned by another. Here is an example. A series of four to six numbers is heard: 3–7–2–9–4. This is within the attention or memory span and is almost certainly not remembered in the sense in which one's telephone number is remembered, for memory of it is immediately wiped out by a succeeding series of numbers. While it is retained in this unstable way, subject to retroactive inhibition, the order of the numbers can be reassorted: 3–7–2–9–4, 3–2–7–9–4, 4–9–2–7–3, and the like. It is as if, in this case, a rhythmic alternation can suppress alternate items, or a direction of arousal can be applied to the partially excited system. Another example which illustrates even more clearly the spatial characteristics of many memory traces is the method of comultiplication, used in rapid mental calculation. In attempts to play a melody backward, we have a further illustration. I find that I can do it only by visualizing the music spatially and then reading it backward. I cannot auditorily transform even "Yankee Doodle" into its inverse without some such process, but it is possible to get a spatial representation of the melody and then to scan the spatial representation. The scanning of a spatial arrangement seems definitely to determine, in such cases, the order of procedure. Two assumptions are implied by this. First, the assumption is that the memory traces are associated, not only with other memory traces, but also with the system of space coordinates. By this I do not mean that the engram has a definite location in the brain; our experiments show conclusively that such is not the case. Rather, when the memory trace is formed it is integrated with directional characters of the space system, which give it position in reference to other associated traces. Second, the assumption is that these space characters of the memory trace can be scanned by some other level of the coordinating system and so transformed into succession.

This is as far as I have been able to go toward a theory of serial order in action. Obviously, it is inadequate. The assumptions concerning spatial representation and temporal representation may even beg the question, since no one can say whether spatial or temporal order is primary. Furthermore, such determining tendencies as the relation of attribute to object, which gives the order of adjective and noun, do not seem to be analyzable into any sort of spatial structure or for that matter, into any consistent relationship. I have tried a number of assumptions concerning the selective mechanism of grammatical form (spatial relations, the relative intensity or prominence of different words in the idea, and so on) but I have never been able to make an hypothesis which was consistent with any large number of sentence structures. Nevertheless, the indications which I have cited, that elements of the sentence are readied or partially activated before the order is imposed upon them in expression, suggest that some scanning mechanism must be at play in regulating their temporal sequence. The real problem, however, is the nature of the selective mechanism by which the particular acts are picked out in this scanning process, and to this problem I have no answer.

Such speculations concerning temporal and spatial systems do little more than illustrate a point of view concerning nervous organization which is, I believe, more consistent both with what is known of the histology and elementary physiology of the brain and also with behavior phenomena than are the more widely current theories of simple associative chains of reactions.

Nearly forty years ago Becher (1911, page 243) wrote: "There is no physiological hypothesis which can explain the origin and relations of temporal forms in mental life; indeed, there is no hypothesis which even foreshadows the possibility of such an explanation." The situation is little better today, but I do feel that changing conceptions of the fundamental organization of the nervous system offer more hope for a solution of such problems than did the physiological knowledge available when Becher wrote. However, we are still very far from being able to form an explicit explanation of temporal structure.

The Fundamental Mechanism of Integration

Neurological theory has been dominated by the belief that the neurons of the central nervous system are in an inactive or resting state for the greater part of the time; that they are linked in relatively isolated conditioned reflex ares and that they are activated only when the particular reactions for which they are specifically associated are called out. Such a view is incompatible both with the widespread effects of stimulation which can be demonstrated by changes in tonus and also with recent evidence from electrical recording of nervous activity. It is now practically certain that all the cells of the cerebrospinal axis are being continually bombarded by nerve impulses from various sources and are firing regularly, probably even during sleep. The nervous activity which they in turn elicit depends upon the current physiological state of the neurons with which they are connected. It is probably not far from the truth to say that every nerve cell of the cerebral cortex is involved in thousands of different reactions. The cortex must be regarded as a great network of reverberatory circuits, constantly active. A new stimulus, reaching such a system, does not excite an isolated reflex path but must produce widespread changes in the pattern of excitation throughout a whole system of already interacting neurons.

The facts of cerebral structure support such a view. The cortex is composed chiefly of neurons with short axons. LeGros Clark (1941) has found for the striate area of the monkey that Marchi degeneration extends for only a short distance from a point of injury. In the striate area of the rat, I have never been able to trace degeneration beyond three or four cell diameters from the margin of a lesion, and I believe that this lack of long transcortical fibers is true of other areas as well as of the visual cortex. Visual perception reveals close integration of different parts of the striate areas in spite of the absence of long association fibers. In the visual cortex of the rat there are only 19 neurons for each afferent fiber. To produce the animal's visual acuity, all of the afferent fibers must be firing continually. There are approximately 34,000 cell bodies in the lateral geniculate nucleus of the rat, and the minimum number of visual units necessary to produce the visual acuity of the rat is actually above this figure. (The acuity is determined by direct experimental tests.) These figures should be of interest in relation to the numerical values cited by Dr. von Neumann. The number of cells in the visual cortex of the rat is only about 10^6, and in some of my experiments where I have removed the greater part of the visual cortex the capacity for discrimination of visual forms has been retained when no more than 20,000 cells of the visual cortex remain. There is also evidence that no part of the cerebral cortex except the visual areas is essential for visual perception and memory.

DR. LORENTE DE NÓ: What is the number of afferents in the optic nerve?

DR. LASHLEY: There are 290,000 afferents in the optic nerve of the rat, and the figure is reduced to 34,000 in the lateral geniculate. The actual numbers are 9,000,000 myoids, 290,000 ganglion cells, and 34,000 cells in the lateral geniculate. That may include cells with short axons also. There are about 125,000 cells in each of the five layers of the cortex. These figures are for one eye and hemisphere.

DR. VON NEUMANN: In the human being the corresponding number is about 125,000,000 for the first, isn't it?

DR. LASHLEY: I know of no figure for that level.

DR. LORENTE DE NÓ: It hasn't been analyzed in any way.

DR. VON NEUMANN: The optic nerve corresponds to the second one?

DR. LASHLEY: Yes. The axons of the ganglion cells pass through the optic nerves. There is an average of 300 visual cells firing into each central pathway. There are fewer than 5 cells in the receptive layer of the visual cortex of the rat for each afferent fiber of the optic radiation and only 19 cells per afferent fiber in the entire visual cortex. Since the visual acuity of the rat requires that all of the 34,000 cells of the radiation be firing constantly, it seems certain that all of the neurons within the striate areas, the visual cortex, must be firing constantly. There is a good bit of evidence that all of the integrative functions of vision are carried out within the striate areas. In the rat, I have removed, from one or another animal, practically every other part of the isocortex without disturbing visual perception or memory. With monkeys I have removed the supposed visual associative areas without producing any significant loss of visual functions.

These facts lead to the conclusion that the same cells in the visual cortex participate in a great variety of activities. Practically all of the cells of the area must be fired by every visual stimulation, and these same cells must be the ones which retain the visual memories. The conclusion follows that differential responses depend upon the pattern of cells which are excited in combination. The visual cortex is a network of cells of short axon without long interconnections between its parts or with other cortical areas. Its integrative functions are an expression of the properties of such a network.

The same conception must be applied to other cortical areas. There are, of course, long association tracts in the cortex, such as the corpus callosum, the superior longitudinal fasciculus, and the temporo-frontal tracts. Once, 26 years ago, I suggested facetiously that these might be only skeletal structures, since I could find no function for them. No important functions of these tracts have yet been demonstrated. Section of the corpus callosum produces only a slight slowing of reaction time, ipsilateral as well as contralateral (Akelaitis, 1941); section of occipito-frontal fibers produces, perhaps, a temporary disturbance of visual attention but no other symptoms. The integrative functions seem to be carried out as well without as with the main associative tracts. The major integrative functions must, therefore, be carried out by the network of cells of short axon. The properties of such networks of cells must be analyzed before the mechanisms of the cerebral cortex can be understood. Something can be inferred from the characteristics of excitability of cells and their arrangement in recurrent loops. If, as seems a necessary conclusion from the histology of the striate area, all of the cells of the network are subject to constant excitation and are firing whenever they recover from the refractory state, then mutual interference of circuits will produce complicated patterns throughout the area, patterns which will stabilize in the absence of differential stimulation, as is perhaps indicated by the regularity of the alpha rhythm. Any new afferent impulses reaching the area can only produce a reorganization of the existing pattern. What happens at any particular point in the system, as at an efferent neuron, is the statistical outcome of the interaction of myriads of neurons, not of the transmission of impulses over a restricted path, of which that efferent cell forms a link. It is possible to isolate parts of the system by operative means or by anesthetics and so to get a one-to-one relation of stimulus locus and responding muscles, from which the reflex mechanism has been inferred. As Goldstein (1939) has pointed out, however, the parts isolated in the reflex are influenced by a multiplicity of effects in the intact organism of which there is little or no trace in the isolated preparation.

I can best illustrate this conception of nervous action by picturing the brain as the surface of a lake. The prevailing breeze carries small ripples in its direction, the basic polarity of the system. Varying gusts set up crossing systems of waves, which do not destroy the first ripples, but modify their form, a second level in the system of space coordinates. A tossing log with its own period of submersion sends out periodic bursts of ripples, a temporal rhythm. The bow wave of a speeding boat momentarily sweeps over the surface, seems to obliterate the smaller waves yet leaves them unchanged by its passing, the transient effect of a strong stimulus. Wave motion is not an adequate analogy because the medium which conveys the waves is uniform, whereas the nerve cells have their individual characteristics of transmission which at every point may alter the character of the transmitted pattern.

The great number of axon terminations on every nerve cell has not been considered in theories of integration. It implies, of course, that the cell can be fired by impulses from a variety of sources. But it also suggests another possibility, more fruitful for understanding of integrative processes. A nerve impulse arriving over a single axon terminal may not fire the cell but may modify its excitability to impulses from other sources. In an elaborate system of neurons such subthreshold effects might establish a pattern of facilitation which would determine the combination of cells fired by subsequent excitations. The space coordinate system and various types of *set* or priming may be pictured as patterns of subthreshold facilitation pervading the network of neurons which is activated by the more specific external stimulus.

Such a view of the mechanism of nervous action certainly does not simplify the problems nor does it as yet provide any clue to the structuring that constitutes the set or determining tendency, or to the nature of such relations as are implied in the attribute-object, opposites, or other abstract concepts. A few relations seem reducible to spatial terms, part-whole, for example, but even for these there is no clear conception of the neural basis of their space properties. These considerations do not, I believe, contradict fundamentally the basic conceptions that have been formulated by Dr. McCulloch. They do, however, indicate a direction of necessary elaboration. The nets active in rhythmic and spatial organization are apparently almost coextensive with the nervous system. The analysis must be extended to the properties of such nets; the way in which they are broken up into reactive patterns in the spread of excitation, to give, for example, directional propagation or its equivalent. I strongly suspect that many phenomena of generalization, both sensory and conceptual, are products, not of simple switching, but of interaction of complex patterns of organization within such systems.

Summary

The problems of the syntax of action are far removed from anything which we can study by direct physiological methods today, yet in attempting to formulate a physiology of the cerebral cortex we cannot ignore them. Serial order is typical of the problems raised by cerebral activity; few, if any, of the problems are simpler or promise easier solution. We can, perhaps, postpone the fatal day when we must face them, by saying that they are too complex for present analysis, but there is danger here of constructing a false picture of those processes that we believe to be simpler. I am coming more and more to the conviction that the rudiments of every human behavioral mechanism will be found far down in the evolutionary scale and also represented even in primitive activities of the nervous system. If there exist, in human cerebral action, processes which seem fundamentally different or inexplicable in terms of our present construct of the elementary physiology of integration, then it is probable that that construct is incomplete or mistaken, even for the levels of behavior to which it is applied.

In spite of its present inadequacy, I feel that the point of view which I have sketched here holds some promise of a better understanding of cerebral integration. Attempts to express cerebral function in terms of the concepts of the reflex arc, or of associated chains of neurons, seem to me doomed to failure because they start with the assumption of a static nervous system. Every bit of evidence available indicates a dynamic, constantly active system, or, rather, a composite of many interacting systems, which I have tried to illustrate at a primitive level by rhythm and the space coordinates. Only when methods of analysis of such systems have been devised will there be progress toward understanding of the physiology of the cerebral cortex.

References

Akelaitis, A. J. 1941. Studies on the corpus callosum. ii. The higher visual functions in each hononymous field following complete section of the corpus callosum. *Arch. Neurol. Psychiat.*, 45, 788–96.

Becher, E. 1911. *Gehirn und Seele*. Heidelberg.

Bethe, A. 1931. Plastizität und Zentrenlehre. *Handb. d. norm. u. path. Physiol.*, 15: 2 1175–1220.

Boring, E. G. 1929. *A History of Experimental Psychology*. New York: Century.

Brown, T. G. 1914. On the nature of the fundamental activity of the nervous centers. *J. Physiol.*, 48, 18–46.

Buddenbrock, W. von. 1921. Die Rhythmus der Schreitbewegungen der Stabheuschrecke Dyxippus. *Biol. Centralb.*, 41, 41–8.

Chamberlain, A. F. 1911. Indians, North American. *Enc. Brit.*, 14, 452–82.

Clark, W. E. LeGros. 1941. Observations on the associative fiber system of the visual cortex and the central representation of the retina. *J. Anat. London*, 75, 225–36.

Epstein, I. n.d. *La Pensée et la polyglossie*. Paris: Payot.

Fournié, E. 1887. *Essai de psychologie*. Paris.

Fritsch, G., and Hitzig, E. 1870. Ueber die elektrische Erregbarkeit des Grosshirns. *Arc. f. Anat. u. Physiol.*, pp. 300–32.

Goldstein, K. 1939. *The Organism*. Boston: Ginn.

Holst, N. von. 1937. Vom Wesen der Ordnung im Zentralnervensystem. *Die Naturwissenschaften*, 25, 625–31; 641–7.

Ingebritzen, O. C. 1933. Coordinating mechanisms of the spinal cord. *Genet. Psychol. Monogr.*, 13, 483–555.

Jacobsen, E. 1932. Electrophysiology of mental activities. *Amer. J. Psychol.*, 44, 677–94.

Lashley, K. S. 1917. The accuracy of movement in the absence of excitation from the moving organ. *Amer. J. Physiol.*, 43, 169–94.

Lashley, K. S. 1942. The mechanism of vision. xvii. Autonomy of the visual cortex. *J. Genet. Psychol.*, 60, 197–221.

Lashley, K. S. 1948. The mechanism of vision. xviii. Effects of destroying the visual "associative areas" in the monkey. *Genet. Psychol. Monogr.*, 37, 107–66.

Max, L. W. 1937. Experimental study of the motor theory of consciousness. IV. *J. Comp. Psychol.*, 24, 301–44.

Pick, A. 1913. *Die agrammatischen Sprachstörungen*. Berlin.

Sherrington, C. S. 1906. *The Integrative Action of the Nervous System*. London: Constable.

Sherrington, C. S. 1929. Some functional problems attaching to convergence. *Proc. Roy. Soc.*, B, 105, 332–62.

Thorsen, A. M. 1925. The relation of tongue movements to internal speech. *J. Exp. Psychol.*, 8, 1–32.

Titchener, E. B. 1909. *Lectures on the Experimental Psychology of the Thought Processes*. New York: Macmillan.

Washburn, M. F. 1916. *Movement and Mental Imagery*. Boston: Houghton Mifflin.

Watson, J. B. 1920. Is thinking merely the action of the language mechanisms? *Brit. J. Psychol.*, 11, 86–104.

25

The Study of Adam, Eve, and Sarah

Roger Brown

In the fall of 1962[1] Ursula Bellugi, Colin Fraser, and I began a longitudinal study of the development of English as a first language in the preschool years of two children, whom we have called Adam and Eve. A third child, whom we call Sarah, joined the company somewhat later. The children were selected from some thirty who were initially considered. Adam, Eve, and Sarah were selected primarily because they were all just beginning to speak multi-word utterances, had highly intelligible speech, and were highly voluble which meant we would not have to sit around forever to get usefully large transcriptions. And because the investigators undertaking primary responsibility for each child (Ursula Bellugi for Adam; Colin Fraser for Eve; Gloria Cooper for Sarah at first, and later Courtney Cazden) felt comfortable with the child and the parents.

All the children were only children at the start of the study. Adam is the son of a minister who lived at first in Cambridge and later in Boston. Eve is the daughter of a man who was at the time a graduate student at Harvard and who lived in Cambridge. Sarah is the daughter of a man who worked as a clerk, at the start of the study, and their home was in Cambridge. The parents of Adam both had college degrees; Eve's father had a college degree and her mother a high school degree; the parents of Sarah both had high school degrees.

The principal data of the study are transcriptions of the spontaneous speech of the child and his mother (occasionally the father and others) in conversation at home. For each child we have at least two hours of transcription for every month, but within these limits the schedules have varied somewhat. For Adam and Eve a two-hour visit every second week was the basic schedule. For Sarah it was one half-hour each week. These are minimum schedules; when interesting things seemed to be happening fast much more speech was recorded. We found that the visits required two persons, the main investigator and one assistant (Richard Cromer, Gordon Finley, Courtney Cazden, and Melissa Bowerman have all served as assistants). One member of the team devoted himself to

From *A First Language: The Early Stages*. Cambridge, Mass.: Harvard University Press, 1973, pp. 51–9. © 1973 by the President and Fellows of Harvard College. Reprinted by permission of the publisher.

a written transcription, on the scene, of the speech of the child and mother (and any others) together with notes about important actions and objects of attention. The other took on the role of playmate for the child and also tended the tape recorder. All conversations were taped. In the case of Adam and Eve the microphone was in a fixed position, and all concerned simply tried to keep interaction within the microphone's range. For Sarah we required a record of higher fidelity because her records were to be phonetically transcribed in a narrow notation including prosodic and paralinguistic expressive features. Accordingly we sewed a microphone into a garment she was always asked to wear, and her speech was transmitted wirelessly to the tape. The final transcriptions, which constitute the primary data of the project, were made by the investigator principally responsible for each child working from the tape recording in conjunction with the on-the-spot transcription to make a single best record. These were made as soon after the visit as possible. Our experience is that transcription from tape of the speech of children at an early age, even when it is relatively intelligible child speech, needs the assistance of memory of the scene and a written record made on the scene.

The transcriptions of Adam and Sarah are simply at the morphemic level, that is, if a meaningful element was sounded well enough to be recognized, it was recorded in normal English spelling with no effort being made to render the particularities of the child's pronunciation. However, the transcribers, Ursula Bellugi and Colin Fraser, took great pains over grammatically significant and phonetically minimal features like inflections, prepositions, articles, and contracted auxiliaries. It is a tribute to their immense care, I know, that the data described in Stage II are so remarkably orderly. Gloria Cooper and Melissa Bowerman did the phonetic transcriptions for Sarah. These have been of considerable value for checking on points where one worried whether the transcriptions of Adam and Eve were accurate. They have always proved to be so, on their own level. Sarah's transcriptions have not been used as yet for a study of the development of phonology but would be valuable for that purpose. Anyone planning to undertake a phonetic record must be warned that it is an immense labor.

During the first year of the project a group of students of the psychology of language met each week to discuss the state of the children's construction process as of that date. The regular participants were: Jean Berko Gleason, Ursula Bellugi (now Bellugi-Klima), Colin Fraser, Samuel Anderson, David McNeill, Dan Slobin, Courtney Cazden, Richard Cromer, and Gordon Finley. We had wonderfully stimulating, light-hearted discussions. Anyone in developmental psycholinguistics looking over the membership of this seminar will realize how bounteous that year was. In the seminar small experiments or near-experiments were often suggested and then tried by the main investigators. The results were sometimes useful but never conclusive; the difficulties of experimentation on language with small children are considerable, and we put the transcription schedule first.

At the end of the first year the project suffered the kind of blow to which longitudinal studies are liable: Eve's family had to move to Nova Scotia, and our 20 two-hour transcriptions were all we would be able to obtain from her. We continued taking data from Adam and Sarah for another four years. But as it happened the fact of Eve's withdrawal has shaped my role in the project even until the present time. I decided to concentrate on just the developmental period for which we had data from all three children. As it happened Eve's speech developed so much more rapidly than that of Adam and Sarah that 10 months of her transcriptions equalled about 20 months for Adam and Sarah.

Long before the end of the first year the children got way ahead of the seminar. Their records were far too rich to be analyzed in a two-hour session. It became clear that a fine-grained analysis was a big job and had to be undertaken by one person. Even then only a fraction of the data could be examined. Still I was determined to make the effort because I had not set out to create an immense archive that no one would ever use.

It is sensible to ask and we were often asked, "Why not code the sentences for grammatically significant features and put them on a computer so that studies could readily be made by anyone?" My answer always was that I was continually discovering new kinds of information that could be mined from a transcription of conversation and never felt that I knew what the full coding should be. This was certainly the case and indeed it can be said that in the entire decade since 1962 investigators have continued to hit upon new ways of inferring grammatical and semantic knowledge or competence from free conversation. But, for myself, I must, in candor, add that there was also a factor of research style. I have little patience with prolonged "tooling up" for research. I always want to get started. A better scientist would probably have done more planning and used the computer. He can do so today, in any case, with considerable confidence that he knows what to code.

Our three children were not at the same chronological age when we began our study; Eve was 18 months; Adam and Sarah were 27 months. We had not equated for age because we knew, from much earlier work, that children acquire language at widely varying rates. We had rather equated them from the length of their utterances, both the mean length (MLU) and the upper bound or longest utterance. The mean length of utterance (MLU) is an excellent simple index of grammatical development because almost every new kind of knowledge increases length: the number of semantic roles expressed in a sentence, the addition of obligatory morphemes, coding modulations of meaning, the addition of negative forms and auxiliaries used in interrogative and negative modalities, and, of course, embedding and coordinating. All alike have the common effect on the surface form of the sentence of increasing length (especially if measured in morphemes, which includes bound forms like inflections rather than words). By the time the child reaches Stage V, however, he is able to make constructions of such great variety that *what* he happens to say and the MLU of a sample begin to depend more on the character of the interaction than on what the child knows, and so the index loses its value as an indicator of grammatical knowledge.

Table 25.1 presents a copy of the rules we used in calculating mean length of utterances (MLU) and upper bound or longest utterance for a transcription. These rules take account of things we learned about child speech in the first year of the study, for example, the fact that compound words are not analyzed as such and the fact that the irregular pasts that occur early are not used with semantic consistency or contrasted with present forms. Still no claim can be made that these are just the right rules. They have, however, served all of us well as a simple way of making one child's data comparable with another's, one project with another, and in limited degree, development in one language comparable with development in another.

When I say that the indices have served us well I mean simply that two children matched for MLU are much more likely to have speech that is, on internal grounds, at the same

Table 25.1   Rules for calculating mean length of utterance and upper bound.

1. Start with the second page of the transcription unless that page involves a recitation of some kind. In this latter case start with the first recitation-free stretch. Count the first 100 utterances satisfying the following rules.

2. Only fully transcribed utterances are used; none with blanks. Portions of utterances, entered in parentheses to indicate doubtful transcription, are used.

3. Include all exact utterance repetitions (marked with a plus sign in records). Stuttering is marked as repeated efforts at a single word; count the word once in the most complete form produced. In the few cases where a word is produced for emphasis or the like (*no, no, no*) count each occurrence.

4. Do not count such fillers as *mm* or *oh*, but do count *no, yeah,* and *hi.*

5. All compound words (two or more free morphemes), proper names, and ritualized re-duplications count as single words. Examples: *birthday, rackety-boom, choo-choo, quack-quack, night-night, pocketbook, see saw.* Justification is that no evidence that the constituent morphemes function as such for these children.

6. Count as one morpheme all irregular pasts of the verb (*got, did, went, saw*). Justification is that there is no evidence that the child relates these to present forms.

7. Count as one morpheme all diminutives (*doggie, mommie*) because these children at least do not seem to use the suffix. productively. Diminutives are the standard forms used by the child.

8. Count as separate morphemes all auxiliaries (*is, have, will, can, must, would*). Also all catenatives: *gonna, wanna, hafta.* These latter counted as single morphemes rather than as *going to* or *want to* because evidence is that they function so for the children. Count as separate morphemes all inflections, for example, possessive {s}, plural {s}, third person singular {s}, regular past {d}, progressive {in}.

9. The range count follows the above rules but is always calculated for the total transcription rather than for 100 utterances.

level of constructional complexity than are two children of the same chronological age. We know that we are going to run into serious inconsistencies and uncertainties with some foreign languages, and these are discussed in Stage I. However, the MLU may be effectively redefined or we may find some other, almost equally simple index, prefer-able. In any case we are getting beyond the point where a single index is vital because we are accumulating knowledge about the acquisition order of general construction types and their meanings, and it is the order of knowledge we really care about.

I calculated the MLU's and upper bounds for all sample transcriptions for all chil-dren. The results when MLU is plotted against chronological age for just the period in which Eve participated in the study appear as Figure 25.1. The values rise quite con-sistently with age, for Eve most amazingly so. It was almost impossible to fail to find an increment every time two weeks had elapsed. As I remember it the one downward jog came on a day when Eve had a cold. This stretch of development, common to the three children, is what I undertook to analyze in some detail – a good many years ago.

How to proceed? There was far too much data in even this interval to be exhaustively analyzed. I decided to divide the total shared developmental stretch at five points as nearly as possible equidistant from one another in terms both of MLU and upper bound (UB) and draw 713 consecutive complete utterances from each child at each point for detailed linguistic analysis. The odd number, 713, was an accidental consequence of the size of the transcriptions from which the first samples were drawn.

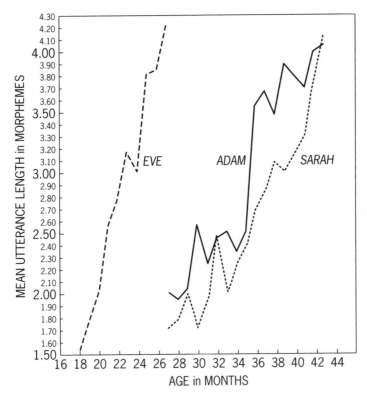

Figure 25.1   Mean utterance length and chronological age for three children.

Table 25.2   Target values and approximations attained for mean length of utterance and upper bounds.

Stage	Target Value		Approximation Attained	
	MLU	Upper Bound	Maximum Distance from MLU	Maximum Distance from Upper Bound
I	1.75	5	.31	2
II	2.25	7	.05	1
III	2.75	9	.25	1
IV	3.50	11	.20	1
V	4.00	13	.06	1.67

Table 25.2 describes my target values which for MLU begin at 1.75 and end at 4.00 with increments of 0.50 (except for III to IV). The upper bounds begin at 5.0 and proceed by increments of 2.0 to 13.0. Of course I could not hit these targets exactly for the samples of varying size from each child. And so Table 25.2 also describes the widest departures from the target values that the data ever forced me to accept. These are never very great.

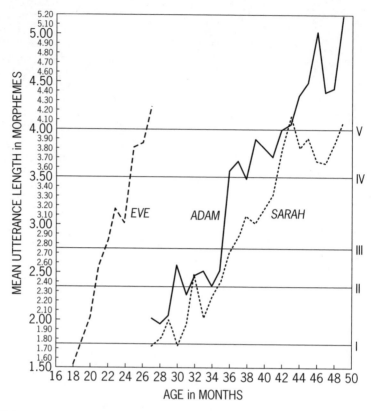

Figure 25.2   Mean utterance length and age in three children.

Figure 25.2 is just like Figure 25.1 except that the Roman numerals I–V and corresponding horizontal lines mark the points at which fifteen 713 utterance samples were
taken. These were my preliminary Stages I to V. Then the work of analysis began. I
decided to press for an explicit generative grammar for each sample but, because I knew
any such grammar would have to remain indeterminate at countless points, I undertook
also to write extensive annotations describing alternative formulations, gaps in the evidence, and so forth. Of course the data of performance have long ago been pronounced
(Chomsky, 1964) an inadequate base for a grammar that attempts to represent competence or knowledge. I agree that it always is but I venture to say that not many people
know how much can be milked from mere performance in the case of small children –
especially conversational performance in which you can track relations between sentences.
I have found the process of grammar writing a continual discovery of new things to look
at, new aspects of the data that could tell me something about the knowledge in the minds
of these three children.

Why write admittedly indeterminate grammars? Simply because the requirement to
be fully explicit and develop rules that will really derive the sentences you have obtained
forces a kind of intense examination and continuing re-examination of the data, and so
is a good way to get to know it very well. The 15 annotated grammars took something
like two months each to do, with the time longer in the later stages. I suppose they are

mostly 50 pages or more long. In the years that this took, linguistic theory, of course, went on changing in response to intuition and logical arguments, and when I saw the point of a change I also shifted my procedure and formal notation. In the end I was left with 15 weighty manuscripts which not more than half-a-dozen people in the world have the *knowledge*, the *patience*, and the *interest* to read; nay, not so many as half a dozen.

In the process I formed a conception of great commonality among these unacquainted children and of a remarkably invariant order in the kinds of things they said. I learned that there were some points on which the data were simply too thin to support any sort of generalization; for example, the order of adverbs. I also formed a conception of the kinds of things about which something might reasonably be said, and these are the five constructional processes described in the beginning of the chapter. The 15 grammars I now regard as a protracted preliminary exploration, not boring to me because of the puzzle properties each one develops. One can stand a lot of sorting and resorting when it is done with hypotheses in mind which make the outcomes exciting. I am personally reluctant to hand this process over to a computer. About two years ago I started to write a new set of Stages I–V, but sticking this time to the kinds of things about which something can be said and hoping to make myself clear to more than half-a-dozen readers.

It remains only to answer a question that was put to me, with some asperity, a few years ago after a talk about child language: "What is this work about really?" It is not about the way the child's mind in fact processes sentences in speaking and understanding. I do not know how that is done. It is about knowledge; knowledge concerning grammar and the meanings coded by grammar. Knowledge inferred, of course, from performance, from sentences spoken, the settings in which they are spoken, and from signs of comprehension or incomprehension of sentences spoken by others. The book primarily presents evidence that knowledge of the kind described develops in an approximately invariant form in all children, though at different rates. There is also evidence that the primary determinants of the order are the relative semantic and grammatical complexity of constructions rather than their frequency or the way in which parents react to them. I believe that this knowledge must somehow be utilized in actual sentence processing, in speaking and understanding, but cannot say how. I hope the volumes will help to establish reasonably firm generalizations about the unfolding of construction knowledge in children, generalizations on which theory can build.

The Expository Plan of this Work

The plan is not quite the same for any two stages but there are several things that are constant throughout.

1. The stages are not known to be true stages in Piaget's sense; that is they may not be qualitative changes of organization forced on the investigator by the data themselves. The original equidistant samples based on MLU were simply a device for sampling the data; a discontinuous sampling imposed upon more continuous data. My divisions I to V were rather like a sociologist's imposition of arbitrary dividing points on a continuous distribution of incomes.

2. The original stages were points on an MLU distribution, but in this work they have become intervals. Stage I, for instance, begins as soon as the MLU rises above 1.0,

when multi-word utterances begin, and ends at 2.0. This is because our discussions are not limited to the data from Adam, Eve, and Sarah. Since we started in 1962, there have been numerous studies of the development of English and other languages which started when the child's MLU was less than 1.75, the target value for Stage I in the original analyses in our study. I have tried to put all this work together, and it is clear that construction begins before 1.75. Stage II extends from 2.0 to 2.50 because we found it possible to deal with all the data in this period in a certain quantitative respect. Other considerations make intervals of all the later stages.

3. A stage is named (Semantic Roles and Syntactic Relations for Stage I; Grammatical Morphemes and the Modulation of Meaning for Stage II; Modalities of the Simple Sentence for Stage III; and so on, either for a process that is the major new development occurring in that interval or for an exceptionally elaborate development of a process at that stage. However, the whole development of any one of the major constructional processes is not contained within a given stage interval. Semantic roles go on developing after Stage I; the modulations of meaning extend from Stage II to beyond even Stage V. The germs of the major modalities of simple sentences (interrogation, negation, the imperative) are to be found even in Stage I in a syntactically rudimentary form, and there are combinations of the modalities, like the tag question, which do not appear until after Stage V. When we discuss embedding in Stage IV we shall have to go all the way back to Stage I to show why certain constructions (the possessive and the prenominal adjective) which appear in Stage I, and are analyzed by many linguists as embeddings, are not such in the child's speech. In general there is something of interest to say about all five major aspects of construction in all five stages. In general the stage discussion deals with the construction aspect for which it is named across the full range of data.

4. As mentioned in passing, not only the data of Adam, Eve, and Sarah but all the longitudinal and experimental data available to me on a given stage are discussed. There is far more information beyond our own, on Stage I, than on any other stage, including longitudinal studies of Finnish, Samoan, Swedish, Spanish, Luo, and German, as well as a number of studies of American English. The data thin out after Stage I simply because most of the investigators in question have not had time to carry their analyses beyond this point.

5. The stages are not simply descriptive but are organized as evidence and argument for and against certain generalizations. In Stage I, for example, the question is, on what evidence, if at all can the constructional meanings of the first sentences be inferred? There is one recurrent theme in all stages, that order of development, conceived in the right abstract terms is invariant across both children and languages and is primarily determined by the relative semantic and grammatical complexity of constructions.

Note

1   The first five years of this work were supported by Public Health Service Grant MH-7088 from the National Institute of Mental Health, and the second five years by Grant HD-02908 from the National Institute of Child Health and Development. We are deeply grateful for the generosity of this support and the intelligent flexibility with which both grants have been

administered. Miss Esther Sorocka has been executive secretary to the project from the beginning, and her importance to the success it has had is very great. The parents of Adam, Eve, and Sarah, and the three children themselves by their unfailing, welcoming friendliness made the whole project possible.

Reference

Chomsky, Noam. 1964. Formal discussion. In Ursula Bellugi and Roger Brown (eds.), *The Acquisition of Language*. Monographs of the Society for Research in Child Development 29, pp. 35–9.

26

Syntactic Regularities
in the Speech of Children

Edward S. Klima and Ursula Bellugi[-Klima]

What we have set as our immediate goal is the overall grammatical capacity of children – their general linguistic competence. The question of course is how to arrive at this competence. The utterances produced – which seem the most direct access to competence – cannot give the total answer. There is really no way to determine which of the child's utterances are grammatically non-deviant in terms of his own grammar. And even if the grammatically non-deviant utterances could be reliably determined, they could only give hints as to the total grammatical capacity of the child, which includes not only what has been produced (or understood) but also what could be produced (or understood). The situation is the same as that involved in describing our own adult grammar if we limited ourselves to what had been uttered over some short period of time and faithfully gave equal weight to everything uttered, no matter how it actually came out. What is actually done, in analysing, is to select. Sentences are selected which are felt intuitively to be most free of deviances, and then one goes beyond the mere corpus to develop a more structured theory that excludes sentences which are wrong grammatically (i.e., present clear deviances) and that explains the status of the other cases. The range of difficulties that face the analyst in describing the language of children on the basis of their utterances should be illuminated by examining a sketch of grammatical structure in adult English.

Approaching the grammar of child language from the other direction answers certain of the problems – that is, from the point of view of the child's ability to understand sentences. Sentences the child understands describe the scope of his grammar more accurately than those he produces, just as with the adult. But if the child's "understanding" of adult sentences is examined, there is some evidence to suggest that the child comprehends sentences according to his existing grammar. Where comprehension involves syntactic characteristics not present in the child's utterances it seems that this does not represent a relatively rich grammar coupled with a much poorer production device, but rather a limited grammar coupled with a liberal perceptual device that sifts out or bypasses unfamiliar material. As an example, we tested children whose speech did not contain

From J. Lyons and R. J. Wales (eds.), *Psycholinguistic Papers*. Edinburgh: Edinburgh University Press, 1966, pp. 183–208. Reproduced by permission of Ursula Bellugi-Klima.

passives on this construction, using pairs of pictures. For instance, one picture showed a cat being chased by a dog, and another, a dog being chased by a cat. When the children were asked to point to the picture of the cat chased by the dog, they pointed to the picture of a cat chasing a dog, and vice versa. We plan to use as much information on comprehension of syntax as possible in investigating the grammar of children.

A striking characteristic of the language acquisition situation is the fact that the particular linguistic ability that develops in the individual child as he gradually masters his native language is grossly underdetermined by the utterances he hears. Not only does he understand, produce, and recognize as perfectly normal countless sentences he has never heard, but he will reject as deviant in some way or other countless utterances that he has heard produced during his linguistically formative years. The child will reject as deviant all the various slips of the tongue, false starts, interrupted completions, and noises that are present in our everyday utterances. Given the external characteristics of language acquisition, the psycholinguist asks: How do any two children – to say nothing of those of a whole speech community – arrive at anywhere near the same language? How does a particular language – each time it is acquired by a child – keep from changing radically? Since language does not change radically in this situation, there must surely be some general principles at work, and it is the principles underlying language acquisition which we want eventually to illuminate.

But first, prior questions must be investigated. If one looks closely at the development of speech in children who have heard totally independent language environments during the early period of language acquisition, it may well be that each will follow an independent path in his grammatical growth and syntactic patterns. And if the limitations on what the child produces have little relationship to his grammatical capacity, one would not expect that a study of children's speech would reveal regularities in the order of appearance of structures across children. We propose to investigate the development of negative and interrogative structures in the speech of three children in order to examine some of these questions.

The Language Acquisition Project

For several years, our research group (Professor Roger Brown and his associates[1]) has been studying language acquisition. We have as data for this research a developmental study of three children. We collected two hours of speech every two weeks in a natural setting; that is, recordings of conversations between mother and child in the home. We supplemented this data by performing small experiments to begin investigation of the children's grammatical comprehension and competence.

With these three children, each was followed by a different investigator; the families were totally unacquainted and independent of one another, and each child heard a different set of sentences as "input". The children were beginning to string words together in structured utterances when we began the study. One child was 18 months old, another 26 months and the third was 27 months old when we began the study. However, all three were at approximately the same stage of language development.

For each child, then, there are two to four sessions of the speech of the mother and child per month as data. These sessions were tape recorded and later transcribed together with a written record made at the time of the recording which includes some aspects of

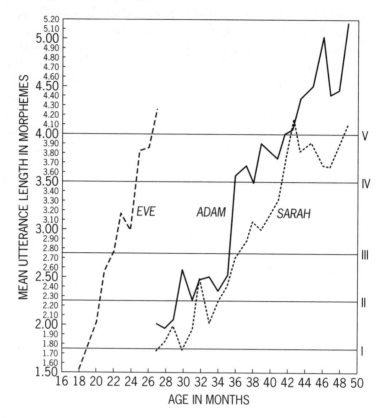

Figure 26.1

the situation which relate to the meaning of the interchange. In order to describe stages in development we picked two end points in terms of mean utterance length; the first stage is from the first month of study for each child; the last is from the month in which the mean utterance lengths approach 4.0 for each of the three children; and the second stage is between the two.

Each stage represents several thousand child utterances. From the total speech we isolated the negative statements and the questions for analysis, and have suggested outlines for a study of the development of these systems in the children's speech. We have used the children's utterances and evidence about the children's understanding of those constructions in the language of others, in attempting to consider the children's developing grammatical capacities.

Negation in English

To begin, it is necessary to specify some of the linguistic facts about the terminal state toward which the children are progressing, that is, the syntax of English negatives and interrogatives. We will consider that *negative* is a morpheme which can combine with other parts of speech to motivate negation in a sentence, and its usual expression is *no* or *not*. With this notion, we can examine the facts about English negation that are relevant to the early stages of language acquisition; there are many complexities that do not occur at all in those early stages, but the basic facts about negation in simple English sentences are all relevant.

Negation and Auxiliary Verbs.   The negative morpheme *no* or *not* appears most commonly in conjunction with the auxiliary verbs in English and is generally contracted with them in speech. Consider first the modal auxiliaries (*will, can, may, must, could, would, shall, should,* etc.) and notice that the negative morpheme is generally attached to the auxiliary of the sentence when there is one, and is located after the first helping verb. Compare these sets of affirmative and negative sentences:

The man will finish today.　　*The man won't finish today.*
The baby can sit up.　　*The baby can't sit up.*
He will have been doing it.　　*He won't have been doing it.*

The negative morpheme is connected with the auxiliary verb *be*, with *be* as a copular verb, and with *have* as an auxiliary and sometimes as a main verb:

They are coming here.　　*They aren't coming here.*
Her face is red.　　*Her face isn't red.*
I have done it.　　*I haven't done it.*

In each case, the contraction of the negative element with the auxiliary is optional. One can say either: *They can not go*, or *They can't go*, although the latter seems more frequent in informal speech.
　　The negative element is not attached to main verbs, nor does it stand in place of an auxiliary; thus we do not say **I wantn't it* or *I not want it, but rather *I don't want it.* The auxiliary verb *do* occurs wherever the affirmative version of a sentence does not have an auxiliary verb, and not only carries the negative morpheme but also the tense marker. *He made one* is the affirmative sentence corresponding to *He didn't make one*, not to **He doesn't made one.* (An asterisk preceding an utterance means that this is not a possible sentence of English.)

Negative Imperative.   There are reasons to consider the imperative sentences of English as having a deleted subject (*you* or an indeterminate *somebody*) and modal auxiliary (*will* or *can*); and the negative imperative then begins with the negative with *do* that co-occurs with *you* followed by a verb phrase:

Don't be late, will you?
Don't trip over that.

and sometimes:

Don't you do that again!

One cannot have imperatives of the following forms: *Can't have it, *Isn't coming, *No go, *Not do it, *Doesn't want it, etc.

Negation and Indefiniteness.   Generally, simple English sentences have only one negation in standard speech. In affirmative sentences the form of the indeterminate pronoun is *some*, as in *I see somebody* and *I want something*. The distributional facts of negative sentences suggest that if a negative element is embedded in the auxiliary of a sentence, the indeterminate form becomes an indefinite. Compare the following sets:

You have some milk.   You haven't any milk.
Give me some more.   Don't give me any more.
I want something.   I don't want anything.

When the negative element appears in conjunction with an auxiliary verb the form corresponding to the indeterminate *some* is the indefinite *any*.

Negative sentences are not only formed by embedding the negative element in the auxiliary of the sentence; the negative element may also combine with a pronoun or adverb, as in *no one, nothing, never*, or with a determiner, as in *no more, no books*, and so on. In this case, there is one negativized element per simple sentence of English, and this does not co-occur with auxiliary negation, but is an alternative.

The negative element is attached to the left-most relevant constituent; that is, the negative occurs as soon as possible in the sentence. Ordinarily it is the subject that is negated: *No one is coming* rather than *Anyone isn't coming*. However, in a passive sentence it is the object that occurs on the left, and that would therefore be negated. Compare the negative active and passive forms:

No one is persuading anyone to do it. (Subject)
No one is being persuaded by anyone to do it. (Object)

The points of concern here are:

1   An indeterminate occurring in a sentence which has a negative element in it will be of the form *any*.
2   Negation tends to occur as early in the sentence as possible, perhaps as a signalling device. It is the word order in the surface structure and not the base structure which determines this tendency.
3   Negation can occur with auxiliary verbs, adverbs, and indefinite pronouns and determiners. Thus we find:

He never did it.
He didn't do it.
No one ever did it.

Negation not included in this study.   The sections described above cover the problems which arise in relation to negatives in the children's speech as far as we have considered it in this study. Symptomatic of sentence negation in adult English is the possible occurrence of an *either*-clause (*I didn't like it and he didn't either*); the negative apposit-ive tag (*I don't like dogs, not even little ones*); and the question tag without *not* (*He's not going, is he?*). None of those occur in the children's speech in the early stages. Negative word-marking does not occur either (*unfortunately, impossible, unmade*), nor do inher-ently negative words like *doubt, reluctant*.

This discussion comprises part of what we mean by the negative system, the inter-rogative system and the auxiliary system in adult English; that is, all the occurrences and non-occurrences involving those parts of the grammar. We will try to capture the nature of these systems by a set of rules something like those on the following pages, although undoubtedly as more is learned about grammatical systems in general and about English in particular, the form of these rules will be different. We feel that in their pre-sent state they do at least capture the spirit of this part of the grammar in a way that is compatible with other aspects of the grammar of English. One can think of the rules as giving some verifiable substance to our claim that these occurrences and non-occurrences fit together in some systematic way.

Rules for Negation in Adult English

The verb phrase has at one level in its derivation the following form:

$$\left[[T - do]_{\text{Aux}_1}(\text{Neg}) \left[\begin{Bmatrix} \text{IMP} \\ \text{M} \end{Bmatrix} (\textit{have-pp})(\textit{be-prp})(\textit{be-pp}) \right]_{\text{Aux}_2} \begin{Bmatrix} V \\ be \\ have \end{Bmatrix} \right] \text{VP}$$

$$\text{or} \left[[T - do(\text{Neg})]_{\text{Aux}_1} \qquad \text{etc.} \qquad \right] \text{VP}$$

This represents the underlying structure after certain transformations (the details of which are not important in this study) have already operated; for example, the positioning of the negative morpheme, the occurrence of the passive auxiliary.

Transformations

I. Replacement of *do*

$$T - do - (\text{Neg}) - \begin{Bmatrix} \text{M} \\ have \\ be \end{Bmatrix} \Rightarrow T - \begin{Bmatrix} \text{M} \\ have \\ be \end{Bmatrix} - (\text{Neg}) - \phi$$

II. Interrogative Inversion

$$Q[X^1 - wh + \text{indet}] - NP - \text{Aux}_1 - X^2 \Rightarrow Q[X^1 - wh + \text{indet}] - \text{Aux}_1 - NP - X^2$$

III.   Indefinite Colouring

    1. $X^1 - \text{Indet} - X^2 - \text{Neg} - X^3 \Rightarrow X^1 - \text{Indef} - X^2 - \text{Neg} - X^3$

    2. $X^1 - \text{Neg} - X^2 - \text{Indet} - X^3 \Rightarrow X^1 - \text{Neg} - X^2 - \text{Indef} - X^3$

    (If Neg is treated as occurring initially in the underlying string, then a simpler formulation is possible.)

IV.   Formation of Negative Pronouns

    1.   Obligatory

$$X^1 - \text{Indef} - X^2 - \text{Neg} - X^3 \Rightarrow X^1 - \text{Neg} + \text{Indef} - X^2 - \phi - X^3$$

    2.   Optional

$$X^1 - \text{Neg} - X^2 - \text{Indef} - X^3 \Rightarrow X^1 - \phi - X^2 - \text{Neg} + \text{Indef} - X^3$$

V.   *Do* Deletion

$$T - do - V \Rightarrow T - \phi - V$$

or, expanded to include imperatives as approximately:

$$T - do - (\text{IMP}) \begin{Bmatrix} V \\ be \\ have \end{Bmatrix} \Rightarrow T - \phi - \begin{Bmatrix} V \\ be \\ have \end{Bmatrix}$$

Negation in Children's Speech

What it is that the child learns in becoming a mature speaker of the language is, of course, the whole system which we have tried to capture by the rules above, and certainly not those particular tentative rules. It should be understood that when we write rules for the child grammar it is just a rough attempt to give substance to our feeling about, and general observations demonstrating, the regularity in the syntax of children's speech.

We have intentionally allowed ourselves much freedom in the formulation of these rules. Even within this freedom we feel that at the very earliest stages perhaps we fitted the language unjustifiably to what we assume to be the underlying structure of adult language. These rules reflect but certainly do not describe completely the utterances produced by the child. Whenever possible we took into consideration comprehension of utterances; but comprehension, like speech, only REFLECTS the grammar. Our aim in both cases is to find basic regularities.

One of the ultimate objectives in describing such regularities is to discover – given the child's own linguistic abilities as they have developed at some particular stage and given the utterances that he hears – what system or possible systems the child will ascribe to the language.

Not very much is known about how people understand a particular sentence or what goes into producing one; but something is known about the systematicity of adult language. It has seemed to us that the language of children has its own systematicity, and that the sentences of children are not just an imperfect copy of those of an adult.

Are there hazards in considering the grammar of a child's language from the point of view of his speech? Of course there are many. One possibility is that the limitations on what is produced have nothing at all to do with the grammar but have to do with factors of memory, immediate requirements of explicitness, and the like. However, if this were the case, one would not expect the order of appearance of certain structures, and in particular certain systematic "mistakes", to be regular across children. We want to emphasize here that we are not dealing with the expression of semantic concepts on the part of the child, or of basic grammatical notions like subject function and transitivity; rather we are concerned with the way he handles lower-level syntactic phenomena like position, permutability, and the like.

Stage 1.   The sentences we want to describe from stage 1, are taken from the protocols of all three children:

No . . . wipe finger
More . . . no
No a boy bed
Not . . . fit
No singing song
No the sun shining
No money
No mitten
No sit there
No play that
Wear mitten no
Not a teddy bear
No fall!

Unless otherwise noted, the sentences included in this report represent large numbers of like utterances in the children's speech, and are not to be considered isolated examples but rather reflections of recurrent structures occurring in the children's spontaneous speech. Notice that there are no negatives within the utterances, nor are there auxiliary verbs. The element which signals negation is *no* or *not*, and this element either precedes or follows the rest of the utterance.

Let us refer to the elements *wipe finger, more, the sun shining,* in the above sentences as the Nucleus. Notice incidentally that there seems to be limited structure to the Nucleus. The sentences consist largely of nouns and verbs without indication of tense or number. Non-occurrences include inflections, prepositions, articles, pronouns, adjectives, adverbs, auxiliary verbs, and so on.

The negation system at stage 1 can be considered as follows:

$$\left[\left\{ \begin{matrix} no \\ not \end{matrix} \right\} - \text{Nucleus} \right] \text{S} \quad \text{or} \quad \left[\text{Nucleus} - no \right] \text{S}$$

At this stage, there is no clear evidence that the child even understands the negative embedded in the auxiliary of adult speech, without at least some reinforcement. The adults at this first stage often reinforce their negative statements, as in, *No, you can't have that*, or as in the following interchange:

Mother: *I'm not sure.*
Child: *Sure.*
Mother: *No, I'm not sure.*

What is striking in the speech of the child at this stage is that he employs extremely limited means for negative sentences in his own speech, and the same system is repeated in all three subjects. In subsequent periods, the rule for negation will have a different form. In those subsequent periods there may indeed be an initial sentence adverb *no*, but this initial element is not a sufficient or even necessary part of negation.

The rule for negation that we have given serves many negative functions in the child's speech at stage 1 which will later be supplanted by other more complex rules, as the following interchanges will suggest:

Adult: *Get in your high chair with your bib, and I'll give you your cheese.*
Child: *No bibby.*
Adult: *Oh, you don't want your bibby?*

———

Adult: *Well, is the sun shining?*
Child: *No the sun shining.*
Adult: *Oh, the sun's not shining?*

———

(An adult leans over to talk to the child. Child looks up and puts up a hand in warning.)
Child: *No fall!*

———

Child: *No.*
Adult: *No what?*
Child: *No, Mommy.*
Adult: *No Mommy what?*
Child: *. . . No.* (as if she is having trouble finding words)
Adult: *No what?*
Child: *No . . . Oh foot . . . foot floor.* (pushes mother's foot onto the floor)
Adult: *Oh, you want my foot on the floor.*

Stage 2.   Some of the sentences we want to describe, again from all three children, are as follows:

I can't catch you.
I can't see you.
We can't talk.
You can't dance.

I don't sit on Cromer coffee.
I don't want it.
I don't like him.
I don't know his name.

No pinch me.
No . . . Rusty hat.
Book say no.
Touch the snow no.
This a radiator no.
No square . . . is clown.

Don't bite me yet.
Don't leave me.
Don't wait for me . . . come in.
Don't wake me up . . . again.

That not 'O', that blue.
He not little, he big.
That no fish school.
That no Mommy.
There no squirrels.

He no bite you.
I no want envelope.
I no taste them.

A characteristic of child language is the residue of elements of previous systems, and the sentences produced might well be described as a coexistence of the rules at stage 1, and a new system. Let us begin with a basic structure something like:

$$S \rightarrow \text{Nominal} - (\text{Aux}^{neg}) - \begin{Bmatrix} \text{Predicate} \\ \text{Main Verb} \end{Bmatrix}$$

where Neg has as possible lexical representatives *can't*, *don't*, *not* and occasionally *no*. The auxiliary verbs can be thought of as occurring in the speech of the children only when accompanied by a *neg*, since it is a fact that the auxiliary verbs do not occur in questions or declarative utterances at this stage. They occur only in negative sentences, and in these limited forms. This first rule can be related to the shape of sentences by the following rules:

$$\text{Aux}^{neg} \rightarrow \begin{Bmatrix} \text{Neg} \\ V^{neg} \end{Bmatrix}$$

$$\text{Neg} \rightarrow \begin{Bmatrix} no \\ not \end{Bmatrix}$$

$$V^{neg} \rightarrow \begin{Bmatrix} can't \\ don't \end{Bmatrix} V^{neg} \text{ restricted to non-progressive verbs}$$

where the particular selection of the negative is determined by the Main Verb with *don't* and *can't* restricted to occurrence before instances of non–progressive main verbs.

Two auxiliary verbs appear in the negative form, *don't* and *can't*. These are considered as lexical representations of V^{neg} since there are no occurrences of *I can do it*, *Can I have it?*, *He shouldn't have it*, *They aren't going*, etc., but only instances of the sort described above. The negative element is also found within the sentence, but not connected to an auxiliary verb, as in *He no bite you.*

There are a number of sentences with neg (*no* or *not*) followed by a predicate. There is a limited class of subjects in this set. The negative imperative has appeared in the speech of all three children, in the form: *Don't leave me.* In the previous stage the imperative form was presumably *No fall.* There is at this stage an affirmative imperative as well, as in *Come here* and *Do it.* There are hardly any sentences with indefinite determiners or pronouns, but there are by now personal and impersonal pronouns, possessive pronouns, articles and adjectives.

It is clear that the child understands the negative embedded in the auxiliary of the sentence by this stage. Some typical interchanges suggesting discourse agreements are:

Mother: *I don't know that song, Adam.*
Child: *Why not?*
_____

Mother: *Well, I can't change your diaper right now.*
Child: *Why not?*

There is also evidence that the child uses negatives to negate a preposition by this stage as in:

Mother: *Did you play in the snow?*
Child: *No, play sunshine.*
_____

Child: *He not little, he big.*

The system which we have suggested for stage 2, then, is the rule for stage 1, and:

$$S \rightarrow \text{Nominal} - (\text{Aux}^{neg}) - \begin{Bmatrix} \text{Predicate} \\ \text{Main Verb} \end{Bmatrix}$$

$$\text{Aux}^{neg} \rightarrow \begin{Bmatrix} \text{Neg} \\ V^{neg} \end{Bmatrix}$$

$$\text{Neg} \rightarrow \begin{Bmatrix} no \\ not \end{Bmatrix}$$

$$V^{neg} \rightarrow \begin{Bmatrix} can't \\ don't \end{Bmatrix} V^{neg} \text{ is restricted to non-progressive verbs.}$$

Stage 3.   A sample of the sentences to be described, again from all three children:

Paul can't have one.
I can't see it.
This can't stick.
We can't make another broom.

I didn't did it.
Because I don't want somebody to wake me up.
I don't want cover on it.
I don't . . . have some . . . too much.
You don't want some supper.
You didn't caught me.
You didn't eat supper with us.
I didn't see something.
Paul didn't laugh.
I didn't caught it.

I gave him some so he won't cry.
'Cause he won't talk.
Donna won't let go.

No, I don't have a book.
No, it isn't.
That was not me.
I am not a doctor.
I isn't . . . I not sad . . .

This not ice cream.
This no good.
They not hot.
Paul not tired.
It's not cold.

I not crying.
That not turning.
He not taking the walls down.

Don't put the two wings on.
Don't kick my box.
Don't touch the fish.

I not hurt him.
I not see you anymore.
Ask me if I not made mistake.

In the speech of the children, the modal auxiliaries now appear in declarative sentences and questions, as well as in negative sentences; so we can now begin with a basic structure like:

$$S \rightarrow \text{Nominal} - \text{Aux} - \begin{Bmatrix} \text{Predicate} \\ \text{Main Verb} \end{Bmatrix}$$

and suggest some rules as follows:

$Aux \rightarrow T - V^{aux} - (Neg)$

$$V^{aux} - \begin{Bmatrix} do \\ can \\ be \\ will \end{Bmatrix}$$

where *be* is restricted to predicate and progressive and is optional, *can* and *do* to non-progressive main verbs.

Transformations

I.   Optional *be* deletion

   $NP - be \Rightarrow NP$

II.   *Do* deletion

   $do - V \Rightarrow V$

In the speech of the children at this stage the negative auxiliary verbs are now no longer limited to *don't* and *can't*, and the auxiliary verbs now appear in declarative sentences and questions, so that the auxiliary verbs can be considered as separate from the negative element of the sentence.

   Indeterminates now start appearing in the children's speech, in affirmative utterances as *I want some supper* or *I see something*. The children's negative sentences have the form, *I don't want some supper* and *I didn't see something*. The negative versions are clearly not imitations of adult sentences, and indicate that the complex relationship of negative and indefinite has not yet been established. Examples of indefinite colouring or negative pronouns are rare, and do not appear with any regularity until subsequent stages.

Rules for Negation in Children's Speech

Stage 1.

$$\left[\begin{Bmatrix} no \\ not \end{Bmatrix} - \text{Nucleus} \right] \text{ S } \quad \text{or} \quad \left[\text{Nucleus} - no \right] \text{ S}$$

Stage 2.

$$S \rightarrow \text{Nominal} - Aux^{neg} - \begin{Bmatrix} \text{Predicate} \\ \text{Main Verb} \end{Bmatrix}$$

$$Aux^{neg} \rightarrow \begin{Bmatrix} \text{Neg} \\ V^{neg} \end{Bmatrix}$$

$$\text{Neg} \rightarrow \begin{Bmatrix} no \\ not \end{Bmatrix}$$

$$V^{neg} \rightarrow \begin{Bmatrix} \text{can't} \\ \text{don't} \end{Bmatrix}$$

where the particular selection of the negative is determined by the Main Verb with *don't* and *can't* restricted to occurrence before instances of non-progressive main verbs.

Stage 3.

$$S \rightarrow \text{Nominal} - \text{Aux} - \begin{Bmatrix} \text{Predicate} \\ \text{Main Verb} \end{Bmatrix}$$

$$\text{Aux} \rightarrow \text{T} - \text{V}^{aux} - (\text{Neg})$$

$$\text{V}^{aux} \rightarrow \begin{Bmatrix} do \\ \text{M} \\ be \end{Bmatrix}$$

where *be* is restricted to predicate and progressive, *can* and *do* to non-progressive main verbs.

Transformations

I.   Optional *be* deletion

   $\text{NP} - be \Rightarrow \text{NP}$

II. *Do* Deletion

   $do - \text{V} \Rightarrow \text{V}$

Interrogatives in English

For questions in adult English, we represent the interrogative nature of the sentence by the symbol Q, with which may be associated some interrogative word(s) (*What will that person make?*) or the element *yes/no* (*Will that person make something?*). In direct questions, the co-occurrence of Q and *yes/no* has no phonological effect, whereas in the corresponding indirect questions *whether* occurs (*I asked whether that person will make something*).

The interrogative words can be thought of as special instances of various constituents of the Nucleus of the sentence. Thus *what* in *What will that person make?* is a special instance of a noun phrase (to wit, the noun phrase functioning as direct object of the verb *make*). To capture the similarity in syntax of the interrogative words on the one hand and the indeterminate and indefinite pronouns on the other, let us represent the interrogatives as *wh* + *indet*. In the presence of an initial Q, one interrogative word may be preposed (*That person will make what?* and *What will that person make?*).

The subject noun phrase of the sentence and the first auxiliary verb are inverted if Q and either an interrogative word or the element *yes/no* occurs before them (*Which person will make it?* but *What will that person make?*) Auxiliary *do* is absent as in negation, unless some element intervenes between *do* and the main verb.

Rules for Questions in Adult English

S→(Q(*yes/no*))Nucleus
Nucleus→NP − Aux − VP
NP→(wh) + indet (provided that Q, but not Q(*yes/no*) occurs before Nucleus)

The verb phrase has at one level in its derivation the following form:

$$\left[[\text{T} - do - (\text{Neg})\,]\text{Aux}_1[\,(\text{M})(\textit{have}\text{-pp})(\textit{be}\text{-prp})\,]\text{Aux}_2 \begin{Bmatrix} \text{V} \\ be \\ have \end{Bmatrix} \cdots \right] \text{VP}$$

Transformations

I.   Replacement of *do*

$$\text{T} - do - (\text{Neg}) - \begin{Bmatrix} \text{M} \\ have \\ be \end{Bmatrix} \Rightarrow \text{T} - \begin{Bmatrix} \text{M} \\ have \\ be \end{Bmatrix} - (\text{Neg}) - \phi$$

II.   Interrogative Preposing (Optional)

$$\text{Q} - \text{X}^1 - [\text{X}^2 - wh + \text{indet}] \begin{Bmatrix} \text{NP} \\ \text{PP} \end{Bmatrix} - \text{X}^3 \Rightarrow \text{Q} - [\text{X}^2 - wh + \text{indet}] \begin{Bmatrix} \text{NP} \\ \text{PP} \end{Bmatrix} - \text{X}^1 - \text{X}^3$$

III. Interrogative Inversion

$$\text{Q} \left\{ [\text{X}^1 - wh + \text{indet}] \begin{Bmatrix} (\textit{yes/no}) \\ \begin{Bmatrix} \text{NP} \\ \text{PP} \end{Bmatrix} \end{Bmatrix} \right\} - \text{NP} - \text{Aux}_1 - \text{X}^2 \Rightarrow$$

$$\text{Q} \left\{ [\text{X}^1 - wh + \text{indet}] \begin{Bmatrix} (\textit{yes/no}) \\ \begin{Bmatrix} \text{NP} \\ \text{PP} \end{Bmatrix} \end{Bmatrix} \right\} - \text{Aux}_1 - \text{NP} - \text{X}^2$$

IV.   *Do* Deletion
$$\text{T} - do - \text{V} \Rightarrow \text{T} - \phi - \text{V}$$
wh + something ⇒ *what*
wh + someone ⇒ *who*

Questions in Children's Speech

Stage 1.   The questions to consider, from all three children, are:

Fraser water?
Mommy eggnog?
See hole?
I ride train?
Have some?
Sit chair?
No ear?
Ball go?

Who that?
Why?
What('s) that?
What doing?
What cowboy doing?

Where Ann pencil?
Where Mama boot?
Where kitty?
Where milk go?
Where horse go?

Again, one can consider the elements *Fraser water, Mommy eggnog, Ann pencil, my milk go,* in the above questions as the Nucleus. As with the negative, in stage 1 there is very limited structure to the Nucleus, which consists primarily of nouns and verbs without indication of tense and number. If one considers the Nucleus of questions, negatives and interrogatives, there are few distributional distinctions which one could make at this stage. The sentences include *Want bibby, Get it, Mom sandwich, Baby table,* and so on.

The questions without an interrogative word can be thought of *yes/no* – nucleus, where the *yes/no* marker is expressed as rising intonation. There are no other identifying characteristics of yes/no questions in adult English, since there are no auxiliaries, and there is no form of subject-verb inversion. From the context of mother-child interchange, it seems that these rising intonation sentences are frequently responded to by the adult as if they were *yes/no* questions. The formulation suggested is:

S: *yes/no* – Nucleus

The *wh* questions can be described as a list which includes only a few routines that vary little across the three children. The most common questions are some version of *What's that?* and *Where Nounphrase (go)?* and *What Nounphrase doing?* It is not at all clear that the *What* in *What cowboy doing?* has any relationship to a grammatical object of the verb *do* (that is, that it is a special case of Q Nucleus where the particular interrogative occurs as the object of *do*). What might be said, with reservation, is that, indeed, there is a relationship in the child's speech between sentences like *go NP* and *Where NP go?* but that the special interrogative form is bound to the particular word *go* and does not at all have the generality of the adult structure. Paraphrases of the above questions for the child might be: *I want to know the name of that thing; I want to know what you call that action;* and *I want to know the location of that object.* One might tentatively suggest a formulation as follows:

$$\rightarrow Q^{what} - NP - (doing)$$
$$\rightarrow Q^{where} - NP - (go)$$

Let us take as an example the interrogative word questions in which the object of a verb is the missing constituent and has been replaced by a preposed *what*. If one looks at the set of what-object questions, which the mother asks the child in the course of the samples of speech, one finds that at stage 1 the child generally does not respond or responds inappropriately, as in:

Mother: *Well, did you hit?*
Child: *Hit.*

Mother: *What did you do?*
Child: *Head.*

Mother: *What do you want me to do with his shoe?*
Child: *Cromer shoe.*

Mother: *What are you doing?*
Child: *No.*

At this stage, then, the children are not producing questions that even superficially resemble what-object questions, and they do not understand this construction when they hear it.

The child's interrogative system at stage 1 may be summarized as:

S→(Q (*yes/no*))Nucleus
 →Q^{what} NP (*doing*)
 →Q^{where} NP (*go*)

Stage 2.   Some of the questions to consider are:

See my doggie?
Dat black too?
Mom pinch finger?
You want eat?
I have it?

Where my mitten?
Where baby Sarah rattle?
Where me sleep?

What book name?
What me think?
What the dollie have?
What soldier marching?

Why?
Why you smiling?
Why you waking me up?
Why not?
Why not he eat?
Why not me sleeping?

Why not . . . me can't dance?
Why not me drink it?
You can't fix it?
This can't write a flower?

There is some development in the superficial structure of the sentences since stage 1. Notably, pronouns have developed, articles and modifiers are more often present, some inflections (present progressive and plurals) occur, and the verb phrase may include a prepositional phrase or preverb. There are no modal auxiliaries in affirmative sentences, and only two negative modal forms (*don't* and *can't*). There are few indeterminates or indefinites.

There seems to be a gradual development of rules and not necessarily the wholesale replacement of one set by another. The same form of constituent questioning is continued as in stage 1. Although the interrogative word *what* appears in sentences which have a missing object, there are frequent occurrences of that interrogative without those conditions. It is perhaps premature to associate this word with a particular deleted element; here, as in other structures in the child's sentences, there is an indication that certain elements have been too closely linked. Certainly there is already an association of what will be referred to as an interrogative constituent with zero form and the interrogative introducer *what*. In the next stage it is quite clear that the association is made. Let us begin with the nounphrase:

NP→(Det) N
N → interrog

where *interrog* may represent any N in a question which is not a *yes/no* question (i.e. in an s of the form Q – Nucleus). The ultimate form of interrog is ϕ:

S→(Q(*yes/no*)) Nucleus
 →*what* – Nucleus
 →*where* – Nucleus

where the nucleus has some interrogative (i.e. a ϕ) in an N – constituent. For example:

What [the dollie have [interrog]N]Nucleus
What [soldier marching] Nucleus

In the *wh*-question, all *wh*-interrogative words are in initial position; the auxiliaries are missing in all questions. The set of *why* and *why not* questions relates this stage to stage 1:

→*why* (*not* (V^{neg})) Nucleus

where the negative *not* is related to the negation in stage 1 and some of the children's sentences still are produced in this way, and the V^{neg} is related to the negation in stage 2. A transformational rule gives the appropriate order:

why not – V^{neg} – Nominal – MV $\Rightarrow$ *why not* – Nominal – V^{neg} – MV

Notice that at no other place in the grammar at this stage do we find multiple negation, and this form is no longer produced by the next stage but may be replaced by complex multiple negation.

By this stage there are appropriate answers to most questions. The responses reflect that the child understands that the object of a verb or preposition is being questioned:

Mother: *What d'you need?*
Child: *Need some chocolate.*

_____

Mother: *Who are you peeking at?*
Child: *Peeking at Ursula.*

_____

Mother: *Who were you playing with?*
Child: *Robin.*

_____

Mother: *What d'you hear?*
Child: *Hear a duck.*

The system which we have hesitantly suggested for stage 2 is:

NP →(Det) N
N →interrog (where interrog may represent any N in a question which is not a *yes/no* question. The ultimate form of interrog is ϕ.)
S→(Q(*yes/no*))Nucleus
  →*what* – Nucleus
  →*where* – Nucleus
  →*why* (*not* (V^{neg})) – Nucleus

Transformation

why not – V^{neg} – Nominal – MV $\Rightarrow$ *why not* – Nominal – V^{neg} – MV

Stage 3.   The questions to consider are:

Does the kitty stand up?
Does lions walk?
Is Mommy talking to Robin's grandmother?
Did I saw that in my book?
Oh, did I caught it?
Are you going to make it with me?
Will you help me?
Can I have a piece of paper?

Where small trailer he should pull?
Where the other Joe will drive?

Where I should put it when I make it up?
Where's his other eye?
Where my spoon goed?
What I did yesterday?
What he can ride in?
What you had?
What did you doed?
Sue, what you have in you mouth?
Why the Christmas tree going?
Why he don't know how to pretend?
Why kitty can't stand up?
Why Paul caught it?
Which way they should go?
How he can be a doctor?
How they can't talk?
How that opened?
Can't it be a bigger truck?
Can't you work this thing?
Can't you get it?

Between the previous stage and this one there is an impressive and sweeping set of developments in the children's grammar. There is now a class of verbal forms that inverts with the subject in certain interrogatives (*yes/no* questions) and may take the negative particle with it. One particular verb, *do*, occurs only in its function as a helping-verb in inverted questions and negatives, seldom in *wh*-questions. At this point, the system that has been developed bears striking similarities to the adult pattern. Notice, however, that the auxiliary verbs are not inverted with the subject nounphrase in *wh*-questions. There are other aspects that set this child's system apart from the adult language, namely the child does not produce the full set of sequences of the adult auxiliary system. In the adult system, the possible sequences are (M) (*have*-pp) (*be*-prp); that is, any combination of these, but always in that order, where tense appears always on the first, or if none of these are present, then with the main verb. The children, at this stage, do not produce any combinations of auxiliaries.

Considerable development is found in the children's grammar by this stage. In addition to the noun and verb inflections appearing in the previous stage, one finds possessive markers, third person singular present indicative, and the regular past indicator. The sentences are no longer limited to simple English sentences. There is considerable development in complexity, and we find relative clauses and other embeddings present for the first time: *You have two things that turn around; I told you I know how to put the train together; I gon' get my chopper for chopping down cows and trees; They don't turn when I get on the floor; Let's go upstairs and take it from him because it's mine.*

Let us begin with the same basic structure as for negatives at stage 3:

$$S \rightarrow (Q) - \text{Nominal} - \text{Aux} - \begin{cases} \text{Predicate} \\ \text{MV} \end{cases}$$

$$\text{Aux} \rightarrow T - V^{aux} - (\text{Neg})$$

$$V^{aux} \rightarrow \begin{cases} can \\ do \\ will \\ be \end{cases}$$

NP→wh + indet

Transformations

I.   Interrogative Preposing

$$Q - X^1 - wh + \text{indet} - X^2 \Rightarrow Q - wh + \text{indet} - X^1 - X^2$$

II.   Interrogative Inversion (for *yes/no* questions only)

$$Q - NP - V^{aux} - X \Rightarrow Q - V^{aux} - NP - X \text{ (provided NP is not } wh + \text{indet)}$$

III.   *Do* deletion

$$do - V \Rightarrow V$$

In *yes/no* questions, we have noted that the children invert the auxiliary component with the subject noun phrase appropriately. Affirmative sentences generally have an auxiliary. In *wh* questions, however, the auxiliary is generally not inverted. The auxiliary form of *be* is optional at this stage, and the auxiliary *do* is not present in the final shape of most of the *wh* questions.

Rules for Questions in Children's Speech

Stage 1.

S→(Q(yes/no)) – Nucleus
  →Q^{what} – NP – ($doing$)
  →Q^{where} – NP – (go)

Stage 2.

NP →(Det) N
N →interrog (where interrog may represent any N in an S of the form Q – Nucleus. The ultimate form of interrog is ϕ.)
S→(Q(yes/no)) Nucleus
  →$what$ – Nucleus
  →$where$ – Nucleus
  →why (not (V^{neg})) – Nucleus
why not – V^{neg} – Nominal – MV ⇒ why not – Nominal – V^{neg} – MV

Stage 3.

$$S \rightarrow (Q) - \text{Nominal} - \text{Aux} - \begin{Bmatrix} \text{Predicate} \\ \text{Main Verb} \end{Bmatrix}$$

$$\text{Aux} \rightarrow T - V^{aux} - (\text{Neg})$$

$$V^{aux} \rightarrow \begin{Bmatrix} can \\ do \\ will \\ be \end{Bmatrix}$$

$$\text{NP} \rightarrow wh + \text{indet}$$

Transformations

I.   Interrogative Preposing

$$Q - X^1 - wh + \text{indet} - X^2 \Rightarrow Q - wh + \text{indet} - X^1 - X^2$$

II.   Interrogative Inversion (for *yes/no* questions)

$$Q - \text{NP} - V^{aux} - X \Rightarrow Q - V^{aux} - \text{NP} - X \text{ (provided NP is not } wh + \text{indet)}$$

III.   *Do* deletion

$$do - V \Rightarrow V$$

Summary

The speech of the three children consists primarily of a small set of words strung together at the earliest stage we have investigated in two and three word sentences. Among the early systematic aspects of child speech in its step-by-step approximation to the adult system are the following: in the early period the negatives and an ever-growing class of interrogative introducers occur first in the sentence, as sentence modifiers in the basic framework. The association of the interrogative word with other constituents of the sentence is very limited at first, restricted at the beginning to a complement of one or two particular verbs (e.g., *go* in *Where NP go*). Only later does the association apply to whole categories, such that the proposing of *wh* + prefixed elements can be spoken of with any generality. The auxiliary verb emerges first (anticipated perhaps by the optional occurrence of the copula *be*) always associated with negatives (as *can't, don't*). Not until afterwards do the modal auxiliary verbs and *do* appear inverted with the subject, and then only in the *yes/no* questions (i.e. the question not introduced by an interrogative word). At the same time, the modal auxiliary verbs, but not *do*, finally emerge independent of interrogatives and negatives. Not until the next stage does the inversion of auxiliary verbs extend to questions introduced by an interrogative word. Negation is embedded in the auxiliary verbs by this third stage, but the complex relation of negative and indefinite is not established yet. We have attempted to capture the regularities which we found in the speech of the three children in the rules which we have suggested for negatives and interrogatives.

Note

1   This group has included also Colin Fraser, Dan Slobin, Jean Berko Gleason, and David McNeill.

27

The Reduction Transformation and Constraints on Sentence Length

Lois Bloom

The formal notation in the grammars proposed for the texts of Kathryn and Gia specified that categories from which subject and predicate constituents were derived were obligatory rather than optional in the underlying phrase structure. It was pointed out that specifying categories as optional – meaning that one or more could occur in final derived strings – would ascribe the ability to exercise all options in a string to the child's linguistic competence when, in fact, such sentences (subject-verb-object) did not occur. In order to account for the differences between the underlying structure of sentences – which accounted for their semantic interpretation – and the reduced surface structure of these sentences as they were actually produced, a reduction transformation was postulated that mapped the richer base form into the reduced surface form.

But there needs to be justification in the data for the existence of categories in the phrase structure in order to be able to specify their deletion in terminal strings. For example, there was no category in the grammar of Eric II with the grammatical function *subject of the sentence* – Eric did not produce nouns in sentence-subject relation to verbs – so the nonoccurrence of sentence-subjects in Eric's earliest sentences could not be attributed to reduction. Whether or not Eric understood the grammatical function of sentence-subjects in the speech he heard, there was no evidence that he could produce sentences with grammatical subjects. Similarly, at Time I, Gia did not produce noun forms in subject or object relation to verbs, so the nonoccurrence of verbs in Noun + Noun constructions could not be attributed to reduction.

The problem of justifying the representation of category components in the phrase structure grammars, so that their nonoccurrence in terminal strings could be accounted for by the syntactic process of deletion, is considered in the following discussion of the evidence in the data that provided support for the specification of reduction rules to account for the reduced form of children's sentences.

From *Language Development: Form and Function in Emerging Grammar*. Cambridge, Mass.: MIT Press, 1970, chapter 6, pp. 135–69. © 1970 by the MIT Press.

27.1   The Nature of Sentence Accretion

Looking at the grammars presented in Chapters 3, 4, and 5 and at the linguistic data for which they were constructed, it appears that, in a general sense, growth in sentence constructing proceeded with a linear concatenation of constituents from right to left. Object-nouns predominated in the children's lexicons and were combined in syntactic constructions with verb forms, modifying forms, subject-noun forms, or pivot forms. At the same time, as a general rule, such object-nouns did not also function as sentence-subjects. Subsequently, subjects or demonstrative pronouns occurred before elaborated predicates.

Going beyond the data presented here and looking at the subsequent texts collected for the three children, it was apparent that the noun phrase construction that appeared in predicate positions was far more complex at every stage than noun phrases that appeared in subject positions. For example, when the children were 3 years old, they could produce such sentences as:

(1)   I want the little green man who rides the truck, or
(2)   That's the little green man who rides the truck,

but such a sentence as:

(3)   The little green man who rides the truck goes on top,

did not occur.

Brown, Cazden, and Bellugi (1969) reported that in writing complete grammars for the children they studied there were differential rules for accounting for noun phrase constructions at the earliest stage studied by them – that the object noun phrase and the predicate nominal noun phrase were more complex than the subject noun phrase. However, contrary to the findings reported here and referred to in the "little green man" example, they observed that "one of the things that happened between I and III [roman numerals refer to the levels at which grammars were constructed for their three subjects] was that the four 'NP' [predicate nominal, direct object, subject of a predicate nominal, and subject of a verb] came to resemble one another closely enough so that a single 'NP' symbol . . . rewritten by a single set of rules, could be entered in all four positions."

There is additional support for the notion of the linear increase in sentence length from right to left in the findings reported by other investigators of children's language. In the "sentence-generating" and "nominal phrase-generating" rules presented by Ervin (1966), a number of optional word-classes have privileges of occurrence, in a specified order, before a required class and the required class occurs in sentence-final position. The rule that Brown and Bellugi (1964, p. 148) proposed for the early development of the noun phrase represented a series of ordered but optional elements preceding an obligatory form in sentence-final position:

$$\text{"NP} \rightarrow (\text{Dem}) + (\text{Art}) + (\text{M}) + \text{N,"}$$

where Dem is "demonstrative," Art is "article," M is "modifier," and N is "noun."

There is evidence of similarity in the direction of sentence accretion in the acquisition of one aspect of Japanese syntax – where the word order of object and verb is the reverse of English order. In a study of the early development of linguistic forms of requests that combined both longitudinal and cross-sectional data, Murata (1961) reported that "verb-forms denoting requests" were "differentiated from the interjectional words" in the second half of the second year. Toward the end of this period "syntactical integrations [of words in an utterance] increased rapidly. Their typical forms were word–chain utterances of requests which were constituted of 'Object + Verb' (Japanese word-order of sentences, which constitutes one of the most striking differences from that of Europeans)."[1] Thus, it appears that the Japanese children produced verbs and then object-verb strings as request forms – extending the original single-word utterance from right to left.

In explanation of the fact that their subjects tended to imitate the most recent words in a model sentence, Brown and Fraser (1963, p. 193) suggested that "perhaps the human mind operates on an unlearned 'recency' principle, and . . . sentences . . . are nicely adapted to this principle in that the least predictable, most informative words usually fall into the final position."

However, the generalization about the direction of sentence accretion is true in only a limited sense. The addition of elements to utterances in forming longer or more complex utterances was not cumulative and, as will be shown, not strictly linear. That is, the children's ability to construct sentences did not proceed sequentially as the following hypothetical paradigm might suggest:

(4)   bridge.
      big bridge.
      a big bridge.
      build a big bridge.
      will build a big bridge.
      Eric will build a big bridge.

The following examples of consecutive utterances, produced within the boundaries of single speech events, illustrated that increase in structure or complexity was not a matter of simply increasing length of utterance by adding structure to structure or adding elements within a structure:

(5)   G:II (Gia taking train cars from the bag of toys) $\begin{bmatrix} \text{more block.} \\ \text{more.} \\ \text{Gia block.} \end{bmatrix}$

(6)   K:II (Kathryn looking at a
      picture of a mother cooking) $\begin{bmatrix} \text{cereal. hmmmmm.} \\ \text{raisin there.} \\ \text{buy more grocery store.} \\ \text{raisins.} \\ \text{buy more grocery store.} \\ \text{grocery store.} \\ \text{raisin ə grocery store.} \end{bmatrix}$

As the children learned certain basic phrase structures that increased the complexity of sentences, there were constraints on the extent to which these structures could be realized in the actual production of a single sentence. This kind of limitation in the surface structure of sentences due to increased complexity or length was most obvious when the child produced such consecutive utterances as "more block. more. Gia block." But it was also apparent that there were missing elements in the single, nonsequential sentences produced by all three children, with occurrence of adjacent constituents that could be accounted for only by postulating unrealized intervening constituents.

27.2   "Telegraphic" Speech

Even the most casual observer is aware that children's sentences are incomplete and fragmented, that elements are omitted that can generally be predicted. These early, incomplete sentences were characterized as "telegraphic" by Brown and Fraser (1963). In their description of the child's imitation of sentences he has just heard, they reported that the child omits some words or morphemes from the longer model sentences. The result is an abbreviated utterance that can be compared to the kinds of sentences produced by an adult who is under pressure to be brief – for example, when sending a telegram or taking lecture notes.

This phenomenon of "imitation and reduction" was discussed by Brown and Bellugi (1964) in describing the processes involved in children's acquisition of syntax. They observed that in the interaction between mother and child the child listens to sentences spoken by his mother; his attempts to reproduce what she has said consist of "highly systematic reductions" of the models. Also, the sentences produced by the child spontaneously, without an immediately previous adult model, have the same "telegraphic" properties.

In describing which forms are retained and which forms are omitted in "telegraphic" sentences, Brown and Bellugi and Brown and Fraser noted that the sentences consisted generally of nouns, verbs, and, less often, adjectives – the substantive, lexical items or "contentives" of the language. Grammatical formatives or "functors" – for example, the articles "the," "an"; verb inflection, "-ing," "-ed," "-s"; possessive noun inflection, "-s" – were the forms generally omitted.

In comparing sentences produced in imitation with sentences produced in spontaneous speech, Ervin (1966) found that both kinds of sentences "were equally predictable" from the same rules for four of the five children studied; that is, that imitated and spontaneous sentences were similar in complexity and characterized by omission of predictable forms. The forms omitted tended to be the unstressed segments – for example, articles, prepositions, auxiliaries, and pronouns, the same kinds of words omitted in the "telegraphic" sentences described by Brown and his associates.

In these studies, the nature of the language that the child was learning was considered to be the dominant influence on the form of his sentences. In addition to the description of sentences in terms of form class membership of constituents, Ervin reported three further characteristics of imitated sentences. The words retained and repeated by the child occurred in the same order and consisted of the words that were most recent and most heavily stressed in the model sentences.

Brown and Fraser (1963) also observed the preservation of original word order and the influence of sentence position and relative stress on the determination of the forms retained in the children's imitation of sentences, and by extension, included in spontaneous sentences as well. They also pointed out that these words (the content words of the language) carry the greatest information value – as the "reference-making" forms in the language. Brown and Bellugi (1964) suggested that the words produced by the child in imitated and spontaneous utterances tend to be those words with which he is most familiar – having "practiced" them as single-word utterances before the development of syntax.

Thus, it appears that the characterization of children's imitated and spontaneous sentences as "telegraphic" depends on the distinction between (1) the substantive, lexical items that receive heaviest stress in production, have semantic correlates and so carry the most information, and are least predictable, and (2) grammatical formatives that are weakly stressed, carry little information value, are most predictable, and tend to occur in sentence-interior positions.

There is an interesting paradox in the literature that describes children's language, on the one hand, as *telegraphic* – consisting only of substantive words with omission of function words – and, on the other hand, in terms of *pivot grammars* – syntactic constructions that consist of a class of function words in juxtaposition with the more diverse and open class of substantive words. Both characterizations have been used by Brown and his associates and by Miller and Ervin. It appears that the distinction between content and function words that underlies the pivot–x-word designation of children's earliest grammars contradicts the general characterization of children's sentences as "telegraphic."

There has been no published discussion of the relationship between pivot grammars and "telegraphic" speech, and the two phenomena appear to coexist in the data reported by Brown and by Miller and Ervin. However, Braine (1963) reported that x-word + x-word constructions (a string of substantive, content words) appeared subsequent to pivot constructions in his data.

27.3   Evidence for the Operation of Reduction

The phrase structure grammars presented earlier accounted for the underlying structure of the obtained sentences; this structure was rarely realized completely in the surface structure of the sentences that occurred. In order to obtain the reduced surface form from the base form, a transformation was postulated that deleted those elements in the base that did not occur in production:

K:I $T_{\text{Reduction}}$
(obligatory)
  (a)   S.D.: $X - Ng - Y$,
        where X and Y are category symbols (which dominate lexical items)
        S.C.: $x_1 - x_2 - x_3 \Rightarrow x_2 - x_3$
  (b)   S.D.: $\# - X - Y - Z$,
        where X, Y, Z are category symbols
        S.C.: $\# - x_1 - x_2 - x_3 \Rightarrow \# - x_i - x_j$,
        where $0 \leqslant i < j \leqslant 3$

It is important to emphasize that the reduction transformation did not account for the "telegraphic" nature of children's sentences as this notion has been described in the literature just reviewed. Rather than operating to delete the grammatical formatives or function words that did not occur in such sentences – *for which there were not representations in the base* as yet – the reduction rules operated to account for the nonoccurrence of the *substantive* forms for which evidence existed to specify their representation in underlying strings. It was not possible to speak of deletion of function words as a syntactic process in accounting for their nonoccurrence in "telegraphic" sentences, because, in the early stages when the reduction transformation operated obligatorily, there was limited evidence for the existence of grammatical formatives in the children's grammars.

The kind of reduction accounted for by the reduction rules occurred in the "buying more raisins at the grocery store" example. Kathryn was apparently constrained to delete the verb "buy" with expression of the object noun in the last sentence in the sequence, "raisin ə grocery store" – for which the presence of the verb was obligatory in the underlying representation to account for the semantic interpretation (the grammatical relationship between "raisin" and "grocery store") of the sentence. The occurrence of such sequential utterances with simultaneous expansion and deletion provided strong evidence for the operation of reduction and the child's inability to handle increased complexity or extended length.

It was more difficult to justify the operation of reduction in the occurrence of an isolated sentence. Evidence for inclusion of elements in the underlying representations of sentences was obtained from two courses: (1) the semantic interpretation of the utterance as described in Chapter 1, and (2) the observed distribution of structures in the entire text. To illustrate the operation of reduction in the distribution of structures, all utterances that included the form "make" have been extracted from the corpus of utterances obtained from Kathryn at Time II and presented in Table 27.1.

Choosing the verb "make" to illustrate the operation of reduction actually distorts the example in favor of nonreduction or the relative completeness of sentences, because the verb was not only very frequent in occurrence but was well learned in contexts with direct object nouns. That is, the verb "make" did not occur as a single-word utterance at Time I or Time II and appeared to have been learned as a form with the syntactic feature [+__Noun], although this claim must be qualified somewhat by noting that no data were collected previous to Time I, when "make" may have occurred as a single-word utterance. Also, "make" was one of the most frequent verbs to occur at Time I, so its existence in Kathryn's lexicon was well established at Time II. The utterances with "make" should have been less vulnerable to deletion, and Kathryn should have had less difficulty using this word in syntactic constructions than other verbs that occurred infrequently – for example, "buy," "bring," "eat."

The mean length of utterance of the total number of 48 utterances was 3.77 morphemes. In comparison, the mean length of utterance of the entire text at Time II was 1.92 morphemes. It is evident that these sentences were among the longest sentences produced by Kathryn at Time II – another factor that distorts the example in favor of nonreduction.

The utterances in which "make" did not appear:

Table 27.1 Sentences with "make" produced by Kathryn at Time II

Description of Speech Event	Kathryn's Utterance
(7) (K taking out train cars) (8)	> making building house. > make ɔ choochoo train.
(9) (K picking up blocks) Shall we build a house? What shall we do?	> make ə house.↑
(10) (K pushed tower of blocks after she had stacked them) (stacked blocks again)	> make ə house again.
(11) (L going to train cars on floor) I'm going to make a train (K joining her) (12) (13)	> make ə tree. > make ə flower. > make ə tree.
(14) (L pushing train under bridge; K going to train and bridge; subsequently pushed it under)	> Kathryn under bridge.
(15) (Bridge collapsed; K asking for another one)	> Lois ə make ə bridge.
(16) (K trying to seat second wire man, after seating first one) (17) (K trying to seat man again)	> made ə sit down again. man sit down. > made this sit down.
(18) (K spilled her blocks on the floor) What shall we do with the blocks? (19)	> Kathryn ə making house. > making train.
(20) (K took the train apart) Let's make the train again. Let's make the train go under the bridge. (L hadn't made bridge)	train under bridge. > make ə bridge.↑
(21) (L pushed the train under the bridge; L picked up the truck) Let's make the truck___ (K interrupting) No make a truck? (K pushing train under)	> no make ə truck. ə bridge. under bridge.
(22) Who's going to go under the bridge? I know who's going under the bridge. (K holding a lamb) What is this? Let's make him go under the bridge. (K taking lamb to bridge)	this under bridge. lamb. > Kathryn ə make ə under bridge.
(23) (K pushed first lamb under bridge; picking up another lamb)	go lamb. > make ə more under bridge.

Table 27.1 *(cont'd)*

Description of Speech Event	Kathryn's Utterance
(24) (Bridge collapsed as K was about to push lamb through) (25)	⎡ > make ə more under more. ⎣ > make another bridge. ⎤
(26) (Bridge collapsed) What happened to it? (K didn't make bridge)	> Kathryn ə make another bridge.
(27) (K picked up bear with a loose ribbon on its neck) (28) (K fumbling with the ribbon) (29) (K "tied" the ribbon; whispered) (K left bear) Did you fix the bear's tie?	⎡ > Kathryn make ə ties. ⎤ > Kathryn bear tie. Kathryn /fɪk/ ə tie. ⎣ Kathryn /fɪk/ ə ties. ⎦ there > make ə bear tie.
(30) (K replacing small block that had fallen out of hole in big block, after she had put it in before)	> Kathryn ə make again.
(31) (L making a bridge with book)	> Lois make ə bridge.
(32) (K snapping plastic beads together)	> Kathryn make this.
(33) (K taking out box of wooden snap blocks)	⎡ > make ə cars. ⎤
(34) (K trying to snap blocks together) (35) (36)	⎡ > make ə foot. ⎤ > this ə make ə foot. ⎣ > make arms. ⎦
(37) (M preparing dinner; opening a box of frozen food) (38) (In response to (37)) Make the vegetables? Make pineapple?	> make ə vegetable. ⎡ no. ⎤ ⎣ > make pineapple. ⎦ yes.
(39) Go get the man with the truck. (K going after man and truck)	> go make ə man truck.
(40) (K picking up a bag of blocks)	> ə want make ə blocks.
(41) (In response to (40)) We can build a bridge with the blocks. (42) (43)	⎡ > make ə block. ⎤ > make ə house. blocks. ⎣ > make ə house. ⎦
(44) (K stacking blocks)	> make another bridge.
(45) (K pushing car under bridge)	> make ə car under bridge.
(46) (K knocked bridge over)	> make another one.
(47) (In response to (46)) Make another one? Will you help me? Will you help me? (L making a bridge)	> making one.

Table 27.1   *(cont'd)*

Description of Speech Event	Kathryn's Utterance
(48) (K picked up a wheel while L was making a bridge with the blocks) That's the green one.	> make another. go slides.
(49) (K starting out of room) Where are you going?	car. /æn/ go gets it.
(K picking up her car)	> make it sit.
(50) (L stacking blocks; K sits on floor to stack blocks also)	> make another one.
(51) (K stacking blocks)	⌈> Kathryn make ə house. that's mine.
(52)	⌊> Kathryn make ə seat. ⌋
(53) (K going into the bathroom; "plop" was K's word for "defecate";	⌈> ə make plop.
(54) subsequently urinated)	⌊> no plop. ⌋

(14)   Kathryn under bridge.
(28)   Kathryn bear tie.
(54)   no plop.

were included in Table 27.1 because of their occurrence in the same behavioral contexts as existed with the occurrence of utterances

(22)   Kathryn ə make ə under bridge.
(27)   Kathryn make ə ties.
(53)   ə make plop.

   Looking at the entire group of sentences, it could be seen that when the subject of the sentence was expressed, either the verb, the object, the adverbial phrase, or more than one of these was not expressed. If all the possible constituent positions were filled, the ultimate result might be the production of such a sentence as

(55)   Kathryn ə want ə make ə more choochoo train under bridge $\begin{Bmatrix} \text{again} \\ \text{more} \end{Bmatrix}$

with at least nine morphemes. No sentence like this in extent of completion was produced in the Kathryn II text. Characteristically, elaboration of what preceded or followed the verbal position was accompanied by a deletion of some or all other constituents. There was deletion of categories as well as deletion within major categories when other categories occurred or were expanded.

It was possible for Kathryn to increase the complexity of sentences without necessarily increasing sentence length, and sentence accretion occurred with hierarchical and not strictly linear effect. That is, the structure of sentences could be represented on more than one hierarchical level with constituents derived from more than one phrase-marker node, as in the following tree-diagram:

```
              S
            /   \
          N      PredP
                /    \
             VB       Comp
                     /    \
                   N       PrepP
```

for the possible derivation of such sentences as

(14)   Kathryn under bridge.
(22)   Kathryn ə make ə under bridge.
(23)   make ə more under bridge.
(45)   make ə car under bridge.

Although the nodes of the tree-diagram were not "filled" in the utterances that Kathryn produced, the existence of the nodes in underlying representations of the sentences would be needed to account for their semantic interpretation, for example, of "Kathryn under bridge" – that is, to account for the relationship between "Kathryn" and "bridge." Kathryn was not under the bridge. Specifying the grammatical relationship between the constituents in "Kathryn under bridge" would imply the existence of nodes VB (directly dominated by the node PredP, predicate phrase) and N (dominated by the node Comp, complement, which in turn is dominated by PredP).

Thus, the notion of *reduction* is presented here as a grammatical process that attempts to explain the surface structure of children's sentences – rather than a notion that describes how children's sentences differ from the adult model.

In his examination of the data collected by Brown and his associates, McNeill (1966) observed that there were limitations on the inclusion of structure within the boundary of a single sentence. However, he concluded that "the child's first grammatical productions are the NP's and PredP's of adult grammar. Most often he produces them independently, though occasionally they are brought together to result in the skeleton of a well-formed sentence." McNeill suggested an alternative set of rules for children's early constructions that would replace, but also include, the "pivot + x-word" and "x-word + x-word" rules. The two rules with which McNeill "assume[d] that the child generated all his sentences" at Time I in the Brown data are reproduced here in the form of their phrase-markers, as presented by McNeill (p. 44), where P is "Pivot":

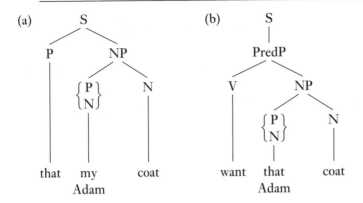

McNeill concluded that "all the child lacks [at this time] is the simultaneous applica-tion of both rules in the generation of a single sentence." According to McNeill, these rules represent the NP and PredP of adult grammar, and McNeill concluded that the frequency of their combination in a single sentence increases as the child matures, prob-ably as a result of "the child's growing memory span." This account implies that the increase in sentence complexity was simply an additive process; two syntactic structures that occurred first as two different "sentence types" were ultimately combined within the same sentence.

Before continuing the discussion of the operation of reduction, a word should be said about the NP generated by McNeill's Rule (a) (actually Rule (7) in the McNeill text). In the grammars proposed for Kathryn and Gia, the NP construction occurred as a predicate nominal or direct object. The forms that occurred in subject position in constructions with predicate phrases were less complex, and, rather than being a noun phrase, these forms consisted of single nouns – most often the names of people or animals – or pronouns. Brown, Cazden, and Bellugi (1969) reported, similarly, that "subject NP at [Time] I never consisted of more than one morpheme – a simple pronoun or noun," and subjects of verbs "were almost always names of persons or animals."

It would appear that there was not an equivalence of subject and predicate NP's (as concluded also by Brown, Cazden, and Bellugi) at this stage, and the NP of McNeill Rule (a) may be the same NP as in McNeill Rule (b), and not the subject NP, as he suggested. Rules (a) and (b) may indeed represent two different sentence types, that is, predicate nominative and verb plus complement.

It is felt that McNeill's account of the acquisition of syntax, as a process of increas-ing structural complexity by adding structure to structure, cannot explain the variable relationships between constituents in the distribution of such sentences as those with "make" in the text of Kathryn II. The analysis of the grammatical functions of the constituents in these sentences was not simply disjunctive – they did not just represent either the subject noun phrase or the predicate phrase of adult sentences.

An account of the development of grammar as an additive process becomes less tenable with consideration of the effect of the syntactic operation of negation on the internal structure of sentences.

27.3.1   Reduction and Negation

The example of reduction with negation will be discussed at length for two reasons: (1) the semantic correlates of negation were relatively clear in the texts, so that the non-realization of constituents in the surface structure of sentences could be demonstrated; and (2) negation was a syntactic operation that entered the grammars at a time when the development of the system was under way, so that its effects on the system could be examined.

All the syntactic constructions with a negative particle ("no") from the Kathryn I text are presented in table 27.2.[2] Looking at these negative utterances and the contexts in

Table 27.2   All negative sentences produced by Kathryn at Time I

Description of Speech Event	Kathryn's Utterance
(56) (K unable to find a pocket in M's skirt)	> no pocket.
(57)	> no pocket in there.
(58) (K waiting for M to make "pretend" socks for her feet)	no sock.
(59) (K unable to nest blocks or fit lambs into blocks; 7 instances of utterance in similar situations)	> no fit.
(60) (K standing in unzipped boots)	> no zip.
(61) (K unable to turn plastic screw in washer)	> no turn.
(62) (K unable to close box)	> no close.
(63) (K picked up clean sock) Oh that's not a dirty one. That just has a big hole in it. It has a big hole in it.	[this sock dirty.] hole. > no dirty.
(64) (K pushing away a piece of worn soap in the bathtub, wanting to be washed with new pink soap)	> no dirty soap.
(66) (K pulling away from L, who had offered to comb her hair)	> no Mommy.
(67) (K protested taking a bath, wanted to go outside)	> no outside.
(68) (K put lamb into block upside down; head was not in round window like the other lambs) He can't see out of the window. Can he see out of the window?	> no window.
(69) (K pushed lambs off the chair) Now why did you do that? They wanta sit on the chair. (K trying to climb on the chair) (M putting lambs on chair) (K pushing lambs off chair) They wanta sit on the chair. (K pushing lambs off)	ə wanta sit down chair. no! no. no. > ə no chair.
(70) (Indeterminate utterance; M washing K's face after lunch) Clean your nose.	milk > no milk.

which each occurred, there appear to be two broad classes of sentences (excluding (70) "no milk," which could not be interpreted). These can be distinguished according to the relation of the surface constituents of the utterance to the negative predication: (1) sentences in which the negative particle preceded an element that was clearly being negated:

(56)   no pocket.
(57)   no pocket in there.
(58)   no sock.
(59)   no fit.
(60)   no zip.
(61)   no turn.
(62)   no close.
(63)   no dirty.
(64)   no dirty soap.
(65)   no sock.

and (2) sentences in which the "no" occurred and the remainder of the sentence was clearly not being negated directly:

(66)   no Mommy.
(67)   no outside.
(68)   no window.
(69)   ə no chair.

With "no pocket," there was no pocket; with "no sock," there was no sock; with "no zip," the boots were not zipped; with "no dirty soap," Kathryn did not want the dirty soap. However, with "no outside," Kathryn wanted to go outside; with "no window," there was a window; and with "ə no chair," Kathryn wanted to sit on the chair.

There were two alternative explanations for the occurrence of "no" in utterances where the segment after "no" was clearly not negated. In (66) "no Mommy" and (67) "no outside," the "no" was anaphoric and applied to a prior utterance (Lois, not Mommy, offering to comb Kathryn's hair, and Mommy telling Kathryn it was bath time, respectively). Anaphoric "no" in these sentences occurred in juxtaposition with an affirmative utterance that expressed a positive alternative to something said by someone else. Although there were only two such examples at Kathryn I, this type of utterance increased in frequency in subsequent samples. For example, the following are two of the eight occurrences of the sentence type *no plus affirmative sentence* at Kathryn II:

(71)   K:II (Kathryn, looking for a book about
       dragons, picked up a book about bears)

$$\left[\begin{array}{l} \text{this.} \\ > \text{no that's ə bear book.} \end{array}\right]$$

       (and dropped it)
(72)   K:II (Kathryn, unable to connect the
       train, giving the cars to Lois)   no Lois do it.

Prosodic features of juncture or stress did not assist in interpreting these sentences. There was not a pause after "no," and "no" did not receive differential stress. Acoustically, these sentences did not differ from negative sentences – for example:

(73)   K:II (Kathryn looking at Lois' bare head)   Lois no hat.

where "no" occurred after the sentence subject and before a negated constituent. Superficially, such sentences as "no that's ə bear book" and "no Lois do it" were ambiguous, and, as discussed presently, only the nonlinguistic cues of context and behavior were available for interpreting the sentences in order to resolve the ambiguity.

The second explanation of "no" in juxtaposition with a segment not being negated applied to (68) "no window," (69) "ə no chair," and the example that follows, in which the surface structure is, at first glance, paradoxical:

(74)   E:II (Eric pointing to the tape recorder
       as Mommy entered the room, after being
       told he could not play with it)   no 'chine.

Looking at these utterances – (68) "no window," (69) "ə no chair," and (74) "no 'chine" – without knowing the accompanying behavior and context in which they occurred, the adult could be misled by his own grammar into interpreting them to mean that there was no window, no chair, and no machine. But the children had demonstrated the ability to use the negative operator to indicate nonexistence – for example, "no pocket" when there was no pocket and "no more noise" (at Eric II) when the noise had stopped. It appeared that the same superficial form was used to express a more complex negative-syntactic relation.

For each of these sentences – "no window," "ə no chair," and "no 'chine" – a semantic interpretation would depend on an underlying structure that specified a semantic relation between the negative element and a constituent intervening between "no" and the sentence complement. It appeared that in these sentences the negative element had immediate effect on an aspect of the sentence that did not get produced in its surface structure. A similar analysis could be made with (64) "no dirty soap" and (65) "no sock," where the semantic correlates of negation were different; for example, the dirty soap was being negated, but indirectly in that Kathryn was negating "using" or "wanting" the dirty soap.

Such utterances as (68) "no window," (69) "ə no chair," and (74) "no 'chine" appeared to represent the reduced form of an implicit, more complex underlying structure. This postulation of *reduction* in linguistic expression of negation was supported by the following observations. First, the children had learned something about the semantics and syntax of negation; that is, they used the negative particle as a syntactic operator, with semantic effect on immediate constituents, as Kathryn did in (56) "no pocket," (58) "no sock," and (60) "no zip." If the child knows that "no" plus a substantive element signals negation of that element, as in "no pocket," then it is reasonable to assume that the child's use of that same superficial syntactic structure with different intent, as in "no window," "means" something else. "No pocket" signaled direct negation of "pocket," but "no window" did not signal negation of "window" in quite the same way. Second, the semantic interpretation of these negative sentences, given the speech events of which they were a part, depended on the postulation of unrealized constituents in more complex syntactic structures than were actually produced. Otherwise, the utterances could not be interpreted as "negative" in the same sense that other utterances with "no" were interpretable at the same time. In each instance, there was negation of a predicative structure but there was expression of only the object complement. "Window," "chair," and "'chine" functioned grammatically as predicate objects in relation to unrealized constituents that were obligatory in the inherent structure of the sentences.

But it appeared necessary for the children to have produced a syntactic construction (conjoining two or more constituents with an inherent relationship between them) in order to postulate the operation of reduction. In the texts of the three children there was frequent occurrence of "no" as a single-word utterance and there were also instances in which the child produced a single word with apparent negative intent, although a negative element was not expressed – for example:

(75)   K:I (Kathryn taking off the lavaliere
            microphone, not wanting to wear it)   necklace.

An argument for the operation of reduction in these two instances – that is, the occurrence of "no" alone or single-word utterances such as "necklace" – would be necessarily weak. The response "no" is an acceptable elliptical response to yes-no questions or imperatives, and grammatical ellipsis is necessarily distinguished from *reduction*. In the other instance, "necklace," the nonlinguistic evidence of negative semantic intent was strong, but so was the possibility for ambiguity. Kathryn could have intended the fuller sentence "off necklace" (an utterance that actually occurred in a different but identical speech event at Kathryn I) as easily as the negative sentence "no necklace," and the context and behavior could support both interpretations.

There were instances of sentence reduction with deletion of the negative element – for example:

(76)   K:II (Lois had said "coffee store?"; Kathryn was
             reminded of having the "coffee 'chine" fixed
             and then said, shaking her head negatively)   ⎡ > me like coffee.   ⎤
             (no longer shaking her head)   ⎢ Daddy like coffee   ⎢
             (shaking her head)   ⎣ Lois ə no coffee.   ⎦
(77)   E:III (Eric unable to find a particular block
             and giving up)   ə find it.

However, the possible deletion of the negative element was less interesting – and somewhat more difficult to evaluate – than the reduction that occurred in the remainder of a sentence when the negative element was expressed. Sequential utterances in a single speech event – where the child subsequently expanded or changed an utterance and reduced it at the same time – provided clear-cut evidence of the effect of the syntactic operation of negation on sentence complexity, as in "Lois ə no coffee" in (76). In the utterances "no window," "ə no chair," "no 'chine," the semantic correlates of negation provided evidence of the nonrealization of constituents, that is, reduction in surface structures of negative sentences (as manifest in the relation of the negative element to the rest of the sentence). However, a more important question with respect to the effect of negation on syntactic complexity was how all the negative sentences compared in syntactic structure with the affirmative sentences that also occurred in the same texts. Was there any evidence that negative utterances were syntactically different?

The structural form of the first negative sentences was a negative particle before nominal or predicate forms. There were certain missing elements in these negative utterances that were irrelevant; for example, the fact that there were no verb and noun inflections was immaterial because verb and noun inflections were not realized in the early grammars at all. However, there were other structural omissions in the negative utterances that were significant in that they did characterize the negative sentences in a way that set them apart from the other, affirmative sentences that occurred.

First, there was no expression of sentence-subject in any of the sentences, except "no Mommy" (in which, it turned out, "Mommy" was not the subject of a negative predication). However, at the same time, the nominal subject was expressed in more than 60 of the total of 397 utterances analyzed in the text of Kathryn I, excluding the occurrence of preverbal /ə/. Second, there were no occurrences of both a predicate complement and a verb in a single sentence with "no," although Kathryn expressed such "complete" verb phrases in more than 40 of the 397 utterances and verb-object phrases were among the most productive constructions in the texts of all three children. These omissions of subject, verb, or object complement were not attributable to lack of vocabulary; Kathryn "had" the words in her lexicon – for example, "want," "see," "boot," "box," "lamb," "Mommy," "Kathryn."

Looking at the rest of the surface structure of these sentences, it was apparent that without the "no" they were comparable to the most primitive utterances that Kathryn produced. However, the more complex underlying structures for these sentences, which would account for their semantic interpretation – for example, "no window": roughly, "X no Y window" (where X and Y represent inferred underlying category symbols with the grammatical functions of sentence-subject and predicate) – could be accounted for by the same grammar that would generate the affirmative sentences that also occurred.

A number of affirmative sentences in the data could be considered semantically reciprocal to, or the affirmative correlates of certain of the negative sentences that also occurred, for example, at Kathryn I: "no turn" and "this turn"; "no dirty" and "this dirty." But it was significant that the negation of "this turn" and "this dirty" did not result in *"this no turn" or *"this no dirty," nor *"no this turn" or *"no this dirty."

At Kathryn II there were two examples of an immediate denial of an affirmative statement in which the affirmative sentence was reduced with the operation of negation:

(78)   K:II (Kathryn sticking out her tongue)
       Whose tongue do I see?
       Who?

$$\begin{bmatrix} \text{that ə Wendy.} \\ \text{no Wendy.} \\ \text{Kathryn. no Wendy.} \end{bmatrix}$$

(79)   K:II (Kathryn going into the bathroom)

$$\begin{bmatrix} \text{ə make plop.} \\ \text{no plop.} \end{bmatrix}$$

       ("plop" was Kathryn's word for "defecate";
       Kathryn subsequently urinated)

The following example from the text at Gia V illustrated the comparative simplicity of a negative utterance in an extended sequence with more complex utterances, several of which appeared to be plausible positive correlates of the negative. At this time Gia produced sentence subjects (usually pronoun forms) frequently, but none appeared in the negative sentences that also occurred at Gia V.

(80)   G:V
       Do you wanta read "Mop Top"?
       (Gia's newest book)   yes
       (Lois picking up the book;
       Gia reaching for it)   > no Mop Top.
       Hm?
       (Gia reaching for it) $\begin{bmatrix} \text{Móp Tòp.} \\ \text{/mædàp/} \end{bmatrix}$
       What?
       (Lois going to the sofa with it;
       Gia following, holding out her
       arms for the book) $\begin{bmatrix} \text{read ə m\_\_/æ · æ}^w\text{/.} \\ \text{I wanta read new /mádə/.} \\ \text{I wanta read ə my book.} \end{bmatrix}$
       (whining)

                                    · · · · ·
       (Lois gave Gia the book; after
       "reading" it, Gia giving it to Lois)   you read wə__Móp Tòp.

One possible explanation for the differences between the surface structures of affirmative and negative sentences might be that they are learned separately; that is, as different sentence patterns, they are accounted for by "different grammars" or different sets of rules. Such an explanation could not be argued very productively; learning separate "grammars" for different sentence types would be inefficient and would increase the child's cognitive tasks. One of the most attractive aspects of the theory of transformational grammar in application to children's language is the specification of the "relatedness" of sentences so that one set of rules is learned that underlies all the sentences of the language. It is more likely that children learn the semantic component of negation as an option in generating sentences so that two kinds of semantic realities – affirmative and negative – can be distinguished. However, exercising the option to include the element of negation in a sentence operates to increase the syntactic complexity of the sentence. It appeared that in negating a sentence it was necessary to reduce it at the same time – that the syntactic operation occasioned the reduction.

There was further support for the notion that the operation of negation *within* a sentence increased its complexity, and thereby necessitated reduction in the surface structure, in the fact that structure of the affirmative sentences with anaphoric "no" (the sentence type "*no*" *plus affirmative sentence*) was more structurally "complete" in all the texts, when compared with the negative sentences that occurred at the same time. Thus, the inclusion of "no" (without juncture) did not affect sentence length when "no" was anaphoric and without effect on the internal syntax of the sentence.

The account of the operation of negation just presented differs from Bellugi's description of the first of five stages in the development of the syntax of negation (Bellugi,

1967; Klima and Bellugi, 1966). In the first stage described by Bellugi, Period A, the mean lengths of utterance of the three subjects she studied were 1.96, 1.80, and 1.74. Comparing these figures with the information in Table 2.1, it can be seen that text collection began with Kathryn, Eric, and Gia somewhat earlier in terms of mean length of utterance, which was less than 1.5 for all three children.[3]

Period A was described by Bellugi as "negation outside the sentence nucleus," where a negative element is attached to a "rudimentary sentence." The grammar of the "rudimentary sentence" or its relation to the children's nonnegative sentences were not specified. Negative sentences were described as having "little internal structure, consisting only of noun phrases or unmarked nouns and verbs."

The negative sentences that Bellugi reported – for example, "no heavy," "no the sun shining," "no sit there," "no more string," "no Mommy read," "no no put glove" – are similar in surface structure to the sentences of Kathryn, Eric, and Gia over the course of several observations. The more complex sentences, such as "no the sun shining" or "no no put glove," are comparable to the surface form of utterances in the texts of Kathryn II, Eric V, and Gia V.

In the phrase structure for the text of Kathryn I, the negative element was an optional semantic choice within the internal structure of the sentence:

$$\text{K:I} \quad S \rightarrow \text{Nom (Ng)} \begin{Bmatrix} \text{NP} \\ \text{VP} \end{Bmatrix}$$

In contrast, Bellugi described the operation of negation in terms of an element "outside" the sentence "nucleus":

$$``\left[\begin{Bmatrix} no \\ not \end{Bmatrix} -\text{Nucleus} \right] S \quad \text{or} \quad [\text{Nucleus}-no] \; S"$$

A grammar is constructed to answer the question of what it is the child knows about the language – the system that underlies the observed behavior. In this sense, Bellugi has characterized this first syntactic operation of negation as a "primitive abstraction which later drops out, having been replaced by a much more complex system of negation" and "not the primitive version of some later structure which adds constituents to form longer sentences." The principal evidence Bellugi provided for placing the negative element "outside" the sentence nucleus was the observation that the "children seldom place the negative morpheme in an internal position in the sentence structure" (for example, "no Mommy read," "no the sun shining"), and here Bellugi was describing *surface* structure only. No evidence of the function of negation or of the relation of the negative element to the rest of the sentence, in terms of content, was presented: ". . . we have stripped the speech of paralinguistic features . . . of information arising from discourse relations by omitting interchanges, and of information from the setting or situation." However, when this kind of information was taken into account in analyzing the texts of Kathryn, Eric, and Gia, semantic interpretation of negative sentences was possible in most cases. Isolating the semantics of these sentences made it possible to analyze the internal structure of the syntax – revealing that inclusion of the negative element operated to replace or delete other forms.

Table 27.3   Utterances with negative element and sentence-subject, without identifying information

(81)	K:ll	Lois no hat.
(82)	K:ll	Kathryn no shoe.
(83)	K:ll	Mommy no picture there.
(84)	K:ll	man no go in there.
(85)	K:ll	Kathryn no /fɪk/ this.
(86)	K:ll	Kathryn no fix this.
(87)	K:ll	Kathryn no like celery.
(88)	K:ll	Lois ə no coffee.
(89)	K:ll	this ə no goes.
(90)	E:V	you no bring ə choochoo train.↑
(91)	E:V	I no reach it.
(92)	E:V	I no like to.
(93)	K:ll	no Lois do it.
(94)	K:ll	no Kathryn want play with self.
(95)	K:ll	no Kathryn playing self.
(96)	K:ll	no my have ə this.
(97)	K:ll	no I my have ə this.
(98)	K:ll	no that's ə bear book.
(99)	E:V	no car going there.
(100)	E:V	no this Daddy.
(101)	E:V	no this ə Mommy.
(102)	E:V	no this Mommy Daddy.
(103)	G:V	no man ride *this* tank car.
(104)	G:V	no now I do ə /dɪt/.
(105)	G:V	no doll sleep.
(106)	K:ll	no Daddy hungry.

   In the earliest sentences, the negative element did occupy the initial position in the surface structure of sentences (except for the few occurrences after /ə/), as also observed by Bellugi. However, this occurred as a consequence of the deletion of other constituents, that is, sentence-subjects, in the earliest negative sentences. In the subsequent texts (Kathryn II, Gia V, and Eric V) there were sentences that contained both sentence-subject and the negative particle, and these later texts could still be described as having occurred in Bellugi's Period A; that is, there were no noun and verb inflections and the form of the negative element was invariant.

   Table 27.3 presents all the sentences that contained both sentence-subject and a negative element in the texts of Kathryn II, Gia V, and Eric V (such sentences did not occur in the earlier texts). These sentences happened to include the most complex negative sentences the children produced – precisely because of the inclusion of sentence-subjects.

   Differentiation of the negative element had not begun at Kathryn II; the only form was "no." Gia, at Time V, produced a few sentences with the form "can't," and Eric, at Time V, had begun to use the forms "didn't" and "doesn't" – but the primitive forms "no" and "no more" were far more frequent in both children's texts. Thus, Kathryn's and Gia's sentences in Table 27.3 could be described as having occurred in Period A – before the use of different forms of the negative element, which characterized the

Table 27.4 Identification of utterances in Table 27.3

(N) Negative Sentences

(81)	K:ll	Lois no hat. (L not wearing a hat)
(82)	K:ll	Kathryn no shoe. (K pointing to her bare feet)
(83)	K:ll	Mommy no picture there. (M reading a novel)
(84)	K:ll	man no go in there. (K holding her toy clown; watching L pack up toys to leave)
(85)	K:ll	Kathryn no /fɪk/ this. (K unable to snap blocks)
(86)	K:ll	Kathryn no fix this. (K unable to snap blocks)
(87)	K:ll	Kathryn no like celery. (K watching M eat celery after not taking celery when M offered it to her)
(88)	K:ll	Lois ə no coffee. (in sequence (76): "me like coffee, Daddy like coffee, Lois ə no coffee.")
(89)	K:ll	this ə no goes. (K trying to fit puzzle piece into the wrong space)
(90)	E:V	you no bring ə choochoo train.↑ (E disappointed because L had not brought the train)
(91)	E:V	I no reach it. (E pointing to the window blind, which he wanted L to open for him)
(92)	E:V	I no like to. (M had asked E if he wanted to go on a roller coaster again)

(A) Affirmative Sentences

(93)	K:ll	no Lois do it. (K, unable to connect the train cars, giving them to L to connect)
(94)	K:ll	no Kathryn want play with self. (K didn't want to play with the slide; L asked, "Shall I do it myself?"; K climbing into her playpen to play with her toys)
(95)	K:ll	no Kathryn playing self. (In sequence with (94))
(96)	K:ll	no my have ə this. (In response to "Kathryn'll have two and I'll have two"; K refusing to give wheel to L)
(97)	K:ll	no I my have ə this. (In response to "Lois'll have this"; L reaching for K's snap block; K holding on to it)
(98)	K:ll	no that's ə bear book. (K, looking for her book about dragons, picked up a book about bears, then dropped it)
(99)	E:V	*no* car going there. (E insisting that he sees a car in a picture in the animal book)
(100)	E:V	no this Daddy. (E had called the boy figure "Daddy"; L asked "Is this Daddy?"; E pointing to the Daddy figure)
(101)	E:V	no this ə Mommy. (E had named all the figures; L pointed to the baby, asked "Is this Mommy?"; E pointing to Mommy figure)
(102)	E:V	no this Mommy Daddy. (E pointing to Mommy and Daddy on the form board, in response to "Is this Mommy?")
(103)	G:V	no man ride *this* tank car. (G pointing to a different car for the man to ride on)
(104)	G:V	no now I do ə /dɪt/. (G had completed a puzzle; L asked "Now can I do it?"; G refusing to let L do the puzzle; did it again herself)
(105)	G:V	no doll sleep. (G had pretended to sleep; getting up and taking her doll to put to sleep)
(106)	K:ll	no Daddy hungry. (This utterance is presented with the context of the speech event in which it occurred in the following discussion)

second stage, Period B, in Bellugi's account. Eric's sentences might be characterized as transitional – occurring somewhere between Periods A and B. Eric's sentences with "didn't" and "doesn't" were not included in Table 27.3.

When presented in this way (as in Table 27.3), in an unordered list without identifying information, the position of "no" in relation to the rest of the sentence appears to be variable. It occurred both before and after the sentence-subject.

However, when the contexts of the speech events of which the utterances were a part were studied, these sentences were seen to fall into two distinctive groups (see Table 27.4). In the first group, (N), the "no" occurred before a predicate that was clearly being negated – for example, "Lois no hat" (Lois was not wearing a hat), "Kathryn no shoe" (Kathryn was not wearing shoes), "Mommy no picture there" (Mommy was reading a novel), "Kathryn no fix this" (Kathryn could not fix the train). In the second group, (A), the "no" was clearly anaphoric and did not apply to the remainder of the sentence, which was an affirmative statement: "no Kathryn playing self" (Kathryn did not want to play with the slide and went into the playpen to play alone), "no Lois do it" Kathryn was giving the train to Lois to fix), "no man ride *this* tank car" (Gia was pointing to a different car for the man to ride), "no doll sleep" (Gia wanted to put the doll to sleep).

There was only one exception in the data to this clear distinction between the (N) negative sentences, where the negative particle followed the sentence-subject, and (A) affirmative sentences, where the negative particle preceded the sentence-subject – the utterance "no Daddy hungry," which occurred as follows:

(106)   K:II (Kathryn looking at a picture of a
family at a dinner table; in the picture
the mother and children are seated at the
table and the father is walking toward the
table carrying a platter of food)

> hungry. hmmmmm.
> girl hungry.
> Daddy hungry. . . .
> \> no Daddy hungry.
> Daddy up.
> Mommy hungry.
> boy hungry.

If the distinction between the two kinds of sentences with sentence-subject and a negative element in the texts of Kathryn, Gia, and Eric did not exist in the Bellugi data, it represents an important difference in the development of negation in the two groups of children. In a personal communication to William Labov at Columbia University (1967), Bellugi described the nonlinguistic context that accompanied the utterance "no I see truck" in a published "section from Adam's first record" (Brown and Bellugi, 1964, p. 135) that would support characterization of the sentence as negative; that is, Adam could not see the truck.

The account of the operation of negation proposed here – that introduction of additional structure in a sentence, such as including the element of negation in its base form, has a limiting effect on production, causing reduction of the sentence with deletion of constituents – contradicts the Bellugi account. If the negative element is outside the sentence in its underlying structure, then, it is presumed, it would not affect the internal structure of the sentence. Such was the case in sentences with preceding anaphoric "no," where the negative element was without effect on the remainder of the sentence.

Further, such a rule as that proposed by Bellugi appears to imply that there are no constraints on sentence complexity or sentence length with the operation of negation – if the choice of negation simply adds an element to an otherwise affirmative utterance. But in the texts of Kathryn, Eric, and Gia, the negative utterances were otherwise among the least syntactically complex when compared with affirmative utterances. There was strong evidence that the inclusion of the negative particle reduced surface form.

Finally, the specification of the negative particle outside the sentence is inconsistent with sentence negation in the adult model of English, where negation is an inherent semantic fact of English sentences. In the fully realized system of negation in the adult grammar of English, the "structural position of the negative element in the sentence" is related to the "scope of negation (i.e., the structures over which the negative element has its effect)" (Klima, 1964, p. 316). And, indeed, the constituents that were most often deleted in these early negative sentences were sentence-subjects, which were not within the immediate scope of negation.

Bellugi (1967) suggested that, in Period A, negation outside the sentence represented a syntactic structure that has no relation to the adult model of the language – "a primitive abstraction which later drops out." In contrast, the development of Kathryn, Eric, and Gia suggested that the earliest system of negation was more similar to the adult model than it was different – but it was a much simpler, fragmented, and far more generalized system.

The evidence for this conclusion included the following observations:

1. The relation of the negative element to the content of the rest of the surface structure of sentences was direct or else, in some utterances, appeared to be semantically paradoxical (for example, "no 'chine," "no window") unless an unrealized element was postulated between the adjacent constituents "no" and "'chine," "no" and "window," on which the negative element would have direct effect in the internal structure of the sentence.

2. The negative element never occurred before the subject of a negative sentence. In the earliest examples, there was no occurrence of sentence-subject in negative sentences, although sentence-subjects were fully productive in affirmative sentences in the texts of Kathryn and Gia. Indeed, even at Time V, when Gia produced the sentences in Table 27.4 with anaphoric "no" and an affirmative sentence that included sentence-subjects, she did not produce any negative sentences with sentence-subject at the same time. When, at a subsequent stage, subjects were expressed in negative sentences, the negative element always followed the subject – preceding the negated predicate.

3. The negative element occurred after /ə/, when a possible source for /ə/ might have been "I" or "it," or when in the absence of semantic correlates, /ə/ was designated in the phrase structure only as a pre-verbal element.

The latter two observations correspond to the attraction of the negative element to the essential verb of a sentence in the adult model. When "the whole combination of a subject and a predicate is negativized – the negative element [is] joined more or less closely to the finite verb" (Jespersen, 1961, p. 438). An objection to this interpretation could be raised when the finite verb did not occur. But it was just this non–occurrence of the verb – for example, "want" or "use" in "no dirty soap," "play" in "no 'chine" – that was an effect of the constraints that operated to reduce the surface structure of the children's early sentences. The sentences could not otherwise be interpretable as negative sentences, given the facts of behavior and context in the speech events in which they occurred.

4. The negative element never occurred before (outside of) a syntactic structure that could be construed as the affirmative correlate of a negative structure. For example, the most frequent early verbal construction in the texts of all three children consisted of /ə/ (or, occasionally, some other noncontrastive phonological element) before a verb form – for example, "ə fit" and "ə turn" – but the negative correlates of these sentences in the same texts were "no fit" and "no turn," not *"no ə fit." Similarly, in other examples already cited, "this dirty" occurred, but "this dirty" plus the negative operator resulted in "no dirty" in the same text, not *"no this dirty."

Negative sentences could not be construed as simply a positive sentence with a negative sign attached, outside the sentence. Rather, the negative element was intrinsic to the structure of the sentence and as such operated to increase its complexity, as in adult grammar. This account has attempted to show that the earliest system of negation in the children's grammar differed from the account of the adult system only in the fact of its essential immaturity.

27.4   Constraints on the Form of Children's Speech

It appeared that pivot and "telegraphic" sentences were often the reduced forms of more complex underlying structures. The results of an experimental study by Shipley, Smith, and Gleitman (1969) provide support for the contention that children's speech may not be isomorphic with what is known about linguistic structure. They reported that "children whose speech is telegraphic readily obey well-formed commands, and less readily obey telegraphic commands" (p. 336), indicating that the children know more about grammatical structure than their speech would indicate.

When the total distribution of sentences in a text was examined, it was observed that sentences were incomplete (in terms of basic subject–verb–object representation), but the pattern was variable. There were subject–verb, subject–object, and verb–object strings, but subject–verb–object strings did not occur. Leopold (1949, Vol. III, p. 28) observed the same restriction on the production of sentences in his daughter's development. At the time (20 to 23 months) that "sentence span was limited to two words," he observed that "where the standard [the adult model utterance] required at least three words because the predicate was not a simple verb, the child was forced to omit one of them." It might be argued that inclusion of "no" in such strings simply increased sentence length beyond the "permitted" two morphemes – that constraint on complexity *is* a constraint on length. But it appeared that reduction was the result of something more than a production limitation on sentence *length*. The evidence presented here suggests that some sort of cognitive limitation in handling structural complexity (such as accompanies sentence negation) *underlies* the constraint on length of children's utterances – that the constraint on sentence length reflects an inherent limitation in linguistic operations. It was clear that the earliest negative sentences did not simply add a negative marker or operator to an otherwise affirmative sentence. Rather, the linguistic operation of negation had a limiting effect on structural complexity and length of utterances.

Thus, the operation of the reduction transformation has been ascribed to a constraint on sentence complexity; with an increase in the underlying complexity of a sentence, something had to give in its production. If this was so, what determined which constituents were deleted and which were retained? The factors that operated to influence the production or deletion of particular forms in a sentence appeared to be related to the nature of the language the child was learning (linguistic constraints) and the basic fact of the immaturity of the cognitive system (cognitive constraints).

27.4.1   Linguistic constraints

Vocabulary.   The nonoccurrence of elements in production often resulted from the fact that the child operated with a primitive lexical system – primitive in the sense that the lexicon was insufficient in the number of words, but also in the sense that the inherent and syntactic features of particular items were rudimentary. "Learning" a word did not imply that the word, with the features that govern its combination with other words in the adult model, appeared full-blown in the child's lexicon. For example, at Kathryn I, "hurt" and "ə hurt" occurred in the text. The following also occurred, in different speech events:

(107)   K:I (Jocelyn, Kathryn's friend, had
        bruised her cheek on the playground
        and cried a few days previously;
        Kathryn reporting this to Mommy
        at lunch)   Jocelyn cheek.
        Jocelyn hurt her cheek.
(108)   K:I (Kathryn's doll "cried")
        What happened to the baby doll?
        Is she crying?   /a/ baby cheek.

Although Kathryn had used "hurt" and "ə hurt" in appropriate contexts (talking about chapped hands), it appeared that she might not have learned the complex symbol features of "hurt" as a verb that can appear in environments before and after nouns. "Hurt" was at least a possible lexical item that might have occurred in the utterances "Jocelyn cheek" and "/a/ baby cheek." But the effect of reduction was the deletion of the intervening (dummy) constituent in the base form of the sentences that accounted for the grammatical relationship between "Jocelyn" and "cheek" and between "/a/ baby" and "cheek" – not the deletion of the lexical item "hurt." The reduction rules did not operate on particular lexical items but, rather, on the categories in the underlying structure from which lexical items are derived. However, the motivation for reduction could have occurred in the fact that a lexical item that could be substituted for the terminal, category symbols (N or V) in a derived string did not exist in the lexicon or existed without the necessary contextual or syntactic features.

Syntax.   Two sources of deletion are not pertinent to this discussion and need to be distinguished. Grammatical ellipsis could have resulted in the production of acceptable sentence fragments that represented full sentences in particular environments – for example, the response "making a house" to the question, "What are you doing?" Eventually, in the later texts, there was also grammatical deletion of elements in sentence embedding – for example, deletion of the subject in the constituent sentence of "I see the man who rides the truck." These grammatical deletion transformations, which are necessary for a linguistic account of such utterances, were not related to immaturity.

If it is true – as it was for Eric and Gia and probably for Kathryn also, although the evidence for Kathryn was incomplete – that children learn predicate-objects (the names of the "things" that can be acted upon, counted, modified, owned) first, then the learning of these forms in complement constructions with verbs and as constituents of predicates that say something about sentence-subjects constitutes the substance of the child's earliest syntactic learning.

Brown, Cazden, and Bellugi (1969) reported that, on the basis of their data, "the child's knowledge of these [grammatical] relations which, in English, are chiefly expressed by order undergoes no development. He seems to express the relations he means to express from the very start." This conclusion was based on the fact that children make few errors in word order; subjects of sentences occur before objects. This order is one of the universals of language reported by Greenberg (1963); with rare exception, subjects precede objects in all languages.

Gia did make "mistakes" in word order. For example, at Time II, Gia produced "book read" and "read book" in virtually identical speech events. At Gia I, object nouns occurred before verbs – for example, "balloon throw" as Gia dropped the balloon as if throwing it – although subjects always preceded objects in Noun + Noun constructions. It appeared that "errors" in word order at Gia I and II were related to the tentative position of verbs as they emerged in the grammar.

The grammatical relations subject-verb-object did not exist in the sentences that Gia and Eric produced in the earliest texts. Gia learned the subject-object relation first; Eric learned the verb-object relation first. Both children subsequently learned the subject-verb relation – the structure that was least productive in the texts of all three children.

The nonoccurrence of sentence-subject in relation to verbs or object nouns in Eric I and Eric II and the nonoccurrence of verbs in relation to nouns in Gia I were not attributed to the operation of reduction rules. Category forms with these functions did not exist in the total distribution of the sentences that occurred. However, in the subsequent grammars – Eric III and Gia II, when Eric began to produce subject-verb strings and Gia began to produce subject-verb and verb-object strings – the previously nonproductive forms appeared to be the forms that were most likely to be reduced in three-term strings.

In the operation of negation, it was observed that sentence-subjects were deleted, and verbs were deleted in negated predicates when the predicate complement occurred. Generally, it appeared that, in the case of negation, the reduction rules deleted elements from left to right. It may have been that deleted elements were somehow those elements that were most vulnerable – sentence-subjects being less productive than, for example, predicate-objects.

The operation of reduction appeared to be systematic. In answer to the question of the factors that determined which constituents were deleted and which were retained with the operation of reduction, the following linguistic factors appeared to be influential: (1) the relative recency of the appearance of the category components that dominated the deleted or retained constituents in the phrase structure; (2) the child's cognizance of lexical items and the relative "completeness" of the semantic and syntactic feature representation of particular items in his lexicon; and (3) in the case of negation, the deletion of constituents that were most often not within the immediate scope of negation, such as sentence-subjects.

At the level represented by Kathryn I, all three children appeared to have learned something about the grammatical relations object-of-verb, predicate-of-sentence, and subject-of-predicate. However, there were lexical and syntactic constraints that interacted with cognitive constraints to limit the production of sentences, so that all three grammatical relations could not occur in the surface structure of a single sentence.

27.4.2   Cognitive constraints

It was more difficult to specify the nature of the cognitive constraints that influenced production. As pointed out by Brown and Fraser (1963, p. 193), some sort of limitation in memory span is almost certainly a factor in influencing length of imitated responses. The role of memory in influencing the length or complexity of spontaneous utterances is less easily defined. Brown and Fraser referred to "a similar limit of programming span for the situation in which the child is constructing sentences"; mean lengths of imitated and spontaneous utterances in their data were highly similar.

What does a child need to remember when constructing sentences? The names for "things" and "actions" are important, but he learns that he can get by without them and begins to use proforms such as "this," "this one," "do," "it," "here" quite early.

The children's ability to remember complex linguistic material was often impressive – as evidenced by the production of stereotype model sentences that had no analogue in the child's grammar; for example, "who has that book?, Kathryn has that book" at Kathryn I. An even more striking example was Eric's ability to "recite" accurately from memory long passages of text in his favorite story books, turning the pages at the appropriate juncture, when he was two and one-half years old. But he was unable to answer specific questions about the text, and certain phrase structures he recited – sentence adverbials, for example – did not appear in his spontaneous utterances. Perhaps there is a relative distinction, in this context, between more or less "immediate" memory. But something more than a memory factor appeared to be operating to account for the reduction of spontaneous sentences. Certainly the children presented no evidence of difficulty in remembering what they had intended to say. On the contrary, their utterances were produced as "wholes" – as if the children assumed reciprocal editing on the part of the listener.

The reduction transformation accounted for the inferred relationship between underlying structure and obtained utterances; evidence of its operation provided insight into the child's ability to handle surface structure. The rule operated on category symbols that were necessary in an underlying representation to account for the inherent relation between two constituents of an utterance, such as between "Mommy" and "pigtail," and between "no" and "chair" (where "chair" was not being negated directly). The number of syntactic operations or the complexity of grammatical relationship within a sentence appears to increase the cognitive weight of the sentence for the child, and his reduced utterance reflects the inability to carry the full sentence load in performance.

When the children played with the train, they had to gather the disconnected cars – engine, dumper, tank car, and tank, as well as all the flat cars – and carry them to a clear space on the floor. This always involved several trips, and each armload of cars deposited on the floor by itself never added up to a "train." The analogy is a simple one but fairly direct. The limitations in linguistic performance reflected an inability to carry the full structural load of the underlying representation. Limitations in linguistic operations appear to interact with limitations in cognitive function to influence linguistic expression in an as yet unspecified way.

Notes

1   Quotations were taken from an abstract, in English, supplied by the author.
2   For the purpose of this discussion, the negative sentences at Kathryn I in Table 27.2 will be used as primary examples, although the discussion and conclusions that have been drawn apply as well to the negative sentences in the data presented and discussed in Chapter 7 (Kathryn II and III, Eric I to VI, and Gia I to VI).
3   It should also be noted that Bellugi's Period A was based on a 10-hour speech sample from each of the children, obtained over a 10-week period for two of the children and over a 20-week period for the third child. The individual observations of Kathryn, Eric, and Gia were spaced over a period of a few days, and obtained every six weeks. Thus, the period discussed as the first stage (Period A) by Bellugi overlaps the first several observations of Kathryn, Eric, and Gia.

References

Bach, Emmon, and Robert T. Harms (eds.) 1968. *Universals in Linguistic Theory*. New York: Holt, Rinehart and Winston.

Bellugi, Ursula. 1967. The Acquisition of Negation. Doctoral dissertation, Harvard University.

Braine, Martin D. S. 1963. The ontogeny of English phrase structure: The first phase. *Language* 39, 1–13.

Braine, Martin D. S. 1965. Three suggestions regarding grammatical analyses of children's language. Paper presented to the Annual Conference on Linguistics of the Linguistic Circle of New York.

Brown, Roger, and Ursula Bellugi. 1964. Three processes in the child's acquisition of syntax. *Harvard Educational Review* 34, 133–51.

Brown, Roger, Courtney B. Cazden, and Ursula Bellugi. 1969. The child's grammar from I to III. In J. P. Hill (ed.), *1967 Minnesota Symposia on Child Psychology*. Minneapolis: University of Minnesota Press.

Brown, Roger, and Colin Fraser. 1963. The acquisition of syntax. In Charles N. Cofer and Barbara S. Musgrave (eds.), *Verbal Behavior and Learning*. New York: McGraw-Hill, pp. 158–97.

Cazden, Courtney B. 1967. On individual differences in language competence and performance. *Journal of Special Education* 1, 135–50.

Cazden, Courtney B. 1968. The acquisition of noun and verb inflections. *Child Development* 39, 433–48.

Chomsky, Noam. 1957. *Syntactic Structures*. The Hague: Mouton.

Chomsky, Noam. 1964a. Current issues in linguistic theory. In Jerry A. Fodor and Jerrold J. Katz (eds.), *The Structure of Language*. Englewood Cliffs, N.J.: Prentice-Hall, pp. 50–118.

Chomsky, Noam. 1964b. Formal discussion. In Ursula Bellugi and Roger Brown (eds.), *The Acquisition of Language*. Monograph of the Society for Research in Child Development, 29, pp. 35–9.

Chomsky, Noam. 1965. *Aspects of the Theory of Syntax*. Cambridge, Mass.: MIT Press.

Chomsky, Noam. 1968. *Language and Mind*. New York: Harcourt, Brace and World.

Chomsky, Noam. 1969. Deep structure, surface structure, and semantic interpretation. Unpublished paper reproduced by the Indiana University, Bloomington.

Ervin, Susan M. 1966. Imitation and structural change in children's language. In Eric H. Lenneberg (ed.), *New Directions in the Study of Language*. Cambridge, Mass.: MIT Press, pp. 163–89.

Greenberg, Joseph H. 1963. Some universals of grammar with particular reference to meaningful elements. In Joseph H. Greenberg (ed.), *Universals of Language*. Cambridge, Mass.: MIT Press, pp. 73–113.

Gruber, Jeffrey S. 1967. Topicalization in child language. *Foundations of Language* 3, 37–65.

Harris, Zellig S. 1964. Discourse analysis. In Jerry A. Fodor and Jerrold J. Katz (eds.), *The Structure of Language*. Englewood Cliffs, NJ: Prentice-Hall, pp. 355–83.

Hymes, Dell. 1964. *Language in Culture and Society*. New York: Harper and Row.

Jakobson, Roman. 1968. *Child Language Aphasia and Phonological Universals*. The Hague: Mouton.

Jespersen, Otto. 1917. *Negation in English and Other Languages*. Copenhagen.

Jespersen, Otto. 1961. *A Modern English Grammar*. Part V. London: George Allen and Unwin.

Klima, Edward S. 1964. Negation in English. In Jerry A. Fodor and Jerrold J. Katz (eds.), *The Structure of Language*. Englewood Cliffs, NJ: Prentice-Hall, pp. 246–323.

Klima, Edward S. and Ursula Bellugi. 1966. Syntactic regularities in the speech of children. In J. L. Lyons and R. J. Wales (eds.), *Psycholinguistic Papers*. Edinburgh: Edinburgh University Aldine Press, pp. 183–208.

Labov, William. 1966. Grammaticality of everyday speech. Paper presented to the Linguistic Society of America.

Lenneberg, Eric H. 1967. *Biological Foundations of Language*. New York: Wiley.

Leopold, Werner F. 1939–9. *Speech Development of a Bilingual Child*. 4 vols. Evanston, Ill.: Northwestern University Press.

Leopold, Werner F. 1961. Patterning in children's language learning. In Sol Saporta (ed.), *Psycholinguistics*. New York: Holt, Rinehart and Winston, pp. 350–8.

Lewis, M. M. 1951. *Infant Speech, a Study of the Beginnings of Language*. New York: Humanities Press.

Lieberman, Philip. 1967. *Intonation, Perception, and Language*. Cambridge, Mass.: MIT Press.

McCarthy, Dorothea. 1954. Language development in children. In Leonard Carmichael (ed.), *Manual of Child Psychology*. New York: Wiley, pp. 492–630.

McNeill, David. 1966. Developmental psycholinguistics. In Frank Smith and George A. Miller (eds.), *The Genesis of Language*. Cambridge, Mass.: MIT Press, pp. 15–84.

McNeill, David, and Nobuko B. McNeill. 1967. A question in semantic development: what does a child mean when he says "no"? Paper presented to the Society for Research in Child Development.

Miller, Wick, and Susan Ervin. 1964. The development of grammar in child language. In Ursula Bellugi and Roger Brown (eds.), *The Acquisition of Language*. Monograph of the Society for Research in Child Development, 29, pp. 9–34.

Murata, Koji. 1961. The development of verbal behavior: III. Early developmental processes of the linguistic forms and functions of requests. *Japanese Journal of Education Psychology* 9, 220–9.

Postal, Paul M. 1964. Underlying and superficial linguistic structure. *Harvard Educational Review* 34, 246–66.

Sapir, Edward. 1921. *Language*. New York: Harcourt, Brace and World.

Shipley, Elizabeth F., Carlota S. Smith, and Lila R. Gleitman. 1969. A study in the acquisition of language: Free responses to commands. *Language* 45, 322–42.

Sinclair-deZwart, Hermine. 1969. Developmental psycholinguistics. In David Elkind and John H. Flavell (eds.), *Studies in Cognitive Development*. New York: Oxford University Press, pp. 315–36.

Slobin, Dan I. 1966. Comments on "developmental Psycholinguistics". In Frank Smith and George A. Miller (eds.), *The Genesis of Language*. Cambridge, Mass.: MIT Press, pp. 85–91.

Slobin, Dan I. (ed.) 1967. *A Field Manual for Cross-Cultural Study of the Acquisition of Communicative Competence*. Berkeley: University of California Press.

Smith, Frank, and George A. Miller (eds.) 1966. *The Genesis of Language*. Cambridge, Mass.: MIT Press.

Weir, Ruth H. 1966. Some questions on the child's learning of phonology. In Frank Smith and George A. Miller (eds.), *The Genesis of Language*. Cambridge, Mass.: MIT Press, pp. 153–68.

Wells, Rulon S. 1963. Immediate constituents. In Martin Joos (ed.), *Readings in Linguistics*. New York: American Council of Learned Societies, pp. 186–207.

Zipf, George K. 1965. *The Psycho-Biology of Language: An Introduction to Dynamic Philology*. 1st ed., Boston: Houghton Mifflin, 1935; 2nd ed., Cambridge, Mass.: MIT Press.

28

The Young Word Maker: A Case Study of Innovation in the Child's Lexicon

Eve V. Clark

Noah: (picking up a toy dog) This is Woodstock.
(He bobs the toy in Adam's face)
Adam: Hey Woodstock, don't do that. (Noah persists)
I'm going home so you won't Woodstock me.

28.1 Introduction

Lexical creativity is widespread in childhood. Children coin new compounds like *plate-egg* and *cup-egg* (for fried and boiled eggs), *tell-wind* (a weathervane), or *fix-man* (a mechanic). They coin agent and instrument nouns like *lessoner* (a teacher), *shorthander* (someone who writes shorthand), *winder* (a machine for making ice-cream), and *driver* (the ignition key of a car). They form adjectives like *toothachey*, *windy* (used in *a windy parasol*, one being blown by the wind), or *bumpy* (used in *a bumpy door*, for a door that was banging). They ask when cocoons will be *flyable*. They form comparatives and superlatives from nouns, saying that food needs to be *salter* (more salty) or describing a bench as the *sliverest seat*. And they use nouns as verbs, talking about cheese that has to be *scaled* (instead of weighed), about *lawning* (for mowing the lawn), or, as in the dialogue between 3-year-olds cited at the opening of the chapter, about actions connected with a toy called Woodstock.

The questions raised by innovations like these are twofold. First, why do children create new words? And second, how do they do it? The answer to the first question may hinge on the communicative function of language. Children may create new words to fill gaps in their lexicon, to express meanings for which they have no ready-made words. (Of course, children might not be aware in this situation that they are creating new words.) The answer to how children do this seems to be that they draw on words and morphemes already known to them. By using word stems in new ways or combining them with other

From Eric Wanner and Lila R. Gleitman (eds.), *Language Acquisition: The State of the Art*. New York: Cambridge University Press, 1982, pp. 390–418. ©1982 by Cambridge University Press. Reprinted with the permission of Cambridge University Press.

stems or affixes, they can express a variety of new meanings. In this chapter I shall argue that children learn very early that the lexicon can be used creatively,[1] and that this knowledge plays an important role in acquisition.

Creativity in the lexicon, though, is not simply a matter of learning which word-formational paradigms are available in a language. This is because the paradigms themselves are open-ended: It is not possible to list all their actual and potential members. For instance, no dictionary lists all the verbs to which the -er suffix can be added in English to form an agentive noun, as in *climber, sitter, goer, maker,* and so on. Similarly, there is no *a priori* limit on the possible relations that can hold between the denotata of any two nouns combined to form a new compound on a particular occasion, as in *fire-dog* for a large yellow dog found at the site of a fire (Pelsma, 1910) or the adult *apple-juice-chair* for the place at table with a glass of apple juice nearby (Downing, 1977). They, too, cannot be listed in dictionaries. Lexical innovations, then, are primarily important not because they show mastery of the word-formation paradigms, but because they suggest that children are learning the *process* required in that language for creating new words.

The fact that children are creative and produce numerous lexical innovations raises three major issues for the acquisition process. First, what is the range of productivity among child innovations and why do children use them? Second, what is the relation between child and adult innovations? The latter are governed by conventions that place certain constraints on the process of innovation, and children have presumably to acquire these conventions. Third, what form does the innovative process take? Children could take a particular term already in their repertoire and construct a new one by analogy, say the pair *jump/jumped* as a model for *bump/bumped*, or they could abstract a rule such as "Add -ed to all verb stems to express past time" and use that.

In examining these issues and particular hypotheses that arise from them, I will take as my data innovations produced by English-, French-, and German-speaking children and focus on one area of the lexicon only – denominal verbs. And since we already know something about adult usage in this domain, I will begin with a sketch of the categories of denominal verbs in adult speech and the convention that governs their use.

Denominal verbs

In a recent study of denominal verbs (E. Clark and H. Clark, 1979), Herbert Clark and I noted that (1) most denominal verbs can be grouped into a small number of categories; (2) these verbs lie on a continuum, with well-established verbs at one end and innovations at the other; and (3) to use new denominal verbs, speakers of English rely on a convention that places certain constraints on the process of innovation itself. I will take up each of these observations in turn.

Most denominal verbs in English can be grouped very roughly into eight categories, five major and three minor ones, with a few leftovers. Their classification is based on the role played in a situation by the entity denoted by the noun from which the verb is formed – the parent noun. *Locatum verbs* consist of those denominal verbs whose parent nouns denote an object that is placed somewhere. Thus, in *He PLASTERED the ceiling* and *She BLANKETED the bed*, the plaster goes on the ceiling and the blanket on the bed. *Location verbs*, in contrast, have parent nouns that denote the place where some object is put.

For instance, in *He STABLED the horses*, we understand that horses are put in a stable. *Agent verbs* have parent nouns that denote the agent of the action, as in *He AUTHORED the books* or *She CAPTAINED the boat*. *Goal verbs* have parent nouns that denote the goal of the activity, as in *They KNOTTED the ropes* (made the ropes into knots) or *He POWDERED the aspirin* (made the aspirin into powder). And *instrument verbs* consist of verbs whose parent nouns denote the instrument used in the activity, as in *She WEDGED the door open* (made the door stay open with a wedge) or *He LAUNDERETTED the clothes* (cleaned the clothes by means of a launderette).[2]

The three minor categories have only a few members. First, *experiencer verbs* have parent nouns that denote the entity experiencing something, as in *They WITNESSED the crime*. *Source verbs* have parent nouns that denote the source from which something is produced, as in *They PIECED the quilt together*. And *duration verbs* have parent nouns that denote a stretch of time, as in *He SUMMERED in Canada* or *They WEEKENDED in the mountains*. Last, there are a few very small clusters of verbs that fall outside the other categories: verbs of consumption with parent nouns that denote meals or food (*to lunch, to snack*), verbs of collection with parent nouns that denote objects that are collected and removed (*to hay, to nut*), and verbs for weather (*to snow, to rain*).

Within these categories, some verbs have a more transparent connection with their parent nouns than others. At the opaque end of this continuum lie verbs whose parent nouns may not even be recognized as such, as in verbs like *lynch* or *boycott*. Next come verbs where the connection between noun and verb is no longer known, as in *to shanghai*, *to slate*, or *to riddle*. Next come verbs where the connection remains somewhat transparent, as in *to park* or *to land* (but consider *land on water*). And further still towards the transparent end of this continuum lie verbs where the connection seems quite clear, as in *to bicycle*, *to skate*, or *to hammer*.

Many denominal verbs are well established in the language. The process of forming verbs from nouns has been going on for hundreds of years in English. This, of course, is one reason why many noun–verb pairs no longer retain a transparent connection in meaning. Well-established verbs belong to the conventional or idiomatic lexicon of a language. In this, they contrast with innovations, newly coined denominal verbs, used with particular meanings on particular occasions.

Innovations are governed by conventions – conventions of language use. The convention on innovative denominal verbs, like other conventions, stems from the fact that many innovative expressions are neither purely denotational (like *dog*) nor indexical (like *he*), but *contextual*. That is, they have the three following characteristics:

1   Contextuals have an indefinitely large number of potential senses. An innovative verb formed from a noun might be used with one sense on one occasion, another on a second occasion, yet another on a third, and so on. There is no limit on the number of senses such a contextual can potentially convey.
2   Contextuals depend for their interpretation on the context in which they are produced. Just as one relies on context to identify the referent of an indexical like *he* or *the dog*, so do facts about the context play an essential role in the interpretation of contextuals.
3   Contextuals demand cooperation between speaker and listener. A speaker must assess what his listener knows or could infer from context, and the listener must use any

clues from context plus any other facts he has reason to assume the speaker expects him to use in arriving at the intended interpretation.

In order to interpret contextuals as intended, the speaker and listener rely on a convention that goes roughly as follows. In using an innovative expression to denote some kind of situation, the speaker expects his listener to be able to arrive at a readily computable, unique interpretation by considering both the expression itself (here, an innovative denominal verb) and the speaker's and listener's mutual knowledge. This convention places limits on both the use and the interpretation of innovative expressions.

The convention can be spelled out more formally as follows:

> *The innovative denominal verb convention.* In using an innovative denominal verb, the speaker means to denote (1) the kind of situation (2) he has good reason to believe (3) that on this occasion the listener can readily compute (4) uniquely (5) on the basis of their mutual knowledge (6) such that the parent noun denotes one role in the situation and the remaining surface arguments of the denominal verb denote other roles in the situation. [E. Clark and H. Clark, 1979, p. 787]

This convention places certain constraints on which nouns can be used innovatively as verbs.

One of its consequences is captured by the principle of *pre-emption by synonymy*. Certain innovations are pre-empted, or counted as illegitimate, if there is a common term in the language with just the meaning the innovation would have had. There are three types of pre-emption by synonymy:

1   Suppletion.   Pre-emption by suppletion occurs when the meaning that would be expressed in context by an innovative verb coincides with the meaning of another verb already in the language. For instance, although most vehicle names can be used as verbs with the meaning "go by *X*" (as in *taxi/taxi, bus/bus*, or *bicycle/bicycle*), the verbs *car* and *aeroplane* are pre-empted by *drive* and *fly*, which have just the meanings the innovative verbs would have.

2   Entrenchment.   Pre-emption by entrenchment occurs where the existence of one denominal verb with an idiomatic meaning prevents the formation of another, with the same meaning, from the same parent noun. Thus the innovative verb *prison*, meaning "put into prison," is pre-empted by *imprison*, and the innovative *hospital*, meaning "put into hospital," is pre-empted by *hospitalize*.

3   Ancestry.   Pre-emption by ancestry occurs when the parent noun is itself formed from a verb with the very meaning that the innovative denominal verb would have. For instance, the denominal verb *baker* is pre-empted by *bake*, just as the verb *farmer* is pre-empted by *farm*, and so on.

Of course, if the innovative verbs contrast in meaning with verbs already in the language, they are quite legitimate. The categories of pre-emption just listed operate only where there is no contrast in meaning. All three reflect the fact that speakers have a strong tendency to avoid creating complete synonyms (see Bolinger, 1977).

Another consequence of the innovative denominal verb convention is captured by the principle of *pre-emption by homonymy*. Here, an innovative verb may be pre-empted by reason not of its meaning, but by reason of its form. For instance, the existence of the verb *spring*, meaning "leap, jump," pre-empts the use of *spring* as in *Jeffrey springed in France*, meaning "spend the season of spring." Pre-emption by homonymy prevents the use of innovative verbs that are homonymous with common verbs already well established in the language. It is not clear how strong pre-emption of this type is compared to pre-emptions by meaning.

28.2   Issues and Hypotheses

Learning conventions

When children acquire their first language, they learn sounds, morphemes, and words, with their various rules of combination. But this is not all. They also learn the conventions that govern uses of particular forms, and among them, they learn conventions for innovation. When, then, do children learn the innovative denominal verb convention? And what part of the convention do they acquire first?

The first part of the convention that we can be sure children have acquired is the device to be used, the denominal verb. They must give evidence of knowing that nouns can be used as verbs before anything can be said about the remainder of the convention. However, if they only know condition (6) of the convention, there will be no reason for children to observe the consequences of the full convention. Their innovations could as well be illegitimate as legitimate, and could fall into any or all of the pre-empted verb types. Thus use of illegitimate innovations would be evidence for knowledge of condition (6) and against knowledge of the other five conditions of the innovative denominal verb convention. Furthermore, as children acquire the other conditions, they should come to use fewer and fewer illegitimate innovations.

The acquisition of a convention for using innovative verbs must of course go hand-in-hand with the acquisition of well-established verbs and verb meanings. It is the well-established verbs that provide the pre-empting forms, the forms that rule out illegitimate innovations. For example, before children acquire *drive*, *kick*, or *slap*, there is no reason why they should not use innovative *car*, *foot*, and *palm*, or *hand*, with just those meanings, to fill these "gaps" in their lexicons. (They might not be understood very easily, however.) But learning the well-established verbs is not enough: Children have also to realize that one of the consequences of the innovative denominal verb convention is pre-emption. In effect, without the convention, there would be nothing to constrain their innovations.

Children's innovative verbs usually allow the listener to arrive at a readily computable unique interpretation. How do the speaker and listener manage this when the speaker is not observing the appropriate convention? One explanation might be that the convention holds by accident for young children. Most or all of their conversation is focused on the here-and-now. This allows their listeners, in most situations, to readily identify a unique activity as the denotation of an innovative verb. In effect, limitation to the here-and-now allows the speaker and listener to operate, by default, with a restricted version of mutual knowledge (see further H. Clark and Marshall, 1981).

As children get older, their earlier accidental observance of the convention no longer holds because they talk more and more about events displaced in place or time from the locus or moment of speech. So for their listeners to grasp their intended meanings, children have to learn to cooperate with their listeners by using the relevant convention. This cooperation is a complex affair. In some situations, children as old as 8 or 9 do not appreciate that what is known to them as speakers is not automatically known to their listeners (e.g., Warden, 1976). Children, then, may well take several years to acquire and be able to use the innovative denominal verb convention in its entirety.

The process of innovation: analogy or rule?

Consider what children must do in order to add a suffix like the past-tense ending in English to a verb. They must first identify the suffix as an element separable from the verb stem, and second work out what meaning it adds. This part of the acquisition process can be represented as follows:

1   Identify the suffix as an element that can be detached from the particular stem(s) it occurs with (e.g., *jump* + *ed*, *walk* + *ed*).
2   Identify the meaning of the suffix (*-ed* picks out a time prior to the time of the utterance).

Once these steps are achieved, children can add the suffix to other verb stems:

3   The suffix *-ed* adds the meaning of completion or past time to verbs.

The general procedure in the first two steps represents the analysis of form and meaning that has to precede extension of that suffix to new verbs. And the statement in the third step represents the modulation of meaning, to borrow Brown's (1973) term, that children can carry out once they have analyzed the meaning of this suffix.[3]

But by what process do children use past-tense forms? Traditionally, there have been two ways of talking about this. The first assumes analogy and would posit that children choose the nearest possible exemplar on each occasion as a model for adding the appropriate past-tense allomorph. For instance, in deciding how to form the past tense of *bump*, children could retrieve a verb with a similarly shaped stem[4] and use it as the model exemplar, for example, *jump/jumped::bump/____*. The second way of talking about such a process assumes rule use. Under this view, one would argue that children rely on a rule that represents a generalization (such as that in the third step just listed) drawn from their experience with a number of different exemplars. Because they have abstracted a rule – say, "Express past time by adding *-ed* to the verb stem" – they would have no need to conjure up a particular exemplar but could simply apply their rule in adding the appropriate suffix to any new verb.

Do children rely on analogy or on rules? Early studies constrasted rote memorization with analogy, not analogy with rule use (e.g., Stern and Stern, 1928). Guillaume (1927), for instance, argued that French-speaking children were relying on analogy when they formed incorrect past participles for third-conjugation verbs like *éteindre*, "switch off." Instead of the adult past participle *éteint*, 3- and 4-year-olds produced *éteindé* (from a first-conjugation model like *donné*)[5] or even *éteindu* (from another third-conjugation model like *descendu*). Such regularizations are incompatible with the view that children learn by memorizing the forms they have heard.

More recent studies have contrasted rote memory with rule use. For example, Berko (1958) showed that children could add appropriate noun and verb endings to new words (nonsense syllables). She argued from this that they could not be relying on rote memorization because (1) they had never heard these new words before, and (2) they consistently chose regular, rather than irregular, forms of the endings added. However, when rule use is contrasted with analogy, it is not clear which position data like Berko's really favor.

MacWhinney (1975b), in his study of Hungarian children's noun plurals, argued that children start out with memorization and then progress via analogy to rule use. At the rote memorization stage, words and their endings are unanalyzed wholes. With analogy, children add new plurals to their repertoire by modeling the plural of a new word on the plural of a known word resembling it. Later still, he argued, children progress to using rules. This is shown by their taking into account the complex conditions that govern the choice of the appropriate plural forms for both real and nonsense stems. But it may be hard to distinguish analogy and rule. Indeed, Park (1978) has questioned whether MacWhinney's data provide evidence for rule use rather than analogy.

There may be no single answer. In deciding how to add word endings, children might well begin by comparing new instances to specific exemplars already in their repertoires. But later, after being exposed to a large number of forms in a coherent paradigm, they should have a plethora of exemplars to work from, and their use of an inflection might take on the form of a general rule. Or they might simultaneously use rules in some domains and analogy in others. Overregular use of the English noun plural suffix *-s* would seem to favor a rule interpretation. But construction of a compound like *coffee-churn*, to designate a coffee grinder, by a child who knew *milk-churn* (Pelsma, 1910), would seem to favor analogy.

To summarize, whether children use analogy or rules is not easy to decide from the data available. Some studies appear to support analogy and others rule use, but few have actively contrasted the two in the domain of language acquisition. Moreover, analogy and rule use appear to lie on a continuum, with analogy based on single exemplars at one end, and rules abstracted over multiple exemplars at the other (see further Brooks, 1978; Kossan, 1978; Medin and Schaffer, 1978). In language, this continuum is such that, whereas instances of analogy could actually be instances of rule use, there should be identifiable instances of rule use that could not be accounted for by analogy. I shall consider this issue further for the case of innovative denominal verbs. If children's innovations conform to the model exemplars offered in adult speech, it may not be possible to decide between analogy and rule use. But if they depart from the exemplars offered, this departure would favor rules over analogy in the process of innovation.

Some hypotheses

There are several hypotheses implicit in the preceding discussion that will be tested against the present corpus of children's innovative denominal verbs. First, if children do not know all the parts of a convention about language use – here, the convention for using innovative denominal verbs – they could produce both legitimate and illegitimate innovations. However, the incidence of their illegitimate innovations should decline with age as they learn (1) other terms that would pre-empt particular innovations, (2) that well-established terms do pre-empt, and (3) how to assess mutual knowledge – the special common ground that people need in order to make effective reference and so on (see H. Clark and Marshall, 1981). These predictions, I assume, should hold equally for all three languages under discussion here.[6]

Second, there are several alternative hypotheses about the sources of children's innovations. One source children might use is the set of well-established denominal verbs available in their own vocabularies. To use these, whether by analogy or rule, children will need to have recognized and analyzed the relation that holds for particular noun–verb pairings. Evidence for this source could show up in two ways: First, the innovations children produce should belong to the *same* categories of denominal verbs as their well-established verbs; and second, the frequency of their types should reflect that of their well-established verb categories.

An alternative hypothesis about the source of children's innovations is that, instead, they base them on adult usage. With this source, there are similar predictions: First, the innovations children produce should all fit into the adult categories of denominal verbs; and second, their frequency should reflect the relative frequencies of the adult categories. Of course, if children's well-established verbs happen to fall into the same categories as adult denominal verbs, these two hypotheses will not be distinguishable.

In either case, if there are parallels between the proposed model and children's innovations, one could probably not decide between analogy and rule. Their innovations could be produced by analogy to specific exemplars in their own vocabulary or in adult speech, or by a rule based on their own or adult speech.

A third alternative, in which the potential role of analogy or rule might be easier to assess, is the following: Children could produce innovations because they need a way to express particular meanings on particular occasions. In this case, all they need notice is the general fact that adults use words that denote concrete objects as terms for talking about states, processes, or acts associated with those objects. This would essentially correspond to part (6) of the adult convention, but would involve use of a more general rule, one not governed by the rest of that convention. Under this view, children's innovations – legitimate or illegitimate – would not necessarily parallel either their own well-established verbs or the verb categories used by adults. For example, children might use one or more categories *not* used by adults. This would be strong evidence in favor of rule use.

Data for the case study

The innovations to be analyzed here consist of 224 denominal verbs produced by young children acquiring English (123 verbs), French (35 verbs), and German (66 verbs). The sources for the English data are several. First, there are my own longitudinal records of 2- and 3-year-olds, plus a long-term collection of more casual observations of children's innovations. Examples cited from this source are labeled with the initials D, H, J, K,

S, JA, SA, and ME in the tables presented later. A second source of English data is Bowerman (1974, 1978b, and unpublished data), indicated by the initials CB and EB. In addition, I have culled a few instances from other published sources: HO and SO (O'Shea, 1907), EP (Pelsma, 1910), RG (Grant, 1915), DH (Huxley, 1970), HL and JW (Kuczaj, 1977), and AK (Kuczaj, 1978).

My sources for French are sparser. I have relied here on instances appearing in published diary studies and discussions by Decroly (1932a), indicated by WD, YD, and XD; Grégoire (1937, 1947), indicated by CG and EG; and Aimard (1975), indicated by LA, VA, and MA. The German data have also been drawn from published sources. The two main studies I have relied on are Neugebauer (1914), indicated by RN, and Stern and Stern (1928), indicated by HS and GS. In addition, I have drawn on additional examples cited by Stern and Stern from other German studies, indicated as follows: AP (Preyer, 1882), DL (Lindner, 1898), FS and SS (Schneider, 1903), Tö (Tögel, 1905), HF and RF (Friedrich, 1906), and Sc (Scupin and Scupin, 1907). The majority of the innovative verbs for all three languages were produced by children between the ages of 2 and 5.

In addition to the English data on innovative verbs, I have also used a comparison corpus of well-established or idiomatic denominal verbs found in the vocabulary of 3-year-olds. This corpus was compiled from seven vocabulary studies by tallying all those denominal verbs for which children also knew the parent nouns (Bateman, 1915; Bohn, 1914; Boyd, 1914; Brandenburg, 1915; Grant, 1915; Nice, 1915; Pelsma, 1910). A second set of comparison data comes from the adult corpus compiled by E. Clark and H. Clark (1979) of over 1,300 established and innovative denominal verbs in English.

Each of the verbs in the corpus of innovations, from all three languages, as well as each of the well-established verbs from English-speaking 3-year-olds, was classified using the schema in E. Clark and H. Clark (1979). For well-established verbs, the classification was based on the adult meanings; for innovative verbs, the classification was based on contextual information about the occasion of use, together with adult glosses of what the child had intended to convey.

To be sure that children are using a noun as an innovative verb, one has to make sure that they are observing certain syntactic constraints that allow identification of the word class of the stem in question. Utterances from the one- or two-word stage clearly cannot be categorized reliably as nouns or verbs because they cannot meet the adult constraints on uses of different word classes (see Stern and Stern, 1928). The child must therefore be using subject-verb-object sequences in his utterances before he can be credited with any innovative denominal verbs. The problem is an obvious one when one-word utterances are considered. For instance, some children made early verblike uses of *door* (an adult noun) that are exactly paralleled by other children's uses of *open* (an adult verb) (see Griffiths and Atkinson, 1978). The same problem lingers with two-word utterances that contain a potential denominal verb: In *Daddy brush*, one could have a sequence of noun-plus-noun, in a genitive relation ("Daddy's brush") or a subject-object relation ("Daddy's doing something to the brush"); noun-plus-verb, in a subject-verb relation ("Daddy's brushing something"); or noun-plus-noun, in a subject–manner adverb relation where *brush* is the instrument used in a particular action ("Daddy's doing something with a brush"). Until children produce subject-verb-object utterances, there is no reliable way to identify the syntactic word class of a particular term.

There are, inevitably, certain problems associated with the use of such data on innovations. Since the sample size for each language is different, the samples may not be truly representative. This problem is compounded by the fact that the data for each language are drawn from several different children, and they in turn may not be representative of children acquiring that language. Despite these problems, the instances of innovations observed in my own data appear very similar to those observed by Bowerman, and they fall into similar categories, as do the data from children acquiring German. Moreover, in the case of German, more recent studies contain observations directly comparable to those noted in earlier diaries (e.g., Augst, Bauer, and Stein, 1977; Panagl, 1977). The French corpus is the smallest and therefore possibly less representative than either the English or German one.

A second source of problems with such data lies in their categorization. As I mentioned earlier, each innovative verb was classified according to the role in the situation of the entity denoted by the parent noun. But how is this decided? Both in my own data and in Bowerman's, detailed contextual notes on what the child was talking about on each occasion and what he intended to convey allow as precise a categorization as for adult innovations. But published sources are not always as detailed either about the context or about the intended interpretation. As a result, some innovations could have been classified in more than one way. (This problem is not unique to child innovations; it also occurs with many adult uses; see E. Clark and H. Clark, 1979.) The adult glosses provided in diaries like Grégoire's (1937, 1947) or Stern and Stern's (1928) vary in the amount of detail provided. Some innovations may be transparent to the observer who knows the child and his routines, while to others the same innovations are opaque. In the relatively few instances that lacked both a context and a gloss, the verb category was determined on the basis of the predominant feature of the entity denoted. If the entity was one normally used as an instrument, for instance, the verb was placed in the instrument category, and so on.

A third problem is related to the sampling issue raised earlier. Comparatively few of the innovative verbs in the corpus are legitimate innovations. In essence, people do not notice when children produce verbs that might as well have been produced by adults, but they do notice when child forms violate adult conventions on innovations. This means that the innovations actually produced by children may be severely underestimated in my data. The criterion of illegitimacy is a very conservative one. And there is a second source of underestimation. In many cases, children may reinvent what for adults are well-established forms. These too should be added to the tally of children's innovations, but there is a detection problem. Reinvention is virtually impossible to distinguish from forms based on observed adult usage. This bias against noticing child innovations, then, will lead to even greater underestimates of innovation in the child's lexicon.

28.3   Innovative denominal verbs

In giving an account of the kinds of innovations typically produced in all three languages, I will go through the verb categories in turn, illustrating them with examples from each language. I will then compare innovative verb categories with well-established ones, and children's denominal verbs with those produced by adults.

Table 28.1   Instrument verbs: some English examples

(1)	S	(2;4, wanting to have some cheese weighed): *You have to scale it first.*
(2)	S	(2;4, reaching for the pocket calculator): *I can button it.* [= turn it on]
(3)	S	(2;7, having hit his baby sister, explaining what made her cry): *I broomed her.* [= hit her with a (toy) broom]
(4)	S	(2;11, not wanting his mother to sweep his room): *Don't broom my mess.*
(5)	S	(2;11, telling his father that his mother nursed the baby): *Mommy nippled Anna.*
(6)	S	(3;0,21, watching a man opening a door with a key): *He's keying the door.*
(7)	S	(3;2, pretending to shoot his mother with a stick): *I'm going to gun you.*
(8)	S	(3;2, asking if the pants his mother is mending are ready): *Is it all needled?*
(9)	S	(3;2, putting on a cowboy hat with a string-and-bead catch for holding it on under the chin): *String me up, mommy.*
(10)	EB	(3;10, taking spaghetti out a pan with some tongs): *I'm going to pliers this out.*
(11)	EP	(4;0, asking for some sticks to be chopped): *Won't you hatchet this?*
(12)	CB	(4;0, rejecting some paper she'd cut her finger on earlier): *I don't think I'll have it because it papers me.* [= paper cuts me]
(13)	CB	(4;4, struggling with the lace on her boot): *How was it shoelaced?*
(14)	CB	(4;6, doing up the seat belt in the car): *I seat-belted myself.*
(15)	HL	(5;0, complaining about the unfairness of woodchopping assignments): *You axed the wood and I didn't axe it.*
(16)	JW	(5;7, hitting a ball with a stick): *I'm sticking it and that makes it go really fast.*

Note: Ages are given in years; months, and (sometimes) days.

Table 28.2   Instrument verbs: some French examples

(1)	LA	(2;0, no context given): *C'est déconstruit, c'est bulldozé.* [It's unbuilt, it's bulldoze(re)d.]
(2)	VA	(3;9, before licking an envelope to seal it): *Je peux la boutonner?* [Can I button (close, fasten) it?]
(3)	VA	(3;10, having heard the word Nixon a lot on the radio): *Ce nixon, c'est pour anixonner?* [This nixon, it's for nixoning?]
(4)	VA	(4;1, wanting to write with a piece of chalk): *Tu as pas une craie? Je voudrais crai . . . ver.* [Have you got a piece of chalk? I'd like to chalk.]
(5)	CG	(4;7,6, talking about raking a path): *On ne rate pas dans les crasses.* [You don't rake in the dirt/filth.]
(6)	XD	(no age given), talking about painting with a paintbrush, used the verb *pincer.* [to paintbrush]
(7)	YD	(no age given), talking about measuring something, used *mètrer.* [to meter]

Instrument verbs.   Typical examples of innovative instrument verbs from children acquiring English, French, and German are given in Tables 28.1, 28.2, and 28.3. The category of instrument verbs comprises those denominal verbs whose parent noun denotes the instrument used in the activity being talked about. Table 28.1 lists instances observed in the speech of several English–speaking children.

Many of the innovations in Table 28.1 are illegitimate for adults, even though they are interpretable in context. Some are illegitimate because they are pre-empted by *sup-pletion* (the same meaning attached to a different form). The child's *scale* is suppleted

Table 28.3 Instrument verbs: some German examples

(1)	RN	(1;11,21), talking about climbing something by means of a ladder, used *leitern*. [to ladder]
(2)	RN	(1;11,21), talking about tying a cord, used *schnuren*. [to cord]
(3)	RN	(2;1,7, talking about a train leaving): *Lekta-sch is forträdelt*. [Electric train has wheeled away.
(4)	RN	(2;1,7), talking about using a whip, used *peitschen*. [to whip]
(5)	RN	(2;2, talking about a buckle): *Wie hannn man das anbroschen?* [Can someone brooch (fasten) this on?]
(6)	RN	(2;2, using tongs to pick things up): *Mutter, was kann ich noch zangen?* [Mommy, what else can I tong?]
(7)	RN	(2;9, rubbing stones by running a small stick over them): *Jetz muss ich die noch stöckeln*. [Now I must stick them again.]
(8)	Sc	(3;6), being sniffed by a dog, used *angeschnauzelt*. [(It) muzzles/snouts.]
(9)	HS	(3;8, to her mother): *Hast du die Schürze vergürtelt?* [Have you girdled (fastened) your apron?]
(10)	HS	(3;9), measuring the length of her necklace, used *metern*. [to meter]
(11)	HF	(3;9,15), talking about sewing with a sewing machine, used *maschinen*. [to machine]
(12)	GS	(3; 11, playing with some glass): *Ich splittre nich. Ich wer mich ja nich splittern*. [I don't splinter. I shan't splinter myself = hurt with splinters.]
(13)	HS	(4;2), talking about sweeping with a broom, used *best*. [(He/she) brooms.]
(14)	AP	(no age given), talking about cutting something with a knife, used *messen*. [to knife]

by adult *weigh*, *broom* (in [4]) by *sweep*, *nipple* by *nurse*, *gun* by *shoot*, *needle* by *mend*, and both *hatchet* and *axe* by *chop*. Other innovations are illegitimate because they are pre-empted by *homonymy* (a different meaning attached to the same form). Thus the child's *button* (turn on by means of a button) is pre-empted by the adult's "fasten with a button," the child's *key* (open with a key) is pre-empted by the adult's "make a key for," and *needle* (mend with a needle) is pre-empted by adult "irritate, annoy." (*Needle* is therefore pre-empted both by meaning and by form.) Other examples of pre-emption by homonymy are *string up* (fasten with a string) beside adult "hang," *paper* (cut with paper) beside "put paper on," and *stick* (hit with a stick) beside "adhere to."

Most of the remaining verbs are legitimate innovations. *Broom* (in [3]) meaning "hit with a broom," *pliers out*, "remove with pliers" (with *pliers* overextended to include tongs), and *seal-belted*, "fasten in with a seat belt," are all legitimate. *Shoelaced*, however, would normally appear in the form *laced* for adults. Since the child was trying to lace her boots, this verb has presumably been formed from an unanalyzed compound, and is pre-empted by the *entrenched* verb *lace* – the same meaning with a different form.

Table 28.2 contains some instrument verbs produced by French-speaking children. As in the English data, a number of these verbs are illegitimate. Several are pre-empted by suppletion, for instance, *boutonner*, "fasten an envelope" (from *bouton*, "button"), is pre-empted by adult *cacheter*. Similarly, *pincer*, "paint (with a paintbrush)" (from *pinceau*, "paintbrush"), and *mètrer*, "measure" (from *mètre*, "measuring tape"), are pre-empted by adult *peindre* and *mesurer*, respectively. There is also one instance of pre-emption by entrenchment: *Rater*, "use a rake" (from *rateau*, "rake"), is pre-empted by adult *ratisser*, derived from the same noun. (In Old French, however, *rater* did mean "use a rake.")

Two verbs are pre-empted by homonymy (the same forms with different adult meanings). *Pincer*, "paint" is pre-empted by *pincer*, "pinch," and *rater*, "use a rake," is pre-empted by *rater*, "fail." These two, then, are pre-empted by both meaning and form.

The only legitimate instrument verbs appear to be *bulldozé*, *anixonner*, and *craiver*, but these forms are not necessarily the ones adults would have created. For example, the parent noun for *bulldozé* is *bulldozer* (borrowed from English). To make this noun into a verb would normally require the addition of the first-conjugation ending in *-er*, resulting in a past participial form *bulldozeré*. *Anixonner* seems to have been created with the child assuming *Nixon* to be the name of a product. Given that, the innovation appears quite legitimate. But *craiver*, "write (with chalk)," ought, strictly speaking, to be *craier* (from the noun *craie*, "chalk"). However, the child may have avoided *craier*, which would be homophonous with *créer*, "create, make." Whether this accounts for the form chosen, though, is not clear. The child may also have been influenced by forms like *écrivez*, from *écrire*, "to write," a semantic neighbor of the meaning being expressed.

Table 28.3 lists innovative instrument verbs from German-speaking children. Again, these verbs can be classified as legitimate or illegitimate. Among the illegitimate ones, there are several instances where the child's verb is pre-empted by suppletion and one instance of pre-emption by entrenchment. Suppletion occurs with *forträdelt*, "leave" (based on the noun *Rad*, "wheel"), pre-empted by adult *fortgefahren*; with *metern*, "measure" (based on *Meter*, "ruler, measuring tape"), pre-empted by *messen*; with *best*, "sweeps" (based on *Besen*, "broom"), pre-empted by *fegen*; and with *messen*, "cut" (based on *Messer*, "knife"), pre-empted by *schneiden*. The latter verb is also pre-empted by homonymy: Adult *messen* means "to measure." Other instances of homonymy are provided by the verb *splittern*, "hurt with splinters" (based on *Splitter*, "splinter, sliver"), which is pre-empted by the adult meaning of "make into splinters," and by *anschnauzen*, "sniff, muzzle at" (based on *Schnauze*, "snout, muzzle"), which is pre-empted by the adult meaning of "talk roughly to."

The remaining innovations all seem to be legitimate. The verb *leitern* (based on *leiter*, "ladder") was intended to mean "climb with a ladder," and although adults normally use *auf eine Leiter steigen* instead, it was transparent in context. The verb *peitschen* (based on *Peitsche*, "whip"), which is actually an established adult verb meaning "whip," was invented spontaneously by RN, who, according to Neugebauer (1914), had never been exposed to it as a verb. *Anbroschen* (based on *Brosche*, "brooch," overextended to include buckles), meaning "fasten (with a buckle)," is legitimate, as are *zangen* (based on *Zange*, "tongs"), *stöckeln* (based on *Stock*, "stick"), *vergürtelt* (based on *Gürtel*, "belt, sash"), and *maschinen* (based on *Maschine*, "machine").

Locatum verbs.   After instrument verbs, locatum verbs are the most frequent innovative denominal verbs in children's speech. Representative examples from the three languages are shown in Tables 28.4, 28.5, and 28.6. In locatum verbs, the parent nouns denote the entity that is being placed somewhere.

Table 28.4 presents examples from English-speaking children. Only two of them are illegitimate. The first, where the meaning is expressed with a different form by adults, is pre-empted by *ancestry*: The verb *decoration* is based on a noun derived from a verb with the same meaning, namely, *decorate*. The other illegitimate innovation is pre-empted by homonymy: The verb *cast* for adults means "make a cast from," not "put a cast on."

Table 28.4 Locatum verbs: some English examples

(1) DH (2;3, talking about getting dressed): *Mummy trousers me.*
(2) J (2;6, asking a teacher to toss a pillow at him during a mock pillow fight): *Pillow me!*
(3) EB (3;4, deciding not to wear her new nightgown outside in the patio): *Mine will dust.*
     Mother: Dust?
     EB: *Mine will get dust on it.*
(4) EB (3;4, talking about her foot that had a Band-Aid put on earlier): *It was Band-Aided.*
(5) CB (3;11, putting crackers in her soup): *I'm crackering my soup.*
(6) JA (4;0, in the role of doctor dealing with a broken arm): *We're gonna cast it.*
(7) CB (4;2, talking about a rag for washing the car): *But I need it watered and soaped.*
(8) CB (4;5, putting first a bead and then a rubber band into the playdough she's kneading):
     'I think I'll bead it. I think I'll rubber band it.
(9) ME (4;11, talking about the Christmas tree): *We already decorationed our tree.*
(10) SA (5;0, to his mother): *Will you chocolate my milk?*
(11) JW (5;7, dressing a doll): *I'm shirting my man.*

Table 28.5 Locatum verbs: some French examples

(1) VA (4;5, wrapped up in a blanket when asked to put on her slippers): *Je vais me pantoufler
     dedans.* [I'll slipper myself inside.]
(2) EG (6;8), talking about some bread with egg on it, used *pain enoeuffé.* [egged bread/with
     egg on]
(3) CG (7;0), talking about bread thickly covered with jam, used *pain enconfituré.*
     [jammed bread/with jam on]
(4) CG (7;0), talking about putting syrup on things, used the verb *ensiroter.* [to syrup]
(5) CG (7;3,19, talking about his plate): *Mon assiette est entartée.* [My plate is covered with
     tart.]
(6) CG (13;0, asking for a cup of hot chocolate): *Chocolate-moi.* [Chocolate me.]
(7) CG (16;0, talking about builders who had been repairing the brickwork): *Ils ont bien briqué
     la maison.* [They've bricked the house well.]

Table 28.6 Locatum verbs: some German examples

(1) RN (2;2), poking with a sharp tool into a hole, used *reinspitzen.* [to point-in/put the point in]
(2) HS (3;0, having drunk enough milk): *Hab genug emilcht.* [(I) have milked enough.]
(3) Sc (3;2, talking about applying a wet bandage, used *handtucheln.* [to towel]
(4) HS (3;6, refusing to use a spoon because it had already been used for soup): *Der Löffel ist
     besuppt.* [The spoon is souped/has soup on it.]
(5) HS (3;6), putting leaves into paper bags, used *einblättern.* [to leaf-in/put leaves in]
(6) FS (3;9) talked about something covered in ashes as *vollgeascht.* [well ashed]
(7) GS (3;11), making a string of beads, used *aufperlen.* [to thread beads]
(8) HS (4;7, talking about having ribbons on that needed tying, used *zugebändst.* [ribboned]
(9) DL (5;6, talking about stripes on something): *Hier ist Gold angestreift.* [This is
     gold-striped/has gold stripes on it.]

The other locatum verbs in Table 28.4 are legitimate innovations. Notice, however, that some, like *rubber band*, may have an unexpected interpretation. Rubber bands are usually used as instruments for holding things together, not as objects to put somewhere. This clearly makes such verbs difficult to interpret out of context.

Table 28.5 lists some French examples of locatum verbs. As with the English examples in Table 28.4, most of these innovations are legitimate. The two exceptions are both instances of pre-emption by homonymy. *(En)siroter*, meaning "put syrup on" (based on *sirop*, "syrup"), is probably pre-empted by the adult *siroter*, meaning "drink with small sips"; and *briquer*, meaning "put bricks on" (from *brique*, "brick"), is pre-empted by adult "clean vigorously." The remaining verbs all appear to be legitimate.

Table 28.6 contains innovative locatum verbs produced by German-speaking children. Again, there are only a few illegitimate innovations. One of them is pre-empted by suppletion: *Angestreift*, "striped," is normally expressed by *gestreift* (another form based on *Streife*, "stripe"). There is also one pre-emption by homonymy: The verb *milchen*, meaning "drink milk," is kept by adults for "yield milk" (from *Milch* "milk").

The remaining innovations are all legitimate. In many cases, they are based on the same parent nouns as other adult verbs but contrast with them in meaning. For example, the child's *reinspitzen*, "put the point in," contrasts with adult *spitzen*, "make into a point, sharpen" (both from *Spitze*, "point"); the child's *einblättern*, "put leaves into," contrasts with adult *blättern*, "turn the leaves (of a book)" (both based on *Blatt*, "leaf"); and the child's *aufperlen*, "thread beads on," contrasts with adult *perlen*, "sparkle" (both based on *Perle*, "pearl").

Location, goal, and agent verbs.   Innovative location, goal, and agent verbs are comparatively rare in children's speech. Some of the few examples observed for each language are illustrated in Tables 28.7 through 28.9. The parent nouns of these verbs denote the location, the goal, and the agent involved in the activity, respectively. There were no instances of agent verbs observed in the French data; this category was also very rare for English and German.

Table 28.7 gives some innovative location, goal, and agent verbs produced by English-speaking children. These verbs are occasionally hard to classify. For instance, *towel* was used for asking to be wrapped in the towel, not dried with it, hence its classification as a location rather than as an instrument verb. (Location and locatum verbs, in fact, often double as instrument verbs: *Net the fish*, for example, means both "put in a net" and "capture by means of a net.") In general, I have assigned such verbs to the instrument class except where the context made clear that they had a location or locatum meaning only (see E. Clark and H. Clark, 1979). Of the verbs in Table 28.7, only one is pre-empted, by homonymy. It is *cement*, meaning "make cement"; for adults, that same form means "put cement on." All the other verbs are legitimate innovations.

Table 28.8 contains innovative location and goal verbs from French-speaking children. Two verbs are illegitimate, both pre-empted by homonymy: *Emboîter*, meaning "put in an envelope" (from *boîte*, "box"), for adults means "nest or encase one box in another." And *bossu*, an adjectival form, means "humpbacked," not "humped," as the child intended. *Bosse* means "hump," but the adult verb has the meaning "fix ornamental humps (bosses) onto." The child's form, then, is illegitimate (quite aside from the auxiliary verb used). The remaining innovations all appear quite legitimate.

Table 28.7   Location, goal, and agent verbs: some English examples

Location
(1)   CA   (4;6, waving a funnel at her younger sister): *I'm going to funnel you. Ff, ff, ff. You're all in there.*
(2)   SO   (ca. 5;0): *I'm going to basket those apples.*
(3)   CB   (5;5, asking her mother to stop her sister from putting popcorn "beads" on her thread): *Mom, will you keep Eva from threading on mine?*
(4)   K   (7;0, asking her mother to wrap a towel round her as she got out of the bath): *Towel me, mommy.*

Goal
(5)   S   (3;1, watching a cement truck with its back revolving): *That truck is cementing.* [making cement]
(6)   CB   (5;6, asking for her hair not to be done in "dogears"): I don't want to be dogeared today.

Agent
(7)   EB   (2;8, after roaring, with "claws" outstretched, at a towel hanging in the bathroom): *I monstered that towel.*
(8)   AK   (5;1, talking about someone dancing in a ballet): *She's ballerining.*
(9)   HO   (ca. 5;0, after overhearing some remarks about a new governess coming): *When is she coming to governess us?*

Table 28.8   Location and goal verbs: some French examples

Location
(1)   MA   (3;3), talking about closing an envelope, used *emboîter*. [to box/put in a box]
(2)   CG   (9;3) described a procession on the water as *une procession eautée*. [a watered procession/on the water]

Goal
(3)   EG   (3;9,29, talking about some plants): *Elles ne sont pas encore grainées.* [They haven't made seeds yet.]
(4)   VA   (4;4, talking about an episode at the swimming pool): *J'ai rencontré une vieille dame qui m'avait mis de l'eau quand je m'avais bossu.* [I met an old woman who poured water on me when I made myself into a hump.]
(5)   EG   (5;8, arming himself with a toy sword and gun): *Je vais m'ensoldater.* [I'm going to make myself into a soldier.]

Table 28.9 presents location, goal, and agent verbs produced by German-speaking children. All three types were comparatively rare. Three of the verbs here are illegitimate. The one agent verb, *dieben*, meaning "steal" (based on *Dieb*, "thief"), is pre-empted by suppletion: Adult *stehlen* has the same meaning. The other illegitimate verbs are both pre-empted by homonymy: *Wassern*, meaning "place in water" (from *Wasser*, "water"), for adults means "alight on the water"; and *lichten*, meaning "produce light" (from *Licht*, "light"), for adults means "make clearings (in a wood)" or "thin trees." *Lichten* is also pre-empted by suppletion since adults express the meaning "produce light" with the

Table 28.9   Location, goal, and agent verbs: some German examples

---

Location
(1)   RN   (2;7,15, dipping a stick into a bucket of water): *Der Stock soll bewassert sein.*
          [The stick is supposed to be in the water.]
(2)   Sc   (3;11), talking about burying something, used *vererden.* (to earth]

Goal
(3)   RN   (2;10, talking about making small cakes): *Da wird er glatt und dann wird er*
          ausgeplätzelt. [Then it's getting smooth and then it's caked/ made into cakes.]
(4)   RF   (3;6,15), talking about showing one's teeth, used *bezähnen.* [to tooth]
(5)   FS   (3;11), talking about playing music, used *musiken.* [to music]
(6)   HS   (3;11), tying something in loops, used *zuschleifen.* [to loop]
(7)   HS   (5;1,15, talking about lights): *Du brauchst nicht zu lichten.* [You needn't light/
          shine a light.)
(8)   HS   (5;4,15, when her brother turned up the lamp): *Günther lichtet mehr.*
          [Günther lighted more/made more light.]

Agent
(9)   GS   (4;4), talking about someone stealing something, used *dieben.* [to thief]

---

verb *beleuchten.* Another pre-emption by suppletion occurs with *vererden* (based on *Erde*, "earth"), "bury," where the adult verb is *begraben* or *beerdigen*.

The remaining verbs all appear to be legitimate innovations. The meaning of *ausgeplätzelt* (based on *Plätzchen*, "small cakes") is perfectly comprehensible. The same goes for *bezähnen* (based on *Zähne*, "teeth"), *musiken* (based on *Musik*, "music"), and *zuschleifen* (based on *Schleife*, "loop").

Characteristic activity verbs.   Characteristic activity verbs, together with locatum verbs, form the largest group of children's innovations after instrument verbs. They denote the characteristic activity done *by* or *to* the particular entity denoted by the parent noun of the verb (E. Clark, 1978a). This class of verb is rare or nonexistent in adult speech for talking about the activities of concrete objects; the only potential exemplars in English appear to be the weather verbs like *rain* or *snow* (E. Clark and H. Clark, 1979). Typical examples from English, French, and German children are shown in Tables 28.10, 28.11, and 28.12. Although there are more instances in the corpus for English and German than for French, the French examples appear very similar to those in the other two languages.

The first half of Table 28.10 comprises activities done *by* the entity named in the verb; the second half comprises activities done *to* the entity named in the verb, by someone else. Among the illegitimate innovations in this table, several are pre-empted by suppletion, for example, *bell* by *ring*, *match* by *light*, *nut* by *crack*, and *deck* by *cut*. The last verb, *deck*, is also pre-empted by homonymy, because adult *deck* means either "put *X* on a deck," as in *He decked his opponent*, or "put a deck on," as in *They decked and masted the ship*. Three other verbs are pre-empted by ancestry. *Buzzer* and *rocker* are both formed from nouns that are in turn formed from *buzz* and *rock*, verbs that denote the activities talked about. And *snowflake* is pre-empted by the simpler adult *snow*.

Table 28.10 Characteristic activity verbs: some English examples

Act of
(1) EB (2;3, when the stove timer went off): *The buzzer is buzzering.*
(2) RG (3;0, wanting a bell to be rung): *Make it bell.*
(3) S   (3;0, watching a truck go by): *It's trucking.*
(4) S   (3;2, looking at a drooping flag that suddenly spread out in a gust of wind): *It flagged.*
(5) S   (3;2, noticing a picture of trees leaning in the wind): *It winded.*
(6) CB (3;11, making dots with a crayon over a person she had drawn): *It's snowflaking so hard that you can't see this person.*
(7) CB (4;0, talking about pictures in a book she's making): *Right now it's storming. Here it's storming too.*
(8) CB (4;4, describing a storm): *It was winding hard and then it started raining.*

Act done to
(9) S   (2;4, to mother preparing to brush his hair): *Don't hair me.*
(10) S   (2;4, eating soup): *I'm souping.*
(11) J   (2;6, seated in a rocker): *Rocker me, mommy.*
(12) S   (2;8,15, hearing his father using the vacuum cleaner in the hall): *Daddy's rugging down the hall.* (Later, going out to help): *I'm helping rug.*
(13) S   (2;9, overheard talking to another child while outside playing with a toy lawn mower): *I'm lawning.*
(14) EB (3;2, talking about another child): *I saw Julie match up a match.*
(15) D   (5;0, looking at a picture revealed by moving a puzzle piece): *They're teaing.*
(16) CB (6;0, bringing her mother two walnuts to crack): *Will you nut these?*
(17) H   (6;0, during a card game, wanting to cut the deck): *It's my turn to deck the cards.*

Table 28.11 Characteristic activity verbs: some French examples

Act of
(1) VA (3;6, talking about the neighbor's cat meowing): *Chez Nan-nan, j'entends miaou . . . miaouner . . . mianouner le chat de Madame P.* [At Nan-nan's, I heard Madame P's cat meowing.]
(2) CG (6;3,17, talking about the weather): *Il grelonne.* [It's hailing.]

Act done to
(3) CG (4;8,15, to his father): *Pipe un peu.* [Pipe/smoke your pipe a bit.]
(4) EG (11;0, discussing with his brother what to do): *Nous argilerons dans la chambre.* [We'll clay/play with clay in the bedroom.]
(5) CG (13;0, responding to his brother's utterance, in [4]): *Et nous allons microscoper.* [And we'll microscope.]
(6) WD (no age given), talking about playing the piano, used the verb *pianer.* [to piano]

The legitimate innovations in Table 28.10 tend to fall into various segments of the "Others" category in E. Clark and H. Clark (1979). *Soup* and *tea* are clearly akin to adult *lunch, breakfast,* and *snack. Wind* and *storm* fall together with adult *rain* and *snow.* There is no obvious reason why other weather terms should not occur as verbs in English. (Indeed, *storm* is used by some speakers, but not by the parents of these children.) *Truck* and *flag* denote the activity of these entities on particular occasions. The nearest uses

Table 28.12   Characteristic activity verbs: some German examples

---

Act of
(1) RN (1;10, talking about the cat): *Miezelt.* [(It's) catting/meowing.]
(2) RN (1;10, talking about bees): *Die Biene hummelt.* [The bee is humming.]
(3) Tö (2;3, talking about a dog): *Der Hund waut.* [The dog is woofing.]
(4) RN (2;4,15, screwing in a screw): *Die Schraube tunndelt durch.* [The screw tunnels through.]
(5) RN (2;4,15, shaking out a cloth): *Jetz haben wir aber (ge)flügelt!* [Now we have winged.]
(6) RN (2;6), watching a barrel organ handle turn, used the verb *mühlen.* [to mill]
(7) SS (2;6, listening to bells): *Es glockt.* [It's belling.]
(8) RF (2;6,15, talking about a caterpillar): *Raupt.* [(It)'s caterpillaring.]
(9) RF (2;6,15, talking about a shrew): *Spitzt.* [(It)'s shrewing.)
(10) GS (3;2, talking about a coffee grinder): *Gemühlt.* [(It) mills.]
(11) Sc (4;0, talking about the weather): *Es windet.* [It's winding/the wind is blowing.]
(12) Sc (5;7), talking about waves flowing down, used the verb *runterwellen.* [to wave-down]
(13) HS (6;6, looking at someone blinking): *Du wimperst ja so schnell.* [You're (eye)lashing so quickly.]

Act done to
(14) RN (1;10), turning pages in a picture book, used the verb *bildern.* [to picture/turn pages in picture books]
(15) RN (2;8, when his mother wiped his nose): *Du näselst.* [You nose/wipe noses.]
(16) GS (2;9, after playing on the piano): *Fettig ewiert.* [Done pianoed.]
(17) HS (3;8, when her mother was drumming her fingers on the table): *Warum kawierst du denn dort?* [Why are you pianoing there?]

---

of these in adult speech are often figurative, as in *The market submarined*, but such figurative verbs do not denote an actual participant in the activity named by the verb. *Hair* represents a use that was maintained by this particular child over eight months or so without any encouragement from his parents. It resembles two other verbs used by the same child, *lawn* and *rug*. Verbs like this do not seem to be represented at all among adult categories of denominal verbs in English.

Table 28.11 presents a few characteristic activity verbs produced by French-speaking children. These verbs seem rarer in French than in English or German and in general are produced by older children. Several are illegitimate. Some are pre-empted by synonymy: *Miaouner* or *mianouner*, based on *miaou*, is pre-empted by adult *miauler*, with the same meaning.[7] Similarly, *grelonner* (based on *grelon*, "hailstone"), meaning "hail," is pre-empted by *grêler*, and *piper* (based on *pipe*, "pipe"), meaning "smoke (a pipe)," is pre-empted by *fumer*. *Piper* is actually pre-empted both by synonymy (the suppletive verb *fumer*) and by homonymy, since the form *piper*, for adults, carries the meaning "deceive." The remaining verbs, *argiler* (from *argile*, "clay"), *microscoper* (from *microscope*, "microscope"), and *pianer* (from *piano*, "piano"), all appear legitimate.

Lastly, Table 28.12 presents some typical examples of characteristic activity verbs from German-speaking children. This table is also divided into two sections, for activities done *by* the entity named in the verb and activities done *to* it. Most of the illegitimate innovations in this table are pre-empted by suppletion. For instance, the three verbs for animal sounds (based on *Mieze*, the name of the cat, *Hummel*, "bumblebee," and *Wauwau*, "woof-woof") are pre-empted by adult *miauen*, *summen*, and *abrinden*. *Tunndelt* (based on *Tunnel*, "tunnel"), meaning "tunnel/screw in," and *flügelt* (based on *Flügel*, "wing"), meaning "shake, flap," are pre-empted by *einschrauben* and *schütteln*, with those same meanings. And *mühlen* (from *Mühle*, "mill"), used for talking about turning the handle of a barrel organ, is pre-empted by adult *drehen*. Another use of *mühlen*, this time for talking about the action of a coffee grinder, is also pre-empted, but by the verb *mahlen*, "grind, mill." *Glocken* (from *Glocke*, "bell") occurs in several different records. One child, for instance, commented that people could "bell" every day: *Die könnten jeden Tag glocken* (HS, aged 4; 11, 15). This verb is pre-empted by *läuten*. *Runterwellen* (from *Welle*, "wave"), meaning "flow down (in waves)," and *wimpern* (from *Augenwimper*, "eyelash"), meaning "blink," are pre-empted by *runterfliessen* and *blinken* or *blinzeln*, respectively. Finally, *näseln*, meaning "wipe one's nose" (from *Nase*, "nose") is pre-empted by homonymy: For adults, this form has the meaning "speak through one's nose."

The remaining verbs in Table 28.12 all appear to be legitimate: They fill gaps in the adult lexicon, either where there is no particular word to express just that meaning or where one would use a phrase rather than a single word. For example, in talking about the typical motion of caterpillars and shrews, the child filled gaps in the adult lexicon by using *raupen* (from *Raupe*, "caterpillar") and *spitzen* (from *Spitzmaus*, "shrew"). *Windet* (from *Wind*, "wind") falls with other weather verbs in German, where the general pattern of use is similar to that in English. All the innovations in the second half of the table appear legitimate: *bildern* (from *Bild*, "picture"), and *ewiert* and *kawierst* (both from *Klavier*, "piano").

Patterns of innovation

The overall patterns of innovation in English-, French-, and German-speaking children are very similar. As the figures in Table 28.13 show, the same categories of denominal verbs were represented in each language, with the largest being instrument, locatum,

Table 28.13 Categories of innovative denominal verbs used in English, French, and German

Verb category	English	French	German	% of total
Instrument	42	26	36	37
Locatum	21	34	18	22
Location	5	14	3	6
Goal	11	9	11	11
Agent	2	0	2	2
Experiencer	0	0	0	0
Source	0	0	0	0
Duration	0	0	0	0
Characteristic activity	19	17	30	22

Note: Data are expressed as a percentage of the corpus for each language, for comparison (123 English, 35 French, 66 German).

Table 28.14   Child innovations, child well-established, and adult denominal verb categories in English

Verb category	Child innovations	Child well-established	Adult
Instrument	42	60	32
Locatum	21	25	25
Location	5	3	14
Goal	11	6	12
Agent	2	0	12
Experiencer	0	0	.2
Source	0	0	.2
Duration	0	0	1
Others (combined)	0	6[a]	3[b]
Characteristic activity	19	0	0

Note: Data are expressed as a percentage of the total types for each corpus (123 innovative, 145 well-established, 1,323 adult).
a All these verbs were weather verbs.
b Weather verbs made up one-tenth of this category, or .3% of the total adult corpus.

and characteristic activity. The relative sizes of the six categories used were also similar, with an average rank order correlation between languages for these categories of .87. The one category missing from the French data, agent verbs, was also the smallest for the other two languages (2 percent of the totals). There appears to be considerable unanimity, then, among children in the categories of innovative denominal verbs they produce.

I also compared children's innovative verbs in English to their well-established verbs, and to adult denominal verbs.[8] These comparisons were designed to answer two questions. First, do the categories of well-established denominal verbs represented in 3-year-old speech correspond to the innovative categories children use? And second, do adult denominal verb categories correspond to the innovative categories children use?

For the first question I sorted the denominal verbs taken from seven vocabulary studies of children aged between 2 and 3 into categories, just as I had done with the innovative verbs. Since well-established verbs might provide a model for innovations, I counted only those denominal verbs whose parent nouns were also present in the children's vocabularies, to make sure that in each case there was a noun–verb pairing available. The percentage of well-established verbs in each category is shown in Table 28.14. Instrument verbs made up the largest group, followed at some distance by locatum verbs. The only other well-established verbs were a few instances of location and goal verbs. There were no verbs in any other categories, with the exception of two "weather" verbs, *rain* and *snow*, listed under Others.

A comparison of the first two columns in Table 28.14 reveals both similarities and differences in the categories represented among innovations and well-established verbs. The proportions of verbs for both in the first five categories were similar, although well-established instrument verbs had a larger share of the total (60 percent) than their innovative counterparts (42 percent). Furthermore, there were no instances of well-established agent verbs, as against 2 percent among innovations. From one point of view, this general positive correlation between innovative and well-established verbs could be regarded as surprising: One might expect the child to innovate mainly in categories where he knew fewer well-established verbs. This is clearly not the case. At the same time, the biggest difference between innovative and well-established verbs was in the last category – characteristic activity verbs. Although these made up one of the three largest categories among innovations (19 percent), they went completely unrepresented among well-established verbs.

For the second question, I examined the categories of denominal verbs represented in adult speech, together with their relative frequency, in a corpus of over 1,300 well-established and innovative verbs compiled by E. Clark and H. Clark (1979). The percentage of verbs in each category is shown in Table 28.14. The first two categories listed, instrument and locatum, between them accounted for 57 percent of the adult corpus, with the next three taking up a further 38 percent (location, goal, and agent verbs). The remaining categories together constituted a mere 5 percent, with no instances of characteristic activity verbs.

When these adult categories were compared to the categories of innovations produced by children, there were again some striking differences. Although adults and children used similar proportions of instrument and locatum verbs, children used fewer location and agent verbs. (This was true for both innovations and well-established forms in the child data.) But the biggest discrepancy was again in the last category: Characteristic activity verbs made up 19 percent of the children's corpus versus 0 percent of the adult one.

Where do characteristic activity verbs come from? There is no obvious model offered either by children's well-established verbs or by adult denominal verbs. The nearest potential candidates that might be considered are weather verbs like *rain* and *snow*, but their claim to the role of models for innovative characteristic activity verbs is at best very tenuous. First, weather verbs cover a very restricted domain of activity compared to the range covered by children's innovations (see Table 28.10). Second, weather verbs are highly restricted syntactically and occur only with subject-position *it*. But children's characteristic activity verbs occurred with animate subjects in the first, second, and third person as well as with *it*. In fact, the *it* used with characteristic activity verbs is rarely the ambient *it* of weather and time expressions (Bolinger, 1977), but is often an *it* co-referential with a non-animate noun phrase. Moreover, in contrast to weather verbs, which are intransitive, there were both intransitive and transitive characteristic activity verbs among the children's innovations.[9] Third, weather verbs made up only a small proportion of children's well-established verbs (6 percent – contributed by only two verbs, *rain* and *snow*) and an even smaller proportion of the adult corpus (0.3 percent). Characteristic activity verbs, then, appear to have no counterpart either in children's well-established denominal verbs or in adult denominal verbs.

28.4   Discussion

Lexical creativity is endemic in children's speech. Children exploit what they already know of their language to create new words. In talking about actions, they appear to draw freely on the stock of nouns they have available to create a wide range of innovative denominal verbs. But why do children create new words with new meanings? And what devices do they rely on in the process of innovation?

Using a rule

The data just considered suggest that in talking about actions, children assume that the noun denoting an entity can be used as a verb for any state, process, or activity associated with that entity. They do this, I argue, because they need the vocabulary to talk about actions with a degree of precision not otherwise available (E. Clark, 1978a). The result of such an assumption is reliance on an extremely general rule for producing new verbs, a rule that is gradually narrowed down in its possible applications as children get older. Let me now spell out the arguments in support of this view of children's innovative denominal verbs.

When young children talk about actions, they appear to face certain difficulties. Their vocabulary for actions typically lags behind that for objects, and they take a relatively long time to work out verb meanings (see, e.g., E. Clark, 1978a; Gentner, 1975, 1978). Naming the entity involved in the action, then, may be a good substitute for finding precisely the right verb. Indeed, many of the denominal verbs children create are pre-empted by specific action verbs already present in the language. *Sweep* normally pre-empts *broom*, *drive* pre-empts *car*, *fly* pre-empts *airplane*, and *shoot* pre-empts *gun*, to take only a few of the attested English examples. For adults, innovative denominal verbs serve the appropriate purpose only where established verbs are lacking. For children, innovative denominal verbs fill more gaps since they do not yet know many of the established verbs that will later pre-empt some of their innovations. Their rule of using a noun as a verb for talking about a precise action serves them well: They want to express precise meanings and they lack other devices for doing so.

Changing a noun into a verb seems to be a very simple business in English. As many linguists have pointed out (e.g., Adams, 1973; Jespersen, 1942; Marchand, 1969), this process has had a very long history in English. Moreover, the noun-to-verb changeover, with no derivational affix to add to mark the change in form class, has virtually no productive competing patterns in English. This presumably makes the creation of verbs from nouns already known particularly easy for children: They do not have to master any special affixes in coining new verbs.

But where does their rule come from? The comparison made between children's innovative verb categories and their well-established denominal verbs showed that the innovations were not simply modeled on their well-established verbs. Nor were their innovations modeled on adult denominal verb categories (see Table 28.14). Adults produced some categories of denominal verbs that did not appear in children's speech, and children created one large class of innovative verbs that was not represented in adult speech.

Their rule might nonetheless be abstracted from observations of adult usage. There are many instances where the noun–verb pairing is transparent, as in *bicycle/bicycle*, *brush/brush*, or *dress/dress*. Children could simply make an over-broad generalization from such cases to come up with a rule that might be characterized as follows:

> Any noun denoting a concrete entity can be used as a verb for talking about a state, process, or activity associated with that entity.

Notice that this rule is essentially equivalent to condition (6) of the adult convention governing innovative denominal verbs. The difference is that children apply their rule too generally because, first (unlike the adult rule), it is not constrained by the other parts of the adult denominal verb convention; second, they lack other (pre-empting) vocabulary; and third, they lack the ability to judge mutual knowledge for their interlocutors.

These data, someone might complain, are really just mistaken part-of-speech assignments. Children are using nouns as verbs, not because they are relying on a rule, but because they do not know that those lexical items are really nouns and not verbs. For instance, one possibility might be that children begin by identifying the word *broom*, say, as a verb and at first never use it as a noun. This misassignment would produce just the kind of data we have been considering. Another possibility is that children first identify *broom* as a noun but are confused about whether it is a noun or a verb and so use it in both ways. A third possibility, the one put forward here, is that children know *broom* is a noun but use it as a verb in order to say things they could not say otherwise.

One consequence of the first two possibilities is that children should use verbs as concrete nouns just as often as they use concrete nouns as verbs. However, the data do not fit this prediction: There is a strong asymmetry in children's usage. My records contain only seven verbs used as concrete nouns in English, for example, *the shave* (lather), *the rub* (eraser). In fact, the process of forming concrete nouns from verbs has always been much rarer in English than the formation of verbs from concrete nouns (Marchand, 1969). Moreover, 3-year-old speech is remarkably free of any other part-of-speech confusions. As Brown (1957) demonstrated, children that age are already very sensitive to part-of-speech information provided by the syntactic context of newly introduced words. Using a noun as a verb, then, represents the setting up of a precise means for talking about actions.

Is this rule really a rule for children, or could they instead be using a series of analogies to arrive at the innovations produced? The evidence as a whole favors rule use over analogy. Although children produced a number of innovative verbs that fell into various adult denominal verb categories (see, e.g., Table 28.1, 28.4, and 28.7), they also produced verbs of a type *not* used by adults – namely, characteristic activity verbs (Table 28.10). Had children been using analogy, it should have been possible to identify potential models for each verb type among either children's well-established denominal verbs or adult verb categories. But even if that had been possible, rule use could not have been excluded as an explanation. Either analogy or rule could have been at work. However, since children did produce, as one of their largest categories, a verb type for which there was no model from which to work by analogy, they must have been using a rule.

Although the evidence favors rule use in the case of innovative denominal verbs, this may not necessarily be true of the acquisition process in general. Children may rely on rote, analogy, and rule, in differing degrees at different stages, depending on the aspect of language being acquired. Generalizations about other types of lexical innovation will have to await further case studies like the one undertaken here.

Notes

1 Even though lexical creativity pervades everyday adult speech, it has seldom been discussed or analyzed in any detail (but see E. Clark and H. Clark, 1979; Downing, 1977; L. Gleitman and H. Gleitman, 1970). Most discussion of linguistic creativity in children has been limited on the one hand to the combining of words to form new utterances, and on the other to the adding of inflections to nonsense words.

2 The actual boundaries between these categories are not always clear-cut. For example, many locatum verbs can also be instrumental. Contrast *He leashed the dog* with *He leashed the dog to the post*. In the former, *leash* would be classified as a locatum verb and in the latter as an instrument verb as well (see further E. Clark and H. Clark, 1979, pp. 778–9).

3 The procedures in the first two steps clearly assume that children do not have to learn each present–past pair by rote. If they did, they should never produce incorrect past-tense forms, and they should be unable to use the generalization described in the third step to form past tenses for "new" (nonsense-syllable) verbs. However, even very young children overregularize verb and noun endings (W. Miller and Ervin, 1964) and readily add endings to nonsense forms they can never have heard before (Berko, 1958).

4 Similarity of phonological shape, of course, is only one of many dimensions of similarity that children (or adults) might use in forming analogies. They could equally well rely on conceptual criteria, for instance, where the action to be denoted is similar in some way to some other action for which they already have a word with a present–past contrast. I give phonological shape as the example here simply for illustrative purposes.

   Notice also that although people may appear to favor analogy in very small paradigms like *throw/threw, grow/grew, know/knew, blow/blew*, or *ring/rang, sing/sang*, when presented with nonsense stems of similar shapes, it is quite possible that these, too, involve rule use. The rules here would simply be more restricted than the one for weak verbs taking *-ed*.

5 According to Grevisse (1964), at least 90 percent of all French verbs belong to the first conjugation.

6 Although there has been no research, to my knowledge, on the form of the conventions governing innovative denominal verbs in French and German. I shall assume that they are similar for conditions (1) through (5) to that for English, and have similar consequences.

7 It is possible that verbs denoting animal noises like this ought to be treated as goal rather than characteristic activity verbs (see also Table 28.12). However, these verbs seem to be just as closely linked to other animal verbs where the characteristic activity is the typical motion rather than the noise produced. They are therefore grouped together in the present analysis.

8 These comparisons were confined to English because there are no published data available for the pertinent comparisons in French and German.

9 The range of characteristic activity verbs in English was also typical for the other two languages considered (see Tables 28.11 and 28.12). Moreover, the syntactic properties of these innovations are very comparable to the English examples, in contrast to the restricted syntax of weather verbs in both French and German.

References

Adams, V. 1973. *An Introduction to Modern English Word-formation*. London: Longman.
Aimard, P. 1975. *Les Jeux de mots de l'enfant*. Villeurbanne: Simép Editions.
Augst, G., A. Bauer, and A. Stein. 1977. *Grundwortschatz und Idiolekt*. Tübingen: Max Niemeyer Verlag.

Bateman, W. G. 1915. Two children's progress in speech. *Journal of Educational Psychology* 6, 475–93.

Berko, J. 1958. The child's learning of English morphology. *Word* 14, 150–77.

Bohn, W. E. 1914. First steps in verbal expression. *Pedagogical Seminary* 21, 578–95.

Bolinger, D. 1977. *Meaning and Form*. London: Longman.

Bowerman, M. 1974. Learning the structure of causative verbs: a study in the relationship of cognitive, semantic, and syntactic development. *Papers and Reports on Child Language Development* (Department of Linguistics, Stanford University) no. 8, pp. 142–78.

Bowerman, M. 1978. Semantic and syntactic development: a review of what, when, and how in language acquisition. In R. Schiefelbusch (ed.), *Bases of Language Intervention*. Baltimore, Md.: University Park Press, pp. 97–189.

Boyd, W. 1914. The development of a child's vocabulary. *Pedagogical Seminary* 21, 95–124.

Brandenburg, G. C. 1915. The language of a three-year-old child. *Pedagogical Seminary* 22, 89–120.

Brooks, L. 1978. Non-analytic concept formation and memory for instances. In E. Rosch and B. B. Lloyd (ed.), *Cognition and Categorization*. Hillsdale, NJ: Erlbaum, pp. 169–211.

Brown, R. 1957. Linguistic determinism and the part of speech. *Journal of Abnormal and Social Psychology* 55, 1–5.

Brown, R. 1973. *A First Language: The Early Stages*. Cambridge, Mass.: Harvard University Press.

Clark, E. V. 1978. Discovering what words can do. In *Papers from the Parasession on the Lexicon*. Chicago: Chicago Linguistic Society.

Clark, E. V., and H. H. Clark. 1979. When nouns surface as verbs. *Language* 55, 767–811.

Clark, H., and C. Marshall. 1981. Definite reference and mutual knowledge. In A. K. Joshi, B. Webber, and I. Sag (eds.), *Linguistic Structure and Discourse Setting*. Cambridge: Cambridge University Press.

Decroly, O. 1932. *Comment l'enfant arrive à parler*. Volume 2. Brussels: Cahiers de la Centrale.

Downing, P. 1977. On the creation and use of English compound nouns. *Language* 53, 810–42.

Friedrich, G. 1906. Psychologische Beobachtungen an zwei Knaben. *Beiträge zur Kinderforschung und Heilerziehung* 17.

Gentner, D. 1975. Evidence for the psychological reality of semantic components: the verbs of possession. In D. A. Norman, D. E. Rumelhart, and the LNR Research Group, *Explorations in Cognition*. San Francisco: Freeman, pp. 211–46.

Gentner, D. 1978. On relational meaning: the acquisition of verb meaning. *Child Development* 49, 988–98.

Gleitman, L. R., and H. Gleitman. 1970. *Phrase and Paraphrase: Some Innovative Uses of Language*. New York: Norton.

Grant, J. R. 1915. A child's vocabulary and its growth. *Pedagogical Seminary* 22, 183–203.

Grégoire, A. 1937–47. *L'Apprentissage du langage*. 2 vols. Paris: Droz.

Grevisse, M. 1964. *Le bon usage: grammaire française avec des remarques sur la langue française d'aujourd'hui*, 8th edn. Grembloux: Editions J. Duculot.

Griffiths, P., and M. A. Atkinson. 1978. A "door" to verbs. In N. Waterson and C. Snow (eds.), *The Development of Communication*. New York: Wiley, pp. 311–19.

Guillaume, P. 1927. Le développement des éléments formels dans le langage de l'enfant. *Journal de Psychologie* 24, 203–29.

Huxley, R. 1970. The development of the correct use of subject personal pronouns in two children. In G. B. Flores d'Arcais and W. J. M. Levelt (eds.), *Advances in Psycholinguistics*. Amsterdam: North Holland, pp. 141–65.

Jespersen, O. 1942. *A Modern English Grammar on Historical Principles*. Part VI. *Morphology*. Copenhagen: Munksgaard.

Kossan, N. E. 1978. Structure and strategy in concept acquisition. Unpublished doctoral dissertation, Stanford University.

Kuczaj, S. A. II. 1977. The acquisition of regular and irregular past tense forms. *Journal of Verbal Learning and Verbal Behavior* 16, 589–600.

Kuczaj, S. A. II. 1978. Why do children fail to overgeneralize the progressive inflection? *Journal of Child Language* 5, 167–71.

Lindner, G. 1898. *Aus dem Naturgarten der Kindersprache*. Leipzig: Grieben.

MacWhinney, B. 1975. Rules, rote and analogy in morphological formations by Hungarian children. *Journal of Child Language* 2, 65–77.

Marchand, H. 1969. *The Categories and Types of Present-day English Word-formation*, 2nd rev. edn. Munich: Verlag C. H. Beck.

Medin, D. L., and M. M. Schaffer. 1978. Context theory of classification. *Psychological Review* 85, 207–38.

Miller, W., and S. Ervin. 1964. The development of grammar in child language. In *The Acquisition of Language*, ed. U. Bellugi and R. Brown. Chicago: University of Chicago Press, pp. 9–34.

Neugebauer, H. 1914. Sprachliche Eigenbildungen meines Sohnes. *Zeitschrift für Kinderforschung* 19, 174–81, 242–6, 362–70.

Nice, M. M. 1915. The development of a child's vocabulary in relation to environment. *Pedagogical Seminary* 22, 35–64.

O'Shea, M. V. 1907. *Linguistic Development and Education*. New York: Macmillan.

Panagl, O. 1977. Aspekte der kindersprachlichen Wortbildung. University of Trier, Linguistic Agency, Paper no. 24 (Series B).

Park, T. Z. 1978. Plurals in child speech. *Journal of Child Language* 5, 237–50.

Pelsma, J. R. 1910. A child's vocabulary and its development. *Pedagogical Seminary* 17, 328–69.

Preyer, W. 1882. *Die Seele des Kindes*. Leipzig: Schaeffer.

Schneider, O. 1907. Die schöpferische Kraft des Kindes in der Gestaltung seiner Bewusstseinszustände bis zum Beginn des Schulunterrichts. *Zeitschrift für Philosophie und philosophische Kritik* 121, 153–75.

Scupin, E., and G. Scupin. 1907. *Bubis erste Kindheit*. Leipzig: Grieben.

Stern, C., and W. Stern. 1928. *Die Kindersprache: Eine psychologiche und sprachtheoretische Untersuchung*, 4th rev. edn. Leipzig: Barth.

Tögel, H. 1905. 16 Monate Kindersprache. *Zeitschrift für Kinderforschung* 10, 156–65.

Warden, D. A. 1976. The influence of context on children's use of identifying expressions and references. *British Journal of Psychology* 67, 101–12.

29

Strategies for Communicating

Eve V. Clark

Language is a tool for communication. While this point has often been lost sight of in the study of language acquisition, children clearly make the most of their resources for communicating from the start. They supplement gestures with words, and they stretch their words to talk about many different situations. Their efforts to communicate even result in systematic misuses of language – both in how they use words and in which words they choose to convey particular ideas. In this paper I outline some of the strategies children seem to rely on for communicating, and, in doing so, I hope to show why it is important to keep the communicative function of language in mind as we study what children say.

The processes of language comprehension and language production make different demands on the language user. In comprehension, listeners try to interpret what they have heard from other speakers. This process, in children, is supported by the actual physical setting of the utterance combined with the children's general knowledge about the objects, events, or relations present. In contrast, in production, speakers try to convey particular meanings to others. This process, unlike comprehension, receives no direct support from the setting, since what is said depends on the speaker's intentions. Instead, it is supported by the child's ability to retrieve from memory the appropriate linguistic or nonlinguistic devices for conveying what he wants to convey (see also Clark and Clark 1977). My focus here will be on young children's strategies in language production – how they go about conveying particular meanings to others.

By *strategy* I mean the choice of a device to communicate a particular meaning. Children might choose a single word, a two-word combination, or a fully grammatical utterance, depending on what they want to convey and how much they know of their first language. Alternatively, they might rely on a gesture or combination of gestures in lieu of words. In illustrating some of the production strategies children rely on during the early stages of language acquisition, I will take examples from how children talk about objects,

From *Child Development* 49 (1978), pp. 953–9. Reprinted with permission of the Society for Research in Child Development.

about spatial relations, and about actions and examine the extent to which they rely on general purpose terms in all three domains.

Talking about Objects

In picking out objects for a listener, young children typically rely at first on deictic gestures: they gaze intently and point at whatever interests them. In the absence of words, this strategy seems to work well enough (e.g., Bates 1976; Carter 1978). Next, these gestures are combined with words, either deictic words or category names. And from this point on, whenever they do not have names available for what they want to talk about, children seem to rely on two general production strategies. The first is to use a general purpose deictic word like *here*, *that*, or *look* (accompanied by pointing) to pick out specific objects or events (Clark 1978; Clark and Sengul 1978). The second is to "stretch" words already known or partly known to cover other things that appear sufficiently similar to the originals to justify use of the same name (Clark 1974).

Children seem to rely freely on both these options as they gradually build up more extensive vocabularies. They frequently depend on deictic words combined with gestures when they do not know what something is called (e.g., Bohn 1914; Kenyeres 1927). And they just as frequently seem to stretch certain words in their vocabularies. For instance, many investigators have noted that 1- and 2-year-olds will apply a word like *doggie* not only to dogs but also to cats, sheep, horses, cows, bears, and so on – all objects that are, roughly speaking, mammal shaped, with a head and four legs. Or they will use a word like *ball* first for a ball and then stretch or overextend it to oranges, cookies, light switches, doorknobs, a cake of soap – all objects that are spherical or round. Overextensions like these have been widely documented: they appear very common in the speech of children 1–2½ years old, learning quite unrelated languages. And, in general, they seem to be governed by the perceptual similarities children notice among the different referents for the overextended word (Bowerman 1976; Clark 1973a).

With the second strategy, children produce a word already in their vocabulary – presumably whichever one they think "fits" best or one that is readily retrievable from memory – and rely on that to guide their listeners. But whenever they overextend a word, they apply it in a way that is incompatible with adult usage. And this, one could argue, shows that they have yet to work out its full adult meaning. By working back from a child's overextensions, then, it is possible to make inferences about what meaning the child may have attached to the word so far. For example, his overextensions might show that for child A the word *doggie* picked out objects that were mammal shaped, while for child B it picked out a furry texture. These two children presumably had different hypotheses about the meaning of *doggie*, hypotheses that were revealed by the kinds of overextensions made. A third child, C, might include both shape and texture in his meaning for *doggie* and, as a result, overextend the word when needed to objects meeting both criteria – shape and texture – or to those meeting either one or the other – shape or texture. The kinds of overextensions that children produce, then, provide a good deal of information about children's meanings and about the process of acquiring meaning (Clark 1975).[1]

Overextensions in production, however, may provide us with an underestimate of how much children know about meanings. For example, children might sometimes over-extend a word deliberately because they have no other word in their repertoire or because they cannot retrieve precisely the right word. But if children do overextend words delib-erately after they have worked out the adult meanings, this should be detectable in an asymmetry between the production of a word (overextended) and its comprehension (correct). And, on occasion, just this type of asymmetry has been observed. Moore (1896), for instance, noticed that at one point her child overextended the word *bird* to any moving animal, yet on hearing *bird* would look around for a bird and not, for example, be satisfied on seeing a cat. In another study, Thomson and Chapman (1977) tested children's comprehension of words they had overextended in production. They found some words were overextended in both production and comprehension, but others were always understood correctly. One child, for example, given the instruction "Show me the dog," only selected pictures of dogs, although in production he applied the word *dog* to all sorts of four-legged animals.

The production strategies of using general purpose deictic words or stretching words already known allow children to talk about many things for which they have not yet acquired the appropriate vocabulary. Moreover, when their production strategies result in overextensions or other misuses of words, they indirectly provide us with ways of finding out what meanings children have attached to particular words. Because children are intent on communicating, they choose whatever word seems to fit best on that occasion, and what fits best will depend largely on what they already know about par-ticular words and word meanings. As they learn more about meanings, and acquire more words as well, their production strategies gradually come to match the adult's. This may take many years, though, since choosing the right words (from the adult point of view) requires a much more extensive knowledge of language than is available to the 2- or 3-year-old.

Talking about Spatial Relations

When children first talk about the location of one object with respect to another, they name the object located and use a deictic term like *here* or *there* for the location ("flower here," "there car"), or they name both the object located and its location ("baby chair," "towel bed") – in neither case specifying the exact spatial relation between the two objects. Very shortly, though, many children begin to use a general purpose locative marker. This marker is linked in some way – as a preposition, a postposition, or a suffix, depend-ing on the language being acquired – to the word for the location. Initially, it seems to be used for a variety of different spatial relations, then it is gradually ousted from cer-tain contexts as children begin to use other spatial terms in its place. The strategy of using one general purpose element for talking about spatial relations is closely akin to the production strategy of using general purpose deictic words in talking about objects. In both instances, children start out by applying only a few terms where adults normally apply many.

Children acquiring English often pick a schwa sound [ə] or a syllabic *n* [n̩] as their general purpose locative marker and simply insert it before any noun phrase denoting a location – for example, "Ball [ņ] table" for "The ball's on/under the table." Other children choose one particular preposition and let it serve, just as a schwa or syllabic *n* does, for every spatial relation. If they choose a preposition like *in*, they will appear to use it quite appropriately as long as they talk about containment ("in the box," "in the house"), but when they stretch it to talk about something being "on" the table, "under" the bed, or "next to" the door, its general purpose status becomes very apparent (Clark, unpublished data).

Interestingly, children acquiring English as their second language appear to rely on a very similar production strategy. Hakuta,[2] for instance, reported that a Japanese-speaking child he followed used *in* at first for containment and then for a variety of other spatial relations, including "at," "off," "out," and "around." Cancino[3] reported a similar phenomenon in a Spanish-speaking child who also chose *in* as her all-purpose locative. In both cases, it is possible that the children were influenced by their first languages. Japanese has a general locative postposition, *ni*, that is attached to the location noun. This general locative marker can then be further specified by the addition of words like *side*, *top*, or *front*. While Spanish does not have a general locative marker like Japanese, it does use one preposition, *en*, to cover a number of spatial relations that have to be distinguished in English – for example: *en la mesa* ("on the table"), *en casa* ("at home"), *en el cuarto* ("in the room"), and so on. However, since children acquiring English as their first language follow the same strategy, it seems likely that, regardless of the language being learned, use of a general purpose locative results more generally from the kind of communicative strategy children rely on when their resources are limited.

The generality of this production strategy shows up in other languages too. In French, children tend to start out by using the preposition that means "at" or "to" (*à*) as a general purpose spatial preposition (e.g., Grégoire 1947; Guillaume 1927). Much the same happens in Danish. Rasmussen (1922) reported that his daughter Sonia, aged 2–6, over-used the preposition meaning "to" for several different spatial relations, including "on." In German, Stern (1924) reported similar overuse of a spatial preposition, this time one meaning "of" or "from" (*von*). Children acquiring Turkish and Serbo-Croatian opt for a similar production strategy and start out using one locative form as a general purpose locative marker (Slobin).[4] And in Russian, Museyibova (1964) observed several children use a single preposition as a general purpose locative for talking about a variety of spatial relations.

Lastly, children whose language acquisition is retarded also seem to rely on this type of production strategy. One 6-year-old acquiring English, for example, used *on* for all spatial relations. However, he would only use this locative marker when under communicative pressure to talk about how different objects were related to each other in space (Hecht).[5]

For spatial relations, then, just as for objects, children rely on certain production strategies to extend the range of what they can talk about. These production strategies, of course, reveal only part of what children know about the meanings they use. When they make mistakes in production, using *on* for *under* or *in* for *beside*, it becomes clear that their words cannot be taken at face value. Children may mean what they say, but they do not always mean what adults mean with the same words. Nonetheless, what they say does tell us something about their word meanings – for instance, that they realize that some spatial term is required for talking about any relation in space (e.g., Kenyeres 1927).

Once this information is combined with what we can infer from their comprehension strategies (Clark 1973b; Clark and Clark 1977), it should become possible to paint a much more detailed picture of the steps children go through in working out new word meanings.

Talking about Actions

Children's earliest words for actions tend to encode the action and its result together or just the result. A particle like *up*, for example, is commonly used for the result of lifting or raising and may be produced when the child talks about any upward or downward displacement of himself – being lifted into his high chair, being put down on the floor, asking to climb into someone's lap, going up or down stairs, or requesting objects that are too high to reach. Other verb particles like *off*, *out*, or *on* seem to be used in a very similar way (e.g., Farwell 1975; Leopold 1949; Gruendel).[6] *Up*, then, is applied to a great many different situations. The same is true of words like *open* or *door*, which may be stretched from talking about a door being open or shut to getting a lid off a box or a jar, to peeling fruit, to turning a light or a tap on or off, to unlacing shoes and unbuttoning coats (e.g., Farwell 1977; Griffiths and Atkinson 1978; Guillaume 1927a). From the adult point of view, the earliest action words, like *up* and *open* (or *door*), are clearly being overextended. This very limited set of terms for resultant states, though, is soon supplemented by a growing number of words that, at least for adults, pick out just the actions themselves.

When children start to talk about actions, they face the same problem they have in naming objects. Their resources are too limited at first to cover all they want to talk about. The solution many children adopt is to use a small number of general purpose verbs for a large variety of different actions. The commonest general purpose verbs in my data are *do* and *make*. They are used for talking about building, writing, opening, knocking over, putting on, cutting out, putting away, picking up, rolling, and so on, actions for which the children at first lacked more specific terms. However, what children are talking about with general purpose *do* or *make* is usually opaque without contextual information. The precise actions being talked about in "I do it again," "The clown do!" and "Make [ə] this" cannot be understood from the utterances alone. *Make*, unlike *do*, is also used in the sense of producing or causing a resultant state, as in "Make it big" or "Make it up" (put it up) (see also Bowerman 1974; Leopold 1949).

In my own research, the youngest children recorded were just over 2, but some diary studies, as well as personal observations, suggest that *do* may be used even earlier with a general purpose function. Pollock (1878), for instance, reported a child aged 1 year 10 months saying "Baby do't" as he watched someone spinning an ivory ring. The child then tried to spin the ring himself, failed, and asked his mother: "More 'gain/Mama 'gain/Mama do't." Grégoire (1947) reported similar uses of French *faire* ("do," "make"); for example, Edmond, aged 2, asked his father to right his fallen chair by saying: "*Papa fais*" ("papa do"). Another child, aged 1 year 9 months, used *do* whenever he came across some new object to manipulate or play with and would sit playing and say: "Rodi do." Actions covered by such uses of *do* included throwing toys down the stairs, twanging a spring doorstop, and opening boxes or jars (Clark, unpublished data).

Table 29.1   Some typical examples of "do," "make," and "go" in the speech of S, aged 2 years 2 months

Verb	Utterance	Context
Do........	I do it again.	Said as knocks over blocks
	You . . . do . . . doing that.	Said as watches O build blocks into a tower
	You do do it, OK?	Asking O to unroll some computer tape, after trying unsuccessfully to do it himself
	You do [ə] that!	Indicating which toy O should take out of a box
	Uh oh. I did.	Said as he turned off the tape recorder by pushing a knob
	The clown do!	Asking O to make the toy clown do what clowns do
Make......	Make name!	Telling O to write his name
	I make a little doggie.	Said as cut a dog shape out of Play-Doh
	Make a dog.	Telling O what to draw next
	Make it go in there.	Asking O to get a crayon back into its box
	Make [ə] that.	Said as pointed to the hand moving on a clock; seemed to be request for O to move the hand on
Go........	It go there.	Talking about a block lying on the floor
	Red went boom.	Talking about a red block that fell on the floor
	They go in the car.	Talking about two storybook characters
	'N turn [ə] go up.	Said as turned a puzzle piece the right way up
	'N go like that.	Said as dropped puzzle pieces on the floor

Note: Examples cited come from the first month of recordings from S, a child taped at weekly intervals for 1 year from age 2–0. The utterances cited occurred without any immediately preceding use of the particular general purpose verb by either the observer (O) or the child's parents.

Table 29.1 lists some typical uses of *do* and *make* from one 2-year-old. The general purpose verbs are on the left and the context of use on each occasion is on the right. Notice that the specific actions picked out by the general purpose verbs seem very obvious with the context supplied, unlike the utterances given earlier, on their own. In addition to *do* and *make*, children seem to use two other general purpose verbs very commonly from age 2 or so onward. The first of these is *go*, with the general meaning of "move" or "travel," and the second is *put*, used a little less frequently, with the meaning of motion of an object to a location. Both *go* and *do* are also used for talking about all sorts of noises from animals, cars, and trains, as well as noises produced as the result of some action. Bloom, Miller, and Hood (1975), not surprisingly, found these verbs were the most frequently used by far for talking about actions and locative actions.

Children acquiring English as their second language appear to use the same production strategy as native speakers for talking about actions: they rely on a small number of general purpose verbs. Spanish-speaking children, for example, commonly opt for *do*, *make*, and *put* for talking about all sorts of actions (Fillmore)[7] – for example: "How do you do dese?" "How do you do these little tortillas?" (= "make," "cook"); "How do you do dese in English?" (= "say"); "How do you make the flower?" (talking about Play-Doh); "How I put the number?" (= "dial"). Similar examples were recorded by Hakuta for a Japanese-speaking child acquiring English who opted for *do* as her general purpose verb. Not all children, though, identify an appropriate general purpose verb.

One child Fillmore studied, for instance, chose *sweep*, which he then used for talking about a variety of actions – sweeping with a broom, wheeling a supermarket cart, making pastry, playing ball, and building with blocks. This persisted for several months before the child began to use more specific – and more appropriate – verbs for these different actions. His strategy, however, seems to have been the same as that of those who used the more usual *do* or *make*.

Although the commonest strategy for talking about actions seems to be to use general purpose verbs like *do*, *make*, or *go*, it is not the only one. At times, some children opt for another one: they use the word for an object or for a resultant state to pick out the particular action in question. Instead of a general purpose verb, therefore, they use a highly specific one. They may choose a word for the instrument used in the action (e.g., "The man is keying the door" [opening with a key]; "I want to button it" [turn off by pressing a button]); a word for the object affected by the action (e.g., "I'm souping" [eating soup]; "They're teaing" [having tea]; "Pillow me!" [throw a pillow at me]), a word for the end state resulting from the action (e.g., "I'm darking the letters" [scribbling over them to make them dark]; "She's rounding it" [making the jump rope into a half circle]; "Can you higher that?" [make it higher]), and so on. Uses like these serve just as clear a communicative purpose as a general purpose verb: they pick out the specific action associated with the object, instrument, or end state in a particular context.

In summary, most children pick up a small number of general purpose verbs fairly early on and use these for talking about a large number of different actions. General purpose verbs are similar in function, then, to the deictic terms *this* and *that* used for talking about objects. Both play an important communicative role in the early stages of language acquisition. Both constitute devices whereby children can stretch their resources to the utmost. While many children rely primarily on the production strategy of using a general purpose verb, others may produce highly specific verbs by naming a role or state connected with an action. These forms are usually transitory in nature, serving to communicate what the child wants to convey on that occasion only. Both these production strategies seem to be put to use by young children after an initial period when they simply overextend whatever primitive action words they have (e.g., *up*, *off*, *open*) to a limited number of situations.

Conclusion

One ingredient that is all too often omitted in discussions of language acquisition is communication. But the strategies children rely on in production are motivated by communicative concerns. In the early stages of acquisition, children have only a very small vocabulary at their disposal, and, while they freely supplement this with gestures and demonstrations, it is only adequate for talking about a limited number of events. They are often faced, therefore, with wanting to talk about things for which they have no words. Their solution is to stretch their resources as far as possible: they rely on one or two general purpose deictic terms to pick out objects (and they also overextend nondeictic words), they make use of general purpose locative markers for talking about locative relations in space, and they rely on a small number of general purpose verbs for talking about actions.

Learning a language is not simply a matter of learning a system of rules for linking sounds and meanings: it is learning how to use such a system for communication. Working out new meanings, then, goes hand in hand with trying to communicate as clearly and as effectively as possible. From the investigator's point of view, what children say is doubly important: first, it reveals what options children usually take in making the most of whatever language they already have; and second, it reveals, through their special uses of certain words, what systems of meanings children are working out as they acquire language.[8]

In this paper, I have concentrated on the first point – the kinds of communicative strategies children rely on in production during the early stages of acquisition when their linguistic resources are limited. But my ultimate interest in such strategies lies with the second point – the fact that children's misuses and errors in speech are potentially revealing of what they know about their language and, in particular, about the meanings it can be used to express.

Notes

1   Although children also underextend some words, using them to pick out only a subset of the adult category denoted, underextensions themselves, like correct usage, reveal comparatively little about children's strategies for communicating with limited resources.
2   Hakuta, K. Becoming bilingual at age five: the story of Uguisu. Unpublished honors thesis, Harvard University, 1975.
3   Cancino, H. Grammatical morphemes in second language acquisition: Marta. Unpublished manuscript, Harvard University, 1976.
4   Slobin, Dan I. Personal communication, 1977.
5   Hecht, Barbara. Personal communication, 1977.
6   Gruendel, J. M. Locative production in the SWU period: a study of *up-down*, *on-off*, and *in-out*. Paper presented at the biennial meeting of the Society for Research in Child Development, New Orleans, March 1977.
7   Fillmore, L. W. The second time around: cognitive and social strategies in second language acquisition. Unpublished doctoral dissertation, Stanford University, 1976.
8   Despite this optimism, notice that apparently adultlike word usage can provide no direct information about children's lexical meanings. It is where their usage diverges from the adult's that we are most likely to be able to use production data fruitfully.

References

Bates, E. 1976. *Language and Context: The Acquisition of Pragmatics*. New York: Academic Press.
Bloom, L., Miller, P., and Hood, L. 1975. Variation and reduction as aspects of competence in language development. In A. Pick (ed.), *Minnesota Symposia on Child Psychology*. Vol. 9. Minneapolis: University of Minnesota Press, pp. 3–55.
Bohn, W. E. 1914. First steps in verbal expression. *Pedagogical Seminary* 21, 578–95.
Bowerman, M. 1974. Learning the structure of causative verbs: a study in the relationship of cognitive, semantic and syntactic development. *Papers and Reports on Child Language Development* (Stanford University) 8, 142–78.

Bowerman, M. 1976. Semantic factors in the acquisition of rules for word use and sentence construction. In D. M. Morehead and A. E. Morehead (eds.), *Normal and Deficient Child Language*. Baltimore: University Park Press, pp. 99–179.

Carter, A. L. 1978. Learning to point with words: the structural evolution of attention-directing communication in the second year. In A. Lock (ed.), *Action, Gesture, and Symbol: The Emergence of Language*. London: Academic Press, pp. 309–49.

Clark, E. V. 1973a. What's in a word? On the child's acquisition of semantics in his first language. In T. E. Moore (ed.), *Cognitive Development and the Acquisition of Language*. New York: Academic Press, pp. 65–110.

Clark, E. V. 1973b. Non-linguistic strategies and the acquisition of word meanings. *Cognition* 2, 161–82.

Clark, E. V. 1974. Some aspects of the conceptual basis for first language acquisition. In R. L. Schiefelbusch and L. L. Lloyd (eds.), *Language Perspectives: Acquisition, Retardation, and Intervention*. Baltimore: University Park Press, pp. 105–28.

Clark, E. V. 1975. Knowledge, context, and strategy in the acquisition of meaning. In D. P. Dato (ed.), *Developmental Psycholinguistics: Theory and Applications*. Washington, DC: Georgetown University Press, pp. 77–98.

Clark, E. V. 1978. From gesture to word: on the natural history of deixis in language acquisition. In J. S. Bruner and A. Garton (eds.), *Human Growth and Development: Wolfson College Lectures*, 1976. Oxford: Oxford University Press, pp. 85–120.

Clark, E. V., and Sengul, C. J. 1978. Strategies in the acquisition of deixis. *Journal of Child Language* 5, 457–75.

Clark, H. H., and Clark, E. V. 1977. *Psychology and Language: An Introduction to Psycholinguistics*. New York: Harcourt Brace Jovanovich.

Farwell, C. B. 1975. Aspects of early verb semantics – pre-causative development. *Papers and Reports on Child Language Development* (Stanford University) 10, 48–58.

Farwell, C. B. 1977. The primacy of *goal* in the child's description of motion and location. *Papers and Reports on Child Language Development* (Stanford University) 13, 126–33.

Grégoire, A. 1937–47. *L'Apprentissage du langage*. 2 vols. Paris: Droz.

Griffiths, P. D., and Atkinson, M. 1978. A *door* to verbs. In N. Waterson & C. E. Snow (eds.), *The Development of Communication: Social and Pragmatic Factors in Language Acquisition*. New York: Wiley, pp. 311–19.

Guillaume, P. 1927a. Les Débuts de la phrase dans le langage de l'enfant. *Journal de Psychologie* 24, 1–25.

Guillaume, P. 1927b. Le Développement des éléments formels dans le langage de l'enfant. *Journal de Psychologie* 24, 203–29.

Kenyeres, E. 1927. Les Premiers Mots de l'enfant et l'apparition des espèces de mots dans son langage. *Archives de Psychologie* 20, 191–218.

Leopold, W. F. 1949. *Speech Development of a Bilingual Child: A Linguist's Record*. 4 vols. Evanston, Ill.: Northwestern University Press.

Moore, K. C. 1896. The mental development of a child. *Psychological Review, Monograph Supplements* 1(3).

Museyibova, T. A. 1964. The development of an understanding of spatial relations and their reflection in the language of children of pre-school age. In B. C. Anan'yev and B. F. Lomov (eds.), *Problems of Spatial Perception and Spatial Concepts*. Washington, DC: NASA.

Pollock, F. 1878. An infant's progress in language. *Mind* 3, 392–401.

Rasmussen, V. 1922. *Et barns dagbog*. Copenhagen: Gyldendal.

Stern, W. 1924. *Psychology of Early Childhood*, 3rd edn.; trans. A. Barwell. New York: Holt.

Thomson, J. R., and Chapman, R. S. 1977. Who is "daddy" revisited: the status of two-year-olds' overextended words in use and comprehension. *Journal of Child Language* 4, 359–75.

Index